$60.00

REFERENCE - - NOT TO BE
TAKEN FROM THIS ROOM

D1801340

DRAMA
for Students

DRAMA for Students

Presenting Analysis, Context, and Criticism on Commonly Studied Dramas

Volume 9

Ira Mark Milne, Editor

Detroit
New York
San Francisco
London
Boston
Woodbridge, CT

National Advisory Board

Dale Allender: Teacher, West High School, Iowa City, Iowa.

Dana Gioia: Poet and critic. His books include *The Gods of Winter* and *Can Poetry Matter?* He currently resides in Santa Rosa, CA.

Carol Jago: Teacher, Santa Monica High School, Santa Monica, CA. Member of the California Reading and Literature Project at University of California, Los Angeles.

Bonnie J. Newcomer: English Teacher, Beloit Junior-Senior High School, Beloit, Kansas. Editor of KATE UpDate, for the Kansas Association of Teachers of English. Ph.D. candidate in information science, Emporia State University, Kansas.

Katherine Nyberg: English teacher. Director of the language arts program of Farmington Public Schools, Farmington, Michigan.

Nancy Rosenberger: Former English teacher and chair of English department at Conestoga High School, Berwyn, Pennsylvania.

Dorothea M. Susag: English teacher, Simms High School, Simms, Montana. Former president of the Montana Association of Teachers of English Language Arts. Member of the National Council of Teachers of English.

Drama for Students

Staff

Editorial: Ira Mark Milne, *Editor.* Elizabeth Bellalouna, Elizabeth Bodenmiller, Angela Y. Jones, Michael L. LaBlanc, Polly Rapp, *Contributing Editors.* Dwayne D. Hayes, *Managing Editor.*

Research: Victoria B. Cariappa, *Research Team Manager.* Cheryl Warnock, *Research Specialist.* Corrine A. Boland, Tamara Nott, Tracie A. Richardson, *Research Associates.* Timothy Lehnerer, Patricia Love, *Research Assistants.*

Permissions: Maria Franklin, *Permissions Manager.* Margaret A. Chamberlain, Edna Hedblad, *Permissions Specialists.* Erin Bealmear, *Permissions Associate.* Sandra K. Gore, *Permissions Assistant.*

Production: Mary Beth Trimper, *Production Director.* Evi Seoud, *Assistant Production Manager.* Stacy Melson, *Production Assistant.*

Imaging and Multimedia Content Team: Randy Bassett, *Image Database Supervisor.* Robert Duncan, *Imaging Specialist.* Michael Logusz, *Graphic Artist.* Pamela A. Reed, *Imaging Coordinator.* Dean Dauphinais, Robyn V. Young, *Senior Image Editors.* Kelly A. Quin, *Image Editor.*

Product Design Team: Cynthia Baldwin, *Product Design Manager.* Pamela A. E. Galbreath, *Senior Art Director.* Gary Leach, *Graphic Artist.*

Copyright Notice

Since this page cannot legibly accommodate all copyright notices, the acknowledgments constitute an extension of the copyright notice.

While every effort has been made to secure permission to reprint material and to ensure the reliability of the information presented in this publication, the Gale Group neither guarantees the accuracy of the data contained herein nor assumes any responsibility for errors, omissions, or discrepancies. Gale accepts no payment for listing; and inclusion in the publication of any organization, agency, institution, publication, service, or individual does not imply endorsement of the editors or publisher. Errors brought to the attention of the publisher and verified to the satisfaction of the publisher will be corrected in future editions.

This publication is a creative work fully protected by all applicable copyright laws, as well as by misappropriation, trade secret, unfair competition, and other applicable laws. The authors and editors of this work have added value to the underlying factual material herein through one or more of the following: unique and original selection, coordination, expression, arrangement, and classification of information. All rights to this publication will be vigorously defended.

© 2000 Gale Group
27500 Drake Rd.
Farmington Hills, MI 48331-3535

Gale Group and Design is a trademark used herein under license.

All rights reserved including the right of reproduction in whole or in part in any form.

∞™ This book is printed on acid-free paper that meets the minimum requirements of American National Standard for Information Sciences—Permanence Paper for Printed Library Materials, ANSI Z39.48-1984.

ISBN 0-7876-4083-2
ISSN 1094-9232
Printed in the United States of America

10 9 8 7 6 5 4 3 2 1

Table of Contents

GUEST FOREWORD
   "The Study of Drama"
   by Carole L. Hamilton ix

INTRODUCTION xi

LITERARY CHRONOLOGY xv

ACKNOWLEDGMENTS xvii

CONTRIBUTORS xxi

ANTIGONE
   by Jean Anouilh 1

THE CHAIRS
   by Eugène Ionesco 28

THE ELEPHANT MAN
   by Bernard Pomerance 41

THE FRONT PAGE
   by Ben Hecht and Charles MacArthur . 83

FUNNYHOUSE OF A NEGRO
   by Adrienne Kennedy 104

THE GHOST SONATA
   by August Strindberg 127

THE GOOD PERSON OF SZECHWAN
   by Bertolt Brecht 169

HOT L BALTIMORE
   by Landord Wilson 196

LADY WINDERMERE'S FAN
    by Oscar Wilde 211

THE LOWER DEPTHS
    by Maxim Gorki 230

MOURNING BECOMES ELECTRA
    by Eugene O'Neill 253

THE PHILADELPHIA STORY
    by Philip Barry 292

RIGHT YOU ARE, IF YOU THINK YOU ARE
    by Luigi Pirandello 309

SERJEANT MUSGRAVE'S DANCE
    by John Arden 330

GLOSSARY OF LITERARY TERMS 355
CUMULATIVE AUTHOR/TITLE INDEX . 389
NATIONALITY/ETHNICITY INDEX . . . 393
SUBJECT/THEME INDEX 397

The Study of Drama

We study drama in order to learn what meaning others have made of life, to comprehend what it takes to produce a work of art, and to glean some understanding of ourselves. Drama produces in a separate, aesthetic world, a moment of being for the audience to experience, while maintaining the detachment of a reflective observer.

Drama is a representational art, a visible and audible narrative presenting virtual, fictional characters within a virtual, fictional universe. Dramatic realizations may pretend to approximate reality or else stubbornly defy, distort, and deform reality into an artistic statement. From this separate universe that is obviously not "real life" we expect a valid reflection upon reality, yet drama never is mistaken for reality—the methods of theater are integral to its form and meaning. Theater is art, and art's appeal lies in its ability both to approximate life and to depart from it. By presenting its distorted version of life to our consciousness, art gives us a new perspective and appreciation of reality. Although, to some extent, all aesthetic experiences perform this service, theater does it most effectively by creating a separate, cohesive universe that freely acknowledges its status as an art form.

And what is the purpose of the aesthetic universe of drama? The potential answers to such a question are nearly as many and varied as there are plays written, performed, and enjoyed. Dramatic texts can be problems posed, answers asserted, or moments portrayed. Dramas (tragedies as well as comedies) may serve strictly "to ease the anguish of a torturing hour" (as stated in William Shakespeare's *A Midsummer Night's Dream*)—to divert and entertain—or aspire to move the viewer to action with social issues. Whether to entertain or to instruct, affirm or influence, pacify or shock, dramatic art wraps us in the spell of its imaginary world for the length of the work and then dispenses us back to the real world, entertained, purged, as Aristotle said, of pity and fear, and edified—or at least weary enough to sleep peacefully.

It is commonly thought that theater, being an art of performance, must be experienced—that is, seen—in order to be appreciated fully. However, to view a production of a dramatic text is to be limited to a single interpretation of that text—all other interpretations are for the moment closed off, inaccessible. In the process of producing a play, the director, stage designer, and performers interpret and transform the script into a work of art that always departs in some measure from the author's original conception. Novelist and critic Umberto Eco, in his *The Role of the Reader: Explorations in the Semiotics of Texts,* explained, "In short, we can say that every performance offers us a complete and satisfying version of the work, but at the same time makes it incomplete for us, because it cannot simultaneously give all the other artistic solutions which the work may admit."

Thus Laurence Olivier's coldly formal and neurotic film presentation of Shakespeare's *Hamlet* (in which he played the title character as well as directed) shows marked differences from subsequent adaptations. While Olivier's Hamlet is clearly entangled in a Freudian relationship with his mother, Gertrude, he would be incapable of shushing her with the impassioned kiss that Mel Gibson's mercurial Hamlet (in director Franco Zeffirelli's 1990 film) does. Although each of the performances rings true to Shakespeare's text, each is also a mutually exclusive work of art. Also important to consider are the time periods in which each of these films were produced: Olivier made his film in 1948, a time in which overt references to sexuality (especially incest) were frowned upon. Gibson and Zeffirelli made their film in a culture more relaxed and comfortable with these issues. Just as actors and directors can influence the presentation of drama, so too can the time period of the production affect what the audience will see.

A play script is an open text from which an infinity of specific realizations may be derived. Dramatic scripts that are more open to interpretive creativity (such as those of Ntozake Shange and Tomson Highway) actually require the creative improvisation of the production troupe in order to complete the text. Even the most prescriptive scripts (those of Neil Simon, Lillian Hellman, and Robert Bolt, for example), can never fully control the actualization of live performance, and circumstantial events, including the attitude and receptivity of the audience, make every performance a unique event. Thus, while it is important to view a production of a dramatic piece, if one wants to understand a drama fully it is equally important to read the original dramatic text.

The reader of a dramatic text or script is not limited by either the specific interpretation of a given production or by the unstoppable action of a moving spectacle. The reader of a dramatic text may discover the nuances of the play's language, structure, and events at their own pace. Yet studied alone, the author's blueprint for artistic production does not tell the whole story of a play's life and significance. One also needs to assess the play's critical reviews to discover how it resonated to cultural themes at the time of its debut and how the shifting tides of cultural interest have revised its interpretation and impact on audiences. And to do this, one needs to know a little about the culture of the times which produced the play as well as the author who penned it.

Drama for Students supplies this material in a useful compendium for the student of dramatic theater. Covering a range of dramatic works that span from the fifth century B.C. to the 1990s, this book focuses on significant theatrical works whose themes and form transcend the uncertainty of dramatic fads. These are plays that have proven to be both memorable and teachable. *Drama for Students* seeks to enhance appreciation of these dramatic texts by providing scholarly materials written with the secondary and college/university student in mind. It provides for each play a concise summary of the plot and characters as well as a detailed explanation of its themes and techniques. In addition, background material on the historical context of the play, its critical reception, and the author's life help the student to understand the work's position in the chronicle of dramatic history. For each play entry a new work of scholarly criticism is also included, as well as segments of other significant critical works for handy reference. A thorough bibliography provides a starting point for further research.

These inaugural two volumes offer comprehensive educational resources for students of drama. *Drama for Students* is a vital book for dramatic interpretation and a valuable addition to any reference library.

Source: Eco, Umberto, *The Role of the Reader: Explorations in the Semiotics of Texts,* Indiana University Press, 1979.

Introduction

Purpose of Drama for Students

The purpose of *Drama for Students* (*DfS*) is to provide readers with a guide to understanding, enjoying, and studying dramas by giving them easy access to information about the work. Part of Gale's "For Students" literature line, *DfS* is specifically designed to meet the curricular needs of high school and undergraduate college students and their teachers, as well as the interests of general readers and researchers considering specific plays. While each volume contains entries on "classic" dramas frequently studied in classrooms, there are also entries containing hard-to-find information on contemporary plays, including works by multicultural, international, and women playwrights.

The information covered in each entry includes an introduction to the play and the work's author; a plot summary, to help readers unravel and understand the events in a drama; descriptions of important characters, including explanation of a given character's role in the drama as well as discussion about that character's relationship to other characters in the play; analysis of important themes in the drama; and an explanation of important literary techniques and movements as they are demonstrated in the play.

In addition to this material, which helps the readers analyze the play itself, students are also provided with important information on the literary and historical background informing each work.

This includes a historical context essay, a box comparing the time or place the drama was written to modern Western culture, a critical overview essay, and excerpts from critical essays on the play. A unique feature of *DfS* is a specially commissioned overview essay on each drama by an academic expert, targeted toward the student reader.

To further aid the student in studying and enjoying each play, information on media adaptations is provided, as well as reading suggestions for works of fiction and nonfiction on similar themes and topics. Classroom aids include ideas for research papers and lists of critical sources that provide additional material on each drama.

Selection Criteria

The titles for each volume of *DfS* were selected by surveying numerous sources on teaching literature and analyzing course curricula for various school districts. Some of the sources surveyed included: literature anthologies; *Reading Lists for College-Bound Students: The Books Most Recommended by America's Top Colleges;* textbooks on teaching dramas; a College Board survey of plays commonly studied in high schools; a National Council of Teachers of English (NCTE) survey of plays commonly studied in high schools; St. James Press's *International Dictionary of Theatre;* and Arthur Applebee's 1993 study *Literature in the Secondary School: Studies of Curriculum and Instruction in the United States.*

Input was also solicited from our expert advisory board (both experienced educators specializing in English), as well as educators from various areas. From these discussions, it was determined that each volume should have a mix of "classic" dramas (those works commonly taught in literature classes) and contemporary dramas for which information is often hard to find. Because of the interest in expanding the canon of literature, an emphasis was also placed on including works by international, multicultural, and women playwrights. Our advisory board members—current high school teachers—helped pare down the list for each volume. If a work was not selected for the present volume, it was often noted as a possibility for a future volume. As always, the editor welcomes suggestions for titles to be included in future volumes.

How Each Entry Is Organized

Each entry, or chapter, in *DfS* focuses on one play. Each entry heading lists the full name of the play, the author's name, and the date of the play's first production or publication. The following elements are contained in each entry:

- **Introduction:** a brief overview of the drama which provides information about its first appearance, its literary standing, any controversies surrounding the work, and major conflicts or themes within the work.

- **Author Biography:** this section includes basic facts about the author's life, and focuses on events and times in the author's life that inspired the drama in question.

- **Plot Summary:** a description of the major events in the play, with interpretation of how these events help articulate the play's themes. Subheads demarcate the plays' various acts or scenes.

- **Characters:** an alphabetical listing of major characters in the play. Each character name is followed by a brief to an extensive description of the character's role in the plays, as well as discussion of the character's actions, relationships, and possible motivation.

Characters are listed alphabetically by last name. If a character is unnamed—for instance, the Stage Manager in *Our Town*—the character is listed as "The Stage Manager" and alphabetized as "Stage Manager." If a character's first name is the only one given, the name will appear alphabetically by the name.

Variant names are also included for each character. Thus, the nickname "Babe" would head the listing for a character in *Crimes of the Heart,* but below that listing would be her less-mentioned married name "Rebecca Botrelle."

- **Themes:** a thorough overview of how the major topics, themes, and issues are addressed within the play. Each theme discussed appears in a separate subhead, and is easily accessed through the boldface entries in the Subject/Theme Index.

- **Style:** this section addresses important style elements of the drama, such as setting, point of view, and narration; important literary devices used, such as imagery, foreshadowing, symbolism; and, if applicable, genres to which the work might have belonged, such as Gothicism or Romanticism. Literary terms are explained within the entry, but can also be found in the Glossary.

- **Historical and Cultural Context:** This section outlines the social, political, and cultural climate *in which the author lived and the play was created.* This section may include descriptions of related historical events, pertinent aspects of daily life in the culture, and the artistic and literary sensibilities of the time in which the work was written. If the play is a historical work, information regarding the time in which the play is set is also included. Each section is broken down with helpful subheads.

- **Critical Overview:** this section provides background on the critical reputation of the play, including bannings or any other public controversies surrounding the work. For older plays, this section includes a history of how the drama was first received and how perceptions of it may have changed over the years; for more recent plays, direct quotes from early reviews may also be included.

- **For Further Study:** an alphabetical list of other critical sources which may prove useful for the student. Includes full bibliographical information and a brief annotation.

- **Sources:** an alphabetical list of critical material quoted in the entry, with full bibliographical information.

- **Criticism:** an essay commissioned by *DfS* which specifically deals with the play and is written specifically for the student audience, as well as excerpts from previously published criticism on the work.

In addition, each entry contains the following highlighted sections, set separate from the main text:

- **Media Adaptations:** a list of important film and television adaptations of the play, including source information. The list may also include such variations on the work as audio recordings, musical adaptations, and other stage interpretations.

- **Compare and Contrast Box:** an "at-a-glance" comparison of the cultural and historical differences between the author's time and culture and late twentieth-century Western culture. This box includes pertinent parallels between the major scientific, political, and cultural movements of the time or place the drama was written, the time or place the play was set (if a historical work), and modern Western culture. Works written after the mid-1970s may not have this box.

- **What Do I Read Next?:** a list of works that might complement the featured play or serve as a contrast to it. This includes works by the same author and others, works of fiction and nonfiction, and works from various genres, cultures, and eras.

- **Study Questions:** a list of potential study questions or research topics dealing with the play. This section includes questions related to other disciplines the student may be studying, such as American history, world history, science, math, government, business, geography, economics, psychology, etc.

Other Features

DfS includes "The Study of Drama," a foreword by Carole Hamilton, an educator and author who specializes in dramatic works. This essay examines the basis for drama in societies and what drives people to study such work. Hamilton also discusses how *Drama for Students* can help teachers show students how to enrich their own reading/viewing experiences.

A Cumulative Author/Title Index lists the authors and titles covered in each volume of the *DfS* series.

A Cumulative Nationality/Ethnicity Index breaks down the authors and titles covered in each volume of the *DfS* series by nationality and ethnicity.

A Subject/Theme Index, specific to each volume, provides easy reference for users who may be studying a particular subject or theme rather than a single work. Significant subjects from events to broad themes are included, and the entries pointing to the specific theme discussions in each entry are indicated in **boldface.**

Each entry has several illustrations, including photos of the author, stills from stage productions, and stills from film adaptations.

Citing *Drama for Students*

When writing papers, students who quote directly from any volume of *Drama for Students* may use the following general forms. These examples are based on MLA style; teachers may request that students adhere to a different style, so the following examples may be adapted as needed.

When citing text from *DfS* that is not attributed to a particular author (i.e., the Themes, Style, Historical Context sections, etc.), the following format should be used in the bibliography section:

"Our Town," *Drama for Students*. Ed. David Galens and Lynn Spampinato. Vol. 1. Farmington Hills: Gale, 1997. 8–9.

When quoting the specially commissioned essay from *DfS* (usually the first piece under the "Criticism" subhead), the following format should be used:

Fiero, John. Essay on "Twilight: Los Angeles, 1992." *Drama for Students*. Ed. David Galens and Lynn Spampinato. Vol. 1. Farmington Hills: Gale, 1997. 8–9.

When quoting a journal or newspaper essay that is reprinted in a volume of *DfS*, the following form may be used:

Rich, Frank. "Theatre: A Mamet Play, 'Glengarry Glen Ross'." *New York Theatre Critics' Review* Vol. 45, No. 4 (March 5, 1984), 5–7; excerpted and reprinted in *Drama for Students,* Vol. 1, ed. David Galens and Lynn Spampinato (Farmington Hills: Gale, 1997), pp. 61–64.

When quoting material reprinted from a book that appears in a volume of *DfS,* the following form may be used:

Kerr, Walter. "The Miracle Worker," in *The Theatre in Spite of Itself* (Simon & Schuster, 1963, 255–57; excerpted and reprinted in *Drama for Students,* Vol. 1, ed. Dave Galens and Lynn Spampinato (Farmington Hills: Gale, 1997), pp. 59–61.

We Welcome Your Suggestions

The editor of *Drama for Students* welcomes your comments and ideas. Readers who wish to suggest dramas to appear in future volumes, or who have other suggestions, are cordially invited to contact the editor. You may contact the editor via

E-mail at: **mark.milne@galegroup.com.** Or write to the editor at:

> Editor, *Drama for Students*
> The Gale Group
> 27500 Drake Rd.
> Farmington Hills, MI 48331-3535

Literary Chronology

1849: August Strindberg is born in Stockholm on January 22.

1854: Oscar Wilde is born to affluent parents in Dublin, Ireland.

1867: Luigi Pirandello is born to affluent parents in a small provincial town in Sicily.

1868: Maxim Gorki was born Alexei Maximovich Peshkov in Nizhy Novgorod, Russia, on March 16.

1888: Eugene O'Neill is born in New York City to a theatrical family.

1892: Oscar Wilde's *Lady Windermere's Fan*, his first produced play, becomes an instant success on the London stage.

1894: Ben Hecht is born on February 28 in New York City, to Joseph and Sarah Hecht.

1896: Philip Barry is born on June 18 in Rochester, New York, to a wealthy Irish-Catholic family.

1898: Bertolt Brecht is born on February 10 in Augsburg, Bavaria, Germany.

1900: Oscar Wilde dies from cerebral meningitis and is buried in Paris.

1902: Maxim Gorki's *The Lower Depths* is produced by the Moscow Arts Theatre on December 18. Konstantin Stanislavsky directs the play and stars in it as Sahtin.

1908: August Strindberg's *The Ghost Sonata* is originally staged at the Intimate Theatre, his 161-seat theatre, which opened its doors in Sweden in 1907.

1910: Jean Anouilh is born in a small town near Bordeaux, France.

1912: Eugene Ionesco is born on November 26, 1912, in Slatina, Romania.

1912: August Strindberg dies of stomach cancer on May 14 at the age of 63.

1917: Luigi Pirandello's *Right You Are, If You Think You Are* is produced.

1928: *The Front Page*, written by Ben Hecht and Charles MacArthur, premieres in Broadway's Times Square Theatre on August 14, and it runs for 276 performances.

1930: John Arden is born in Barnsley, Yorkshire, England, on October 26 to Charles Alwyn Arden, a glass factory manager, and Annie Elizabeth (nee Layland), a schoolteacher.

1931: Adrienne Kennedy is born (maiden name Adrienne Hawkins) on September 13 in Pittsburgh, Pennsylvania.

1931: Eugene O'Neill's *Mourning Becomes Electra* is produced and runs for 150 performances.

1934: Luigi Pirandello receives the Nobel Prize for Literature.

1936: Maxim Gorki dies on June 14 under suspicious circumstances amid speculation that he was assassinated.

1937: Lanford Wilson is born on April 13 in Lebanon, Missouri.

1937: Luigi Pirandello dies of pneumonia.

1939: Philip Barry's *The Philadelphia Story* is produced.

1940: Bernard Pomerance is born in Brooklyn.

1943: Bertolt Brecht's *The Good Person of Szechwan*, worked on as early as the late 1920s, and primarily written from 1939-43 during World War II, makes its debut on February 4 at the Schauspielhaus, Zurich, Switzerland.

1944: Jean Anouilh's *Antigone*, written in 1942, is published. .

1951: Philip Barry dies from a heart attack at the age of fifty-five.

1952: Eugene Ionesco's *The Chairs* is first performed in Paris on April 22—only the third of Ionesco's plays to be produced.

1953: Eugene O'Neill dies. It takes the posthumous revival of *Long Day's Journey into Night* in 1956 to reestablish his esteemed position in the American theater.

1956: Ben Hecht dies of an internal hemorrhage on April 21.

1956: Bertolt Brecht dies as a result of a coronary thrombosis on August 14 in East Berlin.

1959: John Arden's *Serjeant Musgrave's Dance* is produced. Its initial British run at the Royal Court Theatre lasts for only twenty-eight performances.

1964: Adrienne Kennedy's *Funnyhouse of a Negro* makes its debut on January 14 at the East End Theater in New York City—Kennedy's first produced play.

1973: Lanford Wilson's *Hot L Baltimore* opens in February, becoming the first major success for Wilson and his theater company, the Circle Repertory Company. Wilson's play set an Off-Broadway record of 1,166 performances after playing Off-Off-Broadway for a month. Wilson is awarded the New York Drama Critics' Circle award for his play.

1979: Bernard Pomerance's *The Elephant Man* is first produced in London at the Hampstead Theatre. It soon moved to New York and opened Off-Broadway at the Theatre of St. Peter's Church, and then to Broadway and the Booth Theatre. Pomerance's play earned good reviews and a number of awards, including a Tony Award, the New York Drama Critics award, the Drama Desk Award, and the Obie Award.

1980: Lanford Wilson wins the Pulitzer Prize for Drama.

1987: Jean Anouilh dies of a heart attack.

1994: Eugene Ionesco dies in his Paris home on March 28, 1994.

Acknowledgments

The editors wish to thank the copyright holders of the excerpted criticism included in this volume and the permissions managers of many book and magazine publishing companies for assisting us in securing reproduction rights. We are also grateful to the staffs of the Detroit Public Library, the Library of Congress, the University of Detroit Mercy Library, Wayne State University Purdy Kresge Library Complex, and the University of Michigan Libraries for making their resources available to us. Following is a list of the copyright holders who have granted us permission to reproduce material in this volume of *Drama for Students (DfS)*. Every effort has been made to trace copyright, but if omissions have been made, please let us know.

COPYRIGHTED MATERIALS IN *DfS*, VOLUME 9, WERE REPRODUCED FROM THE FOLLOWING PERIODICALS:

America, v. 140, February 24, 1979. (c) America Press 1979. All rights reserved. Reproduced with permission of America Press, Inc.,106 West 56th Street, New York, NY 10019.—*American Literature,* v. 38, 1966. Copyright (c) 1966 Duke University Press, Durham, NC. Reproduced by permission.—*Cahiers Elisabethains,* v. 17, 1980 for ''Shakespearian Reminiscences in Serjeant Musgrave's Dance,'' by Fernand Lagarde. All rights reserved. Reproduced by permission of the publisher and the authors.—*English Studies in Africa,* v. 6, March, 1963. (c) Witwatersrand University Press 1963. Reproduced by permission of the publisher and the author.—*The Eugene O'Neill Newsletter,* v. 6, Summer-Fall, 1982; v. 11, Summer-Fall, 1987. Reproduced by permission.—*The Explicator,* v. XXII, February, 1964, v. XXIV, April, 1966, v. 46, Summer, 1988, v. 54, Fall, 1995., v. 56, Spring, 1998. Copyright 1964, 1966, 1988,1995, 1998 by Helen Dwight Reid Educational Foundation. Reproduced with permission of the Helen Dwight Reid Educational Foundation, published by Heldref Publications, 1319 18th Street, NW, Washington, DC 20036-1802.—*Forum,* v. XXVII, Winter, 1986. (c) 1986 Ball State University. Reproduced by permission.—*The French Review,* v. 41, 1967. Copyright 1967 by the American Association of Teachers of French. Reproduced by permission.—*Literature/Film Quarterly,* v. 13, 1985. (c) copyright 1985 Salisbury State College. Reproduced by permission.—*Modern Chinese Literature,* v. 7, Fall, 1993. Reproduced by permission of Kirk Denton.—*Modern Drama,* v. 10, 1967, v. 14, February, 1972, v. 16, 1973, v. 26, March, 1983, v. 26, September, 1983, v. 40, Fall, 1997. Copyright (c) 1967, 1972, 1973, 1983, 1997 University of Toronto, Graduate Centre for Study of Drama. Reproduced by permission.—*The Nation,* New York, v. 178, May 29, 1954, v. 182, April 21, 1956. (c) 1954, 1956 The Nation magazine/ The Nation Company, Inc. Reproduced by permission.—*Negro American Literature Forum,* v. 9, 1975 for '''For the Characters Are Myself': Adrienne Kennedy's Funnyhouse of a

Negro" by Lorraine A. Brown. Copyright (c) 1975 by the author. Reproduced by permission of the publisher and the author.—*The New Republic,* v. 196, January 5 & 6, 1987. (c) 1987 The New Republic, Inc. Reproduced by permission of The New Republic.—*The New Yorker,* v. 62, December 8, 1986 for "Low Life in Chicago" Brendan Gill. (c) 1986 by The New Yorker Magazine, Inc. All rights reserved. Reproduced by permission of the Literary Estate for Brendan Gill./ v. 74, April 13, 1998 for "Present Absences" by John Lahr. (c) 1998 by The New Yorker Magazine, Inc. All rights reserved. Reproduced by permission of Georges Borchardt, Inc. for the author.—*PMLA,* v. 104, October, 1989. Copyright (c) 1989 by the Modern Language Association of America. Reproduced by permission of the Modern Language Association of America.—*Queen's Quarterly,* v. 78, 1971 for "Serjeant Musgrave's Dance: Form and Meaning" by Barry Thorne. Copyright (c) 1971 by the author. Reproduced by permission of the author.—*Revue Des Langues Vivantes,* v. 4, Summer, 1975 for "Insular Typees: Puritanism and Primitivism in Mourning Becomes Electra" by Ronald T. Curran. Reproduced by permission of the author.—*The Saturday Review,* v. 29, October 26, 1946. (c) 1946 Saturday Review Magazine, (c) 1979 General Media Communications, Inc. Reproduced by permission of Saturday Review Publications, Ltd.—*Scandinavian Studies,* v. 40, August, 1968 for "Strindberg's Biblical Sources for The Ghost Sonata" by Stephen C. Bandy. Reproduced by permission of the publisher and author.—*Theater,* v. 25, 1994. (c) 1994 by Alisa Solomon. Reproduced by permission of Duke University Press.—*World Theatre,* v. XVI, May-June, 1967. Reproduced by permission of Theatre Communications Group, Inc.

COPYRIGHTED MATERIALS IN DfS, VOLUME 9, WERE REPRODUCED FROM THE FOLLOWING BOOKS:

Berry, Jon M. From "Discourse and Scenography in The Ghost Sonata" in *Strindberg's Dramaturgy*. Edited by Goran Stockenstrom. University of Minnesota Press, 1988. Copyright (c) 1988 by the University of Minnesota. Reproduced by permission.—Brown, John Mason. From *Broadway in Review.* W. W. Norton & Company, Inc., 1940. Copyright, 1940, by W. W. Norton & Company, Inc. Reproduced by permission of the Literary Estate of John Mason Brown.—Erlich, Victor. From "Truth and Illusion in Gorky: The Lower Depths and After" in *Freedom and Responsibility in Russian Literature: Essays in Honor of Robert Louis Jackson.* Edited by Elizabeth Cheresh Allen and Gary Saul Morson. Northwestern University Press, 1995. Copyright (c) 1995 by Northwestern University Press. All rights reserved. Reproduced by permission.—Greiff, Louis K. From "Two for the Price of One: Tragedy and the Dual Hero in Equus and The Elephant Man" in *Within the Dramatic Spectrum: The University of Florida Department of Classics Comparative Drama Conference Papers, Volume VI.* Edited by Karelisa V. Hartigan. University Press of America, 1986. Copyright (c) 1986 by University Press of America, Inc. All rights reserved. Reproduced by permission.—Jacobs, Susan Taylor. From "When Formula Seizes Form: Oscar Wilde's Comedies" in *Staging the Impossible: The Fantastic Mode in Modern Drama.* Edited by Patrick D. Murphy. Greenwood Press, 1992. Copyright (c) 1992 by Patrick D. Murphy. Reproduced by permission of Greenwood Publishing Group, Inc., Westport, CT.—Meigs, Susan E. From "No Place but the Funnyhouse: The Struggle for Identity in Three Adrienne Kennedy Plays" in *Modern American Drama: The Female Canon.* Edited by June Schlueter. Fairleigh Dickinson University Press, 1990. Copyright (c) 1990 by Associated University Presses, Inc. Reproduced by permission.

PHOTOGRAPHS AND ILLUSTRATIONS APPEARING IN DFS, VOLUME 9, WERE RECEIVED FROM THE FOLLOWING SOURCES:

Anouilh, Jean, 1971, photograph. AP/Wide World Photos. Reproduced by permission.—Arden, John, photograph, (c) Jerry Bauer. Reproduced by permission.—Bos, Sanneke in "The Lower Depts," photograph. (c) Donald Cooper/PHOTOSTAGE. Reproduced by permission.—Brecht, Bertolt, photograph. Archive Photos, Inc. Reproduced by permission.—Briers, Richard as the Old Man and Geraldine Miewan as the Old Woman in "The Chairs," (c) Donald Cooper/Photostage. Reproduced by permission.—Cukor, George, directing "The Philadelphia Story", with John Howard as George Kittredge, Katharine Hepburn as Tracy Lord, Cary Grant as C. K. Dexter Haven, Cukor is giving the actors a "What for" speech as he explains the action of a scene, 1940, photograph by James Stewart. M-G-M. The Kobal Collection. Reproduced by permission.—Finney, Albert in "Serjeant Musgrave's Dance," photograph. (c) Donald Cooper/PHOTOSTAGE. Reproduced by permission.—Gorky, Maxim, photograph. The Library of Congress.—Hecht, Ben, photograph. The Library of

Congress.— Hurt, John in film "The Elephant Man" (standing alone on a ship deck), photograph. Paramount Pictures/Archive Photos. Reproduced by permission.—Hurt, John in film "The Elephant Man" (standing by a mantle, looking at framed photographs), Paramount Pictures/Archive Photos. Reproduced by permission.—Ionesco, Eugene, photograph. The Library of Congress.—Johnson, Rebecca in "Lady Windermere's Fan," photograph. (c) Donald Cooper/PHOTOSTAGE. Reproduced by permission.—Lemmon, Jack (with Walter Matthau and unidentified actor) in the film "The Front Page", photograph. Universal Studios/Archive Photos. Reproduced by permission.—O'Neill, Eugene G., photograph. The Library of Congress.—Pirandello, Luigi, photograph. AP/Wide World Photos. Reproduced by permission.—Playbill for "Funnyhouse of a Negro." PLAYBILL® is a registered trademark of Playbill Incorporated, N.Y.C. All rights reserved. Reproduced by permission.—Playbill for "Right You Are." PLAYBILL® is a registered trademark of Playbill Incorporated, N.Y.C. All rights reserved. Reproduced by permission.—Playbill for the 1946 production of "Antigone." PLAYBILL® is a registered trademark of Playbill Incorporated, N.Y.C. All rights reserved. Reproduced by permission.—Playbill cover for "Mourning Becomes Electra." PLAYBILL® is a registered trademark of Playbill Incorporated, N.Y.C. All rights reserved. Reproduced by permission.—Stuart, Bill as the husband and Fiona Shaw as Shen Te in "The Good Person (Woman) of Szechuan," photograph. (c) Donald Cooper/PHOTOSTAGE. Reproduced by permission.—Wilde, Oscar, photograph. The Library of Congress.—Willis, Jerome and Linda Marlowe in "The Ghost Sonata," , photograph. (c) Donald Cooper/PHOTOSTAGE. Reproduced by permission. Wilson, Lanford, photograph. AP/Wide World Photos. Reproduced by permission.

Contributors

Liz Brent: Ph.D. in American Culture, specializing in cinema studies, from the University of Michigan; freelance writer and teacher of courses in American cinema. Original essay on *The Hot L Baltimore*.

Clare Cross: Doctoral candidate, University of Michigan, Ann Arbor. Original essay on *The Good Person of Szechwan*.

Lane A. Glenn: Author, educator, director, and actor, Lansing, Michigan. Entry on *The Ghost Sonata*. Original essay on *The Ghost Sonata*.

Carole Hamilton: Freelance writer and instructor at Cary Academy, Cary, North Carolina. Entries on *Antigone*, *Lady Windermere's Fan*, and *Right You Are, If You Think You Are*. Original essays on *Antigone*, *Lady Windermere's Fan*, and *Right You Are, If You Think You Are*

Helena Ifeka: Doctoral candidate, Columbia University, and freelance author. Entry on *The Philadelphia Story*. Original essay on *The Philadelphia Story*.

Jennifer Lynch: Teaches at the Potrero Hill After School Program and the Taos Literacy Program; also contributes to *Geronimo*, a journal of politics and culture. Entry on *The Lower Depths*. Original essay on *The Lower Depths*.

Sheri Metzger: Freelance writer and Ph.D., Albuquerque, NM. Entries on *The Elephant Man*, and *The Hot L Baltimore*. Original essays on *The Elephant Man* and *The Hot L Baltimore*.

Annette Petrusso: Freelance author and screenwriter, Austin, TX. Entries on *The Chairs*, *The Front Page*, *Funnyhouse of a Negro*, *The Good Person of Szechwan*, and *Serjeant Musgrave's Dance*. Original essays on *The Chairs*, *The Front Page*, *Funnyhouse of a Negro*, *The Good Person of Szechwan*, *Right You Are, If You Think You Are*, and *Serjeant Musgrave's Dance*.

Arnold Schmidt: Professor of English, California State University, Stanislaus. Entry on *Mourning Becomes Electra*. Original essay on *Mourning Becomes Electra*.

Antigone

JEAN ANOUILH

1944

Jean Anouilh's *Antigone* is an adaptation of Sophocles' tragic play of the same title. Written in 1942, when Nazi forces occupied France, the story revolves around the conflict between the idealist Antigone and her rigid uncle, Creon, over the proper burial of Antigone's brother, Polynices. The play was also interpreted to represent the struggle of the French Resistance movement against the forces of the Vichy government during the height of Nazi occupation.

Antigone is one in a series of Anouilh's plays based on Greek mythology. Disillusioned and shocked by the events of World War II, he also wrote *Eurydice* (1942) and *Médée* (first performed in 1937; published 1946), which were also adapted versions of the original Greek classics. These plays explored the role of destiny in people's lives.

Often considered his masterpiece, *Antigone* cemented Anouilh's reputation as a dramatist. The play was an instant success when it was first staged in Paris in 1944.

AUTHOR BIOGRAPHY

Born in a small town near Bordeaux, France, in 1910, Jean Anouilh was raised in a middle-class family. As a young man, his family moved to Paris, where Jean attended secondary school and law

school. He abandoned law, however, for a brief career in advertising. In 1931 he worked as a secretary to the actor, director, and producer Louis Jouvet. This experience inspired him to begin writing his own plays.

Anouilh served briefly in World War II; by the end of the war, however, he returned to Paris, disillusioned and distraught over the Nazi occupation of France. His work during this period, such as his well-known work, *Antigone,* was a thinly-veiled attack against all French people that collaborated with the Germans.

His work is divided roughly into two categories: his early, dark plays that explore hypocrisy and evil; and the later lighthearted work that incorporates elements of humor or fantasy.

Anouilh's work has not enjoyed wide popularity in the United States. Critics often disparage his plays as overly verbose and too intellectual; however, in his native France, he has been called "the most distinguished playwright in France, the most literate, the most interesting, the most controversial." He died of a heart attack in 1987.

PLOT SUMMARY

Prologue
At the play opens, the chorus offers brief introductions to the play's main characters: the beautiful Ismene; her sister Antigone; Antigone's lover and cousin Haemon; and Ismene's uncle and Haemon's father, Creon.

The chorus also chronicles the fight between Antigone's brothers, Eteocles and Polynices—a momentous battle that occurred before the play's opening—over control of the region of Thebes. After the brothers killed each other, Creon assumed control of the throne. To restore order, he has ordered a grand funeral for one brother, Eteocles. Considered a treasonous rebel for challenging his brother's rule, Polynices is left to rot as a warning to other rebels.

Antigone and Her Nurse
The nurse discovers Antigone sneaking back into the house at four in the morning. When confronted, Antigone merely reveals that she has had a rendezvous. Ismene enters and debates with Antigone the wisdom of going against Creon's edict to bury Polynices. Out of fear, Ismene sides with convention and tries to convince her idealistic, determined sister to give up her quest to bury their brother properly. The penalty of violating Creon's edict will be death.

Ismene does not realize that Antigone has just returned from burying Polynices' corpse—the deed is already done. They are interrupted by the arrival of Haemon.

Antigone and Haemon
Antigone apologizes to Haemon for a recent spat, then tells him that she will "never, never be able to marry" him. Shocked, Haemon exits.

Ismene enters and reminds her sister that Polynices "was a bad brother" who "was like an enemy in the house." She insists that this is Creon's affair and not theirs; in this way Ismene frames the central conflict from one between allegiance to the state versus allegiance to family, and it shifts Antigone's motivation from a sense of duty to a sense of self-fulfillment. Antigone announces to Ismene that her warnings are too late: she has already buried Polynices. Antigone exits, and Ismene follows.

Arrest of Antigone
Creon is informed by one of his guards that Polynices' corpse has been ritually buried against his orders. No one saw who did it—the only evidence is a child's shovel that was left behind. Realizing the damage this act of defiance will do to his authority, Creon orders his guards to exhume the corpse and to keep the secret on pain of death.

Chorus Interlude
The chorus explains the concept of tragedy.

Arrest of Antigone
After reburying her brother in broad daylight, Antigone is caught and dragged before Creon. The guards fail to recognize her because they are too busy figuring out ways to avoid blame and gain reward. Their buffoonery offers comic relief to offset the tragedy of Antigone's situation.

Antigone and Creon
Creon is shocked to learn that Antigone was the one who disobeyed him. He tries to convince her to renounce her actions, reminding her of the hollowness of religious ritual and the fact that is within her self-interest to go along with him. Antigone rebuffs him and announces that she is ready to die for her transgressions.

Creon urges her to marry Haemon and enjoy her life, for "Life is nothing more than the happiness you get out of it." When she fails to respond to his entreaties, he becomes morose. When Ismene joins them, Antigone taunts Creon. Creon decides not to execute her outright, but to confine her to a cave for the rest of her life.

Creon explains to the Chorus that "death was her purpose," that "Polynices was a mere pretext." When Haemon enters, Creon pleads with him to forget Antigone, explaining that he has tried everything and failed to "condemn her to life." Haemon begs his father to stop the guards from dragging her away, but Creon explains that the mob will not be stopped.

Antigone's Death

Antigone dictates a letter to Haemon. She is taken away. A messenger appears to tell of Antigone's death: it seems that as she was being closed in the cave, a man's moan was heard. In a panic, Creon tears the rocks away with his own fingers, only to find Antigone hung by the cord of her robe and Haemon hanging onto her dead body. Creon begs Haemon to rise, but his son strikes at him, then stabs himself.

Epilogue

In mourning for his niece and his son, Creon is informed by the Chorus that his wife Eurydice has just killed herself. Now alone, Creon anticipates his next task, a cabinet meeting at five o'clock. He and the page exit. The Chorus describes a "great melancholy wave of peace" that descends over Thebes, with the exception of the guards, who simply go on playing cards.

CHARACTERS

Antigone

Antigone, the protagonist, is driven by her fate, compelled even before the play begins, to act out her part till the end. Thus she is really two characters: an actress playing a role, and Antigone, the character she plays. This duality, however, disappears as the events of the play proceed, and it is with the thin and unbeautiful girl that the audience identifies. Antigone is a child-woman, too young, too thin for adulthood, yet too hard-headed to be treated as a child. She repeatedly proclaims that she is far too young for an early death, and the other characters

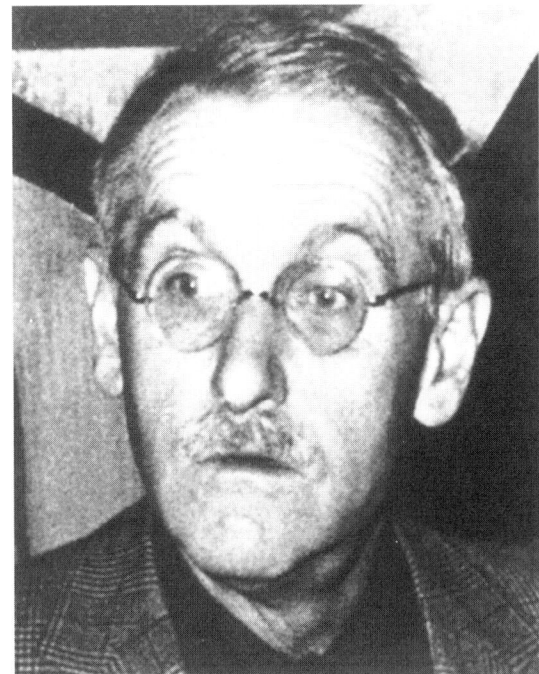

Jean Anouilh

frequently remark on her youth or her thinness, a characteristic of an undeveloped woman. Her childlike qualities also appear in her clumsy attempt at rivaling her sister Ismene's beauty and sophistication by wearing makeup and a dress, and in her use of a child's toy shovel to bury her brother. Antigone stands for the idealism of youth, which cannot survive in a corrupt world. Survival in such a world demands compromising one's values. She is a woman in the sense of her firm stand against the world, and in her integrity. Like her father Oedipus, she pursues truth to the end, no matter the consequence. She carries her integrity to the point of breaking off her engagement to Hamon, to save him from pain. Unfortunately, she cannot save him from pain, since he refuses to return to the world of the living as she dictates. Antigone is such a purist that she refuses her sister's assistance in burying their brother, because Ismene expresses a desire to abide by the law. When Ismene later tries to join her in condemnation, having committed no crime at all, Antigone refuses to accept her companionship. Antigone is too much of an idealist to function in the world. Her foil is Creon, a paragon of such compromise. They debate over what Antigone should do with her life-Creon prescribes getting fatter and producing children with Hamon, which Antigone disdains-in the pivotal scene of the play. In fact, Antigone's role is

MEDIA ADAPTATIONS

- A recording of Jean Anouilh reading *Antigone* was produced by *La Voix de l'Auteur*. There is also a tape of a 1965 Cleveland Touring Company production of the play.

so central to this play that every other character's moral fiber has to be considered in relation to hers, the standard or ideal. Ultimately, she stands for personal integrity as opposed to the expediency of personal compromise, such as those Creon makes in his efforts to maintain the state. Against Creon's compromises, Antigone emphatically states that it is her role to "say no and to die." In her idealistic sacrifice Antigone became a heroic figure in occupied France, providing inspiration to the resistance movement as it fought against the German occupiers.

Choir/Chorus

The Choir includes the Prologue, who initially introduces the characters as players in a play, thus deflating the illusion of theater because the ending is revealed from the first. The Chorus represents the "character" of the playwright, perhaps Jean Anouilh himself. The Prologue explains that Antigone is forced to play her role "till the end." This statement suggests that the characters, just as real persons, cannot escape themselves, even within the made up world of the theater, the world of fantasy and assumed identities. The Chorus appears in the beginning and end of the play, creating a framework that draws attention to the theatricality of the play. Also, in the middle of the play, the Chorus presents a digression on tragedy, another jolt to those who may succumb to the illusion of reality. In their digression the Chorus defines tragedy as "tranquil," since the end is known and inevitable. Its presence and tone add a sardonic twist to the play's events. When Creon deliberates over what to do with Antigone, and nearly convinces himself that she really wants to die, the Choir calls Creon a fool and reminds him that his niece is only a child. In this role, the choir acts like the traditional Greek chorus, as a group of moraling elders.

Creon

Tired and careworn with the heavy affairs of state, Creon issues an edict against burying Polynices merely as a way of cementing his authority and restoring public order after the war. He hopes by this edict to discourage dissenters from rallying around the warrior, while giving a proper burial to the brother challenging his authority. He does not dream of encountering dissent from Antigone, essentially a family member and fellow ruler, so when he discovers her guilt, he tries to talk her out of repeating "ce geste absurde" of the ritual burial. Her stubborn piety (to her brother instead of to the state) exasperates him. For himself, Creon has chosen the path of saying "yes" to duty, "yes" to the world, "yes" to being king, and thus "yes" to compromise. He can see no other way to rule. In his attempt to convince Antigone not to persist with her burials, he discredits Polynices' character, stripping away her last vestige of faith in fellow humans. In return, she forces him to face his own lost hope, reminding him of the idealistic boy he had once been, before he began his lifetime of compromise. At the end of the play, Creon must continue, now without the illusion of doing good, now he merely does.

Guard

The guard and his two cohorts, the other guards, fail in their vigilance over the dead body of Polynices, and while their attention wanders, Antigone dusts ritual dirt onto her brother's body, completing a ritual burial in defiance of Creon's law. Creon warns the guards that they will be killed if another oversight occurs. Therefore, when the guard catches Antigone and brings her to Creon, he cares nothing for her, but rather feels relieved at having redeemed himself. He and the other guards look no further than their own skins. The arresting guard is thirty-nine, with two children—an average family man. He has seventeen years of service and wants nothing to stand in the way of his promotion, due in June. Thus, it takes some convincing from Antigone to bribe him (with a ring) to write a final letter to Hamon, which he botches so badly that Antigone realizes the futility of any final words. At the end of the play, the guards simply go on playing cards, immune to the tragedy around them, because their eyes are focused only on their own dim lives.

Hamon

Hamon, son of Creon, loves Antigone, though he had dallied with Ismene before asking Antigone to marry him. Yet, it is Antigone he loves, most truly. He is so loyal and trusting that he at first keeps his promise not to speak after her announcement that they will never marry. When he fails to avert his father from fulfilling the law to punish his fiancee, he chooses to be buried with her in her cave, and when he finds she has hung herself, he plunges his sword into his own chest and dies.

Ismene

Ismene is Antigone's very feminine and beautiful sister, the woman with whom Hamon danced a whole evening the night before he suddenly and unexpectedly proposed to Antigone. Ismene is cautious, a rule-follower who counsels Antigone to leave their brother unburied and to leave to men the job of dying for one's ideas. In this, Ismene disgusts her sister. When Ismene finally wants to join with Antigone and begs to be punished alongside her for the burial of their brother, Antigone scornfully refuses her company.

Messenger

The Messenger's role is revealed at the beginning of the play by the Prologue. He will announce the death of Hamon, and the gravity of his message preoccupies him as he awaits the start of the play. At the end, the Messenger tells a chilling tale of Hamon's agonized death, and then departs.

Nurse

Antigone affectionately calls this simple woman her old, "wrinkled apple." The Nurse loves and remains loyal to Antigone throughout her ordeals, demonstrating Antigone's humanity and her place in a traditional family. The Nurse adds comic relief from an otherwise rather dismal play. She concerns herself with Antigone's rest and meals, completely unaware of and unable to understand the intricacies and import of Antigone's defiance. The Nurse serves to emphasize the sacrifices that must be made for the sake of honor.

The Page

The Page is a young assistant to Creon, someone who accepts Creon as king and never questions his decisions, and who mindlessly keeps track of the king's duties. The Page stays with Creon after the deaths of all of his immediate family. Even though he has ostensibly witnessed all of the events of the play, at the end he tells Creon that he wants to grow up. The Page represents the bureaucratic machine, ever performing the minor duties that keep the regime running, no matter how corrupt, inept, or misguided.

THEMES

Myth

Anouilh was not the only French dramatist to revive classical myths during the early twentieth century. Jean Cocteau and Jean Giraudoux (whose influence Anouilh acknowledged) both adapted Greek drama, especially that of Sophocles, to the modern French stage. They created a heightened atmosphere of theatricality, thus leading a departure from dramatic realism that until then had been the only mode of the theater.

For example, Anouilh's Antigone has the intellectual abilities to challenge Creon on a philosophical level. Creon attempts to save his young niece from self-destruction by revealing that her brother Polynices does not deserve her dedication. By painting a dark picture of one whom she had admired, he only succeeds in strengthening her resolve to leave the world behind. Thus, Anouilh shifts the focus away from Sophocles' contest for loyalty between state and religion to question faith in anything.

The actual myth of Antigone is well known; one must look to the places where Anouilh has refitted and embellished the myth to discover the unique nature of his message.

Antigone was first produced in Paris in 1944, when northern France was under the yoke of Nazism while a puppet Vichy government ruled southern France. Anouilh used the Greek myth as an allegory to level criticism at the growing legion of collaborators. Like these traitors, Creon rationalizes that to keep control, he must stand ready to "shoot into the mob" the first time anyone defies his authority.

Throughout the play Antigone is called "little," and she herself admits that she is "a little young for what I have to go through"—an obvious allegory for the brave members of the French Resistance, who sought, against impossible odds, to undermine the Nazis through small, everyday acts of sabotage and defiance. Anouilh used Sophocles' myth to bypass the censors and provide inspiration for the French Resistance and its supporters.

TOPICS FOR FURTHER STUDY

- How do the characters of Ismene, Creon, and the Page serve as foils for Antigone?

- How do the changes that Anouilh has made to the basic plot of Sophocles's *Antigone* affect its meaning and impact? Write an essay detailing the changes and why you think he made them. Which version is more appealing to you and why?

- Identify lines or events in the play that correspond to events in France between 1940-1944, the period when the play was written and produced.

- Do you agree with the Chorus's assessment of tragedy as "tranquil"? Is this a tragedy without hope? Support your answer with evidence from the play.

Disillusionment

Antigone is comprised of a series of disappointments. Every character is touched by a moment of overwhelming disillusionment: Antigone is crushed to learn the truth about her brothers; Haemon is devastated to realize that true love will not win out after all; Creon recognizes the compromises and personal sacrifices he made to take power, including exiling his own niece.

STYLE

Theatricalism

Through the words of one of his characters, Anouilh explains his theory of theater: "Naturalness and truth in the theater, my dear, are the most unnatural thing in the world. Don't think that it suffices to find the precise tone of real life.... Life is very pretty, but it has no form. The object of art is precisely to give it one, and through all possible artifices to create something that is truer than truth."

In this way Anouilh rejected dramatic naturalism, which seeks to present a realistic representation of life through sparse staging, lighting, costuming, and props. This style of drama is embodied by the work of Henrik Ibsen.

While the characters may speak and act realistically in Anouilh's play, the story is more concerned with their ideas. In an attempt to scrutinize the modern psyche, playwrights rejected realism and concentrated on the themes of the play—staging was meant to underscore those themes. Constant reminders of the theater's artificiality—such as the nurse anachronistically bringing the modern breakfast of coffee, toast, and jam to Antigone—are meant to disturb the viewer and contribute to themes of disillusionment, disenchantment, and hypocrisy as they are echoed in the set.

Allusions to the theatricality of the story occur regularly, as when Creon hisses to Antigone, "You have cast me for the villain in this little play of yours, and yourself for the heroine." These references to play-acting demystify the theater. However, the subtle references to Antigone's youthful innocence suggest a nostalgia for a more romantic, bygone era.

Chorus

For ancient Greek audiences, the chorus provided necessary background information on the story, interpreted the events of the play, sang philosophical odes, and judged the characters' actions. The Greek chorus evolved from a band of men who sang at religious festivals; this band gradually took on more dramatic function as the theater evolved.

Sophocles was an innovator with this dramatic technique. He increased the number of its members (from twelve to fifteen) and had them voice their opinions on the characters' virtues. Anouilh also provides new uses for the chorus by letting them introduce the characters of the play. In addition, he allows the chorus to meditate on the nature of tragedy.

HISTORICAL CONTEXT

France during the Occupation

In 1940, France was demoralized by its quick defeat at the hand of Hitler's *panzer* division, surrender to Germany, and German occupation. While

COMPARE & CONTRAST

- **Ancient Greece:** In the ancient Greece of legendary Thebes, the king has absolute power. Rulers are in constant danger from assassination attempts and coups.

  1940s: France is invaded by Nazi Germany; a puppet government is set up to rule over the French people. A Resistance movement forms to undermine the Nazis and their collaborators.

  Today: France is a stable democracy.

- **Ancient Greece:** Women hold inferior positions in society, remaining in separate quarters in the household. They are expected to follow their father's or husband's rules, and to be spoken of as little as possible. By the latter half of the fifth century, around the time that Sophocles wrote *Antigone,* women are enjoying a period of emancipation and can exercise greater autonomy.

  1940s: Women enter the workplace in great numbers because of the need for labor and the demands of World War II. Although ninety percent of the military and the Resistance fighters are men, women support the war effort and the fight for French freedom through their work.

  Today: Great strides have been made in the struggle for gender equality in business; in many countries, women's roles are still very limited.

Germany ruled the northern half of France, a puppet French government controlled the southern region from Vichy.

Anouilh had served a short term in the French military, then returned to Paris. From there he supported and participated in the French Resistance movement, which consisted of about 200,000 people who manned an underground army. They sabotaged German operations in France and performed espionage in the service of the Allies. First Great Britain and then the United States, under General Eisenhower, supplied and directed them. Underground Resistance forces also assisted in rescuing downed Allied pilots and secretly helped Jews to escape the Nazis.

When the Germans instituted forced labor conscription, the Resistance movement swelled. Rebels resorted to guerrilla tactics to hinder the German forces. Whether or not the actions of the French Resistance significantly deterred the Wehrmacht (German armed forces), its very existence provided a much-needed morale boost for the entire French nation.

In this milieu, *Antigone* proved an invaluable source of communication. Howard Barnes of the New York *Tribune* wrote that "Men of good will, muted to the verge of silence, discovered that a modernization of a Greek tragedy afforded them elliptical communication with their comrades. Sophocles became an honorary member of the French resistance movement. His stern account of a young girl defying a persuasive tyrant must have needled the Wehrmacht no end in its colloquial translation, but the Germans could do nothing about it."

Modern French Theatre

Throughout the latter half of the nineteenth century, European dramatists sought to depict in objective and precise detail the individual in society. Known as realism (depicting life objectively) and naturalism (focusing on the human at the mercy of his social or natural environment), these movements found expression in Henrik Ibsen's work, which were social dramas about everyday people and problems.

In the 1890s, the theater of anti-realism came into being as an outgrowth of and reaction to realism and naturalism. The new movement reached fruition in 1913 in a manifesto by Jacques Copeau entitled "Un essai de rénovation dramatique...," which outlined his concept of absolute simplicity and the necessity for an absence of artifice. Instead, the plays emphasized and explored psychological themes.

Taking this legacy a step further, Jean Cocteau, Jean Giraudoux, Armand Salacrou, Paul Claudel, Jean-Paul Sartre, Albert Camus, and Jean Anouilh dabbled in dramatic surrealism, where theatrical devices deliberately confute dramatic realism and draw attention to the theater's means of staging a play. Throughout the 1940s and 50s, they experimented with self-reflexive devices and carried forth the theatricalism movement, in drama as well as in the new medium of film, evolving their philosophy to the brink of the *theater of the absurd* of Samuel Beckett, Eugène Ionesco, and Jean Genet.

CRITICAL OVERVIEW

Although Anouilh's *Antigone* enjoyed initial success, it has not endured through the years as well as Sophocles' version. First produced in Paris in 1944, the play ran for more than five hundred performances to popular and critical acclaim. The political climate of Paris during those years made for a receptive audience.

That successful initial run of *Antigone* established Anouilh's reputation in France. According to Leonard Pronko, it "served as a rallying point for the disheartened French, who could see their own struggle reflected in the conflict between the uncompromising attitude of Antigone and the expediency of Creon. They identified Antigone with the spirit of Freedom, and Creon with the Vichy government."

Two years later, the play ran on Broadway, but the performance was not well accepted; it closed after only forty-four performances. Critics considered it too intellectual and lacking in emotion.

Walter Kerr of the *Herald Tribune* damned the play with the faint praise, calling it a "reasonably workable play."

Lewis Nichols of the *Times* complained of "unrationalized talk by characters who are not quite living beings," while Howard Barnes of the *Herald Tribune* called it "remote and dramatically inarticulate," although he could see how it succeeded in Vichy France.

Likewise, Louis Kronenberger of the newspaper *PM* maintained that "as an inspirational figure for an occupied Paris she [Antigone] had her value; as a human being she is quite unreal." The pessimism and the wordiness of the play did not appeal to Americans at that time.

Subsequent productions of the play have proved no more successful. Critics agree that much of the play's appeal is found in its allegorical significance to the French people. As such, although Anouilh is a respected playwright worldwide, his most enthusiastic audiences continue to be French. It is in his native country that the play endures and still is celebrated as a relevant work for the contemporary theater.

CRITICISM

Carole Hamilton

Hamilton is an English teacher at Cary Academy, an innovative private school in Cary, North Carolina. In this essay, she explores the device of storytelling in Antigone *as it is used as a medium for communicating social roles.*

Storytelling is a device of narrative drama used to move the plot along, announcing action that takes place offstage, skipping over time, and revealing intrigues. Anouilh makes efficient use of storytelling from the very start, when his chorus-narrator relates the story of Oedipus and his sons, whose deaths brought Creon to the throne. In this case storytelling informs the audience, allowing the action of the play to jump in at the moment of Antigone's act of defiance against Creon's law.

He also uses storytelling as prophecy and warning, inspiration, and persuading. In these cases, storytelling serves to remind the characters—and the audience—of social roles and the social consequences of ways of enacting those roles. This has been the function of storytelling since its age-old inception, a purpose that predates literature, but that lives on in stories told today, orally around the office coffee machine, or written in the newspapers, in the work of Nobel prize-winning authors, and in every form of human drama.

For Anouilh, however, stories may assign roles, but they fail to reassure that these roles matter. His play about Antigone demonstrates the ruinous delusion of storytelling.

Although storytelling in *Antigone* begins with a simple aim to inform, it quickly takes on more

KATHARINE CORNELL

In Association with GILBERT MILLER presents

ANTIGONE

Adapted by LEWIS GALANTIERE

From the play by JEAN ANOUILH after SOPHOCLES

with

CEDRIC HARDWICKE

BERTHA BELMORE	HORACE BRAHAM
RUTH MATTESON	WESLEY ADDY
GEORGE MATHEWS	KATHARINE CORNELL

Staged by GUTHRIE McCLINTIC

Setting by RAYMOND SOVEY

Costumes by VALENTINA

Playbill of Anouilh's Antigone

---

complex purposes and becomes a tool for persuasion. For example, Ismene relates to Antigone how it will feel to be hounded by the mob after they get caught burying their brother, with "a thousand arms" seizing their arms and "a thousand breaths" breathing in their faces.

Ismene's vivid story resembles the mood of the story Antigone tells when trying to convince the nurse to care for her dog in her absence, painting a pathetic picture of the dog moaning and pining for her missing owner. These "horror" stories are designed to alarm and convince their listeners. They exaggerate the future as a way of avoiding it. However, because the Nurse does not fully comprehend why Antigone tells her the story, the full potential of the warning is lost.

Antigone informs her loved ones—the Nurse and Haemon—that she will leave them, without telling them why. Instead, she relates wistful stories of a future that she herself will destroy. To Haemon she describes the child they might have had, the mother she might have been; she uses the past subjunctive, as though this choice had already passed them by, even though their marriage is set for the future. Her narrative of the traditional family, loving mother with her child, presents a story that will never come to fruition.

When she tells Haemon her story, she does not arrange a surrogate as she did for her dog, but simply destroys the vision forever by immediately announcing she can never marry him. Thus her story can only haunt him as her true intentions are revealed.

The family narrative usually serves as a model for human behavior, assigning roles and behavior patterns to parents and children, so that they can conform their actions to society's structure and expectations. Ismene accepts this, and so she understands Creon's desire to set a good example for his people; she accepts the ban against Polynices as a necessary measure to keep peace in Thebes.

For her part, Antigone objects to Ismene's type of "understanding," which entails accepting Creon's narrative as truth. The sisters disagree over which stories to follow. Antigone, as Ismene chides her, wants her "own stubborn way in everything." Ismene prefers to accept her fate and leave heroics to men, because "It's all very well for men to believe in ideas and die for them. But you are a girl!"

The female narrative only requires a woman to be beautiful, to marry, and to bear children. Creon tells Antigone "You're going to marry Haemon;

WHAT DO I READ NEXT?

- The classic film *Casablanca* (1942), starring Humphrey Bogart and Ingrid Bergman, also concerns making personal sacrifices on behalf of the French Resistance.

- Anouilh's *L'Alouette* (*The Lark,* 1953) focuses on the life of Joan of Arc.

- Mark Twain wrote a novel about *Joan of Arc* (1896) after spending twelve years researching her life and times.

- Albert Camus' *The Stranger* (1946) explores the predicament of a faithless man who commits a senseless murder and contemplates the absurdity of modern existence.

---

and I want you to fatten up a bit so that you can give him a sturdy boy.'' Creon never questioned that Antigone would follow the prescribed life story or script for a woman—in fact, he gave Antigone her first doll, a toy given to young girls to act out and envision their futures.

In a way, Antigone opposes these expectations even more than she opposes the desecration of her brother's corpse. Creon resents her rebelliousness. ''What sort of game are you playing?'' he demands. As a ruler who has had to roll up his sleeves and attend to the ship of state, which was ''loaded to the water line with crime, ignorance, poverty,'' Creon objects to anyone deviating from their predetermined roles.

As the leader of Thebes, he tells her, ''You shout an order, and if one man refuses to obey, you shoot straight into the mob.'' He advocates complete obedience, and ''no matter how many may fall by the wayside, there are always those few left that go on bringing their young into the world, traveling the same road with the same obstinate will, unchanged from those who went before.'' His perspective appalls Antigone and the audience.

Creon is also a victim of his stories. Besides the rigid expectations and roles he has imposed on himself and his city, he sometimes imagines false stories and then acts on them in error. Creon assumes that a child has buried Polynices, and his imagination takes over as it fills in the gaps of a story that is wrong from the start.

Creon sees ''a baby-faced killer,'' a ''martyr,'' corrupted by his enemies, ''leaders of the mob, stinking of garlic.'' His fantasy blinds him to his real enemy and exacerbates his paranoia, leading him to overreact when he does find the culprit.

Yet when Creon finds the real culprit—Antigone—she turns out to be intractable and dismissive. He complains to her that ''You have cast me for the villain in this little play of yours, and yourself the heroine.'' He admits that he will have to play his part ''through to the end'' as well as she, because he of all the characters understands the governing power of stories.

A thirst for story infects every major character in *Antigone*. Stories constitute life scripts, life plans, and to follow a plan gives one reassurance and a sense of purpose in life. Creon clings to his script of city-savior, a story that envisions him as martyr to his lost ideals and to the survival of the city.

Occupation with one's script leaves little time to worry about deep questions; one has to ''sweat and roll up your sleeves and plunge both hands into life up to the elbows.'' Creon's way is to ignore his mind and give his body over to life. He wants a story to quiet his mind so that his body may work.

Antigone's way is to question the purpose of that body: she wants it to have an honorable role, informed by the mind. Her act of burying Polynice's body disrupts Creon's complacency, and he finds it necessary to silence her—to shut her up away from the public in a remote cave.

For Antigone thirst for story equates to faith; when Creon strips away her false perceptions of Polynices's honor, she mourns the loss of her faith. "Would it have been better to let you die a victim to that obscene story?" Creon asks. "It might have been. I had my faith," she answers, despondent.

Creon accuses her of having her father's desire for glory in death. Oedipus could not control his passions, which prompt him to sleep with his mother and kill his father. It was the story that destroyed him, rather than the acts themselves, which were committed without thought and would have gone unheeded had the story not come to light.

His own story both punished and fascinated Oedipus. Creon relates that he "drank in the dark story that the gods had destined him first to live and then to hear." Somehow the narrative grasp of his shameful story, at least for the moment of the telling, overrode the horror of killing his own father and dishonoring his mother.

Stories can wind their subjects into a web from which they cannot escape. Once Antigone's story of reprisal against the king gets out, the story holds her in its clutches and no other stories can help her. Haemon and the chorus suggest alternative stories to tell the angry mob, such as telling them that Antigone is mad, or that the law is changed, but the king cannot make an exception of his niece without losing his authority. The story is bigger than his office.

"The story is all over Thebes," he says. The story sways the mob, who will see that the story gets enacted till the end—they must have closure. Not to close the story would open the door for chaos: without a script, there is no structure. Even though the chorus proclaims that "We shall carry the scar of her death for centuries," the story must unroll to its conclusion.

Antigone's problem is that for her—unlike Creon and the mob—story does not satisfy. Once stripped of the illusion that her brother's honor existed and that she could honor it, she lost her hope in stories. Then she only wanted death—the end to all stories.

Creon finds her lack of faith abhorrent. "Death was her purpose, whether she knew it or not," Creon proclaims. "Polynices was a mere pretext. When she found she had to give up that pretext, she found another one—that life and happiness were tawdry things and not worth possessing. She was bent upon only one thing: to reject life and to die." Creon, though he tries, can offer nothing to appease her.

> "A THIRST FOR STORY INFECTS EVERY MAJOR CHARACTER IN *ANTIGONE*. STORIES CONSTITUTE LIFE SCRIPTS, LIFE PLANS, AND TO FOLLOW A PLAN GIVES ONE REASSURANCE AND A SENSE OF PURPOSE IN LIFE."

The play exposes the meaninglessness, the paucity of stories. The guards have remained apathetic, not caring for a moment whether Antigone succeeded in her mission or avoided her death, for "none of this matters to them." "They go on playing cards," a game that simply repeats, in endless variations, a series of meaningless steps, just as their lives repeat, in endless minor variations, the lives of all citizens.

Antigone asserts that neither the lives nor the stories of kings and heroines, nor of the guards who protect them hold any meaning. Anouilh is a dramatist whose story exposes the malignancy of story, because hope is a "whore" that offers delusion for consolation.

Stripping away illusion, then, is an act of heroism, exposing that we are all, as Creon finally realizes when Haemon kills himself, "wounded to death," and that stories can only obstruct this truth. All that remains is "a fellow-feeling" among the characters, a sense of camaraderie that we are not, at least, alone, and that the heroism of an Antigone is still possible.

Source: Carole Hamilton for *Drama for Students,* Gale, 2000.

William Calin

In this essay, Calin examines the differences in point of view between Antigone and her enemy Creon.

"Le Charme D'Antigone, dans la piece d'Anouilh, c'est le charme de'enfance. . . . On ne comprendrait rien a cette fille maigre et brulante, si l'on ne convenait d'abord qu'elle est une petite fille.'' This statement is to be found in one of the most recent studies on Jean Anouilh. Pol Vandromme is not the first to have pointed out how Anouilh emphasizes the protagonist's childlike purity and idealism, qualities absent from the world of adult society. Anouilh invented the role of the Nurse (*la nourrice*); her appearance in the first scene introduces us to the fact that Antigone has only recently crossed the threshold of adulthood. They speak together of the pranks the young girl played as a child, her fear of the bogey-man and of creatures in the night, her helplessness in the presence of others; the nurse gives orders and tries to direct Antigone's life. Creon too reminds her how only a little while ago he would have punished her with '' . . . du pain sec et une pair de gifles''. For him, as for Nurse, she is *la petite Antigone;* he reminds her that her first doll was a present from him "il n'y pas si longtemps." In Sophocles' *Antigone* we do not know with what instrument Polynices is buried; Anouilh tells us that his heroine uses a child's toy shovel (''une petite pelle d'enfant toute vieille''), Polynice's shovel with which she and her brother used to build sand castles on the beach when they were children. And when Antigone commits suicide, hanging herself by the cord of her robe, the messenger says that these strands ''lui faisaient comme un collier d'enfant.'' In life and in death Antigone remains true to the intransigent vision of youth; she commits the decisive act of rebellion and pays for it as a child.

As a child, Antigone exudes spontaneity and naturalness, and feels close to nature; around her the author constructs a pattern of animal imagery. *La petite Antigone* is assimilated to benevolent small animals. She had loved all the little creatures and wished to possess them all: ''Qui pleurait deja toute petite, en pensant qu'il y avait tant de petites betes, . . . et qu'on ne pouvait pas tous les prendre?'' Nurse calls her *mon pigeon, ma petite colombe, ma mesange, ma tourterelle.* Antigone begs the older woman to take care of her pet dog, to let her into the house and speak to her as one would a person. After her first attempt to bury Polynice is discovered, Creon asks the guards if they are not mistaken, if in fact instead of a person seeking to bury the corpse it was only ''une bete en grattant?'' The guards are not mistaken, as we well know, but Creon has unconsciously discovered a sort of metaphorical truth, for, once Antigone has lost her shovel, she is obliged to crawl on all fours and scrape the earth with her nails, like a small animal. Creon then is quite correct in picturing Antigone as a little bird, a sparrow, or as a small trapped animal (''un petit gibier pris'').

As a child, the princess played pranks on Ismene by covering her with dirt and tying her to a tree. At the age of nineteen she still loves to walk in her garden and in the fields alone at night, far from men's eyes. She runs barefoot in the dewy grass, the wind blowing in her hair; when tired, she drops to the earth to rest and bathes in a cool stream. She chooses the tactical moment to bury Polynice (covering his body with earth): just before the break of day, when she will be hidden by darkness and pre-dawn mists. The young girl finds joy in three of the four traditional universal elements or categories (as reinterpreted by Bachelard): water, air, and earth; her most lyrical outbursts are reserved for the exaltation of Nature. Her hair in the wind, her feet in water, and earth on her dress, Antigone flies like a bird, spiritualized, free from the gross material cares of society. She participates in the eternal feminine embodied by Earth and Water. She is vitally alive, participating in the splendor of the universe, even and especially when the Others are asleep, i.e., dead to the world: ''Qui se levait la premiere, le matin, rien que pour sentir l'air froid sur sa peau nue? Qui se couchait la derniere seulement quand elle n'en pouvait plus de fatigue, pour vivre encoure un pen de la nuit?''.

Her enemy Creon looks upon the universe with different eyes. Only once does he evoke Nature with the intensity usual to Antigone: his great speech on the ship of state. Instead of Antigone's refreshing stream and dew, we find mountains of waves sinking the ship; instead of her gentle, stimulating wind, we find a tempest which snaps the masts. Drinking water, so readily available to the young girl, in Creon's world has been seized by the officers for their own selfish ends. There is no earth on which man can rest. Creon ridicules his niece's thirst for pride, assimilating what he considers to be spiritual hybris to her freely admitted natural desires: ''Quel breuvage, hein, les mots qui vous condamnent? Et comme on les boit goulument quand on s'appelle Oedipe, ou Antigone,'' and she retorts that she will force him to drink her words, whether he will or no. Nurse, who in spite of her love for Antigone, remains a member of Creon's adult world, wishes the girl to wash her feet and cleanse away the dirt before going to bed, and objects to her mistress's dog entering the palace for similar reasons. Nor do the guards on sentry duty relish the chill, darkness, and mist of the night or the sun and wind of the day.

For these people Nature is hostile to man, a negative force destroying all that society holds dear, or an obtrusive quality outside their routine, which can give rise to acts of folly.

In opposition to these blind, anarchical forces, Creon relies upon the every-day world of men in society. The Prologue introduces him as one who "joue au jeu difficile de conduire les hommes." He sees the kingship not as an adventure or game but as a trade, a job to do, a piece of work. To do the job, he takes off his jacket, rolls up his shirt-sleeves, stands with hands in pockets and feet firmly planted on the ground. He says: "il faut suer et retrousser ses manches, empoigner la vie a pleines mains et s'en mettre jusqu'aux coudes".

Creon believes in a calm, ordered, restful world. Long ago he loved music, richly bound books, and whiling away his time in antique shops. He still pictures happiness in terms of a good book, a child at your feet, a tool in your hand, a bench in front of the house. Hemon, too, speaking of his childhood in Creon's home, evokes the memory of books, bread, a lamp in the evening, and the *odeur defendue* of his father's study. Like Nurse and the soldiers, Creon abhors filth: he despises the stench of Polynice's rotting corpse brought by the sea-wind and would willingly close his window and shut it out. Yet for all his disgust with some aspects of nature, or perhaps because of it, it is Creon, not Antigone, who evokes in concrete imagery the physical reality of death. Uncle, niece, and a guard all allude to the punishment prepared for Antigone, execution by immuring, as they say, in a *trou*. But it is Creon and his men who evoke Polynice's corpse in terms of rotten meat putrifying and decomposing in the sun, its vile odor penetrating every nook and cranny. As the guard says, "c'etait comme un coup de massue. J'avais beau ecarquiller les yeux, ca tremblait comme de la gelatine, je voyais plus." Creon views life and death with equal lucidity; he cuts through the haze of sentimental idealism surrounding sacrifice, religion, and personal freedom. He paints death in frightening tones specifically in order to frighten Antigone and dissuade her from an act which will result in her destruction. Yet the images of death (rot and decomposition) and those of domestic tranquillity (bench, book, warm bread) have one thing in common: they are figures of softness and repose, of harmony and security, which form a striking contrast to the imagination—pattern of expansion and energy—the power of the will—we find inherent in Antigone.

> "NATURE IS OFTEN CRUEL, AND IN ANY CASE THE THEBAN PRINCESS IS A HUMAN BEING CONDEMNED TO LIVE AND DIE AMONG HER OWN KIND. CREON TOO FINDS HIS IDEAL WORLD OF THE HEARTH DEGRADED AND HE HIMSELF CORRUPTED BY THE PEOPLE HE LOWERS HIMSELF TO SAVE."

The two protagonists of Anouilh's drama do not exist in a vacuum. They relate to the other characters and participate in a scene of direct confrontation. Each protagonist undermines the other's position, parodies and satirizes the other's point of view. Thus Anouilh points out the weaknesses as well as the strength in Antigone and Creon, the ambiguities inherent in their psychology and respective world-views.

Practicality and Degradation: Creon would have us think of him as the captain of a vessel, struggling alone, defending his crew against the onslaught of a hostile storm. As such, he is an idealist, as heroic as Antigone. Creon also prides himself on having a command of practical affairs in the real world. Thus he explains the motives governing his decision to insult Polynice's corpse, the aspects of *Realpolitik* which compelled his decision: he wishes to make his niece aware of the sordid reality behind the facade of political life, the inner workings of the theater or palace: "Car c'est cela que je veux que tu saches, les coulisses de ce drame ou tu brules de jouer un role, la cuisine." But Antigone applies Creon's metaphor concretely and extends it by accusing him of being a cook in his kitchen: "Tu l'as bien dit tout a l'heure, Creon, la cuisine. Vous avez des tetes de cuisiniers! . . . Tu m'ordonnes, cuisinier? . . . Allons vite, cuisinier!" There is a fundamental contradiction between the image of the captain defending his crew against a tempest and the cook in his kitchen, the sordid reality of the palace or theater. Antigone recognizes that Creon is lowering himself to the level of the masses for whom both he and she have such utter contempt ("Vous avez des tetes de cuisiners . . ."). Thus is he assimilated to those around him who share his views and help implement them. The self-proclaimed captain of the ship of state has no illusions about the pathetic brutes whom he wishes to protect. And in this respect Antigone shares his point of view (a fact more than a trifle embarrassing to those left-wing intellectuals who invoke her as spokesman for their own attitudes on class struggle, *engagement,* the Resistance, etc.). She hates the guards who smell of garlic and red wine, can't stomach being touched by their dirty hands; they are the cooks who surround Creon. She begs him to keep her away from the masses whose faces and voices she wishes to avoid. She prefers never to tell Hemon of her suffering, lest the others know of it too: "Il vaut mieux que jamais personne ne sache. C'est comme s'ils devaient me voir nue et me toucher quand je serai morte." These are the people of whom Ismene speaks to frighten her sister and persuade her to obey Creon: the thousands and thousands of people in the city, with their thousand arms and thousand faces, who will spit in her face and destroy her with their odor and laughter; and the guards with their stupid faces, thick hands, and ox-like stare, who will conduct her to torture and death. The mob and the palace guards are indistinguishable; both follow Creon blindly. It is appropriate for Antigone, child of nature and enemy of society, to fear the people; Creon's contempt is less justifiable in terms of his character and the philosophical position he defends.

Nature and Animals: Antigone, for all we have said above, fears certain aspects of nature—insects in the night—and compares her bourgeois enemies to the dogs who caress whatever and whoever lies on their path. Creon, too, speaks of the hostile crowd howling about the palace. Antigone is called not only a turtledove and a sparrow but also a rat caught in a trap, a little hyena scratching at her brother's grave. She does not want the scraps people toss to good dogs; she recognizes that although animals enjoy the company of their kind, she is a human being and must die alone: "Des betes se serraient l'une contre l'autre pour se faire chaud. Je suis toute seule." When Creon, in an unaccustomed turn of phrase, invokes the laws of nature to convince his niece to accept society's laws and live ("Les betes, elles au moins, sont bonnes et simples et dures"), she treats him and his image with contempt: "Quel reve, hein? pour un roi: des betes!" Antigone assimilates to nature yet cannot be a part of it; she partakes of mankind yet is repelled by all that men are and have created.

Light and Darkness: One might imagine that a child of nature relishes the light of day in all its glory. But no, Antigone prefers the grey of night and compares the reds, yellows, and greens of dawn to a cheap, man-made postal card. At night she succeeds in burying her brother undetected; at high noon she is perceived and captured. And she will be executed in the full light of the sun. Is not the sun (which also causes Polynice's corpse to stink) an eternal masculine principle of justice, Creon's ally, an emanation of him? Yet is not the sun also the source of life?

Beauty and Ugliness: Our protagonist, a child of nature, is herself physically unattractive. Anouilh spares no pains to tell us she is swarthy (*noiraude*), thin, pale, flat-chested, and badly groomed (*mal peignee*). Comparing herself to Ismene, Antigone admits her sister's superiority ("Je suis noire et maigre, Ismene est rose et doree comme un fruit"), is even proud of Ismene's beauty. Yet she recoils from ugliness in others: the mob, her guard, Creon. Antigone attacks Creon by assimilating the presumed ugliness of his deeds to his physical appearance: his wrinkles and fat belly: "La vie t'a seulement ajoute tous ces petits plis sur le visage et cette graisse autour de toi." She may be homely in the flesh, Antigone admits, but Creon's men are morally repulsive, even the most handsome, they all have something ugly at the corner of their eyes and mouths. Men who are afraid are ugly, she say. And for all her homeliness, it is Antigone whom young men stare at on the street, whose hand Hemon seeks in marriage. Something emanates from her. She is beautiful, not like the others, but differently: "Pas belle comme nous, mais autrement", says Ismene.

Society and Solitude: Antigone stands alone against the world. She was sitting by herself in a corner when Hemon asked her to marry him; as the play begins she sits apart from the others, thinking. She buries her brother alone, spurning Ismene's help. Yet she does cherish individual human beings, Hemon for example, and wishes Nurse to love her dog like a human, the way she herself does. She seeks a rapport with her guard, her last *visage d'homme*. In the end Antigone will have achieved a greater communion with mankind than Creon is capable of. The king has the power to snuff out her life, but Hemon her beloved and Creon's wife die with her. Hemon is also alone and can receive no consolation from Creon's world. The king, on the other hand, has lost his son, his wife, and his niece;

his only remaining friend, the page-boy (like Antigone, a child), does not understand him. Deprived of his dead loved ones, this apostle of man's commitment to society and life is condemned to live in solitude among men who do not comprehend.

Anachronisms: Scholars have pointed out that Anouilh's conscious introduction of anachronisms into this as well as other plays creates an aura of universality, making the play valid for our century, creates distance between the characters and their public, establishing a tone of irony, and serves to upset the audience, to give it a sense of broken illusion and manipulated convention. Still another function of anachronism is to create ambiguities, to help undermine the protagonists' points of view and our self-identification with them as "people." Creon tells the story of Polynice's civil war in terms of a twentieth-century youth rebelling against his father, a hoodlum, a *jeune voyou* who frequents low dives and drives fast cars. His description of the funeral rites Antigone seeks for her brother is viewed from the same perspective: "Tu as vu ces pauvres tetes d'employes fatigues ecourtant les gestes, avalant les mots, baclant ce mort pour en prendre un autre avant le repas de midi?" Creon humiliates his niece and lowers her in the public's esteem by dissipating whatever idealism and purity may adhere to the ancient myth (grandeur of distance, the hallowed tradition of Greek literature), by assimilating her myth to the sordid scandals, so common and mundane, of the public press in our own century. Yet the sword of anachronism cuts both ways. When Creon's guards employ a military slang of the 1940s and their pre-occupations are centered on the *bistro* and whorehouse, we are made to sympathize with Antigone's rebellion. The world is coarse and vulgar; Creon does degrade himself by consorting with such people. The very pettiness of everyday life justifies to some extent Antigone's rebellion. Her fondest souvenir is a paper flower Polynice had brought back from one of his evenings on the town. For the modern reader and for Creon, it is only a pitiful anachronism, equally inappropriate in the world of Sophoclean tragedy and in a situation requiring carefully thought-out political decision-making: a cheap bit of fluff which could move only a schoolgirl, an artificial imitation of nature at best. Yet her flower is still less ugly and ignoble than the rotting corpse, drunken guards, and stench of the kitchen that made up Creon's world.

From Anouilh's use of imagery we learn that Antigone and Creon are not two perfect, admirable, triumphant embodiments of opposing philosophies of life. True, Antigone incarnates the virtues of wild nature, Creon those of domestic society. But Antigone is made only too aware of the fact that she can never be a little furry creature in the woods. Nature is often cruel, and in any case the Theban princess is a human being condemned to live and die among her own kind. Creon too finds his ideal world of the hearth degraded and he himself corrupted by the people he lowers himself to save. Antigone and Creon are heroic and vulnerable, majestic and inconsistent, eloquent and irrational—at the same time. We cannot accept the notion, dear to some critics, that Anouilh is on Antigone's side, that she embodies his own socio-political views. Instead, Anouilh's great innovation in treating the Antigone myth is to ennoble the character of Creon, to make him co-equal with Antigone. In the French play we have two protagonists, both worthy of admiration, both suffering from weakness. Anouilh presents both points of view and allows us to choose between them; rather, he presents the human condition in all its sordidness and poetry, the poetry of two gifted people each at grips with the other, with his own self, with society, and with the natural world. We are shown the human predicament, and we behold it with wonder.

Source: William Calin, "Patterns of Imagery in Anouilh's *Antigone*," in *French Review,* Vol. 41, 1967, pp. 76–83.

Peter Nazareth

In the following essay, Nazareth discusses the Truth in tragedy and compares Anouilh's Antigone *to Sophocles's* Antigone.

"When Jean Anouilh turns historian we can take it that truth will be revealed in the light of the emotions—lightly, wittily revealed, in brilliant flashes. But truth is no less true because it comes as a jest in a jewelled sentence." (Caryl Brahmns, in a review of Beckett's *Plays and Players,* August, 1961.)

"With Anouilh now firmly entrenched as purveyor of fancy goods to the entertainment hunters, it is hard to credit that, not so long ago, he was classed as a rebel . . . [Anouilh was] never a major writer, or even a serious thinker . . . *Antigone* will not stand up to scrutiny; [its] factitious and sentimental skating round subjects, in which the real issue is always carefully avoided, is revealed. . . . Anouilh has not only cut history down to size, but larded it with humour of the cheapest kind." (Tom Milne, in a review of *Beckett* in *Encore,* October, 1961.)

> "... ANOUILH'S CREON CONTRASTS WITH SOPHOCLES'S CREON IN ONE PARTICULAR ASPECT, TO CREATE A POSITIVE BY WHICH WE ARE TO JUDGE HIM. ANOUILH'S CREON DOES NOT BELIEVE IN 'ALL THAT FLUMMERY ABOUT RELIGIOUS BURIAL.' BUT SOPHOCLES'S CREON DOES. THIS MAKES US REALIZE HOW MUCH ANOUILH'S CREON HAS LOST SPIRITUALLY. HE HAS NO IDEALS. THERE IS NO GREATNESS IN HIS SOUL...."

When there is such controversy about a contemporary dramatist, it is fruitful to make a detailed examination of at least one of his plays, in Mr Lewis Galantiere's translations. "*Antigone* will not stand up to scrutiny": Let us therefore scrutinize *Antigone*.

Some critics say that *Antigone* is a tragedy. For instance, T. R. Henn begins his analysis of *Antigone* by saying "A critic has said, I think with justice, that M. Anouilh 'alone among modern playwrights is able to wear the tragic mask with ease.'" Note, too, Raymond Williams's analysis of *Antigone*.

However, if we accept the play as a tragedy, we find that we are unable to explain several parts of Anouilh's play. For instance, towards the end of the play, when Antigone is about to be sealed up in a cave, she talks to the guard. The guard then starts talking about himself and the things that concern him:

> If you're a guard, everyone knows you're something special; they know you're an old N.C.O. Take pay for instance. When you're a guard you get your pay, and on top of that you get six months' extra pay, to make sure you don't lose anything by not being a sergeant any more ...

And so on. Antigone is not interested, of course, and interrupts him with, "Listen ... I'm going to die soon." But he is not interested in *her* fate and continues talking about himself. Surely, when the guard talks so much about himself, the tragic mood of the play is destroyed.

Even more striking is Anouilh's use of the chorus. Anouilh's chorus is one man, who leans casually on the proscenium arch while talking directly to the audience. The play opens with the words,

> Well, here we are. These people are about to act out for you the story of Antigone.

He points to Antigone and says,

> That little creature sitting by herself, staring straight ahead, seeing nothing, is Antigone. She is thinking. She is thinking that the instant I finish telling you who's who and what's what in this play, she will burst forth as the tense, sallow, wilful girl whose family would never take her seriously and who is about to rise up alone against Creon, her uncle, the king.

But that is not all. The chorus (in the French version it is the Prologue) goes on to say

> Another thing that she is thinking is this: she is going to die. Antigone is young. She would much rather live than die. But there is no help for it. When your name is Antigone, there is only one part you can play; and she will have to play hers to the end.

This, surely, is an untragic way to begin a tragedy! The chorus insists on explaining to the audience *the fact that they are watching a play*—and explaining at such length that the tragic mood is destroyed.

Later, after Creon discovers that his law has been defied and Polynices has been buried, the chorus says,

> The spring is wound up tight. It will uncoil of itself. That is what is so convenient in tragedy ... Tragedy is clean, it is restful, it is flawless.

In fact, the chorus goes on to make a long speech on what tragedy is.

Many critics take the speeches of the chorus at their face value. Henn quotes part of the chorus's definition at the beginning of Chapter VI of *The Harvest of Tragedy* and accepts it as a genuine definition. Raymond Williams says:

> The convention, both of commentary on the various characters in turn, and of establishment of the play and the characters as action and parts which begin "now that the curtain has risen," *is very impressive*. By the end of Prologue's speech the audience has been firmly introduced to *the conventional nature of the play,* and also to each of the characters ... It is very simple, and *completely convincing*. It gains an immediate dramatic concentration, and the conditions of intensity; it also provides the major resource which the naturalistic drama has lacked, that of commentary. (The italics are mine.)

We notice that Williams takes the speeches at their face value and thinks they are convincing. The fallacy of Williams's comments is obvious when we ask ourselves the obvious question: does naturalistic drama need commentary? What about Chekhov's drama?

Other critics also take these speeches at their face value, but conclude that they are not convincing. The play, these critics say, is pseudo-tragedy, it is sentimental and pretentious. The chorus is defining tragedy so that the audience will be deceived into thinking it is experiencing a great tragedy. Further, Anouilh does not have the courage of his convictions. He wants to write a tragedy, but he is afraid that the audience will accuse him of sentimentality; and so he also laughs with the audience at the play. In other words, he does not take the play seriously; he is intellectually dishonest. This is symptomatic of the vulgarity and lack of culture of the masses. Conditioned by mass-produced television, films, pop songs and advertising, the masses can only accept pseudo-tragedy. They have to be told that they are experiencing a great tragedy, because they are incapable of experiencing true tragedy.

But we must stop to ask ourselves this question: does Anouilh want us to take the speeches of the chorus at their face value? If he were doing so, would he overplay his hand, *or,* if he were attempting aesthetic sleight-of-hand, would he insist that the audience watch the hand he was going to deceive them with? Would he let the chorus say, "In a tragedy, nothing is in doubt and everyone's destiny is known. That makes for tranquility"? Isn't it the natural tendency for the audience to *react against* tragedy because of speeches like this?

If we take the speeches at their face value, we shall be misunderstanding the play. J. L. Styan's comment in his analysis of *Colombe* is relevant and illuminating. He says,

> Because of the play-within-the-play, we are doubly the skeptical audience we were: we simply do not respond sentimentally to the sentiment with which the words are spoken. To believe that the author intended us to would contradict the total meaning of this play, not to mention others.

The speeches of the chorus are a sardonic comment on what tragedy (i.e. a tragic play) is. Anouilh is telling us through the chorus what is *wrong* with tragedy. Tragedy is clean, restful and flawless; *therefore it is not true to life.* It ignores certain issues in life which, according to Anouilh, it should not. Therefore his play cannot be interpreted as a tragedy in the same sense in which we usually understand the term "tragedy." The fact that the chorus is anti-tragic and tells us what is wrong with tragedy is an indication that Anouilh's *Antigone* is "played against" a tragedy. To be specific, Anouilh's *Antigone* is "played against" Sophocles's *Antigone.*

The framework of both plays is the same. Antigone, the daughter of Oedipus, decides to defy the edict of her uncle King Creon and to bury the body of her brother Polynices. She asks her sister Ismene for help, but Ismene refuses to help her. So Antigone buries Polynices herself. She is brought before Creon, who decides to have her killed—even though she is engaged to his son Haemon. After Antigone's death, Haemon commits suicide. When his mother, Eurydice, hears about his death, she also commits suicide.

However, what lies within this framework is different in the two plays. The differences are apparent very early in the plays. When Sophocles's Ismene refuses to bury Polynices, she says:

> We must remember that we are women, and women are not meant to fight with men. Our rulers are stronger than ourselves, and we must obey them in this, and in things more bitter still . . . And so I shall obey those in power, since I am forced to do so, and can only ask the dead to pardon me, since there is no wisdom in going too far.

We feel that Ismene is perhaps weak, but that is all we feel. Now let us look at what Anouilh's Ismene says:

> He [Creon] is stronger than we are. He is the king. And the whole city is with him . . . His mob will come running, howling at us as it runs. A thousand arms will seize our arms. A thousand breaths will breathe into our faces. Like one pair of single eyes, a thousand eyes will stare at us. We'll be driven in a timbrel through their hatred, through the smell of them and their cruel, roaring laughter. We'll be dragged to the scaffold for torture, surrounded by guards with their idiot faces all bloated, their animal hands clean—washed for the sacrifice, their beefy eyes squinting as they stare at us. And we'll know that no shrieking and no begging will make them understand that we want to live, for they are like slaves who do exactly as they've been told, without caring about right and wrong. And we shall suffer, we shall feel pain rising in us until it becomes so unbearable that we *know* it must stop. But it won't stop; it will go on rising and rising, like a screaming voice. Oh, I can't, I can't, Antigone.

The difference between these two speeches is striking. Anouilh's Ismene says the same thing as Sophocles's Ismene, but takes it a stage further. In the second case (Anouilh's), we are presented with a powerful, shocking and realistic picture of the horrible fate that Ismene thinks awaits her and Antigone if they break Creon's law. It is a horrifying picture. Ismene is only human, and we realize most forcefully why Anouilh's Ismene refuses to bury Polynices, as we did not in the case of Sophocles's Ismene.

Creon has passed the edict that Polynices is not to be buried; anybody who defies this edict does so on pain of death. Sophocles's Creon has done this because he thinks it is for the good of the state. After Antigone has defied the edict and buried Polynices, there is a brief exchange between her and Creon. She says that she could not bring herself through fear of one man and one man's pride to disobey the laws of the gods. Creon's pride is hurt because he is unsure of himself. He decides to kill Antigone because "she will be the man, not I, if she wins this victory and goes unpunished." He refuses to listen to the advice of his son, saying finally, "I *am* the state." He even refuses to listen to Teiresias and accuses him of corruption; Teiresias, with whose help he has ruled the state. Too late does he realize his blindness. After the deaths of Antigone, Haemon and Eurydice, he says

> Ah me! the guilt is mine, I know it. I blame no other.

When Anouilh's Antigone is brought before Creon, she insists that Creon kill her. But Anouilh's Creon wants to save Antigone. He does not believe in "all that flummery about religious burial." He asks Antigone,

> Do you really believe that a so-called shade of your brother is condemned to wander forever homeless if a little earth is not flung on his corpse to the accompaniment of some priestly abracadabra?

Until Kitto's interpretation of Sophocles's *Antigone* in *Form and Meaning in Drama* (1956), it was believed that Sophocles's Antigone had to bury her brother because the soul of a dead person was condemned to wander forever homeless if the body was left unburied. Anouilh's *Antigone* was written long before Kitto published his interpretation. It does not matter to Creon which body is buried and which is unburied; in fact, he does not even know whether the body is that of Polynices or Eteocles. Antigone cannot understand him; he then reveals his position clearly. He had to agree to be the ruler of the state, or the state would have collapsed. Sophocles's Creon says:

> My friends, the gods have brought our ship of state safely to port after wild tossing on the stormy seas.

Anouilh's Creon also talks of the state as a ship; but he carries the image much further:

> There had to be one man who said yes. Somebody had to agree to captain the ship. She had sprung a hundred leaks; she was loaded to the water-line with crime, ignorance, poverty. The ship was swinging with the wind. The crew refused to work and were looting the cargo. The officers were building a raft, ready to slip overboard and desert the ship. The mast was splitting, the wind was howling, the sails were beginning to rip. Every man-jack on board was about to drown—and only because the only thing they thought of was their own skins and their cheap little day to day traffic. Was this a time, do you think, for playing with words like yes and no?

Once more we see in stark terms why Anouilh's Creon had to do what he did. We realize clearly the real, factual difficulties in the path of the ruler of the state, which we did not in the case of Sophocles's Creon. Further, Anouilh's Antigone had last seen Polynices when she was twelve years old, and therefore she did not really know him. Creon tells her that both Eteocles and Polynices were "rotten." Both men tried to assassinate their father. Had Antigone considered all this when she decided to bury Polynices?

Anouilh has raised far more factual issues than Sophocles by just taking everything a stage further, and by including "irrelevancies." Everything that Anouilh says could have really happened, but Sophocles does not even touch upon many of these issues.

At this stage I should like to quote extensively from Aldous Huxley's essay *Tragedy and the Whole Truth* (1932), because it is vital to our understanding of Anouilh's play. I do not agree with Huxley's ideas and comments in this essay; I am quoting from it extensively because I suggest that the kind of aesthetic and critical consciousness Huxley reveals in this essay is like Anouilh's creative consciousness, and it will therefore help us understand Anouilh's approach in *Antigone* (The fact that Huxley has long been accepted as a serious writer in France is an indication that his creative consciousness is congenial to the French.)

Huxley distinguishes between two forms of literary art, Tragedy and Wholly-Truthful Literature, and says that the two are incompatible. He gives an example from the *Odyssey*. Six of the best and bravest of Odysseus's companions are lifted out of the ship by Scylla. The survivors could only look on while Scylla "at the mouth of her cave devoured them, still screaming, still stretching out their hands [at Odysseus] in the fearful struggle." Odysseus adds that it was the most fearful and lamentable sight he had ever seen in all his "explorings of the passes of the sea."

Later, the danger passed, Odysseus and his men went ashore for the night, and, on the Sicilian beach, prepared their supper—prepared it, says Homer, "expertly." The Twelfth Book of the *Odyssey* concludes with these words: "When they had satisfied their thirst and hunger, they thought of their dear companions and wept, and in the midst of their tears sleep came gently upon them!"

Homer's . . . is the whole Truth. Consider how almost any other of the great poets would have concluded the story of Scylla's attack on the passing ship. Six men, remember, have been taken and devoured before the eyes of their friends. In any other poem but the *Odyssey,* what would the survivors have done? They would, of course, have wept, even as Homer made them weep. But would they previously have cooked their supper, and cooked it, what's more, in a masterly fashion? Would they previously have drunk and eaten to satiety? And after weeping, or actually while weeping would they have dropped quietly off to sleep? No, they most certainly would not have done any of these things. They would simply have wept, lamenting their own misfortune and the horrible fate of their companions, and the canto would have ended tragically on their tears.

Homer, however, preferred to tell the Whole Truth. He knew that even the most cruelly bereaved must eat; that hunger is stronger than sorrow and that its satisfaction takes precedence even of tears. He knew that experts continue to act expertly and to find satisfaction in their accomplishment, even when friends have just been eaten, even when the accomplishment is only cooking the supper. He knew that, when the belly is full (and only when the belly is full), men can afford to grieve, and that sorrow after supper is almost a luxury. And finally he knew that, even as hunger takes precedence of grief, so fatigue, supervening, cuts short its career and drowns it in a sleep all the sweeter for bringing forgetfulness of bereavement. In a word, Homer refused to treat the theme tragically. He preferred to tell the Whole Truth.

Huxley goes on to say,

To make a tragedy the artist must isolate a single element out of the totality of human experience and use that exclusively as his material. Tragedy is something separated from the Whole Truth, distilled from it, so to speak, as an essence is distilled from the living flower. Tragedy is chemically pure. Hence its power to act quickly and intensely on our feelings.

Compare this to Anouilh's

The spring is wound up tight. It will uncoil of itself. That is what is so convenient in tragedy . . . Tragedy is clean, it is restful, it is flawless.

Huxley says,

Wholly-Truthful art overflows the limits of tragedy and shows us, if only by hints and implications, what happened before the tragic story began, what will happen after it is over, what is happening simultaneously elsewhere (and "elsewhere" includes all those parts of the minds and bodies of the protagonists not immediately engaged in the tragic struggle). Tragedy is an arbitrarily isolated eddy on the surface of a vast river that flows majestically, irresistibly, around, beneath, and to either side of it. Wholly-Truthful art contrives to imply the existence of the entire river as well as the eddy. It is quite different from tragedy, even though it may contain, among other constituents, all the elements from which tragedy is made.

Writers who create Wholly-Truthful art shirk almost nothing. Among other things are the irrelevancies which, in actual life, always temper the situations and characters "that writers of tragedy insist on keeping chemically pure." These irrelevancies would destroy Tragedy.

Consequently, Wholly-Truthful art produces in us an effect quite different from that produced by tragedy. Our mood when we have read a Wholly-Truthful book is never one of heroic exultation; it is one of resignation, one of acceptance. . . But I believe that its effects are more lasting. The exultations that follow the reading or hearing of a tragedy are in the nature of temporary inebriations. Our being cannot long hold the pattern imposed by tragedy.

Compare all this to the chorus's sardonic and ironic comments:

It [tragedy] has nothing to do with melodrama. . . Death in a melodrama is really horrible because it is never inevitable. The dear old father might so easily have been saved; the honest young man might so easily have brought in the police five minutes earlier.

In a tragedy, nothing is in doubt and everyone's destiny is known. That makes for tranquility . . . Tragedy is restful; and the reason is that hope, that foul, deceitful thing, has no part in it. There isn't any hope. You're trapped. The whole sky has fallen on you, and all you can do about it is shout. Don't mistake me: I said "shout": I did not say groan, whimper, complain. That is vulgar; it's practical.

The two accounts are remarkably similar, especially if one substitutes "Wholly-Truthful art" for "melodrama."

Huxley gives another example. He says,

Shakespeare's ironies and cynicisms serve to deepen his tragic world, but not to widen it. If they had widened it, as the Homeric irrelevancies widened out the universe of the *Odyssey*—why, then, the world of Shakespearean tragedy would automatically have ceased to exist. For example, a scene showing the bereaved Macduff eating his supper, growing melancholy, over the whisky, with thoughts of his murdered wife and children, and then, with lashes still wet, dropping off to sleep, would be true enough to life; but it would not be true to tragic art. The introduction of such a scene would change the whole quality of the play; treated in this Odyssean style, *Macbeth* would cease to be a tragedy.

We certainly cannot agree with what Huxley says about our reaction to tragedy. But, as I said earlier, it is his kind of consciousness in this essay that is important, because it is similar to Anouilh's creative consciousness. His distinction between "Tragedy" and "the Whole Truth" *as art forms* is therefore particularly useful to us. He suggests that there is in some writers a consciousness of simple, everyday, commonplace things, which seem on the surface to be irrelevant, but which do, in fact, temper a particular situation. This consciousness leads these writers to create "Wholly-Truthful Art" and not "Tragedy"; this distinction, from the critics' point of view, is only one of *art forms,* because the creative consciousness involved is different. Lionel Trilling tells us in *The Modern Element in Modern Literature,* "It is a commonplace of modern literary thought that the tragic mode is not available even to the gravest and noblest of our writers." I suggest that this is due to the twentieth-century consciousness of "realism" (note also Eric Bentley). A consciousness of "realism" means a consciousness of the "irrelevant" things that are really relevant. Hence one cay say that the dominant mode of writing in the twentieth century is "Wholly-Truthful Art" (or "realism").

It is important at this stage to distinguish between "realism" in drama, as the *form* of a play, and realism as the *effect* (or content) of a play. Anouilh's *Antigone* is realistic in effect, but not in form.

Let us return to a comparison of the two plays (Anouilh's and Sophocles's). Antigone has buried her brother, knowing that her punishment will be death. Anouilh's Antigone, however, seems at first guilty of the fourth temptation of Archbishop Thomas in T. S. Eliot's *Murder in the Cathedral.* Accepting the fact that she will be killed, she seems to look forward with relish to her death. She seems to enjoy the idea of being executed. Creon does not want to kill her—but she insists. She had an ideal when she buried Polynices. But Creon tries to destroy her ideal by telling her, among other things, that both her brothers had been evil. For a moment, Antigone seems destroyed. Up to this point, our sympathy lies with Creon. But then Antigone decides that she will die for the ideal she had. In the eyes of Creon, her sacrifice is completely unjustified. Creon accepts life for what it is, and decides to "make the best of a bad job." But Antigone refuses to compromise with life—she chooses instead to die. We may compare Antigone's action here to the advice Zooey gives Franny in J. D. Salinger's *Franny and Zooey* (Heinemann, 1962)—she acts from a purity of motive. It does not matter that the facts do not fit her ideal; she refuses to let the ideal be destroyed. She says, in a very powerful speech,

> I spit on your idea of happiness! I spit on your idea of life—that life must go on, come what may. You are like the dogs that lick everything they smell. You with your promise of a humdrum happiness—provided a person doesn't ask too much of life. I want everything of life, I do; and I want it now! I want it total, complete, otherwise I reject it! I will *not* be moderate. I will *not* be satisfied with the little bit of cake you offer me if I promise to be a good little girl. I want to be sure of everything this very day; sure that everything will be as beautiful as when I was a little girl. If not, I want to die!

In this speech, our sympathy lies wholly with Antigone.

It is clear, then, that Anouilh's play explores problems that have not been raised explicitly in Sophocles's play. One should not therefore conclude that Anouilh's play is independent of Sophocles's, and that we ought not to identify the two. Huxley tells us:

> In recent times literature has become more and more acutely conscious of the whole Truth—of the great oceans of irrelevant things, events and thoughts stretching endlessly away in every direction from whatever island point (a character, a story) the author may choose to contemplate.

The "island point" in Anouilh's *Antigone* is Sophocles's *Antigone.* Anouilh's *Antigone* follows Sophocles's *Antigone* up to a stage—and then explores certain problems which are realistic, "true-to-life," and which are not improbable in Sophocles's play. But when we see Sophocles's *Antigone* these questions do not strike us. What were the personal problems facing Ismene in her decision not to help Antigone? What would really happen if she did help Antigone? Further, when Antigone decides to bury Polynices, does she consider first whether or not he has been good? Does she think of the problems Creon has to deal with as a ruler? What if Creon had refused to be king; would anyone else have agreed to be king? What would happen to the state if Creon did not face up to his responsibilities as king? Again, when Antigone buries Polynices, is there any personal ideal she wants to live up to? Is Creon's reaction after the three deaths merely a temporary emotional reaction; will he change his mind in his calmer moments and say that he was not really to blame? By using Sophocles's play as a frame of reference, Anouilh solves a major problem the artist of to-day is said to face. This is lack of "contact" between audience and artist, lack of common values. As Stephen Spender tells us,

> The thing written establishes communication between writer and reader . . . The message has to be conveyed at several levels. These might be compared to the wires of a cable . . . One wire is the background of objects experienced in life and having established associations which are common to writer and reader.

By assuming knowledge of a myth or a play that the audience knows, the dramatist creates the common "background of objects." Further, Henn tells us that the twentieth-century revival of interest in Greek myth or fable is partly due to the psychological recognition of the archetypes. The fables thus acquire a new validity in themselves, and can be re-clothed effectively on what is basically the same skeleton. But this is only a partial explanation.

> If such a re-clothing takes place, with a partial re-articulation of the bones, a new field is opened for the exercise of wit, the perception of metaphysical similarities or discordances, and endless over-and-undertones of irony. Out of such parallelisms, close or remote, the dramatist can invite his audience to find "meaning" which is usually a synthesis of factors which are, to a great extent, set in opposition or paradox . . . He can provide a critical edge, at various planes, by explicit comparisons between the two ages; the past whose bones he has discovered, the present whose breath is upon them.

One should mention at this stage that Anouilh's Creon contrasts with Sophocles's Creon in one particular aspect, to create a positive by which we are to judge him. Anouilh's Creon does not believe in "all that flummery about religious burial." But Sophocles's Creon does. This makes us realize how much Anouilh's Creon has lost spiritually. He has no ideals. There is no greatness in his soul; his soul is filled with commonness, as of dust.

Another commonplace of modern literary criticism is that the modern audience is complacent. (Obviously, this must be qualified; there is greater critical activity now than ever before.) Anouilh deals with this problem in the same way as Ezra Pound and T. S. Eliot do in their poetry. He constantly changes the focus in his play, thereby upsetting the mood of the audience and preventing it from getting complacent. He jerks the audience back to awareness. At the same time, this change of focus is used, as in the case of Pound and Mr. Eliot, to make the play all-embracing of various complexities. In Aldous Huxley's *The Genius and the Goddess,* John Rivers says,

> The trouble with fiction is that it makes too much sense... Fiction has unity, fiction has style. Facts possess neither. In the raw, existence is always one damned thing after another, and each of the damned things is simultaneously Thurber and Michelangelo, simultaneously Mickey Spillane and Thomas à Kempis.

By a constant change of focus, by selecting a contraposition from which we are to view his object, Anouilh can include "simultaneously Thurber and Michelangelo, simultaneously Mickey Spillane and Thomas a Kempis."

I suggest that Anouilh is one of the pioneers of what has been called the Theatre of the Absurd. The dramatists of this theatre regard their audience as complacent, apathetic, asleep. With taunts and shock effects, by breaking the continuity of a traditional form of drama, the dramatists hope to jerk the audiences into awareness, consciousness, understanding. Anouilh's *Antigone* has been misunderstood because of the preconceptions some critics have had about drama. For instance, note Montgomery Belgion's criticism of Shaw:

> Realism may be all right, and a stage convention may be all right. But these characters are neither one nor the other. They are pseudo-realistic.

Again, note C. E. Vaughan on Ibsen:

> How far is the scheme of Ibsen's drama, the design as apart from the execution of it, compatible with the highest ends at which tragedy can aim? Are not his details overloaded, his themes depressing, his characters too persistently lacking in the nobler, the more heroic qualities without which our sympathies remain cold?

The criticism often brought against Jonson and Wilde is that their characters are two-dimensional or are counters, and people are not like that. By such conceptions, Anouilh's play must seem false and irresponsible. His method of changing the focus and breaking the continuity is looked upon as irresponsible clowning. (It is interesting to note that this criticism is also levelled against Byron.)

But, as Styan points out, drama is the historic creation of a sequence of suggestions which create impressions in the minds of the audience. The sequence of impressions operates to create in the minds of the audience the total *effect* of the play. (To "minds," we must also add—in the case of most plays—"hearts and souls.") We are not to judge a play by the *methods* the dramatists use; we are to judge it by its *total effect.* (Of course, we are to see how the impressions are created, and whether or not they link together to form the total effect of the play.) We are to see how genuine the total effect is. If in its *total effect* the play presents a distorted view of life, or it distorts psychology, or it offers facile solutions, or it muddies fundamental issues, we reject the play. Yeats tells us that Richard II "is typical, not because he ever existed, but because he made us know something in our minds we had never known of had he never been imagined."

Let us see how Anouilh creates his impressions in *Antigone*. His method is essentially fivefold. First of all, he reacts against the fact—"fact" to Anouilh but not to us—that Tragedy does not present the whole Truth. Through his chorus, he passes sardonic comments on the smooth way tragedy works in order to destroy the idea that tragedy is true-to-life and that his play is a tragedy. Secondly, he brings in several "irrelevancies" which make his play realistic, but untragic. Several examples of this have been quoted earlier in this essay. Another example is when Antigone wants to write a letter to Haemon just before her death. The guard at first refuses. But, by bribing him, she gets him to agree to copy out a letter she will dictate. We then have the following scene:

> *Antigone* Write now. "my darling . . ."
>
> *Guard* (writes as he mutters) The boy friend, eh?
>
> *Antigone* "My darling. I wanted to die, and perhaps you will not love me any more. . ."
>
> *Guard* (mutters as he writes) ". . . will not love me any more."
>
> *Antigone* "Creon was right. It is terrible to die."
>
> *Guard* (repeats as he writes): ". . . terrible to die."
>
> *Antigone* "And I don't even know what I am dying for. I am afraid. . ."
>
> *Guard* (looks at her) Wait a minute! How fast do you think I can write?

This method of "echo" or repetition can be used by different dramatists in different ways. It can be used to make a scene more tragic. It can be used to fill the audience with a chilling sense of foreboding, as Webster uses it in *The Duchess of Malfi*. Anouilh, by means of a disinterested guard, uses it to destroy the tragic mood that would have existed if this play were a tragedy—though it does not destroy the pathos of Antigone's plight.

Thirdly, Anouilh presents Antigone in modest, human terms. For example, Antigone's answer to Ismene's "Don't make fun of me" is

> I'm not, Ismene, truly. This particular morning, seeing how beautiful you are makes everything easier for me. Wasn't I a miserable little beast when we were small? I used to fling mud at you, and put worms down your neck. I remember tying you to a tree and cutting off your hair. Your beautiful hair! How easy it must be never to be unreasonable with all that smooth silken hair so beautifully round your head.

Notice, too, Anouilh's use of the nurse. Not knowing that Antigone has been out to bury Polynices, the nurse concludes that she has been out to meet a lover:

> And we'll hear what he [Creon] has to say when he finds out that you go wandering alone o'nights. Not to mention Haemon. For the girl's engaged! Going to be married! Going to be married, and she hops out of bed at four in the morning to meet somebody else in a field. Do you know what I ought to do to you? Take you over my knee the way I used to when you were little.

The scenes that remind us of Antigone's childhood not only "humanize" Antigone, they also contract the happy innocence of Antigone's youth with the world she now has to face.

Fourthly, as I mentioned earlier, the play raises problems untouched by Sophocles. This is done partly by a discussion between Antigone and Creon. At this stage, *Antigone* becomes a play of ideas. Bentley tells us that the play of ideas is a modern evolution of drama. Of course, "play of ideas" is a vague term. In one sense, Bentley says, there are ideas in all words and therefore in all drama. Tragedy has always suggested ideas concerning the significance of human life—but in most tragedies, "the characters fight, the ideas lie still and unmolested. In a drama of ideas, on the other hand, the ideas are questioned, and it is by questioning—and it could only be by the questioning—that the ideas becom[e] dramatic." The discussion between Antigone and Creon is moving because it is not a "detached" discussion of abstract concepts.

Finally, we must not forget the "modern language and dress." For instance, the scene between Antigone and the guard, mentioned earlier, when the guard is talking about his pay: "they know you're an old N.C.O. Take pay for instance." Much earlier, the chorus tells us,

> There was a ball one night. Ismene wore a new evening frock. She was radiant. Haemon danced every dance with her.

We come now to an important point—Anouilh's negativeness. Anouilh's *Antigone* is not negative, to my mind, because of its historical context. Geoffrey Brereton tells us about *Antigone* "First produced during the German occupation, it has an obvious topical message." "An obvious topical message" is perhaps putting it too crudely; but we can see how the clash between Antigone and Creon could be an intensely true-to-life experience when it was first produced. The setting of the play was really the situation in France. But we find Anouilh offers the same "positive" in other plays; and, in a different context, we cannot accept this positive. Earlier, I compared Anouilh and Salinger. A comparison between them also shows us the difference between their positives. The norm offered in Zooey is, to put it a little bluntly, that one should act out of a purity of motive, even if various elements in life are "impure." But this is important—one should *live* with this purity. Anouilh, on the other hand, suggests in other plays that because life is impure, one should reject it; the longer one lives, the more soiled one becomes. (Of course, this does not apply to comedies like *Ring Round the Moon*.) We find finally that we have to condemn Anouilh for the very negativeness which he accuses Samuel Becket of.

To return to *Antigone*—Anouilh's *Antigone* is to my mind, a good play. Although it is not the same type of play as Sophocles's *Antigone,* there can be little doubt that Sophocles's play is a much greater play than Anouilh's. Anouilh explores many problems that Sophocles leaves untouched; but Sophocles leaves them untouched because they are irrelevant to his tragic conception and his tragic theme. The theme and one form of Sophocles's *Antigone* are different from that of Anouilh's. As Kitto tells us, Greek plays are "constructive." The simplicity of the form of Sophocles's play is for the sake of concentration.

Since Anouilh uses Sophocles's play as a frame of reference, it follows that his play would not exist if Sophocles's play did not exist. Therefore, in a sense, Anouilh's *Antigone* is not a finished work of art. Further, while *Antigone* is a good play, it seems pernicious that its form should be adopted for other plays. Let us see why. It jerks the audience back to consciousness by breaking the continuity of a conventional form. Styan tells us,

> No dramatist can work outside a channel of convention, since only this permits continuity of attention. Even when it is his object to break this continuity, he must begin by moving along one of these channels. It must be an already flowing train of feeling he interrupts if after the break he is to secure that exciting renewal of attention.

The stress is on the fact that the dramatist must interrupt an *already flowing train of feeling*. How long can the interruptions continue before the train of feeling, in a sense, ceases to flow? A few plays of this sort jerk the audience back to consciousness. But many plays like this can unsettle the audience so much that the audience may not be able to accept a convention of drama anymore. Then what will such plays feed on? How long can dramatists continue breaking the continuity before all continuity in drama is broken?

Thus Anouilh's *Antigone* is a paradox: it is a good play which ultimately undermines the whole dramatic idiom.

Source: Peter Nazareth, "Anouilh's *Antigone:* An Interpretation," in *English Studies in Africa,* 1963, Vol. 6, pp. 51–69.

Harold Clurman

In this review of a 1956 revival of Anouilh's play, Clurman examines the political nature of Antigone *while offering a mixed appraisal of the work.*

I never read a French review of Anouilh's *Antigone* but report has it that when it was done in Paris during the Occupation it was considered a covert piece of propaganda urging defiance of the Nazi government. Yet the Nazi authorities permitted its production. It seems to have meant different things to different people.

In the hush of its present revival by a new theatre organization—Mazda Productions—I believe I discern how this case of mistaken identity could occur. Anouilh's *Antigone* defies Creon not because her moral sense has been outraged, but because, having been informed that her brother was a despicable thug by the very reasonable politician Anouilh has made Creon, she sees that life isn't worth living at all. All is corruption: life dulls, coarsens, depraves men's initial goodness, and those who go on living become mere "cooks," compromisers content to come to terms with the shabby routine of ordinary existence. And the police shall inherit the earth. It is better to die pure.

This is a perverse romanticism—typical of much French writing since 1937, the key to Anouilh's ideology, whether he writes in the pink vein of *Thieves' Ball* or in the black one of *Eurydice. The Lark* is a quasi-ironic illustration of the exceptional (saintly) person who redeems the mess that most Frenchmen make.

On a higher level (in Camus' work let us say) the thought may be summed up as follows: life is nonsense, let us revolt against its absurdity and then make some sense of it. It is a desperate manner of thinking and though beguiling theatre patterns may be made of it in the acidly sentimental way of which Anouilh has taken full advantage, I distrust it. Its appeal is to a basic weakness in us. Anouilh's

Antigone is an anti-heroic heroine; in a word, an hysteric.

I think it an error for the ambitious organization on 57th Street to have chosen *Antigone* as its first bill, but I am glad have the organization, and look forward to seeing it produce better work in more suitable plays.

Source: Harold Clurman. Review of *Antigone* in the *Nation,* Vol. 182, no. 16, April 21, 1956, pp. 347–48.

Donald Heiney

In the following excerpt, Heiney examines a number of Anouilh's plays, assessing the playwright's facility with the tragedy genre.

Jean Anouilh (b. 1910) is often considered the leading French dramatist of the postwar generation, even though his reputation is only a dozen or so years old. It was under the peculiar conditions of the Occupation that his drama first attracted widespread public attention; *Antigone* (1942) was interpreted, as it was probably intended, as a thinly-veiled allegory of France under the Vichy regime. In America, where his work has been available since 1945, he is still relatively little known. *Antigone* is occasionally played in this country; *Ring Around the Moon.* Christopher Fry's adaptation of *l'Invitation au château,* has attracted some attention, and an adaptation of *Eurydice* has been presented to Broadway audiences under the title *A Legend of Lovers.* But the leitmotif of Anouilh's work is not widely understood; he is typically treated as a theatrical *prestidigitateur* with the expected "French" charm but with little content. This is the sort of misconception with respect to French drama that Anglo-Saxon critics have nourished even since the heyday of the Vieux Colombier. Anouilh is a psychological dramatist, although not in the modern pseudo-scientific sense; he is also the chief contemporary exponent of tragedy in the drama. Most of his tragedies are based on classic themes; they are simultaneously a modern expression of the Aristotelean tragic principle and a sensitive approach to the portrayal of psychological processes.

To Anouilh humanity is made up of two kinds of people: the anonymous mass of normal and rational nonentities who accept the banality of daily existence, and the heroes. The first group is motivated chiefly by a desire for happiness, not the ecstasy of the saint but the *petit bonheur* of the unambitious. This is the race which populates the earth and performs the daily drudgery which is the price of human existence; which "eats its sausage, makes its babies, pushes its tools, counts its sous, year in and year out, in spite of epidemics and wars, right up to life's end; living people, everyday people, people you don't imagine dead."

The second group rejects this banality. Where the ordinary man realizes the imperfection of the human lot but nevertheless grasps at the petty happiness that is offered him, the hero has the courage to say "no." It is this second race which supplies the world with saints, martyrs, Caesars, artists, assassins, prophets, and above all with tragic heroes; for the man who refuses to say "yes" to life thereby condemns himself to a tragic end. These are "those you imagine stretched out, pale, a red hole in the forehead, a moment triumphant with a guard of honor, or between two gendarmes. . . ." It is not that the hero deliberately chooses this path; he is condemned to it by the nature of his personality. He can no more escape tragedy than the ordinary man can escape banality. The ordinary man and the hero belong to different species, and they are condemned to perpetual misunderstanding, suspicion, and enmity; human existence is an eternal struggle between heroism and happiness. Out of this antithesis Anouilh fashions his dramatic conflict. It is significant that he includes all his Greek plays in the two collections he entitles "pièces noires"; to him classic mythology is indissolubly linked with tragedy and death. . . .

Antigone (1942) treats the same basic theme, but utilizes a different technique. Like most other modern Antigone plays, it is based on Sophocles; the period and décor remain that of classic Greece. But there is an anachronistic, modern element which serves to give the action an aura of timelessness. The drama is played in modern dress; Creon wears evening clothes, and the palace guards wear battle-jackets and carry automatic rifles. Such incidental anachronisms aside, the plot roughly follows Sophocles. To Antigone the burial of Polynices is less a religious ritual than a symbolic act she must perform in order to retain her own integrity. Creon, an intelligent and reasonable Machiavellian, tries to convince her that her project is both destructive and meaningless; one by one he refutes her reasons for wanting to throw her handful of dirt over the corpse of her brother. He forces her to admit that Polynices was almost a stranger to her in her childhood; he proves incontrovertibly that Polynices was a ne'er-do-well and profligate who wasted his money on debauchery and treated his father Oedipus without respect. To clinch his argument he confesses he is by no means sure the corpse rotting on the outskirts of the city is Polynices at all. Moreover he, Creon, has no particular opinions about the virtues of the two brothers, and is not impressed by the superstition that unburied souls are condemned to wander eternally in the nether regions. He believes in any case in letting sleeping dogs lie. He is merely trying conscientiously and doggedly (as was, it might be remarked, Marshal Pétain) to rule Thebes to the best of his ability, and he wants to keep philosophical considerations out of the technical process of government. ''Thebes has a right now to a prince without a history,'' he remarks. ''Me, I'm just Creon, thank God. I've got both feet on the ground, my hands in my pockets, and since I am king I am determined, less ambition than your father, to employ myself simply to make the world order a little less absurd, if possible. There's nothing adventurous about it, it's an everyday job, and not always fun, like all jobs. But since I've been put here to do it, I'll do it. And if tomorrow some mangy messenger should come out of the mountains to announce that he isn't quite sure of my pedigree, I would simply beg him to turn around and go back where he came from. I wouldn't have any desire to go and peer at your aunt in the face or to set myself comparing dates. Kings have other things to worry about than their personal tragedies, my dear girl.''

Antigone replies that for Creon this position is eminently rational and just; it is, in fact, the only position he can logically maintain. He has said ''yes'' to life, and in doing so he has brought upon himself a whole chain of consequences which force him to act as he does. As for herself—''I haven't said yes. What do you think that is to me, your politics, your necessity, your miserable stories? I can still say no to everything I don't like, and I'm the only judge. And you, with your crown and your guards and your panoply, you can only put me to death, because you have said yes.'' Her choice made, Antigone goes to her death and drags Hemon after her because she refuses to tell a useful lie as the price of happiness. As Creon tells Hemon toward the end of the play, Antigone was born to die; even though she herself did not realize it, Polynices was only a pretext. . . .

The essence of tragedy as it was understood by the ancients was that a noble hero came to his downfall through an inherent fault in his character; usually this flaw consisted of an excessive fervor or self-confidence. When the classic tragedy demonstrates that *hybris* brings its inevitable *nemesis*, it is merely reiterating that the Dionysian personality

> IT IS NOT THAT THE HERO DELIBERATELY CHOOSES [HIS] PATH; HE IS CONDEMMED TO IT BY THE NATURE OF HIS PERSONALITY. HE CAN NO MORE ESCAPE TRAGEDY THAN THE ORDINARY MAN CAN ESCAPE BANALITY. THE ORDINARY MAN AND THE HERO BELONG TO DIFFERENT SPECIES. . . .''

carries within itself the seeds of its own catastrophe. This is precisely the nature of the catastrophe which arrives to the heroes of Jean Anouilh: fanatic idealists who will accept no compromise, they come to destruction because they are born into a world in which compromise is the price of existence. Most of the other tragic heroes of modern drama are not tragic in this sense; they are destroyed only because they could not achieve their ends. Anouilh passes beyond this modern pseudo-tragedy to arrive at the essence of the tragic situation, and his technique proves itself in the unmistakable emotion *katharsis* the spectator feels at his plays.

Anouilh himself distinguishes between true tragedy and catastrophic melodrama in a curious passage he inserts into the middle of Antigone. While Creon muses over the mysterious burial of Polynices, the chorus comes forward and analyses the situation with a remarkable scholarly detachment. ''It's nice, the tragedy. It's calm, restful. In the melodrama, with those traitors, those desperate villains, that persecuted innocence, those avengers, those Saint Bernards, those glimmers of hope, it's horrible to die, almost by accident as it were. You might have escaped, the good young man might have arrived in time with the gendarmes. In the tragedy you can relax. In the first place, you're at home—after all, everyone's innocent! It isn't that there is someone who kills and someone who is killed. It's just a question of arrangement. And then, most of all, the tragedy is calm because you know there's no hope, no dirty hope; you're caught, you're caught after all like a rat, it's all on your shoulders, and all you can do is cry out—not groan, no, not complain—to bawl at the top of your voice what you have to say."

Tragedy should speak to us, as it spoke to the Greeks, as a living and contemporary human drama; the action should appear to involve persons like ourselves who are seen in predicaments we can understand. If this feeling of timelessness is not present, if we feel we are viewing a "historical" drama, we cannot believe the tragedy is our tragedy, and the drama degenerates into mere spectacle. Anouilh's dramas, written in modern vernacular and filled with the objects and figures of our own daily life, achieve a universality in time which would be impossible in a mere sterile imitation of the external apparatus of classicism.

Source: Donald Heiney. "Jean Anouilh: The Revival of Tragedy" in *College English,* Vol. 16, no. 6, March, 1955, pp. 331–35.

Joseph Wood Krutch

Noted drama critic Krutch assesses a 1946 Broadway production of Anouilh's Antigone, *examining the parallels between the story and the German occupation of Paris, France, during the play's initial run.*

Antigone is adapted from the adaptation made by Jean Anouilh, played in Paris during the occupation, and more or less put over on the German censors. Though acted in modern costume, the scene was left in ancient Greece, and little essential change was made in either the action or even the motives. In Sophocles's original the conflict is already that between the individual and the state, or, more precisely, between the laws decreed by a supreme secular authority and those of God and of nature. To transform it into a fable for the times, little more than a mere modernization of the terminology was necessary. Make Creon a rationalizing fascist dictator who justifies himself by arguing the need for an established order in the turbulent Greek states, make it clear that Antigone's insistence upon burying her brother springs from her conviction that necessity, the tyrant's plea, is never superior to the claims of fundamental human decency, and you get a play which the Germans could not and obviously did not fail to recognize as a discussion of the current situation.

Lewis Galantière's obviously skilful version— it is not called a translation—is acted by Katharine Cornell and Cedric Hardwicke in modern dress upon a stage bare except for its draperies and in one continuous act, which runs for a bit over an hour and a half. Horace Braham, serving as narrator-commentator, is the chorus compressed into one person, the dramaturgical method is Greek, not modern, and, indeed, even the order of the incidents follows fairly closely that of the Sophocles original; so that what one gets is something perhaps even closer to the Greek in form than it is in thought.

On the whole most of the reviewers seem not to have been very greatly pleased, and *Antigone* got a rather poor press. I find myself agreeing with many of the specific strictures made, but I seem to have been more interested and more moved by the whole than those of my colleagues whose reviews I have read. It is true, I think, that to make the guards neither like Greeks nor like S. S. men but like simple-minded American tough guys is probably a mistake. I agree that though Miss Cornell's performance is excellent—specially and as usual with her, pictorially excellent—acting honors probably go to Hardwicke, whose portrait of the icily reasonable dictator is a genuinely memorable one. Moreover, even at the risk of seeming pedantic, I might add that the modern playwright actually outdoes the Greek in decorum, since though of course Sophocles permits no deaths upon the stage he does have the body of Haemon brought in, and I wonder, difficult as such things are to manage properly, if some such presentation of the bodies might not have added the final scene which the play as it now stands does need. But all these are relatively minor matters. I found none of the play, except perhaps some of the very earliest scenes, uninteresting, and I found the interview between Creon and Antigone, which takes up perhaps a third to a half of the entire running time, both absorbing and moving. One of the boldest of the author's modifications of his text, that in which he makes Creon confess that he is using the dead brother merely as a politically useful scapegoat, seems to me very effective, and Antigone's retort at the climax of the debate is conclusive and tremendous. Creon has launched into a characteristic rhapsody in praise of vitality and the will to live. "Ah," interrupts Antigone, "if men were only animals, what a king you would be!"

Since the German censors could not have failed to recognize that the play was intended as a commentary upon the current situation one wonders why they permitted it at all. One wonders also if they would have permitted a revival of Shaw's "St. Joan," in which the same problem is discussed and in which, though the very presence of Jeanne d'Arc might have been thought intolerable, the claims of the central authority really come off rather better than they do in the American version of *Antigone.* Obviously the Germans decided that they were willing to risk their case on the effectiveness of Creon's presentation of it, and a note in the present program helps make it understandable that they should have done so. The play as we now have it is not quite the play that was performed in Paris during the occupation. No Frenchman, Mr. Galantière assures us, could have come away feeling that Creon's argument was stronger than Antigone's, but, so he implies, a German might have felt otherwise, and in the American version Antigone's case has been somewhat built up, ''not by taking anything away from M. Anouilh's Creon, but by adding something to his Antigone, his chorus, and his Haemon.'' Since a part of the interest in this American production is documentary and historical, I am not sure that Mr. Galantière would not have been wiser to give us the argument precisely as it was given in the French version.

Source: Joseph Wood Krutch. Review of *Antigone* in the *Nation,* Vol. 162, no. 9, March 2, 1946, p. 269.

SOURCES

Anouilh, Jean. *Jean Anouilh: Five Plays, with an Introduction by Ned Chaillet,* Methuen, 1987.

Della Fazia, Alba Marie. *Jean Anouilh,* Twayne Publishers, 1969, 154 p.

Falb, Lewis W. *Jean Anouilh,* Frederick Ungar Publishing Co., 1977.

Kelly, Kathleen W. *Jean Anouilh: An Annotated Bibliography,* Scarecrow Press, 1973.

Pronko, Leonard Cabell. *The World of Jean Anouilh,* University of California Press, 1961.

FURTHER READING

Chiari, Joseph. *The Contemporary French Theatre: The Flight from Naturalism,* Gordian Press, 1970, 242 p.
Traces the development of theatricalism in French theater.

Della Fazia, Alba Marie. *Jean Anouilh,* Twayne Publishers, 1969, 154 p.
A comprehensive study of Anouilh's life and work, with analysis of the major plays.

Harvey, John Edmond. *Anouilh: A Study in Theatrics,* Yale University Press, 1964, 191 p.
A study of the theatricalism of Anouilh's plays, with discussions of his staging and characterization.

Lenski, B. A. *Jean Anouilh: Stages in Rebellion,* Humanities Press, 1975, 104 p.
Analyzes the theme of rebellion in Anouilh's works.

McIntyre, H. G. *The Theatre of Jean Anouilh,* Harrap, 1981, 165 p.
Examines theatrical elements of Anouilh's plays.

The Chairs

EUGÈNE IONESCO
1952

Eugène Ionesco's *The Chairs* is one of the playwright's most popular plays. First performed in Paris on April 22, 1952, *The Chairs* was only the third of Ionesco's plays to be produced. At the time, Ionesco was still a struggling playwright.

Most critics and audiences did not know what to make of *The Chairs*. In the play, an elderly couple sets up chairs and greets invisible guests who have come to hear the Old Man's message to the world. The message is left in the hands of an Orator after the couple commits suicide, but he is deaf-mute and cannot relay it.

In the program for the original production, Ionesco writes, "As the world is incomprehensible to me, I am waiting for someone to explain it." As the idea of a theater of the absurd—a literary form that explored the futility of human existance—evolved, *The Chairs* came to be seen as a seminal example of the genre, highlighting the loneliness and futility of human existence.

By the time the play was revived in Paris in 1956, most critics and audiences lauded Ionesco for his unique staging and profound sense of humor. Since these early productions, *The Chairs* is still regularly performed worldwide.

AUTHOR BIOGRAPHY

Eugène Ionesco was born on November 26, 1912, in Slatina, Romania. When he was still an infant, his family moved to Paris, France, where Ionesco spent much of his childhood.

When Ionesco was thirteen years old, his family moved back to Romania. He attended the University of Bucharest, graduating with a degree in French. It was at this time he began to write poetry and literary criticism. After graduation, he became a teacher of French.

During the 1930s Ionesco moved to Paris on a grant to study contemporary poetry. Instead of working on his proposed thesis, he went to work for a publisher and became a French citizen. During World War II he worked a variety of different jobs.

Ionesco wrote his first play, *The Bald Soprano,* in 1948. A one-act work, it was not produced until 1950 and was initially considered a failure. Still, his reputation as a playwright began to grow.

In 1952 Ionesco wrote *The Chairs*. Critics were confused about the meaning of the play, but its run was relatively successful. In 1954 Ionesco's reputation as a playwright was cemented in France with the success of *Amédée,* his first full-length play. Within a few years, his work was known worldwide.

As a playwright, Ionesco was extremely prolific, writing twenty-eight plays over the course of his career. He was a prominent proponent of the theater of the absurd, a literary form that explored the ridiculous nature of the human condition.

In the 1980s and 1990s, Ionesco stopped writing plays, instead focusing on his love of painting. He died in his Paris home on March 28, 1994.

PLOT SUMMARY

The Chairs opens with the Old Man sitting on a stool looking out the window. His wife, the Old Woman, worries that he will fall out of the window. Finally, she pulls him in and drags him towards two chairs. The Old Man sits on her lap.

The Old Woman works to calm him, reminding him that he has a message to deliver. The Old Man is excited when he remembers this. He gets up and starts to pace. The Old Woman tells him how

Eugène Ionesco

talented he is and that he must tell the world his message.

It is revealed that the Old Man will reveal his message to many important people that evening. The doorbell rings and the first guest arrives.

All the guests are invisible. The first guest is The Lady. The old couple makes small talk with this invisible woman and gets her a chair. Another guest arrives. It is a Colonel, who is seated next to the Lady.

The doorbell rings again and two more guests arrive: Belle and her husband. The Old Woman makes grotesque sexual gestures towards Belle's husband; the Old Man intimates that he had been involved with Belle in the past.

More invisible guests arrive. The Old Woman fetches more chairs, but she cannot keep up. She gets frustrated by the Old Man's demands. The Old Woman does not even know who the guests are, but the Old Man is too busy to explain them to her.

Other invisible guests arrive, some bringing children. This upsets the old couple, but they try to seat them just the same. As more invisible guests arrive, the Old Woman's hunt for chairs becomes comical.

When the Old Woman runs out of chairs, she begins to sell programs and food treats. The invisible guests without chairs are forced to stand against the wall. The crowd is so massive that the Old Man and the Old Woman have to shout to locate each other across the room. They continue, however, to make small talk among their guests, assuring them that the message will be spoken in a few moments.

The Emperor arrives. The old couple is shocked that such an important man is in their house. The invisible crowd gives the Emperor the best seat in the house.

The Orator arrives to announce the Old Man's message. Unlike the other guests, he is a real person and dressed in the garb of a nineteenth-century artist. The Orator mounts the dais, and the Old Man directs the invisible audience to ask the Orator for autographs. He signs them.

The Old Man thanks his guests for coming. He tells the Emperor that his life will not have been in vain after his message has been shared with them. Finally, the Old Man thanks his wife. Then, after one last praise of the Emperor, the Old Man and the Old Woman jump out the window and commit suicide.

The Orator begins to speak, but he is a mute as well as deaf. He can only make throaty noises. To communicate the message, he writes a few meaningless words on a chalkboard. He finally leaves and the noise of the invisible audience marks the end of the play.

CHARACTERS

The Old Man
The Old Man is ninety-five years old and married to the Old Woman. He works as a handyman on the unnamed island where they live. He has waited forty years to unveil his profound message to the world; to that end, he and his wife have invited many important guests and even hired an orator to announce the message.

Yet the Old Man seems confused on the big night: he almost falls out of the window; he sits on his wife's lap; he calls for his mother at one point; and he directly contradicts some things his wife says.

After the Orator arrives, the Old Man commits suicide with his wife, confident that his message will be heard. It is an absurd twist that the Orator is a deaf-mute and cannot express it to the crowd.

The Old Woman
The Old Woman is ninety-four years old and married to the Old Man. A supportive and mothering presence, she believes that her husband is brilliant and could have been much more than a handyman. She is also demanding, making the Old Man repeat stories he has told over and over again.

Although she is supportive of the Old Man, she also can undermine him. Just as the first guest is about to arrive, the Old Woman admonishes him when he shows a moment of insecurity. When she is introduced to an attractive man, she makes inappropriate sexual advances.

Yet in the end, she remains loyal to him and commits suicide with him.

The Orator
The Orator has been hired by the Old Man to deliver his message to the invisible crowd. When arrives, he is silent and signs autographs for the guests. He is dressed like a nineteenth-century artist and makes grand gestures with his arms.

After the couple has jumped out of the window, the Orator unsuccessfully tries to speak. Unable to talk because he seems to be mute, he writes words on a chalkboard. The only identifiable words are ''Angelfood'' and ''Adieu.'' When it becomes clear that he cannot communicate, he leaves.

THEMES

Absurdity
Many of the events in *The Chairs* are absurd, underscoring the loneliness of human existence and the hunger for human contact. The Old Man acts like a child, calling out for his mother as he sits in his wife's lap. The Old Woman makes bizarre sexual gestures as she flirts with one of the invisible guests.

The guests are invisible, though the Old Man and Old Woman talk to them as if they were real. The Old Man is desperate to relay his profound message for the world; yet his invited audience—including the Emperor—is invisible.

The Old Man hires an Orator to relay this profound message. After the couple commits suicide, it is revealed that the Orator is a deaf-mute—he cannot communicate the message to the invisible audience. He tries to write it on the chalkboard, but can only manage a couple of comprehensible words. These absurdities underline the ridiculous nature of human life.

Human Condition/Isolation

Like all humans, the Old Man and Old Woman are isolated from each other and the rest of the human race. They live on an island and seem to have little contact with others. When they finally receive guests in their home, their guests are invisible, emphasizing their isolation.

Only the Orator is more isolated than the elderly couple—he must face the invisible crowd alone. Even more symbolic of his isolation is the fact that he is a deaf-mute. He can only speak in guttural noises, and his attempts to write on a chalkboard yield only a few nonsensical words. Every character in *The Chairs* tries to make contact with other people and overcome their isolation; tragically, these people are invisible.

Communication (or the Lack Thereof)

The play revolves around the Old Man's attempts to broadcast his message to the world. To that end he has invited many important people into his home to hear it. His wife, the Old Woman, tries to discourage him from holding his meeting that night—thus putting off communication with the outside world for another day—but the guests have already begun to arrive.

Yet the guests are invisible; there is no one to hear the Old Man's message. The couple goes through the formalities with these invisible guests—but in reality, they are communicating with no one. They do not even communicate with each other.

The Orator also underscores this theme. A deaf-mute, he communicates with noises and gestures that the invisible crowd does not understand. He tries to communicate through writing, but he can only write nonsensical words. When his attempts to communicate fail, the Orator becomes upset and leaves.

TOPICS FOR FURTHER STUDY

- Compare and contrast *The Chairs* with *Waiting for Godot,* an absurdist play written by Samuel Beckett in 1952. What does each play express about human existence? Which one do you identify with and why?

- Research the rates of and reasons for suicide among the elderly. How do your findings relate to the Old Man and Old Woman's decision to kill themselves at the end of the play?

- What do plays like *The Chairs* say about society at the time it was written? Is the play still relevant? Why or why not?

- Reseach the philosophical writings of Albert Camus (such as *The Myth of Sisyphus*) and Jean-Paul Sartre (such as *Being and Nothingness*), two authors that greatly influenced Ionesco's work. Are there direct parallels between the ideas of those philosophers and *The Chairs*?

STYLE

Setting

The Chairs is a "tragic farce" (as Ionesco describes it), which takes place on a remote island. The play is not set in a particular time or place.

All the action of *The Chairs* takes place in a room with a circular or semi-circular shape. Along the wall are two important elements: a window that overlooks the seas and eight doorways.

The window frames the action of the play. When *The Chairs* opens, the Old Man is leaning far out the window. By the end, both the Old Man and

Irony

Many of the elements of *The Chairs* are ironic, which means that the intended meaning is different from the actual meaning. This sense of irony contributes to the absurd atmosphere. The Old Man has a very important message to give to the world, yet all of his invited guests are invisible.

The Old Man hires an Orator to broadcast his message. Yet the Orator cannot effectively communicate because he is deaf and mute. These and other uses of irony in *The Chairs* underscore the play's thematic concerns.

Sound Effects

Although the guests in *The Chairs* are invisible, sound effects are employed to make their presence known. The sound of boats announces the arrival of guests. The sound of waves reminds the audience of the isolation of the island. The doorbell rings to signal the arrival of guests.

Some sound effects provide a clue to what kind of guest has arrived. For example, when the Colonel appears, a trumpet sounds. There are gate-crashing noises when the Emperor appears. Furthermore, the stomping of feet is audible when the Emperor is announced by the Old Man and Old Woman. When the elderly couple commits suicide, the sound of their bodies hitting the water is heard.

After the Orator leaves, frustrated that he could not make himself understood, the stage is empty—but the audience can hear the sounds of a large crowd talking. These sound effects emphasize the absurd elements of *The Chairs*.

Lighting

The use of lighting is an interesting aspect of *The Chairs*. In the opening scene, the Old Woman lights a lamp that emits a green glow. When the Emperor arrives, a powerful light announces his presence. The lights dim after the couple commits suicide.

HISTORICAL CONTEXT

In 1952, France was still recovering from the devastating impact of World War II, which had ended less than a decade earlier. There was a lingering sense of political, social, and economic uncertainty.

During the German occupation of France during World War II, Germany had exploited much of France's raw materials, food, and severely disrupted their transportation system. There also had been severe restrictions on French citizens and their civil liberties.

After the war, many reforms were put into place. For example, a social security system was implemented.

Governmental instability led to uncertainty in France. For example, in 1952 there were three French leaders: Rene Pleven, Edgar Faure, and Antoine Pinay. There were also economic problems including high inflation, an increasing cost-of-living index, and tax increases. The government asked shops to lower prices in an attempt to halt rising inflation.

While industrial production increased significantly in 1952, it was not until the mid-1950s that the foreign aid from the United States began to facilitate new levels of growth. France also had problems converting from an exclusively private economy, based on independently run businesses, to a deficit-ridden public economy in which certain types of businesses were run by the government.

France's economic problems were compounded by its involvement in the Korean War (as part of the United Nations) and in Vietnam. Vietnam was one of several countries where France still had colonial interests.

After World War II, half of Vietnam was taken over by Ho Chi Minh, a communist. A war resulted, but France's poor economic situation limited its ability to intervene. By the mid-1950s, Vietnam was divided in half.

CRITICAL OVERVIEW

When *The Chairs* debuted in Paris in 1952, many critics did not know what to make of the play. A few praised the production. Reneé Saurel (quot-

COMPARE & CONTRAST

- **1952:** Television is very popular. In fact, 42% of American households own a television set. In the United States, color television is introduced. There are four major networks.

  Today: At least one television can be found in nearly every American home. With the advent of cable and satellite television, there are hundreds of networks available. The average citizen can gain access to the television medium through public access programming.

- **1952:** Numerous countries in the world place restrictions on media and their ability to gather information.

  Today: The Internet and cable television changes the way people get news and information from around the world.

- **1952:** While the American economy is very strong, many countries, including France, suffer from severe inflation and relatively weak economies.

  Today: While the American economy is very strong, the economies of many other countries in the world, especially in Asia, are weakening.

---

ed by Rosette C. Lamont in her *Ionesco's Imperatives: The Politics of Culture*) believes the play is "hauntingly beautiful and perfectly structured under its surface of incoherence."

Most critics were not as kind. Some regarded it as too strange. Others were just confused. A contemporary critic quoted in Ruby Cohn's *From Desire to Godot: Pocket Theatre of Postwar Paris* wrote, "Since the guests are represented by chairs, I didn't understand whether this was a symbol of the author, a dream of the Old Man or a financial economy."

Because of such reviews, audiences stayed away. Sometimes Ionesco, his wife, and daughter were the only spectators in the theater. Still, he was pleased. Allan Lewis quotes the author as saying "If my failures continue on this scale I will certainly be a success."

The critics changed their opinion as the concept of the theater of the absurd became widespread and popular in Europe and Paris. When *The Chairs* was revived in Paris in 1956, many critics praised Ionesco's work.

As quoted by Cohn, French playwright Jean Anouilh wrote in the Paris publication *Figaro*, "I think that it's better than Strindberg because it's dark in the fashion of Moliere, sometimes madly funny, it's frightful and ridiculous, poignant and always true."

English-speaking critics were divided on *The Chairs*. The unnamed critic in *Newsweek* contended: "There are two articulate schools of thought about Eugene Ionesco. One regards him as a gifted charlatan and a practical joker. The other agrees with Kenneth Tynan, the London critic who classifies 'the poet of double-talk' as 'a supreme theatrical conjurer.'"

An anonymous critic in *Time* concurred, maintaining that Ionesco's "work has been about equally hailed for its meaning and hooted for lack of any." Moreover, the critic asserted: "Providing playfully humorous touches and some remarkable stage affects, *The Chairs* is at times both engaging and lightly evocative, but calls for greater imaginative pressure, has no really tragic underside to its surface drolleries."

Many critics shared these divergent opinions. For example, *The Nation*'s Harold Clurman contended: "The point of all this is supposed to be that none of us can communicate with another, but I am

Richard Briers as the Old Man and Geraldine Miewan as the Old Woman in Ionesco's play

not convinced that that is the point. There is a strange humor in the play; it presents an arresting theatrical image. Though weird, it is not depressing. There is about it a light, poignant poesy.''

Henry Hewes of the *Saturday Review of Literature* countered, ''Eugène Ionesco has, I think, theatre importance that extends beyond his ability as a writer. The technique is simple. The characters are general types. The situations are usual. But the action and dialogue follow whatever course will amplify the absurdity inherent in the contradictions of each immediate moment.''

Since these original productions, *The Chairs* has been performed worldwide. While most critics believe the themes have resonated over time, a few disagree. Stefan Kanfer in *The New Leader* wrote: ''Irrational response to a crazy world was de rigueur in the postwar period. Today it seems as adolescent as acne and obsolete as a 1952 Renault.''

Such critical division existed even into the late 1990s. Most share the opinion of Adrian Tahourdin of the *Times Literary Supplement*. He asserted that ''*The Chairs* is a sparkling piece, full of wit, pathos and theatrical invention.''

John Simon agreed: ''The exact meaning of every detail is debatable, but the outline is clear enough. We live in terrifying isolation, companioned mostly by imaginary others. We cannot even voice our final justification.''

CRITICISM

A. Petrusso

In this essay, Petrusso considers The Chairs *a play about self-delusion.*

Eugène Ionesco's play *The Chairs* lends itself to many different interpretations. For example, Allan Lewis asserts in *Ionesco*, ''The Old Man seeks certainty and truth in the midst of the absurd.''

The Chairs explores the lack of truth in the Old Man and Old Woman's life, reflecting the lies humans often tell themselves. Many critics also believe the play is about communication between people. This essay argues that *The Chairs* is about people's deluded communication with themselves, which reflects their innate isolation.

The Old Man is the most delusional of the three characters; his needs direct the course of the play. His delusions are evident from the beginning. After the Old Woman pulls him away from the window,

WHAT DO I READ NEXT?

- *No Exit* (1944), a play by Jean-Paul Sartre, is an existentialist drama that explores the meaning of life.

- *Contact: Human Communications and Its History* (1981) is a collection of essays edited by Raymond Williams. It includes numerous essays on the history of human communication.

- Written in 1956, *The Balcony* is a play by another absurdist playwright, Jean Genet. In the play, clients of Madame Irma get their lifelong wishes fulfilled.

- *The Loves of the Subway* (1952), a play by French avant-garde playwright Jean Tardieu, also concerns a couple and the futility of human communication.

Ionesco writes in the stage directions that "the Old Man seats himself quite naturally on the lap of the Old Woman." The Old Woman treats the Old Man as a child and he acts like one.

A bit later, he calls for his mother and says that he is an orphan. He talks in baby talk, then, as the Old Woman calms him down, he turns back into an adult, claiming "I have a message, that's God truth, I struggle, a mission, I have something to say, a message to communicate to humanity, to mankind."

He is ninety-five years old, with what he believes is an important message to save the world, yet he acts like a child. A child would not have the insight or feel the responsibility to formulate such a message.

Once the Old Man starts acting like an adult again, his untruths are compounded. He tells the Old Woman, "I'm not like other people, I have an ideal in life. I am perhaps gifted, as you say, I have some talent, but things aren't easy to me." These are the statements of an adult rationalizing their life.

Sometimes there is a grain of truth to his deception. He tells the Old Woman, "I have so much difficulty expressing myself, but I must tell it all." To that end he tells his wife he has hired an Orator to relay his message to his invited guests.

The deception becomes physical when the invisible guests arrive to hear his "scientific lecture." The Old Man believes a roomful of guests come to hear his message: women and men of all classes; old friends; and important people like colonels and the "Emperor" (of uncertain origin because France had no royalty at the time of the play's performance). Because the guests are invisible, the conversation is one-sided, mostly of subjects of concern to the Old Man and the Old Woman.

The whole situation is controlled and imagined by the Old Man as well as his wife. This becomes evident when the Old Man talks "to" Belle, a woman from his childhood. In his mind, like many people, he wants to communicate. The Old Man does not talk to Belle as if she, too, is elderly, but much younger. The Old Man has a similar conversation with the Colonel.

The Old Woman encourages the Old Man's delusions. She repeatedly tells him that he could have done more with his life. At one point, she declares, "Ah! yes, you've certainly a fine intellect. You are very gifted, my darling. You could have been head president, head king, or even head doctor, or head general, if you had wanted to, if only you'd had a little ambition in life."

During one of these incidents, the Old Man tries to demure, saying "Let's be modest, we should be content with little." Yet he is not. He believes he is so important that dignitaries must come to his house and hear his message.

Later, the Old Woman reinforces these beliefs, claiming "It's a sacred duty. You've no right to keep your message from the world. You must reveal it to mankind, they're waiting for it–the universe waits only for you.''

When the invisible guests begin to arrive, the Old Woman makes polite conversation, but, more importantly, serves her husband's delusion by fetching chairs, chairs, and more chairs. She runs herself ragged making sure that all the guests he has ''invited'' have chairs.

When the Old Man believes the Colonel has insulted him, the Old Woman defends him, saying ''My husband never lies; it may be true that we are old, nevertheless we're respectable.'' Also, when Belle and her husband bring the elderly couple a gift, the Old Man has to tell her what it is. This is concrete evidence that *The Chairs* is mostly a figment of the Old Man's imagination.

The Old Woman also tries to bring the Old Man back to Earth. She tells him that ''You've quarreled with all your friends, the directors, with all the generals, with your own brother.'' He replies simply, ''It's not my fault Semiramis, you know very well what he said.''

The Old Man doesn't want to hear the truth. The Old Woman tries to postpone the meeting just before it is to begin. Guests arrives before he can change his mind.

The Old Woman also has her own delusions. When the Old Man acts like a child, she does too. She demands that they play make believe and that he ''imitate the month of February.'' Then she demands that he tell her the story of how they arrived on the island seventy-five years ago.

During the story, the Old Man contends that they were in a ''village'' called Paris, but the Old Woman, switching back to her maternal role, says, ''Paris never existed, my little one.'' Her conversations with invisible guests are polite but fantastic. Shockingly, she tries to seduce Belle's husband in a bizarre sexual display.

One scene illustrates just how delusional the whole situation is. When talking with Belle and her husband, the elderly couple contradict each other many times: the Old Woman tells Belle's husband that she has a son who abandoned them, while the Old Man tells Belle that he and the Old Woman had no children; the Old Man tells Belle that he killed his mother, while the Old Woman informs Belle's husband that the Old Man took wonderful care of his family. There is no truth—each believes what he or she wants to believe.

There is no real evidence that the Old Man actually has a real message to convey. The play implies that the Old Man hired the Orator sometime before the play began and gave him the information necessary. Yet the Orator is a deaf-mute, according to Ionesco's stage directions, so the Old Man had to have been aware that the Orator could never speak his message.

Yet when the Orator appears, the Old Man and Old Woman act somewhat surprised. The Old Woman has to touch the Orator before she believes he is really there. The Old Man says, ''He exists. It's really he. This is not a dream!'' then, according to the stage directions, he ''clasps his hands, lifts his eyes to heaven [and] exults silently.''

It is only because the Orator is a real man that the Old Man's delusions became real and truly pathetic. The Orator could be interpreted as a physical manifestation of the delusion because he allows the couple to believe the Old Man's lie.

Now that his life's work is almost complete, the Old Man is ready to die. Yet the delusions continue: he thanks everyone who has ever helped him, though the island's isolation has been emphasized throughout the text. What is evident in the last few moments of the Old Man's lie is that he believes that because his message will be heard, his life has not been in vain.

Many people want to believe such things, though few ever really accomplish this. Yet this is the final delusion. After the couple commits suicide, the Orator is incapable of relaying the Old Man's message. The few words the Orator manages to scribble on the chalkboard are nonsense.

At the end of the play, all the audience is left with is the chairs and the sound effect of a noisy crowd. The chairs remain as empty symbols of the Old Man's hopes and dreams. Ultimately, the Old Man wanted to find and understand his own message himself, and killed himself when he thought, incorrectly, that he had accomplished it.

Source: A. Petrusso, for *Drama for Students,* Gale, 2000.

John Lahr

Lahr reviews a 1998 revival of Ionesco's play in this essay. The critic offers a highly favorable appraisal of the play, labeling it as one of the great dramatic pieces of the twentieth century.

Once, contemplating the survival of his plays, the French-Romanian playwright Eugène Ionesco said,

"It takes a few decades for a work to become brilliant—when it's no longer written by the author, but rewritten by the generations who come after him." Britain's Théâtre de Complicité has restaged Ionesco's one-act *The Chairs* nearly half a century after it was written, in 1952, and has established finally and forever the indubitable poetry and genius of the play, which Ionesco subtitled "a tragic farce." Here, at the Golden, superbly directed by Simon McBurney and aided by the Quay Brothers' water-stained gray-plank surround of towering doors and cornices, Ionesco's ontological void takes the shape of a floating, threadbare island world "on the edge of nothingness," in which two nonagenarians—played by the English comic veterans Richard Briers and Geraldine McEwan—act out the folly, fulminations, and fierce solitude of their dwindling days. The production plunges the audience into a vivid, contradictory world of light and darkness, proliferation and absence. Ionesco originally saw an image of ever-increasing chairs on an empty stage—what he called "present absences"—as a vision of "total absence." The great accomplishment of the Complicité's production is to capture the pulse of the feverish anxiety out of which he wrote—the sense of a metabolism gone haywire, and of what Ionesco referred to as a whirlwind of accumulating emptiness.

A large part of the play's new shine is a result of the fine playing of Briers and McEwan, who know all there is to know about comic timing. At the opening of the show, Briers, white-haired and feeble, stands at the window, casting a hangdog look at the water vastness just outside his front door. The play's first words establish the corrupted world they inhabit: "Please—poppet—shut the window. You're letting the stench of stagnant water in." The Old Man thinks he's seeing boats "like sunspots" in the distance. "There aren't any little boats," the Old Woman says. "There isn't any sun. It's night-time, popsey." The Old Man counters, "There's still the afterglow." It's a terrific joke. They can't agree on what is in the world; nonetheless, nostalgia for it prevails. This is the precise emotional affliction that inspired Ionesco's plays. "I write out of anguish; out of nostalgia . . . a nostalgia which no longer knows its object," he once said. The Old Man and the Old Woman tell each other stories to agree on their history and to keep their insubstantial selves intact. "Your story is my story too," the Old Woman says to the Old Man, and at one point she suggests, "Why don't you 'be' something to cheer us up?" The Old Man replies, "Why don't *you* 'be'

> IONESCO'S ONTOLOGICAL VOID TAKES THE SHAPE OF A FLOATING, THREADBARE ISLAND WORLD 'ON THE EDGE OF NOTHINGNESS,'"

something—it's your turn," and they fall into a vaudeville of recrimination:

OLD WOMAN: Oh no it's not.

OLD MAN: Oh yes it is.

OLD WOMAN: Isn't.

OLD MAN: Is.

Their folderol exudes the distinctive perfume of despair. Later, after being told that he "could've achieved something in life," Briers ends up on McEwan's lap, regressing. "I want my mummy," he says. "Where's my mummy? I'm an orphan." The air is full of regrets and abdications. Grandiosity vies with self-loathing. The Old Man feels compelled to give the world his message; the Old Woman, always the supportive wife, says, "Mankind is waiting. The universe hangs on your lips." A party to broadcast his views is called for that night. An Orator is hired to insure the proper delivery of his message, and before you can say "Hey, Feydeau!" the event, and what Ionesco called "the mechanics of proliferation," gets under way.

Chairs are brought into the room for the imaginary newcomers, and Ionesco's fun machine goes quickly out of control. McEwan turns into a roadrunner, skittering around the stage with chairs in her hands, over her head, collapsing hilariously with her body slumped against the door. Chairs are shoved through the doors, dropped from the ceiling, popped onto cornices. As the old couple go through their social paces with each guest, including the resplendently invisible King of Kings Himself (a spotlight follows His Invisibleness around the auditorium to the place where he resides, beside a pair of white gloves on the balcony railing), their badinage compounds clutter with cliché. The play, well translated by Martin Crimp, is a virtual encyclopedia of dead phrases, which has the weird comic effect of turning language, too, into emptiness. "You can find yourself looking at things that seem to be mere

> "YOU CAN FIND YOURSELF LOOKING AT THINGS THAT SEEM TO BE MERE APPEARANCES, EXPRESSIONS OF NOTHING, FACES WITH NOTHING BEHIND THEM,' IONESCO SAID, AND THIS PROLIFERATING NOTHINGNESS IS WHAT THE PLAY BOTH LITERALLY AND SYMBOLICALLY ACHIEVES."

appearances, expressions of nothing, faces with nothing behind them," Ionesco said, and this proliferating nothingness is what the play both literally and symbolically achieves.

At a certain speed, all things disintegrate: in *The Chairs* the exhausted old couple, separated by the crowd, finally commit suicide by jumping into the sea out of opposite windows. It's left to the ghostly Orator (Mick Barnfather) to deliver the message; inevitably, words escape him. He's deaf and dumb; he speaks in sign language and, finally, in frustration, writes the following punning statements on the doors: "ANGELSWEEP" and "GOD™ISAGONE." In the final coup de théâtre, McBurney actually stages Ionesco's "whirlwind of emptiness." The house appears to be blown away: the doors collapse, the scrim flies up, and the set becomes a gray, skeletal shell, like some bombed war ruin. But Ionesco has one last, chilling laugh. After a few moments of silence, the sound of murmuring laughter and conversation wells up underneath the chairs. As the lights fade, a stationary chair turns in our direction. In that startling moment—not scripted by Ionesco—the production teases one final caprice from oblivion: a theatrical illusion within a universe that to Ionesco was all illusion.

Source: John Lahr. "Present Absences" in the *New Yorker*, Vol. 74, April 13, 1998, pp. 78–80.

James L. Brown

In the following brief essay, Brown discusses the manner in which certain meanings in Ionesco's play can be misconstrued due to differences in language and translations.

Willis D. Jacobs' comment on *The Chairs* of Ionesco (EXP., Feb., 1964, XXII), is certainly very interesting and probably valid for the English text; but his attempt to find a positive message in the orator's writing on the blackboard must be doomed by a consultation of the French. The English translation "angelfood" stands for the French *Angepain*, which is the two words *angel* and *bread* placed side by side. This construction in French does not give adjectival force to the word *angel* as it does in English. The effect might be carried into English better if it were written "angel; bread." Yet as a single word, *angepain* might suggest the adjective *Angevin* just by the sound. Such an adjective in this place would have the value only of an absurdity. The most that could be made of it is that the orator has replaced the phoneme *vin* by *pain*—wine by bread. This scarcely has positive implications.

Next follows the series of letters: NNAA NNM NWNWNW V. These letters were probably chosen because they most resemble pure nonsense scribbling. But if one attempts to pronounce them they suggest the negative "ne" or "non" more than anything else.

Finally the orator writes ΛADIEU ΛDIEU ΛPΛ. The inverted V is there to obfuscate. The message is Adieu Dieu—goodby God. (I have no explanation for the final P; pronounced *pé* in French, it probably would *not* suggest the French word *pet*, pronounced *pè*, meaning the breaking of wind.)

That the play is meant to end on a negative note is indicated by the fact that in its first performances the blackboard was not used, only the nonsense mumbling of the orator being heard.

Source: James L. Brown. "Ionesco's *The Chairs*" in the *Explicator*, Vol. XXIV, no. 8, April, 1966, pp. 73–74.

Willis D. Jacobs

Jacobs discusses the nature of absurdity as it applies to drama. He argues that The Chairs, *rather than being an example of theatre of the absurd, is actually "straightforward and obvious good sense."*

Absurd, absurd, absurd. It's time to put this silly misrepresentation of avant-garde playwrights to rest. As for Samuel Beckett, he is melancholy, hopeless, pessimistic, pejoristic, and this is not absurd. It's a conviction of man's brutality and life's difficulty. Living through obscene poverty and the ferocity of Hitler's Germans, Beckett came to conclusions that are intelligent and sensible, not absurd.

But the case most at point is Eugene Ionesco's brilliant play *The Chairs*. Rather than absurd, it is—at least for the vast majority of our population—straightforward and obvious good sense.

The old couple has just died. The Orator strives to speak. His words are not understood. Then he writes the message left by the old people, and which he himself absolutely believes, upon the blackboard. There it faces us with clarity and force. He capitalizes the words to emphasize their meaning, to make them loud and strong. And the message is incorporated in two words of great obviousness. One is ANGELFOOD. The other is ADIEU. Neither of these words is gibberish. Both are words of meaning—all the more meaning in their context of the death if an aged man and woman. The Orator writes: ANGELFOOD. Where have these two dead old people gone; what has become of them? *They have gone to heaven. They are the stuff out of which angels are made. There is divine love and divine reward.* But the audience, like Mr. Esslin, Mr. Coe, and Mr. Glicksburg, have not yet understood. Impatiently the Orator writes ADIEU ADIEU. These are not nonsense syllables, they are valid words. They mean, literally and emphatically, TO GOD TO GOD. The aged couple have gone to their Creator and Redeemer *There is God, there is heaven, there is divine love and reward.*

The Orator knows that he has delivered an understandable and joyous message. No wonder he looks with stupefaction, then with anger, at an audience too blind to read, too obtuse to understand simple words. For here indeed is a message that can command equally the attention of all people—janitors, bishops, chemists, bankers, intellectuals—a message to which even the Emperor, even God himself, would rightfully lend his presence.

What explains the willful refusal by so many able people to see the joyous, affirmative, profoundly devout declaration by Ionesco is, I suppose, the conventional opinion that all advanced contemporary writers are dark, gloomy, atheistic. Even the Orator stammers in word and in writing as he attempts to speak in other words to our times. But that conventional opinion is wrong and it destroys our understanding of many writers. Ionesco is a religious man. He is a believer. He is orthodox in faith. In *The Chairs* he affirms that there is a consolation to even the meanest life, that even the humblest have something worthy to be heard by any and all of mankind, and that what they have to say is that God exists, the soul exists, immortality exists, heaven exists. We are of the stuff of Angels and we shall all be received within the love of God. God loves and rewards us. Not absurd, maybe; not pleasing to the cynical modern ear, no doubt; but there it is in Ionesco. We are angelfood, all of us, and we shall one day go to God.

> "WHAT EXPLAINS THE WILLFUL REFUSAL BY SO MANY ABLE PEOPLE TO SEE THE JOYOUS, AFFIRMATIVE, PROFOUNDLY DEVOUT DECLARATION BY IONESCO IS, I SUPPOSE, THE CONVENTIONAL OPINION THAT ALL ADVANCED CONTEMPORARY WRITERS ARE DARK, GLOOMY, ATHEISTIC."

Source: Willis D. Jacobs. "Ionesco's *The Chairs*" in the *Explicator,* Vol. XXII, no. 6, February, 1964.

SOURCES

Cohn, Ruby. *From Desire to Godot: Pocket Theater of Postwar Paris,* University of California Press, 1987, pp. 122-33.

Clurman, Harold. A review of *The Chairs* in *The Nation,* July 6, 1957, pp. 186-93.

Hewes, Henry. "'Sanity' Observed," in *Saturday Review of Literature,* January 26, 1958, p. 26.

Ionesco, Eugène. *Four Plays by Eugène Ionesco,* Grove, 1958, pp. 111-60.

———. *Notes and Counter Notes: Writing on the Theatre,* translated by Donald Watson, Grove, 1964, pp. 17-18.

Kanfer, Stefan. A review of in *The New Leader,* April 6, 1998, p. 23.

Lamont, Rosette C. *Ionesco's Imperatives: The Politics of Culture,* The University of Michigan Press, 1993, pp. 69-70.

Lewis, Allan. *Ionesco,* Twayne Publishers, 1972, pp. 40-2.

A review in *Newsweek,* January 20, 1958, p. 84.

Simon, John. "Lost Will and Testament," in *New York,* April 20, 1998, pp. 64-5.

Tahourdin, Adrian. "Sitting Uncomfortably," in *TLS,* December 5, 1997, p. 25.

A review in *Time,* January 20, 1958, p. 42.

FURTHER READING

Coutin Andre and Rosette C. Lamont. "Culture Dreams: A Conversation," in *Grand Street,* Summer, 1998, p. 166-75.
    An interview with Eugène Ionesco.

Dolamore, C. E. J., "Adam at Odds with Eve: Ionesco and the Woman's Mission," in *Journal of European Studies,* December, 1993, pp. 409-26.
    Discusses the female characters found in Ionesco's plays, including *The Chairs.*

Gaensbauer, Deborah B. *Eugène Ionesco Revisited,* Twayne/Prentice Hall, 1996, 177 p.
    Biographical and critical study.

Ionesco, Eugène. *Present Past/Past Present: A Personal Memoir,* translated by Helen Lane, Grove, 1971, 192 p.
    Autobiography of Ionesco.

Lamont, Rosette C. and Melvin J. Friedman, eds. *The Two Faces of Ionesco,* Whitston Publishing Company, 1978, 283 p.
    This collection of essays includes original writing by Ionesco as well as criticism of his work.

The Elephant Man

BERNARD POMERANCE

1979

The Elephant Man was first produced in London at the Hampstead Theatre. It soon moved to New York and opened Off-Broadway at the Theatre of St. Peter's Church, and then to Broadway and the Booth Theatre. Pomerance's play earned good reviews and a number of awards, including a Tony Award, the New York Drama Critics award, the Drama Desk Award, and the Obie Award.

The play is based on the story of Joseph Merrick; in large part, it draws from the book by Frederick Treves, which chronicles Merrick's life story. Critics applauded Pomerance's efforts to depict the conflict that results when Treves saves Merrick from the freak shows only to exploit Merrick himself.

The play was so successful that it was turned into an even more successful Hollywood film in 1980. The film earned several British Academy Awards, including Best Actor (for William Hurt as Merrick) and Best Film.

It also received a number of Academy Award nominations in America, including Best Actor, Best Art Direction, Best Costume Design, Best Director (David Lynch), Best Film Editing, Best Picture, and Best Original Score. The film also starred Anthony Hopkins, John Gielgud, and Anne Bancroft.

AUTHOR BIOGRAPHY

Bernard Pomerance was born in Brooklyn in 1940. He is a very private man and there is very little information about his parents, his childhood, his early education, or his personal life.

Pomerance was a student at the University of Chicago, but then moved to London when he was in his early thirties. After moving to England, he began working with small, innovative theatre groups. With director Roland Rees, he founded the Foco Novo theatre group, which produced Pomerance's early plays.

Pomerance's reputation as a playwright is based on one play, *The Elephant Man,* first performed in 1979 and then made into a successful Hollywood film in 1980. The play initially opened in London at the Hampstead Theatre before moving to New York and eventually opening on Broadway.

After writing two more plays, *Quantrill in Lawrence* (1980) and *Melons* (1985), he finally published his first novel, *We Need to Dream All This Again,* in 1987.

PLOT SUMMARY

Scene I

The opening scene takes place in London Hospital: Dr. Treves, the new lecturer in anatomy, presents his credentials to the hospital administrator, Carr Gomm. A salary is settled upon, and Gomm makes a mysterious reference to the salary serving as an excellent consolation prize.

Scene II

In a store, Ross is collecting money for a viewing of John Merrick, who is described as a freak of nature. Treves enters and says he will not pay if it is all a trick; but after seeing Merrick, Treves pays Ross. They agree that Treves will pay Ross a fee to take Merrick for a day to study his condition.

Scene III

While conducting a lecture, Treves shows slides of Merrick while describing the exact nature of the deformities. Merrick is also present and demonstrates his infirmities when asked. A voice from the audience tells Treves that he cannot permit Merrick to return to the freak show.

Scene IV

In Brussels, the pinheads are being prepared to sing by the Man. Ross and Merrick enter, and Merrick tells the pinheads that he has earned a lot of money, which Ross is holding. Merrick also says he is happy. The Man enters again and tells the pinheads to sing.

At that moment a policeman enters and orders the show stopped. Ross comes back and tells Merrick that he has become a liability. After stealing his money, Ross turns Merrick over to the conductor, who agrees to drop Merrick at Liverpool Station in return for a little money. The scene ends with Merrick saying he has been robbed.

Scene V

Merrick arrives in London, and a policeman and the conductor have to hide Merrick to protect him from the mob. Merrick tries to speak, but his words are difficult to understand; the policeman and conductor think he is an imbecile. They find Treves's card in Merrick's pocket and send for the doctor.

Scene VI

Treves interviews Nurse Sandwich, whom he hopes will be able to care for Merrick. A number of other nurses have been too revolted by his appearances to care for him. Although he claims to have vast experiences in Africa with terrible diseases, Miss Sandwich is just as frightened and bolts from the room.

Scene VII

The bishop and Gomm talk about Merrick's aptitude for biblical instruction. The bishop feels it is his Christian duty to help Merrick with religious instruction. He is also pleased that Treves is a Christian.

Scene VIII

Treves informs Merrick that he has a home for life and that he will never have to go on exhibition again. Treves badgers Merrick to acknowledge how lucky he is. He repeatedly forces Merrick to thank him and to admit that, while there are rules to follow, those rules will make Merrick happy. It illustrates that Treves sees Merrick as a child and not capable of real thought.

Scene IX

Treves brings in an actress, Mrs. Kendal, to meet Merrick. Treves informs her that Merrick is very lonely that he needs to be more socialized. Mrs. Kendal asks about Merrick's disorder and whether his sexual function has been inhibited. Treves is embarrassed to discuss sexual matters with a woman, but he finally admits that Merrick is normal in that way.

Scene X

Mrs. Kendal comes to visit Merrick and they discuss *Romeo and Juliet,* a play she has acted in several times. They engage in a spirited discussion of Romeo and Merrick is revealed to very much an intellectual capable of deep thought.

Mrs. Kendal is very impressed with his ability to explore beyond the obvious and tells Treves that Merrick must be introduced to some of her friends. She shakes Merrick's hand as she leaves and he is heard sobbing in the background as she exits.

Scene XI

Merrick is working on a model of St. Phillip's Church. He is visited by several important members of society, each leaving a Christmas gift for him. After they leave, Treves and Merrick discuss the model he is building and the illusion of perfection.

Scene XII

Several of Merrick's visitors, including Mrs. Kendal, Gomm, and the bishop, think Merrick is like each of them. All of them fail to see that Merrick has a definite personality of his own.

Scene XIII

Lord John and Treves are talking; the details are not given, but it appears that John may be a swindler of sorts. Merrick overhears and is worried that he may lose his home in the hospital if all the money is gone.

Scene XIV

Merrick complains to Mrs. Kendal that he has never even seen a woman's body unclothed. She begins undressing. Merrick turns to look at her just as Treves enters. As a proper Victorian gentleman, he is shocked that Mrs. Kendal has shown Merrick her body and he orders her to cover herself.

Scene XV

Ross returns and asks Merrick to help him; he has read that Merrick has important visitors and he suggests that Merrick begin charging each of these people to visit. Merrick reminds Ross that he robbed him and refuses to be a part of his plan.

Scene XVI

Treves tells Merrick about a patient he operated on and who came back from the dead. Merrick, who is clearly hurt by Mrs. Kendal's being sent away, begins to question Treves about the women he operates on and how he fells about seeing their naked bodies.

When he asks Treves if Mrs. Kendal might return, Treves replies that she would not choose to do so. The scene ends with Treves muttering to himself that he does not want her present to see Merrick die.

Scene XVII

Treves dreams that Merrick has come to borrow him from Gomm and takes him back for examination. Gomm, who is disguised as Ross, describes Treves as a dreamer.

Scene XVIII

The dream continues: Merrick is lecturing and describing Treves as self-satisfied and incapable of truly giving of himself. He also describes Treves as sexually repressed and focused more on controlling his emotions than on being able to empathize with those around him. This scene mirrors the earlier one where Treves presents Merrick at a lecture.

Scene XIX

Treves informs Gomm that Merrick is dying. Treves notes the irony that as Merrick has finally managed to achieve a more normal life, his body is failing him. The bishop steps away from Merrick, where the two have been praying, and tells Treves that he finds the depth of Merrick's religious belief moving.

Treves appears to be in despair over the meaninglessness of his life and grieving for something lost. As Treves collapses into weeping, Merrick places the final piece in the model of St. Phillip's that he has constructed.

Scene XX

Snork brings Merrick his lunch. After he eats, Merrick falls asleep sitting up—only that way will keep the weight of his head from killing him. In a dream, the pinheads enter, singing, and lay him down. Merrick dies and Snork enters to find the body.

Scene XXI

Gomm reads a letter he will send to the newspaper announcing the death of Merrick in his sleep. The letter contains a brief summary of how the hospital attempted to make Merrick's life easier. The remaining funds, previous donated to care for Merrick, will be donated to the hospital's general fund. The play ends with the reading of the letter.

CHARACTERS

The Bishop

The Bishop is concerned about Merrick's religious instruction and offers spiritual guidance. He genuinely believes in doing his Christian duty, but he also appears to forget that Merrick has needs beyond those of religion.

Conductor

The Conductor believes that Merrick is an imbecile. When they arrive in London, he gets help from a policeman to protect Merrick.

Countess

The Countess is one of Merrick's visitors.

Duchess

The Duchess is one of Merrick's many visitors who brings him Christmas gifts.

Carr Gomm

Gomm is the administrator of the London Hospital where Merrick is housed. His care of Merrick always appears to be self-serving. When Merrick dies, Gomm writes the final epitaph for Merrick and decides to donate the money for Merrick's care to the hospital.

Walsham How

See The Bishop

Lord John

Lord John is involved in some shady financial dealings. When a great deal of money is lost, it is implied that John will be leaving town quickly.

Mrs. Kendal

An actress, Mrs. Kendal visits Merrick in order to provide some normal social interaction for him. She is not repulsed by Merrick's appearance. Finding him to be charming and intelligent, she decides to introduce him to society. She visits him frequently and becomes an important part of his life.

When he tells her that he has never seen a naked woman, she removes her clothes. Treves enters and is so outraged that he throws Mrs. Kendal out of the room—and out of Merrick's life.

John Merrick

Merrick suffers from Proteus Syndrome, which has resulted in large, bulbous growths growing from his skull. To explain his nickname, "The Elephant Man," he tells Treves that his mother was beautiful, but she was kicked by an elephant when she was pregnant.

Placed in a workhouse when he was three, he had been part of a freak show for many years. He brings in a lot of money for his "handler," Ross, but then Ross also steals from him. He is incredibly lonely.

After Treves finds Merrick, he is taken to the London Hospital where he is studied and sheltered. While in the hospital, Merrick begins to draw and read, and ultimately he constructs a model of St. Phillip's Church.

Merrick is intelligent and funny, with a normal interest in women. When he tells Mrs. Kendal that he has never seen a normal woman's body, she responds by removing her clothing. When she is banished, Merrick misses her very much.

Pinheads

These are three women freaks with pointy heads. They appear briefly in Brussels as part of a freak show and reappear in Merrick's dream as he dies.

Ross

Ross is the manager of "The Elephant Man," a freak show. He steals from Merrick and sends him back to London. Later, after Ross reads that Merrick has become a celebrity, Ross visits him and suggests that they go back into business again.

Miss Sandwich

Sandwich is the nurse that is so repulsed by Merrick's appearance she runs from the room.

Snork

Snork is a porter who brings Merrick his meals. It is he who finds Merrick's body after he dies.

Fredrick Treves

A surgeon and teacher, Treves brings Merrick to the hospital for study. He also rescues Merrick after Ross abandons him. He appears to genuinely care about Merrick, but he hopes to garner attention from his association with him. Treves is rigid and uncompromising, a Victorian gentleman who is shocked when Mrs. Kendal shows Merrick her body.

In the end, Treves becomes disillusioned in his life and finds no satisfaction in his job or his family. Yet he does seem to understand by the play's conclusion that his life has been changed by Merrick.

THEMES

Alienation and Loneliness

On account of his disease, Merrick is completely isolated from normal society: first in the freak show, and later, in his quarters in London Hospital. When Treves meets him, he is treated as a freak and in dire need of friendship.

Although Treves has kind motives, Merrick remains isolated in the hospital; Treves often treats him as a subject to study; and the burgeoning friendship between Kendal and Merrick is ruined when they become too close. When she is banished, Merrick is left even more lonely—now he knows what he is missing, and it breaks his heart.

MEDIA ADAPTATIONS

- *The Elephant Man* was made into a successful film in 1980. The film starred Anthony Hopkins, John Hurt, Anne Bancroft, John Gielgud, and Wendy Hiller. The director was David Lynch. Pomerance had nothing to do with the film, which was written by Lynch, Eric Bergen, and Christopher DeVore. The video is available from Paramount.

Beauty

In a society that values beauty, Merrick is an outcast: his appearance is so deformed and hideous that people run from him in fear. He serves as an interesting contrast for the beautiful Mrs. Kendal, whose humanity is far greater than her beauty. She is able to look past the deformity and perceive the beauty of Merrick's soul.

Creativity and Imagination

In his artwork, Merrick finds an escape from his problems. Alone in his room at the hospital, he begins to sketch St. Phillip's. There is a beauty in his art that Merrick thinks is missing from his life. Although he is trapped in a body that has betrayed him, Merrick's mind reveals hidden talents.

Fear

When Merrick arrives at Liverpool Station, mobs of people attack him out of fear—scared of what they might become and scared of a disease they do not understand.

Treves has his own fears. Like so many other Victorians, Treves fears sexuality and what it represents: loss of control and the embracing of emotion.

Freedom

Because he is so obviously different and he inspires fear in public, Merrick's movements are severely restricted. The hospital is supposed to be a

TOPICS FOR FURTHER STUDY

- Research the state of medicine in London in the 1880s. What medical options were available for the poor and for those who did not fit into mainstream London society?

- Conduct some research into Proteus Syndrome. (Until recently, Merrick was thought to suffer from neurofibromatosis.) Determine what treatments existed in the nineteenth century and compare them with those that exist today.

- Investigate freak shows and discuss why you think they have remained popular.

- An important theme of this play is humanity versus science. Treves can offer Merrick no cure or treatment, but he keeps him sequestered in a hospital setting. Treves perceives Merrick as a reflection of his own humanity and seeks to impose his values and beliefs on Merrick. Discuss his motives and whether you think he succeeds in redeeming himself by the play's conclusion.

---

safe place, but Merrick gives up freedom for that safety. When Mrs. Kendal is thrown out, Merrick is powerless: he cannot make choices and is dependent on Treves to invite her back. True freedom for Merrick only comes with death, when he becomes free from his bodily constraints.

Human Condition

Treves perceives Merrick as a reflection of his own humanity and seeks to impose his values and beliefs on him. In the process, he ignores that Merrick is a human being with needs of his own. Each of the people who visit Merrick views him as a reflection of his or her own values.

Mrs. Kendal relates that Merrick is gentle, cheerful, honest, almost feminine—just like her. The Bishop thinks Merrick is religious and devout—just like the bishop. Gomm thinks Merrick is practical and thankful for his blessings—just like Gomm. The Duchess thinks Merrick is discreet—just as she is. Even Treves falls victim to this game and thinks Merrick is curious, compassionate, concerned with the world—just as Treves is.

STYLE

Alienation Effect

The alienation effect was proposed by Bertolt Brecht, who thought that keeping the audience at a distance created a desirable effect. Brecht maintained that personal involvement with the plot or characters would inhibit the audience from understanding the political message of the play. Pomerance admired Brecht and modeled the construction of his play on Brechtian ideas about maintaining aesthetic distance.

Melodrama

The Elephant Man is classified as a melodrama, which are plays in which the plot offers a conflict between two characters who personify extremes of good and evil. These works usually end happily and emphasize sensationalism. Other literary forms that employ many of the same techniques are called melodramatic. *The Elephant Man* offers both good and evil in the personifications of Merrick and Ross.

Scene

Traditionally, a scene is a subdivision of an act and consists of continuous action of a time and place. However, Pomerance does not use acts, and so each scene consists of a short interlude that may be separated from previous scenes by distance of time or location.

Setting

The time and place of the play is called the setting. The elements of setting may include geographic location, physical or mental environments, prevailing cultural attitudes, or the historical time in which the action takes place. The primary setting for *The Elephant Man* is Merrick's quarters in the hospital. The action spans an undetermined period of time.

COMPARE & CONTRAST

- **1880s:** Queen Victoria has named herself Empress of India, and British Imperialism is at its height. Great Britain and France occupy Egypt and within a few years, Africa will be partitioned and divided among European interests.

  1979: Margaret Thatcher is the first woman to become Prime Minister of Great Britain.

  Today: Great Britain has ceded control of Hong Kong to China, and Queen Elizabeth is set to celebrate fifty years as British ruler in 2002.

- **1880s:** Impressionist painters create a new movement in art. They hold a major exhibition in Paris in 1874. Within ten years, the form will dominate the art field.

  1979: Philip Johnson exhibits a new painting, *Paintsplats* (on a wall). Performance art becomes the newest art form.

  Today: An exhibition of Jackson Pollack's art at the New York Metropolitan Museum of Art results in long lines as people wait in cold, wet weather to see Pollack's work.

- **1880s:** Louis Pasteur develops a vaccine to prevent rabies. He also develops pasteurization to keep milk from spoiling from bacteria.

  1979: Medicare-funded kidney dialysis costs the government $851 million for 46,000 patients and raises questions about whether such patients should continue to receive such a disproportionate amount of medical funding.

  Today: Questions about physician-assisted suicide plague the country and leads to fears that doctors will simply dispose of those people who are physically or mentally unable to protect themselves.

- **1880s:** Edison announces the success of his incandescent light bulb. He is sure it will burn for one hundred hours. Meanwhile in the United States, arc-lights are installed as streetlights in San Francisco and Cleveland.

  1979: An accident at Three Mile Island results in the evacuation of 144,00 people. Little radiation is released, but the accident fuels fears about nuclear reactors as an energy source.

  Today: Energy is assumed to be an unlimited, available resource—especially in the United States, where energy conservation lags behind that of other countries.

HISTORICAL CONTEXT

The setting for *The Elephant Man* is late Victorian England; an understanding of this period is important for understanding the relationship that John Merrick had with his doctors and the public.

In the nineteenth century, England was enjoying a successful industrial revolution. Yet industry brought social problems as well. As more people moved from the country to the cities, overcrowding resulted. In 1832, the Parliament passed a number of new laws to improve people's lives: the areas of child labor, welfare, and sanitation were all the subject of new laws.

In 1851 the Crystal Palace exposition displayed England's recent scientific and technological advances. The success of the Crystal Palace led to a smug satisfaction among England's aristocracy that lasted most of that decade.

In 1859, Darwin's *The Origin of the Species* created a dramatic controversy by questioning long-standing assumptions about humanity and man's role in the world. His next book, *The Descent of Man,* introduced the theory of evolution. Religious leaders, who felt that Darwin was attacking a literal interpretation of the Bible, were outraged.

The Utilitarian Movement of the mid-nineteenth century also raised questions about the usefulness of religion. If man's existence was subjected to reason, then religion provided little benefit for humans; people should rely more on technology, economics, and science for survival.

However, religion is based on faith, not reason. In many ways, religion was perceived as a luxury that modern men did not need for survival. In this difficult time, John Merrick's embrace of religion can be interpreted as an endorsement of its absolute necessity in the world.

The Second Reform Act in 1867 gave voting rights to some members of the working class. Labor became a prominent political and economic issue, with Karl Marx's *Das Kapital* (1867) igniting a debate about capitalism.

At the same time, a severe economic depression in the early 1870s led to an alarming rate of emigration, as British people fled their country for a better life elsewhere. By the end of the decade, things had improved; by the 1880s, London had become the center of civilization in the modern world.

As for the royal family, Queen Victoria had her hands full with damage control. Edward, Prince of Wales, indulged in a series of fleeting affairs with actresses and singers. The resulting liaisons created many scandals for the royal family.

Pomerance references this when he has Merrick question Mrs. Kendal about Edward's most recent mistress. His escapades must have provided a welcome relief from the many social problems that plagued Victorian England.

CRITICAL OVERVIEW

The Elephant Man initially opened Off-Broadway in January 1979. In one of the first reviews, Jack Kroll contended that the play suffered from Pomerance's "hard and heavy" morality, but "this is a minor fault, and in any case the entire Victorian does seem like an extravagant morality play on the stage of history." Kroll concluded by saying that the "New York theatre is lucky to have *The Elephant Man*."

Edwin Wilson's review in *The Wall Street Journal* lauded the actors and direction, which he felt made up for the play's faults. Among the problems, Wilson asserted

In the last few scenes of the play Pomerance abandons the hard-edged logic of the first part and chases philosophical phantoms, but through most of the evening his astute treatment of this unlikely subject makes *The Elephant Man* one of the best new plays of the season.

A similar sentiment is voiced by Christopher Sharp in his review for *Women's Wear Daily*. Sharp asserted that the play "can compete with any other true artistic effort in the city. It reminds us of what New York theatre can become with a little courage and imagination."

Sharp also noted the strength of the performances, stating that "this is a work that deserves intelligent acting, and it gets it." He concluded by calling the production "a delicious evening of theatre."

Within three months, *The Elephant Man* moved to Broadway with only small changes in the cast. Richard Elder of *The New York Times* noted that the play's second act "has been tightened up" since it moved from Off-Broadway, but that some problems with this act remained.

In part, asserted Elder, this is because "many of the themes that are dramatized at the beginning remain to be expounded at the end." In spite of these problems, Elder viewed Pomerance's play as "an enthralling and luminous play."

Douglas Watt considered many of the same problems in his review for the *Daily News*, but he found that "Pomerance takes us to the very heart of this awesome, true, oft-repeated story."

Like other critics who reviewed *The Elephant Man* on its initial debut Off-Broadway, Clive Barnes maintained that Pomerance's play brought a renewal to a mediocre New York theatre season.

Barnes deemed it a "wonderful, moving play," heaping most of his praise on Pomerance's writing, especially his treatment of themes and characterization.

In concluding his review, Barnes proclaimed that the Broadway production had "taken on a new dimension" and that "to see it is a great experience."

Dennis Cunningham declared that the "first act is the best first act on Broadway this year." Yet he also found that the second act just restates what has been said in the first act. In spite of this "severe

John Hurt in the film The Elephant Man

flaw," Pomerance's play was "the most extraordinary and moving play on Broadway."

CRITICISM

Sheri E. Metzger,

Metzger is a Ph.D., specializing in literature and drama at The University of New Mexico. In this essay, she explores Merrick's humanity in The Elephant Man.

John Merrick lived his last four years in the hospital, a man ennobled by his suffering—never bitter, always forgiving. His was a humanity that transcends that of normal society; yet, it is normal society that Merrick aspired to join.

In Bernard Pomerance's *The Elephant Man*, the protagonist, Merrick, forces his audience to reconsider its definitions and expectations of what is considered normal. As Martin Gottfried observed in his review of the play, "Treves is trying to 'normalize' Merrick by making him like himself."

Yet Treves focuses only on the deformity, and he is unable to see that underneath the growths and protrusions there exists a real human being with desires and needs similar to his own. In this respect, Merrick is as "normal" as Treves.

The Elephant Man, although set 115 years ago and staged twenty years ago, is especially topical because it questions the rights of patients and their quality of life. In Merrick's efforts to lead a normal life, the audience is able to project their own desires for normalcy. Merrick's struggle, then, is akin to our own.

In her essay, which explores the ethics of medical technology on stage, Angela Belli states that "life in an age of ever-increasing dehumanizing forces" threatens to control twentieth-century man. Belli asserts that man has benefited from the technological advances in science and medicine but that these same advances raise concerns about the patient's physical and mental well being. These advances eventually create the sort of "moral dilemmas" that Belli argues the "public [is] largely ill-prepared" for; she is concerned about the quality of life issues that people must now face as men seek to exert some control over their own destiny.

Belli's focus on the contractual rights of patients to exercise control over their own lives is illustrated by Treves's insistence that Merrick be

WHAT DO I READ NEXT?

- *The Elephant Man: A Study in Human Dignity* (1972), written by Ashley Montagu, is a biography of John Merrick.

- Another biography, *The True History of the Elephant Man* by Michael Howell and Peter Ford (1992), attempts to provide a medical diagnosis for Merrick's condition.

- Fredrick Dimmer's *Born Different: Amazing Stories of Very Different People* (1988) contains a chapter devoted to John Merrick.

- Published in 1992, *Articulating the Elephant Man: Joseph Merrick and His Interpreters* was written by Peter Graham and Fritz H. Oehlschlaeger. The book examines how Merrick's story became a phenomenon that captured the attention of so many people.

---

denied access to Mrs. Kendal. Because Treves does not approve of the merest hint of sexual interest—and although nothing improper has occurred—Mrs. Kendal is banished.

Yet, Treves's stated intent was always to bring some semblance of normalcy to Merrick's life. What is more normal than sexual interest in an attractive woman?

Merrick's repeated questions about Mrs. Kendal's absence are ignored or rebuffed, as would be the questions of an inquisitive child. Treves ignores the contractual relationship and assumes a parent-child relationship with Merrick. He is reduced to a child-like state and is unable to assert his needs because Treves assumes total control over Merrick's desires.

Treves's goal is to turn Merrick into a proper Victorian gentleman, a reflection of Treves. In this respect, the doctor is seeking to use science—which as Belli notes—is unable to help Merrick.

Instead, Treves seeks ''to prove that although his patient is beyond any medical cure, science can improve his life by transforming him into a reasonable facsimile of an upper-class Englishman of the Victorian Age.''

Of course, this is an illusion since normalcy, at least in Treves's eyes, is restricted to a non-sexual, superficially normal life. Merrick is a young man, and young men are interested in the sexuality of women. Yet when Merrick reveals his interest in Mrs. Kendal as a sexual woman, Treves is shocked and disgusted. Normalcy is the eunuch-like existence of a child.

Normalcy is an illusion in other respects. In the artificial world of his hospital room, Merrick eventually comes to understand that the ''normal'' life that Treves has constructed is only ''an approximation of the life he longs for.'' As Belli points out, ''Merrick is confined within an environment where normalcy and freedom are merely a pretence.'' That he can ever lead a normal life away from the hospital is an illusion that Merrick is forced to face.

Belli contends that when Treves finally recognizes that the social environment he has constructed for Merrick is illusionary, he is forced to question his own ideas about normalcy and the power of science to cure all problems. This leads to a crisis of conscience and a loss of faith.

One of the most interesting facets of Merrick's attempts to achieve normalcy is in how those around him see themselves reflected in his image. As Janet L. Larson observes, Treves's pride in having established Merrick with Mrs. Kendal creates for the audience an expectation that Merrick will achieve normalcy.

Then, when each member of Merrick's new social circle comes forward to relate how he or she finds a mirror image in Merrick, Treves is forced to question what he has accomplished in constructing this artificial social milieu, which is far removed from normal existence. Treves's efforts to normalize Merrick's existence eventually kill him, Larson argues, as "the accumulated weight of others' dreams—which Merrick has accepted—breaks his neck."

When Merrick's reality is revealed as nothing more than illusion, there is nothing left to do except die. Of course Treves suffers as well. In creating for Merrick what Larson calls a "civilizing fiction of companionship," Treves's "shallow expectations" are completely destroyed, and he must finally question his own values. Merrick's relationships—carefully constructed within a contrived social circle—are all illusionary.

Only during their last visit together does Mrs. Kendal appear to recognize that Merrick needs and wants more. Her efforts to help make the illusion real end in her banishment.

Treves's attempts to create an illusionary normalcy have been the topic of other critics. In their article comparing *The Elephant Man,* the play, and *The Elephant Man,* the movie, William E. Holladay and Stephen Watt argue that Treves encourages Merrick's normalcy, while restricting it at the same time.

Holladay and Watt note that "Treves endorses Merrick's reading of romantic literature and his conversation with women . . . [while] Treves rehearses the importance of rules in the 'home,' denying Merrick any opportunity to express sexual feelings."

Treves's behavior, "of alternately encouraging and then deflating Merrick's desire for knowledge of the opposite sex," is, as Holladay and Watt state, cruel. Treves establishes boundaries that limit Merrick's sexuality; in this case, sexuality becomes an intellectual pursuit rather than a physical one. Treves provides Merrick with the illusion of sexual fulfillment.

The illusion is initiated by Kendal, who uses her acting ability to create normal discourse with Merrick. As Treves explains, she has been brought to meet Merrick because she is an actress, and thus, will not run in fright when she sees him.

This, too, is an illusion, as Vera Jiji points out in her article on *The Elephant Man.* Although Mrs. Kendal tells Merrick that her stage life is an illusion and that her meeting with him is reality, in fact,

> the audience has watched the actress create the self with which she greets Merrick. She has carefully

> "IF NORMALCY IS AN ILLUSION, AS IT IS FOR JOHN MERRICK, THEN IT IS AN ILLUSION THAT MUCH OF MANKIND EMBRACES. THE NEED TO FEEL NORMAL, TO APPEAR NORMAL, IS ALL TOO COMMON."

> practiced several greetings, and so, her initial response is not spontaneous, but carefully rehearsed.

However, neither Mrs. Kendal nor Treves appears to recognize that there is nothing normal about this staged meeting. The meeting between Mrs. Kendal and Merrick is as artificial as the environment in which they meet.

Jiji notes that it is not until Kendal removes her clothes that she ceases to act. In the act of undressing, she finally reveals that she is Merrick's friend. In dropping her clothing, she drops the act, ceasing to be an actor and achieving a new level of humanity.

When the illusion between Merrick and Mrs. Kendal becomes reality, Treves bursts into the room to remind everyone that Merrick's reality is limited. He can maintain an illusion of normalcy, but it too will be limited. One reason the audience is so dismayed at Treves's actions is because the audience can see what Treves cannot—that Merrick cannot be bound by such artificial restraints. His death, soon after, seems inevitable.

In an age where people all too ready to seek out a plastic surgeon for a quick tummy tuck, face lift, or liposuction, Merrick's ability to project his inner humanity forces the audience to look beyond the obvious and the superficial.

His existence also creates obvious questions about quality-of-life issues that plague modern life. If doctors are to be able to "pull the plug" on those who seek this assistance because they no longer fit the model of what society defines as normal, then perhaps, there are lessons to be learned for all of us from John Merrick's life and death.

If normalcy is an illusion, as it is for John Merrick, then it is an illusion that much of mankind embraces. The need to feel normal, to appear normal, is all too common. That mirrors maintain such a prominent place in so many homes should indicate that the need to reassure us of our normalcy is a trait that much of mankind shares. John Merrick was no different.

Source: Sheri E. Metzger, for *Drama for Students,* Gale, 2000.

William E. Holladay and Stephen Watt

In the following essay, Holladay and Watt examine the popularity of both the stage and the film versions of The Elephant Man.

> *Man stands amaz'd to see his deformity in any other creature but himself. [John Webster,* The Duchess of Malfi*]*

John Webster is not entirely correct: men in particular have stood ''amaz'd'' at their own deformity, as the production in 1979 of Bernard Pomerance's drama *The Elephant Man* exemplifies. Based on the life of John Merrick, a famous Victorian sideshow performer hideously disfigured by neurofibromatosis, the play garnered Tony Awards, Obies, the Drama Desk Award, and the New York Drama Critics Circle Award as the best play of the year; but its success in New York, and in London the previous year, can hardly be attributed to the reputation of its little-known author or to the drawing power of the actors in the principal parts. Moreover, some critics, an ungenerous minority, maintained that the play's merit did not originate in Pomerance's superior or even competent craft. John Simon, for example, found the structure imbalanced and accused Pomerance of suspending dramatic action in the later scenes to create a vehicle for anti-imperialist polemic. Pomerance indeed may be less skilled than Bertolt Brecht or Edward Bond at designing engaging drama that at the same time furthers an enterprise of social education, although he is quite obviously influenced by Brechtian theory. But even if Pomerance were Brecht, this metamorphosis would in no way account for the contemporary celebrity of John Merrick: American audiences have seldom given box-office support to materialist drama like Bond's, Brecht's, or John Arden's. Why then were most reviewers and large audiences captivated by the play?

David Lynch's 1980 film *The Elephant Man* (in which Pomerance had no hand) increased viewers' knowledge of Merrick and, like the play, enjoyed both critical acclaim and considerable popular success. Although more filmgoers lined up to see *The Empire Strikes Back, The Blues Brothers,* and *Smokey and the Bandit, Part Two,* audiences were moved by this skillful black-and-white melodrama re-creating the gritty environment of late Victorian factories and back-alley peepshows. Lynch effectively represents industrialized London by deftly adapting the cinematic style of his earlier cult success *Eraserhead* (1977), a style punctuated by montages of urban mechanization, the constant hum of manufacturing noise, and motifs of burning gas jets and clouds of steam.

By the early 1980s, largely because of Pomerance and Lynch, Merrick's story was widely known; but the play and film are only two examples of the flood of publications about Merrick that appeared in the 1970s and 1980s: Ashley Montagu's *The Elephant Man: A Study in Human Dignity* (1971), Fred Shannon's *The Life and Agony of the Elephant Man* (1979), a published version of the Lynch filmscript, Michael Howell and Peter Ford's *The True History of the Elephant Man* (1980), Christine Sparks's *The Elephant Man: A Novel* (1980), and so on. How does one explain this cultural rediscovery of the ''Elephant Man'' nearly one hundred years after his death in 1890? What characteristics of John Merrick and his life are most fascinating today? Further, though both Lynch's film and Pomerance's drama share some textual features, they are so different in crucial respects as to form opposing mythologies of Merrick's history. What differing attractions do the two offer, and how are these attractions bound up in theatrical and filmic spectating?

We contend that Pomerance's and Lynch's versions of the history of John Merrick combine to provide an unusually wide variety of pleasures, some spectatorial and libidinal, others more intellectual or contemplative. That is, Merrick's story has been and can be shaped into various forms, each with its own array of audience expectations and satisfactions. We hope to illuminate these by positing three distinct, albeit at times related and overlapping, sources of pleasure in Lynch's and Pomerance's treatments of Merrick's life: the conventions of melodrama, the psychological gratifications of both cinematic spectating and the viewing of sideshow ''freaks,'' and the critique of powerful Victorian institutions and colonial biases—an element more pronounced in the play than in the film.

The significant differences between the two versions account for Pomerance's more substantial condemnation of Victorian society. One such difference concerns Lynch's restricted focus on Merrick and his physical well-being. Like Victorian melodramatists who thrilled their audiences by situating powerless characters in increasingly desperate predicaments and devising last-minute rescues, Lynch continually places Merrick in danger and then finds ways to save him. In the film Merrick's tranquil existence in his newfound home at London Hospital is constantly threatened by a wide variety of adversaries: his cruel manager, Bytes; an avaricious porter; an angry mob in a train station; an obstreperous member of the London Hospital Governing Committee; and Carr Gomm, governor of the hospital, who initially opposes Merrick's permanent residency. Crueler still, he is flogged by Bytes, imprisoned in a cage near circus animals, and forced to suffer indignities at the hands of the porter's drunken friends. Only near the end of the film—when his place in the hospital is finally secured and he attends the theater to see Mrs. Kendal—is the audience assured of his safety, just minutes before he falls contentedly into a fatal sleep.

Constructed differently, Pomerance's play follows this pattern of engaging action only as far as the fifth scene (it has twenty-one), in which Treves rescues Merrick from a mob at a train station; thereafter little doubt remains about Merrick's well-being. This structure allows Pomerance considerably greater opportunity for social analysis, which is frequently conveyed through Treves, the doctor who befriends Merrick and who dominates the later scenes by seriously examining his own, ostensibly selfless motives for doing so. In the film, by contrast, the one moment in which Treves betrays any self-doubt serves as only a brief respite from the continual melodramatic excitement. Pomerance dispenses with the excitement much earlier so as to interrogate the discourses that construct sexuality in Victorian England.

Another major difference between the two versions involves Merrick's sexual desire, an issue that Lynch deflects by portraying Merrick as a devoted son and associating him, both narratively and cinematically, with prepubescent boys. Using the mise-en-scène to build this theme, Lynch decorates both Treves's parlor and Merrick's room with numerous artistic renderings of mothers and children. Invited to tea at Treves's home, Merrick admires portraits of Treves's family and confesses to Mrs. Treves that as a son he has surely disappointed his mother; when Princess Alexandra resolves the hospital's dispute about keeping Merrick, she quotes Queen Victoria's characterization of him as "one of England's most unfortunate sons." Lynch also trains numerous close-ups on young boys, such as the showman's assistant and the children who harass

> "... IN EXHIBITING FIGURES LIKE MERRICK, THE LATE VICTORIAN PEEPSHOW PRODUCED A PORNOGRAPHIC VIEW BASED ON A DOUBLE DOMINANCE: MASTERY THROUGH GENDER AND THE SUPREMACY OF IMPERIALISM."

Merrick at the station. He establishes this identification most conspicuously at Merrick's death: unable to sleep lying down because of his enlarged skull, Merrick suffocates when he emulates a sleeping child in a drawing that hangs in his room. Pomerance, conversely, elects to treat Merrick as he was when Treves found him, a young adult with corresponding desires. This portrayal is all the more convincing in the play because of Pomerance's dictum that the actor impersonating Merrick not use makeup to replicate the character's deformity. Through the "normal-looking" actor, spectators more easily recognize Merrick's typicality, his similarity to other young men in their twenties. This interconnection between the typical and the particular in the play, a relation central to historical representation, is nonexistent in Lynch's film. With an enlarged skull, fibrous tumors, and the rest, John Hurt as Merrick bears little resemblance to any "typical" young man. This is not to say that Lynch's film lacks a sexual (or political) dimension entirely; viewers of *Eraserhead* and, more recently, *Blue Velvet* are familiar with the oedipal themes in Lynch's work. Nevertheless, in *The Elephant Man* Lynch creates an engaging preoedipal fairy tale and for the most part eschews analysis of Merrick's libido.

In Lynch's screenplay, then, Merrick is a gentle monster caught between a safe harbor and several dangers; in Pomerance's play, he is similarly victimized—but then again so is his rescuer, Treves, who is ensnared in the values of Victorian England's privileged class. Pomerance effaces the boundary between safety and exploitation, adding layers of social realism to various mythologies about Merrick. These differences between the film and play reveal both the many aspects of Merrick's life that intrigue audiences and the systems of viewing within which spectators' responses are formed. For these reasons, after summarizing the melodramatic conventions that constitute Pomerance's and Lynch's dramas, we delineate the spectatorial mechanisms at work in viewing the Elephant Man (along with the pleasures underlying these mechanisms) and consider Pomerance's comparatively richer explanation of the social origins of Merrick's victimization.

[I]

Like much commercial cinema today, melodrama was the most popular form of theatrical entertainment in Merrick's time. More than a source of pleasure, melodrama offered audiences steeped in its conventions a ready vehicle for interpreting Merrick's experiences. His deformities, much like Quasimodo's in *The Hunchback of Notre Dame,* made him an outcast, and the true story of his fortunes and misfortunes—his mistreatment as a show freak and his "rescue" by the eminent young surgeon Frederick Treves—must have read like something one might see at Drury Lane or, more likely, at the Adelphi, famous in London for its melodrama. Quite literally "read," for in addition to the many newspaper accounts of his life, there were a number of reminiscences, since few who had known Merrick could resist writing about him after his death. Strikingly similar in their melodramatic proclivities, these commentators reveal the extent to which their theatrical viewing informed their memories of actual events. Such interpretations of "facts," as Raymond Williams points out, result from living in a "dramatized society," one in which habitual spectating leads to perceiving the events of daily life as mediated by dramatic conventions: "The specific conventions of a particular dramatization . . . are not abstract. They are profoundly worked out and reworked in our actual living relationships. They are our ways of seeing and knowing, which every day we put into practice. . . ." Treves's own memoir of Merrick, a typical example of the way history can be not merely dramatized but melodramatized, serves as the source for most modern representations of Merrick, including Ashley Montagu's book, Pomerance's play, and Lynch's film. What the doctor describes, both playwright and director dramatize, at times amplifying Treves's sentiment and extending the reductive polarizations of his melodramatic account.

Like many contemporary filmgoers, nineteenth-century London audiences were not ashamed to weep at the sight of a villain persecuting a virtuous heroine; they were eager both to have their emotions engaged and to indulge in the sensationalism and spectacle that skillful melodramatists like Dion Boucicault could create. While there were many successful types of melodrama, some elements remained fairly constant. Suffering heroines and sadistic villains are a staple of the recipe, and, as Martha Vicinus observes, melodrama "always sides with the powerless," the noble heroine over the powerful but depraved adversary. Such villains seem wholly possessed by their desires and will do anything to satisfy them. As a result, the heroine and the hero face myriad injustices, but no matter how "helpless and unfriended," the heroine remains virtuous throughout the play. Domestic melodrama routinely rewards such paragons: the hero rescues the heroine, and their adversaries receive appropriate retribution as a larger moral order triumphs over a malign society. The appeal of such an order is obvious, as Vicinus explains: "Much of the emotional effectiveness of melodrama comes from making the moral visible" in the stock characters and in the plot.

Treves evidently knew this paradigm well. When his account and the play are juxtaposed with Michael Howell and Peter Ford's *The True History of the Elephant Man,* his melodramatizing tendencies become apparent. Howell and Ford's somewhat pleonastic title indicates their efforts to distinguish their factual work from several fictions about Merrick, many of them introduced by Treves. They uncover information that Treves either never knew or had forgotten by the time he wrote his memoir in 1923, information that concerns Merrick's life before he entered London Hospital in 1884, a period about which Treves was uncertain since Merrick preferred not to speak of it. Howell and Ford show that Treves exaggerated many events on the side of the emotional or the sensational, turning the true story into the engaging drama that Pomerance and Lynch recreate. For instance, Treves reproaches Merrick's mother for "basely" deserting her son when he was "so small that his earliest clear memories were of the workhouse to which he had been taken." Less melodramatically, Howell and Ford contend that Merrick's mother was quite kind to him until her death, when her son was nearly eleven. Merrick did enter the Leicester workhouse, but at age seventeen and of his own initiative.

An analogous, yet more subtle, "dramatization" of Treves's consciousness produces his account of first seeing Merrick. At this time the doctor did not perceive a future patient or the results of a devastating disease, only a figure of abject misery:

> The showman pulled back the curtain and revealed a bent figure crouching on a stool and covered by a brown blanket. In front of it, on a tripod, was a large brick heated by a Bunsen burner. Over this the creature huddled to warm itself. It never moved when the curtain was drawn back.... This figure was the embodiment of loneliness.
>
> The showman—speaking as if to a dog—called out harshly: "Stand up!" The thing arose slowly and let the blanket that covered its head and back fall to the ground.... At no time had I met with such a degraded or perverted version of a human being as this lone figure displayed. (Montagu)

Here Treves stresses Merrick's degradation and loneliness, later remarking that Merrick was "as secluded from the world as the Man in the Iron Mask," the popular Dumas character seen often on the Victorian stage. Treves's terms for Merrick—the "creature," the "thing," and "it"—betray the same mixture of pity and revulsion that Hugo's Quasimodo or Verdi's Rigoletto might inspire. Though Treves's feelings are more intense, they parallel those of a Victorian audience watching the numerous other deformed or handicapped characters who, according to Peter Brooks, illustrate melodrama's "repeated use of extreme physical conditions to represent extreme moral and emotional conditions," its portrayal of "invalids of various sorts whose very physical presence evokes the extremism and hyperbole" of the melodramatic world. It is in this world that Treves intellectually placed Merrick at first sight.

The doctor also sensationalizes the closing of Merrick's show in Belgium (on the grounds of indecency) and the subsequent return to England, in part by casting Merrick's showman as a stage villain. Treves was not in Belgium to witness the events he depicts, so his penchant for the theatrical was only minimally constrained by the bare facts: "Merrick was thus no longer of value. He was no longer a source of profitable entertainment.... He must be got rid of. The elimination of Merrick was a simple matter. He could offer no resistance" (Montagu). Regardless of what actually happened, Treves transforms Merrick into the helpless victim suffering at the hands of the cruel manager. Not surprisingly, given this transformation, Merrick is cast in a role usually reserved for a woman: Merrick as heroine. He is ideal for the part because of his innocence, helplessness, and suffering. The theatricalizing impulse manifests itself again in Treves's narration of Merrick's return to London, which replicates the conventional harrowing journey of the outcast woman: "[Merrick] would be harried by an eager mob as he hobbled along.... He had but a few shillings in his pocket and nothing either to eat or drink on the way. A panic-dazed dog with a label on his collar would have received some sympathy and possibly some kindness. Merrick received none" (Montagu). This characterization mirrors the portrayal of hapless victims on the Victorian stage, as in W. G. Wills's *Jane Shore* (1875), in which the title character is marched, starving and hounded by onlookers, through the streets of Christmastime London. History becomes melodrama, an exciting dreamworld of black-and-white morality, sensation, and strong emotion.

Pomerance and Lynch continue Treves's melodramatizing practices, though in differing ways and through re-creations of different moments in Treves's memoir. For example, while Lynch elects to omit the workhouse detail, he substitutes lingering shots of the squalor of Merrick's show life. Pomerance, however, further exaggerates Treves's fiction of the helpless child abandoned to life in the workhouse; he has Ross, Merrick's manager in the play, explain, "Found him in a Leicester workhouse. His own ma put him there age of three. Couldn't bear the sight, well you can see why." To complete the image, Pomerance surpasses his source by writing Merrick a moving speech detailing the horrors of the workhouse: "They beat you there like a drum. Boom boom: scrape the floor white. Shine the pan, boom boom. It never ends. The floor is always dirty. The pan is always tarnished. There is nothing you can do...." Perhaps even more today than in the 1890s, the very term *workhouse* signifies abuse, poverty, and despair—the bleak urban world into which the unfortunates of Victorian literature are frequently thrust. In George Moore's *Esther Waters* (1894), for example, the homeless title character wanders London streets carrying her infant son and pondering her destitution: "Why should such cruelty happen to her? The Workhouse, the Workhouse, the Workhouse!... What had she done to deserve it? Above all, what had the poor innocent child done to deserve it?" Like Treves before them, Pomerance and Lynch induce their audiences to ask these conventional questions of domestic melodrama and to experience the pathos of such deplorable injustice.

For other incidents that Treves narrates melodramatically—his first sight of Merrick and the manager's abandonment of Merrick on the Continent—Lynch builds on the emotion of the original.

(Pomerance, by contrast, minimizes the emotionalism of Treves's initial encounter with Merrick, both by keeping the audience outside the show tent and by not giving the doctor any extreme response.) Lynch emphasizes the immediate impact Merrick has on Treves by capturing the overwrought surgeon in a memorable close-up just as tears gather in his eyes and finally trickle down his face. Similarly, even though both Lynch and Pomerance retain Dr. Treves's interpretation of the events in Belgium—the play and film audiences alike see a profit-hungry huckster robbing his charge—Lynch again exceeds the sensationalism of his source. Lynch's scene begins on the grounds of a Belgian carnival. It is a cold and rainy day, with Bytes attracting a small crowd to see his "creature." Merrick, half naked and totally exhausted, answers his "owner's" command—the thumping on the stage of the same cane Bytes uses to beat him—to step forward from behind a curtain. He falls to the floor and, although Bytes jabs the cane into his back, Merrick cannot summon sufficient energy to stand. A disgusted crowd expresses its revulsion at the spectacle, thus infuriating Bytes. Later, inebriated and convinced that Merrick is being deliberately spiteful, Bytes evicts Merrick from the show wagon, imprisons him in an animal cage, and throws his few possessions out onto the ground. Lynch has represented this kind of cruelty before, tincturing it with sexual ambivalence as Bytes refers affectionately to Merrick as his "treasure"—the valued possession whom he brutalizes. It is only through the kindness of other sideshow performers that Merrick is released from his confinement and placed on a ship for England.

Yet when the ship docks in England and Merrick takes a train to London, his troubles are still not over. He has escaped his sadistic proprietor only to be threatened by an angry mob at the Liverpool Street station. In this scene both Lynch and Pomerance surpass their source in working on their audiences' emotions. Typically the melodramatist supplies a hero to save the helpless heroine just when the situation looks bleakest. When Dr. Treves, in his memoir, depicts Merrick's attempts to get back to London, he places the "heroine" in such straits, but the doctor is modest, even perfunctory, in assigning the hero's role to himself: "I had some difficulty in making a way through the crowd, but there, on the floor in the corner, was Merrick.... He seemed pleased to see me, but he was nearly done. The journey and want of food had reduced him to the last stage of exhaustion" (Montagu). Pomerance does not re-create the train journey; rather, he opens scene 5 with policemen barring a waiting room against an offstage mob pursuing Merrick. Ignoring the real Treves's modesty about his own actions, Pomerance at the end of the scene brings his young surgeon onstage with the stride of a hero rescuing an innocent victim:

TREVES: What is going on here? Look at that mob, have you no sense of decency? I am Frederick Treves. This is my card.

POLICEMAN: This poor wretch here had it. Arrived from Ostend.

TREVES: Good Lord, Merrick? John Merrick? What has happened to you?

MERRICK: Help me!

In Pomerance's scene, the starved Merrick has presumably been hounded by onlookers, though we never actually witness their inhumanity; but in Lynch's film we see an angry crowd pursue Merrick through the station and ultimately trap him in a public restroom. As they draw closer, Merrick stops them with a desperate plea: "*I* am not an animal! I am *not* an animal! *I am a human being!*" The crowd backs away momentarily as several policemen come to Merrick's defense and, in the next scene, return him to Treves. Thus, both Pomerance and Lynch, in their different ways, build effective drama out of an incident that Treves invests with only minimal emotion.

In both play and film, this rescue scene concludes with a stage picture analogous to the "big curtain" tableaux vivants of Victorian melodrama, and from then on Merrick's fortunes improve. As in any domestic melodrama in which the helpless woman in dire circumstances finds a home, Merrick finds his in Treves's hospital. Yet for Pomerance there remained one further authorial chore: to complete Merrick's characterization as virginal heroine by establishing his sexual innocence. Treves's account suggests this role by describing Merrick as a woman—and Pomerance supplies a test of Merrick's purity to perfect the fiction his Victorian predecessor began. Lynch, significantly we think, chooses instead to develop Merrick's innocence as a child, skipping over the thornier issue of his sexuality.

Both play and film accumulate evidence for their divergent representations in their early scenes. As the real Treves had done in a lecture to the Pathological Society of London, Lynch's Treves alludes briefly to Merrick's genitals, commenting on their normalcy. Though Pomerance appropriates material from the same lecture, he handles the issue very differently, projecting our curiosity about

Merrick's sexuality onto Mrs. Kendal, who receives Treves's permission to ask an indiscreet question: "I could not but help noticing from the photographs that—well—of the unafflicted parts—ah, how shall I put it?" This inquiry anticipates scene 14, which Merrick opens by noting that, since the prince and the Irishman (Charles Stewart Parnell) keep mistresses, he has "concluded" that he should acquire one as well. Admittedly, some sexual desire motivates this proclamation, but so too does his ambition to conform socially: the most powerful men in society have mistresses; Treves compels him to learn the ways of this society; and the conclusion is obvious—a Victorian gentleman requires the company of a lady. Never having seen a woman's nude body, Merrick eagerly accepts Mrs. Kendal's offer in this scene to allow him to survey hers. But there is, finally, little evidence of desire in this incident: in a spirit of adventure or kindness, she disrobes so that women for him will no longer be, to borrow Treves's expression, "creatures of his imagination." His innocent response to her nakedness—"It is the most beautiful sight I have ever seen"—is supportive of her earlier opinion: Merrick is "gentle, almost feminine."

In both the historical account and the play, Treves uses the same metaphor of femininity in his lecture when he compares Merrick's arms: the badly deformed, almost "shapeless" and "useless" right arm and his hand "like a fin or paddle" contrast with the "anomalous" left arm, a "delicately shaped limb covered with fine skin and provided with a beautiful hand which any woman might have envied." In an elision of Treves's actual lecture, Lynch's character merely remarks, "And his left arm is entirely normal, as you can see." This small deviation from Treves's account suggests Lynch's decision to avoid the feminization of Merrick that both the historical Treves and Pomerance develop. To be sure, Lynch borrows from Treves's memoir and reproduces minor details; the film's motif of burning gas jets, for instance, might be attributed to Treves's recollection of his first view of Merrick, which was illuminated "by the faint blue light of the gas jet" (Montagu 14). But while Lynch passes over the feminine imagery in Treves's account, Pomerance makes good use of it. In the play, Mrs. Kendal sees Merrick as womanlike and supplies him with toilet articles so that he might "make himself" at the mirror "as I make me." In this regard, Pomerance's characters follow their historical models, as Madge Kendal recalls in her autobiography: "Sir Frederick Treves states that his [Merrick's] troubles ennobled him and 'made him as gentle, affectionate, loveable, and amiable as a happy woman.'" Here Merrick's feminine identity is based on prevalent idealizations of Victorian women and girls: the mid-Victorian "cult of domesticity" configured women as "innocent, pure, gentle, and self-sacrificing"—and submissive, totally dependent on men (Gorham). All these adjectives describe Merrick, who is gentle, pure, domestic, and dependent on Treves.

True to the melodramatic convention that involves the "violation and spoliation of the space of innocence" (Brooks), scene 14 depicts Treves interrupting the meeting between Merrick and Mrs. Kendal and repeating the words he had uttered when Merrick was surrounded by the hostile mob: "What is going on here? ... Have you no sense of decency?" Kendal's explanation—"For a moment, Paradise, Freddie"—underscores the analogy between Merrick's room and Eden, the "enclosed garden, the space of innocence, surrounded by walls," invaded, in Brooks's words, by a "villain, the troubler of innocence." This encounter therefore does not undermine Pomerance's depiction of Merrick's innocence; on the contrary, it communicates Merrick's virtue more resonantly by suddenly transforming Treves from hero into villain. Serving as a foil here to his morally superior patient, Treves is unable to separate, as Merrick can, nudity from sexuality. Mrs. Kendal's act provides a sufficient test of Merrick's character, and his purity remains intact.

As treated in all three versions—Treves's, Pomerance's, and Lynch's—Merrick's life assumes the familiar narrative shape of a domestic melodrama. An innocent "woman" has been eking out a precarious living under the hungry eye of an unscrupulous landlord, mortgage holder, or employer. Finally the day arrives when, unable to pay her rent or otherwise satisfy a "lawful" indebtedness, she is turned out into the streets, penniless, soon to face starvation. Although suffering untold agonies as a social outcast, she maintains her honor, even when it is tested in the most severe of environments. Eventually, at the brink of destruction, a strong and equally untainted champion discovers her distress. Evil is crushed, virtue is rewarded, and the heroine becomes an inspiration to all who know her. Change the heroine to John Merrick, and we recognize one of the appeals of viewing *The Elephant Man:* the appeal of melodrama. What was in Treves's memoir the product of a powerful cultural construct becomes in Pomerance's play and Lynch's film a successful dramatic strategy.

[II]

Scene 14 in Pomerance's play, in which Treves interrupts and condemns Mrs. Kendal's exhibition of herself to Merrick, is provocative for reasons other than its association of Merrick with melodramatic heroines. For one thing, it is initiated by a reversal of gender roles: a woman looking at photographs of a naked man, a situation that disrupts the established patriarchal system of seeing and being seen. Or, as Mary Ann Doane has put it, the reason "men seldom make passes at girls who wear glasses" is that "there is always a certain excessiveness, a difficulty with women who appropriate the gaze, who insist upon looking." Following Laura Mulvey's theorizing, Doane and E. Ann Kaplan regard Western culture as "deeply committed to myths of demarcated sex differences, called 'masculine' and 'feminine,' which in turn revolve first on a complex gaze apparatus and second on dominance/submission patterns" (Kaplan). In theories of this apparatus, the gaze is most often posited as male and dominant; the object of the gaze female and submissive. Moreover, as Patricia Mellencamp emphasizes, "More than other senses, the eye objectifies and masters." Such theories of spectation can be enormously helpful in assessing modern audiences' fascination with Merrick and his story, because Pomerance and Lynch not only recognize the kinds of gender demarcation Kaplan mentions but also, through Merrick's powerlessness as a sideshow exhibit, reverse such constructions of maleness and femaleness. These and other spectatorial pleasures are the subject of what follows.

Lynch's introductory sequences in *The Elephant Man* intimate his awareness of what Freud posits as one motive for scopophilia: the pleasure to be derived from seeing private, even forbidden things. Few directors, other than Alfred Hitchcock or perhaps Brian DePalma, understand this desire so well as Lynch does. The initial scenes signal the audience's eventual viewing of a horrible reality just beneath the surface of society. After a thematically rich opening montage, the first London sequence takes place on a crowded circus ground where Treves, who at this point does not know Merrick, wanders toward a sign upon which the camera focuses: "FREAKS." Treves follows a policeman through an opening marked "No Entry," past several exhibits cased in glass and advertised as "The Fruit of Original Sin," through yet another opening marked "No Entry," and finally along a labyrinthine passageway. Past more exhibits and customers, at the very back of the show tent, reside Bytes and Merrick. These shots mark the trail to Merrick with transgressions of natural and moral law ("Original Sin"): deformed sideshow performers are the products not of disease but of some moral lapse, some "sin." They are housed, consequently, on the periphery of the circus grounds, away from the center of activity. Seeing Merrick is also illegal in the fictional space of the movie; as Treves approaches Merrick's tent, the police close the exhibition (as they did in November 1884). The cinematic metaphor here suggests that what we are about to see, Merrick himself, lies on the margins of, or deep within, late Victorian culture. The prospect is horrible, yet enticing. In this scene, further, Lynch not only thwarts Treves's desire to view Merrick but also delays satisfying the audience's similar curiosity. The film thus promises a very special gaze and then withholds fulfillment of the promise, piquing viewers' interest in the spectacle.

The topography of the opening, with its winding passageways leading to Merrick's secluded tent, is crucial in reinforcing the expectation of a forbidden spectacle, so crucial in fact that Lynch repeats it for Treves's second visit to Merrick. A boy appears at the hospital to inform Treves of Merrick's new location, one hidden from the eyes of the authorities. Treves moves down several alleys, past numerous laborers and steaming machines to a grimy, out-of-the-way room. There Bytes meets him and collects a fee, opens a locked door, and guides Treves down several dark hallways to Merrick. As the showman opens the darkened room, the audience catches a shadowy glimpse of Merrick before the camera cuts to an appalled Treves, whose eyes well up with tears. The sight of Merrick is still withheld when Merrick is brought to the hospital for Treves's lecture to the Pathological Society of London. Lynch places the camera behind a screen, revealing Merrick only in silhouette. The first full view of Merrick comes when he is back at the hospital after Bytes flogs him. The manager has had time, with his show closed by the police and his valuable commodity on loan to Treves, to drink himself into a fury, and when Merrick is returned Bytes inflicts such a severe beating that Treves must be recalled to minister to Merrick. The visual motif of remote quarters and darkened passageways is seldom repeated, and soon after Treves returns Merrick to the hospital, viewers are afforded the long, clear look of him they want. Treves has accomplished what both sides of the present feminist debate on pornography can claim as a victory: he has taken something once relegated to the margins of society and exposed it to the bright light of the central arena.

Lynch's analogous articulation of this source of cinematic pleasure in a later film, *Blue Velvet,* seems to corroborate our reading of the cinematic style of *The Elephant Man.* A disturbing, at times horrific, parody of life in an idealized American small town, *Blue Velvet* presents an underlying oedipal drama with shocking clarity. The screenplay features the interactions of Jeffrey Beaumont (Kyle Maclachlan), a college student; Sandy Williams (Laura Dern), a beautiful high school girl; and Dorothy Vallens (Isabella Rosellini), a nightclub singer whose husband and son have been kidnapped by a local criminal, Frank Booth (Dennis Hopper). Like *The Elephant Man,* the film begins by foreshadowing forbidden sights. In the early scenes Lynch embeds two clues, one visual and one verbal, to the sinister events to follow. The opening montage is composed of idyllic shots of small-town life: blue skies, white picket fences, and red roses; children crossing the streets aided by safety guards; and an elderly man watering his lawn while his wife watches a murder mystery on television. When the man, Jeffrey's father, falls from an apparent stroke, however, the camera follows him to the ground and then moves below, where insects battle ferociously. The long take on this subterranean warfare both undercuts the representation of Lumberton, USA, as an ideal community and suggests what is to come: under the surface, just below our normal field of vision, violence resides. Moments later, as Jeffrey takes a shortcut home through a field, he finds a severed ear, which we later learn Frank removed from Dorothy's husband. Jeffrey goes to the police station and explains his discovery: "Coming home through the field, behind our neighborhood, there behind Vista, I, uh, found an ear." Like the opening montage, Jeffrey's statement intimates a penetration of the familiar vista, taking us both beneath and behind it. Viewers are curious about what they will find, and Lynch does not disappoint them.

In addition to the pleasure derived from seeing the private and forbidden, other pleasures are relevant to viewing Lynch's film, pleasures identified by feminist inquiry into cinematic spectation. One of these relates to what Kaplan regards as the oedipal content of much melodrama; another concerns domestic melodrama's construction of a female spectator. Appropriating Peter Brooks's notion that melodrama is concerned "explicitly" with "Oedipal issues," as intimated by characters' assumptions of the "primary psychic roles of Father, Mother, Child," Kaplan argues, following Doane's lead, that melodrama constructs a female spectator who participates in "what is essentially a masochistic fantasy." This participation, one assumes, is effected by the audience's identification with virtue rather than with rapine, with the suffering heroine, not the villain. And in melodrama this virtue is generally rewarded, thereby reinforcing and valorizing the heroine's masochism.

The gratification of female spectatorship is available to the audiences of both Lynch's film and Pomerance's play even though each lends itself to a different psychoanalytic reading. The scene of Mrs. Kendal's banishment in the play, for example, reenacts the oedipal situation, with some interesting variations: Treves, the figure of the law, plays the punishing father, but Mrs. Kendal has the role of transgressing son, with Merrick portraying the virtuous wife-possession. By contrast, the opening montage of the film suggests a somewhat different psychoanalytic interpretation, illuminating the importance of the preoedipal mother-son relationship in Merrick's story. The first shot of the film, a tight close-up of a woman's eyes, evolves into a slow downward shot of her nose and mouth. As the camera pulls away, we see that the woman's face is actually a framed photograph of Merrick's mother. The sequence continues with shots of elephants and of Merrick's mother lying on the ground, screaming an inaudible scream, and writhing in pain. The next shot is of a billowing cloud from which a baby's cry is heard: the "elephant man" is born. In a later sequence, Bytes, in his capacity as barker for Merrick's show, perpetuates the same mythology of Merrick's origin: on an "uncharted African isle," Merrick's mother was "struck down in the fourth month of her maternal condition by an elephant, a *wild* elephant." Throughout the film, Merrick gazes at his mother's photograph, displays it proudly to both Kendal and Treves's wife, and finally returns to his mother in death. The film closes with her face in the heavens, welcoming her son back to her and promising him eternity: "Nothing ever dies." His submissiveness has finally been rewarded and if we have identified at all with his gentleness, his humanity, and his passivity, the "female" construction of the spectator is completed.

While the notion of a female spectator may explain one pleasure of viewing both film and play, the story of the "elephant man" told by Lynch and Pomerance also reveals the more typical operation of the gaze: the construction of a dominant male spectator observing and thereby controlling a submissive feminine object. Lynch develops the issue of voyeurism with rare clarity in *Blue Velvet,* a development related to this source of pleasure in *The Elephant Man*. Jeffrey, obsessed with discovering the mystery behind the severed ear, gains access to Dorothy's apartment and conceals himself in a closet. From here, he watches Dorothy undress until she discovers him and forces him to strip, in a moment that reverses the dynamics of most cinematic spectation. Before she can accomplish a greater reversal—raping him at knife point—Frank is heard at the door, and Jeffrey is compelled to return to the closet. Booth, we now learn, is keeping Dorothy for himself so that she can play "Mommy" to his domineering "baby"—his terms, not ours—a practice that involves not only sexual intercourse but also physical abuse and the fetishistic use of a piece of blue velvet. Integral to this practice is Frank's demand to "see it"—Dorothy's genitals—and his insistence that during the ritual she not look at him. This sadistic oedipal drama plays itself out with Jeffrey watching and Dorothy excluded from the spectation. While the outrageousness of the scene, combined with Lynch's frequent use of parodic devices, distances the audience somewhat, the male empowerment of the viewer remains a predictable source of cinematic pleasure in *Blue Velvet.*

This more common variety of spectating seems integral to Merrick's story, in all its versions, and involves the viewing of both sideshow freaks and scenes of explicit sexual activity: a kind of pornographic gaze. This gaze replicates one pleasure of the cinema, as *Blue Velvet* demonstrates: the "pleasure of using another person as an object of sexual stimulation through sight" (Mulvey). In the typical pornographic representation, women, "for all the graphic display of their body parts, are the excluded term" (Elmer). Merrick, as the denuded object of a stranger's gaze, performs a role usually relegated to women. In Victorian London, Lynch and Pomerance imply, the businesses of pornography and the exhibition of "freaks" often merged, for "natural oddities" like Merrick and scenes of sexual intimacy were commonly displayed together. Proprietors of attractions like Merrick also often managed sex shows, as Lynch's Bytes hints to Treves: "I move in the proper circles for this type of thing. In fact, *anything* at all, if you take my meaning." Legal history confirms the relation between these two entertainments. George Hitchcock, an associate of Tom Norman, Merrick's real manager, was tried with John Saunders on several counts of indecency (*The Queen v. Saunders and Another* [*Hitchcock*]). In May of 1875, Hitchcock and Saunders operated a show tent divided into two peepshows outside the Epsom Downs racecourse. In one booth, Hitchcock presented two "fat ladies"; in the other, a black husband and wife appeared "naked" to "perform" (*Law Reports*). What is the relation between the viewing of obese women—or of John Merrick—and the viewing of sexual performance? For Leslie Fiedler the viewing of "freaks" provokes sexual desire: "All freaks are perceived to one degree or another as erotic. . . . They induce a temptation to go beyond looking to *knowing* in the full carnal sense the ultimate other." Whether or not we agree with Fiedler's analysis, clearly Lynch does—and by extension so does the great body of film theory that locates one pleasure of the cinema in voyeurism and dominance. In Lynch's film, when the porter brings a crowd of onlookers to the hospital to see Merrick, the camera captures and returns to a man who, while he forces two young women to look at and even kiss Merrick, fondles and licks them in perverse sexual arousal.

Because Victorian sideshow and sex-act performers were often taken from one or another of England's colonial possessions, this specular domination is not only physical, in that the objects of the gaze are often naked and certainly defenseless, but also ideological, since they are denigrated as socially or racially inferior—another reason for the mythologies of Merrick's birth in Africa. Pomerance understands the colonial aspect of such viewing and like other contemporary dramatists—Caryl Churchill, Margaretta D'Arcy and John Arden, and David Hare, for instance—probes the racial and sexual dimensions of British imperialism, both Victorian and modern. The emphasis in Pomerance's play follows that of much recent cultural and historical criticism as well. As Abdul R. JanMohamed points out, "the imperialist configures the colonial realm" as "irremediably different," as a "world at the boundaries of civilization" that is therefore "uncontrollable, chaotic, unattainable, and ultimately evil." For Sander L. Gilman, Victorian medicine and iconographic convention joined in representing sexuality as perhaps the most "uncontrollable" and "animallike" difference of the colonial black, as "scientific" studies of exaggerated genitalia complemented paintings of "The Hottentot Venus" and of white prostitutes with their complicitous black servants. Pomerance's Treves betrays a common Victorian method of confronting "otherness" in his seemingly innocuous first question to Ross concerning Merrick: "Is he foreign?" The "pinheads" exhibited with Merrick in the play are advertised as imports from the Congo, "the land of darkness," and Nurse Sandwich remarks later that in Ceylon and on the Niger she has treated horrible diseases, "dreadful scourges quite unknown to our more civilized climes." And if deformity and bestial sexual appetite can be ascribed to the colonized, so too can defective cognition, as a policeman in *The Elephant Man* assumes: "People who think right don't look like that then, do they?" Thus, in exhibiting figures like Merrick, the late Victorian peepshow produced a pornographic view based on a double dominance: mastery through gender and the supremacy of imperialism. More so than Lynch's film, Pomerance's drama illuminates both levels of subjection.

Much of Merrick's intrigue, therefore, is explained by feminist theories of cinematic spectatorship, based as they are on a pattern of dominance and submission. It is possible, as Pomerance shows, to go beyond the gender distinctions inherent in such theories and apply this dynamic to the dominance and submission of colonialism. On the one hand, both film and play empower viewers to occupy a superior position and to enter imperiously the forbidden territory they want to see. On the other hand, as the powerless Merrick attains his moral victory—which, in Lynch's film, crucially involves going to the theater as a spectator, acquiring the specular power that he had been denied—viewers also identify with him and in so doing may occupy his "feminine" space of masochism. In short, Pomerance's play and Lynch's film embrace several levels of spectating and provide several pleasures. Of special interest is the relation between the pornographic and the melodramatic, both of which foreground women and involve the imposition of sexual or other demands by the powerful on the powerless. Like pornography, the cinema and melodrama empower the viewer even as they commodify the viewed object, marking her submission.

[III]

Of course, Lynch's *The Elephant Man* offers more than the emotional satisfactions of domestic melodrama and the voyeuristic pleasure of the cinema. Through the film's narrative content and cinematic style, Lynch advances sometimes indirect and sometimes more overt criticism of industrial conditions and class inequities in late Victorian England.

In the film's first sequence at London Hospital, for instance, Treves is completing an ugly operation on what is presumably a factory worker. The dialogue specifies the cause of the patient's mutilation—unsafe industrial practices—as Treves bemoans, "We're seeing a lot more of these machine accidents.... Abominable things, these machines...." Despite such observations and the shots of sweating laborers and steaming machines, Lynch elects for the most part to focus on personal rather than political issues. Here he differs from Pomerance, to whom we now turn. Again, the differing narrative structures of the film and play account for Pomerance's more substantial critique: while Lynch's audience is emotionally engaged in Merrick's plight, Pomerance's audience is more detached, in part because the issue of Merrick's safety is resolved early in the play. Treves's movement to center stage serves as a catalyst not only for his self-reflection but for the viewers' as well. When Treves begins to express doubts about both modern science and the society that this science serves, he realizes one of the chief ends of the materialist theater: the creation of a moral self-consciousness, what Edward Bond refers to as a "viable knowledge of the self in relation to practical involvement in the world." Although Treves earns this knowledge slowly and painfully, his newly acquired insight may provide the greatest intellectual satisfaction for the play's audience.

Beginning in scene 16 when Treves tries to explain his banishment of Mrs. Kendal, continuing through his soul-searching in the dream sequence of scenes 17 and 18, and concluding with his plaintive "Help me" in scene 19, the dramatic focus of Pomerance's play shifts from Merrick to Treves. Recently, Franco Moretti has compared what he calls a "novelistic event"—one that "to achieve meaning" requires the "fundamentally unchallenged stability of everyday life and ordinary administration"—with a "tragic event" of personal crisis. The differences between the novelistic and the tragic define Treves's crisis of faith:

> The very fissures and chasms which dismantle such stability [the comforting repetitions of everyday life] constitute the most typical instances of the tragic event, whose meaning lies in being a unique turning-point, a sudden illumination after which one's previous existence—one's novelistic existence—appears irredeemably false.

This "moment of truth" precipitates an unveiling of social structure or of fetishization, a "dereification of everyday life" and a consequent repositioning toward society. Merrick finally causes Treves's crisis of faith, his moment of social truth, in Pomerance's play.

Following Treves's admission that "perhaps [he] was wrong" to expel Mrs. Kendal, his dream exposes his entrapment within Victorian class structure. In the dream Treves plays Merrick and Merrick plays an inquisitive doctor who requests Carr Gomm's permission to examine Gomm's "bloody donkey." Gomm, the governor of London Hospital cast in Ross's role as showman, is reluctant to surrender Treves, a "mainstay of our institution": "He is very valuable. We have invested a great deal in him. He is personal surgeon to the Prince of Wales." Nevertheless, Treves is a negotiable commodity in this scene, since he is also a valuable specimen to "Doctor" Merrick. A "gentleman and a good man," as Gomm promotes him, Treves is "exemplary for study," a characterless representative of his social class devoid of any individuality that might skew results. The dream attempts to redress the impoverishment of thought and experience Treves has suffered as a "mainstay" of the institution.

Treves's evolving understanding also allows him insight into science's co-optation by class and colonial domination. That is, Pomerance is especially concerned about seeing, about what viewing Merrick entails and calls into question. In fact, the play contains critiques of several levels of viewing; the most obvious concern is the authority science and medicine grant for presumably value-free objective viewing. The anatomy theater of the London Hospital in scene 3 authorizes scientific viewing, an authority not shared by the storefront in which Merrick is displayed. Yet when Treves sees Mrs. Kendal expose herself to Merrick, she is condemned as having "no sense of decency." Unfamiliar with social legislation concerning appropriate viewing, Merrick asks about Treves's operation on a patient for a "woman's thing": "Did you see her? Naked? ... Is it okay to see them naked if you cut them up afterwards?" Treves replies that his occupation as a surgeon legitimizes this viewing: "That is science.... Science is a different thing. This woman came to me to be. I mean, it is not, well, love, you know." But Merrick does not "know" that his seeing Mrs. Kendal is a "different thing" from Treves's examining his female patients. Similarly, the process Treves has established for allowing Victorian aristocracy to "see" Merrick is institutionally endorsed, whereas Merrick's public exhibitions were closed by London police for indecency.

Hence, one discourse that authorized the public viewing of Merrick was that of Victorian medical science. To further the "interests of science" (Pomerance's expression), Treves displayed Merrick at several medical conventions in the 1880s. One might assume that the viewing audience at such conventions maintained some objective distance, reacting with neither revulsion nor desire but with appropriate detachment. While in *The Birth of the Clinic* Michel Foucault is not discussing Victorian science, the conception of diagnostic viewing he articulates is precisely the one Pomerance's Merrick has so much difficulty comprehending: an objective or "pure Gaze that would be pure Language: a speaking eye." Like other political dramatists—Brecht in *Galileo* or Christopher Hampton in *Savages* (1974)—Pomerance explodes the myth of a pure gaze, revealing its complicity with other powerful discourses, colonialism, for example. In *Savages* Hampton's anthropologist Crawshaw identifies the role objective vision plays in such enterprises as the Brazilian government's extermination of Indians to acquire and develop their land: "[Anthropologists] aren't supposed to make comments on political matters.... They're supposed to forget that the people they're working with are human and treat them as if they were an ancient monument, or graph, or a geological formation. That's what we call science." Like Hampton, Pomerance probes the implications of the "objective" or "diagnostic" gaze, indicating its proximity to the dehumanizing conventions of Victorian colonialism—or, in his more recent play *Melons,* to the exploitation of American Indians by big business.

Transforming Merrick's physical grotesqueness into an analytical metaphor, Treves begins to recognize that above his mostly middle-class patients looms a "deformed" aristocracy, one "bulged out by unlimited resources and the ruthlessness of privilege" and "yoked to the grossest ignorance and constraint." The metaphorical use of Merrick's body continues in Treves's dream when imperial governance is linked to the repression of sexuality. Assuming Treves's place at the podium, Merrick directs our attention to the doctor's displayed body: "The left arm was slighter and fairer, and may be seen in typical position, hand covering the genitals which were treated as a sullen colony in constant need of restriction, governance, punishment. For their own good." The colonial analogy recalls Churchill's aim in writing *Cloud 9,* one of the contemporary theater's cleverest meditations on Victorianism: to show "the idea of colonialism as a parallel to sexual oppression." Similarly, *The Elephant Man* turns sex into an entrapping, self-contradictory discourse: on the one hand, Treves endorses Merrick's reading of romantic literature and his conversation with women; on the other, Treves rehearses the importance of rules in the "home," denying Merrick any opportunity to express sexual feelings. The cruelty of Treves's behavior—of alternately encouraging and then deflating Merrick's desire for knowledge of the opposite sex—is likened in Treves's dream to the repressive state apparatus of colonial government. (And when colonial subjects escape this needed restriction, as we have mentioned, they end up in sideshows like Merrick's, which need to be closed because they are an affront to decency.)

Immediately after the dream ends, the relation between science and identity emerges in Treves's conversation with Bishop How. Building on the implication of his dream, Treves compares gardening with a science that has "pruned, cropped, pollarded, and somewhat stupefied" the human subject: "Is that all we know how to finally do with—whatever? Nature? Is it? Rob it? No, not really, not nature I mean. Ourselves really. Myself really. Robbed, that is. . . . I. I. I. I." In his inarticulateness, Treves realizes that the mastery of nature—which, along with the mastery of human beings, has always been an aim of both science and civilization—exacts a blinding cost on subjectivity. His friendship with Merrick has rekindled Treves's self-consciousness, eroding in the process his belief in science as a phenomenon separable from human society (and in himself as excluded from human participation). His "Help me" echoes Merrick's cry at the train station, and the parallel indicates the depth of Treves's doubts. Affected by the dream and his subsequent questioning of his relationship with Merrick, Treves moves from an incapacity for "self-critical speech," thus an inability to "change," to "despair in fact." The "scientist in an age of science" is now inconsolable, and the daily practice of his vocation offers no relief: "Science, observation, practice, deduction, having led me to these conclusions, can no longer serve as consolation. I apparently see things others don't." In his confession, Treves evinces a newly formed political vision of the ways in which society has determined his scientific labors: "I have so little time . . . to keep up with my work. Work being twenty-year-old women who look an abused fifty with worn-outedness;

young men with appalling industrial conditions I turn out as soon as possible to return to their labors." He recognizes that inhumane labor conditions form the basis of not only his clinical practice but also his research, which includes a pamphlet on the dangers of wearing corsets. Treves approaches a "totalizing" recognition of his position in London society.

At the instant that Treves, at the climax of his despair, begs Bishop How for help, Merrick pronounces, in Christlike fashion, "It is done." While the "it" refers to Merrick's completion of his model of Saint Phillip's Church, his "Consummatum est" also proclaims Treves's redemption. The salvation, though, is not religious but political, for Treves has already rejected the "mere consolation" of "Christ's church." What *is* "done" is the opening of Treves's eyes, the maturing of his dialectical awareness of his participation in society—a realization that, for Fredric Jameson, defines self-consciousness:

> For the Marxist dialectic . . . the self-consciousness aimed at is the awareness of the thinker's position in society and in history itself, and of the limits imposed on this awareness by his class position—in short of the ideological and situational nature of all thought and of the initial invention of the problems themselves.

Like Treves, the play's spectators have been brought to interrogate the interconnections between Merrick's exploitation and the society in which they live. If they experience only a small part of the insight Treves achieves, then they have participated in—and profited from—the critical pleasure of the political theater.

[IV]

So, regardless of John Webster's observation, men do stand amazed to see their own deformity. But why? What was it about Merrick that amazed Victorians and continues to attract contemporary audiences? One answer involves the pleasure derived from seeing the secret or the forbidden, from traveling Lynch's dark alleys. Another originates in the voyeuristic pleasures of sideshows and pornography. But if pornography allows the viewer to objectify and dominate the viewed, so too does melodrama. Both foreground issues of power and powerlessness, of possession and dispossession, of sadism and masochism. In addition to experiencing dominance, this "male" prerogative, spectators who identify with Merrick and take pleasure in the poetic justice of his victory are also psychically endorsing his submission, his "female" qualities. In short, in both Lynch's film and Pomerance's play, Merrick provides viewers with opportunities to play both roles, to occupy both positions.

To these private, libidinal satisfactions, Pomerance adds an intellectually gratifying criticism of Victorian society and its claim to moral ascendancy, and he does so in a generic vehicle that encourages his spectators, those "other Victorians," to contemplate their own cultural superiority. In transforming Victorian culture into a hypocritical, somewhat barbaric counterpart of today's highly evolved and sophisticated society (Progress with a capital P is really now, was never then), Pomerance also implicates modern audiences in the smugness they despise in his Victorians. Not only have they enjoyed a melodrama and identified with the position of the advanced culture—much like the Victorians who felt superior to Britain's colonial peoples—they have paid to see a "freak show." Indeed, their participation in the pornography exceeds the Victorians' in that their gaze actually transforms an actor into a freak. Pomerance forces such viewing by insisting that the role of Merrick be played without makeup; when Philip Anglim contorts himself before the spectators' eyes, the metamorphosis is as much theirs as his. Even more so than Treves, and for reasons not nearly so selfless, the audience is setting Merrick up for private viewing.

Source: William E. Holladay and Stephen Watt, "Viewing the Elephant Man," in *PMLA,* October, 1989, Vol. 104, no. 5, pp. 868–81.

Val Ricks

In this brief essay, Ricks discusses the recurrent imagery that Pomerance has borrowed from Shakespeare's Romeo and Juliet, *arguing that the playwright uses the material to illustrate the nature of social conformity in the world of* The Elephant Man.

Repeated images—the corset, the cathedral model, and the allusion to Romeo and Juliet—represent twists on the idea of illusive and restrictive moral standards in Bernard Pomerance's *The Elephant Man.* The corset first stands as a symbol of mere control or restriction, depending on the degree of irony applied to the image. Ross, the freak show proprietor, uses the corset image to describe Merrick: he is the result of "Mother Nature uncorseted." Ross is trying to say that anything produced by an uncorseted (or uncontrolled) Mother Nature would certainly be freakish. But when one realizes that Mother Nature restricted by a man-made fashion garment would probably bear anything but a "natural" child, the irony of the statement comes blaring forth; one would expect that Ross and the rest of "normal" people are anything but natural.

In close relation to this, the corset also stands as a symbol for moral standards imposed by culture, which restrict. Merrick, as the product of an uncorseted Mother Nature, is not inhibited by the social standards the "normal" characters impose on themselves. As Ross infers that the bulk of mankind is the product of a corseted Mother Nature, the inverse is true in their case, and Dr. Frederick Treves, paragon of societal normality, becomes the perfect portrait of mankind's moral maladies. In moral disillusionment, Treves laments the "grotesque ailments" caused by corsets: his "patients do not unstrap themselves of corsets. Some cannot." Treves's bewailment of the English social system advances the idea that a Mother Nature corseted by mankind cannot produce children who act naturally and with honesty about their own feelings. The other reference to the corset is indirect and appears when actress Mrs. Kendal undresses in front of Merrick. This disregard for cultural morals (and they are cultural; African pygmies run naked) is symbolized by nothing less than taking the corset off.

The model of St. Philip's cathedral symbolizes Merrick's knowledge of Treves's constricting moral standards. Each time Merrick discovers another illusive ethic in Treves's system of thought, he adds another piece to the model. At the moment Treves himself becomes uncorseted from these moral illusions—still suffering the "most grotesque ailments" and in despair bemoaning the futility of society's standards, Merrick fits the final piece on St. Philip's. This symbol closely ties with the allusion to Romeo and Juliet. Merrick states, "When the illusion ended, [Romeo] had to kill himself." Since the cathedral represents Merrick's knowledge of Treves's faulty standards, when the cathedral is completed, the illusion ends, and Merrick dies. Juliet, played of course by Mrs. Kendal, helps by removing the corset to destroy the illusion of Treves' morals; this ties the images of corset and cathedral and the Shakespeare allusion together. Mrs. Kendal's permanent departure from the play represents Juliet's demise and foreshadows the death of Romeo.

Source: Val Ricks. "Pomerance's *The Elephant Man,*" in the *Explicator,* Vol. 46, no. 4, Summer, 1988, pp. 48–49.

John Hurt in The Elephant Man, *standing by a mantle.*

Louis K. Greiff

In the following essay, Greiff compares the tragic elements in Dr. Treves to those found in Dr. Dysart in Equus.

Two highly successful contemporary plays are so alike in conception and design that one description seems to serve for both. A doctor and his patient are the major characters in these plays, with their relationship and conflict quickly becoming the dominant dramatic center. The doctors in both works are professionally prominent and, at least to the audience's initial view, comfortable within the norms and boundaries provided them by society. Their patients, however, are freaks. One suffers profound mental disturbance, to the point of violence, while the other is so physically distorted that few people can stand his presence or sight. The patients, in fact, are pariahs, shunned not only by society but by blood-kin as well. Their doctors nevertheless draw very close to them and, with partial or even complete success, attempt a process of normalization and cure. At the end, however, the cure proves to be double-edged, so that we remain unsure whether patient or doctor has been the more profoundly touched. Both doctors contemplate the final results of their skill deeply unsettled about themselves and their actions. They wonder whether their effort to heal a special patient has really been a tampering with something beyond themselves—an assault upon uniqueness by simple and successful mediocrity.

The plays in question are Peter Shaffer's *Equus* and Bernard Pomerance's *The Elephant Man.* They can be introduced with the same general outline because they are founded upon an identical confrontation between the normal and the extraordinary. What Martin Dysart and Alan Strang, through their encounter and juxtaposition, achieve for the one play, Frederick Treves and John Merrick achieve for the other. My purpose in pointing this out is not merely to reveal surprising parallels for their own sake. Rather, as I hope to show, the dramatic pattern shared by *Equus* and *The Elephant Man* demonstrates something important beyond specific detail. It offers us, I believe, new perspectives on the very old issue of tragedy and, in particular, on the tragic hero as he remains faithful to the contemporary and to the timeless in human affairs.

On initial encounter, Alan Strang and John Merrick do not seem possible candidates for tragedy because their human condition appears perverse and not noble, diminished and not larger than life. The first is a lower middle-class youth whose obsession with horses has finally led him to psychosis and

> TREVES'S BEWAILMENT OF THE ENGLISH SOCIAL SYSTEM ADVANCES THE IDEA THAT A MOTHER NATURE CORSETED BY MANKIND CANNOT PRODUCE CHILDREN WHO ACT NATURALLY AND WITH HONESTY ABOUT THEIR OWN FEELINGS."

violence. The second is destitute and, as a matter of historical record, the world's most extreme case of physical deformity. His appearance has caused men to riot and to attack him in disgust. Yet as is clear from such works as *The Oresteia* or *Philoctetes,* madness, even hideousness, are not disqualifications from tragic stature so long as there is elevation at the same time. For Alan and Merrick alike the source of elevation—the bow which transcends their wounds—is art. Alan, in his madness, spins a private and unique mythology utterly compelling to himself, to his psychiatrist Dysart, and finally to the audience. Merrick builds a replica, or imitation, of St. Phillip's Church which, like Mozart's music in Shaffer's *Amadeus,* represents human effort to rise from the earth and commune with God. In a fascinating parallel between the two plays, Alan and Merrick emerge as artists by virtue of an identical and paradoxical formulation. For both of them, art and the artist are born in the coalescence of squalor and the sublime or holy, what Yeats has called "The uncontrollable mystery on the bestial floor" (Yeats, 1959). Thus Alan makes the hot creatures of the stable into his gods and, through their celebration, becomes a poet and mystic. Thus Merrick finds within his own being and life both the beast which gives him his nickname and the God-urge, both the underpinnings of his church and the inspiration to build its arches and spires. Merrick himself states the artistic equation for both plays in the following exchange with his confidante, Mrs. Kendal:

> MRS. KENDAL: You are an artist, John Merrick, an artist.
>
> MERRICK: I did not begin to build at first. Not till I saw what St. Phillip's really was. It is not stone and steel and glass; it is an imitation of grace flying up and up from the mud. So I make my imitation of an imitation. But even in that is heaven to me, Mrs. Kendal (Pomerance, 1979).

The close kinship between Alan and Merrick does not require them to be alike in the execution and style of their art. Alan is certainly the more original of the two, with Merrick emerging as a kind of mimetic or Aristotelian craftsman. Also, Alan is by far the more emotionally frenzied creator, Dionysian in contrast to Merrick's Apollonian reserve. As a result, Alan's mythic outbursts shock Dysart and the public while, by an opposite process, Merrick builds his church one piece at a time, quietly, all through the second half of his play. Like Dionysus and Apollo, Alan and Merrick are brothers at heart, yet not identical nor even similar on the surface.

Born as artists through the same union of opposites, they are, however, destined to suffer a similar destruction and ordeal. Each is patient to a skilled doctor, also a friend, whose intention is to cure the special figure and as far as possible make him normal. Words like "normal," "average," and "ordinary" saturate both plays, and in the mouths of the two doctors become prophecies for Alan and Merrick. Reflecting the optimism of his age, Frederick Treves reveals the following plan for his patient:

> My aim's to lead him to as normal a life as possible. His terror of us all comes from having been held at arm's length from society. I am determined that shall end. For example, he loves to meet people and converse. I am determined he shall. For example, he had never seen the inside of any normal home before. I had him to mine, and what a reward, Mrs. Kendal; his astonishment, his joy at the most ordinary things (Pomerance, 1979).

Martin Dysart's tone is by contrast bitter and pessimistic, but the likeness of the message remains unmistakable:

> I'll set him on a nice mini-scooter and send him puttering off into the Normal world where animals are treated *properly:* made extinct, or put into servitude, or tethered all their lives in dim light, just to feed it! I'll give him the good Normal world where we're tethered beside them—blinking our nights away in a nonstop drench of cathode-ray over our shrivelling heads! I'll take away his Field of Ha Ha, and give him Normal places for his ecstasy— (Shaffer, 1974).

Equus ends with the implication that Dysart will succeed, and that Alan will return to normalcy and to society. No such hope is possible for Merrick, who dies at the end of his play, in keeping with historical fact. This opposition is misleading, however, because the plays really end alike for their artist-freaks, even on an identical bit of imagery. The final act performed by Alan and Merrick is to fall asleep on stage, implying that a move toward the norm involves artistic paralysis—or worse. Surely Alan's unconscious collapse in Dysart's arms represents his creative death since, all along, his madness has been his poetic source. Now cured, he will never sing of Equus and the other god-beasts again. The three-way equation of normality, sleep, and death becomes even more explicit and literal in Pomerance's play. Here John Merrick dies attempting for the first time to fall asleep in a "normal" position, something his unnaturally heavy head has always made impossible. This death of both the artist and the man has been foretold by Treves in the previous scene when, like Dysart, he begins to doubt his own remedies: "It is just—it is the overarc of things, quite inescapable that as he's achieved greater and greater normality, his condition's edged him closer to the grave. So—a parable of growing up? To become more normal is to die?" (Pomerance, 1979).

Thus in *Equus* and *The Elephant Man,* alike, two exceptional figures fall into the misfortune of normalcy and are destroyed. Before a conclusion is reached that the plays are, therefore, traditional tragedy, their other pair of characters should be examined. The brother-physicians Dysart and Treves, interesting and significant in their own right, may themselves have some claim to the status of protagonist. One clear truth about both of them is their opposition, in every respect, to their patients. Where Alan and Merrick touch the far extremes of dirt and deity, Treves and Dysart exist together on neutral ground between the two. They never traffic with the beasts, but surely never approach heaven or the gods either.

Also in contrast to the creative patients, these two healers are ironically destroyers. In a nearly exact parallel between the plays, both doctors reveal at least a subconscious awareness of their destructive qualities through dreams. Within Dysart's dream, and Treves's, an identical vision of carving and dismemberment functions as the metaphor of self-revelation. Dysart tells his friend Hesther Salomon that in his dream he appears as "a chief priest in Homeric Greece" officiating at a sacrifice of children. He relates that:

> As each child steps forward . . . with a surgical skill which amazes even me, I fit in the knife and slice elegantly down to the navel, just like a seamstress following a pattern. I part the flaps, sever the inner tubes, yank them out and throw them hot and steaming on to the floor. The other two [priests] then study the pattern they make, as if they were reading hieroglyphics. It's obvious to me that I'm tops as chief priest. It's this unique talent for carving that has got me where I am (Shaffer, 1974).

Treves's dream is acted out rather than told, but with no variation to the central image. In it he and Merrick repeat an earlier scene, only with their roles reversed. Merrick now assumes the dream-identity of physician conducting an anatomical lecture, with Treves on display as patient-specimen. Among several revealing (and often amusing) details, Merrick describes "The surgeon's hands [which] were well-developed and strong, capable of the most delicate carvings-up, for others' own good" (Pomerance, 1979).

Any operation or sacrifice performed on victims as dynamic as Alan and Merrick is bound to have its impact upon the performer himself. For Dysart and Treves, together, this proves to be revelation and a profoundly new awareness of life. It is possible to suggest, in fact, that as the doctors lead their patients toward average sleep, they are themselves awakened in the process—to permanent and disturbing perception. Such a turnabout seems most appropriate when one recalls that Alan and Merrick are, after all, artists. They may be victimized by sacrificial cure, but not before having the chance to infect their healers with a bit of the visionary disease.

Again alike, Dysart and Treves find that their newly-gained insight is two fold. First, they both reach some understanding of what it means to live beyond the borders of complacent normalcy, as Alan and Merrick have done. At a key point in each play, the doctor takes the place of his patient to experience what Dysart calls "Pain that's unique" to the very special individual (Shaffer, 1974). In *The Elephant Man* this occurs comically for Treves during the dream-scene, mentioned above, where the patient turns physician and the physician, for once, becomes a freak on display. In the very next scene—with the comedy ended and Treves now feeling his own private pain—the doctor cries out "help me" and weeps, exactly as Merrick did at the start of their relationship (Pomerance, 1979). For Dysart, the taking on of Alan's burden comes during the play's final scene. Purged from the patient's soul and mind, the god-beast now commands the doctor's attention, perhaps permanently:

> And now for me it never stops: that voice of Equus out of the cave—'Why Me? . . . Why Me? . . . Account for Me!' . . . All right—I surrender! I say it . . . In an ultimate sense I cannot know what I do in this place— yet I do ultimate things. Essentially I cannot know what I do—yet I do essential things. Irreversible,

terminal things. I stand in the dark with a pick in my hand, striking at heads! (Shaffer, 1974).

The second side of both doctors' awakening is paradoxically opposite to the first. In the very sharing of their patients' experience, Dysart and Treves also come to know their essential separation from these patients. In their close approach to the extraordinary figure and his uniqueness, the brother-physicians sadly discover their own contrasting and enduring mediocrity. For Dysart, a single word and his preoccupation with it serve to measure this new self-awareness. The slang-term for psychiatrist, "shrink," begins to gain literal meaning during the play, not so much to signify Dysart's effect on his patient but to inform him of his own existence in contrast to Alan's: "Without worship you shrink, it's as brutal as that . . . I shrank my *own* life. No one can do it for you. I settled for being pallid and provincial, out of my own eternal timidity" (Shaffer, 1974). Within *The Elephant Man,* as well, one word figures heavily [in] Treves's developing perception of himself. This time the word is "consolation," and it recurs throughout the play reflecting several of its different meanings (Pomerance, 1979). At the very outset, the hospital administrator Carr Gomm tells Treves that prominence, title, and "100 guinea fees" will prove "an excellent consolation prize" (Pomerance, 1979). Treves does not understand this at first. Once having encountered Merrick, however, he finds the meaning all too clear and inescapable. The world's familiar honors and achievements are merely what most of mankind accepts in lieu of transcendence, in consolation for being average. When, just before Merrick's death, Treves again thinks about consolation, it is with touching awareness that the idea defines his life, yet remains utterly unsatisfying:

> I am an extremely successful Englishman in a successful and respected England which informs me daily by the way it lives that it wants to die. I am in despair in fact. Science, observation, practice, deduction, having led me to these conclusions, can no longer serve as consolation. I apparently see things others don't. I am sure we were not born for mere consolation (Pomerance, 1979).

Peter Shaffer and Bernard Pomerance have thus, together, provided recent drama with a distinct pattern whereby two opposite figures influence one another toward opposite destinies. When the process is complete, an extraordinary person has been lost, while a far more typical person has been led to important insight and self-recognition. If the plays in question are tragedies, then their authors may be providing audiences and readers with something even more noteworthy—a dramatic strategy allowing for alternative protagonists or two tragic heroes in place of the traditional one.

Alan and Merrick certainly approximate the classical tragic hero and preserve a design that is thousands of years old. They are separated from society by drastic flaws, yet also by something exceptional within themselves which elevates and confers uniqueness. Both finally suffer a destructive fall, and all who view it are moved to strong emotion and a sense of major loss. By contrast, Dysart and Treves do not conform to this timeless pattern. They are ordinary men who encounter the extraordinary but cannot attain it, and who become tragic precisely in their recognition of this truth.

In the presence of such differences on stage, we as audience discover a choice of heroes to identify with or, more accurately, find a dual identification with both of them. To witness and thus share the fall of Alan and Merrick is, through an age-old ritual, to commune with our essential humanity, utterly removed from time and social process. The two unique individuals, and their stories, provide ways to celebrate the eternal freak of nature that is man— the half-beast with a lust for transcendence, the imaginative creature so worthy of wonder, yet so easily destroyed. What Dysart and Treves provide, in contrast, is a mirror not for eternity but for today. From the vantage-point of our study or theater seat, we see in them our immediate image and circumstances, the human condition now burdened by history, society, and personal limitation. The two doctors function as effective tragic figures, I believe, because the consolations and diminishments of their lives are immediately recognized as our own. Like them, most of us who view their drama have a share in the world's prestige and some private version of the 100 guinea fee. Confronted with the utterly extraordinary, again like them, we take accurate stock of our own insignificance, too intellectually truthful and sensitive to do anything less. The honest shock of recognition suffered by Dysart and Treves, in short, purifies the tribe as a whole. The emotions awakened through such an experience differ from our response to the unique hero's fall, yet possess an equally compelling poignancy and depth.

At least one of the playwrights here under study has pursued the dual protagonists, and the encounter of normal man with the extraordinary, into his most recent work. As a result, Salieri and Mozart collide and struggle, during Peter Shaffer's *Amadeus,* much the same way the paired characters did in the earlier plays, although with some variations to the basic pattern. Amadeus himself now functions as the artist-creature who, along with Alan and Merrick, moves toward a traditionally tragic destruction and fall. His art is more tangible, and public, than his brothers' largely solitary efforts, yet in essence the same by virtue of being finally God-driven. The squalid along with the sublime resides in Mozart too, only now emerging comically (and somewhat trivially) through the composer's infantile preoccupations with excrement and with beasts. The audience, for example, sees Mozart make his initial entrance pretending to be a cat, and his first spoken line in the play is miaow.

Opposing this figure is Shaffer's Antonio Salieri, like Dysart and Treves all too desperately normal (and successful) by contrast. Salieri is awakened through contact with his inspired creature, as were the physicians, to the nature of transcendence and to its utter absence in himself. Here, however, a difference arises between this play and the first two. Salieri is honest, like the doctors, in taking his own measure against genius yet, unlike them, aroused to rage and malice by the results. Where Dysart and Treves may have revealed destructive traits subconsciously, and despite genuine intentions to cure, Salieri proves to be overtly vicious toward his counterpart. No healer to Mozart in any sense, he vows to destroy the divine creature and thereby to strike a blow against the God who has sold him short.

My purpose in mentioning *Amadeus* here is not to pursue a detailed comparison of three plays, although I am sure this would yield worthwhile results. Rather, I wish to stress a clear pattern for tragic character held in common by this work and the previous two. If the pattern emerged, over the past decade, through the efforts of Shaffer and Pomerance, it surely still persists in a current and highly visible example of drama today. This is as it should be, because the pattern in question represents a unique contribution to recent theater—a tragic mask whose countenance is twofold. One of its faces is familiar since, through Dysart, Treves, and Salieri, it exactly captures the look of contemporary man. Its other more distorted face is that of Alan, Merrick, and Mozart. While hardly average or ordinary, this face unlike the first preserves the essential and the eternal human expression.

Source: Louis K. Greiff, "Two for the Price of One: Tragedy and the Dual Hero in *Equus* and *The Elephant Man*," in *Within the Dramatic Spectrum,* edited by Karelisa V. Hartigan, Lanham, MD: University Presses of America, 1986, pp. 64–77.

Janet L. Larson

In the following essay, Larson contends that Pomerance's play is a parable, informing the audience of truths they don't expect or even want to hear.

What is an elephant compared to a man?
Brecht, *A Man's a Man*

[T]he more we study Art, the less we care for Nature. What Art really reveals to us is Nature's lack of design, her curious crudities, her extraordinary monotony, her absolutely unfinished condition.... Art is our spirited protest, our gallant attempt to teach Nature her proper place. Wilde, "The Decay of Lying"

[Scripture says] that God is a hidden God, and that since the corruption of nature, He has left men in a darkness from which they can escape only through Jesus Christ.... *Vere tu es Deus absconditus.* Pascal, *Pensées*

In 1977 Foco Novo, a radical fringe group named after a play by Bernard Pomerance about South American guerrillas, first produced *The Elephant Man* in England; early in 1979, the play opened in mid-Manhattan at St. Peter's Lutheran Church, a worship space built into the Citicorp Center; a few months later, the production was moved to a Victorian theater on Broadway, where it has enjoyed a long run. This brief production history suggests the broad span of reference in this most recent Pomerance play: beginning in radical politics, it ends in metaphysics, and in between, it directs questions of aesthetics and ethics against show business, theatrical illusion, and all kinds of imitative performance from language learning to orthodox religious discipline and the imitation of Christ.

This thematic range makes for some incoherence: a few critics have justly observed that the play contains too many allusions, without development, too many ideas which the theater audience can scarcely take in. Yet the incomplete web the allusions weave entangles many who have seen this play in a mysterious enchantment that invites interpretation. The very multiplicity of themes and evocations is also essential to the power of a drama that expands its own dimensions through a dynamic of parable. Unfolding through multiple reversals, questioning its own premises while challenging the expectations of its hearers, *The Elephant Man* grows larger as we experience it and invites the audience to enlarge its own critical perceptions and sympathies. In its parabolic movement, Pomerance's play extends itself beyond its leftist critique as well as its absurdist anguish to offer a slender opening for transcendent religious hope. These surprising ex-

> MERRICK REMINDS THOSE WHO ACCEPT A COMMON VERSION OF THE DARWINIAN HYPOTHESIS THAT THEIR BEASTLY ORIGINS ARE NOT SAFELY BEHIND THEM IN THE PREHISTORIC EONS; HE MOCKS THE EFFORTS TO CLIMB UP AND UP OF THOSE WHO GRAFT ONTO THE HYPOTHESIS A PROGRESSIVE SOCIAL DARWINISM."

pansions make *The Elephant Man* of considerable interest as dramatic parable to students of the modern theater.

I

In the history of the freak John Merrick, popularly known as the Elephant Man, Pomerance found a subject that invited both leftist and absurdist interpretations, but finally eluded them. Merrick was first of all the archetypal social victim of the Victorian city—a misshapen child of the workhouse who eventually sought out the circus as the only means of earning his livelihood. Exploited, banned as "indecent," and at length abandoned by his managers, Merrick was fortuitously rescued by the young surgeon Mr. Frederick Treves, then rising in his profession. Treves brought Merrick to the London Hospital to study the incurable disorder (neurofibromatosis) that had made a "chaotic anatomical wilderness" of his body. But the scientist also sought to cure the creature's sense of humiliation and to make him "a man like others."

Treves's *The Elephant Man and Other Reminiscences,* published thirty years after the experience, tells an affecting rags-to-riches story of Merrick's last years at the London Hospital (1886–1890). It is well known that his aristocratic circle of late Victorians studied, domesticated, and exalted the Elephant Man, a strange cult figure altogether suiting the needs peculiar to the *fin de siecle.* Like Little Nell in Dickens's *The Old Curiosity Shop* (which forty years earlier had given impetus in the nineteenth century to this sort of worship), Merrick was perceived as a figure of saintly suffering "ennobled" by troubles which he never resented, always forgave. Treves's account suggests the tone of this worship:

> [the Elephant Man] had passed through the fire and had come out unscathed. . . . He showed himself to be a gentle, affectionate and lovable creature, as amiable as a happy woman, free from any trace of cynicism or resentment, without a grievance and without an unkind word for anyone. I have never heard him complain. I have never heard him deplore his ruined life or resent the treatment he had received at the hands of callous keepers. His journey through life had been indeed along a *via dolorosa,* the road had been uphill all the way, and now, when the night was at its blackest and the way most steep, he had suddenly found himself, as it were, in a friendly inn, bright with light and warm with welcome. His gratitude to those about him was pathetic in its sincerity and eloquent in the childlike simplicity with which it was expressed.

If Treves seems to protest too much, later he allows himself to suggest that the "accidental" death of the Elephant Man by asphyxiation was an act of suicide. This veiled possibility seems to have made it all the more necessary after his death that Merrick become a religious emblem, shoring up his benefactors' belief in themselves as vessels of "the mercy of God," a God whom they did not otherwise honor. Despite his physical and social entrapments, however, Merrick remains an appealing figure. All the accounts, including Ashley Montagu's 1972 book, *The Elephant Man: A Study in Human Dignity,* persuasively present him as an afflicted man who transcended his conditions and possessed his soul.

Out of these materials, Pomerance has constructed an imaginative work that is considerably more than historical drama, although *The Elephant Man* could be studied alone for its remarkable display of late Victorian attitudes: the triumphal spirit of nineteenth-century science, with its undercurrent of anxiety about beastly origins; the hubris of Empire, with its high-minded cant about the "inferior races"; a callous social engineering, pursued in the same spirit of the Mechanical Age that produced social victims like Merrick; the retrenchment of religious orthodoxy, behind invocations to Duty and a hypocritical sexual code; the new idealizing of the sensual Pre-Raphaelite woman; the fatalism of "Hap" in a Godforsaken universe; the poetry of religion replacing religion; the late Romanticist cult of the victimized artist; and the aristocratic voyeurism of the Decadence, with its cultivation of hothouse curiosities and strange behaviors *a rebours.* Oscar Wilde, another elephantine "freak" of the period who suffered from public opinion, had protested in "The Decay of Lying" (1889) his contemporaries' "monstrous worship of facts" and ridiculed the unimaginative writer who "is to be found at the Librairie Nationale, or at the British Museum, shamelessly reading up his subject." Pomerance's reading, on the contrary, is genuine *recherche;* he has drawn upon the Treves/Montagu biographic materials not just to ground his play in their facts, but to discover useable dramatic tensions within their unintended fictions.

As Leslie Fiedler has suggested, the stories we tell about mutations reflect our needs to fit their differences into some apprehensible design. The Elephant Man's benefactors and Merrick himself responded to his freakish nature by designing stories, drawn upon culture myths, that inadequately accounted for it. Pomerance, sensitive to the allure of such coherences, reflects skeptically in his play on the earlier accounts of Merrick's beautiful spirit and of his captors' beneficence; the play also emphasizes certain clues in these accounts in order to heighten the contradictions in the Elephant Man's struggle for survival in society. But if Pomerance goes beyond historical reports in these ways, he confirms unexpectedly the central intuition they share: he too is fascinated by the mystery of Merrick's being. Mingling skepticism with wonder, Pomerance's version of the story is neither the product of late Victorian myth-making nor a further act of twentieth-century demythologizing, but a dramatic parable that seems to have emerged from the playwright's surprising encounter with his "subject."

The evocation of wonder is remarkable, because a "problem-solving" language and method permeate the play. In a largely cryptic interview with the *New York Times,* Pomerance has called his approach to theater "left-rationalist": "If you point out an error and appeal for the reason," he explains, "then that is a step in the right direction." Often the clipped, wry, ironic language of the play employs the forms of logic to expose errors and appeal for reasons. In this idiom, the wise naif Merrick is the dialectical questioner of social injustice; but since he is deformed by this society, he is also put forward himself as "proof," as the central exhibit in the play's argument against the present social order. Yet at the end of the play, the "benighted" Sir Frederick confesses that scientific "observation, practice, [and] deduction" have led him to "conclusions" that expose the inadequacy of his rationalism for providing either truth or consolation.

Without diminishing its political impact (stronger in the London production), the play shows us that a problem-solving logic is insufficient for head or heart.

What, then, does the case of the Elephant Man "prove"? If the playwright's only project were to "point" to Merrick's shaping as "error," the socially deformed man we encounter in the second half of the play would merely have been reduced to an imitation man, and the play would offer nothing more than the cynical conclusions of Brecht's song in *A Man's a Man:*

> You can do with a human being what you will.
> Take him apart like a car, rebuild him bit by bit—
> As you will see, he has nothing to lose by it.

The miracle of John Merrick is that, although he is rebuilt by the social engineers, he is not utterly "robbed" (Treves's word) of the mystery of his being. In communicating this mystery on stage, *The Elephant Man* surpasses its own critical "left-rationalist" formulations.

Interestingly, this self-questioning is one of the ways Pomerance's play seems not to depart from, but to be indebted to the early work of Brecht, who elaborated an elephant/man joke in *A Man's a Man* and *The Elephant Calf.* Both plays, which Pomerance adapted for the Hampstead Theatre in 1975, contain dozens of lines and songs that might gloss the later play on the Brechtian theme of society's tyranny over the individual soul and the destructive shaping of the Model Citizen. In *The Elephant Calf,* Brecht's critical theater playfully undermines itself with the self-conscious admission that "Art can prove anything." Rushing willy-nilly to demonstrate that the baby elephant on trial really "is a man" and a matricide, one character urges:

> it is unprecedented, which I am also ready to prove, in fact I will prove anything you like, and will contend even more than that, and never be put off but always insist on what I see the way I see it, and prove it, too, for, I ask you: what is anything without proof?

The Elephant Calf, with its mockery of a trial that is also a play, is a burlesque of theatrical proof; visually, it is theater "seen from the side," so that backstage business is literally exposed. (Brecht's staging device, with a theater curtain at a right angle to the audience dividing the platform into a visible before/behind theater on the stage, is borrowed for an early circus scene in *The Elephant Man.*) Robert Brustein has argued that Brecht's plays reveal the inadequacy of their own frontal attacks on capitalist society by pointing to errors without providing persuasive reasons:

> On the surface, . . . [Brecht's revolt] is directed against the hypocrisy, avarice, and injustice of bourgeois society; in the depths, against the disorder of the universe and the chaos in the human soul. Brecht's social revolt is objective, active, remedial, realistic; his existential revolt is subjective, passive, irremediable, and Romantic. The conflict between these two modes of rebellion issues in the dialectic of Brecht's plays. . . .

A similar dialectic is present in *The Elephant Man*. This play does not make its impact only as a leftist morality play, but goes behind or under or through this "stage" to reach for unsettling questions about "the disorder of the universe and the chaos in the human soul." Stanley Kauffmann, among others, has identified the play's "most suggestive" theme as "the arbitrariness of existence, posed against a hunger for design." Near the end of the play Pomerance does plant proofs for an absurdist interpretation, but, as I shall argue later, the production undermines these too. To become a dramatic parable with a religious dimension, *The Elephant Man* reaches beyond its own absurdist/leftist dialectic.

Before offering an analysis of the play's structure, let me summarize here my general conclusion and set forth some definitions. Like the heuristic modern fictions Frank Kermode has described in *The Sense of an Ending,* Pomerance's play overturns its own formulas and "disconfirms" audience expectations in order to create the sense that his dramatic fiction, through these repeated reversals, is "finding something out for us, something *real.*" This heuristic pattern is also characteristic of parabolic structures. Here Kermode's more recent writing on parable is less helpful than John Dominic Crossan's theology of story in *The Dark Interval* and *In Parables,* which draws upon the work of Levi-Strauss to offer a rather specialized account of parabolic teaching in the Gospels. Crossan defines parable not only as a form of narrative, but also as a story event: it is an "event" not because something happens in the parable's plot, but because something happens *between* this plot and the story the hearers expected to hear. The parables maker's structure of expression, says Crossan, confronts the hearers' different structure of expectation. (As parable begins to reveal the kind of story it is, a hearer's immediate response may be: "'I don't know what you mean by that story but I'm certain I don't like it.'") Parable, then, requires an audience, is inherently dramatic, and turns on a surprise which draws in the hearers as critical participants. Through their critical participation, they are transformed—or they reject the parable, and effectively exclude themselves from the Kingdom.

Crossan describes parable's structure as beginning with conventional expectations in a setting familiar to the listeners, with accepted values intact. Then an unexpected force (an "advent") enters into the story to overturn its terms of value (such as rich/poor), at that moment reversing the hearers' conventional expectations: their prejudices, common sense, cherished ethics, world view—in a word, their "myths." Reversal challenges the hearers to new action, but the story's ending does not synthesize all its dissonances into an explicit lesson that tells them precisely what to do, as a moral example story would. In the context of Crossan's theology of story, he argues that in the New Testament parables and in parabolic moments of human lives, the Kingdom of God arrives in sovereign freedom to "shatter the deep structure of our accepted world" and open up a "new world" and unforeseen relationships. Crossan acknowledges that people cannot live without "myths," but "To be human and to remain open to transcendental experience demands a willingness to be 'parabled. . . .'"

Underlying *The Elephant Man* is this definition of what it means to be human; to become nonhuman is to live completely enclosed by myths, such as the late Victorian myth of the "Elephant Man." While Pomerance's play cannot be claimed as a Christian parable (even with Merrick as its Christ figure), its dramatic power derives from its internal dynamics of parable (Crossan's dialectic of advent/reversal/action), as well as from its parabolic impact on the theater audience, whose conventional responses of judgment and sympathy are challenged by the play. On stage, Merrick himself is parabolic, overturning the other characters' expectations of him and of themselves; in turn, they are parabolic for him. (As Crossan says, "It takes two to parable.") In Merrick's transforming relationships with Sir Frederick Treves, the actress Mrs. Kendal, and the churchman Bishop Walsham How, established barriers of thought, language, and feeling are shattered—at least briefly—and unforeseen human possibilities emerge for simple kindness, more thoughtful understanding, and sensitivity to suffering as well as to beauty in unexpected places. In the growing compassion of some characters, and in Merrick's rare epiphanies of harmony and loveliness, a barely intimated hope for community is renewed out of the social "swamp," and the mystery of being is momentarily revealed. Through all these transformations, Pomerance's drama becomes parabolic for itself, questioning its own leftist and absurdist formulations which exclude divine presence. Because of these several parabolic dimensions, *The Elephant Man* at length emerges neither as a leftist morality play nor as an absurd drama, but as a kind of modern mystery play through which we glimpse the possibility of a transcendent realm of being. To understand how Pomerance's parabolic structures work to make this happen, we must turn to the text as interpreted in the New York production directed by Jack Hofsiss.

II

The Elephant Man opens with a ridiculously complacent Freddie Treves presenting himself to the audience as a newly arrived surgeon at the London Hospital who relishes his "excessive blessings":

> A happy childhood in Dorset.
> A scientist in an age of science.
> In an English age, an Englishman.

These concords are brutally disrupted as the scene shifts across Whitechapel Road. Before a garish carnival booth, a rotund manager hawks his traveling mutation show as "... Mother Nature uncorseted and in malignant rage!" But the main attraction is the Elephant Man's suffering from exposure to his fellow men. Ross cries out:

> Tuppence only, step in and see: This side of the grave, John Merrick has no hope nor expectation of relief. In every sense his situation is desperate. His physical agony is exceeded only by his mental anguish, a despised creature without consolation. Tuppence only, step in and see! To live with his physical hideousness, incapacitating deformities and unremitting pain is trial enough, but to be exposed to the cruelly lacerating expressions of horror and disgust by all who behold him is even more difficult to bear. Tuppence only, step in and see! For in order to survive, Merrick forces himself to suffer these humiliations, I repeat, humiliations, in order to survive, thus he exposes himself to crowds who pay to gape and yawp at this freak of nature, the Elephant Man.

(Ironically, Pomerance has lifted this barker's spiel almost verbatim from the humanitarian sentiments of Ashley Montagu in his *Study in Human Dignity*.) The voyeuristic appeals of Ross are rapidly succeeded by the subtler cruelty of the brash young lecturer in anatomy, who rents the Elephant Man for the day. Back at the hospital with his anatomical exhibit, Treves lectures while pointing with his cane to projected photographs of the real Merrick (and the past-tense words he uses come directly from the real Sir Frederick's journal):

> The most striking feature about him was his enormous head. Its circumference was about that of a man's waist. From the brow there projected a huge bony mass like a loaf, while from the back of his head hung a bag of spongy fungous-looking skin.... The deformities rendered the face utterly incapable of the expression of any emotion whatsoever.... The right arm was of enormous size and shapeless.... The right hand was large and clumsy—a fin or paddle rather than a hand.... The other arm was remarkable by contrast. It was not only normal, but was moreover a delicately shaped limb covered with a fine skin and provided with a beautiful hand which any woman might have envied.... The lower limbs.... were unwieldy, dropsical-looking, and grossly misshapen.

These opening speeches are worth quoting at length, because they suggest how Pomerance is sensitive to the formative or deforming effects of language in ways his predecessors were not when they told the Elephant Man story. The New York production brings out these effects most vividly. During this lecture-demonstration, waiting in a patch of light to Treves's side, is a handsome actor who is Apollonian in physique, loincloth-clad, and cruciform in posture, with arms angled slightly from his body and palms toward the audience. As the lecture proceeds, the actor begins to "present" the Elephant Man character by slowly contorting his straight form until he has become "crooked," as though under the deforming pressure of Treves's anatomical jargon and its implicit normative values.

If this initiating scene portends Merrick's slow crucifixion by many kinds of civilizing languages in the play, it also intimates that he will somehow survive this torture of conditioning. The twisted posture that the actor maintains throughout the play never allows us wholly to forget the shocking photographs, but what the audience actually sees is an elegant theatrical paradox: a human figure imitating an inhuman creature, or in the Platonic terms the play invokes, the essential Form of a god with the mere Appearance of mortal being. Because Pomerance has chosen not to paint and pad his freak literalistically, Merrick—ever in a double figure—reminds us of the "other" dimension of beauty and wholeness that is nearly absent from the ugly and broken world the play exposes. One cannot choose to see him only as pathetically lamed, twisted, and barely articulate: the actor playing Merrick is also a symbol of transcendence always present on the stage. And it is important to the play's intimation of hope that we look critically *through this symbol* as we watch Merrick's deformation by the other characters, including their appropriation of the Elephant Man as a metaphor for their condition.

Swift melodramatic scenes follow the lecture-demonstration: Merrick, back on the streets, is insulted, deported, beaten, robbed, abandoned. Yet Merrick believes in "happiness," and shows he is susceptible of compassion for other victims and capable of wit in the face of brutality. When he meets up with Treves again, the doctor takes him "home" to the London Hospital to stay. Here Treves teaches the uncouth creature to bathe himself and to repeat such ordering sentences as, "Rules make us happy because they are for our own good." Pomerance's implicit message in this scene is Peter Handke's explicit one in *Kaspar:* "You have a sentence of which you can make a model for yourself . . . which will exorcise every disorder from you." It is just what Merrick needs, one might think, and certainly what his keepers need for this potentially disruptive patient: "You can quiet yourself with sentences . . . ," says Kaspar; "you can be nice and quiet." With some difficulty, Merrick learns to imitate his betters, yet this naif/victim knows too much to succumb totally to the imitation of their sentences or their myths. When Treves defends the peremptory firing of a staring hospital attendant as a "merciful" act for Merrick's good, the freak questions his keeper (in the "left-rationalist" manner): "If your mercy is so cruel, what do you have for justice?" Such early lines seem to promise that Merrick will be the little child who leads the others to transcend their egoistic naivete and civilized barbarism.

From the beginning, John Merrick is a parabolic presence in Treves's life, causing him to revalue his beliefs and at length to abandon them as inhuman and untrue. Other relations too are developing along these lines in the first half of the play. Most important is Merrick's encounter with a woman. Treves has hired the celebrated actress, Madge Kendal, to provide the civilizing fiction of companionship for the Elephant Man, from whom other women less practiced in the arts of illusion have run in horror. Treves's shallow expectations and Mrs. Kendal's are completely overthrown. Despite her initial repugnance, which she controls at first behind a tough professional facade, Merrick's beauty of spirit quickly charms her into authentic response. Their encounters form the most moving scenes in the play. "[S]ometimes I think my head is so big," he confides to her, "because it is so full of dreams. . . . Do you know what happens when dreams cannot get out?" When he shares his strangely wise interpretation of *Romeo and Juliet,* which he has been reading, the actress (as well as the audience) discovers his sensibility to be "extraordinary". Merrick's unaffected humanity forces Mrs. Kendal, who has been a stage Juliet, to abandon her glibly theatrical myth of "romance" for the reality of a courageous friendship, for *agape* if not yet *eros.* Entering the existentially open, potentially dangerous territory of this out-of-bounds relation, Kendal and Merrick have stepped into the uncharted realm of parabolic action. It is taking this step that makes it possible for Pomerance's drama in its first half to move through and past its initial rationalist social analysis. For without love, Merrick asks simply, "why should there be a play?"

When this pair shake hands (in the New York production, when she chooses to take not his well-formed left hand but his right "fin or paddle rather than a hand"), and when they nearly touch again later, the play seems to be reaching for moments of apocalyptic transformation in the marriage of different realms of being. These glimpses of what Kendal calls "Paradise" happen outside the roles prescribed by the London Hospital world, a false Victorian earthly paradise; and the couple's poetic exchanges likewise move beyond the practiced formulas of polite discourse, the routine "I am very pleased to have made your acquaintance" that rings metallically through many social encounters. Yet some kind of society is clearly necessary for John Merrick so that his "dreams" *can* get out, and indeed the others need to know them. "Before I spoke with people," Merrick confesses, "I did not think of all these things because there was no one to bother to think them for. Now things just come out of my mouth which are true." At the close of the play's first half, Treves proudly announces the great "success" of the Kendal-Merrick connection. He does not seem to realize that the human values which Merrick's advent has brought into his world have caused the word "success" to bear a new meaning, even on his lips. With this triumph, the audience's expectations are high for more than Merrick's induction into normality.

As the second half of the production begins, culture myths have begun to reassert their power, and Merrick is dressed for the old success. Artistically gifted, he is building a model of St. Phillip's Church and explicates its Platonic religious allegory: the cathedral "is not stone and steel and glass; it is an imitation of grace flying up and up from the mud. So I make my imitation of an imitation". Yet it is no longer so clear that "up" is Merrick's direction; the "ANXIETIES OF THE SWAMP" (the title of Scene XIII), of this decaying society, are already sucking him in (as they suck in the colonized victims in such early Brecht plays as *In the*

Swamp). As the Hofsiss production conceives the scene (XI), theatrical caricatures of "the best society" now crowd the stage space, diminishing Merrick's presence. The lavish gifts they bear in a Christmas pilgrimage to the London Hospital are useless artifacts meant as theatrical props for the myth of the Elephant Man's humanity, as Kendal observes; the two-dimensional figures are the "best" people whom the excessively-dimensioned Merrick must imitate to become recognized as a man among men. Now in evening dress, Merrick steps respectfully into the background to receive their formulated homage: "I am very pleased to have made your acquaintance"; they are eager to greet the phenomenon they think they have made of him. (As *A Man's a Man* would describe this transformation: "At first, it was a regular elephant, later it was a fake . . . ".)

"Born" into this fake society at Christmas, Merrick seems to have become their domesticated messiah. In this role, he must now accept the others' powerful, contradictory dreams into his bursting head. So one by one the figures come forward to tell just how Merrick seems "almost like me." He mirrors an "Example to us all," says one who feigns to admire models of Self-Help, the preeminent Victorian creed. Mrs. Kendal describes him as "gentle, almost feminine[,] . . . a serious artist in his way"; Bishop How greets him as a devoutly religious doubter, like himself; Carr Gomm, the militantly atheist hospital administrator (a sort of Charles Kingsley for the opposing team), respects John for knowing practically "what side his bread is buttered on" and counting his blessings. To others, Merrick is a "Piccadilly exquisite" or discreet confidant. Treves sees his protege as "curious, compassionate, concerned about the world, well, rather like myself . . . ". But like the others, who come forward in a second cycle of confessions, Treves also acknowledges his darker self in Merrick. If Merrick is the dream-Christ who affirms their complacences, he is also a suffering servant whom they need to show them their other dimensions as human beings. In either role, however, he is an exploited symbol, loaded with their meanings rather than encouraged to speak his own.

In these equivocal roles, Merrick becomes implicitly a critic of their lives, and the impact of this criticism is felt most powerfully at this point through the change in Treves, who emerges as Merrick's double. No longer the caricatured scientific scientist, Treves confides to the audience that John Merrick is "visibly worse than 86–87. That, as he rises higher in the consolations of society, he gets visibly more grotesque is proof definitive he is like me." At the center of the play, the successful doctor and popular patient have arrived at exactly the same point. Sir Frederick's transformation has begun with the advent of Merrick into his world. But the doctor's changing sense of what limited value "proof definitive" has, forces him to admit that he can "make no sense of" their shared condition.

From this point onward, the play could be considered anticlimactic. It might be conjectured that Pomerance, having created in Merrick such a remarkable person, does not then know, any more than his other characters, what to do with him. But it is also possible, and I think more persuasive, to observe at this point in the play that there is a deliberate complication of its issues, even as the stage space becomes more crowded, and that our critical and sympathetic responses to Treves and Merrick become less easy and certain. The beauty which the play does win from its experience of human beastliness emerges only as the drama's contradictions are heightened and important reversals have taken place for the central characters.

Following a Brechtian pattern, Merrick the innocent now becomes even more deeply implicated in the system of exploitation and counterexploitation that has "saved" him. When his old manager, Ross, reappears, down at the heel and apparently starving, to ask for help, Merrick rejects the man's crude propositioning with the elegant cruelty he has learned. In this unsettling moment of *deja vu*, Merrick echoes Treves's earlier defense of injustice when he says, "I'm sorry, Ross. It's just the way things are." And as "proof" of his new manhood, Merrick backs up against the church model he has made. "By god," says Ross. "Then I am lost."

As witnesses to his moral deformation in society, we find it increasingly difficult wholly to approve Merrick, for we see that he has taken on several new double identities since his comparatively simpler state of natural Elephant-Manhood. He accepts the new artificial self that society imposes, but he judges it; his innocence is provoking and even perverse, while his very goodness has evil effects. Yet despite distortion and confusion, he retains an innate sense of just proportion, and from that center of integrity continues to question divine as well as human justice through the rest of the play.

As these complications are developing in the audience's response to Merrick, Sir Frederick is beginning to attract sympathy. Treves has begun to question the adequacy of his materialist assumptions. Increasingly hard pressed to defend his actions, he falls back upon the Victorian sexual standard as a last resource of moral certainty. The play's climax comes after a great blow to this myth of Treves's and to Merrick's innocent faith in those who have saved him.

One afternoon, Treves discovers the lovely Mrs. Kendal shyly unveiling her torso to Merrick, who has never "seen" a beautiful woman before. In the New York version, her red hair cascaded down a white back, and momentarily she became a sensuous Pre-Raphaelite idealization. The confusion of soul's beauty and body's beauty poses no problem for John Merrick: this "beautiful sight" is simply his supreme moment of Paradise in the play. Treves shatters it. "Do you know what you are?" he shouts at John, bursting in. "Don't you know what is forbidden?" The "Woman" is banished, but worse, Treves never answers Merrick's anguished queries about why his Ideal has never returned to the hospital. Treves even allows Merrick to believe she chooses to absent herself. Although this banishment is meant as kindness, it is cruelty to the doubly betrayed and confused Merrick, and his disillusion forces him back upon the absurdist possibility that his body has always presented. And yet, through the ministrations of Bishop How, he still receives the discipline and sacraments of the Church and stubbornly maintains his childlike faith.

It is not difficult for Pomerance to present Treves's outraged decency as the "error" of an indecent moral confidence, for we know that Treves can invoke no personal religious belief to justify parting these two souls. But when Merrick now begins "chipping away at the edges" of this moralism, Pomerance gives another parabolic turn to our view of its victim. "Frederick," Merrick asks soon after the crisis, ". . . do you believe in heaven? Hell? What about Christ? What about God? I believe in heaven. The Bible promises in heaven the crooked shall be made straight." Treves quips dryly, "So did the rack, my boy. So do we all." It is clear that the innocent inquisitor is also becoming Treves's rack when the doctor explodes, "For God's sakes. If you are angry, just say it. . . . Say it: I am angry. Go on. I am angry. I am angry! I am angry!" "I believe in heaven," return the Model Christian.

Is this "cruelty" or "kindness"? The interchangeability of these words portends a moral nightmare. This chaos in values is brought home in the next scene, a parabolic encounter titled "CRUELTY IS AS NOTHING TO KINDNESS." Stepping forward smartly into Treves's nightmare, a transformed Merrick, equipped with top hat and cane, begins to dissect the moral deformities of "the terrifyingly normal" scientist, hunched dreaming in his chair. The reversal of their roles may be Treves's fantasy, but what we see is a heightened version of Merrick's learned vices for which we already have had proof. Even in its dream mode, this Brechtian lecture-scene jars our sympathy for Merrick, our easy tolerance for the victim's earlier imitative failures of compassion. As with old Ross, Merrick as anatomist of Treves is morally "correct," yet lacks moral imagination. His lecture is patently "analysis" of a "left-rationalist" sort about the cruelties of Treves's patronage, his colonization of other persons and his own sexual desires. Merrick counters neatly the scientist's anatomical language with his own impersonal idiom, and he makes his points sharply; but he lacks the self-criticism for which his speech argues, and more important, he lacks compassion. As Merrick himself has taught us to ask, without love, "why should there be a play?"

As the script directs, scene after scene has ended with Merrick silently placing another piece on the model of St. Phillip's. Even as he has constructed this model of transcendent loveliness, he has been deconstructing Treves and his myths. Treves's confession and breakdown come at last. In a scene near the end of the play, he admits that his society does not "know . . . what else to do with" Merrick's or anyone's nature but to "Rob" it; society has made the Elephant Man "a mockery of everything we live by". When the distressed scientist falls into the arms of the Bishop (as Merrick had once collapsed upon Treves) with the half-articulate cry "Help me," John in the background places the last piece on the church and says quietly, "It is done." In this chilling moment, echoing Christ's words on the Cross, the outwardly emotionless Merrick seems not a messiah, but a predatory child-monster, a social victim so brutalized he can excel only in revenge, an aesthete who cares only for his art. At this crux, the model of St. Phillip's seems to represent not the "consolation" of "Christ's church" (as the Bishop would say), but a "cruciform lair" (as Carr Gomm would quip) from which a mildly apocalyptic beast/man who "is not, and yet is" has made his ravaging forays into civilized territory. In light of one category with which the Christian tradition has tried to make sense of the freak of nature, the "monstrous" Merrick has "finished" his circuit through the world to warn (*moneo*) and show forth (*monstro*) God's wrath to a decadent culture.

By this point, the Elephant Man has fulfilled the ominous speculation early in the play that his presence "may be a danger in ways we do not know." The danger is not physical contagion but spiritual scandal in this world, for Merrick is scandalous both in his mutation and in his imitation of the normal. To the guardians of Victorian morals, he represents the shock of their repressed sexuality. As a product of the workhouse, he is a reminder of the savagery on which this society is based and poses the threat of revolutionary upheaval. To the elegant and healthy, he presents the image of ugliness and disease. To the supercivilized, his childlike spontaneity recollects a natural mode of being. Merrick reminds those who accept a common version of the Darwinian hypothesis that their beastly origins are not safely behind them in the prehistoric eons; he mocks the efforts to climb up and up of those who graft onto the hypothesis a progressive social Darwinism. For the scientific investigator, he embodies all that is outside the known scheme of things; for the doctor, he thwarts the ambition to diagnose and cure. And among all the methodically-minded—the builders of Empire, the London police, the method actress, the churchman who seems nearly all form, the systematic atheist administrator—the advent of Merrick disrupts the rational patterns by which men have organized their social existences, structured desires, and protected themselves from the mystery of their own beings.

Pomerance has described his theater as "some form of social memory," bringing back "points that are too volatile, too dangerous to be lived every day—the skeletons in the closet, the guilt." Late in the play, Treves calls Merrick a "parable" (though he means allegory), and indeed Merrick has begun to be a parable in so disturbing his society—not by illustrating a moral, but simply by being what he is, a *momento mori* among systematic people who have excluded the realities of guilt, suffering, and human limits from their most cherished culture myths. But as a parabolic presence Merrick also does more. In Crossan's sense, parable does not stop with the shattering of illusions and complacences of the hearers; parable brings forth as well uncharted possibilities for actions and relationships. Pomerance's play does, I believe, transcend its own disillusionments—but very narrowly, against great odds, and not until the absurdist potential of the Elephant Man's plight has been explored to its limits.

Rapidly following upon the completion of the church model and his mission, Merrick's "accidental" death by asphyxiation occurs. His deformity requires him to sleep sitting up, but during a fatal dream he straightens into a normal sleeping position and the weight of his enormous head crushes his windpipe. For a moment, the church model seems to loom on stage menacingly, like the little house in *Tiny Alice;* and seconds after Merrick expires, an attendant blunders into the room with the words already on his lips: "Arbitrary. It's all so—. . . . " If this death scene seems to give absurd drama the final broken word, certainly the play has all along fostered the questioning of cosmic justice and the "chancy" nature of existence. Opening this half of the play, Merrick had boasted that he built the church "with just one hand" (the graceful, artistic one); but this triumph is yet another reminder of the man's incompleteness, of the other hand resembling a beastly vestige from an earlier evolutionary stage. In making him, Merrick slyly asks, God "should have used both hands shouldn't he?" Does his death, then, provide "proof definitive" of the futility of all architecture, social and cosmic?

Neither Merrick's life nor his death is completely "arbitrary" and meaningless. Pomerance has attacked the modern theater for purveying "the most limited, self-seeking adolescent vices" and things that are "just not true." In particular, he rejects "one peculiar ideology—that we are all pathetic and that pathos is what we all find in the end." It is on this point that *The Elephant Man,* which recalls *Equus* in some ways, strikingly differs from Peter Shaffer's play. Shaffer's doubting psychiatrist, like Treves, is challenged by the advent of the irrational and anticonventional in the form of his patient; but Dysart's parable is incomplete, and he is left in self-pity and "darkness." This ending was rewarded on Broadway by thundering applause, partly because, I believe, the play told its audience what they wanted to hear: that ordinary life is deadened beyond any hope of salvation by human or divine means, and that pathos is all we find in the end. (This seems to be the message also of Shaffer's recent play, *Amadeus.*) In light of the complaint that Jean-Paul Sartre and Georg Lukacs have lodged against some modernist literature, such a conclusion finally encourages complacency through its fatalistic nihilism. *Equus* also wins its popularity through a predictable and shallow social critique, in my view, rather than generating disruptive forces that really would challenge the status quo. In contrast, *The Elephant Man* evokes the very different response of awed silence in its disturbed audience. Pomerance's play tells us, as parables do, things we do not expect and may not want to hear; it poses challenge after challenge to conventional responses, drawing us in as participants in a dialectical process that forces us back as critics of elements in the play and of ourselves; it invites both our skepticism and our wonder. With its powerful symbol of the freak, the play lives on in the memory as a parable does, having involved us ineluctably in the discovery that there are more things in the world than we have dreamed in our philosophies.

Nor are we allowed to stay in a Kafkaesque world where "We are nihilistic thoughts, suicidal thoughts that come into God's head," a world that is "only a bad mood of God, a bad day of His," where there is (as Kafka added ironically) "plenty of hope, an infinite amount of hope—but not for us." This perspective, which Lukacs discusses in his essay "The Ideology of Modernism," directs the anticlimax of *Equus* and is certainly not absent from climactic moments in *The Elephant Man;* but Pomerance does not allow us to remain in the postures of "modern religious atheism," "worshipping the void created by God's absence."

A central theme of *The Elephant Man* that bears upon these difficulties of classifying it is what Merrick calls our "little vocabulary problem." Like the conventional exchanges in the play, our labels are inadequate. The descriptions "arbitrary" and "absurd" are in a number of ways partial and premature, uttered without regard for other dimensions of the play and before all the evidence is in. In the final scenes, Pomerance takes us one step further to remind us of the firm social grounding for a tragedy that is not meaningless, or a cosmic accident. Merrick's death, we recognize, is the culmination of his long, even ritualistic, murder by society. The occurrence of this unattended death in the hospital "home" suggests the carelessness of all society's care for Merrick. Carr Gomm has the play's last spoken words: "It's too late, I'm afraid. It is done. (*Smiles.*)" Gomm's cynical version of the crucifixion motto is ironic in a way different from Merrick's earlier unconscious use of it. Gomm's "FINAL REPORT TO THE INVESTORS" implies that Merrick has been disposed of at last, and now the money gathered to support the Elephant Man can be channeled into the hospital's general funds. If Merrick had first seemed to the disinterested Treves a form of "medical richesse," he remains for some to the end "our capital," as Ross had called Merrick. Yet the capital gains over which the hospital administrator "Smiles" are not quite safely secured: the hospital's star scientist, Sir Frederick Treves, is deeply shaken by events that are not yet "done" in him, and Merrick's influence is not "finished." In this last speaking scene, Pomerance lets us feel the brutal impact of administrative efficiency, while calling into question Gomm's myth of gain, and because Treves is present, reminding us that this myth is broken for good.

Merrick's death is also the instinctive suicide of a deeply disillusioned man—a suicide for which the others too are guilty. In one figure the play proposes for this collective responsibility, the accumulated weight of others' dreams—which Merrick has accepted—breaks his neck. In another, more complicated figure, Merrick, a polished mirror for the others' self-images, eventually discovers that he reflects their nothingness, and therefore (as an early scene title announces) "WHEN THE ILLUSION ENDS HE MUST KILL HIMSELF." As this enthymeme suggests, his death is then a "logical" extension of his earlier theory of Romeo's suicide upon Juliet's death: Merrick had argued, idiosyncratically, that in trying no harder to revive Juliet when the mirror he holds up registers no breath from her lips, Romeo proves his "love" for her is only an illusion, and when the illusion ends.... With the simple logic of a child and the despair of a man capable of passion, Merrick, bereft of his Juliet and seeing no more evidence of spirit in his world, puts down his head to cut off his own breath. Because there has been love in this play, even this suicidal action has meaning in the context of a society that tries to exclude love from its theater of surfaces and mirrors.

The Elephant Man is a cosmic absurdity, a social victim, and a suicide: but the images for his death do not end here, for Merrick was also by all accounts a Model Christian. Pomerance makes him into a model of Christ as well, yet without allowing the Elephant Man to become enclosed in the messiah myth of his Victorian admirers. The way Pomerance handles this powerful image, as well as other Christian symbols, expresses the skeptical faith characteristic of this play, the faith that human life matters because human beings are not cosmically adrift but grounded, and possibly grounded in more than their material conditions. Hope and human value depend upon the transcendence of these conditions, and the consciousness created and delimited by them. If one *can* call this hope a faith in a transcendent realm of being, Pomerance's expression of it is as significantly qualified, and then left open to interpretation, as one would expect in an agnostic parable. What is surprising—and what any account of the play has to come to terms with—is the fact that while the Christian symbols Pomerance evokes are placed, they are not rejected.

In the New York version, Merrick's end fulfills the potential of the earlier stage allusion to crucifixion. When his head tilts back too far and his arms claw the air, his final posture barely suggests a quite literal *imitatio Christi.* Prompted by dream sirens from "Beautiful darkness' empire" to "Sleep like others you learn to admires / Be like your mother, be like your sire," Merrick formally imitates the dead maternal figure (the mother whose photograph he keeps under his pillow) and, more important, the equivocal paternal figure of Jesus/Treves (whose names have been linked). Just as this horrible end releases Merrick from a life of pain, so either "sire" seems both cruel and merciful, while in the background other characters too have been cruel/kind to Merrick. Imitating his equivocal sires, the Elephant Man is a "Both" (to borrow a term from "The Song of the Both," *A Man's a Man,* and his duality complicates our response to his death, just as it was the curse and blessing of his life.

Pomerance's particular way of qualifying Merrick's "crucifixion" is to set it within a suggestive late Victorian context where, we may recall, the artist-as-victim became (as in Wilde's *De Profundis*) the artist-as-Christ. Coming so soon after the completion of his art project, Merrick's end is made complex by its theatrical aestheticism (and therefore not simply by its arbitrary, broken-off quality). For the English *fin de siecle* writers, as Lionel Johnson and the Rhymers said, life is ritual; for Merrick in his time, death too is ritual and, like his life, imitates art in this play. The form that end takes literally embodies an answer to the question Arthur O'Shaughnessy asked: "What is eternal? What escapes decay? / A certain, faultless, matchless, deathless line, / Curving consummate." Ironically, Merrick achieves immortal form in being made at last "straight" in this final rather morbid performance.

Merrick has journeyed a long way to this late Victorian point: in viewing his equivocal achievement, we might compare his whole career in the play to the development of the English Romantic sensibility. At the beginning, he reminds us of Blake's child weeping in the "charter'd street[s]" of London, soon to be oppressed by the "mind-forg'd manacles" of the Victorian mind police, and closed out of his Garden of Love by the spirit of "Thou shalt not." By the end of the play, the Blakean innocent has thoroughly suffered the social, psychological, and metaphysical shocks of nineteenth-century experience. From the decadence of the "moral swamp," he looks for salvation in the manner of Yeats's Last Romantics. Of course, I am not suggesting that Pomerance is interested in making an allegory of literary history; rather, I am proposing that this is the *kind* of "romantic imagination" Pomerance's Merrick has in the late 1880's. These are Treves's words in his final, nonscientific and tentative diagnosis of the patient's *maladie fin de siecle.* As a Last Romantic, Merrick makes a determined protest with his death against what Wilde called "Nature's lack of design." Or perhaps it would be better to say that Pomerance makes his protest in the design of the play. From the perspective of Brustein on Brecht's dialectical tensions, the objectivity of Pomerance's left-rationalist critique has been called into question by his "romantic" revolt.

The poetry of religion in Pomerance's play marks this revolt as the later uncertain Romanticism which "chose for theme," as Yeats wrote, "Traditional sanctity and loveliness." Although Merrick does not dally with High Church attractions in the manner of Wilde and other later Victorians, in choosing this theme Pomerance does let us see Merrick acting a part. Just before the death scene, at the rear of the stage, Merrick enacts a pantomime of confession with Bishop How (who has become less of a caricature by the end of the production), while conversations go forward upstage about the sincerity of John's faith. Should his faithfulness be taken seriously, or is it only an artistic illusion, "a mass of papier-mache and paint" with which Merrick fools himself and others? Or, to use Treves's medical terms, might it be nothing but a "general anesthetic" protecting Merrick from the brutal surgeries of life, numbing the pain of his doubt that God is merciful? Treves tells Bishop How, who seeks to confirm his protege in the Church of England, that Merrick "is very excited to do what others do if he thinks it is what others do." In this late scene, the agnostic scientist surprises us, however, by affirming that he refuses to cast doubt on Merrick's faith.

Even as Treves recognizes the imitative character of the Elephant Man's social acts, he also seems to sense that in Merrick's attraction to "Traditional sanctity and loveliness," an act of faith is concealed that transcends theatricality. For hypocritical conformity and mindless repetition are not the only modes of imitation one can associate with this tradition to which Merrick has been drawn. Perhaps in the absence of "proof" that the God so confidently invoked by the Bishop really exists in the world, Merrick is nevertheless in his last moments instinctively attempting to "follow the way by which . . . [others] began," as Pascal wrote of the famous wager, accepting the sacraments, discipline, and consolations of the Church (and now imitating Christ's death) *as if* he believed in their efficacy.

The pity of Merrick's end is that he seems to have nothing to lose in a wager on faith, and that he can be made straight only in the posture of death. His end also seems to provide Brechtian proof that, whatever other world there may be, in the world we know where people do not live justly and mercifully with one another, a man cannot both be good and survive.

III

The Elephant Man does not end with the death of John Merrick. He is survived by another, equally ironic, symbol of transcendence on the stage: the model of St. Phillip's Church. Pomerance's remarks on what this church signifies are suggestive but laconic. In an "Introductory Note" to the Grove Press edition of the play, he writes: "I believe the building of the church model constitutes some kind of central metaphor, and the groping toward conditions where it can be built, and the building of it are the action of the play." The "conditions where it can be built," Pomerance says elsewhere, are "the right venue he [Merrick] could survive in."

If one thinks of this play as a dramatic parable, these remarks make fuller sense, particularly for the New York production. *Within* the play, this "church" is the community that Merrick miraculously discovers, built in moments of union with others, a real and present church that helps him to transcend his loneliness and difference. More generally, this survival area is the place that Pomerance has managed to build through the writing of his drama about the Elephant Man, who continues to live in new ways in the popular imagination not as a myth fulfilling desire, a refuge church, but as a parabolic conscience disturbing all our enclaves of false "consolation." The broader community that comes into being in the theater audience is the "church" built through the whole action of *The Elephant Man* as dramatic parable.

The apparent paradox that the building of a "church" should be the central action of this critically conscious play might be put into the larger context that Brustein discusses in *The Theatre of Revolt*. The modern dramatist, he writes,

> wants to convert this collective [the theatre audience] into a "chosen people" through the transforming power of his art. . . . In a world without God, he must shape a congregation, invent a liturgy, create a faith. "To kill God and to build a Church," writes Camus, "are the constant and contradictory purposes of rebellion." These contradictory purposes are the foundation of the theatre of revolt, where each dramatist labors to make a new union out of his secession—to make his initial act of revolt the occasion for a new kind of grace.

In his *Times* interview, Pomerance reflects on this mode of church-building. "The most important element in the theater is the audience's imagination," he says, and imagination connects:

> The audience is people. What is in them, is in me. It goes back to the function of memory. . . . I don't mean to tell them something they do not already know. I'm not bringing hot news. My interest in the audience is to remind them of a common thing and, if only temporarily, they do then become a unity, a community.

As his note to *The Elephant Man* text suggests, it is the labor of the play to "[grope] toward conditions where . . . [the church] can be built," and "the building of it" happens only as the audience is gathered as a community through the collective experience of disturbance and transformation.

It is also this problematical "church-building" that marks the critical contrast between the religious dimensions of *The Elephant Man* and *Equus*. Shaffer yokes violence and the sacred in ritualistic enactments of the individual's epiphany with his dark god. Pomerance's whole mode is different: the ambiance is specifically *liturgical*, and includes audience and actors in a community of worship. His theatrical means are appropriate to this different end: the worshipful moments he includes involve more than one person; ritual objects on the stage are ironic symbols; a cellist at the side plays a soft prelude, an offertory at intermission, and a postlude (an aesthetic/religious touch that was part of the original London production). The Broadway cast have also said that performing *The Elephant Man* resembles the conducting of a religious service, requiring for certain scenes reverent silence in the theater. But this ambiance happens in a play with sharply critical moments as well as witty exchanges that make us laugh. The worship, not self-indulgent and narcissistic like that in *Equus,* maintains a self-critical poise.

Pomerance's drama is not a new parable of the Kingdom, but the audience's silence at the end of the performance recalls what John Dominic Crossan calls the silence in the parables, which do not tell us what to do *next*. *The Elephant Man* sends its hearers on their uncharted ways. To effect this kind of dismissal from Pomerance's liturgical theater, the last scene (added in production) provides a final occasion for grace and completes the gathering of the playwright's congregation through the whole action of the play.

In the last silent tableau, the members of the cast gather around the church model to pay their respects to a mystery which they do not understand but to which they inescapably belong. In this ritualistic moment, they/we are no longer problem solvers or critical thinkers in a "left-rationlist" theater, but a "church" gathered to ponder the parable of the Elephant Man, who has ineluctably, perhaps irrevocably, altered our habitual categories of perception, analysis, and emotional response. The ambiance of this ending reminds us that the loveliness Merrick communicated to those he knew has raised the elusive possibility of some "other" kind of existence where love and justice may be no illusion. It is not with a sense of meaningless waste that this modern mystery play leaves its audience, but rather with the dark wonder of Pascal's words in the *Pensees:* "*Vere tu es Deus absconditus.*" The author of this existence, whom Merrick arraigns and admires, hides himself within the play from the Elephant Man and others, but it is not necessary to conclude that he is absent.

Source: Janet L. Larson, "*The Elephant Man* as Dramatic Parable," in *Modern Drama,* September, 1983, Vol. 26, no. 3, pp. 335–56.

Catharine Hughes

Calling The Elephant Man *"easily the best play thus far of the 1978–79 New York theatre season," Hughes offers a brief, favorable review of Pomerance's play.*

The Elephant Man, by Bernard Pomerance, is easily the best play thus far of the 1978–79 New York theatre season. (No one need remind me that that could be taken as a somewhat left-handed compliment.)

Currently at the new Theatre of St. Peter's Church in the Citicorp Building, but about to transfer to a larger, more "commercial" milieu, it has its flaws but offers the most compelling evening of drama in New York today.

Pomerance has based his play on an actual "freak" of the Victorian era, John Merrick, who suffered from a mysterious and incurable illness that caused his limbs to become twisted and resulted in apparently hideous skin excretions. The title, *The Elephant Man,* was the one applied to him during the period when he worked in a traveling freak show in England.

The playwright, who is an American, though the work was first produced in England, shows Merrick being taken into a London hospital in Whitechapel, where he becomes one of the outstanding curiosities of the British society of the period, the 1880s. In 21 scenes, Pomerance portrays how this deformed man (brilliantly played by Philip Anglim) comes under the wing of Dr. Frederick Treves (Kevin Conway) after he is abandoned by his freak-show manager for being too grotesque even for such audiences. Treves is unable to cure him, but writes about him in a manner that makes him almost fashionable and results in philanthropic grants.

Perhaps the worst thing he does, however—and this would seem to be Pomerance's point—is to try to change him into someone who is conventionally acceptable, someone who will be "like us." It obviously cannot work, and the playwright becomes a bit too obvious at moments. But *The Elephant Man* deserves the fine reviews it has received and the attention of anyone who calls himself a "serious theatregoer." The production, by Jack Hofsiss, could do with a little work before it transfers, but this is relatively minor. It offers the sort of challenging drama rarely seen in the New York theatre.

Source: Catharine Hughes. "Capsule Comments," in *America,* Vol. 140, no. 7, February 24, 1979, p. 135.

SOURCES

Barnes, Clive. A review in the *New York Post,* April 20, 1979.

Belli, Angela. "Medical Technology on Stage," in *Ometeca,* Vol. 3, No. 4, 1996, pp. 291-303.

Cunningham, Dennis. A review of *The Elephant Man* on WCBS-TV, April 19, 1979.

Elder, Richard. A review in *The New York Times,* April 20, 1979.

Gottfried, Martin. A review in *Saturday Review*, March 17, 1979.

Holladay, William E. and Stephen Watt. "Viewing *The Elephant Man*," in *PMLA*, Vol. 104, No. 5, October, 1989, pp. 868-81.

Jiji, Vera. "Multiple and Virtual: Theatrical Space in *The Elephant Man*," in *The Theatrical Space*, Cambridge University Press, 1987, pp. 247-57.

Kauffmann, Stanley. A review in *New Republic*, May 12, 1979.

Kroll, Jack. A review in *Newsweek*, February 8, 1979.

Larson, Janet L. "*The Elephant Man* as Dramatic Parable," in *Modern Drama*, Vol. 26, No. 3, September, 1983, pp. 335-56.

Sharp, Christopher. A review in *Women's Wear Daily*, January 16, 1979.

Watt, Douglas. A review in the *Daily News*, April 20, 1979.

Wilson, Edwin. A review in *The Wall Street Journal*, January 26, 1979.

FURTHER READING

Davis, Tracy C. *Actresses As Working Women: Their Social Identity in Victorian Culture,* Routledge, 1991, 200 p.
    A historical and social examination of the issues faced by female actresses.

Howard, Martin. *Victorian Grotesque: An Illustrated Excursion into Medical Curiosities, Freaks, and Abnormalities, Principally of the Victorian Age,* Jupiter Books, 1977, 153 p.
    As the title promises, this book looks at medicine and human abnormalities.

Judd, Catherine. *Bedside Seductions: Nursing and the Victorian Imagination, 1830–1880,* St. Martin's Press, 1997, 211 p.
    Explores the role of nurse in Victorian social and literary history. The evolution of nursing provides insights into gender and class issues of this period.

Ritvo, Harriet. *The Animal Estate: The English and Other Creatures in the Victorian Age,* Harvard University Press, 1989, 347 p.
    Ritvo provides an unusual approach to discussions of class in Victorian England by focusing on the relationship between animals and humans.

The Front Page

BEN HECHT and CHARLES MACARTHUR

1928

Written by Ben Hecht and Charles MacArthur, *The Front Page* is a play that is considered responsible for defining the modern stereotype of a reporter as a hard-drinking, hard-boiled journalist intent on uncovering truth even in the face of danger. The comedy was a smash hit from its premiere in Broadway's Times Square Theatre on August 14, 1928; it ran for 276 performances.

The Front Page was controversial at the time for its use of profane language and references (to such things as sex, prostitutes, and peeping toms) unfit for a decent audience. Modern critics assert that *The Front Page* paved the way for the use of such language in the theater.

Drawn from Hecht and MacArthur's careers as journalists in Chicago in the 1910s, the play is set in the pressroom at Chicago's Criminal Courts Building and concerns a group of reporters covering a controversial execution.

The Front Page has been revived regularly over the years and is regarded as a quintessential American play. Although modern critics deride its outdated language and ideas, it is still valued as an important landmark of the American theater scene.

AUTHOR BIOGRAPHY

Hecht was born on February 28, 1894, in New York City, the son of Joseph and Sarah Hecht. When he was six years old, his family moved to Racine, Wisconsin, where he resided until moving to Chicago in 1910.

In Chicago Hecht began working for the *Chicago Journal* and eventually become a successful journalist. His interests were not limited to reporting; he also wrote a newspaper column, poetry, and plays. By the early 1920s, he was also a celebrated novelist.

Hecht's reputation as a playwright was established in the 1920s. Though he had a play produced as early as 1917, his first Broadway show was *The Egotist* (1922).

His most popular plays were written in collaboration with Charles MacArthur (see below), a fellow Chicagoan with a newspaper background. Their most successful collaboration was *The Front Page* (1928), which drew on both their newspaper backgrounds and established a stereotype of reporters repeated on stage and screen.

In 1926 Hecht launched his Hollywood screenwriting career at the invitation of friend and already established screenwriter, Herman Mankiewicz. Although he wrote more than seventy scripts and was highly respected for his work, he considered scriptwriting as strictly a source of income, not an artistic endeavor.

Hecht directed and produced a number of his own films—several in collaboration with MacArthur. By the 1950s, he also worked in television after being blacklisted for his anti-British activities in the post-World War II era. He was a firm Zionist and supporter of Jewish causes, including independence for Israel. He died on April 18, 1964, in New York City.

MacArthur was born on November 5, 1895, in Scranton, Pennsylvania, the son of William Telfer and Georgeanna MacArthur. He spent his childhood in Scranton, but his family moved to Nyack, New York, while he was a teenager.

He enrolled in the Wilson Memorial Academy in order to prepare for a career in the clergy like his father. Realizing that he wanted to be a writer, he moved to Illinois and began his journalism career at his brother's paper, *Oak Leaves,* in Oak Park, Illinois.

Between 1914 and 1923, interrupted only by a brief stint in the armed services during World War I, MacArthur was a hard-drinking reporter at some of the best papers in Chicago, including the *Chicago Tribune.*

In 1923, MacArthur's life changed dramatically when he moved to New York City. His first produced play was *Lulu Belle* (1926), a commercial hit written with Edward Sheldon.

After a chance meeting with Hecht on the streets in New York City—they were acquaintances from Chicago's newspaper scene—the pair collaborated on what became their defining play, *The Front Page.*

Although MacArthur wrote several plays on his own and in collaboration with a few other writers, his most successful stage works were written with Hecht. Like Hecht, he also had some success as a solo screenwriter.

Hecht and MacArthur also wrote and produced four films together, including *The Scoundrel* (1935). MacArthur returned to journalism in 1947 when he became editor of *Theatre Arts* magazine, a post he held until 1950. On April 21, 1956, he died of an internal hemorrhage.

PLOT SUMMARY

Act I

The Front Page opens in the pressroom of the Criminal Courts Building in Chicago. Several reporters are playing cards, waiting for new information on a major story: the hanging that night of a convicted cop killer, Earl Williams.

The reporters talk about one of their colleagues, Hildy Johnson; though rumor has it that Hildy has quit the newspaper business to get married, none of the reporters can believe it.

Another reporter, Bensinger, calls his boss and reports that Williams will be examined by a psychiatrist before his death. McCue, one of the other reporters, calls his office to report that the Governor is on a fishing trip and cannot be found to give a stay of execution.

A cop, Woodenshoes Eichhorn, stops by for a visit. He tells the reporters that Williams told his priest that he is innocent; he admitted he killed the cop, but believes that he is being executed because of his radical beliefs. The reporters send Woodenshoes to get hamburgers.

Hildy enters and informs his boss, Burns, that he is quitting his job and going to New York City with his fiancee, Peggy, and her mother that night. Hildy tells the other reporters that he is going to work in an advertising agency. After he leaves to say goodbye to others in the building, the reporters express their jealousy over his good fortune.

Mollie Malloy, a hooker who has been romantically linked to Williams, enters. She is angry about the lies the newspapers have published about her. The reporters throw her out of the office.

Sheriff Hartman enters and predicts that there will be no stay of execution. He leaves as Hildy and Woodenshoes return.

After avoiding another call from Burns, Hildy packs and says his final good-byes. His leave is interrupted by the news that Earl Williams has escaped. Hildy decides to work on the story, even though it means trouble with Peggy.

Act II

Twenty minutes later, the reporters reveal that Williams escaped by shooting the psychiatrist. Hildy calls Burns and tells him that Sheriff Hartman gave his gun to the psychiatrist to be used as a prop in his psychological exam.

Peggy enters, angry with Hildy for always putting his job before her. Peggy's mother, Mrs. Grant, comes in; she has been waiting in a cab downstairs during the argument. Hildy tells them to go ahead to the station—he will meet them later.

In the meantime, the Mayor enters and refuses to make a statement on the escape. The Sheriff announces that they know where Williams is hiding; the reporters rush to the scene.

The Mayor asks the Sheriff why Williams escaped. Their conversation is interrupted by the appearance of Pincus, a man from the Governor's office, who has come with a reprieve for Williams. The Mayor bribes Pincus to say that he never delivered the document. Pincus accepts the bribe and the men leave.

Hildy returns to the office. Suddenly, Williams falls through the window into the room. Williams

Ben Hecht

gives Hildy his gun while he explains his actions. Hildy hides him in the bathroom and calls Burns.

Mollie enters, happy to see Williams. They hide him in a reporter's desk. The disappointed reporters return and call their editors with new information: Williams was not in the house; and tragically, another man was shot in a case of mistaken identity.

Another reporter, Schwartz, theorizes that Williams is still in the building. The reporters decide to look for Williams. Hildy suggests they each take a floor. Before they can leave, Mrs. Grant enters, and reveals that Hildy has caught Williams. Hildy denies it, and the reporters do not believe her.

To deflect attention from Hildy, Mollie claims that she knows where Williams is. To avoid the insistent reporters, she jumps out the window. While the reporters rush out to pursue Mollie, Burns comes in and Hildy tells him that Williams is in the desk. Mrs. Grant sees this; to keep her quiet, Burns has an associate, Diamond Louie, take her to a safe place.

Hildy tries to leave to meet Peggy, but Burns will not let him; he convinces Hildy to finish the story while he smuggles Williams out in the desk. While Hildy writes the story, Peggy returns. She accuses Hildy of not wanting to get married. She leaves and Hildy declares that he loves his job.

Act III

Five minutes later, Hildy is still writing as Burns makes arrangements to smuggle the desk and Williams out of the building. Burns reads over what Hildy has written and makes him rewrite it.

Bensinger knocks at the door. Burns lets him in, and before he can get to his desk, Burns hires him to work for the *Examiner* and sends him to the office. Hildy regrets choosing the newspaper over Peggy.

Hildy's musings are interrupted by the appearance of Diamond Louie. He tells them that there was an auto accident while they were transporting Mrs. Grant. Louie does not know what happened to her. Hildy worries that she is dead and starts calling hospitals.

Hildy calls Burns a murderer. More people appear at the door: the Sheriff, two deputies, and several of the reporters. They will not let Hildy leave to find Mrs. Grant. The deputies discover that Hildy is in possession of Williams' gun. The Sheriff tries to arrest Hildy and Burns.

Mrs. Grant appears at the door. She accuses Burns of kidnapping her, and reveals that Burns and Hildy are hiding a murderer. It is revealed that Williams is inside the desk, and the Sheriff drags him out. Burns and Hildy are handcuffed.

Pincus returns and tells the Mayor that he does not want the bribe; instead, he delivers the reprieve. Hildy questions Pincus and discovers the truth about the Mayor. Peggy returns.

Hildy quits, and assures Peggy that he will change. Burns gives Hildy his pocket watch as a wedding present. Hildy and Peggy leave for New York. Burns calls a man and arranges for Hildy's arrest a few hours later for stealing the pocket watch.

CHARACTERS

Roy Bensinger

Bensinger is a reporter for the *Chicago Tribune*. He is the owner of the big, ornate desk; later in the play, Williams hides inside of it. Bensinger is a neat freak, a quality that the other reporters constantly violate by leaving garbage all over his desk.

Walter Burns

Walter Burns is Hildy's boss at the paper. Desperate to keep his star reporter, he will go to any lengths to entice Hildy to stay. When he finds out that Hildy is hiding Williams in the press office, Burns helps to keep the convict hidden so that Hildy can get the exclusive story.

Burns is a cold, calculating man; he is willing to break the law to get an edge. When Mrs. Grant realizes the truth about Williams, Burns kidnaps her. When the truth is revealed and Williams is found, Burns is able to talk himself out of trouble.

Although he encourages Hildy to leave with Peggy at the end of *The Front Page*—he even presents him with his prized pocket watch—he arranges for Hildy to be arrested for stealing the watch.

Diamond Louie

Diamond Louie is a local thug. He works for Burns as a circulation manager. He helps kidnap Mrs. Grant.

Woodenshoes Eichhorn

Regarded as inept and slow, Woodenshoes is a police officer. He believes that Williams has a duel personality and that the convict is hiding out with Mollie Malloy. He tries to share his information with the reporters, including Hildy, but they are dismissive.

Endicott

Endicott is a police reporter for the *Post*.

Mrs. Grant

Mrs. Grant is Peggy Grant's mother. She is suspicious of Hildy and his commitment to Peggy. When Hildy does not appear at the train station right away, Mrs. Grant is the one who reveals that Hildy is hiding Williams. Though Hildy convinces the other reporters that she is confused, she eventually sees the convict hiding in the desk.

In order to keep her quiet, Burns has Diamond Louie drive her to a secluded place; en route, there is an auto accident and Hildy fears that she has been hurt. When she returns at the end of the play, Mrs. Grant discloses what has happened to her and Burns is almost charged with kidnapping.

Peggy Grant

A strong and popular girl, Peggy is engaged to Hildy. Frustrated because he puts his work before their relationship, she constantly asks him to make a true commitment to her. Although Peggy questions if he really loves her, they do leave together at the end of the play. It seems that she has won the battle, if not the war.

Peter B. Hartman

See The Sheriff

Hildy Johnson

Hildy is a star reporter for the Chicago *Herald-Examiner*. He is ready to leave his job and start a new life when he gets caught up in the story of Earl Williams.

Hildy is engaged to Peggy Grant; later that afternoon, he is supposed to go to New York City with Peggy to get married. After the wedding, Hildy is planning to work at an advertising agency.

Yet before he can leave the pressroom and get on the train, he becomes very involved in the Williams case: he hides the convict in the pressroom; lies to Peggy and her mother; and deceives the other reporters in order to get an exclusive story.

In the end, Hildy realizes that he really does want to marry Peggy and move to New York City. There seems to be some question if he has really left his old life behind or whether he will eventually return to it.

Ernie Kruger

Kruger is a reporter for the *Journal of Commerce*.

Mollie Malloy

Mollie is a prostitute in love with Williams. She berates the reporters at the beginning of the play because she believes they published lies about her. To protect Williams she jumps out of the window. She survives the fall, but her fate is unclear at the end of the play.

The Mayor

The Mayor is the corrupt leader of Chicago. There is an election in three days and he wants Williams to be executed to improve his chances of being re-elected: Williams murdered a black cop, and he figures his death will ensure many African American votes.

To that end, the Mayor bribes Pincus to *not* deliver the reprieve. Later in the play, Pincus changes his mind and delivers the reprieve. To save his own skin, the Mayor removes the cuffs from Burns and Hildy and grudgingly implements the reprieve.

McCue

McCue is a reporter for the City News Bureau. He is eager and enthusiastic.

Murphy

Murphy is a police reporter for the *Journal*. He is cocky and contemptuous towards everyone, except reporters. He physically throws Mollie out of the pressroom when she begins to cry.

Irving Pincus

Pincus delivers the reprieve for the execution of Earl Williams. When the Mayor offers him a bribe to not deliver the reprieve, Pincus agrees. Later he

MEDIA ADAPTATIONS

- *The Front Page* was adapted as a film in 1931. It was directed by Lewis Milestone and produced by Howard Hawks. It starred Pat O'Brien as Hildy and Adolphe Menjou as Walter Burns.

- A version was filmed in 1940 by director Howard Hawks under the title *Girl Friday*. It featured Rosalind Russell as a female Hildy and Cary Grant as Walter Burns.

- A television series based on the play was produced from 1949-50. It starred John Daly as Walter Burns and Mark Roberts as Hildy.

- Another version was filmed in 1974. Directed by Billy Wilder, the movie starred Walter Matthau as Walter Burns and Jack Lemmon as Hildy.

changes his mind and delivers the reprieve. He exposes the attempted bribery to the reporters.

Schwartz

Schwartz is a police reporter for the *Daily News*. He is the first to speculate that Williams was hiding in the building.

The Sheriff

The Sheriff is the primary law enforcement officer in *The Front Page*. Not particularly respected, he tries to get along everyone, including the reporters, but his efforts often make him look soft. Because he furnished the gun for the psychological exam, he is also viewed as somewhat inept at his job.

Earl Williams

Williams is the cop killer and anarchist in *The Front Page*. He killed an African-American cop and has been sentenced to die for the crime. He escapes by stealing a gun during a psychological exam; he hides on the roof of the Criminal Courts Building, then in the pressroom. After hiding in a desk for much of the play, his reprieve is finally delivered by the end of the play and his life is spared.

Wilson

Wilson is a police reporter for the *American*.

THEMES

Choices and Consequences

Hildy Johnson has to make several hard choices in the course of *The Front Page*—the most important choice being his old life or a new one. His new life means that he must leave his career behind in order to move to New York City with Peggy and her mother, get married, and work at an advertising agency. His old life is in the pressroom reporting the news.

This choice results in many humorous situations. Hildy repeatedly puts off Peggy and her mother in order to pursue the Williams story. He almost loses his future several times because of this choice. At the end of *The Front Page*, Hildy chooses his new life over the old one by leaving with Peggy to go to New York City.

Because he makes this choice, Burns gives him his pocket watch and later arranges for Hildy's arrest for stealing it. Thus the choice leads to an unexpected consequence.

Loyalty

Loyalty is a recurring theme in *The Front Page*. Despite their constant complaints, the reporters are loyal to their newspapers and their jobs. They do what it takes to get a story, and are content with their way of life. Even Hildy is loyal to his paper and Burns when the chips are down.

The criminal, Williams, is in trouble out of loyalty. A diehard anarchist who killed a police officer when the cop tried to take down his red flag on Washington's Birthday, he does not mind dying for his cause. He believes it is the right thing to do. Mollie Malloy is so loyal to Williams that she jumps out of a window rather than compromise his hiding place in the press room.

In contrast, the Mayor and the Sheriff are loyal to their own self-interests. They believe that Williams's execution will win them the African-American vote in the upcoming election (the officer he killed was black). They are so determined that when a reprieve is issued to stop the execution, they bribe the messenger, Pincus, to say it was never delivered.

All of these loyalties define the characters and their values. Hecht and MacArthur also use these loyalties to inspire humor and drama.

Deception

Several characters in *The Front Page* participate in deception. The primary example is when Williams hides in the pressroom. Hoping for an exclusive story, Hildy helps him.

First, Hildy puts him in the adjacent bathroom, then inside of reporter Roy Bensinger's desk. Then Mollie also helps Williams by jumping out of the window, nearly killing herself. When Walter Burns arrives, he does everything he can to keep Williams's location a secret.

The Mayor and the Sheriff conspire to keep Williams's reprieve a secret by bribing Pincus, the governor's messenger. Although both of these deceptions ultimately fail and the truth is revealed, these incidents show the lengths each side will go to achieve their agenda.

Politics

Politics and political beliefs play a large role in *The Front Page*. Williams is a confirmed anarchist and is convinced that he is to be executed because of his radical beliefs.

The Mayor and the Sheriff conspire to make sure Williams will die so that they will win the upcoming election. When a reprieve is issued, the Mayor views it as a political move against him.

The reporters are not particularly political in the same sense. They use politics and politicians to create good press. They want to expose corruption and exploit it to sell newspapers.

STYLE

Setting

The Front Page is a comedic melodrama set in Chicago. All of the action is confined to one place (the pressroom) and one time (around 8:30 p.m. on Friday night).

The room is rather bare and dirty, with a few tables, chairs, garbage cans, and telephones. There are several windows that overlook the Cook County jail and an adjacent bathroom. The largest piece of furniture is an ornate desk.

By confining all the action to one location, Hecht and MacArthur emphasize the importance of the reporters; after all, it is there that the truth is eventually discovered.

Symbolism

For Williams, the pressroom symbolizes sanctuary from his pursuers. It serves a similar purpose for the reporters; they avoid their wives, their bosses, and the problems of everyday life by hanging out there. Even the Mayor and the Sheriff are able to talk privately there.

For Burns and Hildy, Williams is perceived as a symbol of the corruption of the current political administration. Burns and Hildy want to use Earl as a means of exposing this corruption to the world.

To that end, Earl is hidden in the only nice piece of furniture in the room: the ornate black walnut

TOPICS FOR FURTHER STUDY

- Compare and contrast the Hildy Johnson of the stage version of *The Front Page* with the Hildy Johnson in the 1940 film version, entitled *Girl Friday*. In the latter, Hildy is a woman played by Rosalind Russell. How do these changes impact the dynamics of the play? What does this express about the role of women in 1928 versus 1940?

- Research the history of corruption in Chicago politics. Has the press played a role in revealing corruption and/or getting rid of corrupt politicians?

- How has journalism changed over the years? Research what working at a local newspaper or television news program would be like. Write an updated description of the pressroom that reflects the technological and cultural changes.

desk. Ironically, the desk was once the property of a Mayor of Chicago, Fred A. Busse.

This complex symbolism could be interpreted a number of ways. The desk could symbolize the greater power of the press over politics. The Mayor's desk is the property of the reporter—like the Mayor is meant to serve the public.

The actions of Burns and Hildy, no matter how selfish their agenda, lead to a reprieve for Williams. This reinforces the idea that the desk ultimately represents the power of the press.

Dialogue and Language

Throughout *The Front Page,* Hecht and MacArthur employ overlapping dialogue, especially in the scenes that feature several reporters. In other words, there are several conversations going on in the pressroom at once. Reporters also constantly interrupt and contradict each other. This kind of dialogue gives a speedy edge to the play and makes it seem more realistic.

What the reporters are saying is also important. They speak in a vernacular appropriate to their profession and they say whatever they have to in order to get the story.

HISTORICAL CONTEXT

During the 1920s, America emerged as the world's major economic and cultural force. Under the administrations of Calvin Coolidge and Herbert Hoover, big business flourished. One such business was the automobile industry; by 1930, twenty-two million cars would be on the road. Roads connecting cities were being built. The proliferation of automobiles and roads allowed better transportation and more efficient movement of goods and services.

Skyscrapers were going up in many major cities. Indeed, the first air-conditioned office building was opened in San Antonio Texas in 1928. With such obvious symbols of prosperity and progress, President Hoover believed that the end of poverty was in sight.

Yet all was not well: the economy showed signs of instability; fluctuations in the stock market foreshadowed the crash in October of 1929; government corruption undermined public confidence; and racial and ethnic conflict increased as the differences between rich and poor intensified.

Lynchings of blacks were still common throughout the United States. Schools were segregated, especially in the southern regions of the country. Many homes in rural areas did not have electricity or indoor plumbing.

In 1920 a constitutional amendment prohibited the distribution of alcohol in the United States. (It was repealed in 1933.) Prohibition was hard to enforce, and in 1927, the Prohibitions Bureau was created. Approximately 75,000 people were arrested for violations in 1928.

For women, the decade signaled some positive changes. In general, women received a better education; more women attended college in 1928 than a decade earlier. They had more opportunities, especially for employment.

Entertainment options increased during the decade. Radio became the dominant form of entertainment and information. Radios played more music and serial dramas (the precursor to the television series), and coverage of the first sport events aired. Many people had radios in their homes.

There was an increase in the number of mass circulation magazines. Tabloid papers were introduced and were growing in number. In all of these mediums, advertising became a key source of revenue and the advertising industry exploded.

Television was in the experimental stages, and the first license for a television station was granted in 1928. It began broadcasting in May 1928.

CRITICAL OVERVIEW

When *The Front Page* first opened in New York City in 1928, the play's critical praise was qualified by a controversy over language. Many reviewers considered it harsh and inappropriate.

J. Brooks Atkinson of the *New York Times* summed up the controversy. He asserted, "*The Front Page,* which is one of the tautest and most unerring melodramas of the day bruises the sensitive ear with a Rabelaisaian vernacular unprecedented for its uphill and down-dale blasphemy."

Still, Atkinson found much to praised. "Hilarious, gruesome, and strident by turns, *The Front Page* compresses lively dramatic material into a robust play." Atkinson closed his review with this qualifier: "Quite apart from its authenticity, which may be disputed, it adds a fresh peril to casual playgoing for the purposes of entertainment."

An unnamed colleague of Atkinson's at the *New York Times* came to a similar conclusion. The reviewer maintained: "Wrangling at poker, leering over the political expediency of the execution, abusing the Sheriff and the Mayor insolently, they [the reporters] utter some of the baldest profanity and most slattern jesting that has ever been heard on the public stage. Graphic as it may be in tone and authenticity, it diverts attention from a vastly entertaining play." These issues of authenticity return repeatedly in later years.

A few critics considered what *The Front Page* said about journalism and America in general. Euphemia Van Rensselaer Wyatt, a reviewer for the *Catholic World,* claimed that "*The Front Page,* as an example of American stagecraft is spectacular, as an example of open-hearted coarseness of speech it is outstanding."

She continued, "[T]hough its basic morals are quite sound and its vulgarity lacks innuendo, the

COMPARE & CONTRAST

- **1928:** Fifty percent of American households have radios. Television is still in developmental stages, but would eventually replace radio as a dominant means of entertainment and information.

  Today: At least one television can be found in nearly every American household; many homes have multiple sets. Its primacy as an information and entertainment source is challenged by the Internet.

- **1928:** The first talking film, *Lights of New York,* is released by Warner Bros. It uses the Vitaphone system. Some believe talking films are a fad that will go away. Separately, Kodak introduces color film stock.

  Today: Movies feature increasingly better sound systems that use digital technology. There are also many ways of watching films outside of the theater, including DVD.

- **1928:** Railroads are the primary means of cross-country travel. Commercial aviation is in its infancy.

  Today: Airplanes are the primary means of cross-country travel. Amtrak, the primary American passenger system, needs government subsidies to survive.

---

words used are neither nice nor seemly. The humor, however, is thoroughly American and spontaneous.''

While *The Front Page* did not have a long run, the play has been revived regularly over the years. The controversy over the language basically died down, and many critics debated how the play had aged.

Reviewing a popular New York revival in 1969-70, John Simon wrote in his book *Uneasy Stages:*

> This 1928 play is full of the least attractive ideas of its time: American chauvinism, contempt for culture, condescension to the intellect, sentimental affection for crooks in and out of government. And, vilest of all, the notion that newspapermen are the toughest, shrewdest, meanest and ultimately cleverest guys in the world.

Yet many critics have found aspects of *The Front Page* timeless, if not contemporary.

Walter Kerr maintained that the play aged well because it was not about a specific time. In his book *God on the Gymnasium Floor and Other Theatrical Adventures,* he contended that ''*The Front Page* isn't really faithful to the early twenties or later twenties or to anything in particular. Its authors admitted that at the time.''

Alan Brien of *Plays and Players,* viewed the script as the reason for its agelessness. ''It still works, like an ancient nickelodeon, because of the craftsmenship of its authors.''

In 1986–87, *The Front Page* was revived on Broadway. Critics noticed how the play echoed contemporary America. Robert Brustein of *The New Republic* asserted that ''Mosher believes *The Front Page* to be the finest American play ever written. I'm not prepared to go that far with him, but the Lincoln Center production certainly makes the case with persuasive eloquence.''

Later in his piece, Brustein maintained that ''for all the double crosses, good-nature chicanery, and idiomatic wisecracks, the play provides a glimpse of the seamy side of American politics and press practices that is ferociously contemporary.''

Similar assessments were made about a 1994 revival at Canada's Shaw Festival. Michael A. Morrison of *The Village Voice* points out that ''At times the play shows its age. The misogyny of the reporters and references to the black citizens with the N-word grate on the ear, but the play's satirical flogging of political correctness (half a century before the phrase was coined) is engagingly con-

Jack Lemmon and Walter Matthau in MacArthur and Hecht's The Front Page.

temporary." Similarly, John Bemrose of *Maclean's* writes "Anyone who thinks that current TV programs such as *The Simpsons*—where crude putdowns are the rule—represent a disturbing new trend in American life should consult *The Front Page*."

CRITICISM

A. Petrusso

In this essay, Petrusso examines the role of women in The Front Page.

In recent reviews of *The Front Page*, several critics have contended that the play denigrates the role of women. For example, John Bemrose of *Maclean's* maintained that "the air is perpetually blue with profanity and verbal attacks—some of them directed against blacks and women."

John Simon argued that the reporters "have contempt at best for women lovers, whatever doesn't jibe with their grimy, grubby, ecumenical smugness."

I assert that the negative attitudes towards women in the play are not this simple. While *The Front Page* certainly has sexist elements, the female characters play key roles: defining standards and even saving their male counterparts on occasion.

There are two kinds of women in *The Front Page*: those who work (Jennie and Mollie) and those who marry (Mrs. Schlosser, Peggy Grant, and Mrs. Grant). Though the two types of women are treated somewhat differently by the reporters and the authors, each plays a vital part in maintaining standards of decency. Sometimes their words contradict their actions, and what the male reporters say about them undermines their efforts. Yet each woman triumphs in her own way.

Jennie is the building's cleaning woman, and a relatively minor character. The stage directions call her "slightly idiotic" but when she enters, "[s]he receives an ovation" from the reporters. They tease her, but they appreciate the fact that she keeps their office clean.

Although the reporters believe that Jennie is sometimes in the way—such as at the beginning of the second act—they appreciate her persistence and hard work. She does her job despite Murphy's complaints that she is in the way; this proves that she is not intimidated by his words.

Mollie Malloy plays a much more vital role in *The Front Page*. She is a known prostitute who is

WHAT DO I READ NEXT?

- *All the President's Men* is a nonfiction book written by Carl Bernstein and Bob Woodward in 1974. Written by two journalists, it chronicles their efforts to uncover political corruption during the administration of President Richard Nixon.

- *The Twentieth Century,* a play written by Hecht and MacArthur in 1933, is a farce that examines the theater scene.

- Written by Bruce D. Price, *Too Easy: A Novel* was published in 1994. The story focuses on a murder investigation in New York.

- *1001 Afternoons in Chicago* (1922) is a collection of Hecht's newspaper columns.

- *Hot Copy* (1931), a play written by Willard John Sergel, is a comedy about newspaper life.

---

treated with derision by the reporters. When she comes into the office, she is angry that the reporters have published lies about her relationship with Earl Williams, the convict.

Mollie asserts: "I never said I loved Earl Williams and was willing to marry him on the gallows! You made that up! And all that other crap abut my being his soul mate and having a love nest with him."

She tries to explain that she only invited him up to her room because it was raining the day before the shooting. She felt sorry for him, and they only talked. Mollie yells at the reporters, "I was the only one with guts enough to stand up for him! And that's why you're persecuting me! Because he treated me decent, and not like an animal, and I said so!"

Mollie has touched on something very profound about the play. She realizes—before anyone else—that the reporters use people like her and Williams to sell newspapers. They do not really care about their fate—unless it makes a good story. The actions of Walter Burns proves this point later in *The Front Page.*

Yet the truth is that Mollie does have feelings for him. When Hildy hides Williams in the pressroom, Mollie sacrifices everything for him. She does everything she can within her very limited power to protect him. One reason Mollie does this is because Williams admits he likes her. He tells her "Yeah, I think you're wonderful. I said you were the most beautiful character I ever met."

So when the reporters become suspicious and insist on answers, Mollie makes a bold decision. She jumps out of the window with the words, "You'll never get it out of me I'll never tell! Never!" This succeeds in deflecting attention away from Hildy and the desk for a long time.

Mollie's actions are heroic compared to the rest of the characters in the play. She does not die, but her self-sacrifice says more than enough about the nobility of the female character in *The Front Page.*

The "married" women are not nearly as dramatic; instead, they represent oppression and respectability. The first woman introduced in the play is a minor character, Mrs. Schlosser. She is the long-suffering wife of a reporter, Herman, who works for the *Examiner.* She is angry because she believes that he is out drinking.

Several reporters try to appease her and cover for Herman. She forces them to reveal that he has gone to a Turkish bath. After Mrs. Schlosser leaves in a huff, several reporters berate her behind her back. Endicott muses, "I don't know what gets into women. I took Bob Brody home the other night and his wife broke his arm with a broom."

These reactions reflect the general attitudes of men towards women—and women towards men—depicted in the play. These attitudes are a recurring theme of *The Front Page*. In this case, Mrs. Schlosser is only placated when she talks to Herman's editor, Walter Burns, on the phone and he agrees to deal with the paycheck situation to her benefit. Mrs. Schlosser gets her way in the end.

After Mollie, the two most powerful women in the play are Peggy Grant and her mother. Mrs. Grant functions as Hildy's conscience throughout the play; she realizes the truth and threatens to reveal it. This knowledge makes her so dangerous that Burns feels compelled to kidnap her to keep her quiet. She only goes because she is taken forcibly by Diamond Louie.

The subsequent automobile accident and Mrs. Grant's disappearance from the scene underscore the choice Hildy must make. It forces him to confront questions about why he is pursuing this job and what he wants to do with his life.

Later, when Mrs. Grant reappears, she exposes Burns and Hildy in front of the authorities. She also reveals Williams's hiding place. She proves that women are not pushovers.

The woman who affects the most change is Peggy. Through her ultimatum, she causes Hildy's dilemma: he is forced to choose between his love for her and his love of reporting.

Hildy finds that it is a difficult decision. He is happy with his old job: he loves the excitement, the camaraderie, and the attention. Yet the prospect of moving to New York City, working in advertising, and making more money appeals to him. Peggy realizes how difficult it will be for him to leave his old job; she knows the powerful attraction it still holds for him.

So she is proactive in order to get what she wants. When Hildy does not arrive at a farewell party, she calls while he is saying his good-byes in the building. When Hildy gets on the phone with her, he is contrite and promises her that he will be there. Eventually she has to show up herself. This happens repeatedly throughout *The Front Page:* Hildy makes a promise, does not keep it, then Peggy has to come to confront him.

When Hildy lies to her—like about spending their wedding money on a lead for the story—Peggy keeps him straight and makes him tell the truth. Peggy's actions make Hildy face up to his responsibilities. He cannot lie to her.

Later, there is a showdown of Burns versus Peggy: tyrant versus wife, bad versus good. Burns wants to control Hildy while Peggy wants to make him face himself and his choices. She accuses him: "You never intended to be decent and live like a human being! You were lying all the time!" Though the argument ends with Peggy leaving in tears, Burns pushes Hildy too far. He realizes what he truly wants: Peggy.

When Peggy returns at the end of the play, Hildy has made the choice to be with women instead of men. Though Burns tries to get him to come back to the paper, Hildy tells her:

> Listen Peggy, if I'm not telling you the absolute truth may God strike me dead right now. I'm going to New York with you tonight—if you give me this one last chance! I'll cut out drinking and swearing and everything connected with the God damn newspaper business. I won't even *read* a newspaper.

While Burns may get the last word in *The Front Page* by arranging for Hildy's arrest, he has lost the war. Hildy will probably not want to come back as a reporter after such a stunt.

The women in the play have fought hard for what they want; in many ways, they each get what they want. They play an important role in the course and outcome of the play.

Source: A. Petrusso, for *Drama for Students,* Gale, 2000.

Robert Brustein

Brustein reviews a 1987 revival of Hecht and MacArthur's play at the Vivian Beaumont Theatre in New York. Finding that the play's potent message has endured, the critic offers a favorable review of The Front Page.

Yet another revival of *The Front Page,* Ben Hecht and Charles MacArthur's 1928 play about Chicago newspapermen covering an execution, would not appear to be a particularly original theatrical idea or an especially bold choice to open Gregory Mosher's second season at Lincoln Center's Vivian Beaumont Theater. The play has already enjoyed three movie versions—one of them macerating this hard-nosed farce into a gender-reversed romantic comedy, with Rosalind Russell as a female Hildy Johnson and Cary Grant doing one of his incomparable comic turns as her editor-lover, Walter Burns. It is, besides, a regular feature of resident theater schedules in this country, and in 1972 it was even memorialized by the National Theatre of Great Britain in a version that, stretched to three hours and groaning under labored American accents, was treated with as much reverence as the Wakefield Mystery Cycle.

This new production under the direction of Jerry Zaks is far from reverent. It lasts for two hours that sweep along like one. From the moment the lights came up on Tony Walton's massive rendering of an improvised press room, with its parquet floors, twirling fans, broken-down chandeliers, overstuffed wastebaskets, old Royal typewriters, and upright telephones—all backed by the silhouette of a Chicago courthouse—I was captured by the show, refreshed as if by a new play. This is one of those happy occasions in the American theater when a familiar work of secondary reputation asserts its claim to classic status. Mosher believes *The Front Page* to be the finest American play ever written. I'm not prepared to go that far with him, but the Lincoln Center production certainly makes the case with persuasive eloquence.

The Front Page doesn't have a soft bone in its body. We are told that the authors originally conceived the work as a satire on ruthless reporters and sensationalistic journalism, only to end up with a valentine to the whole newspaper profession. I'm not so sure. These reporters certainly have their engaging side—so do the hack politicians and corrupt cops who serve as foils for their banter. But for all the double crosses, competitive dodges, sardonic backbiting, good-natured chicanery, and idiomatic wisecracks (expressed in that special urban argot that O'Neill kept trying, unsuccessfully, to create), the play provides a glimpse of the seamy side of American politics and press practices that is ferociously contemporary. Earl Williams, an anarchist in an age of "Red Menace" hysteria, is going to the gallows because he has jeopardized the mayor's bid for re-election: he has shot a black policeman, and the "coon" vote in Chicago is crucial. When the governor sends a reprieve in the last days of the campaign—God knows what *his* motives are—the mayor bribes the messenger to say he never delivered it. When the prisoner escapes, the mayor orders him shot on sight.

The fact is that nobody gives a damn about Earl Williams—not Walter Burns, who only wants an exclusive for the *Examiner;* not the reporters, who tailor the facts to suit their purposes; not even Hildy Johnson, who helps to hide him in a rival reporter's desk. Aside from Mollie Malloy, the sentimental hooker who jumps out of a third story window rather than testify, Williams has no value for anyone except as an opportunity for greed, ambition, vanity, or worse. For the press, the highest premium is "the great big Scoop": the reporters want Williams hanged at five in the morning instead of seven, in time for the city edition. For the politicians, whose only motive is perpetuating themselves in office, ideology, conscience, even human life itself are hostages to expediency. *The Front Page* dramatizes

> *THE FRONT PAGE* DOESN'T HAVE A SOFT BONE IN ITS BODY. WE ARE TOLD THAT THE AUTHORS ORIGINALLY CONCEIVED THE WORK AS A SATIRE ON RUTHLESS REPORTERS AND SENSATIONALISTIC JOURNALISM, ONLY TO END UP WITH A VALENTINE TO THE WHOLE NEWSPAPER PROFESSION."

Darwin's survival theory with a breezy sangfroid equalled before only by Ben Jonson and John Gay, and only by Brecht and Mamet in our own time.

Under Zaks's meticulous direction, the play zips along like a hound dog with cans on its tail. Obviously, Zaks responds to plays with an edge (he is equally good with Durang), and this is a remarkable recovery after the blatant audience-fondling of *House of Blue Leaves*. He has cast the newspapermen with performers in the tradition of [1930's] character actors—Allen Jenkins, Edward Brophy, Edward Binns, the old broken-nose school of working toughs—who lounge at their desks playing poker or hugging phones, "sitting here all night waiting for them to hang the bastard." They recall a livelier time in American life, when it was energy not efficiency that flowed from ruthless careerism.

The casting of the major roles (with one debatable exception) is also impeccable: Jerome Dempsey as the rotund, orotund mayor, equipped (by the costumer Willa Kim, whose period designs are characterizations in themselves) with tailcoat and fez, bouncing languorously about the stage like a huge beach ball on the surface of a pond; Richard B. Shull as the persistently deflated Sheriff Hartman, a Klaxon-voiced pol with a permanent sore throat; Bill McCutcheon as Mr. Pincus, the messenger with the reprieve, a sleepy little pink mouse with a passion for peanuts; Jeff Weiss as Bensinger, the fastidious hypochondriac who sprays his telephone receiver for germs; Paul Stolarsky as the pathetic goofball Earl Williams, appealing vainly to be recognized not as a Bolshevik but as an anarchist; Jack Wallace as Woodenshoes Eichorn, the bullheaded cop with phrenological theories of crime; Julie Hagerty as Peggy, the girl who competes with Walter Burns for Hildy's affections, a thin, nervous, high-pitched hysteric in a cloche hat; and, of course, John Lithgow as Walter Burns.

This is surely one of Lithgow's finest opportunities as a character actor, and although he doesn't enter until late in the second act, he makes the part, if not the play, his personal property. Bearing himself like a Junker general, with a brush moustache and military haircut, he towers over Hildy with the authority of one accustomed to absolute power (at one point, he wraps Hildy's head under his arm and pulls him around the stage like a cowboy breaking a steer). Lithgow offers a considerably more ruthless Walter Burns than did his predecessors in the role (Adolphe Menjou, Pat O'Brien, Walter Matthau)—menacing and dour for all his charm. His passion for his newspaper leaves him indifferent to any weaknesses that aren't exploitable. To an ailing reporter he shouts, "To hell with your diabetes, this is important." "I was in love once," he tells us in an uncharacteristic moment of Sir Andrew Aguecheek tenderness, only to add " . . . with my third wife." Like the play, he has a cartilaginous heart, and by the time he barks the play's famous last line—"The son of a bitch stole my *watch!*"—he has created a comic scoundrel unique in the annals of deception.

The casting flaw is Richard Thomas's Hildy Johnson. When he first appears on stage, a slight, youthful figure in a camel's hair coat, it looks as though a stripling has been called in to do the work of a man. Paradoxically, however, Thomas ends up contributing one of the most detailed performances in the production, precisely because he *has* been miscast. Like a repertory company actor challenged by a part for which he has to stretch and transform, he builds his character piece by piece, and with such commitment that he proves he understands the role, even if he doesn't finally claim it. His hair slicked down, his accent washed with a Chicago rinse, dancing about the stage like a cocky young torero making passes, Thomas brings a crackling energy to Hildy that almost makes you forget he lacks the seasoning and the grit. He's the only alloy in an evening of tempered metal. In the way it takes a beady look at human corruption, *The Front Page* suggests how soft we have since become as a people and as a culture.

Source: Robert Brustein, "Headline Hunting," in the *New Republic,* Vol. 196, no. 1&2, January 5 & 12, 1987, pp. 25–26.

Anonymous

While finding some fault in the casting of the lead roles, this critic still contends that The Front Page *has endured as a powerful dramatic work, one that is borne out in this 1986 revival.*

Whenever *The Front Page* is revived, reviewers feel an obligation to apologize for liking the play, and I am no exception. It is indeed a ramshackle affair, flung together with more scaffolding than structure and containing more funny lines than clever ones, but there is also at the heart of its pretense of heartlessness an air of youthful, ignorant high spirits that we cannot fail to find endearing. If its authors, Ben Hecht and Charles MacArthur, had known more about writing plays, they would surely have written a worse one; like two literary Elizas, they keep leaping from one shaky ice floe of plot to the next, always in peril of their lives and yet always laughing. Walter Burns, the second-most important character in *The Front Page,* doesn't make his appearance until the play is two-thirds over—an error that any proper teacher of playwriting would birch his pupils for committing. Nevertheless, our untutored authors have done exactly right by doing wrong: Burns, the dreaded cynical, ruthless managing editor of the Chicago *Herald-Examiner,* would be hard to put up with for an entire evening. As for the chief character, Hildy Johnson, who is the star reporter of the *Examiner* and Burns's slave, he is a vain, noisy, drunken, and unscrupulous lout, and would also be hard to listen to for long, but again ignorance triumphs: Hecht and MacArthur, seemingly unaware of how expensive a big cast is, fill their stage with such a host of characters—twenty-five in all—that we are never given an opportunity to lose patience with any individual among them. Though reputedly drawn from real life, they are without exception one-dimensional; whenever they get a chance to speak, they nearly always say what they said before, or a close variation of it. This economy of language is applied throughout the play without regard to whether the speaker is a slovenly newspaperman, a crooked politician, a bedevilled prostitute, a middle-aged housewife, or a condemned murderer.

If the play is the cobbled-up comic claptrap I have described, how does it happen to have survived so successfully for sixty years? To me, the answer is an unpleasant one, so a second apology is in order for liking the play; this time the reason is not its faulty craftsmanship but the point of view that lies behind its knockabout melodramatics and is the unexamined source of its energy. Which is to say that *The Front Page* is a classic embodiment of the still prevalent American male fantasy about the nature of paradise: a place—whether a pressroom, a locker room, or a club—where men can sit around and drink and tell adolescently dirty stories; a place where a woman, if she should make the mistake of entering it, would be abused and ordered away (when the prostitute in *The Front Page* attempts suicide by jumping from a window of the pressroom, the reporters present feel neither sympathy nor interest: a prostitute committing suicide is not news); and a place, finally, where even the love that boozy middle-aged men may wish to offer one another is expressible only in terms of vulgar pranks.

Having offered this indictment of the construction of the play and of what I see as its lamentable cultural provenance, I am obliged to add that *The Front Page* delights every audience before which it plays—audiences at least half of which are made up of women. (Why women are amused to see themselves depicted as stereotypes—virginal girlfriend, good-hearted prostitute, mindless mother-in-law, and the like—would require a parenthesis far longer than this one.) The audiences at the Vivian Beaumont measure up to the usual standard—or perhaps ought to be said to exceed it, because the production they applaud is not a very good one. The two main characters are radical examples of miscasting. Richard Thomas plays Hildy Johnson as if in imitation of James Cagney playing George M. Cohan, with a cocky strut and a high-strung manner that make it difficult for us to believe in him as a charming, hard-drinking reporter desperately in love with a pretty girl and eager to abandon his career on her behalf. As for John Lithgow as Walter Burns—Mr. Lithgow is a marvellous actor, but a venomous misanthropy that would make Iago blanch is evidently beyond his capacity to depict. Jerry Zaks has directed with an exceptionally heavy hand. Richard B. Shull is funny as the bumbling sheriff, and so is Jerome Dempsey as the crooked mayor, but Mr. Zaks has made no effort to curb their too obvious pleasure in squeezing more humor out of their roles than the roles possess. When Bill McCutcheon, in a small but crucial role as a virtuous nitwit, struggles to understand the simplest instruction, one can almost hear him counting the beats before he changes expression; telegraphy on this scale of obviousness has long been obsolete on any stage.

Also in the cast of *The Front Page* are Jeff Weiss, Julie Hagerty, Mary Catherine Wright, and Jack Wallace. The welcomely realistic set—the pressroom of the old Criminal Courts Building in Chicago (the building has been preserved, though the pressroom has vanished)—is by Tony Walton, the costumes are by Willa Kim, and the lighting is by Paul Gallo.

Source: Anonymous, ''Low Life in Chicago,'' in the *New Yorker*, Vol. 62, December 8, 1986, pp. 134–35.

Jeffrey A. Smith

In the following essay, Smith probes the transformation of lead character Hildy Johnson from a male role to a female role by film director Howard Hawks.

Clearly central to the task which director Howard Hawks sets himself in adapting Hecht and MacArthur's *The Front Page* into his own film, *His Girl Friday,* is the need to reformulate the central character, Hildy Johnson. Hawks has both begun this reformulation and compounded its difficulties by opting to present Hildy as a woman rather than a man. To bring to fruition this initial switch, while retaining the broad outlines of the stage play's plot, Hawks must justify his new Hildy in terms of the demands levied by Hildy's role in the original play. Specifically, he must make his female Hildy believable as what her opposite, Walter (Cary Grant), dubs her in the film: ''The best newspaperman I know.'' At the same time he must establish her as a recognizable, 1940 romantic lead. Hawks seems to aim at building his essentially new comedy around the special irony of a Hildy who is both. That the resulting character may prove to be of a type—the sophisticated, strong-minded career woman Rosalind Russell often portrayed in such films—will only confirm Hawks's success. It is no argument against the peculiarity of the problem to this situation. Hawks, producer and director on *His Girl Friday,* inherits a stage plot turning upon the irreconcilability of professional and romantic life for its (male) Hildy. To transmute that story into romantic comedy on film, he must retain a measure of conflict but finally cause romance and professional obligation to converge. Hawks saw that a female Hildy might accomplish this fusion—but once brought into being, she *must* do so for the comedy to work at all. Thus arises Hawks's central task.

To assess his approach to it, we naturally would look for scenes that focus intimately on Hildy's character. One such scene ensues when Hildy seeks out the condemned man, Earl Williams, for an interview in his prison cell. Hawks's great success in this scene is the creation of an integrated Hildy

> IF REDEMPTION THEMES ARE THE BASIS OF COMEDY, THE CELL SCENE, IN LESS THAN THREE MINUTES' TOTAL RUNNING TIME, HAS ESTABLISHED A COMIC VISION FOR THE WHOLE FILM."

who is credibly "a great newspaperman" precisely *because* she is female—and conversely one who, as newspaperman, is exactly the woman to succeed in the hard-bitten newspaper world, in Walter's life, and in the pivotal role of Hawks's newly forged romantic comedy. Stylistic analysis of the brief scene yields much insight, not only into Hawks's particular strategies but also into the larger issues involved in adapting a theater comedy of one *genre* into a film representative of another.

The "cell" scene does not appear in the stage version. This fact itself, linking the scene with other important sequences written new for the film, makes it characteristic of Hawks's transmutative work. Predictably, given the task as outlined, most of the new material occurs in the first, largely expository half of the film, when characters are established. The cell scene occurs at an important point near the end of this first half. Reasons for its appearance lie in the logic of Hawks's new plot. The Hildy of *The Front Page* falls back into reporting by instinct, in a reflexive response to the crisis of Earl Williams's jailbreak. Walter, to that point, has done nothing to persuade Hildy to come back to work. His incessant browbeating and his single attempt at trickery have earned only Hildy's vow to "walk right up to you and hammer on that monkey skull of yours." Hildy first betrays reportorial instinct only some time after this exchange. By contrast, Hildy's visit to Earl Williams in the film follows from Walter's conniving. Hildy here shows more of conscious calculation than bombast and instinct. Also, of course, she appears manipulable, but this trait derives from her weddedness to newspaper work—and, implicitly, to Walter, who is altogether more visible to us in the film than in the play. As is quite opposite in the play, Walter's influence at this point *is* that of newpapering. Hildy succumbs to both with the same act. The convergence begins.

On the face of it, therefore, the cell scene presents a conscious, more commanding Hildy, one who is on more intimate terms with Walter and thus subject to the grip of her profession through him. The "monkey skull" line does return later to remind us of the story's central conflict. But an eventual resolution of that conflict, something we are not given on stage, has been hinted at in this interweaving of Hildy's romantic and professional predilections.

Stylistically, the cell scene furthers these effects at deeper levels. Composed of eight shots neatly divisible into groups of four, with each half-sequence forming a unity in time, its central action proceeds by showing Hildy's command of situations—her professionalism—and then integrating that commanding quality with compassion: a compassion derivable in part from the ability to command, and in part from Hildy's distinctly "feminine" character.

The first four shots work principally to show her authority. Heretofore, the film has not shown her functioning as newspaperman, nor in any newspaper setting other than the office. But it is "on the beat" that Hildy will unfold as a reporter. (Significantly, the whole sequence takes place between scenes in the newspaper office and in the Criminal Courts press room. By embedding the scene solidly within these journalistic settings, Hawks underscores its key position as a setting for Hildy's action in that world.) Hildy is discovered in the doorway to the prison foyer at the fade-in. She is already there, in our first view of this world, and, by implication, has been all along. Lighting from an off-camera window highlights her in contrast with the guard, Jacobi, who sits in shadow at his desk. She is prominent here; this is her natural element.

That the guard must turn his head from the side opposite Hildy to come to face her is also worth noting. As the second shot brings us in closer, he is about to turn away again, backside to her, as her interview request ends in her assured, perfunctory, "How about a little service?" The fact that her bribe forces him to turn around once more, unnatural though the movement has come to seem visually, shows us her magnetic hold on him—and implicitly, on the whole system. Hildy does not miss a beat during this bit, which occupies the rest of the shot. With virtually the same movement that brought her through the door, she lifts the bribe from her handbag, drops it, stoops to pick it up and, in the process, carries through the dialogue: "Oh, say, is this your money?" "Don't think it is. . . ." "Twenty bucks." "Well, it just may be." "That's what I thought." It is all one motion, a single, coordinated sentence. She has been certain from the moment she entered what to do, ritualistically, each second.

Hildy's left hand still clutches gloves and a handbag, as it did the moment she entered. Thus, the same hand that just effected the bribe now pushes Jacob from his chair, and the words again coordinate: "C'mon, I'm in a hurry." Her attitude is not the pushiness of one anxious or uncertain about getting her way; it is the total assurance of one so practiced as to be able to carry on automatically—with one hand, so to speak.

We must pause here before other elements that influence the larger comedy. The ease with which Hildy bribes Jacob underlines not only her strength, but the whole system's weakness—particularly that of the yet-to-appear Mayor and Sheriff. The sweep of Hildy's hand to the floor and back with the money just as easily sweeps aside the Sheriff's authority (in this case, to keep her from seeing Earl Williams). Subtextual play and comic undercutting of this sort work importantly, we will discover, throughout this scene.

Also, we notice that Jacob is reading a newspaper when Hildy arrives. Newspaperdom, as noted, permeates the setting; that is the setting's point. But the pencil in Jacobi's hand further suggests what *type* of newspapering is involved. A good guess would hold that Jacobi has been busy with a crossword puzzle. The image will be repeated later in the press room, where a dangling newspaper in one reporter's hand shows a comics page to the camera. Jacobi's nonthreatening nature comes home to us as we spot this, but, more importantly, so does that of this whole world. However seriously it may present itself, even on death row the world of Hildy's profession finally appears containable, "fun," lightheartedly comic.

Moving through a barred door into the cell area in Shot Three, Hildy resumes the motion, only briefly interrupted by the inconvenience of the bribe. Her speech and tone are continuous with what has gone before: "Hey, Joe, open up here." Waving aside Jacobi's last protest, she strides in. Her movement up until now has been from right to left, an unnatural direction visually. Death row is an unnatural place. Yet Hildy shows no consternation; the surety in her step overcomes our visual difficulty, as her assured manner generally takes command of, even redeems, this otherwise alien world.

Shot Four develops this last theme. It is a high-angle shot embracing the whole cell room, and thus delimiting it to stand clearly apart from us. We see it from an unlikely angle that gives us a commanding, all-encompassing overview. The effect of the angle is our sense both of alienness and of the fact that this world *can* be encompassed. It sets us up, as have foregoing shots, to witness Hildy take command. Hildy's ability to move, her efficacy, again overcomes a visually unnatural image, and her movement becomes firmly established as a metaphor for control. It stands in contrast both with the stark, unmoving angles and lines and the long shadows of the cell room—dominated by Earl's cage-like enclosure—and with the severely circumscribed, inefficacious "movement" of Earl within the cell, or of the mechanically pacing guard in the background. Hildy moves assuredly where movement otherwise is absent or confined.

Her name, she tells Earl, is "Johnson," a reminder of her professional, unmarried, pre-Bruce Baldwin (Ralph Bellamy) condition. But she addresses her subject as "Earl." Later, her personal touch will seem almost maternally patronizing. That there is in this attitude a contrast between herself and Earl, one as great as the difference in their respective abilities to move, is emphasized by Earl's ironic assent to the interview: "I haven't anything else to do." Hildy, we are certain by now, has much else to do in this film. As proof, the first half-sequence ends with reminders of her composure, as we saw it at the outset. Still clutching objects in her left hand, Hildy executes another deft sweep with her right as she pulls over a chair. The shot fades with her again in motion, stepping toward Earl.

The second half-sequence continues to show Hildy dominate; but now, as the last shot presaged, it reveals her dominance as a force of quiet strength, enabling her to lend others her support in a sympathetic, "feminine" fashion. Her manner is thus distinguished from that of fellow "gentlemen of the press." Hildy's command becomes empathy, as she works to command Earl *for his own benefit*. This further elaboration of her character supplies an "equals" sign between her femininity and her capacity to be "a great newspaperman." The sequence begins with a fade to a two-person close shot—the first close-up in the cell scene. Visually the tone has changed, quieted; Hildy's movement, emphasized in the preceding series of medium and long shots, largely ceases. Despite the heavy cell wire between them, a clear sense of intimacy appears in this close view of Hildy and Earl. The two are visually pushed together by the solid cell door that frames them on the left. Molly's picture in triangulation on the wall behind enhances this sense of intimacy and of a specifically personal bond, a bond based on *feminine* warmth. When she speaks, Hildy seems to have lost the briskness in her voice. She projects a nearly maternal sense of peace and reassurance.

Both other clues remind us that Hildy still commands the situation. Her profile stands in the foreground, fully lit, higher in the frame than Earl's face, and prominent. It stands out against her own dark clothing. Earl's downcast visage, by contrast, seems of a piece with his drab prison outfit. This is the first shot in the film to present Earl at close range, and everything in actor John Qualen's appearance, right down to his little mustache, reassures us that he is harmless, no match for Hildy, and only comically conceivable as the "Red menace" the Mayor's and Sheriff's hysterics make him out to be. Earl's eyes draw us downward to reveal, moreover, that movement still exists. Hildy's hands finger a pack of cigarettes. As movement on her part has come to represent assurance and control, we here sense Earl's awareness of that control—a reminder of it also for us.

In every respect, the dialogue that commences during this shot reinforces the irony present in visual signs of Hildy's and Earl's relative strength. It begins with Earl's protestations to sanity, a self-characterization we would be the last to deny him. If anything, he is banal normalcy run riot, and every bit the "tough luck" character to find himself fired after twenty-two years on the same job. Hildy, who evidently has him all figured out, affirms this impression. When she asks, "You didn't mean to kill that policeman," she need not look at Earl to read an answer. She assumes it, like a forgiving mother toward a child who has misbehaved. In fact, throughout the scene she rarely lets Earl finish a sentence. Earl's response, "It's against everything I've ever stood for," insists on the absurd premise that he has ever "stood for" anything. "It's just—just the world." (Earl, of course, begins to seem a parody of the Marxist the Major and Sheriff want us to believe he is. Here he offers a quasi-doctrine of social conditioning for crime.)

But above these contrasts, the intimate bond between Hildy and Earl draws certain equations between the two. Earl's reference to "the world," a world this scene has been exploring, may implicate Hildy even more than Earl. The suspicion rises that Earl is a "foil" for Hildy. We might reasonably expect it to rise further.

A first visual confirmation that it does so appears in the next shot, which simply mirrors the preceding. Earl comes into the foreground; Hildy's face remains dominant, but the camera now has captured her in Earl's world, through the bars. To cement the bond, Hildy and Earl exchange a cigarette through the cell wire. Had we begun viewing at Shot Five, we might not now know which of the two sat *inside* the cell. Nor does it finally matter. Earl will be free, and Hildy, in the end, will not be—or, she will realize her subconscious choice not to be. That choice is inescapable. She is "imprisoned" herself, though in a world that, as a prison, fails to be very threatening. As a tag to the shot, Hildy calls her femininity to mind again by apologizing for the lipstick on her cigarette.

The scene's last two shots serve as a compressed re-emphasis of the themes thus far developed. Shot Seven, a visual return to Shot Five, makes circular the mini-sequence between Hildy and Earl, just as the final shot closes off the whole scene with another long view of the cell room. The "produced for use" bit completes Earl's depiction as a parody of both a Marxist and a murdering gunman. It comically undercuts the hysteria that later will attend his escape. It is itself the victim of subtextual play focused on the cigarette, which the non-smoking Earl remembers to hand back to Hildy, who crushes it to the floor *un*used. Intimacy also culminates in Shot Seven in the admiring of Molly's picture. As the first stimulus to animate Earl, this exchange suggests that the kindness of women is indeed his life and salvation.

As they rise in the final shot, we notice something we now expect: a visual mark of Hildy's entrapment. She is framed against the barred wall afront the foyer, and even the chair she pushes back, again with one hand, is backed in a way that suggests "bars." Earl's line is, "Goodbye, *Miss Johnson*," another reminder. Hildy is straight, and again brisk and deft, but her glance back at Earl before leaving shows that the bond remains. Her final line, "Good luck"—a favorite with Hawks—was the sort of farewell given aviators in World War One before they undertook dangerous missions. It indicates that the bond is one of collegiality; that, again, Hildy belongs in this professional world. A fade denies us the chance to see Hildy outside the cell room, since, the film says, her existence outside this world really is irrelevant.

Is Hildy not herself "produced for use"—her proper "use" being the newspaper business and married life with Walter? We are led to believe by this scene that she is as stuck here as Earl, and as at home in this incarnation as he comically seems amid his cell's drab but human furnishings. But Hildy does more than passively fit. The composure, command, and compassion she lends the situation work redemptively on her world to make it a fit little "home." If redemption themes are the basis of comedy, the cell scene, in less than three minutes' total running time, has established a comic vision for the whole film. In its own composure and its concentration on two persons, the scene models sanity and humanness of a kind needed for this film, and altogether absent from the frenetic action of *The Front Page*. It discloses Hildy in the integrated wholeness of her being, thus rendering credible her character itself and her eventual reunion with Walter. It shows that the romantic and professional dimensions of her being each help realize the other. As a paradigmatic case of theatre-to-film adaptation, it helps soften and knead the unrelentingly caustic, crazy stage comedy into a proper romantic-comedy shape—exactly what Hawks meant the "feminizing" of Hildy to do in the first place.

Source: Jeffrey A. Smith, "*His Girl Friday* in the Cell: A Case Study of Theatre-to-Film Adaptation," in *Literature/Film Quarterly*, 1985, Vol. 13, no. 2, pp. 71–76.

John Mason Brown

Brown reviews a 1946 production of The Front Page, *appraising the play as a "lusty" piece of writing that accurately captures the era it seeks to portray.*

From the millions of words spoken as dialogue in new American plays during the last quarter of a century, a few sentences here and there refuse to be forgotten. Most of the others, even when they have done their nightly duty as flares, have been swallowed up in the darkness.

The lines I have in mind are different. Beauty is not their strong point. Neither is wit, eloquence, profundity, nor, as a rule, reverence. Yet they have stuck in the memories of playgoers. They have lodged there as summaries and as tags; as vivid reminders of past pleasures. What is more, they have hung on with the insistence of slogans.

Any theatregoer of fair constancy and of a certain age can place them at once. The stagestruck find them as readily identifiable as schoolboys do

> "MR. HECHT'S AND MR. MACARTHUR'S MELODRAMA IS BASED ON THE ASSUMPTIONS AND THE ATTITUDES OF THE PROHIBITION ERA. ITS TONE IS TOUGH WITH A TOUGHNESS BORN OF THOSE TIMES. ITS SPIRIT IS JAUNTY, IMMATURE, UNTROUBLED. IT IS WRITTEN WITH A LIGHTNESS OF HEART WHICH, TRAGICALLY, MAY BE NO LONGER POSSIBLE. . . ."

such military nifties as "We have met the enemy and they are ours," "Don't give up the ship," "Damn the torpedoes!" "You may fire when ready, Gridley," "LaFayette, we are here," or, as spoken at Bastogne, just plain "Nuts." For that matter they are as spottable as such Presidential declarations as "Speak softly and carry a Big Stick," "I do not choose to run," "Too proud to fight," "The return to normalcy," or "The only thing we have to fear is fear itself."

Many of the lines which ring bells immediately in the minds of playgoers are mere phrases. "Dat ole davil sea," for instance. Or "Sign on the dotted line," "I belong, dat's me," "The mountains of Nebraska," or "It's only Mother."

Some—such as "Gangway for de Lord God Jehovah," or (a long pause, please) "I may vomit"—served as memorable entrance cues. Others—such as "Eleven o'clock in Grover's Corners. You get a good rest, too. Good night," and "No! I'm going to be baptized, damn it!"—ended evenings of rare delight.

Among all such lines, I doubt if any have proved more adhesive than those which rang down the curtain on two of the twenties' rowdiest successes. One of these was, of course, the ebullient, "Hey, Flagg, wait for baby!" with which Laurence Stallings and Maxwell Anderson concluded "What Price Glory?" The other left audiences gasping and roaring when the late Osgood Perkins barked it into a telephone. It ran, (and still runs, because *The Front Page* has recently been revived), "The son of a bitch stole my watch!"

This last gun in Ben Hecht's and Charles MacArthur's newspaper comedy came as a jubilant climax to a merry melodrama. It capped the barrage of surprises which eighteen years ago had kept all of us laughing and startled for the whole of a noisy, fast-moving evening. It was a *coup de théâtre;* unexpected, and as hardboiled as the play. It showed us the true character of the managing editor Mr. Perkins acted to perfection. It was his trick to win back to Chicago newspaperdom the star reporter who had dared to fall in love, dared to go on a honeymoon, dared to think of becoming an advertising man in New York.

The editor had just given the newly married reporter the watch in question as a present. The two men, long friends, had, after squabbling sacrilegiously, enjoyed an almost sentimental moment of reconciliation before parting. Yet, no sooner had the reporter and his bride left for the station, than the editor stepped to the telephone. He had hesitated for an instant and heaved a huge sigh. Managing editor though he was, he was at least that human. Then he had proceeded to growl his instructions to his henchman.

"Listen," he had said, "I want you to send a wire to the Chief of Police of LaPorte, Indiana. . . . That's right. . . . Tell him to meet the twelve-forty out of Chicago . . . New York Central . . . and arrest Hildy Johnson and bring him back here. . . . Wire him a full description. . . . The son of a bitch stole my watch!"

Time is the best of all shock absorbers. It can turn a scandalized "Oh!" into an accepting "So!" within an unbelievably small number of years. *The Front Page,* when seen—and heard—today, remains a far, far better play than most. One of the proofs of its skill is that its excellences as a script cannot be obscured by the less than indifferent performance to which it is just now being subjected. It is stoutly built. And, what matters more, it is peopled by an entertaining group of characters; hardboiled members of the Fourth Estate who breathe to swear and swear at every breath.

To their authors these profane news-hawks are obviously the most glamorous of figures. They see them as D'Artagnans in modern dress; as King Arthurs whose scandal-dripping typewriters are their Excaliburs; as Robin Hoods defying the Sheriff, not of Nottingham but of Cook County, in the Press Room of Chicago's Criminal Courts Building. Their lack of sentiment is what makes their creators feel sentimental about them. They are enchanted with their disenchantment. So, may I add, are we.

That these curmudgeons of the press use the language colorfully, no one can deny. Even so, the "tough-guy" speech, which they sport as romantically as Cyrano flourished his plume, no longer astonishes us. The intervening years have robbed the oaths of *The Front Page* of their novelty. The dialogue now tires us at times by its striving, instead of amazing us throughout by its daring.

If ever realism swaggered as romance, or romance masqueraded as realism, it is in Mr. Hecht's and Mr. MacArthur's melodrama. *The Front Page* was the work—more accurately, the play—of two young men who were described by their original producer, Jed Harris, as "the Katzenjammer Kids of the theatre." Their lightheartedness was the measure of their own youth and of the times in which they were lucky enough to be young. This is what Brooks Atkinson meant when, in his review of the present revival, he said, "Today it would be difficult for anybody to write anything so gay in spirit."

As important to any creative work as what is included in it is what is left out. The point of choice is indeed the point where art begins. Darwin may have championed natural selection, but the creative processes depend upon a selection which, regardless of how inevitable it may seem in the finished product, discards irrelevances and chooses with a definite and quite arbitrary purpose in mind.

Often, in a piece of writing as lusty as *The Front Page,* there is more to the play than is captured in the dialogue or suggested in the action. The very omissions speak for themselves. Mr. Hecht's and Mr. MacArthur's melodrama is based on the assumptions and the attitudes of the Prohibition era. Its tone is tough with a toughness born of those times. Its spirit is jaunty, immature, untroubled. It is written with a lightness of heart which, tragically, may be no longer possible but with a worship of the "lowdown" which, fortunately, has become as dated as it is discredited. Though tamer than it once was, *The Front Page* has, as a script, outlasted the days of its writing. It has become a period piece only because it so successfully captures the feeling of its period.

It was George S. Kaufman who first staged the melodrama. He performed a difficult task with a drive which kept the play cracking like a snakewhip in action. The group scenes, where a stageful of reporters must be given their individual chances to talk "tough," were timed with a precision calculated to win a Swiss clock-maker's envy. Everything was kept moving at so insistent a rate that, until the text was published, no one could be certain how self-reliant the script would prove as a play when unaided by its staging.

One of the disquieting faults of the present revival is that it makes us realize the virtues of the writing merely by granting them no assistance. To those never fortunate enough to have seen *The Front Page* before, and who do not keep seeing and hearing Osgood Perkins and Lee Tracy in it now, the comedy may seem satisfying enough. I say "may," though I gravely doubt it. I know only that I found this performance a dreary, inept affair; miscast, slouchily acted; and lacking, above all, in the fire and the precision needed to do the script justice.

In Mr. Tracy's part of the incurable reporter, Lew Parker acts with more effort than effect. He manages to skid on a dry road. His characterization is smudged and blurred, when it cries out loud to be clean and definite. Arnold Moss is totally lost in Osgood Perkin's shoes. Mr. Moss is an excellent classic actor. His Prospero in last year's "Tempest" made this clear. Yet, as should go without saying, almost every characteristic of voice, gesture, and mind which distinguished him in Shakespeare is misplaced in his impersonation of a tough Chicago newshawk. The late Henry Van Dyke trying to write like Ernest Hemingway could not possibly have been more at a loss.

Much as I admire *The Front Page* as a newspaper play, in the presence of the current slow-paced and amateurish revival I found I had one wish uppermost in my mind. I kept wanting to rush to the telephone in the manner of their managing editor, and warn Mr. Hecht and Mr. MacArthur that someone backstage—I only said "someone"—had stolen their watch.

Source: John Mason Brown, "Gentlemen of the Press," in the *Saturday Review,* Vol. 29, no. 43, October 26, 1946, pp. 24–26.

SOURCES

Atkinson, J. Brooks. A review in *The New York Times,* August 26, 1928, p. 1.

Bemrose, John. "Cynics and Sybarites: Attacking a Deficiency with First-Rate Drama," *Maclean's,* June 13, 1994, p. 45.

Brien, Alan. "The Front Page," Plays and Players, August 1972, p. 35–36.

Brustein, Robert. "Headline Hunting," in *The New Republic,* January 5 & 12, 1987, pp. 25-26.

Fethering, Doug. *The Five Lives of Ben Hecht,* New York Zoetrope, 1977, pp. 67-87.

Kerr, Walter. *God on the Gymnasium Floor and Other Theatrical Adventures,* Simon and Schuster, 1969, pp. 176-78.

Morrison, Michael A. A review in *Village Voice,* August 9, 1994, p. 86.

A review in *The New York Times,* August 15, 1928, p. 19.

Simon, John. *Uneasy Stages: A Chronicle of the New York Theater, 1963–73,* Random House, 1975, pp. 246-47.

———. "Satire is Dead in America!," in *New York,* December 8, 1996, p. 113.

Wyatt, Euphemia Van Rensselaer. A review in *Catholic World,* November, 1928, pp. 211-12.

FURTHER READING

Epstein, Joseph. "The Great Hack Genius," in *Commentary,* December 1990.
  A critical biography of Hecht, including analysis of *The Front Page.*

Hecht, Ben. *A Child of the Century,* Simon & Schuster, 1954, 654 p.
  Hecht's autobiography.

———. *The Improbable Life and Times of Charles MacArthur,* Harper, 1957, 242 p.
  An incomplete biography of MacArthur.

Martin, Jeffrey Brown. *Ben Hecht: Hollywood Screenwriter,* UMI Research Press, 1985, pp. 41-56.
  Discusses *The Front Page* as a play as well as a movie. Also compares the play and the movies to other "newspaper" movies.

Zion, Sidney. "The Scoop from Helen Hayes," *The New York Times,* November 16, 1986, pp. 1, 22.
  Provides background on *The Front Page.*

Funnyhouse of a Negro

ADRIENNE KENNEDY

1964

Making its debut on January 14, 1964, at the East End Theater in New York City, *Funnyhouse of a Negro* was Adrienne Kennedy's first produced play. Early on, critics and audiences recognized the importance of the work. It received an Obie Award from *The Village Voice* for most distinguished play and continued to be produced in the United States and abroad throughout the 1960s.

The play chronicles the last hours in the life of Sarah, a young black woman troubled by race and identity. Kennedy's depiction of Sarah's hallucinatory subconscious—struggling with self-hatred, race hatred, and alienation from the larger culture—was regarded as powerful by some critics of the era. Other critics were confused by the staging and subject matter of the work.

Many scholars contend that *Funnyhouse of a Negro* was revolutionary in a number of ways, especially Kennedy's unique portrayal of what it was like to be black and a woman in the United States in the 1960s.

AUTHOR BIOGRAPHY

Kennedy was born Adrienne Hawkins on September 13, 1931, in Pittsburgh, Pennsylvania. She was raised in an ethnically diverse neighborhood in

Cleveland, Ohio, where her father worked as a social worker and her mother was a schoolteacher.

When Kennedy entered Ohio State University in 1949, she experienced racism for the first time. Upon graduation in 1953, with a B.A. in education, Kennedy married Joseph C. Kennedy; the couple had two sons together before their divorce in 1966.

Kennedy began writing plays as early as the mid-1950s. When her husband returned from serving in the Korean War, the couple moved to New York City. She began her graduate studies in creative writing at various institutions and some of her fiction was published in the early 1960s.

To gain entrance into playwright Edward Albee's workshop at Circle in the Square Theatre, Kennedy submitted two of her plays. One was called *Funnyhouse of a Negro,* which was deemed worthy of production in its original form.

Produced in 1964, the play won an Obie Award. Like many of her subsequent plays, *Funnyhouse of a Negro* was influenced by Kennedy's dreams and reflected her own experiences, serving as a social commentary on race, gender, exclusion and identity.

By the late 1960s, Kennedy began receiving commissions to write plays. For example, *Sun: A Poem for Malcolm X Inspired by His Murder* was commissioned by the Royal Court Theatre, London, and produced in 1968. She also began a secondary career as a guest lecturer at many institutions in this time period.

In 1976, Kennedy wrote *A Movie Star Has to Star in Black and White,* about a writer who lives through film actors and the roles they play. A few years later, she adapted two plays by Euripides, *Electra* (1980) and *Orestes* (1981).

In the late 1980s Kennedy branched out into autobiography and fiction. In 1990 she wrote a play based on her college experiences. The central character of *Ohio State Murders,* Suzanne Alexander, appeared in several subsequent plays.

By this time, Kennedy's importance had been recognized by academics and critics alike, and she began receiving numerous accolades for her work.

Based in New York City, Kennedy continues to write fiction and dramas.

PLOT SUMMARY

Funnyhouse of a Negro opens in front of a closed curtain; a wild-haired woman, the Mother, walks across the stage carrying a bald head in front of her. She mumbles to herself, appearing to be in a trance.

After she exits, the curtain opens to reveal the Queen's chamber, with a tomb-like bed at center. In the chamber are two of Sarah's inner selves: the Duchess of Hapsburg and Queen Victoria.

The women look identical and wear royal gowns and ghostly masks. When knocking is heard, the Queen announces that it must be her father looking for her. The Duchess notes that their father is a black man and she wishes he was dead.

They both complain about him; the Duchess accuses him of killing their mother. Victoria claims that he is dead before the loud knocking ends and the lights go out in the chamber.

The Mother returns on stage carrying the head. She announces that she was raped by the black man, Sarah's father, then disappears. On another part of the stage, which features a square wall, Sarah (also known as the Negro) enters with a hangman's rope around her neck and with blood on her face. She carries a patch of kinky hair that is missing from a spot on her head.

Sarah addresses the audience in a monologue: she describes the place where she lives, a room that is located in a brownstone in New York City. Claiming that she idolizes Queen Victoria, she describes her conversations with the Queen. In these conversations, she states that being black is bad.

Sarah also describes her background; particularly her education, interest in poetry, and her desire to live in a room with European antiques. In this scenario, Sarah makes it clear that she wants to surround herself with things from the white world in order to ignore her African American heritage. The pressure of this self-hatred has caused her hair to fall out; she is almost bald. She also has a boyfriend, Raymond; he is a Jewish poet who is interested in African American culture.

As Sarah continues to talk, her four inner selves stand together on stage: in addition to the Queen and the Duchess, a hunchbacked dwarf named Jesus and a black man with a split head named Patrice Lumumba make an appearance.

Sarah claims that she killed her father. Outside of Sarah's room, in the hallway of the rooming house, the Landlady appears. She informs the audience that Sarah's father hung himself inside a hotel in Harlem when Patrice Lumumba was murdered. The Landlady describes Sarah's habit of hiding in her room.

Located above Sarah's room is the funnyhouse—ruled by Raymond, known as the Funnyman. Raymond and the Duchess talk, with the Duchess clinging to Raymond's leg. The Duchess worries about her father's imminent arrival from Africa. Raymond confirms that her father is the man who shot himself when Patrice Lumumba was murdered.

The Duchess describes her father as a man who went to Africa as a Christian missionary in the jungle. She opens the bag she is carrying, which is full of her hair. She describes her father and the rape of her mother. She describes herself as in-between her father's darkness and mother's lightness. The Duchess also reveals that her mother is in an insane asylum.

Patrice Lumumba addresses the audience in a monologue. He lost his hair too. Furthermore, he describes his mother watching her hair fall out strand by strand, because of "black diseases." Inside the Queen's chamber, the Queen discovers that her hair has fallen out too. The Duchess tries to put her own hair back on her head.

Patrice describes his background the same way Sarah did earlier: where he lives, how he majored in English in college, and how he writes poetry. He also wants white friends to go with his room filled with European antiques. But he says he will despise them as he does himself. He also claims to have hit his father, which caused him to lose his hair.

With her inner selves walking around her, Sarah describes how her paternal grandmother wanted her father to be Christ and save his people. Her paternal grandfather believed that his race was not worth saving. His parents did want him to marry Sarah's mother.

When Sarah's parents went to Africa as missionaries, her mother fell out of love with her father. Sarah's mother would not be touched by him, but after her father started to drink, he raped her mother—resulting in Sarah. She announces that she loved her mother more than her father when they lived in Africa.

After her mother's hair began falling out, the family returned to the United States. Sarah says that her father felt like a Judas for driving her mother to an insane asylum, and he once tried to hang himself in a hotel in Harlem.

Inside the Duchess's place (a ballroom with a chandelier), Jesus and the Duchess talk. Jesus is upset that he lost his hair. The Duchess shows him that she is also bald. While the knocking continues, Jesus and the Duchess try to fix their remaining strands of hair. They talk about how their father will not leave them alone.

Outside Sarah's room, the Landlady continues to talk. She describes events from Sarah's father's perspective: he wanted Sarah's forgiveness for being black.

Back inside the Duchess's place, Jesus and the Duchess have fallen asleep. Jesus wakes up and tells God he has tried to escape being black. He decides to go to Africa and kill Patrice Lumumba.

After a blackout, a jungle scene covers the entire stage. Each of Sarah's four inner selves appears, wearing a nimbus. Jesus says that he always believed his father was God. They all describe how they each wanted their father dead, and how their mother died because she was touched by a black man.

Furthermore, the inner selves believe that their father killed their mother and that he is also dead. Yet he continues to knock at the door. They describe a scene in which he begs Sarah for forgiveness, and her mother appears. Sarah hits him with an ebony hand. They four selves laugh and cheer in victory.

A wall drops, and Sarah's room is revealed. Sarah has hung herself, and her father rushes toward her. Outside the room, the Landlady tells Raymond that Sarah has hung herself like her father did when Patrice Lumumba died. Raymond calls Sarah a liar, explaining that her father is a black doctor married to a white woman.

CHARACTERS

Mrs. Conrad
See Landlady

Duchess of Hapsburg
The Duchess is one of Sarah's inner selves, arguably the closest to Sarah's true self. She repre-

sents the aspect of Sarah's subconscious that is racist. She blames her father for her mother's death. Like all the inner selves, she has lost almost all of her hair.

Funnyhouse Lady
See Landlady

Funnyhouse Man
See Raymond

Jesus
One of Sarah's inner selves, Jesus is a hunchbacked dwarf with yellow skin. Sarah describes him as the son of Queen Victoria. He shares the Duchess of Hapsburg's disdain of Sarah's father. Jesus decides to hunt down and kill Patrice Lumumba. Like all the inner selves, he loses almost all of his hair.

Landlady
The Landlady is a white woman who runs the boarding house where Sarah lives. She comments on the action and Sarah's life, providing a needed perspective on what is happening. She believes that Sarah has hidden in her room ever since Patrice Lumumba was murdered and her father hung herself in a Harlem hotel.

The Landlady also says that Sarah's hair has fallen out because of her suffering. She offers insight into Sarah's father's background, and recalls incidents in which he tried to reconcile with his daughter. It is the Landlady who discovers that Sarah has killed herself.

Patrice Lumumba
Patrice Lumumba is one of Sarah's inner selves. He is a black man whose head is split in half; his eyes have blood and tissue in them. He carries an ebony mask.

Patrice seems to represent Sarah's father, though he describes himself in the exact same words that Sarah uses to describe herself. Yet he also introduces the theme of self-hatred in the play. Like all the inner selves, Patrice has lost his hair.

Man
See Patrice Lumumba

The Negro
See Sarah

Queen Victoria Regina
Queen Victoria is one of Sarah's inner selves; she looks exactly like the Duchess of Hapsburg. Sarah describes her as the mother of Jesus. She describes how Sarah's father searched for her. Like the other inner selves, Queen Victoria loses most of her hair during the play.

Raymond
Raymond is a Jewish poet who lives above Sarah in the rooming house. She describes him as a boyfriend who is interested in African Americans.

At the end of the play, Raymond is present when the Landlady discovers that Sarah has killed herself. He informs the Landlady that Sarah's father is a doctor married to a white woman. It seems that Sarah's father never committed suicide.

Sarah
Sarah is the protagonist of the play and is represented on stage by four of her inner selves: Queen Victoria, the Duchess of Hapsburg, Jesus, and Patrice Lumumba.

Only a few facts are clear among the many versions of her "reality." Sarah is the product of an interracial marriage: her mother is white and her father is African-American. She studied English at a college in New York City, writes poetry, and works as a librarian. She lives in a brownstone rooming house in New York City.

Sarah's primary problem relates to racial identity and related issues: she is conflicted about her heritage, especially concerning her father. By the end of the play, it is clear that Sarah has killed herself.

What is not clear is her real relationship to Raymond, who also lives in the rooming house. She may or may not have been involved with him. Similarly, she may or may not have been born in Africa, and her mother may or may not have been committed to an insane asylum. Sarah's inner conflicts form the heart of the play.

THEMES

Identity
At the core of *Funnyhouse of a Negro* is Sarah's internal struggle to understand and accept her identity as an African American woman in the United States. Each of Sarah's four "selves"—her subcon-

TOPICS FOR FURTHER STUDY

- Research the Civil Rights movement of the early 1960s, in particular the effects of the Civil Rights Act of 1964. How do you think this movement impacted the lives of middle-class African Americans like Sarah?

- Review psychological writings on the children of interracial marriages. Discuss Sarah's identity crisis, self-hatred, and subsequent suicide in light of your findings. Has society changed? Would Sarah feel this way today?

- The character of Sarah feels alienated from both her African-American heritage and white heritage. Write an essay discussing your own heritage and what it means to you. Does it help define who you are? What else defines you as a person?

- Compare and contrast the character of Sarah with Clara from Kennedy's 1965 play *The Owl Answers*. Clara undergoes a similar racial identity crisis, which also involves historical figures. Why did Kennedy pick these specific people—what do they represent? What do the historical figures say about Sarah and Clara's individual crises?

scious's way of dealing with her identity issues—represents a facet of Sarah.

Two of her four selves are white European women of royal blood: the Duchess of Hapsburg and Queen Victoria. Sarah also has a large statue of Victoria in her room. This emphasizes her desire to identify more with her mother, who was white or a light-skinned African American depending on differing interpretations of the text. The Queen and the Duchess despise Sarah's dark-skinned father and what she thinks that represents: impurity, beastliness, and evilness.

Two of Sarah's inner selves are men: Jesus and Patrice Lumumba. The latter is an African revolutionary who was the first Prime Minister of the Democratic Republic of the Congo. After he left office, he was assassinated. He represents Sarah's father—the dark side of her heritage and her self-hatred. Through the persona of Lumumba, Sarah claims that she killed her father.

Sarah's fourth self, Jesus, is a dwarf and a hunchback with yellow skin. Jesus represents Sarah's father as a martyr. Through Jesus, Sarah expresses her desire to kill Lumumba and escape being black.

By the end of *Funnyhouse,* Sarah realizes that she cannot get escape her racial identity—though she claims she does not have particularly black features—and kills herself.

Alienation and Loneliness

Sarah's problems with identity in *Funnyhouse of a Negro* lead to alienation and loneliness. Because she is of mixed heritage—and she has confused ideas about what each heritage represents—she feels alienated from both black and white cultures. This alienation leads to loneliness.

It is implied that Sarah's father has made numerous attempts to reach his daughter, but she has rejected him repeatedly. Some of her selves claim that he killed himself. So she rejects that side of herself.

Sarah also rejects the white side of herself. She claims her mother is dead or in an asylum. Her landlady does not understand her. Sarah says she does not love her white Jewish boyfriend, a poet named Raymond. She claims, "He is very interested in Negroes," which implies he is not interested in Sarah for herself, but her racial identity.

Appearances and Reality/ Truth and Falsehood

Both truth and reality are murky in *Funnyhouse of a Negro*. The truth about Sarah's parents—their marriage, courtship, the details of Sarah's conception, if they are alive—is unclear. Each of her four selves, as well as Sarah herself, relates a slightly different story, especially about Sarah's father.

Furthermore, what Sarah really thinks of herself is also not clear. It is obvious that Sarah has problems with her mixed heritage. Yet she really does not express anything positive about either heritage beyond the idea that white is better than black: the reality of her feelings is essentially indiscernible. Even Sarah's landlady and boyfriend do not know the real truth about her—Raymond calls her "a funny little liar" after her death.

Because the play takes place primarily in Sarah's troubled mind, what is true and what is false is not always clear.

STYLE

Setting

Because *Funnyhouse of a Negro* is a surreal play that takes place primarily inside Sarah's mind, only a few aspects of the setting are "real."

Set in the early 1960s, the play takes place in Sarah's room in a New York City brownstone. Her room features a large statue of Queen Victoria, other pictures of British monarchs, books, a bed, and a writing table. Some of the "realistic" action takes place on the landing and inside Raymond's room.

The play has several settings specific to Sarah's four selves. For example, the Queen has her own chamber with a tomb-like mahogany bed, a chandelier, and walls the color of wine. The Duchess has her own space: a ballroom with a chandelier, marbled floor, fake snow, and benches. In the final scenes, a jungle replaces these rooms, altering their symbolic meaning.

Monologue

There is very little action and dialogue in *Funnyhouse of a Negro*; in fact, much of play is in the form of monologues. Kennedy uses the monologue to let the characters speak freely.

Sarah and her four inner selves use their monologues to relate a version of Sarah's family background and emotional crisis. None are exactly the same, which illustrates her inability to come to terms with her life.

In the Landlady's monologues, she relates stories about Sarah's "real" life, as she has observed and understood it. Only Raymond lacks a true monologue. All of his words are part of a dialogue with other characters.

Symbolism/Imagery

Many of the ideas in *Funnyhouse of a Negro* are expressed by numerous symbols and images. Very little is realistic in the play. Even the characters are symbolic.

Sarah's four selves represent different aspects of her identity: the Duchess and Queen Victoria wear masks or mask-like makeup and white clothing reminiscent of funeral shrouds; Jesus is a yellow-skinned hunch-backed dwarf; and Patrice Lumumba carries an ebony mask.

The character of Sarah's mother is even more symbolic—she carries a bald head as she moves across stage several times. While Sarah's mother is mentioned frequently, she speaks only once. Sarah's mother only flits through her daughter's unconscious: she is only to be discussed and interpreted, not really understood.

Kennedy's stage directions calls for numerous physical symbols and complex images. For example, Sarah's room is dominated by a statue of Queen Victoria, a white ideal of purity and royalty that she will never be able to match. Sarah walks around with a noose around her neck and a bloody face before the audience is told that she is dead. This emphasizes her inner pain as well as her eventual fate.

In the segment that introduces Queen Victoria and the Duchess, black ravens circle overhead, which contrasts with their white-tinged faces and bright white light. Raymond's status as the Funnyman is emphasized by the mirrors behind the blinds in his room that he opens and closes repeatedly. These are but a few of the symbols used in the play to underscore Sarah's state of mind.

HISTORICAL CONTEXT

In the United States, the early 1960s were marked by social and political transformations. One of the most important was the Civil Rights movement, which had been fighting for civil rights for African Americans for a number of years.

At the beginning of the decade, the fight for civil rights took several forms: sit-ins at segregated lunch counters; marches through segregated areas; and boycotts of discriminatory businesses. The National Association for the Advancement of Colored People (NAACP) filed several lawsuits to serve a civil rights agenda. Hopes were high that newly elected President John F. Kennedy would fulfill his promises to pass civil rights legislation.

Kennedy never got a chance to fulfill his agenda; tragically, he was assassinated in November 1963. However, his successor, Lyndon B. Johnson, did continue the civil rights agenda. In 1964, he

COMPARE & CONTRAST

- **1964:** The poll tax is eliminated by the ratification of the twenty-fourth amendment to the Constitution. Throughout the summer, many volunteers travel to Mississippi, Alabama, and Georgia to promote voting rights among African Americans. In Mississippi, three civil rights activists are murdered.

   Today: The right to vote is assured to African Americans.

- **1964:** Interracial marriages are banned by sixteen states, mostly in the South.

   Today: No state bans interracial marriages.

- **1964:** Anti-apartheid leader Nelson Mandela is sentenced to life in prison for his activities in South Africa.

   Today: After being imprisoned for twenty-six years, Mandela was released in 1990. He was elected as South Africa's president in 1994. He has since retired from public life.

---

signed into law several bills that guaranteed civil rights for African Americans and other minorities.

The most important was the Civil Rights Act of 1964. It guaranteed equal opportunity for employment and public places (such as hotels, theaters, and restaurants). Access to employment could not be denied based on race, gender, religion or national origin.

The Civil Rights Act also gave the federal government several means to enforce the law. For example, they could cut off funding to any lower form of government that did not comply. The Justice Department could bring lawsuits against those who failed to adhere to the provisions.

Johnson also signed into law the Equal Opportunity Act in 1964, which was designed to create jobs and fight poverty. Organizations like the United Steelworkers followed Johnson's lead. The United Steelworkers and eleven major steel companies signed an agreement to end racial discrimination in their industry.

Despite such efforts, implementation of civil rights was not always easy. Schools and universities had been ordered to integrate as early as the 1950s, but such changes had been resisted, especially in the South. The Civil Rights Act allowed the government to withhold funds if they did not take measures towards integration.

Voting rights were also part of the Civil Rights agenda. State and local governments, especially in the South, had taken legal measures designed to prohibit African Americans from exercising their voting rights, including polls taxes and voter tests. Poll taxes were outlawed by the 24th Amendment to the Constitution in 1964.

Many civil rights activists traveled to Mississippi, Alabama, and Georgia to educate black voters about their rights and get them registered to vote. Many activists were arrested, beaten, and even killed.

Dr. Martin Luther King Jr., an African-American leader in the civil rights movement who advocated nonviolence, won the Nobel Peace Prize in 1964.

The Civil Rights Act of 1964 included a provision for banning employment discrimination based on gender. Though this part of the Civil Rights Act was not enforced for several years, the role of women was already changing in American society.

Women entered the workforce in greater numbers. By the beginning of the 1960s, about one-third of American women were employed—often in part time, low-paying jobs to supplement income or as teachers.

In 1963, Betty Friedan published *The Feminine Mystique,* which suggested that women could find fulfillment in the workplace. That same year, an equal pay bill was passed.

The women's rights movement would intensify and grow by the mid-1960s.

CRITICAL OVERVIEW

Funnyhouse of a Negro has garnered a mixed critical reaction since its original production in 1964. While many critics found something to praise about Kennedy's writing talent, some were not sure what to make of the play. Most reviewers viewed it as an important exploration of race and identity in contemporary society.

Joshua Billings of *The New Yorker* is a prime example of the qualified praise often accorded Kennedy. He wrote, "As a rule, I don't take to Expressionism, partly because its built-in weirdness and distortion tend to make the material it deals with seem more important than it really is. The material here couldn't be much more important to begin with, so that's all right, I guess, and the style does seem appropriate. *Funnyhouse* is a first play and, as such, is quite strong and original."

Other contemporary critics were more straightforward in their praise of the play. *The Nation*'s Harold Clurman wrote, "The play, the general theme of which may be defined as what it may mean to be a colored person in the United States, embraces far more than plays of similar theme when they are couched in terms of pathetic appeals for 'tolerance' and fair play."

Like Billings, many critics felt obligated to contrast the surreal play to mainstream theater. Howard Taubman of *The New York Times* noted: "But if nothing much happens according to conventional theatrical tenets, a relatively unknown territory is explored and exposed. Miss Kennedy, herself a Negro, digs unsparingly into Sarah's aching psyche...."

Critics maintained that the play set the tone for Kennedy's career; she was seen as the vanguard of a movement by many scholars. Yet there remained some debate as to how to classify the play. Some perceived it as an example of ritual theater, while other scholars contended that it was more symbolic and absurdist.

EAST END THEATER

THEATER 1964

Richard Barr   Clinton Wilder   Edward Albee

presents

ADRIENNE KENNEDY'S

FUNNYHOUSE OF A NEGRO

with

BILLIE ALLEN   ELLEN HOLLY
CYNTHIA BELGRAVE   LESLIE RIVERS
NORMAN BUSH   RUTH VOLNER
LEONARD FREY   GUS WILLIAMS

Directed by
MICHAEL KAHN

Settings and Lighting by   *Costumes by*
WILLIAM RITMAN   WILLA KIM

Playbill of Kennedy's Funnyouse of a Negro.

Many commentators asserted that the play provided psychological insight into the identity struggles for African Americans and women. In 1975, Lorraine A. Brown contended: "That we are allowed to experience this play from within Sarah's mind and sensibility and that the form of the play so noticeably aids our understanding of her struggle are only two measures of its fineness. Equally brilliant is the deep probing of the female psyche which reaches an admirable level of universality...."

As Kennedy's significance in the theater world was recognized, her plays were performed again. There were several productions of *Funnyhouse* in the 1990s.

In a 1995 revival in New York City, critics remained divided over the play, in part because of the way times had changed. The racial context had changed and some of Kennedy's ideas seemed dated. As a result, the play has not endured the test of time.

In one review, John Simon of *New York* dismissed Kennedy entirely. He wrote "Not much goes on in *Funnyhouse*.... The author, who here goes by Negro-Sarah, is a young black would-be playwright who—unhappy with her lot—projects herself onto other characters. . . . Each of these is styled 'one of herselves,' and each is a crashing bore.''

Other reviewers had negative assessments of the play. Ben Brantley of *The New York Times*, critiquing both *Funnyhouse* and *A Movie Star Has to Star in Black and White*, maintained: ''It is true that theater doesn't get much more egocentric than these two plays. . . . But Ms. Kennedy has carefully forged an emotional bridge that one cannot avoid crossing, regardless of race, age, or sex.''

Brantley claimed: ''Deeply personal, poetic and nonlinear, they [her plays] would appear to be better suited to academia than to the stage.''

CRITICISM

A. Petrusso

In this essay, Petrusso explores two prominent symbols used in Kennedy's play.

Adrienne Kennedy's *Funnyhouse of a Negro* uses many symbols to underscore the torment that Sarah feels about herself and her racial identity. Nearly everyone and everything in the play has symbolic meaning—from the opening depiction of Sarah's mother wearing a white nightgown to Raymond's smug explanation of what he believes to be the ''truth'' about his girlfriend—because the play is nonlinear and fragmented.

Two of the most interesting and disturbing symbols in *Funnyhouse* are the obsession with hair and baldness throughout the text, and the use of knocking in some scenes.

Hair plays a complex role in *Funnyhouse*. It defines characters and marks their evolution. In addition, it is the prominent physical difference between black people and white people.

Hair also links scenes and illustrates Sarah's inevitable fate. Kennedy's use of hair underscores the idea that Sarah tried to disavow—then kill—the African American part of her background.

The knocking complements the symbolism of the hair. Her father's knocking will not cease because she cannot escape her father's heritage. This essay explores how these symbols are used within *Funnyhouse*.

When the play opens, the first character seen on stage is a representation of Sarah's mother. She is also called Woman, and is described like this: ''Her hair is wild, straight and black and falls to her waist.'' There is critical contention over the race of Sarah's mother because of certain ambiguous phrases used by Kennedy. Some believe that she is a light-skinned African American, while others are of the opinion that she is white.

For the purposes of this essay, it only matters that she is perceived by Sarah to be the epitome of light, white, and purity—elements defiled by her African-American father. Also, this is a version of her mother in Sarah's mind: she may or may not be what Sarah's mother is really like.

Sarah's mother is the only female character inside Sarah's mind who fully retains her hair. Yet when Sarah's mother first appears on stage, she is carrying a bald head, establishing her link between hair and hair loss. What Sarah's mother represents is idealized by her daughter, as can be seen by her hair, which Sarah's mother retains throughout the play.

Yet Sarah also claims that all of her mother's hair fell out when she was unhappily living in Africa where her father was a missionary. Sarah claims that her father raped her mother, which caused the hair loss and resulted in Sarah's birth. Sarah goes so far as to claim that her mother was put in an asylum because of her father.

In Sarah's confused and confusing mind, her mother represents all that is good—but she is still seen by Sarah as a victim of blackness. This leaves Sarah in a dilemma over her own sense of identity.

Sarah attempts to solve this dilemma through four inner selves that she creates. When two of them—Queen Victoria and the Duchess of Hapsburg—are introduced, they each have a full head of kinky hair. In reality, these two women were white, and by the time *Funnyhouse* was written, very dead.

The Queen and the Duchess speak for part of Sarah's subconscious. They are white, but their hair is meant to be black, showing how Sarah perceives her identity conflict. Sarah cannot escape her racial heritage, no matter how white she tries to be.

Their introductory scene is punctuated by a constant knocking. The Duchess points out that they are still tied to Sarah's father even though he is dead. The play is essentially Sarah's realization of

WHAT DO I READ NEXT?

- *for colored girls who have considered suicide/ when the rainbow is enuf* is a dramatic poem written by Ntozake Shange in 1974. Shange explores different facets of her life and struggles, relating a variety of experiences of African American women in the twentieth century.

- *Black, White, Other: Biracial Americans Talk About Race and Identity* (1995) is a book by Lisa Funderburg that features interviews with forty-three biracial Americans. They discuss the impact of being biracial on their lives.

- *The Owl Answers* is a play written by Kennedy in 1965. It chronicles the adventures of a young woman, Clara Passmore, who is troubled by her racial identity. Eventually, Passmore is imprisoned by several figures in British history, including William the Conqueror.

- *Of Many Colors: Portraits of Multiracial Families,* is a collection of photographs and interviews by Gigi Kaeser, Peggy Gillespie and Glenda Valentine published in 1997. The thirty-nine portraits are accompanied by the stories of these multiracial families.

---

this fact, but not her acceptance of it. The door will eventually have to be answered.

Sarah seems closest to the Duchess, the most prominent inner self. When Sarah visits her white boyfriend Raymond (in her mind), it is in the persona of the Duchess. While she talks to him and acts seductively towards him, she also describes her unexpected hair loss. Indeed, she brings her hair in a red bag to the room. She frantically tells him that when she awoke that morning, most of it was gone. Sarah/Duchess shows her white boyfriend that she has lost her most obvious African-American feature. This event is disturbing to her.

Later, Queen Victoria's hair falls out while she is asleep, though she does not reveal this in words. She acts it out in pantomime during a break in Patrice Lumumba's monologue. After the Queen loses her hair, the Duchess tries to put her replace her hair. She fails. Sarah can't have it both ways: to not be black and to be black at the same time.

Sarah has a number of inner male selves. Like the Queen and the Duchess, these inner selves are historical figures who are dead by the time the play begins. One male inner-self, Patrice Lumumba, is black. He was an African revolutionary leader who was murdered around the time the play was written. Although the stage directions do not specify his physical hair loss, Lumumba describes and further illuminates hair/hair loss as a symbol in the play.

When Lumumba is introduced as "Man," the knocking returns for the first time since the Queen and the Duchess made their initial appearance. He describes how all his hair fell out in the morning, in terms similar to those used by the Duchess.

Lumumba does the same thing when he describes his life. He uses the same terms as Sarah did describing her life, but uses language that is much harsher. He also relates a version of how Sarah's mother's hair fell out until she was bald. Sarah cannot totally immerse herself in her Lumumba self. He represents her father and what he stands for: blackness and everything she hates.

Yet Lumumba is given the lines that reveal what may be the secret to hair in the play. He says, "For if I did not despise myself then my hair would not have fallen and if my hair had not fallen then I would not have bludgeoned my father's face with an ebony mask." While this statement may not be literally true, it shows the pivotal role hair plays in the play.

Sarah seems more sympathetic to another male inner-self—Jesus—than to Lumumba. She says that "Jesus is Victoria's son," and she definitely favors

"SARAH LONGS TO FIT INTO WHITE CULTURE, TO BE PALE, EVEN GOING AS FAR AS TO CLAIM THAT HER FATHER IS DEAD (HE HUNG HIMSELF IN A HARLEM HOTEL ROOM, AMONG OTHER SCENARIOS) BUT HIS LEGACY KEEPS HER AT A DISTANCE. ALL OF HER HALF-TRUTHS ABOUT HIM AND HIS FATE SHOW HOW DESPERATELY SHE HAS TRIED TO AVOID HER HERITAGE."

white royalty. Jesus is a hunchback, a dwarf, and yellow-skinned, the latter the same term Sarah uses to describe herself.

In his major scene with the Duchess, Jesus shows her how all his hair has fallen out. The Duchess explains to him how she tried to put it back on, then comforts him. They comb each other's remaining hairs: a gesture of futile solidarity since their hair continues to fall out. During their closeness, the knocking returns again, reminding Sarah of what she must face.

Later Jesus talks of wanting to kill Lumumba, the closest thing to Sarah's father. Though Jesus only appears briefly, he seems to be how Sarah really sees herself: stunted, deformed, and needy. He is the last of her inner selves to lose his hair. When he succumbs, Sarah's fate is sealed.

Sarah's relationship to hair is more complicated than the other characters since *Funnyhouse* takes place primarily in her mind. During the play, Sarah says that her "wild kinky hair" is the only part of her physical make-up that would identify her as black.

When she makes her first appearance on stage, a patch of hair is missing from her skull and she wears a hangman's noose. She carries the patch in her hand. This implies that no matter what goes on during the course of the play her fate is inevitable: suicide is her only recourse. When she or any of her inner selves lose their hair, they may be divorced from Sarah's physical racial identity—but it does not make her any less black.

Sarah repeatedly says that she wants to "escape the jungle"—implying that she wants to be more white. Like her mother before her, she has lost her hair because of the jungle. Sarah says that her mother spent her time in Africa combing her hair after she fell out of love with Sarah's father. Sarah's mother's hair began falling out after he raped her.

This rape may not be literal, but Sarah believes it to be the only explanation for her anger. Hair equals beauty for Sarah, and she cannot forgive her father's legacy.

Sarah longs to fit into white culture, to be pale, even going as far as to claim that her father is dead (he hung himself in a Harlem hotel room, among other scenarios) but his legacy keeps her at a distance. All of her half-truths about him and his fate show how desperately she has tried to avoid her heritage.

Yet Sarah idealizes whites—including royalty like Queen Victoria who believes that blacks are evil—even though she knows that they are flawed. She wants to be royalty, but the type of hair the Queen and the Duchess have in her subconscious proves that she knows the truth. They do not provide the solace she seeks. Her "real" white friends, at least depicted here, also do not provide comfort.

The prime example of a white friend is her boyfriend, Raymond. He is a Jewish poet who only likes her because of her race. Sarah says, "I would like to lie and say I love Raymond. But I do not. He is very interested in Negroes."

In the last lines of play, Raymond thinks he knows the truth about his girlfriend: Sarah was a liar, her father is an African-American doctor who is alive, and that he has a white wife (who may or may not be Sarah's mother as depicted in the play). According to Raymond, the truth is that Sarah's father lives the life Sarah says she wants. Perhaps Sarah sees its emptiness and can find no other way to live her life.

At the end of *Funnyhouse,* each of Sarah's four selves wears a halo and talks about what Sarah's father means to them. When she reaches a breaking point, all four of them scream in victory. The knocking is incessant by this point because the real truth is knocking at Sarah's door. For many reasons, she cannot answer it.

Sarah kills herself. The reasons are explained by the use of hair in *Funnyhouse of a Negro*. She did everything she could to get rid of the black part of herself—her hair. Until she took her own life, it would not go away.

Source: A. Petrusso, for *Drama for Students,* Gale, 2000.

Claudia Barnett

In the following essay, Barnett discusses Kennedy's play in terms of the psychological theory of projecting one's hope's and fears onto others. This makes others into ideal or persecutory objects respectively, and focuses on treating others as objects rather than as a unified whole.

Adrienne Kennedy's characters speak obsessively of their own births as well as the births—which are so often the deaths—of their children. Their monologues focus on rape and incest, miscarriage and child murders. Such preoccupations psychologically paralyze the characters, fixing them at—and regressing them to—a primitive stage in development which Melanie Klein, a psychologist of the British object relations school, calls [in *Introduction to the Work of Melanie Klein* by Hanna Segal] the "paranoid-schizoid position," an infant stage which normally precedes integration. According to Klein, the life instinct and the death instinct, which are both present in the infant from birth, create a polarity of anxieties that the infant deals with through splitting and projective identification; that is, the infant learns to split external objects into representations of good and evil, projecting hopes and fears away from the subject and onto the object. In later phases, the infant learns to unify such splits and to deal with whole objects. Kennedy's characters, however, rarely reach this point of integration: they never progress beyond the paranoid-schizoid position. These characters remain prisoners of object relations, their worlds disordered by irrational, irrevocable splits.

The infantile ego, in terms of Klein's description, deflects the death instinct outward to an external object, the persecutory object, which "is felt to be bad and threatening to the ego, giving rise to a feeling of persecution." At the same time, it projects the libido, or life instinct, outward, thereby creating an ideal object:

> The infant's aim is to try to acquire, to keep inside and to identify with the ideal object, seen as life-giving and protective, and to keep out the bad object and those parts of the self which contain the death instinct. The leading anxiety in the paranoid-schizoid position

> "THESE WOMEN ARE BOUND BY THEIR ROOTS; AND THEIR BOND REFLECTS NOT ONLY LOVE, BUT HATE. FOR IN THE WORLD OF THESE PLAYS, BLOOD IS A SIGN OF GUILT AND BIRTH IS A RESULT OF RAPE. SARAH WISHES TO EXTRICATE HERSELF FROM HER ROOTS, BUT SHE SIMULTANEOUSLY ENMESHES HERSELF IN THEIR WEB. THE PAST— LIKE EVERY ASPECT OF HER LIFE— EMBODIES BOTH PERSECUTORY AND IDEAL."

> is that the persecutory object or objects will get inside the ego and overwhelm and annihilate both the ideal object and the self.

Klein, according to Hanna Segal, calls this stage the paranoid-schizoid position because the infant's fears demonstrate a paranoia which is characterized by splitting. Kennedy's characters, likewise, attempt to order their anxieties by splitting and projecting them onto persecutory and ideal objects.

Funnyhouse of a Negro, Kennedy's first-published and most famous play, vividly reflects Klein's theories of object relations. The cast of characters includes "Negro-Sarah" and the four "selves" she creates through projective identification: the Duchess of Hapsburg, Queen Victoria Regina, Jesus, and Patrice Lumumba. Other characters include Sarah's Jewish-poet-boyfriend, Raymond, and her landlady, Mrs. Conrad. Sarah's mother appears as an apparition crossing the stage. An author's note at the beginning of the text suggests: "*Funnyhouse of a Negro* is perhaps clearest and most explicit when the play is placed in the girl Sarah's room. The center of the stage works well as her room, allowing the rest of the stage as the place for herselves.... When she is placed in her room with her belongings, then the director is free to let the rest of the play happen around her." Sarah, thus, has split into four majestic selves who occupy the space around her and seemingly take over her world.

When Sarah first appears in the play, she is "*a faceless, dark character with a hangman's rope about her neck and red blood on the part that would be her face.*" In the final scene, "*we see her hanging in [her] room.*" Rosemary K. Curb suggests [in "Fragmented Selves in Adrienne Kennedy's *Funnyhouse of a Negro* and *The Owl Answers*] that this play, "set in the central character's mind, portray[s] the elusive, almost timeless moment just before death, when horrifying images and past events replete with monotonous conversations kaleidoscopically flash through the memory and imagination of the protagonist." *Funnyhouse of a Negro* is a surrealistic vision of death and oppression, operating on the level of morbid fantasy to depict the mind of a young woman who cannot distinguish the persecutory object from the ideal.

The "action" of the play consists of a series of monologues spoken by Sarah's selves. Even when two appear together, they fail to engage in dialogue; instead, one continues a haunted monotone at the point at which another leaves off. Queen Victoria and the Duchess of Hapsburg meet in the Queen's chamber, but their identities seem questionable: they seem not to know who they are. They speak the lines of Sarah's selves, of British royalty appropriated by a schizoid African-American woman who both represses and projects. They speak of themselves as Duchess and Queen but they speak too of their father in the jungle and the harm he has done their (Sarah's) mother. In subsequent scenes, the selves appear in various combinations, contradicting and corroborating one another's narratives. Sarah's inner world is unstable; the characters who exist outside it, however, are reductive and unresponsive. Mrs. Conrad reduces Sarah's projections to a mundane insanity, offering rational explanations for Sarah's seemingly irrational behavior. Like Mrs. Conrad, Raymond exists both within and outside of Sarah's hallucinations. The "*funnyman of the funnyhouse,*" he tortures Sarah's selves with coldness. His clinical distance borders on sadism and characterizes his attitude throughout the play. In the last scene he discovers Sarah's body and tersely comments: "She was a funny little liar"—leaving the audience to wonder whether or not she was a liar at all. Raymond fully embodies the persecutory object, but the four internalized selves present more equivocal positions: they cannot be neatly categorized.

Much has been written of Sarah's "choices" for her projections; most critics agree with Herbert Blau's assertion [in "The American Dream in American Gothic: The Plays of Sam Shepard and Adrienne Kennedy"] that Sarah's is "a psyche formed by white culture which she finds not contemptible but beautiful, more maybe than black is beautiful," and that, as a result, she finds the Queen and Duchess enviable and Patrice Lumumba frightening. "It is [Lumumba]," writes Robert Scanlan [in "Surrealism as Mimesis: A Director's Guide to Adrienne Kennedy's *Funnyhouse of a Negro*"], "who separates Sarah from her white ancestry and the white European royalty she so admires. The Duchess of Hapsburg and Queen Victoria are figures of white and female power she would like to identify with, were it not for her Negro hair." Lorraine A. Brown follows this same line of reasoning [in "For the Characters Are Myself: Adrienne Kennedy's *Funnyhouse of a Negro*"]: "If [Sarah] has chosen Victoria and the Duchess of Hapsburg to escape the sense of powerlessness, she has also chosen them, we suspect, to escape the implication of debased sexuality attached to a Black girl." Curb corroborates these theories, writing of all Kennedy's characters: "They are mentally and emotionally torn between their real external Black selves and the glorious dream White selves which they imagine and desire." And Werner Sollors further develops the distinctions between the black and white selves and finds the selves "in sharp, deadly conflict" [in "Owls and Rats in the American Funnyhouse: Adrienne Kennedy's drama"]:

> [Kennedy] portrays her central character not as unified or whole but as a collage of multifaceted and contradictory selves (who are not only black and white, or male and female, but also father's daughter and mother's daughter, ruler and martyr, stoic and revolutionary, dead and alive, carnal and spiritual, young and old, hairy and bald, glamorous and humble, or proper and lascivious). The antithesis between Victoria and Lumumba may thus be seen as that between empire and anticolonialism; Jesus and the Duchess of Hapsburg may relate to each other as love and lust; the Duchess and Victoria may represent the conflict between a scandalous and a proper woman; Lumumba and Jesus may embody militancy and forgiveness.

These critics see Sarah's selves as antitheses; they see her inner turmoil caused by the inherent conflicts she embodies. Curb calls Sarah "the battlefield for warring forces forever opposed and terrified of invasion." These theories coincide with Klein's model of splitting and projective identification in which objects are split between good and bad, ideal and persecutory. Sarah splits not objects but selves, to which she attributes both attractive and repulsive qualities. However, Sarah's splitting is not as decisive as she might wish and it is ultimately unsuccessful.

Splitting and projective identification are methods used to order experience, to break it into manageable pieces. Like the infant who divides and deflects, Sarah too strives for integration: "She is attempting to reintegrate by simple assertion a shattered sense of self." Scanlan calls Sarah's story "a heroic attempt at psychic survival" and explains that through her monologues, she attempts to define herself: "She is composing her life with words." Sarah, however, cannot compose herself; she finds integration impossible. Her splitting process differs from that of the normal infant: "In situations of anxiety the split is widened and projection and introjection are used in order to keep persecutory and ideal objects as far as possible from one another, while keeping both of them under control." If Sarah's selves could be divided into bad and good, then she might maintain their separation from one another and control them. In her inherent confusion, however, Sarah cannot separate bad from good, and the manifested selves become no less complex than the original. She projects both persecutory and ideal qualities onto each self, finally causing them to implode and self-destruct.

In Sarah's first monologue she explains that her room is Queen Victoria's chamber: "Partly because it is consumed by a gigantic plaster statue of Queen Victoria who is my idol and partly for other reasons." When she is the Duchess of Hapsburg, she says, she sits opposite Victoria and they talk: "Victoria always wants me to tell her of whiteness. She wants me to tell her of a royal world where everything and everyone is white and there are no unfortunate black ones." Queen Victoria represents both self and other: sometimes Sarah speaks to her; sometimes she *is* her. The statue itself is an ideal object, one which Sarah wants "to acquire, to keep inside and to identify with"; thus she has purchased the statue, brought it home, and built three steps as its shrine. It is also, however, "bad and threatening to the ego, giving rise to a feeling of persecution"— for this statue speaks of eliminating the "unfortunate black ones" of whom Sarah is one. "Raymond says it is a thing of terror, possessing the quality of nightmares, suggesting large and probable deaths. And of course he is right," says Sarah. One death it suggests is her own, and she knows that. Yet she is attracted to the Queen for her power, her propriety, her heritage. Libido meets death in Queen Victoria—in a statue which unifies Sarah's greatest fears and desires and embodies them in "*astonishing repulsive whiteness*"—a whiteness signifying both honor and death.

Each of Sarah's four selves is equally multifarious. Patrice Lumumba, an African nationalist leader, was the first prime minister of the Democratic Republic of the Congo (subsequently Zaire); he was assassinated shortly after being forced out of office. Kennedy personally mourned his loss [in *People who Led to My Plays*], which affected her own sense of identity: "Just when I had discovered the place of my ancestors, just when I had discovered this African hero, he had been murdered. . . . Even though I had known him so briefly, I felt I had been struck a blow. He became a character in my play . . . a man with a shattered head." To Kennedy, Lumumba represents the African hero; to Sarah, he represents both the African hero and her father. The Lumumba she projects—"*a black man. His head appears to be split in two with blood and tissue in [his] eyes. He carries an ebony mask*"—combines her visions of both martyr and oppressor. Like her father, Lumumba is a "*large dark faceless Man,*" and like her father he has attempted to save the African people. However, in his hand he carries her father's murder weapon, as he himself admits: "I [have] bludgeoned my father's face with the ebony mask." In this self, then, Sarah combines her aggressions and her affections toward her father and her African heritage; she does not divide them into two distinct selves. In terms of Sarah's sanity, Lumumba becomes a failed projection; he does not provide separate outlets for pleasure and pain.

Like Lumumba, the Jesus Sarah projects is also maimed. He is characterized as a dwarf (which Scanlan proteste as "reprehensible exploitation of a medical condition"). Jesus is physically diminutive and deformed (by his hunchback). Furthermore, his "*yellow*" skin implies impurity, as if he has been "infected" by jaundice or blackness. Throughout his scenes on stage, he seems to scream as much as talk, and when his hair falls out, he is described as "*hideous.*" This Jesus seems physically impotent; one might assume the same of his spirituality. Yet Jesus is considered a savior, even within the context of the play; Sarah's grandmother had wanted her son to *be* Jesus, "to walk in Genesis and save the race." And Sarah wants to be saved. She sees in Jesus her father's dreams but she cannot project these visions into an ideal object. Her father's noble dreams have turned to nightmares, just as

Jesus has transformed into a hunchbacked, yellow-skinned dwarf.

The Duchess of Hapsburg, the wife of Austrian archduke Maximilian, is the most ambivalent historical self. Maximilian was appointed Emperor of Mexico, having been duped into thinking the Mexican people wanted a monarchy. When Napoleon III withdrew his troops from Mexico, the Hapsburgs were left at the mercy of the revolutionaries, penniless and desperate. The Duchess set sail for Europe to ask Napoleon III for aid, and when he refused her, she went to Rome to ask the Pope. "In the Vatican, [she] collapsed, drifted away into a nightmare world of schizophrenia" [according to Dorothy Gies McGvigan in *The Hapsburgs*] Back in Mexico, Maximilian was shot as a traitor. These events are dramatized in the 1939 film *Juarez*, in which Bette Davis plays Carlotta and Brian Aherne, Maximilian. The film, which Kennedy admired so much that she took her family to visit the Hapsburgs' home in Mexico, emphasizes the Duchess's power over her husband but also her failures. It was she who had encouraged him to accept the throne of Mexico and it was she who connived in persuading him into keeping it once he discovered the adverse sentiment of the people. Yet she remains a sympathetic figure for two reasons: the first, that she loves her husband immeasurably; the second, that she accepts total responsibility for her actions. When she finds out she cannot bear children, she offers to leave her husband so he can find a wife who can; and when she realizes how Napoleon has turned on them, she sees it as her duty to confront him. The truth, however, is too much for her to bear, and she spends her last days envisioning her husband's death and shrieking his name. The Duchess of Hapsburg seems an odd choice for a figure of female power. She was beautiful and powerful but she was also childless, miserable, and ultimately insane. Onto this conflicted figure Sarah projects her nightmares and fantasies, appropriately united in a figurehead who has flourished and failed.

In the early scene in the Queen's chamber, ravens fly about the room as the two women stand by the bed. They wear royal white gowns to match the white satin curtain, of which we are told, "*parts of it are frayed and look as if it has been gnawed by rats.*" They wear white headpieces that fall over their faces, and from "*beneath both their headpieces springs a headful of wild kinky hair.*" Sarah's split perception is evident from this image of deathly white and living black. The faces are grotesque:

They look exactly alike and will wear masks or be made up to appear a whitish yellow. It is an alabaster face, the skin drawn tightly over the high cheekbones, great dark eyes that seem gouged out of the head, a high forehead, a full red mouth and a head of frizzy hair. If the characters do not wear a mask then the face must be highly powdered and possess a hard expressionless quality and a stillness as in the face of death.

The Queen and the Duchess, in light of this description, hardly seem enviable. They may once have been "glorious dream White selves," but by now they have been mutilated along with the rest, their deaths more prominent in Sarah's mind than their lives. The fact that they look exactly alike—neither like Bette Davis nor Queen Victoria, but both mangled white corpses with bright red lips—implies that Sarah has lost sight of who they once were. Rather than absorbing the Queen's and Duchess's personalities into herself, she has projected herself onto them. In their voices she hears her worst fears and in their faces she sees her death. "I want not to be," says Sarah. "I ask nothing except anonymity." Rather than embellishing herself with the regal powers of these women, she imposes on them her own negation.

Sarah's desire "not to be" seems at odds with her projections, four figures etched into history by both heritage and achievement. Yet in choosing them, she effectively erases them, stripping their identities and their pasts. Death is part of their attraction, for Sarah wishes she too were dead. "My white friends, like myself, will be shrewd, intellectual and anxious for death. Anyone's death," she says, and Patrice Lumumba repeats her words almost exactly. She associates whiteness with death—from the expressionless alabaster faces of the Duchess and Queen to the frayed satin nightgown of her mother. The imagery throughout the play is white and black (with red exceptions: the Queen's and the Duchess's lips, the bags of hair, the comb), even the lighting in the Queen's chamber: "*It is set in the middle of the Stage in a strong white LIGHT, while the rest of the Stage is in unnatural BLACKNESS. The quality of the white light is unreal and ugly.*" The statue of Queen Victoria is also described as white: "*The figure of Victoria is a sitting figure, one of astonishing repulsive whiteness, suggested by dusty volumes of books and old yellowed walls.*" White is a sign of death, suggestive of corrosion and decay. But black is also a sign of death: black ravens fly about the Queen's chamber and the death mask Lumumba carries is ebony. The rooms of Sarah's mind are filled with death; visually, they offer no possibility of life; even the red signifies hair loss, the onslaught of madness.

When Sarah first introduces herself and describes her four rooms, she explains: "These are the places myselves exist in. I know no places. That is, I cannot believe in places." Place, for her, suggests a concreteness which implies potential connections—impossible connections:

> To believe in places is to know hope and to know the emotion of hope is to know beauty. It links us across a horizon and connects us to the world. I find there are no places only my funnyhouse. Streets are rooms, cities are rooms, eternal rooms. I try to create a space for myselves in cities, New York, the midwest, a southern town, but it becomes a lie.

Sarah feels neither linked nor connected to the world; she feels she does not exist in a concrete place with other people but only in her mind, her "rooms," her funnyhouse. The physical world is closed to her, much as her rooms are closed to the world. Although she physically exists in Mrs. Conrad's rooming house, she does not recognize that location. "Sarah, whose ancestors are all out of place, found herself in a kind of limbo, unable even to 'stay in her place' because there was not one for her." [according to Linda Kintz in *The Subject's Tragedy: Political Poetics, Feminist Theory, and Drama.*] She has begun to erase place as she has begun to erase herself (and herselves), creating a continuum of rooms which, like herselves, are contaminated objects—neither ideal nor persecutory, but both ideal and persecutory, the deadly combination. The very spaces suffocate her.

Julia Kristeva [in "Women's Time," in *The Kristeva Reader,* edited by Toril Moi] discusses time and space as respective male and female realms: "And indeed, when evoking the name and destiny of women, one thinks more of the *space* generating and forming the human species than of *time,* becoming or history." She recalls that for Freud "hysteria was linked to place" and suggests,

> Subsequent studies on the acquisition of the symbolic function by children show that the permanence and quality of maternal love condition the appearance of the first spatial references which induce the child's laugh and then induce the entire range of symbolic manifestations which lead eventually to sign and syntax.

Maternal love, then, is a precondition of spatial awareness, laughter, and language. In the context of Kennedy's play, this theory can be directly applied: Sarah's mother never loved her, never recognized her as her own, and Sarah is severely lacking in the skills cited by Kristeva. Her language and her laughter are severely impaired: she finds herself unable to communicate in spite of her speeches, and the laughter in her world is replaced by screams. Space, for her, has become an internal arena, no longer reflective of the external.

Her rejection by her mother and her subsequent social sufferings align Sarah with the characters of Samuel Beckett: "The urge to get 'unborn,' to shrink back to nonexistence... pervades his oeuvre." [according to Bennett Simon in "The Fragmented Self, the Reproduction of the Self, and Reproduction in Beckett and in the Theater of the Absurd," in *The World of Samuel Beckett,* edited by J.H. Smith]. Mouth, the speaking character in Beckett's *Not I,* shares a great deal in common with Sarah. The deficiencies Kristeva describes are prominent in Mouth, who does not differentiate between signifiers and their referents: if the mouth is hers, it is her. She projects her whole self onto this "object" much as Sarah projects her whole self—and not merely the ideal or the persecutory—onto herselves, so that, like Sarah, Mouth has no chance for integration. Beckett's old woman, like Sarah, is a prisoner of object relations; she has split herself in two, reducing herself to an incessantly speaking Mouth and a silent Auditor. Bennett Simon, in his discussion relating Bion's theories of object relations to Beckett's plays, concludes [in "The Imaginary Twins: The Case of Beckett and Bion"]: "Bion's theory-making is instigated by the problems posed by patients who cancel out the distinction between animate and inanimate by making everything inanimate and concrete. These patients practise the opposite of primitive animism—they infuse all living things with the quality of death." In support of this theory, the old woman splits herself into two "objects" which forebode death: the detached mouth and its silent, hooded auditor. Likewise, Sarah bedecks herselves with death masks and blood; however, hers is a two-step process. She must bring her historical figures to life before she can kill them.

"The counterpoint between stage and text," writes Paul Lawley [in "Counterpoint, Absence and the Medium in Beckett's *Not I*"] of Beckett's *Not I,* "enacts the play's fundamental conflict: between the need to deny the imperfect self and to maintain, even in agony, a fictional other, and the wish for oblivion which would come with the acknowledgment of the fragmented self." This sentence could apply equally well to *Funnyhouse of a Negro,* in which Sarah's denial of herself (of her past, of her guilt) conflicts with her creation of herselves. Lawley argues that the striking stage image of Beckett's play contradicts the Mouth's desire not to be: there she is. She is, however, much reduced. Sarah, on the contrary, has been multiplied. While trying to erase herself, she has instead created four repetitions. Sarah's hallucinations are of a grand scale while Mouth's are minuscule. Yet they share a common goal of self-obliteration, and they share a common sadness that they were not aborted before birth. In his essay "The Fragmented Self, the Reproduction of the Self, and Reproduction in Beckett and in the Theatre of the Absurd," Simon focuses on such processes of splitting and fragmentation as peculiar aspects of modernism: "[I]n the twentieth century... the self is disintegrated, deconstructed, shadowed, fragmented, submerged, unstable, and scarcely able to tell a coherent story." He correlates these self-destructive processes with modern and postmodern concerns about reproduction: "The modern problematic of the self goes hand in glove with a set of modern concerns and anxieties about conception and contraception." Such anxieties, which clearly dominate the writing of both Kennedy and Beckett, link together playwrights of absurdist drama: "The theatre of the absurd is a dramatic culture that has been marked from its beginning with a preoccupation with birth and reproduction."

"*Funnyhouse of a Negro*... grows out of the absurdist and expressionist traditions yet forges a style of its own." [according to David Willinger in the Review of *Funnyhouse of a Negro*....] Kennedy's writing is ultimately original, incorporating absurdist elements yet creating something very different. Her play lacks the humor and the sense of the ludicrous which characterize the absurd; her characters' detachment is not ironical but imposed. Their world is not fundamentally without meaning, but such meaning is deliberately withheld. Here, feelings of detachment are not philosophical but physical, resulting from mortal violence. "An important part of the absurd," according to Simon, "is the sense of being cut off from the roots and, as a usually unstated corollary, of having no branches, no offshoots, no descendants." Kennedy's characters, to the contrary, feel very much attached to their roots—roots which shackle and suffocate them. They have too many roots, knotted, tangled roots which pull them in opposing directions, like the life and death instincts which divide them. These women are bound by their roots; and their bond reflects not only love, but hate. For in the world of these plays, blood is a sign of guilt and birth is a result of rape. Sarah wishes to extricate herself from her roots, but she simultaneously enmeshes herself in their web. The past—like every aspect of her life—embodies both persecutory and ideal.

Sarah transforms her world into a house of mirrors where she watches herselves in the glass; she becomes an outsider observing her life. She speaks objectively and emotionlessly about herself and seems detached from her past even as she recreates it, never mentioning the noose on her neck or her imminent death. She speaks in the present tense of what was and gives her past to her four historical projections in hopes of self-eradication. Instead, her voice is multiplied by four, her image refracted by funnyhouse mirrors which trap her amidst their reflections.

Source: Claudia Barnett, "A Prison of Object Relations: Adrienne Kennedy's *Funnyhouse of a Negro*," in *Modern Drama*, Fall, 1997, Vol. 40, no. 3, pp. 374–84.

Susan E. Meigs

In the following essay, Meigs treats Sarah's multiple selves as masks that represent an imprisonment that keeps Sarah, like many African-American women, from having the power "to resolve the chaotic elements of their black female identities."

> *I know no places. That is I cannot believe in places. To believe in places is to know hope and to know the emotion of hope is to know beauty. It links us across a horizon and connects us to the world. I find there are no places only my funnyhouse*
> —Adrienne Kennedy, *Funnyhouse of a Negro*

In 1960, while dramatists were forging a rhetoric of black theater from the emerging black power movement, twenty-nine-year-old Adrienne Kennedy travelled to Africa with her husband and son. The trip would prove to be the catalyst for her career as one of America's most complex contemporary playwrights. At the time of her trip, Kennedy had been writing stories and plays for nearly ten years and had received virtually no public attention. Her failure to establish herself as a writer was made more discouraging by the recognition her husband Joseph Kennedy received for his work in social psychology at Columbia. She felt increasingly [in *People Who Led to My Plays*] that she "was just accompanying another person as he lived out his dreams" and that she had acquiesced "to another person's desires, dreams and hopes." As she struggled to maintain her identity as a black woman author and attempted to invest herself in the Western literary tradition she embraced, Kennedy grew conscious of a buried African heritage. Africa opened to her a world of black artists and leaders, like Congo Prime Minister

Patrice Lumumba, to match and challenge the Western literary figures and rulers she admired. The conflict between these two ancestral traditions would become one of the primary themes in Kennedy's complex, surrealistic psychodramas.

Although her rhetoric maintains a political agenda, albeit one aimed more at expressing black women's struggles, Kennedy's method draws from the mythic elements of traditional African ritual drama, particularly the Kuntu form described by Paul Carter Harrison. Ritual drama empowers its participants as they negotiate their roles within its theatrical community. Kennedy discovered, however, that these roles, designated like those in many black protest groups by men, fail to allow female participants self-determination. This dissonance in the fragmented black family/community impedes the collective expression of harmony required of ritual theater. "Having been fractionalized, [the black American's] rituals are often played out in a spiritual vacuum, [her] energies dissipated without the generative feedback of a stable society." [according to P.C. Harrison in *The Drama of Nommo.*] Kennedy's plays address the cultural and political fragmentation of black Americans that occurs when a dominant (white) social structure interrupts efforts to construct a black community.

Kennedy uses this damaged social identity in her plays as a symptom of the deeper psychological fragmentation black women suffer. Kennedy particularly uses the mask, a traditional symbol of power and mystery, as a device to develop what Michael Goldman [in *The Actor's: Toward a Theory of Drama*] calls "the double movement of dramatic elation—both escape from self and self-discovery." Kennedy undermines this empowerment and elation, however, and transforms the mask into an image of imprisonment and terror. Many of her characters become trapped in the mask's freakish impersonality and are unable either to discover themselves fully or to escape from the horrifying selves they do discover.

In three of Kennedy's plays, *Funnyhouse of a Negro* (1964), *The Owl Answers* (1965), and *A Movie Star Has to Star in Black and White* (1976), the protagonists are black women who fail to unite the fragmented elements of their identities into harmonic, dynamic wholes. Their equally fragmented communities have failed to provide them with the ritual means for locating themselves and have made them feel guilty for recognizing the extra measure of alienation assigned to black women. These char-

"SARAH, ULTIMATELY POWERLESS TO RECONCILE AND INTEGRATE HER CONFLICTING SELVES AND INCONGRUENT HISTORICAL NARRATIVES, CHOOSES TO ABANDON THE WHITE FUNNYHOUSE. THAT SARAH RECOGNIZES NO ESCAPE OTHER THAN SUICIDE TESTIFIES TO THE INSIDIOUSNESS OF HER TRAGEDY."

acters represent the community of women, largely excluded from the political mechanisms of black protest, who are nonetheless expected to sacrifice gender issues for racial concerns. In these three one-act plays, Kennedy exposes how black Americans, especially women, having been denied a social context and history, are therefore powerless to resolve the chaotic elements of their black female identities.

In *Funnyhouse of a Negro,* Sarah seeks to find herself among four historical figures who share her voice: Queen Victoria, the Duchess of Hapsburg, Jesus, and Patrice Lumumba. Although she lives in a brownstone with her Jewish boyfriend, she mentally inhabits the expressionistic settings suggested by these figures. After her mad mother introduces the play's action, Sarah and her selves confront her fear that her father will find and rape her as he did her mulatto mother. She imagines his various fates, including one in which she bludgeons him with an ebony mask. Herself a mulatto, Sarah's conflicting racial histories are illustrated but never resolved by the figures that serve as her masks. Far from empowering her, these character masks trap Sarah in a role of self-hatred, fear, and the inability to integrate her personality that leads to her suicide.

Kennedy introduces the mask motif in the play's first sequence. Sarah's mad mother passes before the closed curtain wearing an eyeless yellow mask that renders her not only blind but faceless. She gropes across the stage in a dreamlike state we later learn is death, separated from the "life" of the play only by the rat-eaten shroud of a white stage curtain. She carries before her a bald head, an image of weakness that recurs as Sarah's selves lose their wild, kinky hair throughout the play. Although Kennedy later introduces a bald head that drops and hangs from the ceiling to indicate the martyrdom of Christ and Lumumba, the baldness of Victoria and the Duchess is more "hideous" and frightening because it links them to Sarah's dead mother. For Sarah, baldness indicates not only death but also a life of repulsion, vulnerability, and madness. As her female selves lose their hair, the threat of her father's return, of a confrontation with her irreconcilable blackness, grows imminent. Unable to cope with the jungle's darkness, Sarah attempts to hide herself in a white city.

During the course of the play, two historical characters who represent her white heritage assume Sarah's psychological narrative. These alter-egos, Queen Victoria and the Duchess of Hapsburg, also wear white, expressionless death masks and are cast in a strong white light that contrasts with the stage's unnatural darkness. These other selves express Sarah's thoughts while the connotations of their historical identities comment on them. The sense of power and authority evoked by the two European rulers cannot be appropriated properly by Sarah, who is neither white nor black. Their imperialistic implications comment on the extent of Sarah's psychological oppression, one history a victim of the other. Nonetheless, she spends her days writing poetry that imitates Edith Sitwell's and dreaming of living in a white, European culture. She attempts to efface her black heritage not only by "killing" her father but by injecting herself into white society. She claims [in *Funnyhouse of a Negro*] to need these white figures "as an embankment to keep me from reflecting too much upon the fact that I am a Negro. For, like all educated Negroes . . . I find it necessary to maintain a stark fortress against recognition of myself." The expressionless masks of the two rulers serve both to identify an aspect of Sarah's historical identity and to alienate her from it. In the play's final scene, Sarah is discovered hanging from the ceiling of her "funnyhouse" as the lights come up on the white plaster statue of Queen Victoria. Enshrined in Sarah's room, she is finally reduced to a voiceless, immobile image of "astonishing repulsive whiteness." When Sarah dies, the masked figures that have given body to her voice are stripped of their narrative power. They become hollowed references to a history that is finally unavailable to Sarah.

The persona of Patrice Lumumba, whom Sarah both adopts and associates with her father, differs from the first two in that he is black and carries rather than wears his ebony mask. Because Lumumba acts as a bridge between Sarah and her father, he represents both the black man's noble efforts to save his race and her inescapable and damning blackness. Lumumba, murdered by African radicals who smashed his skull, appears in the play with a split and bleeding head. At one point, as Sarah explains how she killed her father, she confuses him with Lumumba: "No, Mrs. Conrad, he did not hang himself, that is only the way they understood it, they do, but the truth is that I bludgeoned his head with an ebony skull that he carries about with him. Wherever he goes, he carries out black masks and heads." Sarah's previous statements about her desires to integrate into white society are repudiated by an unidentified black man who recalls Lumumba because he too carries his mask: "I am a nigger of two generations. I am Patrice Lumumba. . . . I am the black shadow that haunted my mother's conception. . . . It is my vile dream to live in rooms with European antiques and my statue of Queen Victoria."

Because Sarah is a mulatto, she cannot wear the masks of both the Negro and the white woman simultaneously. As the mask signifies the character's fragmented identity, the mulatto bastard becomes a metaphor for the black woman's alienation from her gender and her race. Sarah attempts to reconcile her identity as a mulatto by claiming to have murdered her black father. She is unable to conceal her hatred of him for literally blackening her family. Sarah conflates her story with his story as she recalls how her grandmother encouraged her father to become a black Messiah. Sarah believes he betrayed her wish and his future family by marrying a light-toned woman with "hair as straight as any white woman's." His mother "hoped he would be Christ but he failed. He had married [Sarah's] mother because he could not resist the light. Yet, his mother from the beginning in the kerosene lamp of their dark rooms in Georgia said, 'I want you to be Jesus, to walk in Genesis and save the race, return to Africa, find revelation in the black.'" To fulfill his mother's vision, he takes his white wife to Africa to pursue mission work. There she "falls out of live" with him and slowly goes mad, symbolized by her gradual hair loss. He rapes her when she denies him access to the marriage bed because he is black and creates a legacy of violence, madness, and failure for their daughter Sarah. "'Forgiveness for my being black, Sarah. I *know* you are a child of torment.... *Forgive my blackness!*'" her father pleads. But Sarah can neither accept nor escape her own blackness: "before I was born," she laments, "he haunted my conception, diseased my birth."

Sarah seeks to neutralize her blackness by living with her white boyfriend, Raymond Mann, whom she wishes she could love but doesn't, in an apartment run by a white landlady, Mrs. Conrad. These two white characters in Sarah's "funnyhouse" are modelled after the looming clownlike figures that guard an amusement park in Kennedy's hometown, Cleveland. The set for the scene in which Raymond and the Duchess of Hapsburg engage in a bizarre exchange includes a backdrop of mirrors, revealed only as Raymond alternately opens and closes the blinds that conceal them. The flashing mirrors recall the disorienting nightmare quality of what is ironically called a funnyhouse. Raymond and Mrs. Conrad laugh, in accordance with their roles as funnyhouse guards, at Sarah's bewilderment and failure to distinguish herself from her historical reflections. They mock her attempts to gain self-knowledge and control over the conflicting elements of her persona. When she is unable to do so, Sarah hangs herself. After discovering her body, Mrs. Conrad and Raymond suggest that Sarah's father is not dead but lives in a white suburb with a white prostitute. He and his "whore" join the other white characters in the funnyhouse who, in refusing to understand or sympathize with Sarah's internal struggle, derive ironic amusement from her desperate suicide. "'She was a funny little liar,'" Raymond comments as he observes her hanging figure. Mrs. Conrad can only offer the unsympathetic remark, "'The poor bitch has hung herself!'" Sarah, ultimately powerless to reconcile and integrate her conflicting selves and incongruent historical narratives, chooses to abandon the white funnyhouse. That Sarah recognizes no escape other than suicide testifies to the insidiousness of her tragedy. Unable to move beyond feebly articulating her oppression, Sarah can neither appropriate the power of her masks, as Harrison might suggest, nor follow the mandate of Amiri Baraka's militant theater to create white-free spaces for blacks. To excise her whiteness would leave Sarah vulnerable to a terrifying blackness she cannot control....

Source: Susan E. Meigs, "No Place but the Funnyhouse: The Struggle for Identity in Three Adrienne Kennedy Plays," in *Modern American Drama: The Female Canon,* edited by June Schlueter, Fairleigh Dickinson University Press, 1990, pp. 172–183.

Lorraine A. Brown

In the following essay, Brown sees the play as a world in which "Blackness, femaleness, and education are equally important isolating factors."

For the days are past when there are places and characters with connections with themes as in the stories you pick up on the shelves of public libraries.... There is no theme. No statements.... For the statement is the characters and the characters are myself.

These words spoken by Sarah, the young Negro student, in Adrienne Kennedy's play, *Funnyhouse of a Negro,* apply both to Sarah's own troubled personal world and to the felicitous form of the play itself. An ornate dramatic image, reflecting kinship with and absorption of the work of Samuel Beckett and Jean Genet, this original and penetrating play makes use of surrealistic and expressionistic modes to explore the mind and emotions of an educated Black girl. The play projects a world, in fact, where Blackness, femaleness, and education are equally important isolating factors. This exploration is accomplished structurally by the creation of a rich montage of images and impressions which appear, fade, and recur. The action takes the form of separate scenes made up of monologues, dialogues, or pantomimes, and identical grotesque figures dressed up in cheap white satin also move across the stage, sometimes shouting, sometimes screaming, carrying their bald skulls before them. The scenes occur at various levels and specific areas of the stage, which are illuminated and blacked out as the play proceeds. All of the characters except for Sarah and her father appear in white face, and the stage directions indicate the use of masks or yellow-white makeup to suggest a "hard expressionless quality" (Kennedy)—a stillness akin to death. The nightmare effect thus created by the expert use of these various dramatic resources provide the ideal means to depict the increasing terror, anguish, and fragmentation of Sarah's hallucinatory world.

When the play opens, Sarah's personality is split into four characters who represent various sides of herself: Queen Victoria, the Duchess of Hapsburg, Jesus, and Patrice Lumumba. Sarah, like Genet's characters, has chosen powerful roles which reflect political as well as spiritual dimensions. In her room, however, her creative energies find an outlet in the solitary and fruitless task of filling white pages with poetry in imitation of Edith Sitwell. Sarah's strenuous efforts to achieve wholeness and

> "THIS INTENTION TO MURDER LUMUMBA IS EXPRESSED, SHE SAYS, WITHOUT FEAR, FOR WHATEVER SHE DOES SHE DOES IN THE NAME OF GOD, ALBERT SAXE-COBURG, AND QUEEN VICTORIA—A SIGNAL THAT HER FANTASY LIFE HAS WON OUT, THAT SHE IS UNABLE TO ACCEPT HER BLACKNESS, AND THAT HER SUICIDE IS NEAR."

identity, and her concurrent contest with paranoia, self-hatred, and the will to self-destruction, ultimately result in a disintegration of her personality. But before that occurs, we observe the considerable force of her will, reminiscent of Samuel. Beckett's Winnie who also struggles so valiantly to stay in control and fend off madness. That we are allowed to experience this play from within Sarah's mind and sensibility and that the form of the play so noticeably aids our understanding of her struggle are only two measures of its fineness. Equally brilliant is the deep probing of the female psyche which reaches an admirable level of universality; Miss Kennedy demonstrates that Sarah's struggle is the struggle of all women in a world which not only mocks and rejects Blackness but femaleness as well. For the play is not about Sarah's Blackness alone, but about the combination of Blackness, femaleness, and education, which together create insurmountable barriers to wholeness and psychic balance. For each of these aspects of her consciousness only serves to increase her sense of herself as an outsider and outcast.

Central in her struggle for psychic health is the conflict which stems from her attachment to parental figures. In the first scene in the play, Sarah, as Queen Victoria, tells us that she is "tied to a black Negro" who is her father. He haunted her conception and diseased her birth, she says, and in her fantasies he returns from the jungle to find her. The father is associated in the play with bestiality, the death of her mother, and "a nigger pose of agony," but his Blackness is also identified in her mind with Africa and the need for "the Black man to make a pure statement" (Kennedy) and to rise from colonialism. One of the sides of herself is Patrice Lumumba, an indication that she has reflected on and imagined a central role for herself in the African struggle for independence. That the role is a masculine one obviously complicates the problem. For she must determine just what role an educated American Black woman has in the changing African world. Identification with this powerful male also reflects her desire to escape the powerlessness and passivity associated with being a woman. Again the problem of identification is complicated by the fact that her mother's whiteness was counteracted by her sex and her father's sex by his Blackness. This dilemma helps to explain the existence of both Queen Victoria and Patrice Lumumba in her fantasy life, a dialectic involving the widely divergent worlds of Victorian England on the one hand and the jungles of Africa on the other.

In vivid contrast to the ambivalent feelings associated with her Black father, Sarah's preoccupation with memories of her mother leads her toward the world of whiteness and concern with her own physical resemblance to that fair-skinned, gray-eyed woman with hair as straight as any white woman's. Her mother, too, haunts her. She returns in Sarah's nightmares, her bald skull shining, claiming that her baldness is a result of her rape by Sarah's father. "My Mother was the light. She was the lightest one. She looked like a white woman," Sarah-Victoria says (Kennedy). But for the girl with pale yellow skin, it is clear that identification with her mother and whiteness and rejection of her father (her one defect, she tells us, is her "unmistakably Negro kinky hair" [Kennedy]) is a move toward death. Such identification ties her to her memories of the past, helps her to evade the question of her own identity, and inhibits any growth or development. Instead it encourages her to isolate herself, to hide in her room where she dreams of living in rooms with European antiques, photographs of Roman ruins, and oriental carpets. The language Sarah uses to describe this dream reflects her tension and her straining for extreme control. The images she uses describes a state of siege: white friends to act as *embankments* to protect her from reflecting on her Blackness; a *stark fortress* against recognition of herself. However, even these white friends she distrusts, for they, like she, are preoccupied with death, anyone's death.

In her more intimate relationships, Sarah's search for love and acceptance in the white world offers her no solace or comfort. She admits she doesn't love the Jewish poet, Raymond, and he doesn't love her. He is only "very interested" in Negroes. In the scene with Raymond, when Sarah is the Duchess of Hapsburg, always freer in her behavior than Victoria, Miss Kennedy adeptly portrays Sarah's masochism. She responds wildly to Raymond's embrace, even though he is unmoved by her fears and torments, as she hears her father returning from the jungle to find her. During the scene she sits before him partially disrobed and clings to his leg, while he laughs, stares at her, and opens and closes the blinds. Disarmed and unprotected, an archetypal fallen woman, she pleads for love from the "ghostly thin" poet with black sores on his face. At other times Raymond becomes in her mind a huge grotesque amusement park funnyman who, together with her white landlady, mocks her and fills the funnyhouse world with contemptuous laughter.

If Sarah lacks significant relationships, she also lacks places to live. For to believe in places is to know hope and to know beauty, and beauty, she reasons, links one to the world and life. She disowns such connections; she prefers isolation. Consequently, Sarah knows only the places her selves exist in: a chamber in a Victorian castle, a Hapsburg chamber, the jungle, and the room where she killed her father. Her own small room is "consumed" by a seated figure of Queen Victoria, "a thing of astonishing whiteness, possessing the quality of nightmare" (Kennedy). Three steps lead to the statue, which presides opposite her door, and the room is filled with dark old volumes, a narrow bed and, on the wall, old photographs of castles and monarchs of England. The irony of Sarah's identification and empathy with the literary and historical traditions of England is brought out even more fully and explicitly in Miss Kennedy's play *The Owl Answers*. There Clara Passmore, a soft-spoken Negro school teacher from Savannah, who identifies with her white father, is cruelly rejected by Chaucer, Shakespeare, and William the Conquerer when she tries to gain entrance to St. Paul's chapel to retrieve the body of her white father. As guards, these three significant figures in Western culture (William the Conquerer had been her father's favorite) call her bastard, and ask her why, if she is Negro, she has any claim to her white father, the richest white man in Jacksonville, Georgia. This episode dramatizes most effectively the dissonance created by the devoted espousal of the cultural heritage of her white father and her own humiliating experiences of rejection and scorn from those she most venerates. We remember the forlorn figure of Clara Passmore standing alone outside of the locked Tower gates which have just been slammed shut in her face. The image describes just as effectively Sarah's isolation and alienation from the white cultural world.

Sarah's own choice of the awesome figure of Queen Victoria as one of her selves strikes us, as Samuel Beckett's Winnie would say, as being "in the old style." If she has chosen Victoria and the Duchess of Hapsburg to escape the sense of powerlessness, she has also chosen them, we suspect, to escape the implications of debased sexuality attached to a Black girl. One of Clara Passmore's selves, for instance, is the Virgin Mary, and yet in the summer in Harlem, she picks up strange men on the subway and takes them to her room to love—a dramatic internalization, one suspects, of stereotyping which divides women into saints and whores, and just as automatically attributes the role of whore to Black women. In her discussions and associations with Victoria, Sarah momentarily escapes this stigma by rejecting all Blackness. As the Duchess of Hapsburg, she actively seeks debasement by wooing Raymond.

Sarah's own spiritual link with God is, interestingly, Jesus Christ, and not the Virgin Mary. It is the second instance in the play of her identification with a male role, but this time Jesus is a yellow-skinned hunchback dwarf dressed in white rags and sandals. Sarah's ambivalence about him is reflected in her treatment of him as the Duchess of Hapsburg. In her chandeliered ballroom with its black and white marble floor, the Duchess uses the same indifference and coldness as Raymond used to reject her earlier in the play. Later, as the snow falls outside, they sit on a bench in the chamber combing each other's hair, growing hideous together. In their last scene together, Sarah, as Jesus, admits to attempting flag to escape being Black by claiming God as her father, and she vows to go to Africa to kill Patrice Lumumba because she recognizes that her father was a Black man. This intention to murder Lumumba is expressed, she says, without fear, for whatever she does she does in the name of God, Albert Saxe-Coburg, and Queen Victoria—a signal that her fantasy life has won out, that she is unable to accept her Blackness, and that her suicide is near.

Symbolically then the appropriate place for Sarah's final disintegration is the jungle. The stage directions indicate that "the jungle has overgrown all the other chambers and all the other places with a violence and a dark brightness, a grim yellowness'' (Kennedy). The scene, the longest in the play, moves slowly, as in the last stages of a dream. All of Sarah's selves appear, Jesus arriving first, a nimbus above his head. The other selves wear nimbuses, too, and they wander about speaking at the same time, repeating each other's words, chanting motifs connected with Sarah's suffering, until the tension reaches fever pitch. After an intense silence a reenactment of her father's murder occurs: the light grows bright and Sarah's mother comes smiling toward her as Sarah bludgeons her father with an ebony head. At this point the selves suddenly run about, madly laughing and shouting, creating by their words and actions a terrifying image of her complete collapse.

Miss Kennedy brings us back, in the final scene of the play, to Sarah's room, where her figure of Queen Victoria presides in all of its repulsive whiteness. There sounds again the eternal knocking which has echoed and re-echoed in the play, and suddenly her father's Black figures "with bludgeoned hands rush upon her" as the lights go dark (Kennedy). When they come up again, the laughing landlady is visible, as well as Sarah's hanging figure. Joined by Raymond, the landlady remarks, "the poor bitch has hung herself" (Kennedy). Their brutal exchange establishes at that moment an astonishing counterpoint to our own feelings of shock and outrage. The image of Sarah, that young yet ancient Negro figure, hanging amidst her dusty volumes and old yellow walls, is one that remains long in the mind. For her inability to resist the pressures of society and to resolve the conflicts which raged within her is a vivid reminder of the fragile nature of all psychic balance. Her death also emphasizes the perils of wish-fulfillment, evasion, and escape as methods of alleviating the anguish of the present moment. Even if such impulses stem quite understandably from the enormity of the problems and the intensity of the suffering, they are addictive and crippling, and Miss Kennedy reminds us of the age-old necessity of possessing one's own soul. Her view that the modern world is oblivious, if not downright hostile, to spiritual struggles links her work to that of many others writing for the contemporary theater. That her plays have gone unheralded and unappreciated is unfortunate, for Miss Kennedy is undoubtedly one of the foremost playwrights in America today.

Source: Lorraine A. Brown, "'For the Characters Are Myself': Adrienne Kennedy's *Funnyhouse of a Negro*," in *Negro American Literature Forum*, 1975, Vol. 9, pp. 86–88.

SOURCES

Billings, Joshua. A review, in *The Nation*, January 25, 1964, p. 79.

Brantley, Ben. "Theater Review: Glimpsing Solitude in Worlds Black and White," in *The New York Times*, September 25, 1995, p. C11.

Brown, Lorraine A. "'For the Characters Are Myself': Adrienne Kennedy's *Funnyhouse of a Negro*," in *Negro American Literature Forum*, 1975, p. 86.

Clurman, Harold. A review, in *The Nation*, February 10, 1964, p. 154.

Simon, John. "Playing with Herselves," in *New York*, October 9, 1995, p. 82.

Taubman, Howard. "The Theater: *Funnyhouse of a Negro*," in *The New York Times*, January 15, 1964, p. 25.

FURTHER READING

Binder, Wolfgang. "A MELUS Interview with Adrienne Kennedy," in *MELUS: The Journal of the Society for the Study of the Multi-Ethnic Literature of the United States*, Fall, 1985, p. 99.
    This interview with Kennedy includes a discussion of race, culture, and her artistic development.

Bryant-Jackson, Paul K. and Lois More Overbeck, eds. *Intersecting Boundaries: The Theatre of Adrienne Kennedy*, University of Minnesota Press, 1992, 254 p.
    A collection of critical essays on Kennedy's plays.

Farber, David R. *The Age of Great Dreams: America in the 1960s*, Hill & Wang, 1994, 296 p.
    A historical overview of the 1960s, Farber's book covers political, social, and cultural history, including the civil rights movement.

Kennedy, Adrienne. *People Who Led to My Plays*, Alfred A. Knopf, 1997, 125 p.
    A nontraditional autobiography that uses vignettes and photographs from Kennedy's life to explore her influences and interests.

The Ghost Sonata

AUGUST STRINDBERG
1907

The Ghost Sonata is one of August Strindberg's "Chamber Plays," a series of short, simple dramas he wrote for his 161-seat Intimate Theatre, which opened its doors in Stockholm, Sweden in 1907. The plays were inspired by the chamber music of composers like Joseph Haydn, Wolfgang Amadeus Mozart, and Ludwig van Beethoven. Strindberg created *The Ghost Sonata* with Beethoven's *Geistertrio,* Opus 70, No. 1, in D Major in mind, and the play echoes the style of the music. It creates an atmosphere by repeating various themes, rather than developing a story through conventional portrayals of character and a linear plot. The themes of *The Ghost Sonata* mainly relate to secrets, illusions, and the disappointments and tragedies of life, and it is the revelation of these terrible details of the characters' past lives that form the action of the play.

The Ghost Sonata does not take place in the real world; or at least not in a world most people would recognize as reality. Strindberg originally subtitled his play "Kama-Loka," the name of a mystical dream world through which some mortals have to wander before reaching the kingdom of death in the afterlife. Accordingly, the characters in *The Ghost Sonata* speak, move and act as if they are part of a dream—or a nightmare. One sees glimpses of the future, another embodies tragedies from the past. There are literal ghosts and vampires in the play, as well as a mysterious woman known as the Mummy.

The world Strindberg created in *The Ghost Sonata* was one he found in his own tortured imagi-

nation. On stage, his vision of an alternate reality was a forerunner to later twentieth century experiments in non-realistic dramatic literature, such as Expressionism, popular in Germany in the 1920s, and the Absurdist movement of the 1950s, made popular by writers like Samuel Beckett, Eugene Ionesco, and Jean Genet. When the play was originally staged at the Intimate Theatre in 1908, its strange, avant-garde style and grim view of the world made it unpopular with critics. It wasn't until the famous director Max Reinhardt staged the play in Berlin in 1916, then toured it to Strindberg's native Sweden in 1917, that it won acclaim from audiences and reviewers. Reinhardt's production toured central Europe through the 1920s, and the play was produced by Eugene O'Neill's Provincetown Players in New York in 1924 and at the Globe and Strand Theatres in London in 1926. In 1930 it was turned into an opera with music by Julius Weissmann and performed in Munich, and the British Broadcasting Corporation aired a television production of *The Ghost Sonata* in 1962. Reviewer Maurice Richardson noted that, even though the television production was probably seen by fewer than a million people, "it was probably a larger audience than the total number of people who had ever seen it before."

AUTHOR BIOGRAPHY

August Strindberg is now considered to be one of Sweden's finest dramatists and among the most important contributors to the modern theatre. His life and career at the turn of the twentieth century, however, was a twisting path of minor successes and major public humiliations, of deep psychological and spiritual turmoil, and of a love-hate relationship with women that scarred his mind and inspired him to some of his best writing. Strindberg was an author whose life was an open book. Everything he experienced and felt, from unhappy memories of his childhood to marital strife and battles with madness and despair found its way into his many novels, short stories, poems, essays and plays.

Strindberg was born in Stockholm on January 22, 1849. He was the son of a steamship agent whose family was once part of Sweden's wealthy aristocracy. His mother had been a waitress. His parents had three children—all sons—before they were married. They wed just before August was born, and had several more children, eight of whom survived. By his own admission, Strindberg felt the world was unjust toward him, that his birth into this once noble, now impoverished family was a mistake. In his autobiography *The Son of a Servant* (1886), he blames his father for marrying beneath him, reflects on the family's bankruptcy, his mother's tuberculosis and death, and the sexual conflicts he felt when his father later married the family's housekeeper. These conflicts—an attraction toward motherly figures that might provide him with the affection he craved, and a repulsion from strong, domineering, sexual women—appear repeatedly in his later plays.

Although Strindberg studied at the Swedish University of Upsala on and off for several years, he constantly experienced financial troubles and was unable to complete a degree. Still, he managed to build a wide-ranging resume. As a young man in Stockholm he worked as a teacher, a journalist, and a librarian. He briefly studied chemistry in the hope of attending medical school, but upon failing his entrance examinations he decided to become an actor. After struggling in a minor part, someone advised Strindberg that he should train at the Dramatic Academy to improve his skills. Offended at the suggestion and frustrated by his lack of respect and success, Strindberg attempted suicide by swallowing an opium pill. Instead of dying, though, he awoke from the effects of the drug with vivid memories of his childhood, which he turned into his first three plays in 1869, *The Freethinker, A Nameday Gift,* and *Hermione*.

With this early work, Strindberg earned a little recognition as an artist, but no money to support himself. For a few years he worked at various jobs while continuing to write poetry and plays, then landed a position as an assistant librarian at the Royal Library of Stockholm. He spent eight years at the library, from 1874-1882, reading and writing constantly. During this time he met his first wife, Siri von Essen. She was married to Baron Wrangel, an older man, and already had a young daughter. Strindberg frequently visited the couple, and had begun to view them as parental figures, all the while falling in love with Siri. For her part, Siri was enchanted by romantic notions of the theatre and wanted to leave her dull family life and become an actress. She divorced the Baron and married Strindberg in 1877, a scandalous move that was widely publicized.

Strindberg's marriage to Siri lasted 15 years, during which time he produced a popular autobiographical novel, *The Red Room* (1879), and several historical works that drew sharp criticism for their attacks on Sweden's establishment, causing the author to leave his country and spend the next six years in self-imposed exile, living in France, Switzerland, Germany, and Denmark. In 1884 he published *Getting Married,* a collection of scandalous short stories that drew charges of blasphemy back in Sweden. Strindberg faced a trial and was acquitted, but remained bitter about his treatment at the hands of his fellow countrymen.

While his relationship with Siri was deteriorating, and his bouts with mental illness growing more severe, Strindberg produced some of his best-known plays. *The Father* was staged in Denmark and Sweden in 1887, followed by *Miss Julie* in 1888. Strindberg divorced Siri in 1892 and married Austrian journalist Frida Uhl in the following year. He was forty-four and she was twenty-one. She left him within three months and, though she returned and they had one child together, their relationship ended permanently in 1895.

For the next few years Strindberg lived in Paris, traveled in artistic circles, and dabbled in science, the occult, and alchemy. He actually tried to discover a chemical secret for producing gold and, in the process, injured himself severely and spent several months in the hospital. In 1900 Strindberg met and married the Norwegian actress, Harriet Bosse, who was 29 years younger than him. During the year they were together, he wrote *The Dance of Death* (1900) and *A Dream Play* (1901). For the next few years Strindberg wrote nothing and many of his plays were ignored by Swedish theatres. Abroad, however, his work was being discovered by well-known authors like Henrik Ibsen, Anton Chekhov, and George Bernard Shaw.

In 1907 Strindberg founded his own Intimate Theatre in Stockholm. He wrote his four "chamber plays" for the small, 161-seat performance venue, including *The Ghost Sonata* (1907). None met with particular success, and for the last three years of his life Strindberg wrote only short articles about religion and politics. He died of stomach cancer on May 14, 1912, at the age of 63.

August Strindberg

PLOT SUMMARY

Scene One

The Ghost Sonata begins the morning after a terrible disaster. A house collapsed in Stockholm, Sweden, where the action of the play is set, and a poor student, named Arkenholz, witnessed the tragedy and spent all night tending to the wounded and dying. He appears the next morning, filthy and rumpled, at a public drinking fountain outside of an expensive city apartment house.

The Student meets a milkmaid at the fountain and tells her about his experience of the night before. The Milkmaid, it turns out, is actually an apparition, seen only by the Student. She is the first of several "ghosts" in the play. Still, she listens to him and even hands him a cup of water and helps him rinse his face with a cloth. Not far away, Jacob Hummel, an old man in a wheelchair, watches the scene and listens to the Student speak, apparently, to thin air. The Old Man has been reading about the accident, and the Student's heroics, in the newspaper, and recognizes the boy as the son of a man he once knew.

The Old Man approaches the Student and asks him questions about his life and family. The Student confesses that his father was, indeed, the merchant the Old Man remembers, though they each have a different story about the relationship the two men shared. The Student recalls his father as bankrupt and ruined, and remembers him blaming his misfortune on the Old Man. For his part, the Old Man insists it was the merchant himself who squandered his fortunes, then robbed him of his life savings. Confused about what to believe, the Student agrees to help the Old Man with "a few small services." In exchange, the Old Man will help the Student take advantage of his heroic actions and become well-known, wealthy, and happy.

The first task the Old Man assigns the Student is to attend an opera performance of "The Valkyrie" in order to meet the Colonel and the Girl, who is allegedly the Colonel's daughter. The Colonel and his daughter live in the beautiful house near the fountain—the very building the Student has been passing by each day and jealously admiring. He has had dreams of living in such a home, with a wife, two children, and a generous income. The Old Man, amused by the Student's fantasies, tells him a little about the house and describes each of its inhabitants one by one as they appear.

There is a statue of a beautiful woman, seen through a window, that represents the Mummy who lives inside. Once a lovely, radiant young lady, the Mummy is now, according to the Old Man, a half-crazed recluse who lives in a closet and worships her own statue. Seated at the window of another room is the Fiancee, a white-haired old woman who was once engaged to the Old Man. Outside on the steps are the Lady in Black and the Caretaker's Wife. The Lady in Black is the daughter of the Caretaker's Wife and the Dead Man, a former government official whose ghost now haunts the house.

Because the Student is a "Sunday child," the Old Man explains, he is able to see things others cannot. This supernatural ability allowed him to see into the future the night before, and save the inhabitants of the house that collapsed. With his second sight, he also saw the apparition of the Milkmaid at the fountain, and is now able to see the ghost of the Dead Man walk out of the house and around the corner to see how many people have come to pay their respects. The Dead Man, the Old Man explains, was a "charitable scoundrel" who gave generously to the poor in order to increase his own stature. Now the poor are lined up around the house, mourning his passing.

The house the Student so desperately wants to enter is filled with this odd collection of characters and one other figure who attracts his attention more than anyone else: the Girl. The Old Man and the Student watch as she returns from a morning of horseback riding and enters the house. The Student is struck to the soul by her beauty, and more determined than ever to do whatever the Old Man wants in order to meet her and enter her house.

The Old Man's servant, Johansson, returns from an errand in time to wheel his master around the corner of the house to watch the beggars mourn the Dead Man. While the Old Man is entertaining himself in this macabre way, Johansson returns for a brief conversation with the Student, who tries to learn more about his new benefactor. Johansson compares the Old Man to the god Thor, riding in his wheelchair chariot, and says he has the power to build and destroy both homes and lives. It is no mere coincidence that the Old Man encountered the Student and has convinced him to do his bidding. The Student suspects the Old Man has some kind of sinister plan for the inhabitants of the mysterious beautiful house, and he is ready to walk away and leave it all behind him when the Girl suddenly drops a bracelet out of her window, once again drawing the Student's rapt attention.

His mind once again occupied with thoughts of the Girl, the Student decides to stay and do whatever the Old Man asks. As if on cue, the Old Man returns, standing up in his wheelchair, which is being pulled along by a group of beggars. He shouts to the residents of the nearby homes to clap their hands, cheer and celebrate the deeds of the Student, who risked his life to save the lives of others in the accident of the day before. The Old Man boasts that, like a Sunday child, he too has the gifts of prophecy and healing. Once, he claims, he brought a drowned person back to life.

Suddenly, the Milkmaid reappears. She is making motions like a drowning person and only the Student and the Old Man can see her. Mysteriously, the Old Man is horrified at her appearance. He collapses and shouts at Johansson to quickly take him away.

Scene Two

That evening, inside the house, Bengtsson and the other servants are setting up for the inhabitants' traditional "ghost supper." Johansson has joined them as a waiter. Bengtsson explains to Johansson that they all call the event the "ghost supper" because everyone who attends looks like a ghost. They have been meeting for tea and biscuits in the same room, with the same people, sitting in silence or saying the same things for twenty years. No one ever says anything new, Bengtsson explains, for fear that their secrets will be discovered.

While revealing some of the mysteries of the house, Bengtsson introduces Johansson to the Colonel's wife, who they call the "Mummy." Once a beautiful young lady called Amelia, the Mummy has gone crazy and retreated to a closet, where she lives in the dark, hiding from the world. She cannot stand "cripples or sick people," including her own daughter, and cackles like a parrot when she speaks.

Johansson quickly realizes that this mansion, the "paradise" that the Student so desperately wanted to enter, is really a house of horrors, filled with dreadful secrets and frightening people. It is too late, though: the Colonel and the Girl met the Student at the opera, just as the Old Man planned, and they invited him home for dinner.

The Old Man (out of his wheelchair and hobbling along on crutches) arrives uninvited and demands to be let in to see the Colonel. Bengtsson runs off to fetch his master, and the Old Man sends Johansson away, leaving himself alone in the room with the statue of Amelia as a young lady. As he stands admiring the shapely marble form, he is startled to hear the parrot-like voice of the Mummy, the older Amelia, calling him from the closet.

Amelia emerges from her hiding place and explains, in a normal voice, that she lives there to avoid life, to avoid "seeing and being seen." Jacob, the Old Man, tells her he has come to see the Girl, Adele, who is actually their child from an affair they had years ago, and to take revenge on the Colonel who once stole his fiancee from him. Amelia warns Jacob that if he harms the Colonel, now the Girl's father, he will die in that very room, behind a black Japanese death screen that is standing near a couch.

The Old Man does not fear his own death, however, and explains that he must complete his revenge. He has in mind that he will help the Student become rich, and that the Student will marry the Girl, and all he needs to carry out his plan is an invitation to the ghost supper being held that evening.

The Mummy leaves to join her daughter, the Girl, in the "Hyacinth Room" next door as the Colonel arrives to speak with the Old Man. It is the moment the Old Man has been waiting for. He explains to the Colonel that he has gone around and bought up all of his promissory notes—the debts the Colonel has accumulated in order to keep up his wealthy standard of living. Now, everything the Colonel owns belongs to the Old Man, and he plans to take control of the Colonel's house.

Taking away his belongings, however, is only the beginning. One at a time, the Old Man strips the Colonel of everything he holds dear. He tells him his noble family name has actually been extinct for a century—that he is no longer a nobleman—and shows him a document of proof. He reveals that he is not actually a Colonel, since the American Volunteer Force in which he once served was disbanded and all its titles abolished. The Old Man even points out that the one-time Colonel wears a wig and false teeth and was actually once a kitchen lackey.

The Old Man's revenge, however, is not complete. He orders the Colonel to allow the ghost dinner to go on as planned so he can tear apart the entire household. One-by-one the guests arrive—the Student; Miss Beatrice von Holsteinkrona, the Old Man's former fiancee from upstairs; Baron Skanskorg, whom the Old Man recognizes as a jewel thief; and Amelia, the Mummy. When they are all seated in a circle, the Old Man reveals his plan: The Girl, his daughter, has been suffering from a mysterious illness, he explains. The sickness has actually been caused by the crimes in the air of the house, and once the crimes are exposed, and the criminals driven away, the Student and the Girl may marry and start a new life together in the house that he will give them. He tells them all their time will be up when the clock strikes.

Suddenly, the Mummy reaches up and stops the clock before it can chime. She has, symbolically, stopped time itself. Now it is she who takes control. She tells the Old Man that, in spite of their crimes, everyone in the house is good at heart, and better than him, because they regret their sins and have been long-suffering because of them. Jacob, on the other hand, denies his own crimes and pretends to be virtuous. Once, she says, he stole her heart with false promises, and they had a child together that he abandoned. Furthermore, she explains, he murdered the Consul, the Dead Man who was buried that day, by piling him with debt, and he lied to the Student about his father's debts in order to get him to do his bidding.

Bengtsson remembers the Old Man, too. Years ago the Jacob lived in Bengtsson's house like a vampire. He ate all of the nourishing food and left Bengtsson's family with watery broth, so that they nearly died of starvation. Later, he encountered the Old Man in Hamburg, where he had become a money-lender and was charged with the murder of a young girl, the Milkmaid. The Milkmaid had seen him commit a crime, and to prevent her from reporting it he had lured her out on thin ice, and she fell into the water and drowned.

Crushed by the weight of his crimes brought to light, the Old Man gives up. He hands over the Colonel's promissory notes. The Mummy now strokes Jacob like a parrot, and he cackles as she once did. She directs him to crawl into the closet where she has spent the last twenty years repenting her sins, and hang himself by the rope he has so often used to strangle the life out of others. The Old Man does as he is told, Bengtsson drags the death screen in front of the closet door, and the group of ''ghosts'' pray as the Old Man dies.

Scene Three

The final scene of the play takes place a few days after the funeral of the Old Man. The Student and the Girl are again in the Hyacinth Room, where the Girl spends all of her time when she is not outdoors. There are hyacinths of every size and color in pots and vases all around the room. Still, though the room looks beautiful and perfect, it is called the ''room of ordeals'' because it is really full of defects. It is cold and drafty, and she cannot light a fire because the chimney smokes. There is a fine writing desk that wobbles, and a pen-holder that is constantly covered in ink.

The Girl explains all of this to the Student, who is amazed by the imperfections of the house he once thought was paradise. Worse yet, she explains, are the servants who tend to the family. The Cook is from ''the Hummel family of vampires.'' Like the Old Man when he lived with Bengtsson, the Cook boils all of the nourishment out of the family's food before serving it to them. She drinks the soup stock herself and feeds the family watery broth. She drinks the coffee and leaves the family only grounds, and drinks the wine and fills the bottles with water. She refuses to leave, and is nearly starving the family to death.

The family also keeps a housemaid who dirties the house more than she cleans it. Every day, the Girl must tend to the stove, wash the dishes, re-make the beds, wipe the chimneys and tend to the candle wicks, because the maid does such poor work. According to the Girl, the broken house and vampire servants, who sap the family's strength and will to live, are the penalties they all pay for the sins they have committed.

The Student makes a desperate attempt to save the Girl from her poisonous environment. He asks her to become his wife, and tries to convince her that, together, they may yet find beauty and truth in the world. It is too late, though. The Student realizes that madness and suffering often lie behind beauty and the promise of life. As he laments what an awful, evil place the world is, the Girl collapses and begins to die.

Bengtsson brings the death screen from the other room and arranges it in front of the Girl while the Student welcomes the arrival of Death, who he calls the ''Liberator,'' and hopes the Girl finds peace in an afterlife that is not flawed like the mortal world of ''illusion, guilt, suffering and death.'' The lights fade, the room disappears, and an image of Arnold Bocklin's painting ''The Island of the Dead'' appears, symbolically, in the distance.

CHARACTERS

Adele

Although the Colonel believes Adele is his daughter, she is actually the child of the affair Amelia had with Jacob Hummel. Along with the Student, Adele is one of the few ''innocent'' people in the play, but she must suffer along with all of her guilty family. She has a mysterious illness which saps all of her strength. When she goes out, which is rarely, she likes to go horseback riding. When she is home, she spends her time tending her flowers in the Hyacinth Room. As Hummel finally reveals, Adele's sickness is caused by the lies and crimes of the people in the house that are polluting the air. If they were to confess all their sins and leave the house, she would be saved. It is too late, however. Despite Hummel's attempts to drive everyone from the house, and the Student's efforts at wooing her and trying to convince her there is beauty in the world, Adele collapses and dies at the end of the play.

Amelia

Amelia is the Colonel's wife. As a young lady, she was beautiful. Even at 35, she convinced the Colonel she was only 19, which is when he first married her. The Old Man tells the Student that Amelia once left the Colonel, that he beat her, and that she returned to marry him again. She went crazy and began to think she was a parrot. For twenty years she lived in a closet because her eyes could not stand the light, and her skin became pale and wrinkled, like a mummy's. During the ghost supper, when the Old Man is prepared to reveal everyone's secrets and run them out of the house, Amelia stops time by holding back the hands on the clock, and turns the tables on Hummel. Instead of allowing him to ruin them, she confronts him with all of his own crimes, and forces him to crawl into her closet where he hangs himself.

The Aristocrat

See Baron Skanskorg

Arkenholtz

Arkenholtz is a student and the son of a merchant. His father was ruined by Jacob Hummel while Arkenholtz was a very young boy. Initially, he is happy and idealistic, but by the end of the play he has learned some brutal lessons about life's lies, disappointments and tragedies. He possesses special powers because he is a "Sunday child." His supernatural birthright gives him glimpses into the future, and allows him to see ghosts where others see only empty air. This ability allowed him to save the inhabitants of an old house moments before it collapsed, and for his heroics Hummel claims he will make him a wealthy and famous man. Even more importantly, the Old Man convinces the Student he will get him introduced to the beautiful Girl, Adele, who lives inside the rich house Arkenholtz has been admiring.

Arnkenholtz is confused by Hummel, youthfully naive, and smitten with the Girl, so he agrees to help the Old Man with his strange plans to get inside the house. He is in the Hyacinth Room with Adele when Hummel attempts to ruin the Colonel and his friends, so he does not hear about everyone's crimes, or see Hummel's undignified death. After the Old Man's funeral, Arkenholtz returns to the house and tries to save Adele from her suffering and convince her to be his wife. She has been exposed to the foul air of the sinful house for too long, though, and even as he attempts to play music and sing for her, anything to break the mysterious spell that grips her, she grows weaker, and dies before him. In the end, Arkenholtz finally recognizes that the world is not always what it seems; that guilt, suffering and death often lie behind the doors of beautiful homes, and that paradise may only exist in a life after death.

Bengtsson

The Colonel's butler, Bengtsson, has seen many ups and downs in his life. He has been both master and servant to the Old Man. Once, the Old Man lived in Bengtsson's house as a vampire who tried to starve Bengtsson's family to death. Years later, Bengtsson encountered the Old Man in Hamburg, where he was a villainous money-lender who murdered the Milkmaid in order to prevent her from reporting a crime he had committed. It is Bengtsson's testimony about the Old Man's crimes at the ghost dinner that finally defeats him, and saves the inhabitants of the house from being revealed and evicted.

MEDIA ADAPTATIONS

- A television version of *The Ghost Sonata*, translated by Michael Myer and directed by Stuart Burge, was aired by the British Broadcasting Corporation on March 16, 1962. Afterward, the same production was broadcast in the United States and Australia.

- In 1930 the play was turned into an opera, with music by Julius Weissmann, and performed in Munich. The operatic *Ghost Sonata* appeared in Duisburg and Dortmund in 1956.

The Caretaker's Wife

The Caretaker's Wife helps tend the house. She once had an affair with the Consul, the Dead Man who was buried on the day the play begins. Their child is the Dark Lady.

The Colonel

As a young man, the Colonel was actually a poor kitchen servant who stole Jacob Hummel's fiancee from him. Since then, he has falsely acquired his military title and noble family name, and has borrowed large amounts of money in order to maintain a wealthy lifestyle. He married Amelia, the Mummy, when she was 35, thinking she was really a young girl. He believes the Girl is his daughter, though she is actually the child of Jacob Hummel, who had an affair with his wife, Amelia. Though he has built his entire life on a series of carefully constructed lies, he willingly and honestly admits his mistakes as the Old Man reveals them one at a time during the ghost supper.

The Cook

The Cook is somehow related to Jacob Hummel, the Old Man. As the Girl explains to the Student, she "belongs to the Hummel family of vampires." The Cook is slowly starving the Girl and her family to death by feeding them only watery broth and meat boiled clean of all nourishment. Despite the family's protests, the Cook refuses to leave, and the family is powerless and cannot drive her out. She is, the Girl claims, part of the price they all must pay for their past sins.

The Dark Lady

See The Lady in Black

The Dead Man

Described by the Old Man as "a benevolent scoundrel whose only aim in life was to have a magnificent funeral," the Dead Man was a consul who loved the uniforms, ribbons, medals and ceremonies involved with his public life as a government official. He had an affair with the Caretaker's Wife, and their daughter is the Dark Lady.

The Fiancee

See Miss Beatrice von Holsteinkrona

The Girl

See Adele

Jacob Hummel

Jacob Hummel is 80 years old and wheelchair-bound, but he has been many things in his lifetime. His servant, Johansson, describes him as "a horse-thief in the human market," someone who "steals human beings in all sorts of different ways." His main motivation in the play is revenge: Years ago the man who now calls himself the Colonel apparently stole Hummel's fiancee from him. Later, Hummel had an affair with Amelia, the Colonel's wife, and they had a daughter, Adele. Now Hummel has returned to exact his full revenge. His plan is to lie to the Student and use him to get inside the Colonel's house. Once there, he will ruin the Colonel by revealing all of the lies he has built his life on—his wealth, his noble name, his military title, and the girl he believes is his daughter. He also plans to reveal all of the crimes committed by the people in the house, and chase them all away. In the end, he hopes, Arkenholtz will marry Adele and they will live in the newly purified house together.

What Hummel does not count on, however, is his own criminal past coming back to haunt him. First Amelia stands and accuses him of lying to her, of lying to Arkenholtz, and of murdering the Dead Man by piling him with debts he could not repay. Then Bengtsson recognizes him as the man who once tried to starve his family to death, and later murdered the Milkmaid to prevent her from revealing a crime he had committed. Finally, in defeat, Hummel crawls into the Mummy's closet where he hangs himself.

Johansson

Johansson is an educated man, a bookseller who committed some kind of crime, and would have gone to jail if he had been discovered. But the Old Man knew about his indiscretion, and instead of turning him over to the law, he has made a servant out of him. Johansson serves the Old Man in exchange for food and the small amount of freedom he is allowed.

The Lady in Black

The Dark Lady is the daughter of the Dead Man and the Caretaker's Wife, and she is engaged to Baron Skanskorg.

The Milkmaid

The Milkmaid is a silent character in the play. She is the ghost of a young girl murdered in Hamburg by Jacob Hummel. She witnessed a crime Hummel committed, and to avoid being caught he lured her out onto some thin ice, and she fell through and drowned. She appears from time to time throughout the play to terrify Hummel's guilty conscience.

The Mummy

See Amelia

The Old Man

See Jacob Hummel

Baron Skanskorg

The Aristocrat, Baron Skanskorg, is the son-in-law of the Dead Man. He was once Amelia's lover, and he is now engaged to the Lady in Black, though he is still married to a wealthy baroness. His wife is divorcing him and presenting him with a stone mansion just to get rid of him. When he arrives at the ghost supper, the Old Man recognizes him as a jewel thief.

The Student

See Arkenholtz

Miss Beatrice von Holsteinkrona

The Fiancee is introduced by the Colonel as Miss Beatrice von Holsteinkrona, a reasonably wealthy, and very religious woman who lives in one of the apartments above the house. As a young woman, she was engaged to Jacob Hummel, the Old Man. The Colonel apparently seduced her away from Hummel, and the Old Man has spent the rest of his life seeking revenge.

THEMES

Illusion vs. Reality

Strindberg liked to view himself as a continual seeker of truth, as an artist who could present the sin, suffering and degradation of the world on the stage and unmask all of the world's liars, hypocrites and criminals. Several of his plays attempted to reveal what he felt were the hidden secrets of his society—its institutions and individuals. In a letter to his friend Emil Schering dating March 27, 1907, Strindberg wrote of *The Ghost Sonata*, "It is horrible, like life, when the veil falls from our eyes and we see things as they are. Secrets like these are to be found in every home. People are too proud to admit it; most of them boast of their imagined luck, and hide their misery."

The secrets of *The Ghost Sonata* are terrible indeed, and they are initially hidden behind an illusion of wealth, nobility and respect, inside the walls of a beautiful house. At the beginning of the play, the Student thinks the house is some kind of paradise. He tells the Old Man, "I often stop to look at it. I passed it yesterday when the sun was shining on the window panes, and I imagined all the beauty and luxury in there." He is willing to do anything to get inside, and to meet the lovely young girl who dwells in the house's Hyacinth Room. The Student also thinks he has found a generous benefactor in the Old Man.

What he doesn't know, however, are the past indiscretions of the people in the house, and the terrible crimes committed by the Old Man, who is now intent only on revenge. The Colonel, it is revealed, actually has no claim to a noble family or to any military titles, and all of his apparent wealth is really a pile of tremendous debts he has amassed over the years. The Colonel's wife, Amelia, was once young and beautiful, and she had an affair with the Old Man when he was a youth called Jacob Hummel. Their child was Adele, the Girl who lives in the Hyacinth Room, and thinks her father is the Colonel. The weight of Amelia's sins overcame her, and she has spent the last twenty years living in a closet, becoming pale and wrinkled like a mummy. Everyone else in the house has a similar dark past to hide. The Dead Man, the Aristocrat, the Fiancee and even the Caretaker's Wife all have built illusions to hide the dreadful reality of their lives.

It is the Old Man who tries to strip all of the illusions away and disclose the truths everyone has tried to hide, though he himself is the guiltiest of all. He seduced Amelia then abandoned her. He murdered the Dead Man by burdening him with debts he could not repay. He lied to the Student about his

TOPICS FOR FURTHER STUDY

- In literature, a symbol is something that represents something else, and is often used to communicate deeper levels of meaning. In Nathaniel Hawthorne's famous novel *The Scarlet Letter*, for example, the red letter "A" worn by Hester Prynne is a symbol not only of her supposed crime (adultery), but also of her neighbors' bigotry and her own courageous pride. Strindberg incorporates many symbols into *The Ghost Sonata* in order to communicate deeper levels of meaning to his audiences. Consider the importance of the Old Man's wheelchair, the Girl's hyacinth flowers, and the pendulum clock as symbols in the play. What might each one represent? How are they viewed by different characters? How do they affect your understanding of the *plot* of the play? What are some of the play's other important symbols and how are they used?

- The form of *The Ghost Sonata* is modeled after a particular type of chamber music. A "sonata" is a three- or four-part composition that consists of independent movements that vary in key, mood and tempo. Typically the first section of a sonata is exposition, in which a theme is introduced, followed by a section that develops the theme, and ending in a recapitulation of the theme. Listen to one of Mozart's many piano or violin sonatas, Haydn's sonata number 19 in D-major, or Beethoven's D-minor piano sonata and determine ways in which Strindberg's play is constructed like this chamber music form. Consider the number of scenes and the flow of action in *The Ghost Sonata*, as well as the play's themes and the way they are woven into the plot and "recapitulated" near the end.

- A "motif" is a theme or an idea that occurs again and again in a work of art. In *The Ghost Sonata*, *death* seems to be a dominant motif. What are the many ways that death is discussed, or that images of death appear in the play? What message or messages regarding death do you suppose the playwright is trying to communicate to his audience?

- Several characters in *The Ghost Sonata* are referred to simply by descriptive titles instead of proper names. Why do you suppose Strindberg chose to call some of the most important characters in the play "The Student," "The Old Man," "The Milkmaid," "The Colonel," and "The Girl," instead of giving them individual names? How does this affect the way you view the characters? Would you prefer that they be called by proper names? Why/why not?

- *The Ghost Sonata* has often been compared to absurdist plays of the mid-twentieth century. Read a play by the famous absurdist author Samuel Beckett, such as *Waiting for Godot* (1952) or *Endgame* (1958). How are the characters in each play alike? How does each play view serious subjects like human relationships and death? Can you find examples of humor appearing in unlikely places in both plays? What effect does this have?

---

father in order to get him to do his bidding. Worst of all, he once committed a crime and murdered the only witness, an innocent Milkmaid, to prevent her from reporting him. The Student is slow to learn all of these things, and slower still to apply them to the way he views the world. But by the end of the play his optimism and idealism have turned to cynicism, like the Old Man. He understands reality better, and refers to the world as a place of "illusion, guilt, suffering and death," and now hopes only for a better place in the afterlife.

Betrayal

Several of the characters in *The Ghost Sonata* betray one another in some form. Years ago, the Colonel seduced Jacob Hummel's fiancee away from him. In retribution, Hummel later had an affair with the Colonel's wife, Amelia, that produced a daughter the Colonel believes is his. Then he betrayed Amelia, and left her behind to live with her sin. Even the minor characters of the play live on a merry-go-round of betrayal. The Caretaker's Wife had an affair with the Dead Man that produced a daughter, the Lady in Black. Now the Lady in Black is engaged to Baron Skanskorg, an aristocrat who must first divorce his current wife before marrying his new love.

Coming of Age

One of the most significant changes in the play occurs with the Student, who begins as a heroic, optimistic, idealistic youth, and ends as cynical and disappointed as any of the actual sinners and criminals in the play. The dreams he has of finding paradise in a beautiful house, with a lovely wife, a generous income, and happy children, are dashed when he discovers that the real world is often filled with unexplainable rejection and disappointment, and he watches the girl he loves die in front of him. Still, like any responsible adult, he must formulate a new way of looking at the world and move on with his life. Mature now, he understands the world can be evil, and looks forward to a happier life after death.

Human Condition

One of the most important recognitions in the play is that no one is perfect—all people are flawed in some way or another. Part of being alive and being human is making mistakes—sometimes very big ones—then finding ways to learn from them and recover. Amelia, the Mummy, for example, made a large mistake when she fell for Jacob Hummel, had an affair with him and produced a daughter. She has felt guilty about her mistake ever since, and has locked herself away from the world in a closet where she dwells on her sins and becomes less and less human with each passing day. Jacob's appearance in the house, however, sets her free from her prison. After twenty years she realizes she has paid enough for her mistake, which was really quite human, and now has the strength to turn the tables and accuse Jacob for the crimes he has committed.

Another, even more painful, aspect of the human condition revealed by *The Ghost Sonata* is the terrible suffering human beings must face in life.

The play begins the night after a random disaster. A house collapsed, killing and seriously injuring many people. Though the Student, with his second sight, was able to save some of the inhabitants and tend to the wounds of others, he could not prevent Death from claiming the lives of a few. Everyone else in the play suffers eventually. Bengtsson, Johansson and the other servants suffer with their menial positions. The Colonel suffers all the lies he has told to create the illusion of a happy, prosperous life. The Milkmaid is a silent, suffering ghost who died innocent, and before her time. Hummel, the Old Man, ultimately must answer for his various crimes, and suffer a humiliating death in front of those he would have destroyed. Most tragic of all, the Girl suffers because of the sinners and criminals around her. They have fouled the air she breathes with their corruption and, in spite of the Student's efforts to save her, she dies.

STYLE

Sonata

The form of *The Ghost Sonata* is modeled after a particular type of chamber music called a "sonata." The sonata traces its roots to the fifteenth century, when it was used to describe a variety of selections of purely instrumental music for individual instruments, trios or ensembles. Its most recognizable form, however, began to take shape in the mid-eighteenth century. During the Enlightenment era, sonatas started to take the form of three- or four-part compositions, often for solo pianists or violinists.

The classic sonata consists of independent movements that vary in key, mood and tempo. Typically the first section of a sonata is *exposition*. The exposition establishes one musical theme in a principal key center, called the tonic, then produces another theme in a secondary key center, called the dominant. The two themes intermingle and bridge into the second section, known as the *development* portion of the sonata. During the development stage, the themes presented in the exposition are played in new ways, with new combinations and variations that may include minor keys not found in the exposition. Finally, in the *recapitulation* section, the themes are again played in their original order, but only in the tonic key.

Like the classic sonata musical form, Strindberg's *The Ghost Sonata* is divided into three distinct sections. In the first scene, the exposition stage of the sonata, he presents the beautiful house and all of the people in it as they *seem* to be, and he introduces his two major themes: the Student's youthful idealism and love and longing for perfection, and the Old Man's cynicism, hatred, and longing for revenge. In the second scene, the development phase, Strindberg moves inside the house, and these themes interweave as all of the masks and lies are stripped away from the people and the house is seen for what it really is: an abode for less-than-perfect people, sinners who have spent years paying for their crimes. In the third and final scene, the recapitulation, both of the themes presented in the exposition are proven faulty and destructive. The Student by himself, forming the tonic key, plays both through both themes and finally arrives at a sort of coda to the composition. A new, hopeful theme emerges: the faint hope for the final salvation of mankind in an afterlife free of the miseries and disappointments of the mortal world.

Expressionism

Strindberg is considered to be one of the most important influences on an avant-garde artistic movement called *expressionism* that became very popular in Germany in the 1920s. While writers of realism at the turn of the century tried to produce plots that mirrored real life events and characters who seemed to talk, move and act like real people, expressionist writers, like expressionist painters, tried to portray life as they saw it, altered by strong inner emotions, and modified and distorted by the artist's vision of reality. As a result, expressionist plays are often disjointed, nightmarish scenes that bear little resemblance to the real world.

Strindberg's *The Ghost Sonata* contains many elements also found in later twentieth century expressionistic dramas. For example, his characters are types, rather than individual people. They are known by labels, like "The Student" or "The Old Man," rather than by names, and sometimes they do not even have distinct personalities. The play is filled with symbolic imagery, like that often associated with dreams. The pendulum clock, the Mummy, the "vampires," the Old Man's wheelchair, and the house itself, where the characters have their "ghost supper," are all symbols representing abstract ideas like time, fear, guilt, shame, power and corruption.

Like a dream, the play does not follow a straight line of cause-and-effect actions. Time is ambiguous, and can even be stopped like the hands of a clock, and the characters act in strange, unpredictable ways. Perhaps most important of all, *The Ghost Sonata* projects the feelings and attitudes of its author through the words and actions of his characters. As a style, expressionism is meant to convey the inner workings of the artist's mind. Strindberg's own tortured psyche is on display throughout the play. He was, by his own admission, compulsively neat, and he required an orderly, clean environment. Little wonder, then, that the Girl in *The Ghost Sonata* is so dismayed by a housekeeper who dirties more than she cleans. Reportedly, Strindberg also feared cooks, and often suspected them of poisoning his food, which may explain the appearance of vampire-like kitchen servants in his play. And, given the dark, dismal entries he left behind in his journals and letters, there is little doubt he spoke through the Student at the end of the play when he mourned "this world of illusion, guilt, suffering and death, this world of endless change, disappointment, and pain. The lesson Arkenholtz learns—that the world can be a cold, cruel place—is one Strindberg seemed to live, and desperately wanted to express in *The Ghost Sonata.*

HISTORICAL CONTEXT

Dream Plays and Psychoanalysis

Strindberg began his successful literary career in the 1880s writing the kind of realistic dramas that were made popular by playwrights like Henrik Ibsen and Anton Chekhov. *The Father* (1887) and *Miss Julie* (1888) are both considered to be masterpieces of realism, depicting natural characters in mundane, ordinary surroundings. By the turn of the century, however, Strindberg was reshaping reality on the stage to correspond to his own tortured, nightmarish vision of life. In "dream plays" like *To Damascus,* a trilogy produced between 1898-1901, *The Dream Play* (1902), and *The Ghost Sonata*

COMPARE & CONTRAST

- **1907:** Gustav V becomes King of Sweden. During his 43-year rule the Social Democratic Party created many progressive reforms, including extension of voting rights, the introduction of an eight-hour workday, public child welfare, and state-subsidized housing.

    Today: A new Swedish Constitution in 1975 dissolved all of the powers of the king. Sweden is now governed by a Prime Minister and a Parliament, and, like many industrial nations, is in the process of deregulating the economy, privatizing formerly government-owned industries and businesses, and cutting government spending on welfare programs.

- **1907** Many countries around the world, including the United States, do not allow women to vote, or to serve in public office.

    Today: In 1994, Swedish Prime Minister Ingvar Carlsson led a Social Democratic Party government in which half of his cabinet, and 41 percent of the entire parliament, were women, the highest percentage of women lawmakers in any government in the world.

- **1907** Marriage in most western cultures is viewed as a religious vow and a civil contract, and separations, or divorces, are hard to obtain. In Great Britain and the United States, for example, a separation decree could only be granted if one spouse could prove that the other had somehow caused injury, through such means as adultery, habitual drunkenness, impotence, committing a felony, abandonment, or severely abusive behavior. Men and women who divorced were often viewed as immoral, and treated as outcasts. Out of almost one million marriages conducted annually in the United States, fewer than 100,000 (less than 10%) end in divorce.

    Today: "No-fault" divorce laws in many states have made divorces much easier to obtain. "Irreconcilable differences" is a common, simple, and acceptable reason cited as the reason many spouses separate. Each year, 2.5 million people marry in the United States, and nearly half of those marriages are expected to end in divorce.

- **1907** The early years of flight: On December 17, 1903, Orville Wright first flew a heavier-than-air craft under its own power for 12 seconds at Kitty Hawk, North Carolina. A year later, he and his brother, Wilbur, had constructed an "airplane" that could stay airborne, turn and bank.

    Today: The wartime uses for airplanes helped speed the development of the transportation technology. By the 1950s, more people were crossing the Atlantic Ocean in airplanes than on ships. In the 1970s, Britain and France developed the Concorde, a jet plane that allows travelers to fly faster than the speed of sound, and reach the United States from Europe in only a few hours. In 1995, airlines worldwide flew an estimated 1.26 billion passengers.

- **1907** Although "penny arcades" had been showing short motion pictures to individual viewers since Thomas Edison demonstrated his "kinetoscope" in 1894, it wasn't until photographer George Eastman and inventor Thomas Armat combined flexible film with a projector that mass audiences could sit in one room and watch "movies" together. The first movie theatre opened in 1905, and by 1909 there were 8,000, each seating about 100 people, offering short film attractions. D.W. Griffith's *The Birth of a Nation* (1915) proved that the new medium could compete with the style of realism popular in the live theatre, and soon the film industry surpassed the theatre as the world's favorite form of entertainment.

    Today: Multimillion-dollar blockbuster films may now be purchased or rented, taken home, and viewed on a television with the help of a videocassette recorder (VCR) or digital video disc (DVD) player. Many films are made and released directly to the new tape or disc format, or aired on one of many cable television stations. The television is the late-twentieth century's private kinestoscope, and fewer than 10% of the population attends live theatrical events.

(1907), time and location are often vague and unpredictable. The characters are personality types rather than individuals, and they are mainly alienated, lost human beings struggling with the sins of the flesh while seeking some kind of spiritual fulfillment.

Strindberg's accomplishments in these plays prefigure such major avant-garde literary movements as expressionism and the Theatre of the Absurd, and were generated, at least in part, by his own terrible relationships, bouts with mental illness, and spiritual crises. At the same time, however, a widespread interest in the human mind was developing in Europe, owed partly to the psychoanalytic theories of Sigmund Freud (1856-1939). In *The Interpretation of Dreams* (1900) and *Three Contributions to the Theory of Sex* (1905), Freud tried to describe the structure of the mind, analyze how it functioned, provide reasons for human behavior and suggest ways of dealing with mental illness. In his work, Freud emphasized the importance of the unconscious mind, a place where dreams may be interpreted as the key to understanding suppressed desires. At its root, Freud's psychoanalytical theories are a prescription for seeing past the illusions to the realities beneath the surface—the single most common theme in Strindberg's ''dream plays.''

Women's Rights

August Strindberg was married and divorced three times in a society that did not favor the rights of women, and held the vows of marriage sacred. Each time he was probably mismatched with his mate. Strindberg claimed to cherish domesticity and a ''traditional'' family life, but each woman he wed was outgoing and career-minded. He met Siri von Essen, his first wife, when she was married to a nobleman, Baron Wrangel. He viewed them as mother and father figures, but nevertheless fell in love with Siri and lured her away. In a highly publicized and scandalous move, she divorced the Baron, and married Strindberg in 1877. They spent fifteen years together, battling each other over his increasingly eccentric personality, while she tried to become a successful actress.

They divorced in 1891, and Strindberg married Frida Uhl, and Austrian journalist, in 1893. She was twenty-three years his junior. In the year that they were married, they actually only spent a few months together—just long enough to have one daughter together. After a stretch of a few years during which Strindberg scorned the company of women, he married for the last time in 1901. His relationship with Harriet Bosse, a famous Norwegian actress 29 years younger than him, lasted only a little longer than his time with Frida. They were married for three years, though they separated frequently, and they had one child together before divorcing in 1904.

Sweden, like most of the countries of the western world, did not allow women to vote in the nineteenth century. In fact, it was not until 1919—the year before American women were first allowed to cast ballots—that women in Sweden were granted suffrage. During Strindberg's lifetime, the rights of women were restricted, and often given to them legally and socially through the marriage contract with their husbands. In many countries, women could not legally borrow money or even own property without their husbands' permission. While the industrial age had brought many women out of the home and into the workplace, the jobs available to them were mainly unskilled, menial tasks that required long hours for little pay. Other than housecleaning or repetitive, sometimes dangerous factory work, women might become teachers or clerical assistants, but not much else. The women Strindberg married—a journalist and two actresses—may have been considered adventurous, even improper, for their time.

Divorce was available (and Strindberg relied upon it frequently), but only if both parties agreed, and if there was a strong, just cause, such as infidelity, criminal activity, physical incapacity or insanity. In any event, divorcees were stigmatized by society, and relatively few couples opted to separate. More often, unhappy couples remained together in misery, true to their vows, but false to their hearts.

Realism

The Realism movement in the theatre that shaped Strindberg's early writing owes a great debt to Henrik Ibsen, the Norwegian playwright who produced works like *A Doll's House* (1879), *Ghosts* (1881), *An Enemy of the People* (1882), and *Hedda Gabler* (1890). Like his fellow realists George Bernard Shaw, Anton Chekhov and Maxim Gorky, Ibsen sought to portray characters, actions and the environment in a realistic way on the stage. Unlike the open, emblematic staging of Shakespeare's plays during the Renaissance, or the painted, two-dimensional "realism" of the German Romantic theatre of the late eighteenth century, realist writers of the late-nineteenth century paid great attention to detail in an effort to reproduce the actual world for audiences. Playwrights and designers took great pains to describe and build complicated, three-dimensional rooms, complete with walls, doors, furniture, working lights, and even ceilings. Characters in realistic plays are affected by both heredity and environment, and respond in natural ways to psychological and physical conflict. Additionally, the themes employed by realist writers are common, everyday problems with significance to many people. Ibsen wrote about marital problems, disease, poverty, inter-class conflict and many other issues faced by his audiences in the 1880s and 1890s. Just after the turn of the century, facing competition from the novel new form of entertainment called "movies," the theatre began to turn away from Realism and toward more experimental styles such as Symbolism and Expressionism.

Jerome Willis and Linda Marlowe in Strindberg's Ghost Sonata.

CRITICAL OVERVIEW

The Ghost Sonata was first produced at Strindberg's Intimate Theatre in Stockholm on January 21, 1908. The play followed *The Storm* and *The Pelikan* as Opus No. 3 of Strindberg's "chamber plays," which he wrote specifically for his tiny theatre. Like these two previous productions, however, *The Ghost Sonata* was attacked and ridiculed by critics who did not, or would not, understand the symbolic dream worlds Strindberg was attempting to portray on the stage.

After the failure of *The Ghost Sonata,* Strindberg wrote no more great plays. In 1908-09 he produced a few historical dramas of little note, then spent his last few years writing only essays about religion and politics. The real accomplishment of *The Ghost Sonata* was not widely understood, and the playwright himself was not universally appreciated until after his death in 1912.

Max Reinhardt's production of the play in Berlin in 1916 was the first to meet with popular and critical success. Reinhardt toured the show to the Lorensberg Theatre in Gothenburg, Sweden, then on to the Royal Opera House in Stockholm, where Strindberg's play finally received the acclaim from his countrymen he had so desperately sought. Afterward, Reinhardt's production traveled to Munich, Vienna, and Frankfurt, and he mounted other productions in cities across Europe into the 1920s.

Other famous directors have approached the play, including Olaf Molander, a lifelong devotee of Strindberg's, who mounted *The Ghost Sonata* at the Royal Theatre of Stockholm in 1942, and Ingmar Bergman, who produced the play twice, once in Stockholm in 1941 and once in Paris in 1962 for the Theatres des Nations festival. The play was first produced in England at the Oxford Playhouse in 1926, and appeared in America for the first time at Eugene O'Neill's Provincetown Playhouse in New York in 1924. The Provincetown production fared miserably. Attendance was low, critics complained, and the show closed after only 24 performances.

Over the years, *The Ghost Sonata* and a few of Strindberg's other "dream plays" have appeared occasionally on the stages of universities and community theatres in Europe and the United States. By themselves, they have never achieved tremendous popularity, but as forerunners to some of the great artistic movements of the twentieth century, and as models for some of the great modern dramatists to follow, they are now viewed as monumental turning points in the history of dramatic literature. Antonin Artaud, the famous French director and playwright, credited Strindberg's work as an important precursor to his own "Theatre of Cruelty." Randolph Goodman, in the introduction to his English version of the play in *Drama on Stage,* writes, "His [Strindberg's] influence is clearly discernible in the work of Luigi Pirandello, Eugene O'Neill, and Sean O'Casey, to name but a few of the masters. In more recent times such cynical social commentators as Brecht, Ionesco, Beckett, Pinter, and Genet have raised a superstructure of raucous laughter, of cabaret and farce, on the somber foundations laid down by August Strindberg."

No less a critic than the great British historian Allardyce Nicoll proclaimed in *World Drama,* "Three things in especial Strindberg did. First, in the supreme concentration of the dramas of his middle period, he showed how much even the closely packed realistic plays of Ibsen lacked of essential dramatic economy. Secondly, he came as near as any man towards creating a modern social tragedy. And, thirdly, in his latest works he achieved what might have seemed impossible—producing theatrical compositions that in effect are wholly subjective. In the long range of his writings his hands touch now the early romantics, now the realists and naturalists, now the expressionists, now the surrealists, and now the existentialists. There is no author whose range is wider or more provocative. In him the entire history of the stage from 1800 to the present day is epitomized."

CRITICISM

Lane A. Glenn

Lane A. Glenn is a Ph.D. specializing in theatre history and literature. In this essay he discusses the influence of Emanuel Swedenborg on August Strindberg's life and work, and analyzes The Ghost Sonata *in light of Swedenborg's notions of life, death and the afterlife.*

August Strindberg spent much of his life on a quest for psychological and spiritual fulfillment. Contemporary accounts written by friends, family and colleagues, as well as the playwright's own journals and letters, describe Strindberg as a man who was eccentric, almost always unhappy, and constantly battling mental illness.

Over the course of his lifetime, his madness took many forms. As a boy, he resented his mother for her lower class background, yet still fought for her attention among seven brothers and sisters. She died when he was only thirteen, and his father married their housekeeper. For the rest of his life Strindberg experienced a strong attraction toward women he thought of as pure, motherly figures, and a repulsion from women he damned as promiscuous sinners. As often as not, he felt both feelings toward the same woman, seriously complicating his relationships and contributing to his three failed marriages.

Besides his sexual conflicts, Strindberg also suffered from a severe obsessive-compulsive disorder, frequent bouts of paranoia, hypochondria, delusions, and hallucinations. There were times in his life when he would write for days on end, producing volumes of prose or dramatic text; and there were other, less fertile periods when he would sit, stare into space, and ponder for hours, oblivious to anyone around him. During his darkest hours, while living alone in Paris from 1894-96, he claimed that severe electric shocks were passing through his body, and that hostile "Powers" were pursuing him, bent on his destruction. He turned to pseudoscience, and worked feverishly with chemical experiments designed to produce gold. Recognizing how close he was to the edge of sanity in the summer of 1896, he wrote to Anders Eliasson, a doctor who had been treating him, "I do not especially fear the madhouse, for it would be interesting to see these people whom I believe to be possessed by demons and not sick or senile. And I would regard it as a new education for a new life."

Arguably, what ultimately saved Strindberg from a complete nervous breakdown that summer was his discovery of a new spiritual faith. As a boy, Strindberg detested religion, and vehemently denied the existence of God. As an adult, however, and after experiencing some of the disappointments and tragedies of life, the troubled artist found himself searching for solace in the spiritual realm. In his quest for faith in some kind of higher power, Strindberg turned to Buddhism, occultism, existen-

WHAT DO I READ NEXT?

- In a career spanning forty years, August Strindberg wrote 60 plays. Many were never very popular, and are no longer performed, even in the author's native Sweden, but some have become classics of modern dramatic literature. Try reading *The Father* (1887), *Miss Julie* (1889), a short one-act play called *The Stronger* (1889), or his "dramatic lyrical-fantasy in fourteen scenes," written partly in prose and partly in verse called *A Dream Play* (1901).

- *The Ghost Sonata* is often considered an early form of twentieth century experimental drama like Expressionism or Absurdism. Consider reading *The Emperor Jones* (1920), an expressionistic drama by American playwright Eugene O'Neill, or Samuell Beckett's 1952 absurdist play *Waiting for Godot*.

- Like a handful of other great European writers during the last decades of the nineteenth century, Strindberg was profoundly affected by the movement toward Realism in drama. His *Miss Julie* (1889), for example, is a realistic drama, interwoven with symbolic imagery. Norwegian playwright Henrik Ibsen's *A Doll's House* (1880) and Russian writer Anton Chekhov's *The Three Sisters* (1901) are two other examples of turn-of-the-century European Realism.

- A dominant theme of *The Ghost Sonata* becomes the disappointment and pain the world causes, and the search for relief in the afterlife, an idea familiar to Existentialist thinkers and writers of the late nineteenth and early twentieth century. To learn more about Existentialism and its effects on literature, try a critical history like Walter Kaufmann's *Existentialism from Dostoevsky to Sartre* (1988) or go right to the source with Soren Kierkegaard's *The Concept of Dread* (1844) or *Fear and Trembling* (1846).

- There is a Gothic horror quality to the characters and plot of *The Ghost Sonata* that resembles the work of the American short story author Edgar Allan Poe. Check out Poe's "The Fall of the House of Usher" (1839) and "The Cask of Amontillado" (1846), two horror tales with creepy characters and unsettling stories.

- Like many prolific and successful playwrights, Strindberg occasionally shared his insights on his craft in essays he wrote about the theatre and the art of playwriting. One such essay, "On Modern Drama and Modern Theatre" (1889), appears in *Playwrights on Playwriting* (1960), a compilation of essays by such notable dramatists as Henrik Ibsen, George Bernard Shaw, Eugene O'Neill, Bertolt Brecht, and Arthur Miller.

tialism, mysticism, and Theosophy, before discovering his own unique form of religion, based largely on the doctrines of Emanuel Swedenborg (1688-1772), the eighteenth century Swedish scientist, philosopher, and theologian. From the summer of 1896 forward, Strindberg's life and work, including the 1907 *Ghost Sonata,* were indelibly marked by the playwright's newfound religious beliefs.

In Swedenborg, Strindberg found the balance he was seeking between traditional Western Christianity, Eastern mysticism, and the waking supernatural realm of the occult that he had been exploring, and living, for many years. Strindberg identified with and understood such works as Swedenborg's *Arcana Coelestia,* which emphasized a supernatural vision of the afterlife existing parallel to the mortal world, and acknowledged the unavoidable presence of sin, terror and suffering among all people. In Swedenborg's, and Strindberg's, view, the mortal world was a place for humans to work off their debt of Original Sin, pay the penance of guilt, mental anguish and physical pain, then pass into the afterlife, where their souls would be treated accordingly.

> "IN SWEDENBORG'S, AND STRINDBERG'S, VIEW, THE MORTAL WORLD WAS A PLACE FOR HUMANS TO WORK OFF THEIR DEBT OF ORIGINAL SIN, PAY THE PENANCE OF GUILT, MENTAL ANGUISH AND PHYSICAL PAIN, THEN PASS INTO THE AFTERLIFE, WHERE THEIR SOULS WOULD BE TREATED ACCORDINGLY."

Goran Stockenstrom summarizes the central tenet of Swedenborg's teachings in "The Journey from the Isle of Life to the Isle of Death: Reconciliation in *The Ghost Sonata*." Stockenstrom writes:

> After death men are transported to the spiritual world or the lower earth. After their arrival the appearance of the newly fledged spirits remains unaltered and they can still conceal their thoughts and feelings as they could in life. Therefore many believe that they continue to reside in earthly existence. When after a while the external condition is unveiled by the internal one, the human spirits can no longer hide their thoughts. As feature after feature is stripped away, all hypocrisy dissolves, and the exterior is transformed into a mirror-image of the interior condition. The ultimate objective of this differentiation of spirits is to unmask the person's true self, so that there emerges a complete correspondence between the outer appearance and the inner reality. It is not a question of a judgment in the usual sense, for to Swedenborg God is absolute love. Rather than submitting to judgment, the evil and the good spirits unite with their equals by their own free will in order to be finally dispatched to one of the different societies in heaven or hell.

The place where this unmasking occurs is a sort of purgatory for souls on the way to heaven or hell. The Theosophists of the nineteenth century, who also drew upon the works of Swedenborg, called this place "Kama-Loka," a phrase Strindberg used as the original subtitle for *The Ghost Sonata*. In the play, as in Swedenborg's purgatory, Kama-Loka, masks, lies and illusions are slowly stripped away, baring the naked souls of the people underneath. Life begins with promise and ends, as often as not, in humiliation, degradation and, eventually, release.

The promise of life in *The Ghost Sonata* is found, of course, in the Student, Arkenholtz. Young, heroic and idealistic at the beginning of the play, Arkenholtz has not yet seen enough of the world to know that what he wants—paradise on earth—is unattainable, that it doesn't exist. There is little doubt that the author saw a great deal of himself in his character. Milton Mays notes in "Strindberg's *Ghost Sonata:* Parodied Fairy Tale on Original Sin," "Like Strindberg, the Student is an innocent trying to believe in an unfallen world in the face of the horrors of real existence."

Arkenholtz has rescued people from a collapsed building, catches glimpses of the future with the second sight granted him as a "Sunday child," and has just discovered a mysterious benefactor who is prepared to introduce him to the life he has dreamed of living in an elegant city apartment house. "Think of living up there in the top flat," he has said to his companion, "with a beautiful young wife, two pretty little children and an income of twenty thousand crowns a year."

A bourgeois lifestyle, however, does not begin to pay for Original Sin, and the Student, along with all of the other characters in the play, must begin the process of transformation from sinner to penitent to saved soul. Jacob Hummel, the Old Man, is prepared to force them all along that journey. In the first scene of the play, outside the house, Hummel seems omniscient and all-powerful. He gulls the Student into doing his bidding, knows everything there is to know about the strange inhabitants of the house, and orders his servant, Johansson, about like a slave, because he holds his freedom in his hands.

The building up of opportunity and power in the first scene, though, merely sets the stage for the ritual of soul cleansing that is to follow. Like the mortal souls that enter Kama-Loka, everyone in the house must be stripped of masks, illusions and artifice. Their true natures must be laid bare, so their souls can be separated into the good and the evil.

Initially, the Old Man presides over the unmasking. Once he has worked his way into the house, on the premise of attending the evening's "ghost supper," Hummel sets about taking his revenge on its inhabitants by revealing all of their secrets. The telling of truths begins when he encounters the Mummy, Amelia, who was once his lover. She was young and beautiful, until she lied about her age, married the Colonel, and had an affair and a daughter with Hummel. Since that time, twenty years ago, she has lived in shame and isolation in a closet of the house, where she avoids the light of the sun and the light of public scrutiny, and her skin turns white and wrinkled like a mummy's.

Together, Hummel and Amelia discuss the crimes and secrets of the rest of the household. Baron Skanskorg is divorcing his wife in order to marry his lover, the Dark Lady. This mysterious Dark Lady is the daughter of the Caretaker's Wife, who had an affair with the Dead Man, who was in turn another of Amelia's lovers. Hummel's former Fiancee will be attending the ghost supper. She was seduced away from him by the Colonel, Amelia's husband. It is, as Hummel jokes, "A select gathering." Adulterers, thieves and, as it later turns out, murderers, are on the guest list of the ghost supper. "Crime and secrets and guilt bind us together," Amelia mourns, "We have broken our bonds and gone our own ways, times without number, but we are always drawn together again."

The secrets kept for so long by the weird inhabitants of the house are not uncommon ones, or so the playwright would have his audience believe. Although the world his characters inhabit is clearly not the world most people recognize as real, it is meant to be a parallel world where people like us, yet not like us, live the way we do, and suffer the way we suffer. As Strindberg famously wrote about *The Ghost Sonata* in a letter to Emil Schering in 1907, "It is horrible like life, when the veil falls from our eyes and we see things as they are. It has shape and content; the wisdom that comes with age, as our knowledge increases and we learn to understand. This is how 'The Weaver' weaves men's destinies; secrets like these are to be found in *every* home. People are too proud to admit it; most of them boast of their imagined luck, and hide their misery."

Hummel, the would-be "Weaver," saves his deadliest ammunition for the Colonel, who he has been plotting against ever since the younger man stole his fiancee years before. Hummel now owns all the Colonel's debt, and reveals that the wealth he has surrounded himself with is all borrowed goods. His family name, too, is borrowed. While the Colonel truly believed himself to be a nobleman, Hummel provides him with a document that strips him of his titles. Furthermore, the Old Man presses, he is not even a Colonel, since the army he once served in disbanded and abolished all its titles. The relentless Hummel pins the broken Colonel in a chair and warns him that if he removed his wig, his false teeth and his moustache, he find underneath all the lies a miserable lackey who once served in a kitchen.

Hummel's intention is to methodically strip the masks away from all the guests at the ghost supper, "to pull up the weeds, to expose the crimes, to settle all accounts, so that those young people [Arkenholtz and Adele] might start afresh in this home, which is my gift to them." What the Old Man does not count on, however, is that he, too, is mortal, and like all mortal souls to Swedenborg and Strindberg's way of thinking, he must face his own reckoning.

Amalia abruptly breaks out of the trance that has held her for twenty years and turns the tables on the group's accuser. "We have erred and we have sinned, we like all the rest," she rails at Hummel, "We are not what we seem, because at bottom we are better than ourselves, since we detest our sins. But when you, Jacob Hummel, with your false name, choose to sit in judgment over us, you prove yourself worse than us miserable sinners." In the Swedenborgian realm, Amelia is warning, they have suffered for their sins, but now their souls are prepared for a rewarding afterlife. Hummel's, on the other hand, will continue to suffer after the sorting of his sins.

The list of Hummel's crimes runs long. He stole Amelia's heart with false promises, murdered the Dead Man by burying him in debt he could not repay, and conned the Student by lying to him about his father. Worse yet, he once lived as a sort of vampire in Bengtson's home, nearly starving his family to death, before moving on to Hamburg where he committed crimes and murdered an innocent Milkmaid who might have exposed him. In the end, Hummel is reduced to the gibbering parrot Amelia once was, and crawls into her closet to hang himself.

Despite the seeming justice of Hummel's end, and the suggestion that the sinners of the house have suffered enough, and order will now be restored, the still-innocent young people in the play who were viewed as the hope for tomorrow do not fare any better than their guilty parents. The Girl, Adele, has lived too long in the polluted air of the house, and now suffers like a vicarious sinner in her Hyacinth Room where everything seems perfect, but is really damaged and dying. For his part, Arkenholtz tries to save her. He woos her, even proffers marriage, but she is not to be moved. He tries to play her music, but even the harp will not sound in her room where nothing is what it seems.

Finally, she droops, and dies at his feet. The Student prays for her, wishing for her the best fate that anyone can achieve while passing from this world of misery into the afterlife of the unknown. "The Liberator is coming," Arkenholtz announces, "Welcome, pale and gentle one. Sleep, you lovely, innocent, doomed creature, suffering for no fault of your own. Sleep without dreaming, and when you wake again, may you be greeted by a sun that does not burn, in a home without dust, by friends without stain, by a love without flaw."

This world, the Student now recognizes, is a world of "illusion, guilt, suffering and death." It is a world of "endless change, disappointment, and pain," and only a merciful god in the afterlife can offer any balm to soothe the suffering souls of all of mankind.

Some critics have found fault with Strindberg's variation on a fundamental Christian principle that is reflected in the Student's new outlook. As Stephan C. Bandy explains in "Strindberg's Biblical Sources for *The Ghost Sonata*," "Instead of looking to Christ for release from his unhappy existence, the Student in fact redefines Christian salvation in his own terms. At the center he places not an abstract God, but the Self. And thus it appears that Strindberg has presented us with nothing less than a modern-dress, thoroughly up-dated parable of redemption—but a redemption stripped of its Christian idealism and optimism."

Nevertheless, as bleak and hopeless as the play may make the world seem, there is intended to be a note of optimism in its characters' suffering. Despite the trials and tribulations of life in the mortal realm, Swedenborg suggested, and Strindberg believed, that the hereafter could be different. For Strindberg, writing *The Ghost Sonata* and his other "chamber plays" that addressed the sin, guilt and terror of life was a form of therapy. He alleviated some of his own anxiety and misery by expressing his feelings, and promoting his religious beliefs, in his art. "What has saved my soul from darkness during this work has been my religion," he wrote to Schering, "the hope of a better life to come; the firm conviction that we live in a world of madness and delusion from which we must fight our way free."

Source: Lane A. Glenn, for *Drama for Students*, Gale, 2000.

Jon M. Berry

In the following essay, Berry presents how Strindberg uses the dialogue and staging of The Ghost Sonata *to develop his concept of reality as a*

"single and unified fabric consisting of a homogeneous blend of matter and mind."

August Strindberg's *The Ghost Sonata* is the most produced of his Chamber Plays. Its complexity and depth allow a great many directorial approaches and absorb countless interpretations. Perhaps this is one reason for its popularity: expressionism, symbolism, and realism can all be found in the work and can each, when used as a major production style, produce valid, powerful results. From the realistic interpretation given the play by Olof Molander, to the divergent expressionistic approaches taken by Max Reinhardt and Ingmar Bergman, *The Ghost Sonata* has been proven to be a remarkable play capable of communicating its complex ideas through many voices.

Part of the play's success in this regard may be a result of the form of the work itself—a form that combines realism and symbolism to create a tension between the material and the immaterial concerns of the drama. Such a tension enabled Strindberg to make a difficult theme not only dynamic but also dramatic and allowed him to complete a theatrical experiment in which he had been engaged for years. As Evert Sprinchorn has pointed out, Strindberg, through his scientific experiments beginning in 1891, searched for the great coherent principle in nature and so attempted to "combine the realms of inorganic and organic matter in one grand synthesis in which the universe would display a kind of order without having any teleological end." Further, Strindberg expanded his pursuits to include not only matter but also mind. In his own terms, his intention was to eliminate "the frontier separating matter from what was called mind." In his later works, including *The Ghost Sonata,* one finds a further attempt to eliminate not only the frontiers separating matter from mind but those separating matter, mind, and spirit.

Consequently, Strindberg strove in his scenic experiments to expand even the concept of reality until it was seen to be a single and unified fabric consisting of a homogeneous blend of matter and mind, material and spirit, subjective and objective modes of perception. All phenomena would thus be seen to exist concurrently and coproductively. As with Freud, the map of reality is enlarged. But for Strindberg, it has become all-inclusive, leaving nothing outside its boundaries.

The Ghost Sonata represents a major step in Strindberg's theatrical experiments in staging this broadened reality. In it, realism plays a large role in the staging, but it is a realism that is inclusive rather than exclusive of spiritual and metaphysical concerns. The first scene establishes the context of the play visually as well as verbally. The audience is induced to view the drama from a broadened perspective—a perspective that Strindberg may have regarded as being a primary state of awareness before abstractions are enforced.

Indications for this perspective are immediate. Note, for example, Strindberg's changes within the layout of the set. From the opening moments of the play, one is not looking out upon a street or an exterior environment from inside a drawing room, as was customary, but is looking in upon the interior action from an exterior advantage. The view is from "the other side," both literally and figuratively, and quickly establishes an important context: one enters the house—the small interior world of humanity—from the far side of life; and one's interpretations of the subsequent action will be partially determined from this bias.

Thus, the standard or the norm by which one will view the scene will be that of the world of the Milkmaid—that outer realm that interpenetrates the inner. This does not mean, however, that this play is simply a dream play. It is a dream play and much more. For the world of the Milkmaid is complex and multidimensional. She exists in several realms that operate simultaneously. The Student can see her at the fountain although Hummel cannot. This is possible because she is of the spirit world, visible only to the Sunday child. Neither can Hummel see the dead Consul. Yet, moments later when Hummel boasts of having saved a drowning girl in Hamburg, the Milkmaid appears to him. She is now of the world of dreams—of the drama of mind—and it is Hummel's conscience that "sees" her.

Had Strindberg chosen to present the Milkmaid in verbal discourse alone, or had he not been careful to have her enter the scene, fully visible to the audience, *before* the Student, and to have her use the physical fountain because she feels the heat of the day, her role in the opening scene and the perspective that she represents may have been reduced to that of a psychological aberration—a sign of strain on the mind of the Student. Moreover, had the Milkmaid been visible only to the Student and not to Hummel (who we know is not a Sunday child), her citizenship in multiple worlds would not have been depicted. The audience sees her in several connections, and her reality is therefore a more complete

> "... THE REALISTIC DEPICTION OF THE MATERIAL SCENE PROVIDES A THEATRICAL VEHICLE FOR THE CHARACTER OF THE HUMAN SOUL WHOSE VEHICLE IS THE LANGUAGE OF THE DIALOGUE."

one. Hers is that wide realm in which all partial "realities" (material, spiritual, and psychological) are merely modes of one whole reality.

The play takes on a semidreamlike quality, to be sure, for there are a number of private dreams staged; and, more importantly, one is not used to viewing the world in the way that Strindberg shows it. One is more inclined to believe in the "reality" of Hamlet's murdered father stalking the parapets than in that of a drowned milkmaid wandering the streets of Stockholm. The one reality is theatrical, but the other—Strindberg's—oversteps its theatrical bounds. Strindberg does not ask, as does Shakespeare, that one willingly *suspend* one's disbelief, he asks that one actually *change* one's beliefs to accord with his own. That is, Strindberg seems to require that his audience accept his personal vision (minus a modicum of artistic exaggeration, of course) as a true depiction of the way things are. How is one to make this change? The Milkmaid herself is not ready to accept the reality of this interpenetration of realms. She is not so much frightened at seeing the Student as at being seen and spoken to by him. He is special. He has an expanded vision almost like that of the audience, who will now view the whole of the real world at once rather than piecemeal. The action of the first scene not only establishes the relationships between characters and the exposition of antecedent action needed for the audience to better understand the play but also determines the way in which the play will be viewed. It eases the otherwise unwilling audience into the proper frame of reference.

When this context is established, the audience finds itself peering into a new house, probing into the lives of living people, descending into the material depths. Appropriately, the guide for this stage of the journey is Hummel, for he is alive, rooted firmly to the material mode, and complexly related to the other people in this living inferno. He leads the Student and the audience through an examination of the house and the people within it.

This house is one of many houses talked about in the play; but because of its similarity to the others, it comes to represent society at large. We know that one house has collapsed—the house of the elder Arkenholz is in shambles—and we realize that this one may someday end in the same way. Societies come and go, as do families and nations, and this new house in a new style is no exception. For the moment, however, it seems to resist decay. It appears so perfect and so inviting. The student remarks with an unabashed ardor:

> I have already looked at it—very carefully.... I went by here yesterday, when the sun was glittering on the panes—and dreaming of all the beauty and luxury there must be in that house, I said to my friend, "Imagine having an apartment there, four flights up, and a beautiful wife, and two pretty kids, and twenty thousand crowns in dividends every year."

The Student has looked at the house. He says he has looked very carefully. But he has not looked into it. He has seen only the outside of the house and the few objects visible to him through an open window—objects of luxury and elegance that are also visible to the audience at the opening of the curtain: *"When the curtains are drawn and the windows opened in the round room, one can see a white marble statue of a young woman surrounded by palms and bathed in sunlight. On the windowsill farthest to the left are pots of hyacinths—blue, white, pink."* The house itself is finely decorated: *"Through the door can be seen the hall and the staircase with marble steps and balustrade of mahogany and brass. On the sidewalk on both sides of the entryway are tubs with small laurels."* If appearances mean anything, this is a place to be desired. It is a scene of material perfection, both beautiful and opulent, into which everyone dreams of entering—the beggars at the back door, the Student, and Hummel.

To this vision are added the peeling bells and distant organ tones of a Sunday morning. Ships' bells in the harbor signify the beginning and end of different journeys. The atmosphere early on is reminiscent of that at the close of Goethe's *Faust*. For salvation is in the air, and the best that life has to offer stands bathed in sunlight on a glorious morning. If appearances mean anything, the Student has stumbled into an earthly paradise. But unlike Faust's kidnapping from the mouth of hell, any salvation that will be open to Strindberg's seeker after knowledge lies on the far side of hell. He must first descend into its depths, experience pain, love, confusion, and anguish; his eyes and his mind will be opened until he can no longer bear to see or to know. When his knowledge and his vision crush him, and his love crumbles away, he will have discovered both the reason and the need for faith. Like the outside of this modern new house, the Student will find the promise of this particular Sunday morning a mere façade behind which something rots.

As the ships' bells toll, the Student's journey into the house of Man begins. He has gone through one passage and approaches another. As he grows to physical and spiritual maturity, he leaves the vanished child behind and presses on through *The Valkyrie* into the round room and the room of ordeals. Hummel has come full circle to the end of his own journey. Life and death meet in the person of the Milkmaid; and the theme is reiterated in the scene. Even in this radiant place where every detail breathes success, *"Hanging on the railing of the balcony on the second story are a blue silk bedspread and two white bed pillows. The windows to the left are covered with white sheets signifying a death in the house."* As spruce twigs are scattered on the ground, one journey through this life is accomplished, and another begins.

Overtly symbolic of this rhythm of comings and goings, life and decay, is the statue of the Colonel's wife. "Was she so wonderful?" inquires the Student. Then, in a non sequitur that belies his own love of beauty for beauty's sake, he adds, "Did he love her so much?" Hummel replies: "Suppose I were to tell you that she left him, that he beat her, that she came back again and married him again, and that she is sitting in there right now like a mummy, worshiping her own statue. You would think I was crazy." In the idealistic Student's eyes, something is crazy. For how could ugliness reside in beauty? How could the truly beautiful decay? He does not understand, as yet, the rhythms of life.

In the first scene of *The Ghost Sonata,* matter and mind, life and death are depicted as a confluence of realms interdependent on each other. The action in one sphere defines the action in another; and causes and effects are so interwoven that no amount of analysis could ever unravel them into their separate strands. This complexity of causation and relationship has grown from its initial articulation in the preface to *Miss Julie* to include every conceivable kind of determinism. After Hummel tries to give the Student an idea of the interconnections among the persons in the house, he adds, "Complicated, don't you think?" To which the Student can only respond, "It's damned complicated!" Indeed it is, to borrow Hummel's words, inside and outside. The complicated outside of *The Ghost Sonata*—the context—is established.

Unlike the first scene, the second presents space and the objects within it in the convention of the bourgeois drama. The atmosphere of this interior scene will be darker and more terrible than that of the exterior scene; but, perhaps with the exception of the death screen, the scenery will not be. The darker mood will be established through action, characterization, and language rather than through the visual symbolism of Strindberg's scenography.

The scene is the round room, a conventional drawing room whose furnishings are indices of a particular time and place. The place is an upper-class set of apartments in Strindberg's own Stockholm. The milieu, as many have pointed out, is highly specific; and if the universal can be found in the particular, the universal might be found here. For Strindberg has brought along the baggage and the trappings of naturalism. He does not, however, treat the properties and the setting as mere decoration. The objects in the round room will not function simply as indices of time and place, class and taste, nor will they be, for the most part, overtly symbolic. The objects will play the role of objects in the material world. As characters in the drama, they will represent that material world in the same way that human characters represent humanity. Furthermore, these objects will function as that material stuff through which the human characters must battle.

In terms of the set, the round room is pierced with several doors that lead into other rooms with other doors. There is always a way into or out of a room in this labyrinthine drama of passage and passages. Life is lived in a series of interconnected spaces. In this connection, the role of the Mummy's closet takes on a special function. There is a door, a passage, which leads into a closed room. The purpose of this room is for storage; it was never intended to be a place to live. Much like the psychological niche into which the Mummy has retreated, the closet is a cul-de-sac. It is part of the round room and is not. The parrot-character is in this world and is not. Thus the Mummy lives on the fringe of life and passes now this way, now that, through the papered door—now taking refuge in oblivion, now returning of necessity to eat or to drink in the great round.

Resuming my discussion of the physical objects within the scenic space, the realistically individuated properties of the rich interior constitute a repetition of "things" to which the inhabitants of the house are inextricably wed. Ironically, these inhabitants are both masters and prisoners of their own possessions. In the context of the multiple dimensions established in the first scene, this statement is both sociological and ontological. Sociologically, these bourgeois characters are tied to the objects that support them in their station. The humans are thus defined by their property to such an extent that they would cease to be what they are if their material worth were at all diminished.

For example, in verbal discourse, the Colonel is stripped by Hummel of his stations as a noble and as a military man. These have been the credentials upon which the Colonel has been able to extend his credit, accumulate the hallmarks of his apparent wealth, and move up in the world. Without them, he would have been nothing; and to lose them destroys even his ability to rebuild. He has lost his possessions to Hummel and, by extortion, his ability to recover from the loss.

Yet Hummel does not stop at this. He continues. "Take off that wig of yours and have a look at yourself in the mirror. And while you're at it, take out those false teeth and shave off that moustache and let Bengtsson unlace your metal corset." Much of what appears to be the Colonel is a fabrication, in a literal sense, laid upon the animal. His appearance is supported by objects that have become a part of his character. The Colonel and the other members of his household are indeed trapped in a deteriorating social structure, as Maria Bergom-Larsson has suggested; but they are also trapped in the world of things, of physical objects and a physical being, from which they cannot escape. Societies change, a person's dreams may be altered, but the human condition as Strindberg so often depicts it, is rigid. For the round room is also *Kama-Loka,* the realm of desires, the world of flesh and material need. In this more ontological context of the scene, the human characters are bound to the physical matrix of the great round of life; and they cannot be freed from that bondage without physical death. Strindberg plunges his characters into the agony of an existence they can in no way alter. As Harry Carlson puts it: "The pain in this world of lies and illusions is not simply a result of social injustice, it is existential. Social evils must be remedied, but the great round of life creates and devours in a rhythm that is not governed by human concepts of order and justice."

Ethics, it would seem, are a manufactured sociological expedient that have no permanent place in the natural world.

There is, however, a great difference between total capitulation to the material mode of reality and the recognition of that mode as *Maya*— a veil over a deeper and more complete reality. Hummel has capitulated. He has given himself over not only to satisfying survival concerns but to taking into himself every good thing that crosses his path. Perhaps no character in the play is so deeply rooted in the physical as is Hummel. One of his first acts in the round room after banishing the servants is to roam about that room fingering objects. In one respect, he is taking inventory after having purchased all the Colonel's debts. His action thus sets up the next scene in which he strips the Colonel. In another respect, however, he is making love to the house, touching it, petting it—stimulated by the sight of the statue of the woman who had come to represent for him all of this wealth. He took *her* when he could not take *it*. Now he has returned to take *it*. Hummel becomes, for the audience, the incarnation of lust and greed that he threatened to become in Johansson's introduction of his character to the Student in the first scene:

> —All day long he rides around in his chariot like the great god Thor. . . . He keeps his eye on houses, tears them down, opens up streets, builds up city squares. But he also breaks into houses, sneaks in through the windows, ravages human lives, kills his enemies, and forgives nothing and nobody. . . . Can you imagine that that little cripple was once a Don Juan?

If the world were simply material, Hummel and his ilk would not be in the wrong. Survival of the fittest would be the only ethic.

There is, however, something more to life, and the Mummy points this out when she turns on Hummel in the climax of the supper sequence: "We are poor miserable creatures, we know that. We have erred, we have transgressed, we, like all the rest. We are not what we seem to be. At bottom we are better than ourselves, since we abhor and detest our misdeeds." Hummel has been, like everyone else, in the "wrong." But the Mummy does not come to this conclusion simply because she is on the losing end of a material battle. Rather, she has discovered the value of human cohesion after having come to recognize the realm of desires for what it is. That realm is *Maya;* and *Maya* in *The Ghost Sonata* is the clutter of the physical mode—the illusion created by both pretense and the "reality" of physical objects. It is the shroud that hides the individual soul from its true, nonmaterial nature.

The round room up to this point has stood as a symbol for the great round of life—the cycle in which all living things feed on one another. We see now, however, that the round room has a secondary symbolic meaning tied to late T'ang Buddhist philosophy—that of the Round Enlightenment and its consequent defilements of the real. On the path to Round (perfect) Enlightenment, all *Maya* must be removed to escape the realm of *Kama-Loka;* and the participants in the ghost supper are doing much more than waiting upon all-conquering death to liberate them. They are engaged in sloughing off their bondage to the material mode and to the illusions that they have constructed through a lifetime of ignorance and misunderstanding.

In the Mummy's phrase "at bottom we are better than ourselves," the human existence is split. The Mummy is voicing a concern of the soul, the eternal portion of the human. The recognition of the physical aspect as *Maya* is made from this more spiritual perspective; and once *Kama-Loka* is revealed for what it is in truth, the individual soul, in Strindberg's syncretistic blending of Buddhism and Christianity, can move to make reparations with its fellow souls. Reconciliation is sought with both human beings and God. Although complete reconciliation waits upon death, preparations must be made.

When Hummel points to the clock, which he uses to signify finite human nature—when he points to linear time, which winds down and brings all things to a close, the Mummy ripostes by offering a different perspective: "But I can stop time in its course. I can wipe out the past, and undo what is done. Not with bribes, not with threats—but through suffering and repentance." She cannot stop material time, this woman who wears its ensign more than any other character in the play; but she speaks from a vantage point of timelessness, from a knowledge that the physical life is just one ordeal to be passed through. She stops time in the sense that she knows that it too is *Maya*. This life will end for her, and therein lies hope. The first stage in the movement toward perfect enlightenment is accomplished in the banishing of lust and greed made manifest in the destruction of Hummel. This act is the initial step in the deconstruction of all *Maya* .

Although the human characters in this scene are more than physical and possess eternal souls, the realm of *Kama-Loka* is no illusion. As one has seen in the first scene, the existence of one mode of reality does not negate the existence of all others. The realistic properties in the round room play the role of a very tangible *Maya*. For it is the people and their language (their verbal discourse) and not their material environment that is half in and half out of *this* world. It is verbal discourse that makes the environment appear to be illusory: for it is through that discourse that the soul voices its aphysical nature. To pit the world of objects against the world of the soul, the scenographic discourse is borne out realistically in the tradition of the illusionistic theater. In this way, the major conflict in the scene is recognized as being not between Hummel and all others, nor between the characters and a fictive life, but between the human soul and the necessity of living in a material body in a material world. The harsh character of this material world advances through the realistic staging.

Scene 3 is played in the hyacinth room, and one discovers quickly that the ordeals borne in this place are extensions of those so graphically depicted in the last scene. The theme is repeated, although the point of attack is much earlier—closer to the moment when innocence comes face to face with decay. Yet, even though the theme is reiterated, the third scene is not merely a repetition of the second. The second scene has served, in combination with the first, to prepare the audience for the difficult concepts and discourse of the final movement of the sonata. Leitmotivs have surfaced and resurfaced to foreshadow what will become the dominant strain of the third scene.

The scenographic depiction of the realm of desires is also reiterated when the language of the two human characters parades before the mind's eye a series of psychological scenes in which the material mode seems to act in direct opposition to the human will. That will is the will of innocence to create the best of all possible worlds, and Strindberg shows that such a world cannot exist in the corrosive presence of realistic detail. Although there is little to unmask in either the Student or the Young Lady, an unmasking does in fact take place. It is the unmasking of the scene, which not only serves to reveal the true nature of the hyacinth room but also operates as the dramatic event by which the Student and the Young Lady are led to the transcendence of a world of *Maya*.

The scene is initially "transported" by the presence of objects symbolic of transcendence. Strindberg's stage directions treat these objects simply:

A room decorated in a bizarre style, predominantly oriental. A profusion of hyacinths in all colors fills the room. On the porcelain tile stove sits a large Buddha with a bulb of a shallot (allium ascalonicum) *in its lap. The stem of the shallot rises from the bulb and bursts into a spherical cluster of white, starlike flowers. . . . The Student and The Young Lady (Adele) are near a table, she seated at her harp, he standing beside her.*

A room in a bizarre oriental style breathes a mysticism that is reinforced by the Buddha with his shallot. The hyacinths splash the stage with color. A harp echoes the final tones of an unheard song. The scene is at once transported in time, place, and mood from the grimness of the preceding scene.

Yet that grisly scene lingers: "*In the rear to the right, a door leads to the round room. The Colonel and The Mummy can be seen in there sitting motionless and silent. A part of the death screen is also visible.*" This is a haunting reminder that one has not left the earth, that one has not been transported to Shangri-La, and that, as yet, love has not been able to conquer all. Paradise, or at least a small touch of heaven-on-earth, is juxtaposed to the hell-on-earth of the previous scene. To the rear at the left, like an umbilical life-support for the human beings in this other-worldly plenum, is the door to the kitchen. Strindberg has left no doubt about the context in which this third scene will be played.

As the action begins, the Student tries to leave things as they appear to be. He and the Young Lady, like Dante and Beatrice before them, stand atop purgatory in an earthly paradise looking into heaven. To heighten the reality of their situation into this dreamworld, the Student constructs some symbolism. "Is this the flower of your soul?" he asks. The flower in question is the hyacinth; and by linking it to the Young Lady's soul, he develops a resonance between it and the transcendent nature of her spirit. The mood darkens momentarily as the Student recognizes another resonance. The flower was created, according to legend, in the commingling of blood and earth—in the death of Hyacinthus, whose brains were dashed out by a discus hurled by his lover Apollo and blown awry by the jealous Zephyr. This unspoken legend foreshadows the Young Lady's death in the final moments of the play, but the Student has another reason for avoiding it. He is still determined to put the best face on their situation. He hastily drops the subject and proceeds to create another myth—a symbolic meaning for the flower and a symbol of hope for himself and his companion.

First you have to interpret it. The bulb is the earth. . . .
Here the stalk shoots up, straight as the axis of the world, and here at its upper end are gathered together

the six-pointed star flowers.... It's an image of the whole cosmos. That's why Buddha sits there with the bulb of the earth in his lap, watching it constantly to see it shoot up and burst forth and be transformed into a heaven.

The Student has settled on the dominant metaphor of the Buddhist "emptiness" philosophy—*K'ung-hua*, "the flower in the air as the symbol of an empty mirage of a flower (*hua*) grounded on empty space (*k'ung*)." The Student, however, transposes empty Nirvana to a heaven—something more approachable by the Christian Young Lady and her Christian audience. This world, symbolized by the flower, may someday become a heaven. The young couple is excited about this prospect as if in the creation of such a myth they could make the idea it represents become a reality.

As they re-create the world in the light of their own hopes, the young couple surround themselves with a tentative Eden. They are insulated form an oppressive reality by symbols, flowers, music. They console each other with the notion that earth can indeed be made into a heaven. After this act of creation, the Student proclaims, "We have given birth to something together. We are wedded."

As with the original tenants of Eden, knowledge will be this couple's undoing. The Young Lady's reply, "No, not yet," picks at the thread that begins the unraveling of this make-believe universe. To be truly wedded (as well as to be truly enlightened), time, testing, and patience are required. The testing has begun. From this point on, the scene of beauty will be stripped away in a protracted analysis of the environment. A tension is created between symbolism and reality—that is, between the object as it is used symbolically and the same object in its material function. In this way, the objects in the scene end by working as all objects do: to subdue, to constrain, to poison the ideal with the real. Clearly, the fabrication of a symbolic transcendence *within* a material existence cannot hold for long. For the imposition of symbolic nature upon an object interrupts only briefly its material function, and the materials used to signify spirituality soon decay into those functions.

In this room of ordeals, as the Young Lady calls it, examples of this fact abound. The Young Lady takes the Student on a verbal tour of the room and of her trials and tribulations within it. She speaks of the furniture, the stove, the windows, the laundry, and so on, through a chorus of things and chores that keep her battling to "keep the dirt of life at a distance." An example of the imperfections within the room is the writing desk, which, even though it is verbally presented in only a matter of seconds, encapsulates the nature of all the household objects and symbolizes the plight of the Young Lady herself. "Do you see that writing table?" she asks the Student. He replies, "What an extraordinarily handsome piece!" The Young Lady continues: "But it wobbles. Every day I lay a piece of cork under that foot, but the housemaid takes it away when she sweeps, and I have to cut a new piece. The penholder is covered with ink every morning, and so is the inkstand, and I have to clean them up after her, as regularly as the sun goes up." Her tale of woe is not merely an indication of the untidiness of a maid who ought to be dismissed; it is a parable about the problem of living. Although the writing table is a beautiful piece of furniture, it is also an artifact with a utilitarian function. Its defect, its one short leg, does nothing as yet to impair its beauty but does impair its function. The table wobbles. Therefore, its functional aspect must be ministered to regularly. But its use as a writing table impairs its beauty, for because it is used, its top gets messy and must be constantly cleaned.

Like everything else in the room, the writing table has a functional aspect (a material aspect) that works against its symbolic or aesthetic aspect. Moreover, the functional aspect of each object is imperfect. It is difficult to write on the table. It is nearly impossible to keep a fire going in the stove. It is impossible to marry and have children with the Young Lady.

The symbol enlarges metaphorically: the Young Lady is beauty or the keeper or repository of it. She also has a functional self. Beauty, here equated with purity and innocence, coexists with utility in a combative relationship within the same person. On the ontological level, the functions of the human woman in her daily life compel constant ministering to keep beauty alive. Sociologically, the household and the Young Lady's way of life can be maintained only at great cost. She has been buoyed up upon a sea of people who have labored to support her in her pristine state. But as the sociological structure breaks down, and as the Hummel family of vampires eats away at the foundations, the Young Lady gets ever closer to the filth that is the basis of all material life. In the first scene, the Student claims he had marveled at an apartment that was four flights up. One no longer wonders why that apartment is now on the ground floor.

The worldly paradise tentatively established by the young couple crumbles back into purgatory and the inferno. The Student rages at a world of appearances that kills the individual (the idealistic individual) with its insidious realities. He ends by stripping away even those insulatory secrets that the Young Lady had asked him to let her keep:

> It was a Sunday morning, and I stood looking into these rooms. I saw a colonel who wasn't a colonel. I had a magnanimous benefactor who turned out to be a bandit and had to hang himself. I saw a mummy who wasn't one, and a maiden who—speaking of which, where can one find virginity? Where is beauty to be found? In nature, and in my mind when it's all dressed up in its Sunday clothes. Where do honor and faith exist? In fairy tales and plays for children. Where can you find anything that fulfills its promise? Only in one's imagination!

Indeed, the illusions of reality are a construct of the Round Enlightenment mind. But as the *Maya* gives way to understanding and emptiness, *Kama-Loka* falls away. Likewise, as the Young Lady comes under the blows of the Student's revelations—as she is confronted with the truth against which she no longer has any defense, her hold on life is loosened. Her sickness "at the very core of life" kills her psychologically because she cannot bear the oppression of living while knowing that her life is borne upon pretense. It physically kills her because, without the hope that the pretense had given her, she is no longer strong enough to keep tying that knot that binds her body and her soul together. She is freed spiritually as her mind and body pass into oblivion. To borrow words used by Yeats in another connection, "the ceremony of innocence is drowned"—drowned first in the wash of a decaying civilization and a decaying body and then drowned in the knowledge of its own impermanence. The Young Lady's soul escapes her body and leaves the room of ordeals behind.

In the final sequence of *The Ghost Sonata,* the material mode of reality is passed through. But the clarity of the vision of the life beyond is obscured. How is this vision of the purely immaterial to be expressed in a physical theater without using clichéd images of the afterlife? And if the Buddhist motif is still used, how would one depict "emptiness"? Strindberg knows not to portray too much. His initial intent was to deny the eye any concrete image on which to focus. The lessons of the third scene would teach this much. Therefore, the senses are transported to another level. All visual signs blur, when the walls of the house fall away, into pure light—a radiantly white incandescence. Likewise, speech and all other auditory signs pass into music. The movement of the senses is thus from an object plane to an ephemeral plane. This would have been the more powerful ending to the play.

Strindberg could not, however, use the magnesium light that he wanted, so he called for his set to dissipate into a two-dimensional vision—a painted backdrop of Böcklin's *Isle of the Dead* seen as a continued mode of reality. One sees the Young Lady moving across a Stygian stretch of water into another portion of her life in which the earthly *Kama-Loka* is finished.

Once it is clear that the material mode is to be traversed—that is, lived through rather than capitulated to (as in the case of Hummel) or avoided (as in the case of the Mummy in her closet) or poetically dressed in its Sunday best—then the *Maya* falls away and nonrealistic staging takes over. To get to this point, however, the realistic depiction of the material scene provides a theatrical vehicle for the character of the human soul whose vehicle is the language of the dialogue. Since conflict can exist only between characters that are truly opposed, Strindberg has, in *The Ghost Sonata,* brought both characters face to face. He has pitted humanity's spiritual nature against its physical nature.

Source: Jon M. Berry, "Discourse and Scenography in *The Ghost Sonata,*" in *Strindberg's Dramaturgy,* edited by Goran Stockenstrom, Minneapolis: University of Minnesota Press, 1988, pp. 316–29.

Gerald Parker

In the following essay, Parker discusses Strindberg's use of the play's visual components in a way comparable to his polyphonic or symphonic arrangement of the oral components.

The divergence of critical response to Strindberg's *The Ghost Sonata* is adequately represented by Eric Bentley and Maurice Valency. Bentley writes: "For all the heterodoxy of style and the fantasy of the action, the play is simple in structure and straightforward in its symbolism. The three compact scenes constitute a statement, a counterstatement, and a conclusion." Valency, on the other hand, states that "Unquestionably the play has many faults. Its underlying narrative is fantastically complex. The relation of its three movements is neither close nor entirely apparent." The play, Valency concludes, is "a momentary glimpse of the world through the eyes of madness." Although it has frequently proved a temptation to locate, in Strindberg's art and vision, more of the apoplectic than the apocalyptic, to overemphasize, or indeed to take refuge in psychoanalysis rather than criticism, the extraordinary sense of form which is apparent in much of Strindberg's art would seem to argue that Bentley's sensitivity to the overall clarity of design in *The Ghost Sonata* is valid.

From his earliest plays on, Strindberg was subject to a deeply felt to urge objectify the interior life so as to give it shape. Like others of his epoch, he endured the abrupt disappearance of the gods and the resultant sense of dispossession. However, as Wallace Stevens observed, "There was always in every man the increasingly human self, which instead of remaining the observer, the non-participant, the delinquent, became constantly more and more all there was or so it seemed; and whether it was so or merely seemed so still left it for him to resolve life and the world in his own terms." For Strindberg, as perhaps for most others suddenly in exile, a complete resolution of the self and the world was never possible. Nonetheless, Strindberg attempted to meet the challenge "to resolve life and the world in his own terms." Something of this attempt is evidenced in the various prefaces, letters and essays from the Preface to *Miss Julie,* through "The New Arts, or the Role of Chance in Artistic Creation" to *Open Letters to the Intimate Theatre;* together, these works reveal in Strindberg a mind seriously determined to forge a new and a vital aesthetic of the theatre, an aesthetic responsive to an ever-changing vision of the self and the world. The "heterodoxy of style" in some of the late plays is to be seen as the direct expression of this ever-changing vision—a vision characterized by a moral and intellectual turbulence well beyond the sense of a relatively calm and logical response which might inform the more conventional sequential dramatic structure implied by Valency. On the the other hand, although Bentley's sensitivity to the controlling shape of *The Ghost Sonata* is surer than Valency's, there is little evidence to support the rigidity of his formula: statement, counterstatement and conclusion. The structure of the play is, as Bentley suggests, "simple" and "straightforward"—but for important reasons other than those his analysis proposes.

By the time of the writing of *The Ghost Sonata,* Strindberg was clearly beyond the realist *conventions* which informed such achievements as *The Father, Miss Julie* and *The Bond*—although he continued his intense concern with the problems of guilt and the class-sex struggle with which those and other plays dealt. By as early as the writing of *Master Olof* (1872–6), Strindberg was experimenting with his concept of polyphonic composition, which he considered "a symphony, in which all the voices were interwoven (major and minor characters were treated equally), and in which no one accompanied the soloist." This concept of polyphonic composition was, early in Strindberg's dramatic career, expanded to embrace the functioning of the non-verbal "aesthetics of the theatre" in production. There is no lack of evidence to indicate the great care which Strindberg gave to the crucial substantive functions of the *mise en scene.* As Strindberg's vision reached beyond the more narrow restrictions of realism, elements in the *mise en scene* were orchestrated in strikingly new ways, and given additional vitality and dramatic purpose.

The most significant indication of this new vitality is the increased substantive role of the visual components of the *mise en scene* in *To Damascus* (1898–1904). The complex episodic form of this trilogy looks back to the sequential tableaux arrangement of medieval drama, to the literature of quest and pilgrimage generally (*Piers Plowman, Pilgrim's Progress*) to Romantic drama (Shelley's *Prometheus Unbound,* Goethe's *Faust,* Ibsen's *Peer Gynt*) and, perhaps more significantly, to Büchner's *Woyzeck* which itself was influenced by the genre painting techniques of the *Sturm and Drang* movement. More importantly, the form of *To Damascus* looks forward to the basic principles of montage in the modern film (for instance in the work of Eisenstein, and in the juxtaposition of subjective and objective vision in Bergman's *Wild Strawberries* and *Persona*) as well as to the episodic structure of the plays of Brecht. Elements in *To Damascus* also appear to foreshadow the techniques of radical visual and auditory juxtaposition in such plays as Artaud's *Jet of Blood,* and Ghelderode's *The Chronicles of Hell.*

Strindberg was not unaware of the technical problems in the staging of *To Damascus.* Shortly before the composition of the first two parts of this play he had become interested in the drama of Josephin Peladan. What seems to have impressed him most was the carefully controlled visual simplicity of the outdoor productions of Péladan's tragedies in France. Similar techniques were employed by Emil Grandison in his production of *To Damascus.* Referring to Grandison's production, Strindberg notes the effective simplicity of the set which employed backgrounds not dissimilar to modern projected scenery. Such arrangement permitted uncluttered visual representation which would not interfere with language and gesture, which would unobtrusively (as in medieval stage practice) contribute symbolic visual reinforcement to the complex drama of a spiritual journey. Strindberg, in his relations with his designers Grandison, Karl Ludvig Grabow and August Falck, insisted upon the primacy of the spoken word over the "machinery" of visual display, and yet his varied notes on the production problems of *To Damascus* and *A Dream Play* give clear evidence of a desire to orchestrate an effective and meaningful balance of sight and sound. He did not sanction the more radical implications of, say, Gordon Craig's manifestoes in *The Mask* which championed an almost autonomous aesthetic of the theatre, an aesthetic foreseen by Hegel when he wrote, of developments in the arts of the theatre:

> that which in the first instance had merely the force of an assistant and accompaniment, becomes an object on its own account, and receives the appearance in its own domain of an essentially independent beauty. Declamation passes into song, action into the mimic of the dance, and scenery in its splendor and pictorial fascination itself puts forward a claim to artistic perfection.... [Thus can develop a theatrical art which] liberates itself from the exclusive precedency of articulate poetry, and accepts as an independent end what was previously, to a more or less extent, a mere accompaniment or instrument, and elaborates the same on its own account.

Strindberg insisted that the visual components of the *mise en scene* exist to serve the dramatic dialogue with "the force of an assistant and accompaniment;" nonetheless, the visual dimensions of *To Damascus* challenged the resources of his small theatre, and led ultimately to the encouragement of a new theatre aesthetic wherein the visual could contribute more substantively.

The grotesque banquet scene at the beginning of *To Damascus,* Part One, Act Three, illustrates the brilliance of Strindberg's control and use of the visual. In this scene, there is a striking sense of bizarre incongruity between the assembled luminaries and the poor, an incongruity immediately registered in the visual details of opulence and ostentation on one hand and of squalor on the other. In the course of the scene, the candelabras, flowers, splendid platters of peacock, pheasant, lobster and melons are replaced by plain earthenware mugs; the ceremoniously attired dignitaries give place to grotesque ragged figures, "figures of the night, and disagreeable looking women." Finally, after this visually managed transformation is completed, the scene dissolves first into complete darkness, then into a "conglomeration of scenery, representing landscapes, palaces, and interiors" from which there at last emerges a prison cell, illuminated by a

> ON THIS LEVEL, THE FORM OF *THE GHOST SONATA* IS A CONTINUOUS MODULATION OF SOUND AND SILENCE, OF INTENSIFICATION AND RELAXATION, OF A SENSE OF EVANESCENCE AND 'TOO MUCH PRESENCE.'"

solitary sun beam casting a white spot on a wall on which hangs a large crucifix. This gradual transition from bright colour to semi-darkness, from irradiated material magnificence to isolated austerity, from a scene containing about thirty people to the solitary presence of the Stranger and the semi-lit crucifix is a single movement, a complete pattern the rhythm of which unmistakably contributes to our immediate apprehension of the radical cadence of the Stranger's consciousness.

This cadence can perhaps best be described in terms of Schopenhauer's doctrine concerning the various stages in the objectification of the Will. In Thomas Mann's words, this Will

> as the opposite pole of passive satisfaction, is naturally a fundamental unhappiness, it is unrest, a striving for something—it is want, craving, avidity, demand, suffering; and a world of will can be nothing else but a world of suffering. The will objectivating itself in all existing things, quite literally wreaks on the physical its metaphysical craving; satisfies that craving in the most frightful way in the world and through the world which it has brought forth, and which, born of greed and compulsion, turns out to be a thing to shudder at. In other words, will becoming world according to the *principium individuationis,* and being dispersed into a multiplicity of parts, forgets its original unity and although in all its divisions it remains essentially one, it becomes will a million times divided against itself. Thus it strives against itself, seeking its own wellbeing in each of the millions of its manifestations, its place in the sun at the expense of another.

As Mann goes on to say, "Plato's 'ideas' have in Schopenhauer become incurably gluttonous." This "gluttonous" struggle of will and passion is most evident in Strindberg's handling of the Stranger's "pilgrimage" through the phenomenal world. In this banquet scene the bizarre juxtapositions of rich and poor, plenty and paucity, colour and darkness, underscore the turbulence and blindness of the Will's objectification, present us with the illusive "veil of Maya:" a world of appearances, a "thing to shudder at."

The scenic arrangement here is carefully contrived to augment the motifs of struggle and phenomenal complexity which the dialogue exhibits. In the theatre, the visual presentation reveals directly the controlling rhythm of the Stranger's consciousness: the physical details of the *mise en scene* are orchestrated with a degree of expressive fluidity permitting Strindberg's drama of the soul a more concrete realization than could be acquired through dialogue alone. It was in this way that new and meaningful vitality was given to the visual in production.

II

"I propose, then, a theatre in which violent physical images crush and hypnotize the sensibility of the spectator seized by the theatre as by a whirlwind of higher forces." Thus does Antonin Artaud proclaim for the theatre a radical function. The true vitality of the theatre, Artaud claims, "consists of everything that occupies the stage, everything that can be manifested and expressed materially on a stage and that is addressed first of all to the senses instead of being addressed primarily to the mind as is the language of words."

It is most evidently in this direction that the plays from *To Damascus* on are tending, despite Strindberg's insistence upon the primacy of language. Indeed, the language itself is frequently, as Artaud advocated, "like a dissociative force exerted upon physical appearances." That is, the language throughout many scenes in Strindberg's later plays (including the banquet scene just discussed) loses in the verbal complexities of speech its efficacy as a means of rational discourse but gains new expressiveness as mere sound, as "intonation." Artaud advocated the "concrete value of intonation in the theatre . . . this faculty words have of creating a music in their own right according to the way they are pronounced, independently of their concrete meaning and even going counter to this meaning— of creating beneath language a subterranean current of impressions, correspondences, and analogies. . . ." In this way, language becomes itself as "physically" expressive as are the visual components of the *mise en scene*. For instance, in the banquet scene, speech is employed in such a way as to reinforce the transition from bright opulence to dark austerity. Rather than operating primarily as the sign or symbol of the psychology beneath (as, say, in the drama of Ibsen, or in *Miss Julie*) language is established as a spectacle in itself designed to act "physically" upon the spectator much as do the visual juxtapositions. The speeches delivered by the Professor, The Stranger, the Father and the Beggar come to occupy what Artaud termed theatrical "space," to function within the complex visual context as *mere sound*. The spectator clearly apprehends that the theatrical event is not being played out on the conventional level of discourse or "discussion," that the speeches do not in themselves function as *rational* vehicles of dramatic action, as would be the case in Ibsen or Shaw. As the visual pattern gains a momentum culminating in a conglomeration of images, so does the language rapidly dissolve into a *melange* of voices, until both the visual and the auditory are silenced and stilled by a darkness which serves as a release from the multiplicity of divided and warring *parts* in a world born of the *principium individuationis*.

The Ghost Sonata is a much simpler, less theatrically ambitious work than *To Damascus;* however, the controlling rhythm and form of this work owes much to the sense of a revitalized *mise en scene* that we find in many parts of the earlier play. Both the visual aspects and the language of *Ghost Sonata* are orchestrated in such a fashion as to make theatrically lucid the underlying motifs and to establish on the sensory level alone an experience of extraordinary range and effectiveness. That is to say, the *mise en scene* operates meaningfully with "the force of an assistant and accompaniment," helping to embody the rhythm of thought and feeling which the main action manifests; and the *mise en scene,* as a totality, possesses a certain sensual quality which, as sub-textual, autonomously elicits a response not unlike that demanded by music and painting.

For this reason, although Strindberg has carefully fused in this play "vision" and form, the structure of *Ghost Sonata* possesses a certain duality. On the one hand, there is the straightforward pattern of spiritual action: the Student's entrance into a house wherein he discovers first of all as an observer (in Scenes One and Two) and secondly as an active participant (in Scene Three through his relationship with the Girl) the "curse" which "lies over the whole of creation, over life itself." This action is cadential, tending, as Susanne Langer puts it in her analysis of the tragic rhythm, "to an absolute close." This "close" is the death of the

Girl, and the Student's acquiescence to what is unmistakably a Schopenhauerian awareness of the hellishness of life. Again, in Thomas Mann's words, "every expression of the will to live has always something of the infernal about it, being itself a metaphysical stupidity, a frightful error, *the* sin." The action of the play is, then, on this primary level of "idea" entirely spiritual, and, as in the case of *To Damascus,* the controlling pattern is that of a quest. In Schopenhauer's terms, the first two scenes embody the *principium individuationis* with all its turmoil and divisions: here we are made to share the observing Student's apprehension of hell on earth. In the last scene, the Student fails to "save" the Girl, fails to effect through *action* in the phenomenal world any sort of redemption. However, in the last moments of the play, a kind of "elevation" is manifested, not through action, but in "being." Schopenhauer describes the "Nirvana" of his vision thus: "What lends to everything tragic, in whatever form it may appear, its peculiar impetus to elevation, is the dawning realization that the world, that life cannot grant any true satisfaction, and hence they do not deserve our attachment: in this consists the tragic spirit: hence it leads to resignation."

Such fearful resignation is the emotion informing the Student's concluding prayer to the Liberator death (considered as a sleep) and to the "wise and gentle Buddha," as well as his total awareness of "this world of illusion, guilt, suffering and death, this world of endless change, disappointment, and pain." If Schopenhauer's philosophy is of some assistance to the illumination of such spiritual action, likewise is the Oriental concept of the tension between the qualities of *Samsara* and *Nirvana,* a concept with which Strindberg was likely familiar, indeed, which is hinted at through the presence of the seated Buddha. Nirvana is a state reached "when a man becomes annihilated from his attributes" and thus "attains to perfect subsistence." Samsara, on the other hand, is the wheel of birth and death, the realm of "eternal succession and coincidence of evolution and involution." The Student acquires through observation in Scene Two a growing awareness of the overpowering force of this realm, and, as expressed in the *Vimala-kirti Sutra,* rather than initially shrinking from experience, he "plunges himself into the ever rushing current of Samsara and sacrifices himself to save his fellow creatures from being eternally drowned in it." His efforts, however, are futile, and his defeat is registered in a despair from which the concluding resignation springs.

Although this primary pattern of action is distinctly spiritual, the play, particularly in the first two scenes, and mainly through the appearance of the Cook in the third, is as fully expressive of the tensions of the material-social world as are the earlier realist plays by Strindberg. The spiritual action is lucidly portrayed through the gradual disappearance of the social context so evident in the opening scenes, especially in the complicated exposition by Hummel. As in Ibsen's late plays, the spiritual quest is firmly located in the familiar context of class and family strife, economics, and sex. And, as in such plays as *The Master Builder* and *When We Dead Awaken,* this context is gradually transcended—largely because it represents the scene of personal choice and action which prove ineffectual as redemptive sources in the light of the appealing "metaphysical stupidity" of any expression of the will to live, that is, the will to choose and act. To a considerable extent, the three scenes depict this transcendence of the phenomenal world of action and choice by way of the gradual elimination of characters until only the Student and the Girl remain in a softly lit room visited occasionally by the vampire-like Cook.

Valency remarks that the "underlying narrative is fantastically complex. The relation of its three parts is neither close nor entirely apparent." There is certainly no denying the truth of this first assertion if we centre upon the bizarre complications of Hummel, the Colonel, the Colonel's wife ("White and shrivelled into a Mummy") and the Girl in the Hyacinth Room. These complications are related by Hummel to the Student in Scene One, and are revealed further in the ghostly gathering of Scene Two. Hummel admits the "fairy-tale" quality of his narration to the Student, admits the near impossibility of disentangling the threads of earlier action and the current relationships among the characters. "My whole life's like a book of fairy stories," he says; "And although the stories are different, they are held together by one thread, and the main theme constantly occurs." This main theme is the stultifying stagnation of lives buttressed by lies, deceit, crime, sin and sorrow—lives fettered in every direction by subjugation to the soul-destroying forces resulting from the *principium individuationis* and the world it has brought forth, "born of greed and compulsion . . . a thing to shudder at." The "underlying narrative" *is* complex in the telling, but perfectly lucid as the embodiment of this main theme. Like the Student, we are under no obligation to deliberately sort through the complications and arrive at a clear pattern of *temporal* action: we are meant, surely, to share his confusion, his admission to Hummel "I don't understand any of this." In the theatre, the exposition by Hummel in the first scene and the more public admissions of crime and guilt in the second have a cumulative *sensory* effect; the complications become too involved for immediate rational comprehension and become, theatrically at one level, "mere sound." We are reminded of this use of language in the banquet scene of *To Damascus,* and, perhaps, of a similar use of language and complicated exposition in the plays of Ionesco.

Despite this grotesquely abstruse temporal level of action, the more important spiritual pattern of action is never lost sight of. This spiritual pattern is made evident through the gradual transcendence of the social context, and through the arrangement of the visual elements in the total *mise en scene.* Evidence of the movement from the familiar to the strange, from the temporal to the spiritual, is provided by the visual pattern which tends from the opening out-door, sun-lit scene with the façade of a house, a street complete with drinking fountain, bench and advertisement column, to the Round Room of Scene Two with familiar (though oddly juxtaposed—as in surrealist art) interior objects (a stove, pendulum clock, candelabra, cupboard) and the almost claustrophobic impression of enclosure, to, finally, the Hyacinth Room with its general "exotic and oriental" effect, its clusters of vari-coloured hyacinths, and the dominating presence of a large seated Buddha.

In the course of this visual movement, the highly detailed and more overtly social context of the opening gives place to interior settings: first of all to the almost surreal Round Room, which, in a sense, functions like the single room setting of such plays as *Miss Julie* or Ibsen's *Ghosts* (that is, as a room which seems symbolically to portray the environmental dimensions and entrapment of modern man), and secondly, to another, but stranger interior which is far more "cosmic" in its symbolic implications. The sun-lit effects of Scene One, with shadows giving emphasis to the angular shapes produced by the house façade and the various street details (not to mention the array of objects seen within the house) give place to, first of all the darkly grim second scene, and then to the more subtly orchestrated harmony of coloured flowers and the striking effect of the Buddha from whose lap "rises the stem of a shallot (*Allium ascalonicum*), bearing its globular cluster of white, starlike flowers."

If the first scene is reminiscent of the visual effects of such a realist painting as Degas' *Cotton Market in New Orleans,* the final scene is reminiscent of Gaugin's *Where do we come from? Where are we? Where are we going?* (1897)—a picture, incidentally, which seems to reflect something of the spiritual quest dimension of *Ghost Sonata.* In each of these scenes we never completely lose sight of the others. Scene One portrays vague interior details which become visually clearer in each of the following. In Scene Two, hints of the Hyacinth Room appear off to one side, where we see the Girl reading. In Scene Three, the door to the Round Room is lelt open, and we see the seated Colonel and Mummy, "inactive and silent," and have a slight glimpse of the death-screen used for Hummel. Thus the transitions are not, visually, totally abrupt. Finally, all these visual presentations, which correspond so well to the general pattern of action described earlier, are made to dissolve into a single effect, which in a carefully devised production might pick up certain forms and colours already impressed upon our eyes. As the Student's last prayer is concluded, Böcklin's *Isle of the Dead* appears, the small solitary figures, gloomy shadows, isolated gold-lit temples of this painting displacing the varied impressions of both familiar and strange which the three scenes visually manifested.

In addition to such an overall visual pattern is the pattern of sound which likewise reinforces, "with the force of an assistant and accompaniment" the main action of the play. Apart from the wide range of voices (as sounds or intonations) throughout the play, this pattern is composed of the sound of bells, an organ, a clock, street noises, a harp, the loud pounding on a table. Like the visual details, these sounds are orchestrated to reflect the movement from the "familiar" to the strange and spiritual. In the course of the play, the bells, organ and general street noises of Scene One give place to the more discordant sounds of Scene Two (produced mainly by the voices) and, finally, to the more lyrical sounds of Scene Three, which is framed by the harp-accompanied song, "I saw the sun." The final sound is that of "music, soft, sweet, and melancholy" as the Böcklin picture slowly pervades the entire visual plane. Undoubtedly, Artaud is right in his production plans for this play in suggesting a considerable magnification of sound effects. For instance, to reinforce the steamship bells which are heard at the beginning (an image which, incidentally, is echoed in the small boat carrying passengers in Böcklin's painting) Artaud suggests that "A constant noise of water will be heard, loud at times, to the point of obsession." Artaud also suggests that the return of Hummel with the Beggars, in Scene One, should take place "in a great din. The old man will begin his invocations from very far off, and the beggars will answer him in several stages. At each call the crutches will be heard knocking rhythmically, sometimes on the ground, sometimes against the walls, in a very distinct cadence. Their vocal calls, and the beat of their crutches will be punctuated towards the end by a bizarre sound, as of a monstrous tongue violently knocking against a hole in the teeth."

The play affords many such instances when exaggerated sounds could be employed effectively. The close of Scene One is, perhaps, the most striking instance of an unnerving violence in the play. The relative calm of the opening dialogue in this scene rises rapidly into a crescendo of voices and excitement. The ghostly figures in the house rise and gesture, announcing their real presence, as Hummel stands in his wheel chair, drawn and followed by the beggars, screaming "Hail the noble youth!" Such a crescendo is repeated twice more in the play. In Scene Two, the silence of the group is suddenly broken by Hummel as he begins to function more formidably as the exposer of lies and crimes. His speech is punctuated with silences of varying length, until he rises again—as in Scene One—to a crescendo augmented by the magnified sound of the clock ("ticking like a deathwatch beetle in the wall"), and by the horrendous striking of the table with one of his crutches. This crescendo is broken by the Mummy who stops the clock and in a normal voice proceeds to expose Hummel himself. The scene then subsides in intensity as Hummel gradually loses his forceful manner, and becomes, himself, a grotesque parrot. In Scene Three, after a most lyrical beginning, the disturbing sounds of Scene Two are echoed first of all by the Cook's presence and the Student's violent reaction to her, and secondly, the crescendo is apparent in the course of the Student's relation of the events of the earlier scene to the Girl.

Generally speaking, these deliberately spaced crescendo rhythms together with the various auditory juxtapositions (particularly of the lyrical and the dissonant) contribute to a total sound pattern of wide range and expressiveness; in addition, the overall pattern of sound functions as does the visual in the manner of an assistant and accompaniment to the main spiritual action. The auditory and the visual together constitute "beneath language," as Artaud advocated, "a subterranean current of impressions, correspondences, and analogies." As components of the *mise en scene,* they assist the main action, and they possess a certain sub-textual quality which elicits a response not unlike that demanded by music and painting. In no other single play by Strindberg is there such clear evidence of an advanced aesthetic to a considerable degree expressive of Ionesco's assertion that "The theatre is visual as much as it is auditory. It is not a series of images, like the cinema, but a construction, a moving architecture of scenic images."

Ionesco once wrote that

> For me, a play does not consist in the description of the development of a story—that would be writing a novel or a film. A play is a structure that consists of a series of states of consciousness or situations, which become intensified, grow more and more dense, then get entangled, either to be disentangled again or to end in unbearable inextricability.... All my plays have their origin in two fundamental states of consciousness: now the one, now the other is predominant, and sometimes they are combined. These basic states of consciousness are an awareness of evanescence and of solidity, of emptiness and of too much presence, of the unreal transparency of the world and its opacity, of light and of thick darkness.

An account of a play's structure in such terms will first of all indicate the theatrical functioning of such auditory and visual components of the *mise en scene* as have been discussed; and secondly, will give clearer definition to that movement and rhythm of a play which operates in the theatre somewhat independently of the principle narrative thread or action. Frequently in Strindberg's plays, certainly in such a work as *The Inferno,* we can appreciate a sense of form based upon such a rhythm of "states of consciousness" as Ionesco describes. In *The Ghost Sonata,* the close of Scene One, the exposing of Hummel in Scene Two, and the Student's narration to the Girl in Scene Three are three significant instances of "states of consciousness" which "become intensified, grow more and more dense, then get entangled, either to be disentangled again or to end in unbearable inextricability." The exposition by Hummel in Scene One surely induces in the Student—and in the audience—a sense of "unbearable inextricability" not unlike the "expository" passages in Ionesco's *The Bald Soprano* or the accumulation of questions in *The Lesson* (where the Student responds physically to words which have become like solid objects enclosing her). The close of Scene One also possesses something of the gradual rhythm of intensification and relaxation of tension that we find in *The Chairs.* On this level, the form of *The Ghost Sonata* is a continuous modulation of sound and silence, of intensification and relaxation, of a sense of evanescence and "too much presence." Such a modulation is theatrically orchestrated through tension and release which is related to, yet also independent of the more lucid and "straightforward" spiritual action of the play.

Source: Gerald Parker, "The Spectator Seized By the Theatre: Strindberg's *The Ghost Sonata*," in *Modern Drama,* 1971, Vol. 14, pp. 373–86.

Stephen C. Bandy

In the following essay, Bandy argues that "the play is anchored to a strong underlying structure," which "consists of a series of tightly interlocking allusions to incidents recorded in the Bible.*"*

Readers and audiences generally agree that August Strindberg's *The Ghost Sonata* is a highly provocative play. It is assuredly one of his most popular. Yet, even the most thoughtful critics are hard pressed to explain exactly what this play is about, or to make much coherent sense of the action onstage. As fairly typical of present-day thinking, we may take this comment from an anthology widely-used in introductory literature classes:

> The play is not, as far as reader or spectator can discover, based on any rational system of thought. It asserts, or, rather, it shows—it does not prove. On the other hand, that Strindberg has not philosophized his vision renders it immune to rational criticism.

But before we capitulate altogether to the irrational (encouraged as we are by current theatrical fashions), we might do well to examine *The Ghost Sonata* from a fresh point of view. That point of view is, as my title suggests, Biblical; and the results of the examination may alter our ideas about the presumed absurdity of *The Ghost Sonata.*

It is true that most efforts to devise a "meaning" for *The Ghost Sonata* have been—as perhaps such endeavors ought to be—vague and disappointing. We well know that when we reduce the play to an obvious homily on greed, or age, we have no more a paraphrase of *The Ghost Sonata* than of *King Lear.* Yet we persist in our habitual search for order, attempting to unite character and action into a significant whole, despite the fact that such a design does not readily appear in this play. We are naturally reluctant to accept the intricate web of human relationships which is such a conspicuous feature of *The Ghost Sonata,* as, finally, of no particular importance or relevance. Our expectations as an audience are properly outraged by such prodigal expense of character and dramatic situation, to no purpose.

We need not despair, however. There is a good deal more order in *The Ghost Sonata* than we may at first observe, for the play is anchored to a strong underlying structure. And that structure consists of a series of tightly interlocking allusions to incidents recorded in the *Bible.* Nothing is more probable than this, of course. Strindberg was, in his peculiar way, constantly preoccupied with all manner of religious literature and doctrine. His eclectic tastes in reading included not only the *Bible,* but also writings of theologians of every stripe—pre-eminent among whom was Emanuel Swedenborg. And from this rich background, Strindberg no doubt drew the materials which he has assembled to produce *The Ghost Sonata.* The clues are, to my mind, explicit and unmistakeable. And if they do not clarify *all* the dark sayings in the play (for that would demand a great deal more of them than is necessary to prove their presence), they do at least bring its main actions into a common focus, to offer us a coherent philosophical outlook.

As the play begins, we observe the Student asking the evanescent Milkmaid to give him a drink of water from the well. He then begs her to bathe his eyes with his handkerchief. When she does not respond to his request, the Student unwillingly reveals that he has just returned from an attempt to rescue persons trapped in a burning house. Consequently, his own hands are soiled from contact with wounds and corpses. At length, after he has drunk, the Student pleads: "Vill du vara den barmhartiga samaritanskan?" To understand the Student's question, at this crucial early point in the play, as implying no more than "Will you be my Good Samaritan?"—as English translations customarily render it—may be seriously misleading. For those particular words recall only the familiar parable of the Good Samaritan, on the road to Jericho, whose great act of mercy was his rescue of the man who had been set upon by thieves (*Luke* X:30–37).

Yet there is another possible Biblical allusion embedded in this question, one which is of much greater ultimate pertinence to the play than the parable could be. Because of the absence of specifically feminine inflections in English, our term "Good Samaritan" neutralizes an ambiguity inherent in the Swedish "samaritanskan." That is, the Milkmaid cannot, strictly speaking, be a Samaritan at all—she is rather a Samaritan-ess. My purpose in raising this point is not simply to provide an exercise in comparative philology, but to lead to a further suggestion. We must remember that the Samaritan of the parable is by no means the only member of his tribe to figure prominently in the life and teachings of Christ. There remains yet another Samaritan—and this one is a woman—whom Christ himself met at Jacob's well. Several details of that meeting, the telling of which takes up the greater portion of a chapter in the *Gospel According to St. John,* are reflected to a striking degree in the opening lines of *The Ghost Sonata.*

In this Biblical story, we recall, Jesus has passed through Samaria while traveling from Judea to Galilee. In the city of Sichar, he pauses by the well. The narrative continues in this manner (I quote from the King James version):

> There cometh a woman of Samaria to draw water: Jesus saith unto her, Give me to drink. (For his disciples were gone away unto the city to buy meat.) Then saith the woman of Samaria unto him, How is it that thou, being a Jew, askest drink of me, which am a woman of Samaria? for the Jews have no dealings with the Samaritans. Jesus answered and said unto her, If thou knewest the gift of God, and who it is that saith to thee, Give me to drink; thou wouldest have asked of him, and he would have given thee living water. The woman saith unto him, Sir, thou has nothing to draw with, and the well is deep: from whence then hast thou that living water? Art thou greater than our father Jacob, which gave us the well, and drank thereof himself, and his children, and his cattle? Jesus answered and said unto her, Whosoever drinketh of this water shall thirst again: But whosoever drinketh of the water that I shall give him shall never thirst; but the water that I shall give him shall be in him a well of water springing up into everlasting life (*John* IV:7–14).

Jesus remained with the Samaritans for two days afterwards, during which time he converted many: "And many more believed because of his own word; And said unto the woman, Now we believe, not because of thy saying: for we have heard him ourselves, and know that this is indeed the Christ, the Saviour of the world" (IV:41–42).

This, then, is our first Biblical allusion. Simply on the face of it, the opening scene of *The Ghost Sonata*—in both its action and its setting—has a far stronger affinity with this meeting at the Biblical Jacob's well, than with events which took place on the road to Jericho. But now let us look more closely at this well, which the Samaritan woman has identified as the gift of the father of Israel. It is surely no accident that both the Jewish patriarch, and the evil Hummel of *The Ghost Sonata,* bear the same name: Jacob. Hummel is, of course, the patriarch of the

> "AND THUS IT APPEARS THAT STRINDBERG HAS PRESENTED US WITH NOTHING LESS THAN A MODERN-DRESS, THOROUGHLY UPDATED PARABLE OF REDEMPTION— BUT A REDEMPTION STRIPPED OF ITS CHRISTIAN IDEALISM AND OPTIMISM."

"Hummel family of vampires," and it follows that the well from which the Student drank is as much "Jacob's well" as that from which Christ drank.

With this parallel in mind, we might search for further similarities between Jacob Hummel and his Biblical prototype:

1) The patriarch's first wife was named Lia. Hummel's first wife was Amalia.

2) The homely and "tender-eyed" Lia (*Genesis* XXIX:17) was put away by Jacob in favor of her sister Rachel. Hummel's abandoned natural-wife Amalia, now a grotesque mummy, is shut up in the closet because "her eyes can't stand the light."

3) Jacob was tricked into marrying Lia, whom he did not love, because it was necessary that she be wed before her younger sister. Hummel accuses Amalia of having falsified her birthdate, and accuses the Colonel of having stolen his true fiancee.

4) Jacob and Lia are parents of a single daughter (though of many sons), Dina, who is later ravished. Hummel and Amalia are parents of Adele, who expires in the final scene.

5) Jacob first unfairly gained from Esau his birthright, and then, by disguising himself as his brother, stole his paternal blessing. The Mummy says that Hummel's "whole life has been falsified, including his family tree."

6) In stealing Esau's paternal blessing, Jacob was to become master of all: "Let people serve thee, and nations bow down to thee: be lord over thy brethren, and let thy mother's sons bow down to thee: cursed be every one that curseth thee, and blessed be he that blesseth thee" (*Genesis* XXVII:29).

Hummel, despite his wickedness, exerts incredible power over all others in the play, by keeping them in his debt.

7) Though Esau hates his brother for his deeds, he is told by Isaac that he must serve Jacob until "it shall come to pass when thou shalt have the dominion, that thou shalt break his yoke off thy neck" (*Genesis* XXVII:40). Hummel is finally exposed by the servant Bengtsson, whose words precipitate his collapse: "Yes, I know him and he knows me. Life has its ups and downs, as we all know, and I have been in his service, and once he was in mine. To be exact, he was a sponger in my kitchen for two whole years."

8) Jacob was made lame by his wrestling with the angel of God, who "touched the hollow of Jacob's thigh in the sinew that shrank" (*Genesis* XXXII:32). Hummel too is a cripple, who says of his condition, "... some say it's my own fault—others blame my parents—personally I blame it all on life itself...."

I have no doubt that we could discover other ways in which the history of the Jewish patriarch is reflected in the activities of the Hummel family, for the lives of both Jacobs were extraordinarily eventful. I am not especially troubled by the fact that we find no ladders leading to heaven, or pillows of stone, in *The Ghost Sonata*. Nor that, on the other hand, there are no milkmaids, or parrots, or mummies (so far as I can tell) in *Genesis*. It is tempting, but unnecessary, to seek out a Biblical analogue for every detail of *The Ghost Sonata*. For example, could not the fact that Jacob stayed at home and "sod pottage"—the pottage for which Esau gave up his birth-right—have some connection with Hummel's beginnings in Bengtsson's kitchen, as well as with that *alter ego* of Hummel, the Cook? But Strindberg certainly did not intend to write simply a paraphrase of the Biblical story. Moreover, we must make due allowance for the possibility of private symbols, such as would not readily translate into Biblical terms. (I suspect that the Milkmaid, for example, is one of these.) And indeed, the recurring motif of Buddha and hyacinths, in particular, should caution us against becoming overly-rigid in the application of the formula.

Of all the parallels between the two Jacobs, perhaps the most arresting—aside from the duplication of names—is the lameness of both men. It is interesting to observe the opinion of Swedenborg in this matter. As I have suggested, the writings of this Swedish theologian were seldom far from the mind of Strindberg, and citations from Swedenborg appear frequently in the works of the latter. It is not difficult to imagine (though it is, of course, unprovable) that Strindberg may have, at some time in his life, pondered Swedenborg's explanation of the "internal sense" of Jacob's injury:

> ... as this happened to Jacob, it is signified that this nature passed from him to his posterity, and thus was hereditary. That the nerve of that which was displaced signifies falsity, may be seen above; here falsity from hereditary evil.

A few paragraphs later, Swedenborg more fully describes the nature of "hereditary evil":

> Hereditary evil derives its origin from every one's parents and parents' parents, or from grandparents and ancestors successively.... But what hereditary evil is, few know: it is believed to be doing evil; but it is willing and thence thinking evil.... That hereditary evil could not be eradicated from the posterity of Jacob by regeneration because they would not admit it, is likewise manifest from the historicals of the Word....

There remains a final aspect of these interconnecting allusions which we have not yet explored fully, though it may be the most important, so far as the "message" of *The Ghost Sonata* is concerned: the Student as a symbol of Christ. We gather that Hummel, who says he has "an infinitely long life behind me...," has been expecting the Student, and knows all about him and his heroism in the burning house, without having to be told. It was likewise Jacob the patriarch who first prophesied the coming of the Messiah: "The sceptre shall not be taken away from Judah, nor a lawgiver from between his feet, until Shiloh come; and unto him shall the gathering of the people be" (*Genesis* XLIX:10).

After he had struggled with the angel, Jacob's name was changed to "Israel," for his sons were to found the tribes of that nation. Appropriately, then, Jacob Hummel says to the Student: "Our destinies are tangled together through your father—and other things," for Christ was of the house of David and literally descended from Jacob. In just those words does the prophet Isaiah predict the coming of the Messiah: "And I will bring forth a seed out of Jacob, and out of Judah an inheritor of my mountains..." (*Isaiah* LXV:9). And much of the prophetic writing of Isaiah speaks of the coming of Christ as the salvation of Israel: "... thy Saviour and thy Redeemer, the Mighty One of Jacob" (LX:16).

The identification of "Christ-figures" in ostensibly secular literature has, of course, long been a favorite scholarly pastime, and the attendant danger of permitting one's zeal to overbalance one's judgment is notorious. But the early resemblance in *The Ghost Sonata* of the Student to Christ is confirmed, I think, by another mention of Christ—this time explicit and fully developed—at the very conclusion of the play. Here, the Student ponders that similarity:

> There are poisons that seal the eyes and poisons that open them. I must have been born with the latter kind in my veins, because I cannot see what is ugly as beautiful and I cannot call what is evil good. I cannot. They say that Christ harrowed hell. What they really meant was that he descended to earth, to this penal colony, to this madhouse and morgue of a world. And the inmates crucified Him when He tried to free them. But the robber they let free.

These words forcibly remind us, once more, of the life of Christ, again in close conjunction with the life of the Student. And, if one cares to press the analogy with the sonata-form (for there is much evidence that Strindberg intended us to do so: the three-part structure of the play, or the final coda, in which the Student restates all of the events of the play), he may see a certain aptness in this return to the initial theme of the first scene. In this closing meditation of the Student, we are pointedly reminded that Christ's purpose in entering hell (ironically realized in his rejection as the Messiah come to earth) is to harrow that region and to liberate the souls of men imprisoned there. It is logical to consider these final words of the Student in the light of what has gone before: we may view the collapse of the house of Jacob Hummel (that is, the "Hummel family of vampires") as, in effect, apocalyptic. Just as the Student attempts to save the life of the daughter, so is Christ to redeem mankind in the last days.

But if this parallel is intended, there is something badly amiss in the Student's *imitatio Christi:* the daughter, instead of embracing her savior, droops and dies. Similarly, the Messiah was rejected by the house of Jacob, or Israel. Moreover, we recall that Christ is traditionally described by the prophets as the "Bridegroom" who comes to wed the lovely "daughter of Zion" (*Isaiah* LXII), a figure of speech which would appropriately describe the course of the Student's powerful, but unconsummated, longing for Hummel's daughter. Indeed, the Student's present inability to rescue anyone at all from the Colonel's house was forecast (perhaps "prefigured" is the better word) by his earlier experience in the burning house. As the Student tells Hummel: "The next moment the house collapsed.... I escaped—but in my arms—where I thought I had the child—there wasn't anything...." Is not this to be precisely the fate of the Colonel's house? We mark the words of Johansson, Hummel's servant, as he explains to the Student that his master's method is one of "Eavesdropping on the poor.... Planting a word here and there, chipping away at one stone at a time—until the whole house falls—metaphorically speaking."

Metaphors within metaphors, we might rather say. But, call it what we will—the Colonel's house, the burning house, the house of Jacob Hummel, or the house of Jacob-who-is-Israel—the symbolic burden of this edifice is clear: the house which is collapsing is, in its largest sense, all of unredeemed mankind, bound together as a family by their common guilt and parasitism. One might detect in this formulation a doctrine of correspondences altogether Swedenborgian.

Thus do the actions of the Student, onstage and off, continually rehearse the long-awaited coming of Christ—but always in a manner oddly distorted and inverted. The significance of this tangle of events and allusions may be summarized by words of the Student: "It's remarkable how the same story can be told in two exactly opposite ways." Remarkable indeed! In the eyes of the believer, the betrayal of Christ may represent a triumph of God's mercy and a promise of hope to all mankind—but not so for the Student. He is a "Sunday child," as we are often told, and is able to see what others cannot see: that the tragic sacrifice of Christ is in no way beautiful or noble.

Unquestionably, Strindberg has written much autobiography into *The Ghost Sonata* (the almost ludicrous vampirism of the Cook is commonly recognized as an echo of his own difficulties with domestics at the time). And to this extent, his technique accords with what we have come to regard as a characteristic practice of "Expressionism": a systematic interpretation of all experience through the subjective filter of the Ego. But we are not wise to ascribe such practices to Strindberg without considerable hesitation. We often tend to pigeonhole Strindberg as a precursor of this movement; but Expressionism, as an aesthetic philosophy, was unknown to him, and it came to full flower long after his time. The great danger of this classification is, of course, that it encourages one to cultivate certain critical attitudes toward Strindberg's work, perhaps to the neglect of other, equally valid, view-points. Hence, if we can label Strindberg a card-carrying Expressionist, we then have no difficulty at all in believing *The Ghost Sonata* incapable of analysis. But, with due regard for these pitfalls, we would not go too far to suggest that in *The Ghost Sonata* Strindberg has turned inside-out the traditional meaning on the passion of Christ: he transforms it into an eternal image of the Student's bitter disillusionment. Instead of looking to Christ for release from his unhappy existence, the Student in fact redefines Christian salvation in his own terms. At the center he places not an abstract God, but the Self.

And thus it appears that Strindberg has presented us with nothing less than a modern-dress, thoroughly up-dated parable of redemption—but a redemption stripped of its Christian idealism and optimism. Though we recognize the fundamental similarity to Christ at Jacob's well when the play begins, we are soon aware of a profound departure from the model. Christ converted the Samaritans, but the Student saves no one. Yet we should not be startled by his failure: the Student has already warned us that the same story can be told in two exactly opposite ways. The "living water" which Christ offered to the Samaritans flows from a source which, so far as the universe of this drama is concerned, has run quite dry. The Student cannot reconcile himself to the fact that, although Christ revealed himself as the Messiah whom Jacob had foreseen, he was nonetheless sacrificed. The Student's eyes are now opened to the truth—when he strikes the golden harp with the invocation "Sursum Corda," the strings do not sound.

In a final irony, the Student, far from preserving any of the self-destructive and doomed "Hummel family of vampires," is perhaps himself converted by them. He is, after all, of their seed; and their fleshly sins weigh on his soul as well. So does the Mummy accuse Hummel: "You have stolen the student, and shackled him with an imaginary debt of his father's, who never owed you a penny. . . ." In the same way, the Student later comes to realize, was the Messiah destroyed by those whom he meant to save.

Even though the question is somewhat outside the boundaries of this study, we might now ask what purpose is served by those several conspicuous references to Buddha throughout *The Ghost Sonata*. They seem, at first glance, singularly out-of-place in a play so largely taken up with intramural debate over Judeo-Christian theology. But it may be that Buddha and the legend of the hyacinths are to provide a resolution of that debate. Strindberg seems to balance the values of an exhausted Western tradition, against the more inward-looking values of Eastern philosophy. It is no matter that Strindberg fails to offer a very definite idea of Buddhism, as it appears in the play. Rather, the mention of Buddha seems to serve in *The Ghost Sonata* chiefly as the antithesis of the deadly self-seeking which possesses the intimates of Jacob Hummel. It would be rash to infer that Strindberg is recommending mass conversion to Buddhism; yet he does seem to hold out the hope, not unusual among Western thinkers, that there is a solace to be found among the religions of the East, of a sort which is no longer possible in Western culture. It is clear that in the world inhabited by Jacob Hummel, the mystifications of Christianity are merely a cruel deception. The Student therefore concludes that the only possible liberator from the hell of life is death—whose features strangely resemble those of the "pale Galilean": "Befriaren kommer! Valkommen, du bleka, milda!"

Source: Stephen C. Bandy, "Strindberg's Biblical Sources for *The Ghost Sonata*," in *Scandinavian Studies,* August, 1968, Vol. 40, no. 3, pp. 200–09.

Milton A. Mays

In the following essay, Mays contends "that The Ghost Sonata *takes as its main structural mode the fairy tale, that it is in fact a parodied fairy tale of sorts, and that this form is the means of saying something about Original Sin."*

Despite a good deal of interest in Strindberg's *The Ghost Sonata,* critics, as Evert Sprinchorn puts it, "seem reluctant to declare that the play possesses any great coherence." There has been, in fact, a marked willingness to take the dodge that "dreams needn't make sense": doubly specious, since plays are not dreams, however "dreamlike," and even dreams have, if not a logic, a psychologic. The many readers who find *The Ghost Sonata* one of the most exciting pieces in modern drama—however much avoided by pusillanimous directors—are surely correct. The play, that is to say, for all its admitted redundancies and even symbolic nonsequiturs, must have a thematic and symbolic coherence. The thesis here advanced—which by no means explains everything—is that *The Ghost Sonata* takes as its main structural mode the fairy tale, that it is in fact a parodied fairy tale of sorts, and that this form is the means of saying something about Original Sin.

Strindberg's was a basically religious consciousness, and a fascination with the concept of Original

Sin would seem a natural corollary of his known obsessive fascination with guilt, especially marked in the chamber plays. *The Burned House,* which immediately precedes our play in the group, and is closely associated with it in the writing, turns on a question of the guilty past, and is full of allusions to the Garden, the Tree of Knowledge, and the loss of an (equivocal) childhood innocence. *The Ghost Sonata,* with that hallucinatory clarity peculiar to the surrealistic work, focuses on the universality and inescapability of guilt, bearing down on ''innocent'' and ''sinful'' alike in a debacle which seems fully as terrible as the pagan retribution rejected by the play—and this despite the concluding unction of the Student's words on patience and hope, accompanied by ''a white light,'' Bocklin, and ''soft, sweet, melancholy'' music.

Early in Scene I when the Old Man begins to open out the insanely complicated relationships binding the inmates of the Colonel's house, the Student says, ''It's like a fairy story.'' Hummel, in replying, ''My whole life's like a book of fairy stories . . . held together by one thread, and the main theme constantly recurs,'' seems to corroborate their genre and hints that his story—and our play—is about something specific. Seen in broad relief, *The Ghost Sonata* contains all the elements of the fairy story, and it is this which gives it a kind of structural cohesiveness not found in the other chamber plays, which seem to spill their symbols into a void. We have a poor but heroic youth, and one, moreover, especially blessed or singled out by destiny (a ''Sunday child'' with the gift of second sight). Our Student is enraptured of a beautiful and highborn maiden, who lives in a ''castle'' imagined by the Student to enclose all his life's desires. He thinks his suit is hopeless, but a ''fairy godfather'' with an aura of immense and mysterious powers appears and promises him an entrée to ''doors and hearts.'' In Scene II we discover, as we might have expected, that there are ''ogres'' in the castle who have the maid in thrall; but the fairy godfather is prepared to do them battle. In the third scene we would further expect the fairy princess and hero to be united and ''live happily ever after.'' Just how true— and false—to the facts of the play this outline is should be apparent; yet in the play's relation to this submerged paradigm, I am suggesting, lies much of its meaning.

For the fairy tale, after all, is a projection of the return-to-Paradise wish. Whatever his ill fortune (symbolic of the fallen world), the hero's desert is always good (he is naturally good, an erect Adam),

> "... LIKE STRINDBERG, THE STUDENT IS AN INNOCENT TRYING TO BELIEVE IN AN UNFALLEN WORLD IN THE FACE OF THE HORRORS OF REAL EXISTENCE. . . . BUT HE IS A FAIRY TALE HERO EJECTED FROM HIS FAIRY TALE WORLD—AND A CRUELLY PARODIED HERO AT THAT."

and the powers that be, somehow always recognizing this, return him and his Eve, the princess (who has suffered her trials as well), to Paradise, shutting the golden doors of ''they lived happily ever after'' firmly before our inquisitive eyes. In *The Ghost Sonata* Strindberg uses parody and distortion of the fairy tale to make it say the opposite thing: that guilt is contagious, innocence non-existent, or, if in some sense real (the girl), it is ''sick'' and ''doomed,'' ''suffering for no fault'' of its own. In Adam's fall, sinned we all. Nor is there any Paradise to be regained in the last act. The Student says of the girl's house: ''I thought it was paradise itself that first time I saw you coming in here.'' But the flowers in the ''paradise'' are poisonous; it is in fact a place of ordeals, where no dreams come true. In sum, despite the vague appeal of the Student (who seems in these last moments of the play to have stepped out of the character of hero and into the function of *raisonneur*) to a ''Liberator'' who will waken the innocent girl to ''a sun that does not burn, in a home without dust, by friends without stain, by a love without a flaw''—despite this perhaps rather sentimental gesture, the force of the play is compacted into a metaphor for Original Sin: it is expressive of the agony of ''this world of illusion, guilt, suffering, and death . . . endless change, disappointment, and pain.''

Strindberg's meaning in the play is put both abstractly and concretely: both in discursive ''talk,'' such as we have rather too much of in the Student's last speeches, and in the most vivid symbols, such as the vampire cook—a disturbing contribution of paranoia to art. The Student *says* that ''The curse lies over the whole of creation, over life itself''; but this allusion to the fallen world is only effective because we have seen the ''haunted'' old house, in which the very air is tainted, ''charged with crime,'' so that its inmates, guilty and innocent alike, are withering away.

It has been said that ''the fairy tale's miracles occur on the material plane; on the spiritual plane (affections; characters; justice; love) law abides.'' *The Ghost Sonata* is a fairy tale parodied and distorted. We have not witnessed this play for long before getting a disturbing sense that nothing is quite right, that even a ''spiritual logic'' is being tampered with. Is the Old Man, Hummel, a benefactor, or a self-serving user of other people, after power—or what? That is, is he good fairy or wicked witch? There are abundant hints to shake our confidence in Hummel, the most startling of which is the first sounding of the vampire-motif when Hummel takes the Student's hand in his icy hand, and the Student struggles to free himself, saying, ''You are taking all my strength. You are freezing me.'' Variations on this theme occur throughout the play, of course: ''vampirism'' is a multiplex symbol for vicarious gratification (''enjoy life so that I can watch, at least from a distance''), for enslaving others by a knowledge of their guilty secrets (Johansson, the Colonel), or by a sense of obligation (the Student) or by usury. Hummel is a ''bloodsucker'' both metaphorically, on the surreal level of ''sucking the marrow out of the house,'' and economically (the debts of the Consul and the Colonel).

There is, if anything, a redundancy of suggestion of evil identity for the Student's ostensible benefactor: he is a pagan god in a chariot, a wizard, an ''old devil.'' Hummel's Mephistophelean character is underlined by his saying to the Student, ''Serve me and you shall have power.''

STUDENT. Is it a bargain? Am I to sell my soul?

And when the Student, after hearing something disturbing about Hummel from Johansson, his servant, decides to escape from him, the girl drops her bracelet out of the window, the Student returns it, and there is no more talk of escape. The girl serves Hummel's purpose in a sense as Gretchen does Mephisto's. (And both women are destroyed, though I am not suggesting the parallel be taken any further.)

The question of the essential nature of Hummel remains a difficult one. He is clearly the most dynamic character in the play, the one who seems to make everything happen. With the Student as the ''arm to do [his] will'' Hummel will enter the Colonel's house and ''expose the crimes'' there so that the girl (his daughter by the Colonel's wife), withering away in the evil atmosphere, can live again in health with the Student. All is for the young couple; Hummel's cleansing revenge is to involve the ''ghosts'' only. But by Scene II we are as suspicious of Hummel's intention as is the Mummy. In any case, realistic criteria of character consistency and continuity of action are mostly irrelevant in this play. If we are unsure what Hummel's ''real'' purpose with regard to the ''innocents'' is, we are no more sure how his defeat by the Mummy has influenced the outcome of the play in Scene III. Are the Mummy, the Colonel, and the others versus the Old Man two groups of equally evil figures who mutually destroy each other? This would seem to leave the field clear for the blossoming of young love, the ghost house purged. But before we can understand more fully why this is not the case, the Student must be considered.

The role of the Student in *The Ghost Sonata* also has its curious features. Does the play's conclusion leave him saved or damned? A survivor—the only one—or a victim? Or is he, by the conclusion of the play, not a protagonist at all, but dramatist's *raisonneur,* as suggested above? It seems to me that in his final speeches he does assume the function of authorial surrogate, but that there is a certain fitness to this: like Strindberg, the Student is an innocent trying to believe in an unfallen world in the face of the horrors of real existence. He is an Adam-figure, a ''Sunday child,'' who, when he first saw the house of his beloved on Sunday morning—the ''first day of creation''—thought it was paradise. But he is a fairy tale hero ejected from his fairy tale world— and a cruelly parodied hero at that. His dream of bliss is all bourgeois: ''' Think of living up there in the top flat, with a beautiful young wife, two pretty little children and an income of twenty thousand crowns a year.''' The conclusion of Scene I is also parodistic, and splendid theater: Hummel, standing in his wheel chair which is drawn in by the beggars, cries: ''Hail the noble youth who, at the risk of his own life, saved so many in yesterday's accident. Three cheers for Arkenholtz!'' This scene is followed by a nice tableau of the beggars baring their heads, the girl waving her hankerchief, the old woman rising at her window, and the maid hoisting the flag. Strains of a bizarre slapstick are found throughout the play; the audience should laugh, but not over-confidently.

The girl and the Student—fairy tale hero and princess—do not figure in Scene II, where the ogres or witches fight. At least one consequence of Hummel's defeat follows the fairy tale pattern: Johansson, his servant, is "freed from slavery" by his death, as the victims of the enchanter or wicked witch always are. Alone with his beloved in the Hyacinth Room in Scene III, the Student's expectations are clearly for speedy achievement of his heart's desire. "We are wedded," he says; but his Eve must disillusion him. This place is not what it seems; it is no paradise, and no fairy-tale "ever-after," but is "bewitched"—"bedeviled" we might more literally call the post-lapsarian world. Hummel—"old Adam" as well as "old Nick"?—may be dead (literally by his own hand, as Adam was in effect), but his influence lives on after him. "This room is called the room of ordeals," says the girl; "It looks beautiful, but it is full of defects." We are placed on earth to work out our salvation; and earth's beauties are no end in themselves, but illusory, mutable ("defective"). The metaphor for this in *The Ghost Sonata* is domestic—if insane. The Student's "paradise" was domestic; his fate is the domestic demented; instead of "they lived happily ever after," we see the fairy princess at the kitchen sink, in effect. It is not the real world, but the domestic-surreal, this house with servants who unclean, cooks who un-feed; but the surreal can be taken as measure of the recoil of the tender soul (Strindberg, the Student) from real life. As the Student says in closing, only in the imagination is there anything which fulfills its promise. The Student, rather like his creator, is Adam who refuses to accept his ejection, symbolically as well as psychologically the child who refuses to grow up. ("Where are honor and faith? In fairy-tales and children's fancies.") "I asked you to become my wife in a home full of poetry and song and music. Then the Cook came . . ." says the Student. "What have we to do with the kitchen?" he asks the girl, who replies, "realistically," "We must eat." The Student reflects Strindberg's neurotic fastidiousness, well known, toward the "lower functions"; and eating, by the mechanism known to psychologists as "displacement," can represent the sexual function, also profoundly disturbing to Strindberg: "It is always in the kitchen quarters that the seed-leaves of the children are nipped, if it has not already happened in the bedroom." The Student wants to live in a garden with his bride, but this garden is "poison": "You have poisoned me and I have given the poison back to you," says the Student. But perhaps the "sickness" is in fact the "Student's": It is the recoil of a pathological romanticism upon itself which sees the earth as "this madhouse, this prison, this charnel house." Strindberg, like his surrogate, the Student, desires the fairy-tale princess in a "home full of poetry and song and music"—a home with no "kitchen quarters," only conservatory. That this whole fairy-tale gone crazy is a projection of the Student's we may take as admitted in his saying that he is a man born with one of those "poisons that open the eyes"—or does it "destroy the sight"?—"for I cannot see what is ugly as beautiful, nor call evil good."

As the girl enumerates all the tasks which weigh her down, the Student cries out again and again for "Music!"—music to drown out the sounds of real life. But it is no more possible to do so than it is for Strindberg to ring in "soft, sweet, and melancholy" music at the end of his play in order to effect a resolution. The emotion we depart with is fear trembling on the brink of hysteria, the image that of the grinning vampire cook. No vague promises of a "Liberator," a waking to a "sun that does not burn, in a home without dust, by friends without stain, by a love without a flaw" can salve over the fact, of which *The Ghost Sonata* is the gripping symbol, that "a curse lies over the whole of creation, over life itself." Out of his own conflict between paradise and the fallen world, fairy-tale and reality, Strindberg has made stunning drama.

Source: Milton A. Mays, "Strindberg's *Ghost Sonata:* Parodied Fairy Tale on Original Sin," in *Modern Drama,* 1967, Vol. 10, pp. 189–194.

SOURCES

Bandy, Stephen C. "Strindberg's Biblical Sources for *Ghost Sonata,*" in *Scandinavian Studies,* August, 1968, Vol. 40, no. 3, p. 208.

Goodman, Randolph. Introduction to *Drama on Stage* [his English language version of *The Ghost Sonata*], Holt, Rinehart and Winston, 1978, pp. 428-437.

Hampton, Wilborn. A review of *The Ghost Sonata,* in the *New York Times,* May 9, 1995.

Lide, Barbara. A review of *The Ghost Sonata,* in *Theatre Journal,* March, 1992, p. 109-111.

Nicoll, Allardyce. *World Drama: From Aeschylus to Anouilh,* Harcourt, Brace and Company, rev. ed., 1976, p. 563.

Richardson, Maurice. A review of the BBC television production of *The Ghost Sonata,* in the London *Observer,* March 18, 1962, reprinted in *Drama on Stage,* edited by Randolph Goodman, Holt, Rinehart and Winston, 1978, pp. 439-441.

Sinclair, Clive. A review of *The Ghost Sonata,* in the *Times Literary Supplement,* June 12, 1992, p. 18.

Strindberg, August. Letter to Edvard Brandes, c. June 12, 1885, excerpted in *File on Strindberg,* edited by Michael Meyer, Methuen, 1986, p. 51.

Strindberg, August. Letter to Anders Eliasson, July 11, 1896, excerpted in *Strindberg,* by Michael Meyer, Secker and Warburg, 1985, p. 341.

FURTHER READING

Meyer, Michael. *Strindberg,* Secker and Warburg, 1985.
A thorough biography of playwright August Strindberg, including a complete history of his childhood, his several marriages, his 1884 trial for blasphemy in Stockholm, his investigations into the occult, and his immense body of writing, including plays, novels, stories and essays. Also contains several pages of photographs and illustrations from Strindberg's life and the production of his plays.

Meyer, Michael, ed. *File on Strindberg,* Methuen, 1986.
A collection of excerpted comments and criticism about Strindberg's plays, taken largely from theatre reviews, letters from Strindberg's friends and associates, and writings by the author himself. Also includes a chronology of Strindberg's work and a bibliography of other research sources.

Nicoll, Allardyce. *World Drama: From Aeschylus to Anouilh,* Harcourt, Brace and Company, rev. ed., 1976.
In a book that describes trends in dramatic literature from the Ancient Greeks to the twentieth century, Nicoll places August Strindberg alongside Ibsen and his other Scandinavian contemporaries in an essay titled "Strindberg and the Play of the Subconscious."

Strindberg, August. *The Son of a Servant,* translated by Claud Field, G. P. Putnam's Sons, 1913.
Strindberg's autobiography, in which he details his unhappy childhood as one of eight surviving children born to a bankrupt father who was once part of an aristocratic family and a mother who was once a waitress.

Tornqvist, Egil. *Strindbergian Drama: Themes and Structure,* Humanities Press, 1982.
Tornqvist notes that several authors and critics have assembled biographies of August Strindberg, and attempted critical discussions of the ideas found in his plays and where he fits into late nineteenth century theatre history, but that little has been written about the actual *structure* of his plays, and how his formal style is different from that of his contemporaries. *Strindbergian Drama* examines ten of Strindberg's plays, from *The Father* to *A Dream Play* and *The Ghost Sonata,* and considers the importance of imagery, plot, language and borrowed forms to their creation.

The Good Person of Szechwan

BERTOLT BRECHT
1943

Bertolt Brecht's parable *The Good Person of Szechwan* is one of the playwright's major plays, popular and regularly produced because of its universal themes. Many critics believe the play is one of the best examples of Brecht's epic theater because it challenges the audience. Although Brecht worked on the idea behind the play as early as the late 1920s, it was primarily written from 1939-43 in various European countries and the United States while in exile from his native Germany during World War II. Brecht tried to get *Good Person* produced in the United States in 1941, but the play did not make its debut until February 4, 1943, at the Schauspielhaus Zurich, in Zurich, Switzerland. The play was produced throughout Europe in the 1940s. The first English-language production of *The Good Person of Szechwan* in the United States took place in either Cleveland's Eldred Theater or Hamline University in St. Paul, Minnesota, in 1948. Many American colleges and universities put on the play after this date. *The Good Person of Szechwan* was first produced professionally in New York City in late 1956, shortly after Brecht's death.

The play has continued to be performed throughout the world to the present day, in part because it seems to be a modern parable about a basic human issue: how to be a good person in an imperfect, money-centered, class-divided society. Because of this focus, the play does not seem to be intended to be a reflection of the actual social, cultural and political life in China at that time, although the play

uses some conventions of Chinese theater and is set in China. Brecht's original setting for the play was Berlin, and some recent productions have adapted the story to reflect the time and location of production. As John Fuegi wrote in *The Essential Brecht,* "The profound metaphysical question of why evil is permitted, indeed encouraged, in the world has seldom been asked with such force."

AUTHOR BIOGRAPHY

Bertolt Brecht was born on February 10, 1898, in Augsburg, Bavaria, Germany. He was the son of a Catholic father, Friedrich Brecht, who worked as a salesman for a paper factory, and a Protestant mother, Sofie. Brecht grew up in a middle-class household, and was precociously intelligent in school. He began writing poems while still in secondary school and had several published by 1914. By the time Brecht graduated, he was also interested in the theatre. Instead of continuing on this path, however, he studied science and medicine at university to avoid the draft. It did not work, and he was drafted in 1918 at the end of World War I. He served as an orderly in the military hospital in Augsburg.

Both his upbringing and his experience in the military profoundly affected Brecht and his writing. He rejected the bourgeois values of his youth, and had a keen understanding of the differences between Catholics and Protestants. The turmoil of war that Brecht saw in the hospital led to his life-long pacifist views. He began writing plays as early as 1918 (*Baal*) and joined communist organizations in 1919. After finally giving up his sporadic university studies, Brecht became the dramaturge at a theater in Munich and was writing full time by 1920.

Over the next 13 years, Brecht published several short stories and poems, and successfully staged many of his own plays. Brecht collaborated with composer Kurt Weill on several musical plays, including one of his best known works, 1928's *The Three Penny Opera.* By 1930 Brecht's plays had become increasingly political, espousing his belief that communism would solve many of the world's problems. When the Nazis came to power in the early 1930s, Brecht and his works were banned. Brecht and his family fled the increasingly hostile environment in 1933 and went into exile for the next fifteen years.

During his exile, Brecht lived in the United States and in various countries in Europe and continued to write. In addition to a novelization of *The Three Penny Opera,* Brecht composed numerous plays that were critical of the Nazi regime and the world's political situation. Though he began *The Good Person of Szechwan* as early as 1928, Brecht completed it in exile between 1939 and 1943, when it was first produced. Though *The Good Person of Szechwan* was not as overtly political as *Mother Courage and Her Children* (1939), Brecht hoped it would be produced in the United States.

After the war ended and Germany was divided into East and West, Brecht was invited home. He decided to settle in East Germany, in part because they offered him a theater and funding. Brecht formed the Berliner Ensemble, which debuted in 1949. That same year Brecht wrote his last original play, *The Days of the Commune,* as he devoted all his time to running the theater and working as its stage manager. He continued to write poetry and adapt other playwrights' work for his theater, however. By the mid-1950s, the importance of Brecht's plays had been realized and they became popularly recognized. Brecht died as a result of a coronary thrombosis on August 14, 1956, in East Berlin.

PLOT SUMMARY

Prologue
Wang, an impoverished water seller, tries to find lodging for three prominent gods, who have come to Earth to find good people. Wang's request is refused by everyone. Wang himself lives under a bridge and has no home to offer. He finally asks the town's prostitute, Shen Teh, who agrees to take them in. The next morning, Shen Teh tells the gods that she cannot make a living though she tries to be good. The gods decide to pay her for lodgings when they leave.

Scene One
Shen Teh uses the gods' payment of a thousand silver dollars to buy a small tobacconist business. She hopes to do good through her shop, but people start to take advantage of her. The former owner, Mrs. Shin, begs for rice and money. An elderly couple, who were the first people to take Shen Teh in when she moved to the city but who evicted her when she had no money, ask for shelter for themselves and six relatives. The elderly couple criticize

Shen Teh for being too nice. They tell her she should put people off by saying a relative actually owns the store. She is forced to use this excuse several times, including when the landlady, Mrs. Mi Tzu, demands six months rent in advance. The elderly couple's relatives convince the landlady that Shen Teh's cousin, Shui Ta, is really in charge. The elderly couple believe that Shen Teh will soon be out of business, but they continue to take advantage of her hospitality. Shen Teh is worried that she will lose her shop.

Interlude

The gods charge Wang with looking after Shen Teh and informing them of her progress.

Scene Two

In the morning, the elderly couple's family wonders where Shen Teh is. In her absence, her cousin, Shui Ta, enters with a carpenter. Shui Ta says that Shen Teh will not be coming back and demands that they leave. Shui Ta disposes of several business matters and has the elderly couple's family arrested. When Shui Ta cannot convince the landlady to exempt Shen Teh from paying six months' rent in advance, a policeman suggests that Shen Teh marry to raise capital for the shop. A personal ad is composed to attract someone appropriate.

Scene Three

In a public park, Shen Teh comes upon a young pilot, Yang Sun, preparing to hang himself. It starts to rain, and Sun and Shen Teh seek shelter together. Sun reveals that he cannot find a job, while Shen Teh reveals she has worked as a prostitute. Sun begins to appreciate Shen Teh, but he tells her that he could never love her.

Interlude

The gods visit Wang for a progress report. Wang tells them that Shen Teh is in love with Sun, and has remained good. Wang mentions that Shui Ta has been uncharitable, and the gods are not pleased with the cousin's actions.

Scene Four

Several people whom Shen Teh has helped wait for her outside her shop. Shen Teh had spent the night with Sun and forgotten that she needs to pay the rent on her shop. A carpet dealer and his wife lend her the 200 silver dollars that she needs. When

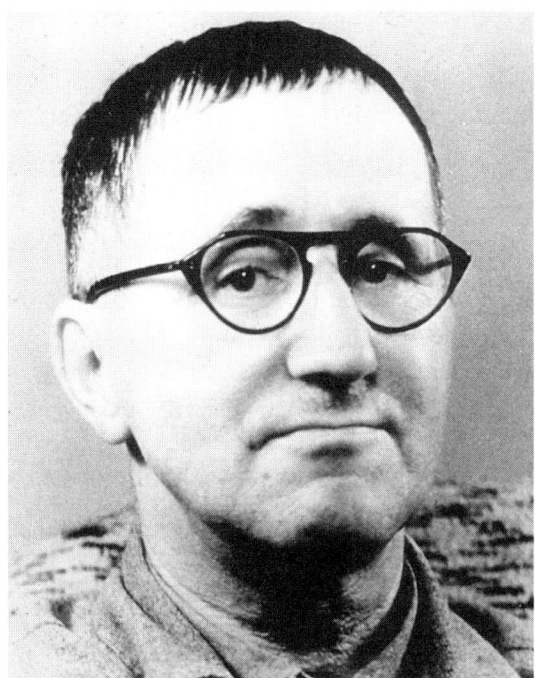

Bertolt Brecht

she leaves the carpet dealer's shop, Wang shows her his hand, which has been broken by the rich barber, Shu Fu. Though there are many witnesses to Shu Fu's crime, none will corroborate Wang's story. Shen Teh becomes angry at those waiting and tells them to leave. Sun's mother, Mrs. Yang, approaches her, because Sun needs 500 silver dollars to get a pilot's job. Shen Teh immediately gives her the 200 silver dollars that the carpet dealer gave her, and pledges to get the rest.

Interlude

Shen Teh reveals that she is really Shui Ta.

Scene Five

Shui Ta is running the shop when Yang Sun shows up. The young pilot wants the remaining 300 silver dollars so he can get his job. Yang Sun even says that he will marry Shen Teh. Shui Ta suggests that he give back the 200 silver dollars and help Shen Teh run the tobacconist business, but Sun insists that they sell the shop for 300 silver dollars instead. Shui Ta agrees until Sun reveals that he intends to leave Shen Teh behind with nothing to live on when he goes to his job. Shui Ta asks for the 200 silver dollars back, but Sun refuses. Shui Ta realizes that Sun does not love Shen Teh.

Mrs. Shin brings the barber, Shu Fu, to the shop. Shu Fu has been admiring Shen Teh and offers the use of some empty buildings to house her homeless guests. When Wang and a police officer enter the shop, Shui Ta denies that Shen Teh witnessed the crippling of Wang. After they leave, Shui Ta tells Shu Fu that Shen Teh is no longer involved with Sun, and will be gone for a few weeks. Then Shui Ta goes into the back room. Shu Fu makes it known that he wants to become involved with Shen Teh, and when Yang appears at the shop, the barber informs him that he (Shu Fu) and Shen Teh will be married. But when Shen Teh emerges from the back room, Yang Sun manages to talk himself back into her affections, and Shen Teh admits she loves him, not the barber.

Interlude

Shen Teh is in her wedding dress. She tells the audience that the carpet dealer is ill, and his wife desperately needs the money back. Shen Teh loves Yang Sun, who now has the money, but is torn over what to do.

Scene Six

At the wedding, Yang Sun complains to his mother that Shen Teh has asked for the 200 silver dollars back. Mrs. Yang assures him that she has sent for Shui Ta. Shen Teh believes all is well until she realizes that Yang Sun and his mother are holding the wedding up for Shui Ta. Yang Sun does not have the 200 silver dollars she asked for, and he is angry that Shui Ta will not be bringing the 300 silver dollars. Shui Ta never comes and the couple do not marry.

Interlude

The gods appear to Wang in a dream. Wang is worried that Shen Teh has lost love because she tried to be good, but the gods dismiss his concerns, believing that goodness will win out.

Scene Seven

Shen Teh prepares to sell her business so she can pay back the carpet dealer. Shu Fu offers Shen Teh a blank check so she can stay in business, but Shen Teh refuses to use it. Shen Teh reveals that she is pregnant, and worries about her child's future. Still, Shen Teh gives Wang her cart, one of the last things she owns, so that he can sell it and go to the doctor.

Some members of the elderly couple's family ask if they can leave some ill-gotten tobacco in her back room. Shen Teh agrees. Later Shen Teh decides that if her child is to survive, she will have to become Shui Ta again. Shui Ta, her alter ego, takes charge of the situation, and puts an end to Shen Teh's charity. He decides to open a tobacco factory, using the elderly couple's tobacco for stock and the homeless guests as workers. Shui Ta uses the blank check to save the business.

Interlude

Wang tells the gods that he has seen Shen Teh in distress in a dream, but the gods are not sympathetic.

Scene Eight

Shui Ta's tobacco factory is thriving. Mrs. Yang tells the audience how Shui Ta saved her son, giving Sun a job in the factory and deducting the 200 silver dollars still owed to Shen Teh from wages. Although Sun does not like the work at first, he excels and eventually becomes the overseer.

Scene Nine

Still running Shen Teh's shop, Shui Ta is very fat because of Shen Teh's pregnancy. Shui Ta/Shen Teh has repaid the carpet dealer and his wife, although they have already lost their shop. Mrs. Shin now knows that Shui Ta is Shen Teh. Sun enters, commenting on how moody Shui Ta has been, tries to get Shui Ta to talk about business, but is put off. Wang enters, asking about Shen Teh's whereabouts, because he is worried that she has met with an ill fate. When Wang inadvertently reveals to Sun that Shen Teh is pregnant, Sun becomes angry. Shui Ta has gone into the back room and cries like a girl. Sun overhears the weeping, believes that Shui Ta is holding Shen Teh prisoner in the backroom. The police come and arrest Shui Ta.

Interlude

Wang tells the gods that Shen Teh is gone, and her cousin has been arrested. They decide to intervene.

Scene Ten

Inside the courtroom, the three gods oversee Shui Ta's hearing. Everyone in attendance believes Shui Ta will get off because he is well-connected. All present tell the gods about how good Shen Teh is. While several people claim Shui Ta is a good and honorable businessman, most say he has ruined them. The merits of Shui Ta and Shen Teh are debated by all whose lives have been touched by them. Shui Ta decides to confess, but only if the courtroom is emptied of everyone but the gods. When they are alone, Shen Teh takes off the masks and clothing that makes her Shui Ta. She explains to them how hard it was to survive as Shen Teh because everyone took advantage of her. The gods are not sympathetic, and wish her luck as they return to heaven. They tell her if she is good, all will turn out well. Shen Teh is left to go on alone.

Epilogue

A player appears in front of the curtain and apologizes to the audience that the ending is not neat and tidy.

CHARACTERS

The Carpet dealer and his wife

The Carpet dealer and his wife run a shop near Shen Teh's tobacco shop. When Shen Teh is joyous because of her relationship with Yang Sun, she buys a shawl from their shop. The couple is supportive of Shen Teh, and when they learn, she does not have enough money to pay her rent, they lend her the funds. This loan becomes problematic for Shen Teh. She does not pay them back until after the carpet dealer has fallen ill, and the couple loses their shop when they cannot pay their taxes. Like many of the people who meet them both, they appreciate what Shen Teh has done, and are afraid of Shui Ta.

Elderly couple

The elderly couple were Shen Teh's first landlords when she moved to the city from the countryside. They made her leave when she ran out of money. However, as soon as Shen Teh opens her tobacco shop, they appear at her door with six relatives and demand lodging. They take advantage of Shen Teh's generosity, though they also try to protect her. When creditors and beggars come into her shop, it is they who suggest making up a relative so that Shen Teh can put them off. Their suggestion leads to Shen Teh creating her "cousin," Shui Ta. Shui Ta later has them and their family arrested, and puts some of their family to work in her tobacco factory. For the most part, the elderly couple only likes Shen Teh because they benefit from her kindness, and dislike Shui Ta because he is tough on them.

Shu Fu

Shu Fu is a wealthy barber who runs a shop near Shen Teh's tobacco business. Shu Fu has both good and bad points. He attacks Wang with curling tongs, breaking his hand. Shu Fu does nothing to help the man he injured. On the other hand, Shu Fu is enamored by Shen Teh. He donates several buildings on his property to her so that she can house the homeless. He offers to marry her to save her business, though she ultimately declines. Shu Fu suffers at the hands of Shui Ta, however. When Shu Fu gives Shen Teh a blank check, Shui Ta takes advantage of the situation and writes in 10,000 silver dollars. Shui Ta turns the buildings Shu Fu donated into his tobacco factory. Ultimately, Shu Fu is a businessman, and as such, he is more like Shui Ta than Shen Teh would have liked.

The Man

See Elderly couple

Mrs. Shin

Mrs. Shin is the woman from whom Shen Teh buys her tobacco shop. The sale makes Shin a pauper, and she demands rice and money from the prostitute. Shin is not fond of Shui Ta, and seems to like Shen Teh more after meeting him. Though Shin takes advantage of Shen Teh's goodness, Shin becomes Shui Ta/Shen Teh's confident. Shin she figures out that they are the same person and that Shen Teh is pregnant. Shin keeps this secret as well.

Yang Sun

Yang Sun is an unemployed pilot with whom Shen Teh falls in love. Yang Sun uses her feelings to better his own situation: he never really seems to love her, though he impregnates her. When Yang Sun needs 500 silver dollars to obtain a pilot's job, he convinces Shen Teh to give him the 200 silver dollars she just obtained from the carpet-dealer and his wife. He almost persuades her to sell her shop to get the other 300 silver dollars. However, Shui Ta learns that Yang Sun plans to leave her behind when he takes the job and does not really love her. Though Shen Teh still loves him and tries to marry him, the event is never consummated because Yang Sun and his mother only want the 300 silver dollars. Yang Sun eventually goes to work for Shui Ta to pay back the 200 silver dollars he owes Shen Teh, and thrives under the ruthless businessman. At the end of the play, he does seem to have some feelings for Shen Teh. When he believes Shui Ta has somehow hurt her, he gets the police to arrest him. Yet Sun stands up for Shui Ta in court. Yang Sun is only concerned with survival at any cost, and uses anyone he has to.

Shui Ta

Shui Ta is the male persona Shen Teh takes on when she needs to be a tough businessman. Ostensibly her cousin, Shui Ta stands up to those Shen Teh cannot. He tells the carpenter, Lin To, that he will only pay 20 silver dollars for his shelving and fixtures instead of the 100 that Lin To demands. Shui Ta gets rid of the elderly couple and their relatives when they take too much advantage of her. As *Good Person* goes on, Shui Ta stays for longer and longer periods of time. After Shen Teh discovers she is pregnant, she becomes concerned with her child's survival and Shui Ta makes an extended appearance. He turns Shen Teh's charity into a business, a tobacco factory, and employs all those who Shen Teh helped for free before. Shui Ta is not without a heart however. He finally repays the 200 silver dollars Shen Teh borrowed from the carpet-dealer and his wife, though the couple has lost their business by that point. After Shui Ta is arrested for Shen Teh's disappearance and appears in court, it seems this persona will not be used by Shen Teh in the future.

Shen Teh

Shen Teh is the good woman (person) that the title refers to. She is a prostitute who give the gods lodging in her home when no one else will. Shen Teh gives up a job that would pay her much needed money. When the gods leave the next morning, Shen Teh tells them that it is hard to be good when poor. They give her a thousand silver dollars. She uses the money to buy a tobacco shop. As soon as she does, many people take advantage of her kind nature. Though she gives rice to people like Mrs. Shin, the woman also demands money. To save herself, Shen Teh invents a cousin, Shui Ta, who is a hard-nosed businessman. As the play progresses, she finds herself slipping into this persona more often and for longer periods of time.

In the second half of the play, one reason Shen Teh feels she has to be Shui Ta is because of her troubled relationship with Yang Sun. She is in love with him, but he is mostly using her. They do not marry because Shui Ta does not come to their wedding and pay out 300 silver dollars. Shen Teh also becomes pregnant by Yang Sun, and feels she must provide for her child. The only way to do this is to be Shui Ta. At the end of the play, many people she has helped wonder where she has gone to. To that end, Shui Ta is arrested. Before the gods, who act as magistrates in the court, Shen Teh admits she is Shui Ta, and tells them it is next to impossible to be good and survive. The gods are happy that she is still good, but provide no solutions to her problems. Shen Teh is again alone and has to find her own way in the world.

Lin To

Lin To is the carpenter who built the shelving and fixtures in Shen Teh's tobacco store. Though he built this woodwork for the previous owner, Lin To claims Shen Teh owes him 100 silver dollars for the work. Shen Teh does not have the money, and it is only when she becomes Shui Ta that she can force a lesser fee on him. This leads to bankruptcy for the carpenter. Lin To and his family move into the buildings that Shu Fu donates to Shen Teh, and later works for Shui Ta in his tobacco factory.

Mrs. Mi Tzu

Mrs. Mi Tzu is the owner of the building which houses Shen Teh's tobacco shop. The landlady demands six months of rent (200 silver dollars) in advance when she learns of Shen Teh's reputation. This is another factor in the creation of the Shui Ta persona, though Shui Ta cannot talk Mi Tzu out of the price. At one point, Shui Ta considers selling the shop's stock to Mi Tzu so that Yang Sun can get his job, but it is then that Shui Ta learns that Yang Sun does not really love Shen Teh. Later, Shui Ta makes a deal with her to rent workshops and expand the tobacco factory. Mi Tzu is one of the only characters to stand up for Shui Ta in court at the end of the play.

Wang

Wang is the impoverished water seller who helps the gods when they first arrive in the city. Realizing their importance, he goes from house to house, person to person, trying to find them lodging for the night. Wang finally leads them to Shen Teh, who takes them in. After the gods leave, they tell Wang to report Shen Teh's progress to them. Wang visits Shen Teh regularly, and like many characters, likes her very much and dislikes her cousin, Shui Ta. When Wang's hand is broken by Shu Fu, the barber, Shen Teh is the only one to stand up for him, even though she would perjure herself. Shui Ta will not do it for him. Later Shen Teh gives him her cart to sell so that he can go to a doctor. Wang is one of the characters who gets the police when Shen Teh is gone for a long time. He tells the gods that Shen Teh may have been killed by Shui Ta, ensuring the gods will finally come back to check on her.

The Woman

See Elderly couple

Mrs. Yang

Mrs. Yang is the mother of Yang Sun. She is the one who originally asks Shen Teh for the 200 silver dollars so that he can obtain his pilot job. Though she is not impoverished, she takes advantage of Shen Teh as well, though always for her son's benefit. Mrs. Yang prefers Shui Ta to Shen Teh. She holds up her son's wedding waiting for Shen Teh's cousin to arrive. When he does not, the wedding does not happen. Later, Mrs. Yang believes that Shui Ta saves her son when he hires Yang Sun to work in the factory. Mrs. Yang champions Shui Ta to the very end of the play.

The gods

The three gods are prominent gods who have come to earth to find at least one good person, otherwise the world will not go on as it is. Their quest has led them to this city, the capital of Szechwan. Here, Wang finds them a good person, Shen Teh, who is only one to offer them lodging in her home for a night. They give Shen Teh a thousand silver dollars so that she can continue to do good. After they leave the city, they continue on their quest, but to no avail. They monitor Shen Teh's progress via Wang, but refuse to help her when times get tough. At the end of the play, they serve as magistrates in Shui Ta's hearing over Shen Teh's disappearance. Though Shen Teh tells them how hard it is to be good, they leave her and the earth, content that she is trying. They offer no solutions to her problems.

THEMES

Success and Failure

Shen Teh wants to succeed at being a good person. The gods give her 1000 silver dollars, and

TOPICS FOR FURTHER STUDY

- Compare and contrast Shen Teh with Anna Fierling, the title character of Brecht's *Mother Courage and Her Children* (1941). Both are women trying to survive in difficult circumstances via their businesses, but make very different choices. What do their choices say about their circumstances?

- Discuss the duality of Shen Teh/Shui Ta in terms of the Ying-Yang principle in Chinese philosophy and/or the psychology of schizophrenia.

- Research Brecht's idea of epic theater, perhaps through his book *Writings on Theater*. Is *The Good Person of Szechwan* an example of epic theater? Why or why not?

- Brecht was an avowed Marxist. Research Karl Marx and Marxism, and discuss the themes of *Good Person* in Marxist terms.

she buys a small tobacco shop with it. Shen Teh hopes to help others through the shop by spending profits on such things as food for the hungry. But most of the people whom she is trying to help take advantage of her generosity. They want food, money, shelter, and constant service. Many of them do not care that their demands are causing the business to fail; they are only concerned with their short-term gain. Shen Teh finds it difficult to succeed at being a good person under these frustrating conditions.

To ensure the success of her business and to secure some hope of being able to do good, Shen Teh invents a male persona, a cousin named Shui Ta. Shui Ta is unlike Shen Teh, less compassionate and more ruthless or hard-nosed. He kicks out the elderly couple's family who have been imposing themselves on her. He does not support Wang's claim against Shu Fu. He becomes a successful businessman by taking advantage of others. For example, he appropriates tobacco belonging to the elderly couple's relatives in order to start his tobacco factory business. However, Shui Ta does do some good. For example, he employs the previously jobless relatives of the elderly couple, albeit in unfavorable working conditions. By scene nine, in Shen Teh's absence, Shui Ta has paid her debts (to the carpet dealer and his wife) and has put out rice for the hungry, as Shen Teh used to do.

At the end of the play, Shen Teh is left to ponder whether being a successful business owner can succeed at being good as well.

Identity

When the gods leave Shen Teh with 1000 silver dollars, they inadvertently create an identity crisis for her. At the beginning of the play, she is simply a local prostitute who is nice enough to turn down business so that the gods have a place to stay for the night. But after she receives money so that she can continue to do good, Shen Teh's identity changes. She is now a local businesswoman and a source of charity. She becomes known as the "Angel of the Slums" for her good deeds. The shift in identity brings a shift in expectations. Many of the poor make demands on her—from her old landlords, the elderly couple, and their extended family asking for shelter to the landlady, Mrs. Mi Tzu, who wants six months rent in advance. They nearly drive her into bankruptcy. Even the man she loves, the pilot Yang Sun, wants her money so that he can take a job as a pilot. Yang Sun does not care if she loses her business in the process, and Shen Teh is so in love with him that she almost gives the shop up for him. The only way to preserve her charitable ambitions and her family is to take on yet another identity.

Shen Teh invents a male cousin, Shui Ta. This male alter ego is essentially the opposite of Shen Teh. He is much more hard-nosed about business and life. He is not above kicking out those who have taken advantage of Shen Teh's generosity. Shen Teh originally intends for Shui Ta to appear only when times are difficult. However, by the last third of the play, Shui Ta is present so much that other characters believe that he has somehow harmed Shen Teh. But the Shui Ta identity has had to remian prominent to ensure a future for Shen Teh and her unborn child. When Shui Ta is arrested for the disappearance of Shen Teh and appears in court before the three gods, the gods do not see how their generosity in support of her good side have forced her to create this alternate identity just to survive. She tries to explain how both Shen Teh and Shui Ta are part of her, but they will only accept the good.

When the gods depart, they tell her to continue to be good, and to use the Shui Ta identity only once a month. Shen Teh is essentially left to resolve the crisis of her identity on her own.

Economic Circumstances/Wealth & Poverty

Economic circumstances, primarily poverty, drive much of the action in *Good Person*. Only a few characters in the play have any wealth to speak of. Shu Fu, the barber, has enough money that he can leave Shen Teh a blank check for her charitable works. The landlady, Mrs. Mi Tzu, owns the building that houses Shen Teh's tobacco shop. The Yangs also seem to have some money, though not enough for Yang Sun to buy his pilot's job. But the other character have suffered financial setbacks, and most are poor by the end of the play. Mrs. Shin has sold her shop to Shen Teh. The elderly couple and their extended family are homeless. At least one of them turns to prostitution to support the family. The carpenter and the carpet dealer and his wife lose their businesses during the course of the play. Wang cannot afford a home, and lives under a bridge. Shen Teh used to work as a prostitute, but becomes a member of the merchant class through a gift of money from the gods. Her newfound wealth attracts many who want her help. She has to become the consummate businessman Shui Ta to ensure a future for her business, herself, and her unborn child. Poverty drives them all to desperation, and the gods generally seem indifferent to how this affects both the good and the bad.

STYLE

Setting

The Good Person of Szechwan is set in the capital city of the Szechwan province of China. The time of the play is not specified, in part because the play is a parable (a story which intends to teach a lesson). Though there is little that is specifically Chinese about the play, Brecht set the play there so that he could employ several ideas from Chinese theater. The action of the play is primarily confined to an impoverished part of the city, including city streets and the area in and around Shen Teh's tobacco shop. Many of the interludes take place where Wang sleeps: under the bridge near a dried up river. This is where the gods appear to him in his dreams. The final scene of the play takes place in a courtroom, where the gods sit in judgement of Shui Ta but make no real decision.

Songs/Verse

Almost every major character in *The Good Person of Szechwan* sings a song or recites some verse that could be sung. Brecht uses these moments to directly inject his philosophical ideas into the text, as well as reveal more about the characters who speak them. One example is "The Song of the Smoke" sung by the elderly couple and their family, who force themselves upon Shen Teh in scene one. The song expresses bitterness over their lives while making a greater political statement. Brecht accomplishes similar goals with songs such as Wang's "The Water-Seller's Song in the Rain" and Shen Teh's "The Song of the Defencelessness of the Gods and the Good People." Shen Teh, especially, comments on action while revealing more of herself in off-handed moments of verse.

Monologues/Characters Directly Addressing the Audience

While some of the songs in *The Good Person of Szechwan* address the audience in a direct fashion, especially Shen Teh's "Song of the Defencelessness of the Good and the Gods," there are several instances in which the actors directly speak to the play's viewers. On these occasions, the audience is informed of what is going to happen and the characters' feelings about these events. These moments also underscore the themes of the play and give Brecht a forum to put forth his political, philosophical, and social ideas. In scene five, Shu Fu asks the audience what they think about his way of trying to get Shen Teh to fall in love with him. First he plans to talk only about ideas with her, then have her fall in love with him. Scene eight has a number of monologues. Mrs. Yang tells the audience how Shui Ta saved her son by giving him a job and allowing him to thrive. As she speaks, the whole story is acted out. First she tells the audience what happens, then she steps back into the action as it occurs.

The most important monologues in *The Good Person of Szechwan* are found at the very beginning and end of the play. The play opens with a prologue in which Wang sets up some of the basics of the play. He is waiting for the three gods to arrive so that he is the first to meet them in the city. When they finally arrive, the monologue stops. In the epilogue, one of the actors steps in front of the curtain and apologizes to the audience for not having a neatly closed ending. Brecht uses this opportunity to make the audience think rather than to just entertain them.

HISTORICAL CONTEXT

World War II (1939–1945) ravaged Europe, and deeply affected life in the United States. Nazi Germany was led by Adolph Hitler, who had been in power for several years and was embarking on a campaign of European domination. Even before the outbreak of the war in 1939, many people (including Brecht and his family) with political views not in agreement with Hitler's views had become political refugees, fleeing the country to avoid persecution and/or death. As Germany invaded country after country in Europe, many more fled. Many of those who were left behind suffered. There was much poverty and uncertainty as economic infrastructures were compromised. Many, such as people of Slavic descent, were put to forced labor as a consequence of the Nazi beliefs in the superiority of their own race and the inferiority of other races.

The United States began supporting Great Britain with armaments as early as the summer of 1940. The Lend-Lease Act of 1941 gave Franklin Delano Roosevelt, the American President, the authority to give Britain, as well as China and the U.S.S.R., defense and information, at a cost to be determined later. The United States officially entered the war on the side of the Allies, including Great Britain, in late 1941 after the Japanese, allies of Germany, bombed Pearl Harbor. By the summer of 1942, the Allies had turned the tide of the war, and in 1943 were making significant gains against the Germans. Much of the year was spent trying to push the Germans back from territory that they had conquered, including Sicily and parts of southern Italy.

While Europeans were suffering, the demands of the war also changed life in the United States. The Great Depression of the 1930s ended as factories geared up for war production. By 1943, some Depression-era legislation was challenged by Congress. The New Deal was questioned by Republicans, while the WPA was ended entirely because the war created many new jobs and the maximum use of resources. Jobs were easier to obtain and more numerous. To support the war effort, women began doing what was considered "men's work" in domestic factories and also served in the armed

COMPARE & CONTRAST

- **1943:** Tobacco cigarettes are advertised as healthy in the United States.

  Today: Tobacco companies are sued for false advertising as it has been revealed in court that they have known for many years that cigarettes cause cancer.

- **1943:** In China, a woman's fertility is unregulated. In many rural areas, especially, women produce large families to provide labor for farms.

  Today: In an effort to control an exploding population, the Chinese government has decreed that each woman is limited to one child, though those who live in rural areas might petition for permission to have two, if the first is a girl.

- **1943:** About one-third of women between the ages of 18 and 64 in the United States are employed in war-related work. Many take on jobs considered "men's work," but are forced to give up their positions to returning soldiers when the war ends.

  Today: Many American women work in nearly every occupation previously considered only appropriate for men. However, there is a glass ceiling in many business sectors which limits women's opportunities to reach the highest executive levels.

- **1943:** Nazi Germany uses millions of prisoners of war and workers from occupied countries as involuntary laborers to support their war effort.

  Today: Companies such as Nike use cheap, sweat shop-type labor in Asia and South America to manufacture goods in a situation many consider near slavery.

---

forces. This ultimately changed the way that people thought about work. It also led to better educational opportunities for women, including more co-educational colleges.

Though jobs were plentiful, and President Roosevelt ordered a minimum 48-hour work week in war-related factories, workers were unhappy in 1943 for several reasons. Prices were rising, and workers wanted higher wages. The federal government worked to control inflation, but that did not change the fact that every day items were rationed. There were also several labor strikes (primarily in the mining industry), threats of strikes, and labor-related riots. Congress outlawed strikes in industries vital to the war effort.

China also suffered during World War II, though for the most, they were not directly involved in the conflict. China had been at war with Japan since 1937, after Japan conquered Manchuria in 1932. War was not officially declared against Japan until late in 1941. Japan was successful in taking over several parts of the country, forcing the ruling Nationalist government to set up in different cities. There was also internal strife in China, between the Nationalists and the upstart Communists, led by Mao Zedong (Mao Tse-Tung). The Communists fought a guerilla war with Japanese while feuding with Nationalists. After the United States declared war on Japan in 1941, China and the United States became allies, though Japan continued to win in the Far East for some time. The war in China created a desperate refugee situation in China, similar to that in Europe. Those most affected by the war with Japan, from eastern and central China, were forced to retreat westward. Such circumstances might have led Brecht to question whether goodness could exist in the world.

CRITICAL OVERVIEW

From the earliest production of *The Good Person of Szechwan* in Zurich, Switzerland's Schauspielhaus Zurich in 1943, many critics have found much to praise. Since that time, however, many critics have also found the play to be exceptionally long in performance, usually running about three to three and a half hours, which sometimes lessens its impact. Many also agree that *The Good Person of Szechwan* is difficult for directors to interpret, often resulting in stylistically inconsistent productions. However, the play is often pointed to as one of the more accessible examples of Brecht's concept of epic theater, entertaining and nonsentimental, though others believe it is too detached. In addition, the ideas in *The Good Person of Szechwan* have been appreciated more and more over time.

At the time of the first production in New York City, Brecht's ideas about theater and the episodic structure of *The Good Person of Szechwan* were still considered unusual. Many critics commented on these aspects of the play. Comparing the play to Voltaire's *Candide,* Brooks Atkinson of *The New York Times,* wrote ''It is strange in form, nonsentimental in theme, and stimulating from several points of view.'' His sentiments were echoed by Tom F. Driver of *Christian Century.* Brecht, he wrote, ''invigorated the modern theater by establishing a stage technique which does away with theatrical illusion and appeals directly to the imagination and the intellect.''

This production, at New York City's Phoenix Theatre, featured a controversial translation by Eric Bentley, who also directed the production. Robert Hatch in *The Nation* was especially critical of the translation, and how it affected the play: ''Eric Bentley translated the play with what sounds to my ear like a warm appreciation of its flavor, but he has displayed it in the theatre as though he were dressing a museum.'' Hatch believed ''The production commits the worse sin of the theatre—it is boring. I think the fault is with the production. . . .'' Henry Hewes of the *Saturday Review* agreed with Hatch. Hewes argued, ''there is much in it [his translation] that is awkward. . . . And lines that might have been funny in the original lose their humor. . . .'' Many scholars have commented on the inherent humor in *Good Person.* Some have pointed out that this humorous quality is often overlooked.

By 1970, when a new professional production in New York City's Vivian Beaumont Theater opened, Brecht's ideas had been widely discussed and studied. Though Brecht may have been better understood, many critics still believed it was difficult to do a good production of *The Good Person of Szechwan* with a unified style. Critics did not find

Bill Stuart as the Husband, standing on a chair expostulating, Fiona Shaw as Shen te, standing in a dark floral dress.

this in the new production. Clive Barnes of *The New York Times* wrote ''*The Good Woman* is a play that should dance across the stage with a gentle mocking smile; it is one of the lightest of Brecht's plays.'' His colleague Walter Kerr, also of *The New York Times,* believed ''Brecht still hasn't been proved out, if that's a proper phrase, in this country; we still wait for a director who will make it all come true.

Beginning in the mid-1970s, there were numerous productions of *The Good Person of Szechwan* in the United States that were highly stylized (a trend that would continue into the 1990s). Critics of the 1975-76 productions of the play at La Mama in New York City debated old questions, such as how important *The Good Person of Szechwan* was in Brecht's canon. Stanley Kauffmann of *The New Republic* was one of the few who placed it in the lower echelon. He wrote ''*The Good Woman* is lesser Brecht. His best plays crystallize some aspects of the modern consciousness in new dramatic modes; his lesser ones are explicit, didactic, linear and relatively unresonant.''

In the late 1990s, many critics noted that American productions of *The Good Person of Szechwan* were being adapted to contemporary, familiar settings, and new scores were being written. Most praised these changes, in part because it made this play more accessible to modern audiences. Of a 1992 production at Emory University, *Atlanta Journal and Constitution* critic Roderick Robinson wrote "This isn't a show that will appeal to *Three's Company* zealots, but Brecht's monumental questioning of humankind's ways still has plenty to bite. The production has fine touches of wit. . . ."

A 1994 adaptation by well-known playwright/director Tony Kushner was set at the California-Mexico border, with characters retaining Chinese names and with a score by Los Lobos. Don Braunagel of *Variety* hit on one long-term issue with the production. He wrote, "La Jolla Playhouse's extraordinary synergy with Bertolt Brecht continues with this superlative presentation, with Lisa Peterson demonstrating why the playwright, directed properly, is timeless." A 1999 production at the Oregon Shakespeare Festival featured a different translation, but was similarly American in its feel. Steve Winn of the *San Francisco Chronicle* believed the play remained relevant: "*The Good Person of Szechwan* feels a lot like life in the '90s."

CRITICISM

A. Petruso

In this essay, Petruso responds to the ending, which invites the audience/reader to interpret to the play. Though many critics believe the play ultimately argues for the merits of goodness, Petruso counters that Brecht shows no positive results for goodness.

The epilogue of Bertolt Brecht's *The Good Person of Szechwan* apologizes for the lack of a true, closed ending to the play. In the last scene, Shen Teh's dilemma of how to be a good person in a harsh world is left unanswered by the gods and Brecht. Instead, the audience is asked to think for themselves. Brecht writes "Indeed it is a curious way of coping: / To close the play, leaving the issue open. / Especially since we live by your enjoyment." Thus everyone is supposed to propose their own interpretation to the problem.

For the most part, critics believe the play supported the idea of goodness, while showing the difficulties in living such a life. Clive Barnes of *The New York Times* believed "*The Good Woman of Setzuan* is a parable about the impossibility of human purity. For its very existence, good has to coexist with evil, riches bring poverty and even to fly man has to cheat." In the epilogue, Brecht seems to support such interpretations. He writes "There's only one solution that we know: / That you should now consider as you god / What sort of measures you would recommend / to help good people to a happy end."

Yet there is not one instance of goodness rewarded in *Good Person*. Every time Shen Teh or several other characters try to do good, their actions come back to haunt them. They end up suffering somehow, whether it be economically, emotionally, or otherwise. Far from arguing that goodness has its merits, Brecht shows how much it negatively affects people's lives. The reason goodness fails, however, is not because of goodness itself. It is because other people take advantage of the good. They are driven to it for reasons such as the capitalist economy reflecting Brecht's Marxist bias). While the lines from the Epilogue quoted above show that Brecht supports the ideal of good people, the play shows the impossibility of being good in such a society.

In addition to Shen Teh, several minor characters struggle greatly after acts of kindness. Wang, the water seller, is not particularly honorable. He has a false bottom in his cup, meaning he cheats those to whom he sells his product. But Wang chooses to wait for the gods at the entrance to the city, hoping to talk to them. They enlist him to help them find lodging for the night, their way of trying to find one good person. Wang is repeatedly turned down, and he finally takes them to Shen Teh who takes them in. Yet Wang becomes confused and runs away after he believes he has failed the gods. His act of goodness leads to personal stress. Wang hides, fearing their wrath. Even after they reassure him, they come to him in his dreams for updates on Shen Teh. His one good deed leads to ever greater obligations.

Wang's problems are minor when compared to the carpet dealer and his wife. In scene four, Shen Teh enters their carpet shop, which is near her shop, to buy a pretty shawl. She has just returned from an evening with Yang Sun and is very happy. The couple reminds her that she must pay her rent soon, but Shen Teh knows she is out of money. Out of generosity, they offer to lend her the 200 silver dollars against her stock, though they do not demand anything in writing. This act of goodness ends up hurting them deeply. Shen Teh promptly gives

WHAT DO I READ NEXT?

- *The Caucasian Chalk Circle,* a play written by Brecht in 1948, is also a parable about survival based on a Chinese myth.

- *Concubines and Bondservants: a Social History,* a nonfiction book written by Maria Jaschok in 1999, explores the history and social impact of prostitution in China.

- *No Exit,* a play written by Jean Paul Sartre in 1944, shows the reactions of four people stuck in an impossible situation who are forced to explore who they really are.

- *The Threepenny Opera* is a play written by Brecht in 1928. It answers the question of whether goodness pays in the world with a negative answer.

- *Dilemmas of a Double Life: Women Balancing Careers and Relationships* is a collection of essays edited by Nancy B. Katreider and published in 1997. It discusses the problems of working women in the United States trying to meet the demands of work and family life.

- *Life of Galileo,* a play written by Brecht in 1943, explores the double life of the scientist who tries to invent while supporting himself as a teacher of rich, unintelligent students.

---

the loaned funds to Yang Sun so he can get his pilot's job.

During the interlude between scenes five and six, Shen Teh reveals that the carpet dealer needs the loaned money back. He is ill over his act of goodness, and does not trust her cousin, Shui Ta. Shen Teh promises to give them the money back, but cannot retrieve it from Yang Sun. Though Shen Teh feels guilty about the situation, the carpet dealer and his wife are left none the richer because of their goodness. Eventually, they lose their store because the loan put them in the position of not being able to pay their taxes. By scene eight, when Shui Ta has almost exclusively taken the place of Shen Teh, the carpet dealer and his wife have been repaid by the hard-nosed alter ego. However, the couple had lost their store by then. Their generosity resulted in greater poverty.

Though Shu Fu, the barber, is not poor like Wang, nor does he lose his business like the carpet dealer and his wife, several of his generous acts end up hurting him. Shu Fu is by no means a nice person. He breaks Wang's hand with his curling tongs, and does not do anything to help him. But because Shu Fu is enamored with Shen Teh, he does some good things to try and assist her. In scene five, he offers the use of some of his buildings to her via Shui Ta. She uses them to house those without homes, until scene seven when Shui Ta gets tough and decides to build a tobacco factory business out of stolen property. Shu Fu's charitable act is twisted into something that hurts those Shen Teh intended to help.

Shu Fu also suffers in more direct fashion. In scene seven, when Shen Teh is in danger of losing her business and cease her charitable ways, Shu Fu writes her a blank check so that she can save herself. Shen Teh declines to use it, but Shui Ta is not above taking advantage of the situation; he fills in an absurd amount, 10,000 silver dollars. Shu Fu does not go bankrupt over the check, but it is hardly what he intended when he tried to do good. Shu Fu also never ends up winning over Shen Teh, so all of his goodness was for naught.

The character who suffers the most because of her goodness is Shen Teh, the title character and the only one with pure motivations. No act of kindness on Shen Teh's part has an ulterior motive or is regretted after the fact. Yet all her goodness drives her deeper and deeper into debt and despair. Each successive good deed is met by greater demands. She is forced to split herself in two to deal with the expectations created by her goodness. Only through

> ONE WAY TO LOOK AT WHAT BRECHT REALLY THINKS OF THE GOOD IN *GOOD PERSON* IS TO EXAMINE WHO IS KIND TO SHEN TEH."

a male alter ego, Shui Ta, is Shen Teh able to be as cruel as the world is and ensure her (and later in the play, her unborn child's) survival.

Shen Teh's problems begin in the Prologue when she gives up an appointment with a client so that the gods have a place to stay for the night. They tell her to continue to be good, but she counters that it is hard to be when she is so poor. They give her money which she uses to start a tobacco shop. If the gods had not given her money, as they were initially inclined not to, Shen Teh would still have been good but not so pressured to do more than she already had been doing. As it stands, the money forces Shen Teh to be consciously, if not detrimentally, good.

In scene one, Shen Teh cannot refuse anyone's request. The elderly couple, who gave Shen Teh her first home when she moved to the city, imposes greatly upon her. Members of their extended family trickle in throughout the scene, taking advantage of Shen Teh's goodness. They demand food, service, a place to sleep—all without regard to Shen Teh or her shop. Two get in a fight and break some of her shelving. Though the couple actually kicked Shen Teh out when she could not pay her rent a long time ago, they have no problem paying her nothing and giving her no respect.

Such impositions on Shen Teh occur throughout *Good Person*. When she starts giving out cigarettes and rice, people like the unemployed man and Mrs. Shin come to expect it. No act of kindness can be just what it is. Everyone wants something more. The one character who wants the most from Shen Teh is Yang Sun. After she essentially saves him from a suicide attempt and falls in love with him, he treats her poorly. He only promises to marry her when she give him 200 of the 500 silver dollars he needs so that he can become a pilot. Then Yang Sun expects her to sell the shop for 300 silver dollars so he can get the rest of the money he needs. When Shen Teh wants the 200 silver dollars back so she can repay the carpet dealer and his wife, Yang Sun will not (and as it turns out, cannot) do it. Shen Teh's wedding day is ruined when Yang Sun and his mother hold up the ceremony waiting for Shui Ta to show up with the 300 silver dollars and some common sense. They are sorely disappointed and Shen Teh does not marry him.

To deal with the demands created by being good and somewhat prosperous (with the gift from the gods), Shen Teh is compelled to create a heartless, male alter ego, her "cousin" Shui Ta. He corrects situations that Shen Teh cannot. He kicks out the freeloading elderly couple and their family, just in time to save Shen Teh's reputation. He learns the truth about Yang Sun and ends up making Shen Teh accept it. Shui Ta protects all of Shen Teh's interests, and by scene nine, it is clear he has been doing some of Shen Teh's charitable works. However, Shui Ta is a realist. He has also taken advantage of the situation Shen Teh has set up with Shu Fu and others. Shui Ta uses the buildings Shu Fu has given Shen Teh for the needy to start a tobacco factory/sweatshop. Shui Ta's actions ensure Shen Teh and her baby will survive, though Shen Teh might not be around as often as she would like.

One way to look at what Brecht really thinks of the good in *Good Person* is to examine who is kind to Shen Teh. Mrs. Shin seems nice after she learns and keeps the secret that Shen Teh and Shui Ta are the same person. But nearly everyone else fears Shui Ta and treats Shen Teh poorly, without much regard to her as a person. Shu Fu is in love with her, and is rebuffed, but acts only out of this feeling. If Shu did not have feelings for her, he would not be nearly as nice.

Only the gods and Wang seem to be good to Shen Teh with no strings attached. The gods want her to be good, but cannot tell her how to stay that way. Wang only asks for lodging for the gods, and nothing else. He will not even let her commit perjury to the magistrate when Shu Fu breaks his hand and all the witnesses refuse to back him up. Perhaps Wang is the most realistic expression of good the play: something of a combination of Shen Teh and Shui Ta. Wang wants to do good, but is afraid of the gods. He scrapes out a living, tries to stay out of trouble, and helps out Shen Teh whenever he can. Trying to be good without exception while protecting one's self is the best Brecht hoped for us to do. Goodness itself gets Shen Teh nowhere fast.

Source: A. Petruso, for *Drama for Students,* Gale, 2000.

Clare Cross

Cross is a writer specializing in modern drama. In the following essay, Cross discusses the play's presentation of love as a commodity.

In the 1960s, the Beatles sang, "I don't care too much for money. Money can't buy me love," thus encapsulating society's idealized view of romance: love and money are separate and have nothing to do with each other. Reality, of course, is a bit more murky. Though most people in Western cultures would probably find fault with what is commonly called "marrying for money," money plays at least a small part in many "romantic" decisions. For instance, a person who is unemployed or has serious financial troubles is likely to have more difficulty finding a partner, while a person with a high income will probably be seen as more desirable. Still, the belief that love and money at least "should" be separate persists. In matters of love, it is the heart that is supposed to rule, not the head.

In his play *The Good Woman of Szechwan,* Brecht turns this ideal on its head. The play presents a world in which love is always linked in some way to money. In fact, one title Brecht considered for the play was *Die Ware Liebe,* which can be translated as *Love for Sale* or *The Commodity Love.* One could argue, of course, that much of the time what is bought and sold in Brecht's play is not love, but sex. After all, Shen Te begins the play as a prostitute. Romantic love and sex, however, can only neatly be divided in theory. Obviously, romantic partners who have sexual relationships are assumed to be in love. Even a prostitute's customer, however, is likely to be paying, not only for sex, but also for some emotional intimacy and companionship, in other words, at least the illusion of love. The American language also reflects the connection between love and sex; today, the term "making love" is most often used as a euphemism for sex. In short, love and sex exist, not as separate entities, but on a continuum. This essay will use both words, but with the understanding that the division between them is necessarily artificial.

Brecht establishes the theme of "love for sale" at the beginning of the play. Shen Te is first referred to by Wong as "Shen Te, the prostitute," with the word "prostitute" appearing as if it is part of her name and thus her essential identification. Trying to keep the gods from realizing that Shen Te sells herself, Wong explains to the audience, "They

> THROUGHOUT *THE GOOD WOMAN OF SZECHWAN,* BRECHT EMPHASIZES THE IMPOSSIBILITY OF BEING GOOD IF ONE IS TO SURVIVE IN A CORRUPT WORLD AND, IN THE FINAL SCENE, THIS IS WHAT SHEN TE TRIES TO TELL THE GODS, WHO TURN A DEAF EAR."

mustn't see her gentleman or they'll know what she is." It should be noted here that Wong refers to what Shen Te *is,* not what she *does.* She may be a daughter, a sister, or a friend, but in breaking society's rules, she is first and foremost a prostitute, and thus not fit for polite society, even though she needed the money to live. After the gods give money to Shen Te, she is able to open a tobacco shop, but her former practice of a less "respectable" profession haunts her when her landlady, Mrs. Mi Tzu, learns about her past and demands that she pay the rent six months in advance, thus punishing Shen Te for selling sex. When Shen Te, as Shui Ta, discusses the matter with a policeman, the policeman presents society's idealized view, that sex for love is acceptable, but sex for money is not: "... love isn't bought and sold like cigars, Mr. Shui Ta ... it isn't respectable to go waltzing off with someone that's paying his way, so to speak—it must be for love! ... as the proverb has it: not for a handful of rice but for love!" In other words, sexual activity is acceptable only in connection with love, and neither love nor sex should have anything to do with money.

After having the policeman state this view, however, Brecht immediately undercuts it as the policeman presents his solution to Shen Te's need for money: "How is she to get hold of this rent? ... It's just come to me. A husband. We must find her a husband!" Marriage has been called by some "legalized prostitution," and that is clearly the view that Brecht presents here. The policeman continues, making the connection between marriage and prostitution even more explicit: "We need capital. And how do we acquire capital? We get married ... We can't pay six months rent, so what do we do? We marry money." The policeman then writes an advertisement for Shen Te, further cementing the connection between marriage and business. In addition, the advertisement he writes emphasizes that Shen Te wants to marry for money: "What respectable man with small capital . . . desires marriage into flourishing tobacco shop?" Shen Te's accepts the policeman's "respectable" solution, but it is clear to the audience that she is once again selling herself in order to survive.

When the audience next sees Shen Te, she is on her way to meet the stranger she has agreed to marry, but at this point she meets the pilot Yang Sun. At first he is brusque with her, even cruel, but as the two talk, he seems to become kinder, and Shen Te, for the first time, falls in love. On her part at least, this is the idealized roman tic love that society at least outwardly supports. Yang Sun is unemployed and dressed in rags, but to Shen Te that doesn't matter; he is "a brave and cleaver man." Shortly after this meeting, Shen Te begins staying with him all night. At one point, when she returns to her shop after spending the night with Yang Sun, the old woman, upon learning that Yang Sun has no money, asks Shen Te how she will pay her rent. Shen Te replies, "I'd forgotten about that." Because she is so wrapped up in idealized romantic love, she cares little about money.

Brecht, however, does not allow the audience to get caught up in the romance of the situation. Almost immediately, Yang Sun's mother arrives and tells Shen Te that he needs five hundred silver dollars in order to bribe his way into a pilot's job. Shen Te immediately gives Yang Sun's mother the money she needs for the rent on her tobacco shop, the money loaned to her by the old woman. Caught up in emotion, Shen Te does not seem to reflect enough to realize that without the money, she will almost certainly lose her shop, and thus her only income. Brecht shows more here, however, than a woman's love untainted by thoughts of money. First of all, it is clear that Shen Te's love for Yang Sun, like her goodness in helping her neighbors, will, left unchecked, lead to financial ruin. Secondly, Yang Sun has known from the beginning of his relationship with Shen Te that she has a shop. "My son has told me everything," Yang Sun's mother says before telling Shen Te of her son's need for money. It seems fairly certain that Yang Sun has sent his mother to Shen Te. In a later scene, however, the situation becomes even clearer. Yang Sun comes to Shen Te's shop and demands more money. Shen Te, now disguised as Shui Ta, agrees to sell her tobacco shop for three hundred silver dollars, knowing that in addition to losing the shop, she will be unable to repay the old woman, who cannot afford to lose the money. In love with Yang Sun, Shen Te is willing to sacrifice everything else. Yang Sun, however, lets Shui Ta know that he wants Shen Te's money, not Shen Te herself. "I'm leaving *her* behind," he says. "No millstones round my neck!" Although Yang Sun may have initially loved Shen Te, here he makes it clear that he too has become a prostitute, selling an illusion of love to Shen Te.

Upon discovering that Yang Sun does not love her, Shen Te, again desperate for money and still disguised as Shui Ta, turns once more to selling herself, this time to Mr. Shu Fu, the barber who has cruelly injured Shen Te's friend Wong. Upon finding Mr. Shu Fu agreeable to the proposition, Shen Te betrays Wong, refusing to support him in his quest for justice against the barber. This plan, however, is short-lived. Yang Sun returns and, when by her silence Shen Te acknowledges that she has been told he is bad, asks her, "Does that make me need you less?" It should be noted here that he does not speak of love for her, but of his own need. He continues in his attempt to persuade Shen Te to return to him, reminding her of their first romantic encounter, but concluding by asking her is she remembers that she "Promised me money to fly with?" Even though Yang Sun does not say he loves her, Shen Te agrees to go back to him, telling the audience, "I want to go with the man I love . . . I don't want to know if he loves me." Thus even as she agrees to return to him, Shen Te seems to know, at least on some level, that she is buying his love.

Soon, however, Shen Te seems to forget Yang Sun's interest in her money. In the following scene, on the way to her wedding, she herself notes that "The things [Yang Sun] said to Shui Ta had taught Shen Te nothing." As if to prove the truth of these words, Shen Te tells the audience, "He loves me." Upon arriving at the wedding, however, she discovers that Yang Sun will not allow the ceremony to be held until Shui Ta arrives—with the money that will allow him to work as a pilot. Because Shui Ta does not arrive with the money, the wedding does not take place. Once again, it is clear that Yang Sun acts as a prostitute, not a lover. He is interested in Shen Te only for her money.

Once more abandoned by Yang Sun, Shen Te finds herself in serious trouble. Mrs. Shin sums up her situation: "No husband, no tobacco, no house and home." Soon, however, Mr. Shu Fu returns to the shop. Still maneuvering to buy Shen Te's love, he gives her a blank check. At first she will not cash it. Mrs. Shin is surprised: "What? You're not going to cash it just because you might have to marry him? Are you crazy?" Mrs. Shin here assumes that Shen Te is willing to sell herself again. This time, however, Shen Te chooses not to marry for money. Disguising herself once again as Shui Ta, she does cash the barber's check, but with no apparent intention of giving him anything in return. In addition, she sues Yang Sun for breach of marriage and is able to force him to work off the money she has already given him. No longer will she sell herself or buy love. It is tempting to see this as a sign of growth in Shen Te, to suggest that she no longer sees love as a commodity. Brecht, however, shows that this is not the case. As Shui Ta, Shen Te still trades in love. Yang Sun becomes her foreman and informs her that the factory is in dire need of Mrs. Mi Tzu's buildings. Shen Te responds by saying that she cannot pay Mrs. Mi Tzu's price, but Yang Sun answers, "If she has me to stroke her knees she'll come down." Once again, Yang Sun shows his willingness to act as a prostitute. Shen Te's first response is to say, "I'll never agree to that," but in a meeting with Mrs. Mi Tzu, Shen Te becomes her former lover's pimp, effectively agreeing to sell Yang Sun in exchange for lower rent. Even though she no longer sells herself, when desperate for money, she turns to selling others.

Throughout *The Good Woman of Szechwan,* Brecht emphasizes the impossibility of being good if one is to survive in a corrupt world and, in the final scene, this is what Shen Te tries to tell the gods, who turn a deaf ear. Goodness, however, is not the only casualty of the world's imperfections. Idealized romantic love, love separate from money, is not possible either. Shen Te is able to pay her rent as a prostitute and could survive economically as a rich man's life, but her love for Yang Sun turns out to be a luxury she cannot afford. That love nearly leads her to disaster. As Shui Ta attempting to sell Yang Sun to Mrs. Mi Tzu, Shen Te abandons emotion and treats love as a business transaction. In a corrupt world, one must buy and sell what one can in order to survive, and so in Brecht's play, even love is for sale.

Source: Clare Cross, for *Drama for Students,* Gale, 2000.

Alisa Solomon

In the following essay, Solomon reinterprets Brecht's play, giving emphasis to the qualities of epic theater, and pointing out the value of the work for feminist arguments.

Like most social activists who believe in theater as an instrument of change, feminists have both claimed and rejected Bertolt Brecht, joining in the critical tug-of-war that has characterized his reception in America since the Theatre Union introduced him to this country with its ill-conceived (and disastrous) production of *The Mother* in 1935. Brecht has been described as the great poet whose plays no longer work, the dramatic genius whose theatrical theory doesn't fit, the artist whose politics hardly matter, the idealist who decayed into an opportunistic creep. Feminist critics, going further, have pointed out a series of seeming contradictions to prove or discount Brecht's usefulness: Most of his major plays feature female protagonists; he portrayed women stereotypically. He assumed (though hardly stressed) the emancipation of women as part of socialism; he paid little attention to the vibrant women's movement of the Weimar period. Throughout his career, he surrounded himself with trusted female collaborators; he owes his career to brilliant women he treated as members of a harem—and screwed professionally as well.

All this invoking, dismissing, extolling, and reviling has often missed the deepest feminist implications of Brecht's epic theater. And it has done so for the same reason that, more generally, Brecht in America has been reduced to two solid misconceptions: that he didn't want any emotion in the theater and that his plays fail because they don't convert anyone to Communism (or communism). These caricatures, long elevated to the status of unshakable cliche, rely, as do many feminist quibbles with Brecht, on a simplification that culminates in smarmy certainty about the "Brechtian"—a grungy, grudging didacticism produced through a predictable set of stage effects (projected scene titles, bright lights, music hall band, scowling actors). This conception has little to do with the plays themselves or with the intricate performance style Brecht built into them, and elaborated in his theoretical writings.

While the Berliner Ensemble toured London in 1956, and again in the late 1960s, inspiring a generation of politically engaged playwrights like Howard Brenton, Caryl Churchill, and Steven Berkoff, here in America Artaud and Grotowski were inflaming a generation of theatrical shamans without the counterbalancing weight of Brecht's "scientific" approach. Along with the Method mania of the mainstream, these gurus could support a

> ALL THIS INVOKING, DISMISSING, EXTOLLING, AND REVILING HAS OFTEN MISSED THE DEEPEST FEMINIST IMPLICATIONS OF BRECHT'S EPIC THEATER. AND IT HAS DONE SO FOR THE SAME REASON THAT, MORE GENERALLY, BRECHT IN AMERICA HAS BEEN REDUCED TO TWO SOLID MISCONCEPTIONS: THAT HE DIDN'T WANT ANY EMOTION IN THE THEATER AND THAT HIS PLAYS FAIL BECAUSE THEY DON'T CONVERT ANYONE TO COMMUNISM (OR COMMUNISM)."

presumption that would leave no room for Brecht: intellect—and thus Brecht's critically based work—does not belong in the theater.

To this day, reviewers—and worse, directors—of American Brecht productions approach his work with received ideas that are at best limited, and limiting. America's—and American feminists'—ability to skim Brecht for confirmation of the old platitudes and leave the rest for waste depends, in sum, on a fundamental failure to recognize the complex achievement of Brecht's dramatic art.

Nowhere is this failure more apparent than in recent readings of the play most frequently cited by feminists, *The Good Person of Szechwan,* in which Shen Teh, "the prostitute who can't say no," opens a small tobacco shop with money she receives from three gods in search of a good person, after she puts them up for a night; when freeloading neighbors exploit her generosity, Shen Teh transvests into her male cousin, Shui Ta, whose entrepreneurial shrewdness should enable her to make ends meet—and remain good. These critics—among them John Fuegi, Iris Smith, Gay Gibson Cima, Anne Herrmann—scold Brecht for the play's "stereotypical" portrayals of femininity as good and masculinity as evil, see only a "metaphor" in Shen Teh's "cross-dressing," or suggest a biographical reading that casts "Brecht lookalikes" as the First God and Shen Teh's lover, Yang Sun, and his many mistresses as multiple Shen Tehs. But they have neglected to examine the play's dialectical action in any but the most superficial of ways. This knee-jerk approach, laying a tendentious template over a work of art to see where it lines up, is particularly frustrating in the case of Brecht because it is so unnecessary. Epic theater's basic effort to make the familiar strange, show the world as alterable, hold events at a temporal distance, and, as Brecht writes, reveal the human being as "the sum of all social circumstances" contains a profoundly feminist impulse (even if the social relations defined by gender were not the ones that particularly interested Brecht).

One call for a feminist refashioning of *Good Person* actually misses the play's theatrical crux, "The Song of Defenselessness of the Gods and the Good People." In a 1991 article in *Theatre Journal,* Iris Smith complains of "the *unseen* creation of the male figure, who seems to appear *sui generis* on the stage." She goes on to suggest that "At some point, perhaps in Scene 7... the costuming of Shui Ta could be done in full view of the audience." Of course, Shen Teh *does* costume herself as Shui Ta in full view of the audience in "The Song of Defenselessness," which follows scene four. Moreover, this careful, complicated scene offers important clues about epic acting, the relationship between gender and epic acting, and indeed about gender *as* epic acting.

The song comes nearly halfway through the play, several scenes *after* we've seen Shen Teh disguised as her shrewd cousin. Its function is not to *reveal* that Shui Ta is Shen Teh's invention, but to show how that invention is assembled, how the contradiction described in the song—that goodness can come about only if militarily enforced—both demands and defeats the use of the disguise, how dramatic character (and, by extension, social character) is artificially manufactured, how our sympathies and antipathies can be evoked and manipulated. The *construction* of Shui Ta, demonstrated through the action of a baleful and defensive song, *deconstructs* notions of character, social role (including gender), dramatic inevitability, and the easy distinction between good and evil. Most important, the interlude substantiates, through the actor's combined action of delivering a song and putting on a costume, the play's elemental disjunction: one actor stirs both our empathy with Shen Teh and our disgust with Shui Ta. Thus, the interlude calls attention to our own dialectical activity in the epic theater, the act of complex seeing, which demands that we perceive things as they are and, at the same time, as other than they are.

The song immediately follows a busy scene in which all the intertwining threads of the plot get tangled up: Shen Teh, newly in love with the pilot Yang Sun, praises the "glorious" morning, cheerfully dishes out rice to the freeloaders who exploit her generosity, and buys a shawl from an old couple with a longstanding marriage. But her romantic haze is ironically framed: before her entrance there's malicious gossip in her shop about where Shen Teh has been all night, and the barber, Shu Fu, smashes Wang the Waterseller's hand; after her entrance, the old woman reminds Shen Teh that she owes rent to the exacting Mrs. Mi Tzu. Worse, the freeloaders refuse to testify for Wang against Shu Fu, which prompts Shen Teh to declare, in verse, "Oh you wretched people! / Your brother suffers violence and you close your eyes." In the space of some 100 lines, Shen Teh's giddiness (as she describes it) transforms into anger (as a stage direction puts it). Yet Shen Teh is not as thoroughly good and kind as charged by those who accuse Brecht of flattening her into an object lesson: early in the scene she's so absorbed in her infatuation that she fails to notice Wang's suffering. (Later, she betrays Wang more directly.)

In the same compact space, the play complicates its representation of love as an economic transaction, and of men's commodification of women. (An early working title was *Die Ware Liebe, Love for Sale* or *The Commodity Love;* playing on the pun of *Ware* and *wahre,* the title could also mean *True Love.*) In one of Brecht's many ironic undoings of the self-conscious dramatic archetype, the prostitute, Shen Teh does not get ripped off by a man until she gives herself to him. In exchange for his love, Yang Sun demands a trip to Peking and the price of a bribe for a pilot's job. At the end of scene four, Shen Teh hands over to him $200, lent her for rent money by the old couple.

Playing against this inverted romance, this scene also introduces the idea of the wealthy barber, Shu Fu, as a husband for Shen Teh. Seeing her in the rosy splendor of the morning—when she's flushed with love for Yang Sun—Shu Fu falls in love with her. In addition to setting up the later transaction between Shen Teh and the barber, this moment also reminds us that Shen Teh met Yang Sun while on her way to a tete-a-tete with a marriage prospect— one who could cough up the rent money. Here, and in the later negotiations with Shu Fu, marriage is compared to the whoring Shen Teh thought she could leave behind by becoming a businesswoman—or businessman. Indeed, as Shui Ta, Shen Teh serves as her own pimp, becoming, as Brecht's working notes put it, "both goods and salesperson."

To sum up, scene four ends with Shen Teh in love with a man and disappointed in humanity, standing under an accelerating cascade of troubles: the rent, and now the old couple, still owed; Wang injured and abandoned; the freeloaders ever demanding; Shu Fu waiting to pounce. The audience is left in a frame of mind to urge, like the freeloaders in the first scene, "Cousin! Cousin!" But rather than simply satisfy this by-now obvious response to Shen Teh's problems, Brecht interrupts (to use Walter Benjamin's word for the process of epic development) the action, casting into relief our mounting empathy for Shen Teh's plight and uncovering the conditions that lead to her extreme solution.

"Shen Teh enters," the stage direction reads, "carrying the mask and clothes of Shui Ta, and sings 'The Song of Defenselessness of the Gods and the Good People.'" After the first verse, "She puts on Shui Ta's clothes and takes a few steps in his manner." After the second, "She puts on Shui Ta's mask and continues to sing in his voice."

Who sings this song? That is, what stage persona commits the action of—in Brecht's words— *zeigen gestus* ("handing over") "The Song of Defenselessness"? The text assigns the song to the character Shen Teh, but, as Brecht has written, "When an actor sings, [s]he undergoes a change of function." This is doubly true here. At the most literal level, the singer presents a character in transition, changing her function from portraying Shen Teh to portraying Shui Ta. But we see something more than one character changing into the costume of another. The actor's function changes also because by singing, "[s]he who is showing should [her]self be shown." The actor demonstrates how she performs both the role of Shen Teh and the role of Shui Ta. And at the same time she demonstrates how she performs another role, which parallels her pointed-to actorly effort: Shen Teh *playing* Shui Ta. In other words, revealing the process by which she takes steps in Shui Ta's manner and sings in his voice, the actor calls attention to the analogy between her activity and Shen Teh's.

The song achieves this dialectic because, through the analogy it draws to all acting, it grants Shen Teh and Shui Ta the same level of credibility. We always perceive Shui Ta as an impersonation performed by Shen Teh; simultaneously, we understand that Shen Teh is herself an impersonation created by the actor; therefore, she elicits no more unexamined empathy than does the less affecting Shui Ta, despite her more appealing nature.

This equilibrium is maintained through a sly paradox of acting: Shen Teh's character, in conventional theatrical terms, is "unbelievable"—could anyone really be so naive, we have to ask in the face of her unmitigated generosity toward the exploitative freeloaders. But Shui Ta's character, the familiar ruthless businessman, is completely believable (*because* it is so familiar). Indeed, in a 1970 *New York Times* review of a Lincoln Center production starring Colleen Dewhurst, Walter Kerr chides the play for precisely this contrast: explaining that "we lose patience with these figureheads [the freeloaders] long before the lady does," Kerr concludes, "if we ever side with anyone, we tend to side with her tough-minded 'cousin.'"

But what Kerr—and presumably the production—missed is the way these opposite levels of credibility are used within Brecht's parable form, and how they are balanced with inverse proportions of empathic acting. Acquiring intimacy with the audience through soliloquies, and given downright sentimental speeches about love and motherhood (which are soon punctured by various ironic devices) Shen Teh demands more "Aristotelian" pity than does Shui Ta; he never addresses the audience, and remains emotionally at arm's length because of our double awareness of him as an effective figure in the parable, and as Shen Teh's creation. The *type* of character Shui Ta represents is more believable than the *type* Shen Teh represents, yet we experience Shui Ta from a greater distance.

To keep wide this distance from the evil character we can so easily compass—and to close the distance on the good character we can hardly accept—Brecht repeatedly reminds us that Shui Ta is being played by Shen Teh. In the first scene, it's the freeloaders who come up with the idea that a wily cousin could get Shen Teh out of her jam with the unpaid Carpenter, and then with the landlady, Mrs. Mi Tzu: "My dear Shen Teh, why don't you turn the whole matter over to your cousin?" After repeated promptings, Shen Teh relents: "slowly, with downcast eyes," the stage direction reads, Shen Teh declares, "I have a cousin." (Michael Hofmann's 1989 translation of the Santa Monica version of *Good Person* goes so far as to have a freeloader think up the name Shui Ta.) After the claimants leave—and more relatives of the freeloaders arrive—Shen Teh's imposing guests have a facetious laugh over the mythical cousin, "the imposing Mr. Shui Ta." The scene ends with more knocking on the door, threatening that still more relatives will overtake Shen Teh's shop.

When knocking is heard again, at the top of the next scene, it announces the quick-fix to the rapidly multiplying relatives: "a young gentleman," as the stage directions say, Shui Ta. At first the freeloaders dismiss him: "But that was a joke." But almost at once they come to grant him the authority of his imposing presence. As an onstage audience to Shen Teh's performance, they offer one model of a response to her acting: for them, the performance of Shui Ta is "Aristotelian," they believe in it completely and are swept away by it; for us, the performance is epic, always experienced with complex seeing. The onstage audience's reaction works like a lens that intensifies our double vision—and that mirrors our more sympathetic response to Shen Teh.

Later in the scene, after Shui Ta wheedles the Carpenter out of his fee, the freeloaders repeat the event, quoting—in a style reminiscent of the acting Brecht calls for in "The Street Scene: A Basic Model for an Epic Theatre"—the dialogue that just took place. Their merriment is ended only when Shui Ta's virtuoso performance is turned on them: he tells them to get out. What happens in their little imitation is complicated. We see a performance reenacted with a particular attitude—gloating amusement, like the attitude of fans recounting how their team routed another in a ball game. This action drives home the freeloaders' smug selfishness at the same time that it reminds us that Shui Ta is a performance, one that could be presented and received from various points of view. In this moment, of course, like Walter Kerr, we have to side with Shui Ta, cheering his rejection of the freeloaders. But part of the reason we cheer him is that we see Shen Teh within Shui Ta, and recognize that she is standing up for herself. More important, our recognition of Shen Teh behind the mask of Shui Ta (and of an actor behind Shen Teh) encourages us to consider *other* points of view from which Shui Ta (and Shen Teh) might be presented. At the same time, if we feel like satisfied backers of a winning team when Shui Ta throws the freeloaders out, it's because it looks like justice is prevailing, and Shui

Ta will temper Shen Teh's mercy, enabling her to live and do good.

But, of course, we can't hold on to this hope uncritically. The contradiction has already been set forth: Shen Teh can't do good unless Shui Ta does well. And if cheating the Carpenter is what enables Shui Ta to do well—no matter how much it entertains the freeloaders—we see at once its dubious merit. The "Street Scene"-style performance by the freeloaders sharpens our awareness of this bind by placing before us our own emotional reactions to Shui Ta. Will we, like the freeloaders, have a laugh over Shui Ta's cold treatment of others? And if so, what does that laugh show us? That we judge the freeloaders harshly (no sentimental portrait of the poor and downtrodden for Brecht!), that we appreciate the comic device of reversal, that we grasp the central contradiction to be expanded upon in the play—that one can't be good without having means, and acquiring means prevents one from being good.

Other ironic reminders of Shen Teh's performance of Shui Ta function in similar ways. In scene three, Shen Teh responds to Yang Sun's challenge, "You're not much of an entertainer," with the line, "I can play the zither a little and imitate people." Then, the stage directions instruct, "She speaks in a deep voice, imitating a dignified gentleman," saying, "'Good Lord, I must have forgotten my pocketbook!' But then I got the shop. The first thing I did was give away my zither. I said to myself, now I can be a deadhead, and it won't matter." Here, Shen Teh switches to verse: "I'm rich, I said to myself. / I walk alone. I sleep alone. / For a whole year, I said to myself/I'll have nothing to do with a man."

At one level, of course, this is so much flirtatious banter. But again, even at this curiously romantic moment, Brecht reminds us of the cousin not merely waiting in the wings, but lurking within the performer we hear speaking "in a deep voice." What's more, Shen Teh can mention getting rid of her zither as a humorous throw-away; to say that she will have nothing to do with a man requires heightened speech because, not only is her evident attraction for Yang Sun contradicting this pronouncement, but her impersonation of Shui Ta suggests that being rich necessitates having *everything* to do with a man, even if it's one she embodies herself.

Similarly, in scene five, right after "The Song of Defenselessness," Shui Ta sits in the tobacco shop reading the paper. When he hears Yang Sun's voice outside, the stage directions command, "Shui Ta runs to the mirror with the light steps of Shen Teh and is about to arrange his hair when he sees his mistake in the mirror. He turns away with a soft laugh." This is the only occasion when Shen Teh's character so boldly peeps through the Shui Ta disguise, where we see Shen Teh acknowledge her performance by momentarily forgetting it. (Still, the stage directions refer to *his* hair, *his* mistake.) Several things are accomplished by this self-conscious action. First, Brecht increases the disdain with which we react to Yang Sun's coarse treatment of Shen Teh, by reminding us of her romantic enthusiasm and showing how thoroughly love has swept her away. At the same time, it asks us to prick up our double vision, increasing our ironic pleasure in registering how wrong Yang Sun is to think he is shooting the breeze with one of the guys. Once again, the double character ignites our dialectical attention, making us simultaneously more empathetic and more critical. All this raises the stakes for the moment, later in the scene, when Yang Sun reveals that he has no intention of taking Shen Teh to Peking with him.

Yang Sun assumes a macho stance when Shui Ta says that Shen Teh will not go along with his decision: "You're going to appeal to her reason? She hasn't got any reason." Some critics point to this line as an indication that Brecht is reinforcing a misogynistic stereotype of femininity. But that is to disregard the play's theatrical dynamics. Yang Sun's remark is not endorsed; its appalling nature is pointed to by our recognition of Shen Teh's hidden presence. Yang Sun is unmistakably an ambitious lout, not, as Gay Gibson Cima suggests, a sanctioned mouthpiece for conveying Brecht's attitude toward women. That it turns out to be true, in terms of the plot, that Shen Teh pays little mind to her reason—she runs off with Yang Sun after all, because, as he puts it, "I've got my hand on her bosom"—does not mean that the play doubts the intelligence of women. Rather, Brecht calls forth a familiar (and derogatory) image of women in order to make it strange, because, after all, the familiar cannot be rendered strange without first being established as *familiar*. By means of the *Verfremdungseffekt*—the central mechanism of which is the Shui Ta disguise—Brecht lets us take a look at the conditions that give rise to this image of love and the commodified, irrational woman. (That Shen Teh so abandons herself to lust contradicts several critics who complain that Brecht denies this female character her "desire.")

Shen Teh next refers to herself as Shui Ta in scene six, the wedding scene. Her marriage to Yang

Sun is delayed—pathetically in terms of our feeling for Shen Teh; comically in terms of the gag of making the flow of wine the celebration's hourglass—because Yang Sun and his mother await Shui Ta, who, they hope, will bring money. Shen Teh asserts: "My cousin cannot be where I am." Why is this line here? We in the audience already know this; Yang Sun and his mother aren't meant to—and don't—understand what she means. Like Benedick's stating the-obvious remark, "This looks not like a nuptial," in *Much Ado About Nothing*, Shen Teh's line pulls the scene away from the precipice of melodrama. It signals us: Don't get so carried away by this bittersweet episode that you forget to employ your complex seeing; the double character once more forces an epic interruption, refocusing our attention.

The wedding ends, of course, without Shui Ta's arrival; like St. Neverkin's day described in Yang Sun's song— "when the poor woman's son will ascend the king's throne" and "life on earth will become a sweet dream"—Shui Ta will never, *can* never, come, at least not until a vexing contradiction can be resolved. In this scene, waiting is the central *gestus:* for the wedding, for Shui Ta, for the good times. The ending stage direction has Shen Teh, Yang Sun, and Mrs. Yang sitting together, "two of them looking toward the door."

But, of course, Shui Ta does come, in scene seven. In fact, Shui Ta dominates the last portion of the play, the "tobacco king" replacing the "angel of the slums" almost as thoroughly as Jeriah Jip overtakes Galy Gay in *Man Is Man*. The mechanism that both retrieves and eventually undoes Shui Ta is Shen Teh's pregnancy; it instigates Shen Teh's most thorough—and least sustainable—transformation.

Even though Brecht's image of motherhood here is not exactly sweet and touching—Shen Teh says she'll treat others like a "tiger and a wild beast"—and even though the image is distanced by an ironic reversal—becoming a bad man enables her to be a good mother—some critics point especially at this scene to nail Brecht with their charge of misogyny. In a much-quoted essay, Sarah Lennox asserts, "a major virtue of [Brecht's] mother figure is her willingness to be instrumentalized, serving others while ignoring her own subjective needs." Anne Herrmann goes further: "By placing the mother in the female subject position, Brecht not only desexualizes her, but also insists on biological differences as they were used and misused by both the sex reformers of the Weimar Republic and the Nazis of the Third Reich." Of course, Shen Teh occupies this "subject position" for seven-eighths of the play before she becomes a potential mother. And while Brecht may use as a plot device the unavoidable biological difference that women can get pregnant, its epic presentation certainly reveals rather than reinforces essentialist propaganda about a woman's proper role. The formal verse of Shen Teh's "big speech" is one clue that the scene must be played for distance. And the about-to-be-enacted costume change is a further reminder that Shen Teh's gender is as provisional as it is providential.

Shen Teh's pregnancy brings about another transformation: it marks the pivotal point where one expectation is exchanged for another. Up until then, we wait for Shui Ta, knowing just when he'll appear to bail Shen Teh out; after, we wait for Shen Teh, hoping (though knowing better) that she'll come back and set things right. Like the freeloaders, we undergo a change. They transform from exploiting loafers to exploited workers; we change the direction in which we yearn for a resolution.

This action of transformation is essential to the play's story and its procedure—and essential, too, to the very purpose of epic theater. The central transformation of Shen Teh into Shui Ta provides a standard against which other transformations can be regarded: of the exploiting into the exploited, of the tobacco shop into a factory, of unemployed flier into unrelenting foreman (that is, labor into management), of the gods into judges—and most of all, the transformation theater enacts, of actor into character, stage into setting. By making the act of theater-viewing strange, Brecht subjects all the transformations in the story to a parallel interrogation: Do they have to happen? In that way? How do I, as a spectator taking part through a kind of imaginative complicity, enable these events to take place?

This dramatic motif, echoed by the theatrical process, is not just a game of self-referentiality. Brecht's metatheatrical pointings direct our attention to the possibility of change and to our role in effecting it. Herein lies the revolutionary nature of Brecht's dramaturgy. His intention was not to provide a recipe for socialism, but to offer spectators the pleasurable experience of practicing and honing their critical attitude in the epic theater, so it could be applied more successfully in the world.

The whetstone in *Good Person* is what Brecht called "the continual fusion and dissolution of the two characters," Shen Teh and Shui Ta. Brecht sought to achieve the same ebb and flow of sympathy and antipathy with many of his protagonists—Mother Courage as victim and villain, Galileo as scholar and cheat, Puntila as humanist and misanthrope, Azdak as wiseman and bum. Walter Sokel calls these "split characters," but they are more double than split, as we always experience one side of the character through the memory and expectation of the other. Brecht was drawn to this device, no doubt, because it steadfastly requires complex seeing; the double character serves as a focal point for the heightened, self-conscious perception we must engage in the epic theater. In turn, this double character reinforces the way in which we perceive everyone on stage—as characters *and* as actors showing them to us. Shen Teh/Shui Ta is not only Brecht's most literal use of this division, but also the one that most effectively and evocatively attaches the dialectic of theater to the dialectic of moral life.

What "The Song of Defenselessness" says parallels this stage action. As the first stanza tells us, "the gods are powerless," suffering from "defenselessness"—or in a more literal translation of *Wehrlosigkeit*, "weaponless-ness." And we know from the prologue that the gods are disheveled and incompetent; even if they had weapons, they couldn't effect the transformation the song calls for any more than they can produce a *denouement* at the end of the play. The implication is that *people* have to accomplish what all-powerful gods are incapable of. That, in a way, is what Shen Teh tries to do by taking on the guise of Shui Ta. (It is also the "Good People" who lack weapons.) His mask and costume, then, are her armor, his manner—the ruthlessness of an empire-builder—her weapon. Yet the inherent contradiction of the song—combined with the complex seeing demanded by the costume change—indicates that Shen Teh's effort is doomed to fail. Thus, at the very moment when the plot promises the transformation as the solution to Shen Teh's predicament, the song declares that it will not work. Bringing about a climate in which goodness can thrive requires a more fundamental change than acting can accomplish.

The song, then, has a complicated *gestus*. Primarily it is a song of justification, much like Macheath's summing-up anthem at the end of *The Threepenny Opera*. Shen Teh *must* do this in order, merely, to survive. (Indeed, the recapitulation of Shui Ta's action in the trial scene at the end of the play provides rationales for his cruel behavior that are difficult to refute.) But this *gestus* provokes a sense of lament and refusal because the song contains—and displays—the inadequacies of its own argument.

The more the song ratchets up the need for the disguise, the more Shui Ta is brought to life—both in the completion of his costuming, and in the way the song's point of view comes to express one we would associate more with his character than with Shen Teh's. As she takes on his appearance, she takes on his attitude. Thus, the transformation reflects the Marxist imperative so central to Brecht's epic theater—that social being determines thought. This principle, of course, is an underpinning of epic acting, which reverses the Stanislavskian process by which an actor builds action from character, proposing instead that the actor derive character from action—especially so that character can be shown to be a product of social forces.

Any critique of Brecht's use of gender in *Good Person* must begin with this principle—but few of them do. Most feminist readings of the play call for a materialist feminist assessment, but pay no attention to the most significant materialist fact: that the play is meant to be performed, in epic style, on a stage before an audience. (One might think that Brecht's inability to stage *Good Person* in his lifetime contributes to this tendency to neglect the idea of the play in performance. But these same critics, despite Brecht's extensive revisions, clarifying notes, and *Modelbuch*, write in the same abstract manner about *Mother Courage and Her Children*.) John Fuegi, for example, is right that Shen Teh as a woman is "virtually a personification of feeling while Shui Ta as a man is made virtually a personification of reason or calculation." But he's right only up to a point because he doesn't credit the play with pointing out and using that critical conclusion. *Good Person* not only *exploits* prejudgments about the "nature" of men and women, it forces us to confront those prejudgments for what they are. How can we hold onto the belief that Shen Teh is kind and emotional *because* she is female when we are repeatedly reminded that she is Shui Ta? And how can we maintain that Shui Ta is hard and self-serving *because* he is male when we are repeatedly reminded that he is Shen Teh? Besides, the meanness of Mrs. Mi Tzu and the decency of Wang—among others—make it difficult to maintain that the play is awash in moral sexual stereotyping.

To insist that Shen Teh represents a misogynistic stereotype is also to overlook that the play is a parable. Shen Teh is good not because she is female, but because it is her function in the parable to be good. It's astonishing how frequently critics lend Shen Teh psychological depth more fitting to an entirely different genre. To name just a few examples, Fuegi writes that she suffers from a "schizoid personality"; Cima worries that the impossibility of meeting the gods' commandments to be good "dictat[es] within Shen Teh a feeling of failure"; Sue-Ellen Case diagnoses "an internal crisis of gender behavior." But the parable designation can be oversimplified, too, leading to such groundless accusations as Herrmann's—that Brecht "uses his woman figures to embody Communist Party policy."

Good Person was written over a long period, primarily during Brecht's exile in Scandinavia. But the idea first surfaces in his journals in the late 1920s, and he attends to it on and off for some 20 years, announcing the play's completion in 1941. Brecht's notes on *Good Person* are often sketchy, but in the movement from a European to a Chinese setting, from the story of a prostitute disguising herself as a man "in order to help her sisters," to one who "dresses as a man in order to pose as [a cigar store's] proprietor while continuing to practice as a prostitute," to the nuanced structure he finally settled on, one can trace Brecht's movement toward his dialectical theater. In some sense, he practiced the association of a double character with the paradox of goodness in his satire on bourgeois morality, *The Seven Deadly Sins of the Petit-Bourgeoisie* (1933), a collaboration with Kurt Weill. Its protagonists, the sisters Anna I and Anna II, travel the world trying to raise money for their family to buy a house. One, the salesperson, conveys their travails in words; the other, the goods being sold, through dance. Each scene illustrates a sin that must be avoided if one is to make a buck—but each of these, of course, is really a virtue. Scene by scene, the house takes shape on stage, walls rising as each sin is debated and avoided. Meanwhile, a quartet of men representing the family—father, mother, two brothers—offers comments from a platform to the side. (The mother pronounces pieties in basso profundo.)

In the same year, Brecht worked with some of the *Good Person* themes in a short story called "The Job, or In the sweat of thy brow shalt thou fail to earn thy bread." The story is based on a true account of a woman who posed as her husband after he died, in order to take a job promised to him. The story's opening lines announce that it shows "the barbaric condition to which the great European countries had been reduced by their inability to keep their economies going except by force and exploitation" after the first World War. The barbarity turns out to be not that the woman so masquerades, but that, when discovered, she is fired, even arrested, and her job given to "one whose legs chanced to have between them the organ recorded on his birth certificate." The story treats gender as an artificial construction that serves male dominance, which Brecht seems to regard as an auxiliary to capitalism. "In a few days," the story reads, "the woman became a man, in the same way as men have become men over the millenia: through the production process." Like Marx, though, Brecht doesn't much factor women's unpaid labor into his definition of production; his protagonist sets up house with a woman who cares for the watchman's two children and looks after their home. Nonetheless, Brecht's story wryly challenges capitalism's enforcement of gender distinctions.

Good Person, to a large extent, amalgamates these two 1933 works, combining a critical use of the cross-dressing "progress narrative" (one that doubts the nature of progress) with a comparison of the dialectics of capitalist ethics to the dialectics of a divided character. Drawing on the lessons of the *Lehrstucke,* and on increasingly sophisticated—and theatrically tested—epic theory, Brecht briefly picks up the 1934 sketch of *Die Ware Liebe* in Denmark in 1930, pokes at it again in Sweden, and then turns fuller attention to the play once he's settled in Finland. What enables him to move ahead on "the play that gave me the hardest time" is his working out the form that could bring his parallel concerns together: the parable. *Good Person* was the first play to which Brecht assigned this label.

Brecht once described the parable as "far more artful than other forms. Lenin used the parable, not as an idealist, but as a materialist. The parable allowed him to unravel complicated things. To the dramatist it offers the perfect solution, because it is concrete in abstraction: it makes the essential obvious." Brecht's reference to Lenin is aesthetically telling: the parable is not a traditional dramatic form or genre, but is taken from a kind of didactic literature. The label has New Testament overtones as well. Thus, the parable is distinguished from its theatrical cousins, allegory and symbolist drama, in which what is presented to the audience is meant to stand for something else (and which can easily slide into dreaded expressionism). For Brecht, the parable is a condensed, intensified poetic form, at once concrete and indirect, that enables him to evoke familiar characters and situations quickly, so that he can then go about the epic task of making them strange.

G. W. Brandt has suggested that Brecht created "negative parables" that "illustrate a *wrong* state of affairs." He adds, "The negative parable does not imply there is no such thing as right conduct, but the audience is not spoon-fed with a moral." This is an important corrective to those who add Brecht's Marxism to his invocation of the parable to conclude that his plays are ideological vehicles, Communist object lessons. Rather, the parable form enables Brecht to subject such doctrines to pleasurable critique. *Good Person* doesn't merely declare that a moral life is incompatible with capitalism; it lets us observe this tenet from a variety of angles, and asks us to consider its accuracy, cause, meaning, value.

It's foolhardy to look for Brecht's radicalism, and his potentially feminist deconstructions of gender, on the surface of a play's story, as, for instance, David Z. Mairowitz does when he complains, "There is no challenge in Brecht to the arrangement of traditional sex roles." Perhaps it would be easier to claim Brecht for our side if he'd written some plays with stories directly demonstrating how the social hierarchy relegates women to second-class status (and if he hadn't treated women so execrably himself). But Brecht's challenges to social arrangements come through epic process, not through traditional dramatic show-and-tell. Indeed, if one considers Brecht's attitude toward identification and heroes, it seems downright ludicrous to look to him, as Iris Smith does, for "desiring and desirable behaviors modeled on stage . . . so that the feminist spectator could find herself there and project herself into the future."

In one telling comment, recommending rehearsal exercises that would help epic actors build their parts, Brecht suggests, "it is also good for the actors when they see their characters copied or portrayed in another form. If the part is played by somebody of the opposite sex, the sex of the character will be more clearly brought out." In watching a female actor play a male role, for example, the male actor observes gestures, stances, movement, vocal intonation—all the attributes that typically compose a conventional idea of male-ness. By separating them from the body to which these characteristics are thought to be fused, the actor reveals how gender behavior is constituted. In this exercise, then, the male actor learns how to act male, how to detach his character's gender from the assumption that it naturally resides in and issues from his body.

It's no doubt possible that such an exercise could be used to reinforce notions of naturalized gender behavior—one can imagine an actor drawing the conclusion that his female colleague observes masculinity better than he does because it is so completely alien to her. But that's not the case with epic acting, which demands that all aspects of character be shown "inquotations." For, as Janelle Reinelt has argued, "The Alienation effect hollows out and denaturalizes behaviors which are actually socially constructed, enforced through power relations and the myopia which results from habitual positioning within them." Applying this process specifically to gender, Elin Diamond points out, "by alienating (not simply rejecting) iconicity [the semiotic observation that the actor's body resembles the character to which it refers], by foregrounding the expectation of resemblance, the ideology of gender is exposed and thrown back to the spectator." As a result, "gender is exposed as a sexual costume, a sign of a role, not evidence of identity" and "the spectator is enabled to see a sign system *as* a sign system." In sum, Diamond asserts, "Understanding gender as ideology—as a system of beliefs and behavior mapped across the bodies of females and males, which reinforces a social status quo—is to appreciate the continued timeliness of the *Verfremdungseffekt.*"

Diamond offers the most sophisticated feminist reading of Brecht to date, but even she stops short of locating the gender-revealing *V-effekt* in Brecht's plays. Her failure to do this leads her to call for nuances of epic performance that Brecht had, in fact, developed. Diamond imagines a Brechtian-feminist practice that would build on epic acting, fashioning a performer who, "unlike her film counterpart, connotes not 'to be looked-at-ness' [a quality of fetishized female presence elaborated by Laura Mulvey]. . .but rather 'looking-at-being-looked-at-ness.'," Brecht had a name for this: the *gestus* of showing, the performer acknowledging that she is being watched and enjoyed. In addition, Diamond's performer would be "paradoxically available for both analysis and identification, paradoxically within representation while refusing its fixity." This, too, is precisely what already occurs in Brecht's epic theater—and never more clearly than in the character of Shen Teh. As already noted, the *V-effekt* depends on first establishing the familiar to make it strange; similarly, Brecht throws events into critical relief *after* drawing us into them. There's no smug anti-Brechtian point to score by saying that Shen Teh (or Brecht's other characters) inspires a wide range of feelings in us. That's a given; what matters is that we notice ourselves having them—and question why.

Shen Teh herself serves as a countermodel of this process: she runs off with Yang Sun, because, by her own reckoning, she is carried away "in a surge of feeling" (much like Filch in *The Threepenny Opera,* when he falls for the phony beggars). This is just what spectators of the lulling "Aristotelian" theater do, abandoning reason to the heedless, easily manipulated stirrings of the heart. We can't follow suit by getting caught up in Shen Teh's predicament; the Shui Ta disguise and the epic pointing to the familiar, socially bound nature of that predicament serve as a guardrail over the brink of sentimentality.

The play offers a more profound lesson than the moral to which it's usually reduced—in John Willett's words, for instance, "In a competitive society goodness is often suicidal." Beyond that, *Good Person* teaches the spectator what kind of engagement is required for considering this simple-sounding dilemma. It demands nothing less than a new way of perceiving.

This, no doubt, is the reason Brecht first appealed to feminist theater-makers in America, though many of his champions took inspiration from the spreading myth that Brecht was the great genius of agitprop. Indeed, the more Brecht was reduced to being a bearer of Marxist messages, the more he could serve as avatar for the feminist theaters that mushroomed across America in the 1970s; the more incompletely or imprecisely Brecht was understood, the more easily he could be latched onto as an icon of radical theater practice. Thus, theaters as different as At the Foot of the Mountain in Minneapolis and the Women's Experimental Theater in New York were described as "Brechtian" simply because they promoted a political agenda and produced non-naturalistic plays.

Still, if such theaters—or their critics—overlooked certain complexities of epic theater in claiming Brecht, they were right to find an affinity between the *V-effekt* and the great "aha" mechanism of their own work, consciousness-raising. In both, as Brecht said of epic theater, "What is 'natural' [has] the force of what is startling." Such devices as putting a pregnant man desperate for an abortion at the center of a drama, as Myrna Lamb did in *What Have You Done for Me Lately?,* or telling the story of the *Oresteia* from the point of view of the women involved in the myth, as the Women's Experimental Theater did, certainly provoked a reassessment of the old way of looking at things. Nonetheless, Lamb's play probably owes more to *commedia dell'arte* than to Brecht; W.E.T.'s probably has more in common with symbolist drama than with epic theater.

One reason, of course, is stylistic. Another is tone. For C-R not only afforded the famous "click" experience, after which nothing looks the same again, it also was a means of affirming solidarity and welcoming a recruit into the fold. As an essay by Kathie Sarachild in an early feminist pamphlet points out, "Consciousness-raising was seen as both a method for arriving at the truth and as a means for action and organizing." This is completely at odds with the truth-scorning critical analysis provoked by the *V-effekt* and with the more generally anti-authoritarian spirit of Brecht's writings.

More recently, as feminist theater (and to a large degree, feminism itself) has moved into the academy, Brecht has been subjected to psychoanalytic, poststructuralist, and deconstructionist readings. It's impossible to characterize all of these assessments with a few broad strokes, but it's fair to say generally, I think, that the more Brecht has been scrutinized through these postmodern lenses, the more epic theater practice has gone out of focus.

Feminists, most of all, must not allow this to happen. Now that the cold war is over, Communism can no longer serve as the great clobbering epithet for conveniently dismissing Brecht. Perhaps now more than ever, we can come to appreciate the dramatic poetry of Brecht's plays and the profound radical and feminist impact they promise—if only we would learn to recognize them.

Source: Alisa Solomon, "Materialist Girl: *The Good Person of Szechwan* and Making Gender Strange," in *Theater,* 1994, Vol. 25, no. 2, pp. 42–55.

SOURCES

Atkinson, Brooks. "Brecht Play Is Staged by Eric Bentley," *The New York Times,* December 19, 1956, p. 41.

Barnes, Clive. "The Theater: Brecht's *Good Woman,*" *The New York Times,* November 6, 1970, p. 51.

Braunagel, Don. A review of *The Good Person of Szechwan,* in *Variety,* August 8, 1994.

Brecht, Bertolt. *The Good Person of Szechwan: A Parable Play,* translated by John Willett, Arcade Publishing, 1955.

Driver, Tom. F. "Over the Edge," *The Christian Century,* January 30, 1957, p. 138.

Fuegi, John. *The Essential Brecht,* Hennessey & Ingalls, 1972, p. 133.

Hatch, Robert. A review of *The Good Person of Szechwan,* in *The Nation,* January 5, 1957, p. 27.

Hewes, Henry. "Trying to Like Eric Bentley," *Saturday Review,* January 5, 1957, p. 24.

Kauffmann, Stanley. A review of *The Good Person of Szechwan,* in *The New Republic,* March 13, 1976, p. 28.

Kerr, Walter. "Will Brecht Ever Come True?," *The New York Times,* November 15, 1970, section 2, p. 1.

Robinson, Roderick. "Theater Emory Pulls off Brecht with Bit of Verve," *The Atlanta Journal and Constitution,* March 20, 1992, p. D2.

Winn, Steven. "Adding Szechuan to Shakespeare," *The San Francisco Chronicle,* March 2, 1999, p. E1.

FURTHER READING

Fuegi, John. "The Alienated Woman: Brecht's *The Good Person of Szechwan,* in *Essays on Brecht: Theater and Politics,* edited by Siegfried Mews and Herbert Knust, The University of North Carolina Press, 1974, pp. 190-96.

> This essay explores the evolution of Brecht's ideas on *The Good Person of Szechwan,* and the prominent woman character, Shen Teh.

Kleber, Pia. *Exceptions and Rules: Brecht, Planchon and The Good Person of Szechwan,* Peter Lang, 1987.

> This book describes the influence of Brecht on a Roger Planchon, a French director and playwright, including a discussion of his three different stagings of *The Good Person of Szechwan.*

Lyon, James K. *Bertolt Brecht in America,* Princeton University Press, 1980.

> This is a critical biography of Brecht during his time in exile in the United States. Work on *The Good Person of Szechwan* was completed in this time period.

Schoeps, Karl H. *Bertolt Brecht,* Frederick Ungar Publishing Co., 1977, pp. 280-97.

> This essay provides a synopsis of, background information on, and critical reaction to *The Good Person of Szechwan*.

Hot L Baltimore

LANFORD WILSON
1973

Opening in February 1973, *Hot L Baltimore* was the first major success for Wilson and his theater company, the Circle Repertory Company. Critics and audiences loved Wilson's play, and it set an Off-Broadway record of 1,166 performances after playing Off-Off-Broadway for a month.

In the play, the actors mill about in the lobby of a dilapidated old hotel, from which the "e" in the hotel sign is missing—hence the name, *Hot L Baltimore*. The play is comprised of a series of conversations between the residents of the hotel, who are contemplating an uncertain future after the hotel is condemned and scheduled for demolition.

Wilson's play won the New York Drama Critics Circle Award for the Best American Play of 1972–73. It also won an Obie Award for best Off-Broadway play, an Outer Critics Award, and the John Gassner Playwriting award. The play was also sold to ABC and adapted as a situation comedy.

AUTHOR BIOGRAPHY

On April 13, 1937, Lanford Wilson was born in Lebanon, Missouri. When he was five years old his parents divorced and his father moved to California; he lived with his mother until 1956.

Wilson attended Southwest Missouri State College (1955–56) and San Diego State College (1956–

57). When he was nineteen, Wilson moved to Chicago. He fell in love with big city life and got a job at an advertising agency doing illustrations.

At that time he began writing plays and enrolled at University of Chicago to learn more about the theater. After he moved to New York in 1962, Wilson became an active participant in the Off-Off Broadway movement.

Several of his early plays were produced at the Caffe Cino or at La Mama Experimental Theatre. These early one-act plays were followed by a succession of full-length works, beginning with *Balm in Gilead* (1965).

In 1968, Wilson co-founded the Circle Repertory Company, where most of his works premiered. Strong character development has become a hallmark of Wilson's work. His characters often exist on the fringes of society, but as the play progresses, they demonstrate that they are capable of growth and change.

Wilson has been the recipient of several awards, including the New York Drama Critics Circle award in 1973 for *Hot L Baltimore* and in 1980 for *The Migrants*. He also received the American Institute of Arts and Letters Award in 1974; in 1980 he received the Pulitzer Prize for Drama.

PLOT SUMMARY

Act I

The play opens at 7 a.m. on Memorial Day. The hotel is being torn down and the residents are being notified that they have one month left before they must move.

As Bill notifies the hotel's residents, Mrs. Bellotti enters looking for Katz, who has refused to allow her son to move back into the hotel. Millie begins a conversation with the Girl about ghosts.

April complains about several things: the sunlight, her inability to sleep, the change to daylight savings time, and the state of the water in the hotel. Mr. Morse enters and loudly complains that his window does not close tightly and that he may well become sick from the draft.

Jackie and Jamie enter, and Jackie immediately begins looking for Katz. Jackie goes up to Morse's room to fix the stuck window. Katz finally enters and is accosted by the entire group with their complaints.

Jackie returns to the lobby to ask Katz to co-sign a loan she needs; he refuses. In the middle of their conversation, Suzy enters with a customer. Katz tries to stop the man from going upstairs with Suzy, but she claims that he is a friend who is going upstairs to have a drink with her.

Mrs. Bellotti pleads with Katz to allow her son to return to the hotel. Katz will not consider it, claiming that Bellotti's son is a thief. Mrs. Bellotti tells everyone that her husband has recently had his leg amputated because of diabetes and that he will not allow the son to return to their home. Jamie, who has been playing checkers with Morse, offers to help Mrs. Bellotti pack her son's belongings.

The Girl receives a phone call from her pimp and sets up an appointment with a customer, which bothers Bill. Suzy's customer comes downstairs, followed by a naked Suzy, who is complaining that the man beat her and locked her out of her room. At that moment, Jamie is descending the stairs and sees Suzy, minus her towel. He is so startled that he drops the box he is carrying.

Act II

Later that afternoon, Paul is badgering Mrs. Oxenham for help in locating his grandfather. Jamie and Morse are playing checkers. The Girl enters and begins to complain about the lack of hot water; she finally realizes that Katz has no intention of fixing the hot water.

Jamie and Morse fight about the checker game. It escalates into a physical brawl. After Morse hides in the closet out of embarrassment, Jamie feigns injuries to lure Morse from the closet.

Jackie enters, complaining that all the pawnshops in town are closed. The Girl asks Paul about his grandfather and learns that he has spent two years on a work farm for selling drugs.

Meanwhile, Jackie brags about the land she bought from a radio ad and about the organic food she is going to grow. The other residents realize that she has been conned. Millie talks about her childhood home.

Morse announces that he has been robbed—all his wife's jewelry is missing. The residents realize that Jackie is the thief and Katz tells her that she must leave immediately or he will have her arrested.

Lanford Wilson

Millie informs Paul that she is sure his grandfather is still alive.

Act III

At midnight, April is complaining about her customers. Bill has had the hot water fixed. The Girl searches through receipts looking for information about Paul's missing grandfather.

The residents realize that Jackie has abandoned her brother. Suzy comes downstairs with all her luggage and announces that she is moving to a new apartment that her new friend (her pimp) has arranged for her.

After a glass of champagne, Suzy leaves. When the Girl informs Paul that she thinks she can find his grandfather, Paul tells her not to bother; he is no longer interested. As the play ends, April takes Jamie by the hand and begins to dance with him.

CHARACTERS

Mrs. Bellotti

Mrs. Bellotti is the mother of a former tenant. Described as a whiner and complainer, she tells the audience that her husband just had a leg amputated because of diabetes. When Katz makes it clear that her son will not be allowed to return, she goes upstairs and begins to pack his belongings.

The Girl

A nineteen-year-old prostitute, the Girl is caring and concerned about the other residents. She goes to great effort to help Morse. It is she who tells Jackie that she has bought worthless land.

Paul Granger III

Paul is a college student who was arrested for selling drugs. He has recently been released from a work farm. He comes to the hotel to look for his grandfather.

April Green

April is one of the prostitutes in the play. She is described as large, pragmatic, quick to laugh, and pretty. She is protective of Suzy.

Jackie

Jackie is a hustler traveling with her brother, Jamie. She needs money and tries to get Katz to co-sign a loan so they can go Utah to grow health foods on a worthless piece of land she has bought. She steals jewelry from Morse's room, but is caught and ordered to leave. She tells Jamie that she is going to buy gas, but never returns to pick him up.

Jamie

Jamie is Jackie's nineteen year-old brother. He is described as being a bit slow. In the last act, Jamie is abandoned by his sister, who simply drives off and leaves him to manage on his own.

Mr. Katz

Mr. Katz is the hotel manager. A balding, tired man, he resists Jackie's pleas for money. He gives the residents one month's notice because the hotel is to be torn down.

Bill Lewis

Bill is the night clerk at the hotel. He has a difficult time communicating and covers by talking too loudly. Bill is interested in the Girl and is more tolerant with her than the other hotel employees.

Millie

Millie is a retired waitress. Considered eccentric, she believes in ghosts and lives in a world more imagined than real. She tells the other residents that she grew up in a mansion. She is a caring person who tells Paul that she knows that his grandfather is still alive.

Mr. Morse

An elderly man, Mr. Morse is loud and demanding. He plays checkers all day and gets into arguments with other residents. When he and Jamie come to blows over a checker game, Morse hides in the broom closet and will not come out until he is convinced that he won the fight. He is robbed by Jackie.

Mrs. Oxenham

Mrs. Oxenham is the desk clerk and phone operator at the hotel. She is tough and tries to keep the prostitutes' customers out of the hotel.

Suzy

Suzy is a prostitute. In the opening act, she brings one of her customers to the hotel; she accuses him of beating her and locking her out of her room.

MEDIA ADAPTATIONS

- *Hot L Baltimore* has never been made into a film, but the play was adapted to television in 1975 by ABC.

She is tough but also romantic in her search for happiness with a new pimp.

THEMES

Choices and Consequences

There are several instances where it becomes clear that in choosing prostitution, the women in the play face the dangerous consequences of their choice.

Suzy is beaten and locked out of her room by a customer early in the play. Later, she announces that she is moving into an apartment with her new pimp. Her friends are concerned that this man will treat her as badly as the previous one did.

Although April makes fun of her customers' fetishes, she has been put at risk by freaky and dangerous customers. Wilson does not emphasize it, but it is clear that prostitution is a risky way to make a living.

Human Condition

Jamie's abandonment is a tragic situation that underscores the precarious nature of the human condition. The young man is almost helpless without Jackie to care for him; his ability to think and rationalize is limited. It is unclear how he will be able to survive without his sister to help him.

The picture of this teenage boy bringing all his possessions to the lobby is heartbreaking. The other residents know that Jackie will not return, and the audience knows it as well. The last image in the play is of April trying to distract Jamie as she teaches him to dance.

TOPICS FOR FURTHER STUDY

- Wilson is interested in what he considers to be an American disregard for the remnants of the American past. Research the history of the American city and decide if his concerns are warranted. Are cities too quick to tear down the past and modernize with new structures? Is there too little regard for historical buildings and areas?

- Prostitution is often described as a victimless crime. In areas where prostitution is legal, is the occurrence of violent crime any worse? Or does ignoring prostitution free police for more serious crimes? Does prostitution encourage organized crime? Provide statistics to support your answer.

- Investigate the history of prostitution. How have communities throughout history handled prostitution? Has the profession changed throughout time?

- Determine the number of Americans who get conned by radio, television, and solicitations into buying worthless land each year. What kind of people choose to buy land they have never seen? What are the current laws against this type of con?

Memory and Reminiscence

The majority of the conversations between the residents concern their memories of the past. Millie tells the other residents about her childhood and the large mansion that was inhabited by ghosts. The Girl talks about her travels around the United States.

These pleasant memories help to alleviate anxiety over an uncertain future. It is particularly important to focus on the past when in a short time they will all be homeless.

Morality

Wilson treats prostitution as just another profession. There is certainly no moral judgment about these women's choice of careers. April's descriptions of her customers and their desires is intended to amuse and evoke pity, but at no point is the audience expected to criticize her actions. She is simply working and trying to earn a living.

The same is true for Suzy and the confrontation with her customer. The audience is expected to laugh at Jamie's shock, but there is no expectation that she will call the police.

The only critical comment comes from Bill when the Girl is called with a job. Yet it is understood that he is likes her and wants to protect her. Wilson never makes a moral judgment about these women, and he does not allow any of the characters to do so either.

Wealth and Poverty

Paul Granger's story about his missing grandfather creates a dichotomy between wealth and poverty. Paul's parents are wealthy, but his grandfather was a working man. His parents are ashamed of him. Initially Paul searches for his grandfather because he wants to offer him a home. Later, he loses interest in locating him.

Wilson never suggests a reason for Paul's sudden disinterest. Perhaps the hotel provides insight into the kind of existence that his grandfather has lived and he realizes how different his grandfather's life has been from his own. Paul may realize that his parents are correct and there is no room in their lives for a poor old man on a railroad pension.

STYLE

Act

Acts are the major divisions in a drama. In Greek plays the sections of the drama are signified by the appearance of the chorus; they are usually divided into five acts. These five acts denote the structure of dramatic action: exposition, complication, climax, falling action, and catastrophe.

The five-act structure was followed until the nineteenth century when Henrik Ibsen combined some of the acts. *Hot L Baltimore* is a three-act play. However, there is little plot in the play; hence the structure of dramatic action is not applicable.

Character

The actions of each character are what constitute the story. Characters can range from simple stereotypical figures to more complex multifaceted ones; they may also be defined by personality traits, such as the rogue or the damsel in distress.

Characterization is the process of creating a lifelike person from an author's imagination. To accomplish this the author provides the character with personality traits that help define who he will be and how he will behave in a given situation.

Wilson does not create complex characters in his play. Most of what the audience knows is provided in brief vignettes. Characters tend to be stereotypical, such as the good-hearted prostitute or the street-tough youth.

Comedy

There are two types of drama: tragedy and comedy. *Hot L Baltimore* is a comedy. The purpose of comedy is to amuse. It has many forms, such as farce and burlesque, and may also include satire and parody. For instance, Wilson is using comedy to point out the problems that occur when cities are too eager to destroy debilitated buildings just because they are old. He sees historical wealth and social value in their preservation and renewal.

Setting

The time and place of the play is called the setting. The elements of setting may include geographic location, physical or mental environments, cultural attitudes, or the historical time in which the action takes place. The location for *Hot L Baltimore* is the lobby of a seedy hotel. All of the action occurs between 7 a.m. and midnight on Memorial Day.

HISTORICAL CONTEXT

In the early 1970s satellite transmissions meant that Americans could watch history unfold as it happened. Because more Americans were watching, television branched out and offered live coverage of important news events.

In the early part of the decade, the Vietnam War as well as the protests over the war across the country were televised into American homes. In a very real sense, it was the images of American men dying on camera that helped fuel much of the opposition to the war.

Television viewers also watched the shooting of four student protesters at Kent State University and the deaths of two more a week later at Jackson State University, events that led to protests at more than 1,200 other colleges and universities—most of which were also covered by television cameras.

Certainly, television changed the way America fought wars. By early 1973 the last of American ground troops were finally pulled from Vietnam in 1975. The televised roof-top evacuation of the American embassy in Saigon was a haunting final image for American viewers.

Other dramatic events made for good television too. The moon landing in 1969 drew millions of viewers all over the world. A year later, the troubled mission of Apollo 13 reminded Americans that there was nothing routine about space flight—viewers were glued to their sets, praying the astronauts would make it home safely.

In 1972, the murder of several Israeli athletes shocked viewers of the Olympic games. Throughout the 1970s, air hijackings and hostage situations escalated, often as a protest against American foreign policy.

When Arab countries, protesting American support of Israel, imposed an oil boycott that resulted in gasoline shortages and higher prices, it was television that brought the images of long lines into American homes. Helping Americans deal with the inconveniences of the embargo was another role for television, which brought the president's warnings about conserving energy.

It was television that broadcast the Watergate hearings—as well as the live image of President Nixon waving goodbye as he left the White House after his resignation from office.

CRITICAL OVERVIEW

Hot L Baltimore was very popular with both critics and audiences on its debut in February 1973. After a month, Wilson's play moved to an Off-Broadway theatre, the Circle in the Square Theatre, where it opened March 22, 1973.

Amongst critics, a sense of nostalgia prevailed. As Douglas Watt noted in his review, "It's no place

COMPARE & CONTRAST

- **1973:** Senate hearings begin in Washington into the break-in at the Democratic National Committee Headquarters in the Watergate building. The hearings would eventually lead to the resignation of President Richard Nixon.

    Today: The nation is still recovering from the impeachment proceedings against President Bill Clinton. During the impeachment trial and its aftermath, televised coverage—network, cable, and the Internet—was continuous and comprehensive.

- **1973:** The Arab oil embargo pushes the price of gasoline to new highs as severe shortages result in mile-long lines at the gas pumps. Consumers are encouraged to conserve energy, and alternate energy sources become more prominent.

    Today: Oil is plentiful and inexpensive. As a result, gas-guzzling SUVs become a popular vehicle.

- **1973:** The median sales price of an existing single-family home in the United States reaches $28,900.

    Today: While the prices of new homes have stabilized in recent years, the median price of a new home now exceeds $130,000 in most areas. In part this results from an increased demand for larger homes.

---

to live, but it's worth a visit.'' Watt discussed the setting, a crucial element of this play: ''Time stands still in seedy hotels. The locations may change, and the people's names; but today's castoffs are the same as yesterday's, giving their own kind of continuity to life. They're the ones you meet in Lanford Wilson's quietly affecting three-act play.''

According to Watt, ''nothing much happens ... [but] we become part of their small world.'' The audience becomes interested in these characters, although there is no plot or action, just dialogue.

Watt asserted that the characters are timeless; there is nothing that establishes them as from 1973, except for their clothing and the music playing in the background. ''There are false notes and awkward moments,'' said Watt, ''but Wilson is a gifted and appealing playwright.''

One of the aspects of the play that apparently appealed to Watt was the absence of gunmen, cops, heroes, villains, and melodrama. In conclusion, Watt maintained that ''you wouldn't want to room there, but *Hot L Baltimore* is an interesting place to visit on a quiet day.''

Another critic, Martin Gottfried, lauded the play: ''The *Hot L Baltimore* is first-class Lanford Wilson, and that is as good as you will find in the American theatre.''

He praised Wilson's ability to find beauty in American stories:

> Wilson was one of the first of our playwrights to seek an American beauty and an essential mythology in our national roots; one of the first to deal with that subject in a style of heightened, poetized reality; one of the first to return to language while fashion was still demanding minimalism and noncommunication. The *Hot L Baltimore* shows him still at the peak of his mastery over these qualities.

He also contended that Wilson's ''writing is superb, a triumph of inspiration and craftsmanship.'' After praising Wilson's ability to create believable characters, Gottfried concluded that ''Wilson builds a magnificently detailed concerto for humanity.''

Richard Watts offered a mixed review. He deemed the play ''as odd and original a play as you are likely to see all season.''

After noting the lack of plot, Watts considered characterization the strength of this play, since Wilson is not trying ''to make any particular points'' but is interested in exploring people and their lives.

Wilson's characterization was also praised by Jack Kroll in his review for *Newsweek*. Referring to Wilson's work as "so old-fashioned in its humanity that it's the freshest play—the best American play— I've seen this season," Kroll wrote that Wilson "dares to remind us of what writers once were in this country."

The strength of character development was also noted by Leonard Probst in his television review of Wilson's play. Probst contended that "the people are alive and real" and the set is "so real that you feel that you're in the Hotel Baltimore." Probst also considered the lack of plot, but added, "the play is completely engrossing."

Probst maintained that "the play has a wonderful sense of humanity, a feeling [sic] of the loss of passion as we, our cities, and our institutions grow weary, and too wise to do anything about it."

CRITICISM

Sheri E. Metzger

Metzger is a Ph.D., specializing in literature and drama at The University of New Mexico. In the following essay, Metzger discusses the creation of character in Hot L Baltimore.

The 1970s were a decade of protests: protests over the war in Vietnam, protests for women's rights, and protests about racial inequities. It was a decade to rethink our nation's history. It is only right that Lanford Wilson's play *Hot L Baltimore* focuses on the importance of preserving America's cities, while embracing each character's personal history, since he presents the notion that history is worth remembering and savoring.

It is primarily the individual characters that bring Wilson's play to life. He manages to imbue each one with a unique spirit that makes it especially difficult for audiences to select a favorite. Each character—whether a prostitute, the forgotten elderly, or the soon-to-be-unemployed hotel staff— brings a humanity to his or her role. It is primarily the setting and the characters that deliver this play's message.

In an interview with Gene A. Barnett, Wilson perceives his strength as writing dialogue for his plays. After first mentioning that he became a playwright because he always wrote dialogue better than he wrote narrative, Wilson asserts that dialogue "was always something that I had under control and had always been attracted to—juxtaposed sounds and rhythms of characters—and so it was really natural." It is the natural sound of the character's dialogue that captures his audiences— and the critics—attention.

Reviews of *Hot L Baltimore* invariably cite the play's greatest strengths as the realism of the characters and the flow of dialogue. In his review for *Women's Wear Daily,* Martin Gottfried asserted that Wilson's

> writing is simply superb, a triumph of inspiration and craftsmanship. He has created 17 [actually 15] individual characters with specific speech patterns and personalities, and has orchestrated them. Each weaves his strand through the play, maintaining his individuality yet part of the whole ... With such language, with such real and yet mythic characters, with such a clear conflict between life's rulers (the hotel personnel) and its victims ... with such poetic ambiguity (a cry for convictions by people whose convictions are doomed), Wilson builds a magnificently detailed concerto for humanity.

Gottfried is not alone in commending Wilson for the richness of his characters or for his appeal to his audience's humanity. Richard Watts' review for *The New York Post* also focused on Wilson's ability to create interesting characters. In fact, he credited the play's success to the characters, finding the plot not worth mentioning.

Watts maintained that "the important thing is that they [the people in the hotel] are entertaining and friendly people, though a little crazy, and their thoughts, woes, confidences and self-revelations make an engaging and sympathetic play." It is the character's stories that pull the audience in and holds its attention.

Each of the hotel's residents is an outcast, living on the fringes of society in a hotel that is on the fringe of existence. In her review of Wilson's life and works, Ann Crawford Dreher asserted that "all the people at the Baltimore are either hurting each other or helping each other." This "delineates a pattern of the human ability to go on feeling and striving in the midst of a crumbling world."

Although each of these people is a societal outcast, each has something to contribute toward the common goal of survival; thus they make their own place in a society that would consider them

WHAT DO I READ NEXT?

- *Talley's Folly,* one of Lanford Wilson's most successful plays, was first performed in 1979. Set in 1944, this play is about the romance between a Midwestern spinster and a Jewish tax accountant.

- Lanford Wilson's *Balm in Gilead* was written in 1965 and is set in New York City. It features characters who are considered outcasts: prostitutes, thieves, and the elderly.

- *Serenading Louie,* Lanford Wilson's 1976 play, is about alienation, estrangement, and death. The focus is on two couples, neighbors who are enduring crises.

- Anton Chekhov's *The Cherry Orchard* (1903) explores what happens when something old and beautiful is destroyed to create something new.

- *The Time of Your Life* (1939), written by William Saroyan, is a series of vignettes about people doing ordinary things.

---

eccentric or foolish. In his article on Wilson's plays, Henry I. Schvey contended that many of Wilson's works "have large casts and are essentially peopled by characters who have no definite place in society."

Of *Hot L Baltimore,* Schvey maintained that Wilson's focus is not solely on the characters as outcasts; instead he is attracted to "the world as it is (dramatically conveyed by the shabby decaying hotel), and a community of people who need to believe in something—whatever the odds."

These people refuse to give up. Their strength and humanity appeals to the audience. Whether or not they are losers, they convey the notion that they are survivors, and American audiences want to cheer for winners.

Schvey asserted that nearly all of the characters are searching for something— but that something is, according to Schvey, "either worthless or fraudulent." Perhaps that is their attraction to audiences, who can identify with the character's fears, while remaining thankful that they, too, have managed to avoid those particular traps.

However, Schvey claimed that in spite of the play's "almost unanimously favourable reviews and wide public appeal ... its simple message wears thin, and its characterization is ultimately superficial." The play's "upbeat message of hope is not sufficient" and Wilson's play could not bear comparison to other works that also focus on similar ideas, such as Chekhov's *The Cherry Orchard,* which has a complexity that Wilson's play lacks.

Martin J. Jacobi would disagree that the characterization in Wilson's play is inadequate. In his article on Wilson's comic vision, Jacobi argued that Wilson's plays

> move from bleakly naturalistic portraits of ineffectual outcasts who have little connection to their group, through pessimistic portrayals of outsiders who might have saved themselves from destruction but do not, to realistically optimistic views of individuals who challenge societal prejudices but still find acceptable places within it. They develop from pathos and incipient tragedy to true, and not sentimental, comedy.

This is far different from an assessment of the characters as superficial. Jacobi viewed Wilson's ability to "identify important traditions and cultural values" as a major contribution in his characters' development. Although they are society's outcasts, each has something to give to the other members of the group.

For example, the play's conclusion demonstrates that while April wants to help Jamie survive his sister abandoning him, he is capable of being on his own. Jamie may be flawed and different, but he is capable of surviving.

This idea is picked up by Jacobi, who noted that "Wilson professes to his audience that people can be individuals, sometimes eccentrically so, and still be good members of their group.'' This is a reassuring message for the audience, and it clearly belongs in a decade that valued individualism and rebellion as did the 1970s.

Often times, writers write to explore ideas, to help them develop a better understanding of an issue. In an interview published by Jackson R. Bryer, Wilson contended that ''writing is the process of understanding what you're feeling.''

Writing also offers Wilson a chance to experiment with creating different ideas and different characters. In providing his characters with eccentricities, Wilson makes them more appealing. It is worth noting that the 1970s were a time of self-expression, of outlandish clothing, of experimentation with drugs, and of sexual adventures.

Wilson told Gene Barnett that he wanted to create characters who were more vibrant, exciting, and unusual. He wanted to move out of ''that suburban rut that I'd gotten into.''

The characters in *Hot L Baltimore* are especially unusual and vibrant. Millie's belief in the spirit world and her family history of eccentricity make her one of Wilson's most interesting characters. And the Girl's inability to pick a name echoes a common theme, often unexpressed beyond childhood, that each individual should be able to select his or her own name.

Each of the other two prostitutes is an individual, moving beyond conventional description into the extraordinary. April's candid descriptions of her customer's proclivities provide some of the funniest lines in the play. And Suzy's humanity inspires the audience's sympathy.

There is no reason for the audience to invest itself in one of Wilson's characters. None of them is what audiences would consider the star of the show. And yet, the audience is mysteriously drawn in and forced to care, even when it does not wish to do so.

In part, this is because there is a sort of timelessness about Wilson's play. The setting is 1970s Baltimore, but it could be any decade and any city. There have always been the poor, the downtrodden, the illicit members of any society. And they have always been the object of urban renewal.

Douglas Watt noted in his review of *Hot L Baltimore* for the *Daily News* that this ''slice-of-life

> THE INHABITANTS OF WILSON'S HOTEL SHARE THE AUDIENCE'S INSECURITIES, BUT THEY ALSO SHARE THEIR DREAMS AND HOPES FOR A BETTER LIFE.''

might have taken place 30 years ago but for the trivial facts that the clothes are different, the country music has a rock beat and April sends out for pizza instead of hamburgers or danish.''

Yet in truth, these characters are representative of what city government often hopes to eliminate when they decide to tear down a seedy hotel, a tenement building, or whatever else they consider an example of urban blight. These are the people who cannot afford something better.

Except for Suzy, whose quest for a better living arrangement may ultimately hurt her, Wilson never suggests a solution for his characters. They do not have to search for a place to live—not yet. And the audience does not have to face the fact that in a month these people will be homeless.

In many ways, Wilson's play is as topical in 2000 as it was more than twenty-five years ago. The homeless clog big city streets, and the working poor are often only a paycheck away from sharing the same fate.

The inhabitants of Wilson's hotel share the audience's insecurities, but they also share their dreams and hopes for a better life. The hotel may be torn down, but life will provide for the people, and the audience is forced to cheer for their survival.

Source: Sheri E. Metzger for *Drama for Students,* Gale, 2000.

Liz Brent

Brent has a Ph.D. in American Culture, specializing in cinema studies, from the University of Michigan. She is a freelance writer and teaches courses in American cinema. In the following essay, Brent discusses the themes of loss and nostalgia in Wilson's play.

Langford Wilson's play *The Hot L Baltimore,* set in the lobby of a soon-to-be demolished hotel, currently a flophouse, focuses on the interactions between a motley set of hotel tenants in exploring deeper themes of loss, death, and nostalgia. The setting of the play is itself steeped in nostalgia. Opening descriptions of the hotel, as well as the nearby railroad station, paint a picture of faded elegance.

> Once there was a railroad and the neighborhood of the railroad terminals bloomed (boomed) with gracious hotels. The Hotel Baltimore, built in the late nineteenth century, remodeled during the Art Deco last stand of the railroads, is a five-story establishment intended to be an elegant and restful haven.

A description of the once-grand interior renders its imminent destruction sharply poignant: "Its history has mirrored the rails' decline. The marble stairs and floors, the carved wood paneling have aged as neglected ivory ages, into a dull gold. The Hotel Baltimore is scheduled for demolition." Wilson's description of the theater setting in which the play should be produced echoes this theme of decayed elegance: "The theater, evanescent itself, and for all we do perhaps itself disappearing here, seems the ideal place for the representation of the impermanence of our architecture." Later in the play, the Girl expresses nostalgia, not just for the Hotel Baltimore, as it once was, but for the city itself, as it once was: "Baltimore used to be one of the most beautiful cities in America."

Wilson sets the time period of the play as "a recent Memorial Day," and provides the directions that the music from the radio should "incorporate music popular during production." The playwright sets his story in a "recent" time, with contemporary music, in order to emphasize the immediacy of the moment, thereby rendering the sense of nostalgia for the past all the more powerful to the audience. Furthermore, characters in the play are continually asking, being informed of, and discussing the time of day. This preoccupation with the theme of time creates an atmosphere in which all of the characters are painfully aware of the passage of time. They learn that they have only one month left before they are evicted and the hotel is demolished. This literal anxiety about the passage of time echoes with the play's theme of nostalgia for a past which can never be recovered.

The Girl, the young prostitute who has not yet decided on a name for herself, seems of all the characters to have the strongest sense of nostalgia about both the decline of the railroads and the imminent demolition of the old hotel. The Girl is obsessed with the train schedule, continually listening for the sound of the trains passing which can be heard inside the hotel lobby. She is obsessed with the fact that the trains are always behind schedule, and imagines that they once ran on time. This concern with time expresses both a nostalgia for the railroad system she imagines to have once been grand and precise, and a sense of anxiety over the passage of time, of time passed, of time lost which can never be recovered. Her interest in the past is expressed directly when she tells Paul that, in high school, "I was pretty good in history." The Girl's fascination with a lost past is expressed in her musings about the hotel's history: "We probably walk right under and right past the places where all kinds of things happened. A tepee or a log cabin might have stood right where I'm standing." This interest in the past takes on a strong aura of nostalgia when she concludes that, "Wonderful things must have happened on this spot."

The setting of Memorial Day provides a frame for the play's theme of death, loss and mourning. The title of the play, in fact, is derived from the loss of the "e" from the original "Hotel Baltimore" sign, so that it reads "Hot₁ Baltimore." The loss of the "e" establishes the theme of loss incurred due to the ravages of time. The character of Paul, who first appears in Act Two, most directly addresses the theme of loss of loved ones appropriate to Memorial Day. Paul, a young man, appears in the hotel lobby in search of his grandfather, not knowing if he is alive or dead. Mrs. Oxenham, one of the tenants, comments that "We're not a missing persons bureau." In questioning the hotel tenants and employees, Paul himself brings up the possibility that his grandfather may be dead, inquiring, "Would you remember if he fell dead in the lobby?"

The theme of loss is also brought up in several more or less minor elements of the play and offhand comments by various characters. Mrs. Bellotti, whose son lives in the building, mentions that her husband, who is a diabetic, has "lost" his leg, as it had to be amputated. After the Girl borrows Jackie's magazine, Jackie makes a point of getting it back from her, stating, "I don't want to lose that." Jackie later says, out of the blue, "Did you know the first two hours after you pick them, green beans lose twenty percent of their vitamin C?" The loss of objects and the loss of loved ones seem to pile up as the play goes on. When Mr. Morse accuses Jackie of stealing from him, he makes a direct association between the loss of his wife, who is dead, with the loss of her jewelry, claiming that Jackie, "Took my wife's things. That's all I have in this world." When questioned, he explains, "My things! My wedding cuff links and my necklace that belonged to my wife! And my mother!'' The elision between the loss of objects associated with a loved one and the death of a loved one is suggested by Jackie's defensive response that, ''Yeah, well, I didn't take his fucking mother.''

Amidst the overwhelming sense of loss which envelopes these characters, they each struggle with what they do and don't *have*. As mentioned above, Mr. Morse exclaims that his wife's ''things,'' her jewelry, are ''all I have in this world.'' Jackie, accused of the theft, retorts that, ''I have *dreams*!'' But the Girl later points out to her that, ''You have nothing,'' referring to the worthless land Jackie has been suckered into purchasing. The Girl, who herself has nothing—not even a name—is especially sympathetic to others who ''have nothing.'' She tells Bill that she can't bear to think of people wanting things and not having them.

Death, loss and nostalgia are combined in the discussion of ghosts and spirits among the hotel residents. The Girl explains that Millie, a retired waitress, ''sees things, knows things, she sees ghosts and auras and things.'' Millie later expresses a nostalgia for old buildings, akin to the play's expression of nostalgia for the old hotel, in describing her childhood home, ''a huge old Victorian house outside Baton Rouge; an amazing old house, really.'' Millie goes on to describe, again nostalgically, the ghosts which resided there:

> Millie: When you ask about spirits—oh, well, you couldn't keep track of them all. Banging doors, throwing silverware, breaking windows. They were all over the house. There was a black maid—slave girl, I suppose, and a revolutionary soldier and his girl, and a Yankee carpetbagger, and a saucy little imp of a girl who sashayed about very mischievously. She'd been pushed out of a window and was furious about it. Storming through the upstairs, slamming windows shut all over the house. It was quite an active place.

Millie later explains that ''Spirits are very peaceful, of course. They don't act up unless there's tension in a household.'' The Girl, in keeping with her strong sense of nostalgia for the historical past, is the most fascinated and excited by the idea of ghosts. She exclaims excitedly that ''I want them to come up with absolute scientific proof that there are spirits and ghosts and reincarnation. I want everyone to see them and talk to them. Something like that! Some miracle. Something huge! I want some major miracle in my lifetime!'' Since a ghost represents a person who has died, yet still exists, the Girl's enthusiasm for, in effect, the return of the dead to some form of life, some ''miracle,'' is an

> "WHILE THE GIRL'S EXPRESSION OF HOPE FOR THE PERPETUAL REPARATION OF LOST LIFE, LOST BUILDINGS, AND LOST TIME SEEMS TO BE NEGATED BY ALL OF THE LOSSES WHICH EMERGE THROUGHOUT THE PLAY, IT IS SHE WHO EXPRESSES THE PLAY'S MESSAGE REGARDING THE THEMES OF LOSS AND NOSTALGIA."

expression of a desire to negate the ravages of time and the inevitability of death, as symbolized by the demolition of the hotel, which have thrown all of these characters into crisis. Likewise, the mention of ''reincarnation'' expresses a desire for those who have died to come back in another life, and therefore never really be lost to the world. In the closing scene, the Girl again expresses the desire, or belief, that life can never really be lost, when she tells Paul, who has given up on finding his grandfather, that ''Nobody vanishes.''

While the Girl's expression of hope for the perpetual reparation of lost life, lost buildings, and lost time seems to be negated by all of the losses which emerge throughout the play, it is she who expresses the play's message regarding the themes of loss and nostalgia. Frustrated by Paul Granger's decision to give up on looking for his lost grandfather, the Girl blurts out, ''That's why nothing gets done; why everything falls down. Nobody's got the conviction to act on their passions.'' This assertion rings poignantly true in the case of Bill, who is unable to ''act on his passion'' for the Girl. In the final moments of the play, as she is on her way upstairs to take a bath, the stage directions state that, ''Bill looks off after her, aching.'' April, observing this, attempts to motivate Bill into action; she ''Snaps her fingers lightly at him. One. Two. Three. Four,'' saying, ''Hey. Hey.'' But April's attempt to get Bill to snap out of his torpor, and express his longing for the Girl, ultimately fails, and April concludes that ''Bill, baby, you know what your trouble is? You've got Paul Grangeritis. You've not got the conviction of your passions.'' The urgency of the need to ''act on the conviction of your passions'' expresses the play's message of how to approach life in spite of the inevitability of death, loss and decay, a piece of advice frequently summed up by the well-known Latin phrase (not used in the play itself): *Carpe Diem!* Seize the day!

Source: Liz Brent, for *Drama for Students,* Gale, 2000.

Sheri E. Metzger,

Metzger is a Ph.D., specializing in literature and drama at The University of New Mexico, where she is a Lecturer in the English Department and an Adjunct Professor in the University Honors Program. In the following essay, Metzger asks if Lanford Wilson's play Hot L Baltimore *can correctly be defined as comedy, or if the urban theatre is a euphemism for tragedy.*

At the conclusion of Lanford Wilson's *Hot L Baltimore,* the inhabitants face eviction, and for many of them, homelessness. Some of them face even more uncertain futures. Suzy, beaten in the first act by a customer, leaves the hotel to live with a new pimp. Pimps have abused her in the past, and there is every reason to suspect that this alliance will end in the same way. All three prostitutes face similar futures and the possibility of violence. Another resident, James, who is incapable of caring for himself, has been abandoned by his sister. James' sister, Jackie, has bought into a land swindle and is headed into a future that does not really exist, something she probably suspects. But her prospects are so bleak that she has no choice but to pursue this empty future. Other characters will leave the hotel with disappointed prospects and diminished dreams. *Hot L Baltimore* is comedy, and there are plenty of laughs, but the characters, their lives, and the bleakness of their futures all point to a play that is more tragic than comic in its presentation.

Traditionally, comedy was defined as drama with a happy ending, as in Dante's *Divine Comedy.* Later, in the evolution of comedic form, Shakespearean comedies concluded with a wedding, or even three, as in William Shakespeare's *A Midsummer Night's Dream.* The weddings in Act V provided a resolution to the story, granting a happy ending that tied up all the story lines and offered a blissful future for the characters. While part of the enjoyment of comedy comes from the near misses, the mistaken identities, and the incongruity of language, much enjoyment is also derived from the slapstick nature of physical comedy. Plays depend on performance to be completely understood. The audience needs to hear and see how the lines are delivered, since this delivery may convey as much meaning as the author's words. It is the body's movements, the expressions on the actor's face, and the intonations of voice that turn the play into comedy. But beyond the words is the subject matter, and the subject of Wilson's play is the plight of homelessness, the loneliness of the individual, the need for compassion, and a desire to hold onto a happier past. Comedy is designed to make the audience smile, to make us laugh, and to help create an escape from the real world. *Hot L Baltimore* manages the first two goals easily, but there is no escape from the reality of the world outside the theatre. The problems that plague large cities—homelessness, crime, prostitution, and hopelessness—are all present in the theatre and on the streets outside. Wilson's play brings the streets and their sometimes bleak future into the theatre. As a result, it is difficult to label *Hot L Baltimore* as comedy.

Wilson originally intended to write comedies, and he has said that even if his plays ''didn't hold out much hope for the world and its people, at least they were a pleasant experience while you [the audience] were going through it.'' But, as his work has progressed, Wilson's approach to theatre has changed. In an interview with John DiGaetani, Wilson notes that he doesn't want to think of his plays as comedies anymore, and while he still wants to entertain, he also wants to explore what he calls ''darker themes.'' This exploration of darker themes is certainly evident in *Hot L Baltimore,* which is really on the edge of tragedy throughout the plot. Wilson is certainly reflecting changes in society, which will be mirrored in performance and theatre. Just as the 1960s and 1970s signaled a period of social unrest and a desire for social reform, theatre of this period could be used as a weapon to create social reform. Playwrights, like Wilson, used their plays to promote new goals and to illuminate the problems of the world. Wilson acknowledges that he recognizes that a play ''impinges on the people.'' But the effect on the audience cannot always be determined until the play is performed; as DiGaetani observes, ''you can see what works in the theatre.'' Because a play always needs revising, Wilson states that in his experience, ''a play never seems to be really completed.'' Although Wilson is speaking strictly of rewrites, sometimes a play with no resolution can appear unfinished, without having been completed. This is the case for Wilson's play, since at the conclusion of *Hot L Baltimore* the audience is left wondering what will become of these characters. There is a feeling that Wilson has brought to life individuals who will have a life after the play concludes: their stories do not end, and the play is simply a brief episode in their lives.

Wilson has said that *Hot L Baltimore* derived from his brief experience as a night clerk at a hotel. Were the people Wilson met this lonely and this sad? Were they also abandoned and in need of one another? It is possible, but Wilson had other sources for his writing, as well. The inhabitants of the Hotel Baltimore are as dark as the society that Charles Dickens depicted in his nineteenth century novels. Wilson's director, Marshall Mason, has said that Wilson devoured Dickens during rehearsals for his play. In an interview with Philip Middleton Williams, Mason remembers Wilson reading "Dickens after Dickens," with characters immersed in greed and poverty, and moral stories that inspired the playwright. Dickens' novels are dark, often with an element of hope, but mostly depicting the exploitation of individuals. They are not comedies, and if Wilson used Dickens to inspire his work, as Mason alleges, than certainly Wilson's play will center more on the dark aspects of the world, rather than the happier ones. It is true, as Mason suggests, that "while Wilson created a cast of social misfits, he broadened their appeal with the comedic approach and nearly farcical staging." The characters are appealing. The audience wants to like them and wants them to succeed. In truth, there are comedic moments and physical humor to lighten the issues underlying the play, but the problems of prostitution, loneliness, and abandonment help to stifle the laughter. The audience likes the characters too much to permit complete surrender into laughter.

It is the characters who capture the audience's imagination and who evoke both laughter and tears. The wise-cracking April creates much of the laughter, but her laughter is also an attempt to ignore the reality of her life. She is the stereotypical whore with a heart of gold who populated so many Hollywood westerns of the twentieth century, now magically transported to 1970s Baltimore. Her familiarity makes it easy for the audience to identify her and to identify with her, and she makes it easy to laugh. The audience does not have to think about her occupation and the danger that prostitutes face on the street. The slow-witted James is an entirely different matter. At the play's conclusion, April will take him into her arms and begin to dance with him. She is meant to appear as his rescuer, and so, the audience can leave reassured that he will be safe—

" THE LOSS OF ONE MORE DERELICT HOTEL WILL NOT MOVE THE CITY TO RESCUE ITS POOR, BUT WILSON DOES ILLUMINATE THE SERIOUSNESS OF THE PROBLEM, AND IN DOING SO, HE MOVES *HOT L BALTIMORE* FURTHER FROM COMEDY AND CLOSER TO SOCIAL COMMENTARY."

and perhaps they will all be safe, all of the characters who are soon to be thrown into the streets. But Wilson's world on stage deals with easy solutions. In the real world April will not protect James. The James of the world all too often end up as the homeless, lying on the streets. There is no resolution, no comedy at the play's conclusion. These characters drift in and out of the action, as the homeless drift in and out of our lives. The loss of one more derelict hotel will not move the city to rescue its poor, but Wilson does illuminate the seriousness of the problem, and in doing so, he moves *Hot L Baltimore* further from comedy and closer to social commentary.

Upon its debut, *Hot L Baltimore* was the first big hit for both Wilson and for the Circle Repertory Company. Critics and audiences loved the play, and it set an Off-Broadway record of 1,166 performances after first playing Off-Off-Broadway for a month. *Hot L Baltimore* won the New York Drama Critics Circle Award for the Best American Play of 1972-73. It also won an Obie Award for best Off-Broadway play, an Outer Critics Award, and the John Gassner playwriting award, and was included in the Burns Mantle/Guernsey *Ten Best American Plays* volume for that season. *Hot L Baltimore* has continued to be very popular, with numerous productions staged every year. This play appears to speak to people, and perhaps it says something about our country and our past. But instead of advertising a Lanford Wilson comedy, perhaps this play might better be advertised as an urban drama, a play that explores modern city life. There is comedy certainly, and the audience will laugh and be entertained, but the inhabitants of the Hotel Baltimore will also evoke a thoughtful response to a problem that haunts many large cities. In the quest to tear down the past, what will take its place and where will those inhabitants of the past find their future?

Source: Sheri E. Metzger, for *Drama for Students,* Gale, 2000.

SOURCES

Barnett, Gene. "Recreating the Magic: An Interview with Lanford Wilson," in *Ball State University Forum,* Vol. 25, No. 2, Spring, 1984, pp. 57-74.

Bryer, Jackson R. "Lanford Wilson," in *The Playwright's Art: Conversations With Contemporary American Dramatists,* Rutgers University Press, 1995, pp. 277-96.

diGaetani, John L. *A Search for a Postmodern Theatre: Interviews With Contemporary Playwrights,* Greenwood Press, 1991, pp. 285-293.

Dreher, Ann Crawford. "Lanford Wilson," in *Dictionary of Literary Biography,* Volume 7: *Twentieth-Century American Dramatists,* edited by John MacNichols, 1981, pp. 350-68.

Gottfried, Martin. A review, in *Women's Wear Daily,* March 23, 1973.

Jacobi, Martin J. "The Comic Vision of Lanford Wilson," in *Studies in the Literary Imagination,* Vol. 21, no. 2, 1988, pp. 119-34.

Kroll, Jack. A review in *Newsweek,* February 26, 1973.

Probst, Leonard. A television review on NBC, March 22, 1973.

Savran, David. "Lanford Wilson," in *In Their Own Words: Contemporary American Playwrights,* Theatre Communications Group, 1988, pp. 306-20.

Schvey, Henry I. "Images of the Past in the Plays of Lanford Wilson," in *Essays on Contemporary American Drama,* edited by Hedwig Bock and Albert Wertheim, Hueber, 1981, pp. 225-40.

Watt, Douglas. A review, in the *Daily News,* March 23, 1973.

Watts, Richard. A review, in the *New York Post,* March 23, 1973.

Williams, Philip Middleton. *A Comfortable House: Lanford Wilson, Marshall W. Mason and the Circle Repertory Theatre,* McFarland & Company, 1993.

FURTHER READING

Bryer, Jackson, ed. *Lanford Wilson: A Casebook,* Garland, 1990, 271 p.
This collection of critical essays examines several of Lanford's plays.

Busby, Mark. *Lanford Wilson,* Boise State University, 1987, 52 p.
Short biography of Wilson.

Dean, Anne M. *Discovery and Invention: The Urban Plays of Lanford Wilson,* Fairleigh Dickinson University Press, 1994, 139 p.
Study of Wilson's work that seeks to prove the validity of his work as poetry and it place in the American literary canon.

Kahn, David and Donna Breed. *Scriptwork: A Director's Approach to New Play Development,* Southern Illinois University Press, 1995, 193 p.
A detailed sourcebook for producing plays. The forward is by Wilson and it contains an interview with him.

Williams, Philip Middleton. *A Comfortable House: Lanford Wilson, Marshall W. Mason and the Circle Repertory Theatre,* McFarland & Company, 1993, 211 p.
Examines the collaboration between Wilson and director Marshall W. Mason.

Lady Windermere's Fan

OSCAR WILDE

1892

Lady Windermere's Fan was Oscar Wilde's first produced play, and it was an instant success on the London stage. Chronicling a series of misunderstandings and deceptions in the high society world of Victorian London, critics and audiences alike were charmed by Wilde's trademark wit and intelligence.

In the play, Lady Windermere considers leaving her husband of two years when she believes he's been unfaithful with a woman—who turns out to be her own mother. Remarkably, it will be the mother who sets her straight without ever revealing her identity.

In his letters, Wilde claimed that he did not want the play to be viewed as ''a mere question of pantomime and clowning''; he was interested in the piece as a psychological study. Although the play has been deemed outdated by recent critics, *Lady Windermere's Fan* continues to entertain audiences all over the world.

AUTHOR BIOGRAPHY

In 1854 Oscar Wilde was born in Dublin to affluent parents. His father was a prominent surgeon and archaeologist; his mother was a witty poet, Irish nationalist, and feminist.

Wilde excelled at the Portola Royal school and then at Trinity College, where he took the Gold Medal for Greek. In 1878 he won a scholarship to Magdalen College at Oxford.

Wilde attracted a crowd of admirers for his witty, intellectual lectures and his outrageous cult of "aestheticism." He believed in art-for-art's-sake, a philosophy he had learned from his association with John Ruskin, an art critic and Oxford don.

A very successful lecture tour of America in the early 1880s on "The Principles of Aestheticism" earned him much-needed income as well as an international reputation.

His marriage to Constance Mary Lloyd in 1884 produced two children; it was during this time he wrote his best works: *The Picture of Dorian Gray* (1891), *Lady Windermere's Fan* (1892), *A Woman of No Importance* (1893), *An Ideal Husband* (1895), and *The Importance of Being Earnest* (1895).

These works brought him financial success and the admiration of the literary circles. His reputation as an insightful, witty, and urbane playwright was established worldwide.

In the early 1890s, at the peak of his career, Wilde entered into a destructive romantic relationship with Lord Alfred Douglas, nicknamed "Bosie." After Bosie's disapproving father, Lord Queensbeery, insulted Wilde, the playwright foolishly sued for defamation of character. Queensbeery's return suit for "depravity" resulted in Wilde's conviction for sodomy—and a two-year jail sentence.

After serving his sentence, Wilde emerged from jail bankrupt, scandalized, and spiritually bereft. He lived alone in France until his death from cerebral meningitis in 1900. His remains are buried in Paris.

PLOT SUMMARY

Act One

The play opens in Lady Margaret Windermere's home, where she is arranging roses for a party later that evening in celebration of her birthday. Lord Darlington visits, and Margaret chides him for flirting with her. He contends that a woman whose husband of two years is unfaithful has a right to "console herself."

Lady Windermere fails to recognize his oblique reference to her husband, and calls herself a Puritan with "hard and fast rules" for fidelity. Lord Darlington continues to flirt with her, but she ignores him.

He leaves and the Duchess of Berwick and her daughter, Lady Agatha Carlisle, enter. The Duchess cattily reports that Lord Windermere has been spending time and money on a Mrs. Erlynne, whose social status is questionable. The Duchess admits that her own husband has had his "little aberrations," and assumes all men are immoral.

Yet the Duchess is anxious to marry off her daughter Agatha, saying "a mother who doesn't part with a daughter every season has no real affection."

After they depart, Lady Windermere looks through her husband's desk and discovers payments to Mrs. Erlynne in his secret bankbook. When he comes in and finds her looking at it, he gets angry. He demands that his wife invite Mrs. Erlynne to their party in order to help the woman back into society. Lady Windermere flatly refuses.

He addresses an invitation to Mrs. Erlynne himself. Outraged, Lady Windermere threatens to hit the infamous woman with her new birthday fan when she arrives. Lord Windermere protests and she storms offstage.

As the curtain drops, he agonizes over what to do about the situation. Apparently there is something to his relationship with Mrs. Erlynne, for he groans "I dare not tell her who this woman really is. The shame would kill her."

Act Two

The Windermere's party is in full swing, and the guests are being announced. The Duchess of Berwick has advised Agatha to dance with Mr. Hopper of Australia, a prospective suitor.

Lord Augustus Lorton, brother of the Duchess, asks Lord Windermere how Mrs. Erlynne can gain respectability. It seems that Lorton hopes to marry her. He is reassured by her invitation to tonight's ball, for it paves her way into "this demmed thing called society."

Mrs. Erlynne appears and smoothly makes her way from guest to guest, especially the men. Their wives glare indignantly. In the meantime, Lady Windermere remains cold to her husband, and seeks comfort from Lord Darlington, who takes advantage of her mood by confessing his love and offering to take her away.

At first shocked, Margaret asks for time to see if her husband would return to her. Defeated, Lord Darlington announces that he will leave England the next day and bids her goodbye.

As the music stops and guests come back into the room, the Duchess of Berwick talks approvingly of Mrs. Erlynne to Margaret, yet advises her to get her husband away from the woman.

Agatha whispers to her mother that Mr. Hopper has proposed. With her goal in hand, the Duchess now takes full charge, insisting that the couple remain in London rather than return to Hopper's home in Sydney.

Two gentlemen offer alternate views to Mrs. Erlynne's presence at the ball: one says that Lady Windermere must have "common sense," while the other credits Lord Windermere with cleverly hiding his indiscretion in the open.

Mrs. Erlynne informs Lord Windermere that Lord Lorton has proposed; in addition, he has asked for 2000 to 2500 pounds a year from him. Annoyed but compliant, Windermere exits with her to the terrace to discuss the details.

As the music strikes up again, Lady Windermere decides to run away with Lord Darlington and leave her husband. She leaves a farewell letter on her desk. Mrs. Erlynne enters and reads it.

She lies to Windermere about the letter's contents and calls for her carriage. Lord Augustus enters with a bouquet for Mrs. Erlynne and proposes. Without responding, she instructs him to take Windermere to his club until morning, and he complies.

Act Three

Alone in Lord Darlington's rooms, Lady Windermere vacillates between staying and going back to her husband. When Mrs. Erlynne arrives, Margaret recoils in contempt of her rival. Mrs. Erlynne pleads with her to return to her husband, denying any relationship with him.

Lady Windermere is moved when Mrs. Erlynne reminds her of her duty to her child. She tearfully decides to go home, but upon hearing voices, they both hide behind the curtains. Lord Augustus ("Tuppy" to his friends), Lord Darlington, Dumby, Cecil Graham, and Lord Windermere arrive, having been turned out of the club.

The men speak cynically of women and society as they settle into a game of cards. This scene

Oscar Wilde

displays Wilde's wit as the men banter back and forth. Then Cecil sees Lady Windermere's fan on a table. He shows it to Tuppy for a chuckle at Darlington, who has been moralizing, for apparently he has a woman in his rooms.

Windermere's reaction to seeing his wife's fan, however, is dramatic. He threatens to search Darlington's rooms. Darlington refuses. Only the sudden appearance of Mrs. Erlynne, stepping out from behind the curtain, stops a probable fight. She pretends to having taken Lady Windermere's fan by mistake. The men respond variously with contempt, astonishment, and mockery, as the curtain falls.

Act Four

Back at home, Lady Windermere lies on a sofa, wondering why Mrs. Erlynne disgraced herself to save her reputation. Lord Windermere comes in and sympathetically suggests a visit to the country. He also expresses a change of heart about Mrs. Erlynne, whom he now considers "as bad as a woman can be."

His wife defends her and insists on seeing her once more before they depart. Lady Windermere almost confesses the truth, but Parker interrupts them. He is carrying Lady Windermere's lost fan and Mrs. Erlynne's card on a tray. Margaret tells Parker to invite her up, in spite of her husband's protest.

Mrs. Erlynne enters, and apologizes for taking the fan. She announces that she is leaving England and wants a photograph of Margaret with her child. While Lady Windermere goes upstairs to find one, Lord Windermere confronts Mrs. Erlynne for causing his first quarrel with his wife, and for misrepresenting herself. It is revealed to the audience that Mrs. Erlynne is Margaret's long-lost mother.

It is true that Mrs. Erlynne had been extorting money from him, but she has had a change of heart, too. She fails to convince him of her new sincerity, but revels in her new relationship with her daughter—who never learns that Mrs. Erlynne is her mother.

Before leaving, Mrs. Erlynne offers Lady Windermere a piece of advice: not to tell Arthur of nearly leaving him. Lord Augustus arrives and accepts Mrs. Erlynne's explanation that she was only looking for him at Darlington's home. He proposes to her again. Margaret comments that he is, indeed, "marrying a very good woman."

CHARACTERS

Agatha
Agatha is the daughter of the Duchess of Berwick. She is passive and only interested in getting married.

Lady Carlisle
See Agatha

Caroline
See Lady Jedburgh

Mrs. Cowper-Cowper
Mrs. Cowper-Cowper is one of the society ladies who attends Lady Windermere's ball.

Lord Darlington
Lord Darlington is in love with Lady Windermere, and hints of her husband's apparent infidelity in order to gain her affection. When she does not return his love, he leaves town.

Duchess of Berwick
A manipulative woman, the Duchess of Berwick thrives on the pettiness of high society. She is the one who initiates the series of misunderstandings between Mrs. Erlynne and Lady Windermere by gossiping about Mrs. Erlynne and Lord Windermere.

At the same time, she masterfully orchestrates the marriage of her daughter to Mr. Hopper, an Australian visitor. Once she snags the young man, she begins her next project of making sure the new couple stays in London rather than going to Sydney.

Margaret Erlynne
The mysterious Mrs. Erlynne is Lady Windermere's long-lost mother—a fact that is not revealed until the late in the play. Lady Windermere never learns her true identity.

Mrs. Erlynne wants desperately to be accepted within her daughter's social circles. She has a reputation as a woman with a shady past, a "divorced woman, going about under an assumed name, a bad woman preying upon life." In other words, she seems to be a woman with no substantial income, and therefore no right to socialize with the Windermeres and their circle.

However, Mrs. Erlynne reveals herself to be a woman of quality, who puts aside her own interests in favor of protecting her child. Having found herself capable of a mother's devotion, she decides to escape in order to spare her daughter further embarrassment. Fortunately, Lord Lorton still loves her and offers his hand in marriage.

Cecil Graham
Cecil Graham is a cynic who trades witty barbs with his pals Windermere, Dumby, and Lorton. He is described as the experienced man about town. He is the one who discovers Lady Windermere's fan in Darlington's rooms.

Mr. Hopper
Mr. Hopper is an Australian man who proposes to Agatha. Although he hopes to take her home to Sydney, the Duchess wants them to remain in England.

Lady Jedburgh

Lady Jedburgh is Cecil Graham's dowager aunt.

Lord Augustus Lorton

The brother of the Duchess of Berwick, Tuppy is a rather simple fellow. He is in love with Mrs. Erlynne and is greatly relieved to learn that she has received an invitation to Lady Windermere's ball, since this serves as an invitation into high society.

He is a very trusting man; he accepts Mrs. Erlynne's excuses and does not rescind his marriage invitation after the scandal.

Parker

Parker is the Windermeres' butler.

Lady Plymdale

Lady Plymdale is the wife of Mr. Dunby. She disapproves of Mrs. Erlynne and of her husband's visits with her.

Rosalie

Rosalie is Lady's Windermere's maid.

Lady Stutfield

One of the society ladies who enjoy the social season.

Tuppy

See Lord Augustus Lorton

Lord Arthur Windermere

For most of the play, it seems that Lord Windermere is having an affair with Mrs. Erlynne. Like his wife, Windermere is a sincere and generous person. He is also loyal: even when it is in his self-interest to tell his wife the truth, he keeps Mrs. Erlynne's secret. His goodness and straightforward manner is symbolized by his plain way of talking.

Lady Margaret Windermere

Margaret is a beautiful, intelligent, and honorable woman who nearly leaves her husband because of a vicious rumor. At first, she rebuffs Lord Darlington's advances and believes that her husband is not having an affair with Mrs. Erlynne. However, she prepares to leave her husband when it appears that the gossip about her husband's relationship with Mrs. Erlynne is true.

MEDIA ADAPTATIONS

- *Lady Windemere's Fan* has been adapted in two silent films: a 1917 version by Ideal Film, and a 1925 Warner Brothers production called *The Fan* by director Ernest Lubitsch.

- Otto Preminger remade *The Fan* with sound in 1949.

- Librettist Don Allan Clayton adapted the play for an Off-Broadway musical comedy called *A Delightful Season* in 1960.

- A recording of the play exists in a 1997 audiotape version with Michael Sheen speaking the part of Lord Darlington.

THEMES

Hypocrisy

Hypocrisy can be defined as pretending to be something one is not or feigning to believe in something one does not. Most of the characters in Wilde's play accept hypocrisy as a necessary component of their social world. People in high society must pretend, must conform to the social norm in order to maintain their position. Hypocrisy is the glue that holds together a complex web of relationships; if the truth were to come out, these relationships would fall apart.

Lies are a necessary tool to avoid conflict. For example, Dumby agrees with Mrs. Stutfield that the season has been "delightful," and in the next breath agrees with the Duchess of Berwick that it has been "dreadfully dull." Likewise, the Duchess of Berwick tells Lady Windermere that her nieces never gossip, then later declares that they always gossip.

TOPICS FOR FURTHER STUDY

- Explore and discuss the role of wit in *Lady Windemere's Fan*. Is it necessary to the play's meaning? Why or why not?
- Is Mrs. Erlynne a "good woman?" Support your answer with evidence of her deeds and words.
- Research the genre of "comedy of manners." What are the characteristics of such a play? Can you think of a recent play or movie in that genre?
- Could such a situation as that in *Lady Windemere's Fan* happen today? Write an essay describing what you would change to make the situation more modern.

Hypocrisy is distinguished from virtuous lies, which are told to protect someone else. To ease the comfort of others—even though this might require lying—was part of the upper class code of conduct. Encouraged by Tuppy's remark that women with a past are "demmed interesting to talk to," Lord Windermere withholds the truth of Mrs. Erlynne's past in order to protect his friend from a truth that would ruin his marriage plans.

Mrs. Erlynne rises above hypocrisy when she sacrifices her own reputation for her daughter's. Although she has lived a life of hypocrisy, and she is desperately trying to get back into the society that once rejected her, she throws it away out of love.

The Bad Mother

The role of women was changing in Victorian society. Women were seeking greater independence, and they were entering the workforce in increasing numbers. The suffragist movement attracted many supporters, as women petitioned for the rights to vote and own property (any money or property of the wife belonged to her husband upon marriage).

This greater independence for women was opposed on all fronts: politically, socially, and culturally. Soon, the independent woman was being portrayed as a bad wife and a bad mother.

Many plays, stories, poems, and articles featured the image of the "bad mother": the woman who abandons her children to pursue some selfish interest, such as a love affair or career. Such entrepreneurial social behavior was portrayed as dangerous and threatening to society in general.

Wilde's play is unusual for its time in allowing the "bad mother," Mrs. Erlynne, to make peace with her daughter (although without recognition of her motherhood) and to pursue her own life.

STYLE

Screen Scene

A *screen scene* is a scene in which an actor hides behind a drape or furniture and overhears the other actors. Melodrama, with its emphasis on secrets and their revelation, often makes use of the screen scene to allow a character to discover a secret. This discovery is a turning point in the plot.

In *Lady Windermere's Fan*, Lady Windermere's eavesdropping convinces her of her husband's fidelity. Also Mrs. Erlynne's sacrifice of her own reputation convinces her of the older woman's virtue.

Part of the purpose of the screen scene is to allow a character to discover information he or she is not supposed to hear. At the same time, the risk of being discovered in the act of eavesdropping adds to the dramatic intensity of the scene.

Further adding to the dramatic intensity, the play often has the eavesdropper leave something behind in the room. The other characters see and recognize a glove, a fan, or other personal item. Only a clever diversion such as that undertaken by Mrs. Erlynne can prevent the eavesdropper from exposure.

Comedy of Manners

During the Restoration period (1660–1699), fashionable audiences flocked to comedies that poked fun at the foibles and witticisms of high society. Pompous characters were held up for ridicule as they indulged in the misbehaviors and pretensions of the sophisticated set.

During the Victorian era, more serious plays came into style. Therefore, Wilde's comedy of manners was a refreshing change of style that revitalized comedy and set the stage for modern comic theatre.

COMPARE & CONTRAST

- **Victorian London:** Industrialization leads to a migration from the country to towns and cities as thousands of workers toil in British factories.

  Today: More and more workers are part of the "service" and high-tech economy as opposed to manufacturing and industry. It is more economical to build factories in Third World countries.

- **Victorian London:** The railroad revolutionizes travel as well as the movement of raw materials and finished goods. The middle and working class could afford excursions to seaside resorts and to the towns and cities for entertainment.

  Today: The Internet puts information and entertainment into the hands of a computer-literate society. From art and literature to stock trading and shopping, the Internet offers many options for its users. People gather in virtual chat rooms instead of drawing rooms, parlors, and music halls.

- **Victorian London:** The mail is delivered up to three times per day in London. For those who could afford it, a message could be sent across town in the morning and a response received that evening.

  Today: People can send messages instantaneously by phone, electronic mail, instant messaging, and teleconferencing.

HISTORICAL CONTEXT

Aestheticism Movement

The late nineteenth century "art-for-art's-sake" movement was promulgated by Walter Pater (1839–1894), an Oxford don who tutored Oscar Wilde. Wilde became a living example of his teacher's theory, which placed style and beauty above moral and social responsibility. Wilde's adherence to this theory earned him the name "The Great Aesthete."

According to Pater, the aesthete appreciated beautiful things and beautiful literature. Interest in art was facilitated by the rise in leisure time for the upper and middle class. The middle class adopted the values of the upper class and viewed the appreciation of art as part of their social training.

The aestheticism and Pre-Raphaelite movements opposed the Victorian obsession with industry, engineering, and efficiency. When Oscar Wilde declared to customs officials in America that "I have nothing to declare but my genius," he alluded to the refinement of character that he nurtured for its own sake.

Wilde surrounded himself with art and sought to exemplify Walter Pater's concept of the true critic, one with "a certain kind of temperament, the power of being deeply moved by the presence of beautiful objects." Pater looked to the Renaissance era for a model of obsession with style.

Aesthetics valued the completely innocent person, such as the character Dorian Gray in Wilde's novel, *The Picture of Dorian Gray* (1891). Gray was both pure and physically beautiful until corrupted by an older man.

Lady Windermere is another beautiful and simple character with a natural ability to appreciate art and true sentiment.

Victorian Society

Three years before Oscar Wilde's birth, England celebrated the triumphs of industry in The Great Exhibition of 1851, which was housed in the magnificent Crystal Palace. Inside, observers viewed the highest technical achievement of every nation, and England's contributions put her in the forefront of scientific achievement.

The exhibition demonstrated the benefits of progress. England was at the height of prosperity, with income increasing exponentially through the efficiencies of industrialization. With a growing economy, a burgeoning middle class began to aspire to the fashions and habits of high society.

By the end of the nineteenth century, the newly affluent class was beginning to shoulder its way into formerly forbidden regions—in politics, clubs, and the workplace.

It was also a time of budding feminism, as women took more and more aggressive steps to win suffrage. In the magazine he edited for two years, *The Women's World,* Wilde ran articles by women on both sides of the women's suffrage issue. Wilde had also changed the title from *The Lady's World* out of respect for the blurring lines between social classes.

CRITICAL OVERVIEW

Wilde's *Lady Windermere's Fan* garnered much popular and critical controversy on its debut at the St. James Theatre in February 20, 1892. The audience was filled to capacity with the literary stars of the time: Frank Harris, Henry James, actress Lillie Langtry, and a host of critics.

However, according to Vyvyan Holland in the introduction to *The Complete Works of Oscar Wilde,* Wilde caused a furor of resentment when he came onto the stage with a cigarette in his gloved hand and his signature green carnation in his lapel and told the audience,

> Ladies and Gentlemen. I have enjoyed this evening *immensely.* The actors have given us a *charming* rendition of a *delightful* play, and your appreciation has been *most* intelligent. I congratulate you on the *great* success of your performance, which persuades me that you think *almost* as highly of the play as I do.

The reviews the next morning focused on the playwright's impertinence. Beckson states that Clement Scott accused Wilde of "condescension" and trying to "take greater liberties with the public than any author who ha[d] ever preceded [him] in history."

In an interview, Wilde took full responsibility for deviating from the expected humility of the author: "I have altered all that. The artist cannot be degraded into the servant of the public: humility is for the hypocrite, modesty for the incompetent. Assertion is at once the duty and the privilege of the artist."

The play ran for five months, then made a tour of the provinces and returned to London for another successful run. Although Henry James called the performance "infantine . . . both in subject and form," George Bernard Shaw, who had not yet made his name in theater, admired it.

Beckson declares that A. B. Walkley maintained that the "plot is always thin," that it is "full of . . . glaring faults" but was nevertheless a "good" play. Those who enjoyed the plethora of witty epigrams compared Wilde to Congreve and Sheridan, even though, in Wilde's play, "all the men talk like Mr. Oscar Wilde."

The play was produced a year later in New York City by Maurice Barrymore, but Wilde was not happy with the production because Lord Darlington was presented as a villain—not as a person intent on saving Lady Windermere from an unfaithful husband. The New York production ran for several successful months.

More recent critics have explored gender issues relating to Wilde's homosexuality. Only recently Wilde's plays have been treated as separate from his personal life.

The deconstructionist view (of the 1970s and 1980s) perceived an inversion of the Victorian melodramatic conventions. Others have focused on the possible influences on his work.

Lady Windermere's Fan, with its somewhat outdated concern for the errant mother and its staging requirements (actors capable of sophisticated social banter and elaborate costumes and sets), is not often produced today. It is viewed as a period piece.

CRITICISM

Carole Hamilton

Hamilton is an English teacher at Cary Academy, an innovative private school in Cary, North Carolina. In the following essay, Hamilton explores how the wit in Lady Windermere's Fan *contributes to the structure and meaning of the plot, while also investing the play with a satirical jab at high society.*

True to the legacy of the Irish raconteur, Oscar Wilde was a master of wit, famous for clever conversation peppered with epigrams. With his rolling, mellifluous voice, he was the center of attention at social gatherings, and is still considered one of the greatest conversationalists of his time.

Rebecca Johnson in the title role of Lady Windermere's Fan.

Lady Windermere's Fan, his first play, was expected to follow on the heels of the success of his novel, *The Picture of Dorian Gray*—and it certainly did.

However, many critics, such as a reviewer at the *Westminster Review,* objected to the number of epigrams in the play. These critics complained that wit so overshadows plot in *Lady Windermere's Fan* that the result is "scarcely a play at all" and that the characters do little more than "serve as mouths to enunciate the author's exquisitely funny remarks on society."

Another critic called Wilde the prophet of "great God Paradox," and maintained that "Mr. Wilde's puppets chant his litany" in a dramatic world where all its inhabitants are "equally cynical, equally paradoxical, equally epigrammatic."

This condemnation troubled Wilde, who wanted his work to be dramatically fresh and interesting and also psychologically true to life. He openly paraded his genius at conversation, but he also held greater ambitions for his plays than as mere platforms for his wit.

In response to the criticism that his play was superficial, he snidely pronounced the opinion of the British public not "of the slightest importance."

They did not understand the depth of the final act, even though he considered it to be deeply "psychological" and "the newest, most true" moment of the play.

In the summation he wrote while at the nadir of his literary life and career—in prison and rejected by even his closest friends—he expressed confidence in his plays, and wrote that he had successfully produced "comedies that were to beat Congreve for brilliancy and Dumas *fils* for philosophy, and I suppose everyone else for every other quality."

Even Wilde himself failed to notice that not only was *Lady Windermere's Fan* a unique combination of brilliant dialogue and philosophical depth, but that he organized the plot through the syntactic structure of wit. He does this through the structure of the paradoxical epigram, which is a statement that contains two opposing ideas in a balance.

The plot elements are a balanced structure of opposing elements, as though Wilde used the pattern to compose his plot as he did to compose his witty sayings.

Epigrams are pithy sayings that compress two antithetical ideas into one polished sentence. The best epigrams contain concise language that pre-

WHAT DO I READ NEXT?

- Richard Sheridan's *The School for Scandal* (1777) is a comedy of manners concerning a wife who nearly betrays her older husband.

- Henrik Ibsen's *A Doll's House* (1879) depicts a mother who feels constrained and unhappy in her limited role. As a result, she leaves her husband and children.

- *Mrs. Warren's Profession* (1898), written by George Bernard Shaw, views the theme of the wayward mother with marked parallels to Wilde's play.

- A play by Moises Kaufman about Wilde's trial for homosexuality, *Gross Indecencies: The Three Trials of Oscar Wilde*, offers insights into Wilde and the social world of Victorian London.

---

sents two antithetical ideas in a mirror-image format. For example, in *Lady Windermere's Fan,* Cecil Graham exclaims, "whenever people agree with me, I always feel I must be wrong."

Here the antithetical ideas are Cecil's opinions versus what people think of his opinions. Graham is saying that when his ideas meet with universal approval, he, paradoxically, decides to disagree with the majority—and disavow his own idea. Underlying his statement is a satire of the people whose opinions Graham so disrespects that their very agreement with him changes his mind.

Almost every character in Wilde's plays and other works occasionally speak in epigrams. Wilde does not simply throw them in to display his own cleverness, but uses them to convey character and mood, and even to structure the plot itself.

The most simplistic of these is to establish character. The characters who use epigrams the most are Cecil Graham, Dunby, Lord Darlington, and Mrs. Erlynne. These characters are shown to be clever and haughty through their use of epigram.

For example, Lord Darlington and Cecil Graham banter about the contrast between a cynic (one who knows the price of everything but the value of nothing) and the sentimentalist (who sees an absurd value in everything and doesn't know the market price of any single thing). Their definitions are humorous and cynical, establishing them as part of the "smart" or sophisticated set.

Lord Darlington's comment that "so many conceited people go about society pretending to be good, that I think it shows rather a sweet and modest disposition to pretend to be bad" also establishes him as a "smart" character, who finds it entertaining to be "bad." His epigrams led at least one director to fail to see Lord Darlington's sympathetic side.

In the 1893 New York production, Maurice Barrymore cast Lord Darlington as a villain. Wilde objected, saying, "Darlington is *not* a villain, but a man who really believes that Windermere is treating his wife badly, and wishes to save her." In this case, the character's witticisms caused him to be typecast.

On the other hand, not speaking in epigrams is a marker of sincerity. One clue that Lord Windermere is virtuous is that he *never* speaks paradoxically. His comments are straightforward and genuine.

His counterpart, Lord Darlington, is not always so sincere. Darlington's style changes from being cynical to being sincere—symbolized by going from epigrammatic speech to more prosaic speech.

In the first scene, he appears as a dandy, with his blithe, epigrammatic sayings and suave compliments. Only when he begins to woo Lady Windermere in earnest does he drop the mask of cleverness and speak in a relatively straightforward manner.

However, his move toward sincerity is gradual. In the midway point, he uses the antithetical format, as when he suggests that "between man and woman there is no friendship possible. There is passion, enmity, worship but no friendship."

In this phrase he still maintains the formal distance of the clever dandy wooing with words. When he drops even the antitheses, he is at his most sincere, simply telling Lady Windermere that he loves her. At this moment, the audience's estimation of Lord Darlington increases.

Contrasted to Darlington's development is Lady Windermere's descent into paradox. She begins in earnest, telling Lord Darlington that she is a Puritan for her beliefs that rules must be hard and fast. Just as her in beliefs, her speech does not tolerate the ambiguity of paradox.

Yet the moment when she begins to distrust her husband, she begins to speak in paradox; she tells Lord Windermere, "You are jealous of Mrs. Erlynne's honor. I wish you had been as jealous of mine." Though she still views her world in black and white, she now pairs her phrases in the form of the epigram, with antithetical elements at odds in the same way she sees her husband's attention to Mrs. Erlynne at odds with his duty to her.

She proceeds to duel in verbal paradoxes with her husband, and when she leaves him, she justifies her actions with another paradox, "He broke the bonds—I only break the bondage." Ironically she is wrong about his having broken the bonds, and it will take another reversal on her part not to break the bonds herself.

Later, her conversation with Mrs. Erlynne is not epigrammatic, but intense and heartfelt; this conversation saves her. Then, as though she needs one last moment of darkness to appreciate her happiness, she indulges in a few more paradoxes while waiting for her husband's return: "What a pity that in life we only get our lessons when they are of no use to us!"

She drops this mode of thought once she feels assured of her husband's affections. Speaking in epigrams indicates a character is angry, or cynical, or insincere. It is as though the epigram speaker judges things from the safe distance of the uninvolved.

Wilde uses wit to reveal a character's internal state of mind in other ways, too. Mrs. Erlynne's comment on the London fog ("whether the fogs produce the serious people or whether the serious people produce the fogs, I don't know") at the end of the play reveals that Mrs. Erlynne has regained her confidence after the fiasco of the evening be-

> "ANOTHER PARADOX LIES IN THE FACT THAT SHE IS BROUGHT TO HER SENSES BY THE VERY WOMAN WHO HAD BETRAYED HER AS A CHILD. BEING SAVED BY THE ONE WHO ABANDONED HER IS A REVERSAL, OR PARADOXICAL PATTERN."

fore, when she sacrificed her own reputation by stepping out from behind the curtain as a diversion so allow Lady Windermere to slip away undetected.

Her comment about the fog and seriousness not only shows her in witty form, but also contains her excuse for leaving town—it is too cold, both literally and metaphorically, in terms of her reception in society. In other cases, witty paradoxes comprise "epigrammatic duels" between characters.

These occur between Lord Darlington and Lady Windermere, between Lady Windermere and her husband, Lord Windermere, and, finally, between Mrs. Erlynne and Lord Windermere. In each case, the exchange ends in a barb aimed at the first speaker, whose character is called into question.

For example, Lord Windermere exclaims to Lady Windermere, "How hard good women are!" and she retorts, "How weak bad men are!" But besides being a verbal clue to their moods, the very syntax of the statements provides a pattern for reading their relationship. An extreme misunderstanding threatens the couple's relationship: they are at polar odds.

Moreover, Lady Windermere's comment is ironically inaccurate, in that Lord Windermere is not being weak, but strong—and is not bad, but good. This dramatic inversion is the basis of dramatic irony that underpins the whole play.

Lady Windermere's Fan is about people who misunderstand or mistrust each other, whose opinions and trust lie at polar opposites, and who must maintain equipoise in the balance of a society that does not easily allow these differences to be aired.

Cecil Graham, an ancillary character whose only apparent purpose is to exemplify the generalized nature of male hypocrisy, proffers a clever definition of scandal, as "gossip made tedious by morality." Here the paradoxical statement contributes to the play's theme by voicing a criticism of a society that makes it difficult for people to trust and be trusted.

The message is presented by one of the most cynical characters in the play. This instance of an ironic paradox that seems like a toss-away comment is really one more perspective on the society the play satirizes.

Epigrammic speaking is "unnatural" in the sense that it sets up antithetical statements that seem not able to coexist (but do). The structure is comforting because of its symmetry; and disturbing, because of the internal tension between its elements.

In the same way, a character who reverses his or her opinions causes discomfort. The Duchess of Berwick at one moment proclaims her curiosity and pleasure in Australia and its darling kangaroos—until her daughter gets engaged to an Australian. Then she announces that she has no intention of letting her daughter go to that "vulgar" place with "horrid kangaroos." Her character reversal is a "character paradox," a signal of an insincere and untrustworthy character.

The syntax of character paradox is the same pattern as the epigram: antithetical ideas in balance causing tension. The character paradox makes one wary, because it cannot be predicted whether the character will reverse again.

The pattern of the paradox is repeated in the plot as well. Wilde's play contains a series of internal plot paradoxes, in a kind of nested box structure. Lady Windermere thinks of life as a sacrament, and discovers that her husband has betrayed that belief, but she is really wrong—a paradox.

Her response—to betray him—is an ironic dramatic reversal, another paradox. That she might do so with a man she doesn't even love is a reversal of character, because she had professed the values of the Puritan, who considers life a sacrament.

Another paradox lies in the fact that she is brought to her senses by the very woman who had betrayed her as a child. Being saved by the one who abandoned her is a reversal, or paradoxical pattern.

Mrs. Erlynne's status is also a grand reversal. She begins as a social outcast desperate for acceptance into society, and ends as one who leaves it willingly.

Furthermore, her second "abandonment" of her daughter is a boon, not a betrayal. The audience, too, undergoes a reversal in its opinion of Mrs. Erlynne. The paradox is a pattern that organizes not only the witticism, but also the plot and the characters. The epigrams are not extraneous, but integral to a full comprehension of the play.

Perhaps Wilde's natural penchant for epigrammatic speaking was a habit so deep that it formulated the structure of his plays and stories, just as it formulated the witty sayings he produced in his brilliant conversation.

Source: Carole Hamilton for *Drama for Students*, Gale, 2000.

Christopher Nasser

In the following essay, Nasser argues that George Bernard Shaw modelled his Mrs. Warren on Wilde's Lady Windermere.

After *Lady Windermere's Fan* was first performed on 20 February 1892, Oscar Wilde found himself a famous playwright. At the time, George Bernard Shaw was struggling to establish himself on the British stage after having failed as a novelist. *Mrs. Warren's Profession,* his third play, was written in late 1893 and early 1894. Shaw's play is a Shavian reworking of Wilde's, an attempt to squarely face the issues that Wilde sidestepped. In a nutshell, it is *Lady Windermere's Fan* intellectualized.

The situations of the two plays are remarkably similar, both built around confrontation between a bad mother and an innocent daughter. In both plays, the mother lives on the Continent and the daughter in England, and in both the daughter knows little about her mother and indeed harbors illusions about her. Both daughters confront the danger of becoming like their mothers, and both withdraw from the precipice after a brief period of confusion. In both plays, society is presented as corrupt, and morally innocent individuals are out of place.

In Wilde's play, after leaving her husband and daughter, Mrs. Erlynne spends 20 years on the Continent with no visible means of support except her good looks. Lord Windermere calls her "a divorced woman, going about under an assumed name, a bad woman preying upon life" (act 4, 458). We are never told how she lived, but the assumption is that she seduced rich men like Lord Augustus and took their money. Certainly, she is presented as an accomplished seductress in the play, but Wilde bows to Victorian morality and leaves this aspect of her life obscure. A question forms in the reader's or viewer's mind: What did Mrs. Erlynne do during her 20 years on the Continent? Shaw picks up the question and answers it mercilessly in the figure of Mrs. Warren, who also uses an assumed name Miss Vavasour. Shaw bluntly unmasks Mrs. Warren as a prostitute who made a fortune in her profession.

Maupassant's tale *Yvette* and Pinero's *The Second Mrs. Tanqueray* are often cited as sources of Shaw's play, and rightly so, but the chief and hitherto unrecognized source is *Lady Windermere's Fan*. Toward the end of 1893 Wilde was taking the London stage by storm (his second social comedy, *A Woman of No Importance,* was first produced on 19 April 1893, and was also successful); the struggling Shaw must have felt a tinge of envy. The suspicion of envy is reinforced by Shaw's negative review of *The Importance of Being Earnest* in 1895 and his attempt some years later to re-create Lady Bracknell in the figure of Lady Britomart, Major Barbara's mother. His reaction, then, in 1893–94 was to attempt to remold *Lady Windermere's Fan* along Shavian lines.

There are many parallels and counterpoints between Lady Windermere and Vivie Warren. At the beginning of their respective plays, both women are innocents with a corrupt mother in the background whose corruption they are unaware of, and both have a strict set of morals. Lady Windermere's values, however, are presented as too rigid, and as the play unfolds she becomes more lenient and forgiving. Vivie moves in the same direction, and by the end of act 2 she has forgiven her mother and accepted her as a persecuted woman who defeated terrible poverty in the only manner open to her. But Vivie soon realizes that her mother was wrong, reasserts her own values, and prefers isolation and poverty to Mrs. Warren's tainted money. By the end of the play, Vivie is if anything more puritanical than at the beginning. Nor does Lady Windermere ever realize how corrupt her society is, whereas Vivie comes to realize "that fashionable morality is all a pretence" (act 4, 57) in capitalist Britain.

Finally, in both plays, society as a whole is presented as corrupt. "I will have no one in my house about whom there is any scandal" (act 1, 424), asserts Lady Windermere, but when we meet her guests, it is clear that they are all immoral, from Cecil Graham, to Dumby, to Lady Plymdale and the others.

> THERE ARE MANY PARALLELS AND COUNTERPOINTS BETWEEN LADY WINDERMERE AND VIVIE WARREN. AT THE BEGINNING OF THEIR RESPECTIVE PLAYS, BOTH WOMEN ARE INNOCENTS WITH A CORRUPT MOTHER IN THE BACKGROUND WHOSE CORRUPTION THEY ARE UNAWARE OF, AND BOTH HAVE A STRICT SET OF MORALS."

Whereas *Lady Windermere's Fan* defines morality in primarily sexual terms, in *Mrs. Warren's Profession* sexual corruption is part of the economic corruption that permeates every corner of British society and that only Fabian socialism can uproot. Money is a concern in both plays, but Wilde never questions the origins of Lord Windermere's or anybody else's fortune, whereas Shaw makes the origin of all fortunes his chief concern.

Given all these similarities and counterpoints between the two plays, then, it is fair to assert that Shaw's play is a direct response to Wilde's.

Source: Christopher Nasser, "Wilde's *Lady Windermere's Fan* and Shaw's *Mrs. Warren's Profession*," in *Explicator*, Spring, 1998, Vol. 56, no. 3, pp. 137–38.

Christopher Nasser

In the following essay, Nasser suggests that Wilde reworks the four stages of Dorian Gray's life by embodying them in the four main characters of Lady Windermere's Fan, *but this reworking is set within the framework and atmosphere of social comedy.*

In *The Picture of Dorian Gray,* Dorian develops from childlike innocence to a state of serious depravity in four states. The first stage is when he is still twenty and posing for Basil Hallward. Here he is the innocent young man who has not yet come in contact with evil. The second is when he is in love with Sibyl Vane. At this state evil has entered his life, but he is still largely innocent. The third is what might be called the "limited corruption" stage. Basil and Wotton become the opposing forces within him. Although he clearly leans toward Wotton, he is still balanced between good and evil, for his conscience is still alive and there are certain crimes, such as deliberate murder, that he would shrink from committing. In the fourth stage, all control is lost. He murders Basil, then tries to kill his conscience, which he identifies with his picture. Instead, he himself dies: human nature is "gray" and no one can become completely evil.

In *Lady Windermere's Fan,* Dorian Gray is fragmented and reincarnated in the four main characters, each of whom embodies one of the aforementioned stages, but within the framework and atmosphere of social comedy. Wilde often based his works on earlier works of his. In *Dorian Gray,* Dorian's development mirrors the drift of Victorian life and art toward corruption. In *Lady Windermere's Fan,* this same drift is shown in the juxtapositon of the four main characters, but it is simultaneously obscured by being cast in the mold of social comedy.

Dorian's first stage, childlike innocence, is embodied in Lord Windermere. Although he exists in a corrupt late-Victorian environment, Windermere is wrapped in a cocoon of early-Victorian morality that is never penetrated by his immoral surroundings. He is the object of much slander in the play, and even his wife becomes convinced that he is having an affair with Mrs. Erlynne. But he remains moral from beginning to end. His interest is in "saving" Mrs. Erlynne and in protecting his wife.

The art he admires is also that of spiritual innocence and purity. In act 4, he attacks Mrs. Erlynne for having drifted away from a miniature of herself that his wife "kisses every night before she prays.—It's the miniature of a young innocent-looking girl with beautiful *dark* hair." This miniature typifies the kind of art that D. G. Rossetti produced in the 1850s and that Basil Hallward created in the picture of Dorian before it began to change. The Victorians have drifted away from such art, however, toward Pater's *Mona Lisa,* decadence, and Dorian's picture after its corruption. But Windermere has not developed with the age. He remains frozen at the state of purity and innocence.

In Lady Windermere we see the second stage of Dorian's development, which began when he fell in love with Sibyl Vane and ended when he rejected her and she committed suicide. Dorian's picture registers the change in him by adding lines of cruelty around the mouth, but it remains otherwise unaltered.

When we meet Lady Windermere, she is still pure and innocent, but during the play she rejects her husband, decides to become Lord Darlington's lover, then draws back from this immoral decision and—with the help of Mrs. Erlynne—is able to return to her previous life and preserve her marriage. It is significant that as soon as she steps into the world of corruption she is overwhelmed by a sense of guilt and decides to withdraw: "No, no! I will go back, let Arthur do as he pleases. I can't wait here. It has been madness my coming. I must go at once." Mrs. Erlynne's role is to open the trap and allow her daughter to slip away.

This episode changes Lady Windermere irrevocably. She becomes aware of an immoral streak in herself and as a consequence becomes more forgiving and stops categorizing people as good or evil. At the end of the play, she is tainted but still basically pure, much like Dorian's picture after the suicide of Sibyl Vane. Her sense of guilt parallels Dorian's after Sibyl's death. And like Dorian, she hides her secret from the world.

In his recent biography of Oscar Wilde [entitled *Oscar Wilde*], Richard Ellman observed of Lord Darlington:

> Lord Darlington, who has been taken as a man about town, and who talks like Lord Henry Wotton, differs from Wotton in his possession of deep feelings.... When the play was given in New York with Maurice Barrymore ... in the role, Wilde complained that Barrymore had failed to see that "Darlington is *not* a villain, but a man who really believes that Windermere is treating his wife badly, and wishes to save her. His appeal is not to the weakness, but to the strength of her character (Act II): in Act III his words show he really loves her." It is because of her that he is leaving England for many years; he is a better man than Windermere.

Darlington may not be a better man than Windermere, but there is more goodness in him than people have generally recognized. He sums up the third stage in Dorian's development, and there is within him a very delicate balance between goodness and corruption. The two opposites struggle in Darlington throughout the play, and the battle is not resolved at its end.

As the play begins, Darlington is in love with Lady Windermere, a married woman, and wants her for his mistress. But his great paradox is that he loves Lady Windermere for her purity and innocence: through her, he wants to recapture his own lost innocence. He says of her: "She is a good woman. She is the only good woman I have ever met in my life." And: "This woman has purity and innocence. She has everything we men have lost." The moral situation of Darlington is captured in act 3, when he says to Cecil Graham and Dumby, "We are all in the gutter, but some of us are looking at the stars."

But Darlington's problem is that he cannot recover his lost innocence through Lady Windermere. She is already married, and if he wins her, he will only be dragging her into the gutter and corrupting her. Definitely not a fool, he realizes the impossibility of his situation but corruptly continues to pursue her. And yet part of the reason he appeals to her to leave her husband in act 2 and to go with him is quite moral: he is thoroughly convinced that Windermere is a monstrously corrupt man who does not deserve her for a wife. Darlington's motives are a very complex and fascinating fusion of goodness and corruption, for black and white are mixed inextricably in him.

His final decision to leave England is ambiguous: he leaves as much for Lady Windermere's sake as for his own. It is true he decides to leave after her apparent rejection of him, but it is also true that she is at her most vulnerable at the end of act 2 and that his chances with her have never been better. Indeed, that same night she reverses her decision and goes to his rooms. His hasty departure is both selfish and self-sacrificial. At least in part, he leaves because his stormy conversation with her leads him to realize how painful social disgrace would be for her. On the other hand, he does not want her to come to him mournfully, in tears, but with a smile and courageously or not at all. Even Lord Darlington's name is ambiguous, marking him both as a dandy and a "darling."

Mrs. Erlynne represents the final stage in Dorian's development. Although she does not commit any action quite as drastic as murder, she is nonetheless an immoral woman, devoted to leading a life of pleasure. In the play she discovers the goodness in herself and makes a major sacrifice to save her daughter. But she discovers that motherly love is too exhausting and strange an emotion for her, and she returns to the life of pleasure. She declares to the shocked Windermere: "I have no ambition to play the part of a mother. Only once in my life have I known a mother's feelings. That was last night. They were terrible—they made me suffer—they made me suffer too much." And: "No—

> "MRS. ERLYNNE REPRESENTS THE FINAL STAGE IN DORIAN'S DEVELOPMENT. ALTHOUGH SHE DOES NOT COMMIT ANY ACTION QUITE AS DRASTIC AS MURDER, SHE IS NONETHELESS AN IMMORAL WOMAN, DEVOTED TO LEADING A LIFE OF PLEASURE."

what consoles one nowadays is not repentance, but pleasure" (act 4). Far from being the conventional fallen woman of Victorian melodrama, Mrs. Erlynne deliberately rejects the goodness in herself and returns to a life of corruption. As Ellmann has observed, " *Lady Windermere's Fan* is a more radical play than it appears.... Wilde ... shelves the stereotype of the fallen woman: Mrs. Erlynne is singularly impenitent." Wilde regarded this point as so basic that he wrote, in one of his letters, that her character is "as yet untouched by literature."

Mrs. Erlynne's rejection of motherly love parallels Dorian's attempt to destroy his conscience by stabbing his picture. Far from dying, however, she tricks the infatuated Lord Augustus into marrying her and travels with him to the Continent. She also retains an affection for her daughter, albeit from a distance: human nature being "gray," the goodness in Mrs. Erlynne cannot be eliminated.

In *The Critic as Artist,* Wilde wrote:

> To an artist as creative as the critic, what does subject-matter signify? No more and no less than it does to the novelist and the painter. Like them, he can find his motives elsewhere. Treatment is the test.... [Criticism] works with materials, and puts them into a form that is at once new and delightful. What more can one say of poetry?

Treatment, then, or form, is what is vital in all art, not subject matter. In *Lady Windermere's Fan,* Wilde applied this principle quite successfully. He took the raw subject matter of his novel and gave it a new form. The result was his first successful play.

Source: Christopher Nasser, "Wilde's *The Picture of Dorian Gray* and *Lady Windermere's Fan,*" in *Explicator,* Fall, 1995, Vol. 54, no. 1, pp. 20–24.

Susan Taylor Jacobs

In the following essay, Jacobs examines Wilde's use of fantasy in exploring the question of cultural identity.

Though fantasy has been dismissed by many academics as a genre of marginal literary value, it attracts artists as well as readers. Indeed, one reason why a consensual definition of literary fantasy eludes us is that authors working in many genres draw upon it, smudging generic boundaries. Oscar Wilde was one of these writers.

Wilde appreciated the mind's power to make its own meanings, and he was skeptical of epistemologies, including his own. He used fantastic techniques, particularly those underscoring epistemological questions, although for him problems of knowing the phenomenological world were less interesting than problems of understanding a literary text. Given the complex, irrational subjectivities of authors and readers, he argued, no literary work could be perfectly understood. Moreover, the ultimate inability of a reader to perceive an author's exact meaning represented opportunities for both in expression and aesthetic pleasure. Wilde pursued such opportunities even in such seemingly conventional forms as the plays that made his fortune, temporarily, in the first half of the 1890s.

This discussion covers some of those plays. Often called Wilde's comedies, they actually conform to conventions of the "well-made play" (sometimes called "society" drama) and a related type, the problem play. The typical well-made play involved the inexorable disclosure of secrets. The problem play, in the hands of an Ibsen, could be made to challenge the status quo; in it, a character facing a moral dilemma would examine his or her heart, which may have been obscured by a life spent subservient to social convention. Wilde's imagination responded to the most conventional elements of these types of plays, particularly their sentimentalization of human nature while formally and ideologically suppressing it.

A discussion of the uses Oscar Wilde made of fantasy in these plays should clarify the differences between fantasy and any genre that is its host, yet critics disagree on fantasy's definition. Fantasy is metamorphic. Like literature in general, it takes on issues and symbols that matter most to an author and her culture, so that many descriptions and prescriptions of fantasy are contaminated by ethnocentricity. Traditionally, fantasy has been defined, as it is in Holman and Harmon's *A Handbook to Literature*, as a genre whose stories contradict reality by describing impossible events, creatures, and places. Such a definition does address what most readers intuit is fundamental to fantasy literature, yet "reality," either as a word or concept, is an unstable criterion. Our understanding of the world is influenced by our education, our experience, and the religious and scientific axioms of our particular culture or society. Some critics concur with Jean-Paul Sartre [in "*Aminadab*, or the Fantastic Considered as a Language,"] that magic and otherworldy settings are not essential to fantasy:

> So long as it was thought possible to escape the conditions of human existence through ascesticism, mysticism, metaphysical disciplines or the practice of poetry, fantasy was called upon to fulfill a very definite function. It manifested our human power to transcend the human. . . . After the long metaphysical holiday of the post-war period, which ended in disaster, the new generation of artists and writers . . . had returned, with much ado, to the human. This tendency had an effect on fantasy itself . . . [which] in order to find a place within the humanism of our time . . . is going to become domesticated, will give up the exploration of transcendental reality and resign itself to transcribing the human condition.

Rosemary Jackson and Leo Bersani are among those to offer psychological, structural, and formal examination of nontranscendental fantasy.

Some critics and writers of fantasy regard it as a disruption of, or conflict between, rhetorical structures. For instance, Eric Rabkin describes fantasy as a text that introduces, then contradicts, ground rules governing how the reader interprets the fictional world. Drawing on Huizinga's theory of play, W.R. Irwin defines a fantastic "world" as a place designated by a rigid set of rules and distinguished from those defining the reader's culture. The focus of recent critics like these on the rule-making mind allows us to explore the operations of fantasy even where there is no magic or bizarre other world, as in Wilde's comedies.

Lady Windermere's Fan, produced in 1891, made Wilde's fortune and enhanced his reputation. It is the story of a woman's encounter with the mother who had abandoned her. Lady Windermere's mother has come back, calling herself Mrs. Erlynne and blackmailing the husband, Lord Windermere, who wishes to spare his wife the truth about her mother. Believing that the two are having an affair, the angry Lady Windermere resolves to elope with an admirer, Lord Darlington. Mrs. Erlynne discovers her daughter's plan, follows her to Darlington's empty apartment, and convinces her to return home. Before they can leave, Darlington enters with his friends, including Lord Windermere and Lord Augustus, Mrs. Erlynne's suitor. The women hide, but Lady Windermere leaves her fan behind. When the fan is discovered, Mrs. Erlynne comes out of hiding, allowing everyone to assume she has come to Darlington for an assignation, and explains that she had taken it by mistake. Wilde undermines the impact on the audience of this sacrifice when she mollifies the resentful Lord Augustus the next day. She and her ''protector'' depart for Paris without revealing her identity to her grateful daughter.

Though this plot contradicts certain clichés, it does not disorient us or contradict the world view of any but the most authoritarian and rigorous of puritans, and so it is not in itself fantastic. In fact, the plot enacts an assumption conventional to both the problem play and the well-made play, that human beings have an essence, an identity, often concealed behind social masks. To uncover this essence, the plot delivers Mrs. Erlynne's moment of maternal protectiveness, supported by some of the stage directions: ''For a moment she reveals herself'' and ''Hiding her feelings with a trivial laugh.'' The woman, uncovered, is loving, distressed by her alienation from the human community but brave enough to resist a temptation to claim a love that would cause the beloved pain.

If we look more closely at Mrs. Erlynne and some of the other characters, however, we find that their identities may not have been uncovered after all. Lady Windermere, the one character on stage who comes to see Mrs. Erlynne as good, is untrustworthy. As Morse Peckham has observed [in ''What Did Lady Windermere Learn''], Lady Windermere's change of heart is superficial: ''She is one of those who cannot tell the difference between ideals and illusions . . . and she is therefore incapable of true moral growth.'' Moving Mrs. Erlynne over into the category of goodness does not change Lady Windermere's puritanical division of people into good and bad. She merely excuses Mrs. Erlynne's past, rather than confront and understand it. This morally immature character, kept in the dark to the last on the grounds that she does not have the temperament for truth, brings the play's very axioms into question, since the only character to unmask an identity does so in the unexamined, narrow terms of her idealistic culture. Wilde does not emphasize this irony, and so many spectators simply understand the play's conclusion as further manifestation of Mrs. Erlynne's generosity. Yet the

> MRS. ERLYNNE'S DRAMATIC FUNCTION IN THE PLAY SIMILARLY DECONSTRUCTS AND NOSTALGICALLY HOLDS ONTO THE CULTURE'S IDEALISTIC ASSUMPTIONS ABOUT IDENTITY.''

coexistence of ironic and traditional structures examining identity, or character, creates an epistemological ambiguity common in fantasy, for neither human nature nor the nature of the play can be decided.

Mrs. Erlynne's comments further undermine the traditional epistemology of this kind of play. Rejecting the characterization of her that the plot has been making, she cavalierly denies that the moment when she nearly sacrifices herself to save her daughter defines her: ''I lost one illusion last night. I thought I had no heart. I find I have, and my heart doesn't suit me, Windermere.'' We can read ''my heart doesn't suit me'' as a pathetic cynicism, a protest against the pain that comes with living, but ''my heart doesn't suit me'' has another implication. Though she does not regret saving her daughter (partly because she does not suffer materially), she is openly repelled by her spontaneous gesture, which, ironically, threatens to encapsulate her— inside an identity. ''I want to live childless still,'' she cries, denying the power of physical fact to force an identity on her. What she did was an emotional impulse, and impulses, she insists, do not necessarily define oneself.

The lack of identity that Mrs. Erlynne preserves is, like her childlessness, an emptiness that is filled incessantly by experimental play. That is, she is a fantasist, responding to the lack implied in the ideal Victorian identity by creating a character for herself the audience would consider impossible, a woman who is all potential because she is without essence. Repeatedly she alludes to herself as a role-player. Gazing at a picture of herself as a young woman, she muses, ''Dark hair and an innocent expression were the fashion then, Windermere!'' To the spectator, experienced in the kinds of assumptions about human nature promulgated by this sort of play, that photograph is a memento of authenticity, lost when the ingenue entered a hypocritical, dangerous society. But Mrs. Erlynne only claims to see a frame and a pose. To her mind, frame and pose record her as accurately as she can be recorded, for she has no identity, only epochs. Mrs. Erlynne underscores the artificiality of theatrical conventions that purport to disclose the essence of human nature: ''Oh, don't imagine that I am going to have a pathetic scene with her, weep on her neck and tell her who I am, and all that kind of thing. I have no ambition to play the part of a mother.'' The crafty and witty demimondaine may be a mask, but so is the weeping, loving mother that the audience has been expecting to see emerge as the ''real'' Mrs. Erlynne.

Certainly the play encourages us to see Mrs. Erlynne as revealing a deeper, better self. Yet Mrs. Erlynne's refusal to be a Stella Dallas cannot be entirely dismissed as mere denial. Though in some ways pathetic, deprived of family and dependent economically on men, she is also creative. Hers are the metamorphoses we have seen in myth and fantasy; she makes herself an ingenue, a demimondaine, a powerful mother, and, yes, a Stella Dallas. What Leo Bersani says about ''fantasy as a phenomenon of psychic deconstruction'' [in *Baudelaire and Freud*] applies to Wilde as well: ''he can be located at that critical moment in our culture's history when an idealistic view of the self and of the universe is being simultaneously held onto and discredited by a psychology (if the word still applies) of the fragmented and the discontinuous.'' Mrs. Erlynne's dramatic function in the play similarly deconstructs and nostalgically holds onto the culture's idealistic assumptions about identity.

Mechanisms of fantasy often operate through Wilde's epigrams, which can deny the play's premises by creating a bizarre world dominated by surface and style, not heart, or identity. In the Windermere world human nature is constrained by ''an idealistic view of the self.'' Windermere language acknowledges only certain experiences and events, interpreting them only from certain (moral) perspectives. The spontaneous revelation of self that people believe they see in the Windermere world is thus a delusion. The heartlessness, in *The Importance of Being Earnest,* that Mary McCarthy complained of is here as well, but not in a moral sense. Heartlessness in the epigrammatic characters is an impersonal wit, with surface and style elevated, in fantasy's exaggerated way, in response to the Windermere idea of heart.

Wilde's contemporary A. B. Walkley noticed [in the Review of *Lady Windermere's Fan*] that the conversation of dandies in Darlington's rooms took place in a secondary world within the play. Action ceases during the scene, he reported, ''but you do not notice its length, for it is a perpetual coruscation of epigrams. Just before the epigrams get boring, the action returns.'' When action freezes and epigrams take over, the epistemology gestured to by the framing play is replaced by another. The dandies form a community based on epigrams, their conversation a ritual during which they touch and acknowledge one another without learning anything about one another's personal histories or sentiments. There are two exceptions: Lord Darlington, whose love for Lady Windermere has suddenly made him open and earnest, and Lord Windermere, troubled by his blackmailing mother-in-law and furious wife. Neither man speaks or interacts with the other dandies.

An otherwise minor figure, Cecil Graham, underscores the difference between the ludic dandy world and the world of the play enclosing it. When the play is staged rather than read, Graham's importance is clear; besides generating the greatest number of epigrams, he takes up a great deal of space. Starting with the directions ''Cecil Graham comes toward him laughing,'' Wilde sets the character off on peregrinations the principals do not follow. He moves back and forth, lights a cigarette, puts a hand on another man's shoulder, and preens in front of the fireplace. The audience follows his movements, a choreographed display of meaninglessness, and listens to epigrams that reveal nothing about the man inside. During this time, the plot is suspended: Windermere sits thoughtfully, while Darlington writes letters, philosophizes to himself, and finally exits. Only Graham and his frivolous cohorts seem animate in the world that has suddenly come into being, where wit and style, but not heart, dominate. It is the restless Graham who finds the fan and turns it over to Windermere, who exclaims melodramatically over it. Thus the play is handed back to its principals and its principles. Graham moves away and grows still, smirking—perhaps maliciously—from the sidelines.

If Wilde had any reason for giving Graham the name of the friend who commits suicide in ''The Portrait of Mr. W.H.,'' it is that both are alienated from the perspective that informs *Lady Windermere's Fan.* One Graham, the suicide, devotes himself to Shakespeare's poetry and to a theory that articulates stylishly the aesthetic merits of Shakespeare's presumed pederasty. The second, sunny-tempered Graham has an appreciation of comic style that replaces the preoccupations of the rest of the play. Spouting his silly epigrams, this Graham exalts a well-timed jest over moral earnestness and the search for a human essence. The scene at which he is the central figure is thus more than a collection of amusing epigrams: it is a fantastic world insubordinate to the culture's will to define identity, or heart.

At times, then, *Lady Windermere's Fan* contradicts all that the conventional plot encourages us to believe. The play's epistemology is undermined by the fantastic vision that, intruding into it, perceives its subjects from different angles, introduces different assumptions into the story, and in general subverts its structure and direction. The plot concerns a quest for identity, while other elements in the play suggest that identity, at least as it is imagined by the plot, neither exists nor matters. Only the audience's self-delusion, fostered by the more sentimental conventions within the play, can let it believe that at the end it has seen past the facades of the Windermeres and Mrs. Erlynne. . . .

Source: Susan Taylor Jacobs, "When Formula Seizes Form: Oscar Wilde's Comedies," in *Staging the Impossible: The Fantastic Mode in Modern Drama,* edited by Patrick D. Murphy, Greenwood, 1992, pp. 15–29.

SOURCES

Beckson, Karl, ed. *Oscar Wilde: The Critical Heritage,* Alfred A. Knopf, 1970, 434 p.

Wilde, Oscar. *The Complete Works of Oscar Wilde; with an introduction by Vyvyan Holland,* Harper & Row, 1989 (1966).

FURTHER READING

Bloom, Harold, ed. *Oscar Wilde,* Chelsea House, 1985, 146 p.
 An anthology of recent scholarship on Wilde, with a brief commentary by Bloom in which he concerns himself with the "anxiety of influence" (Bloom's term for a writer's struggle to create something fresh and new) in Wilde.

Coakley, Davis. *Oscar Wilde: The Importance of Being Irish,* Town House, 1995, 246 p.
 Explores the role of the Irish raconteur in Wilde's family and in his social life.

Ellman, Richard. *Oscar Wilde,* Alfred A. Knopf, 1988, 632 p.
 The definitive Wilde biography.

Freedman, Jonathan. *Oscar Wilde: A Collection of Critical Essays,* Prentice-Hall, 1995, 257 p.
 Essays, brief biography, and selected bibliography.

Holland, Vyvyan Beresford. *Oscar Wilde: A Pictorial Biography,* Viking Press, 1960, 144 p.
 An intimate biography written by Oscar Wilde's son.

Knox, Melissa. *Oscar Wilde: A Long and Lovely Suicide,* Yale University Press, 1994, 185 p.
 A psychoanalytic biography that explore Wilde's childhood experiences and their effect on his later life.

McCormack, Jerusha, ed. *Wilde the Irishman,* Yale University Press, 1998, 205 p.
 Essays on aspects of Wilde's works.

Powell, Kerry. *Oscar Wilde and the Theatre of the 1890s,* Cambridge University Press, 1990, 204 p.
 Places Wilde into a literary and historical context.

Raby, Peter, ed. *Cambridge Companion to Oscar Wilde,* Cambridge University Press, 1997, 307 p.
 Examines the defining themes of Wilde's work.

The Lower Depths

MAXIM GORKI

1902

The Lower Depths is Maxim Gorki's best known play, widely considered both a masterpiece and an extremely problematic work. Subtitled *Scenes from Russian Life,* the play was a huge success from its first performance. The idea for the play was conceived in 1900, and it was written during the winter of 1901 and the spring of 1902. It was produced by the Moscow Arts Theatre on December 18, 1902. Konstantin Stanislavsky directed the play and starred in it as Sahtin, and as it was one of his earliest successes, it became a hallmark of his work, the Moscow Arts Theatre, and Russian socialist realism. The play is a portrait, without much overriding plot, of a destitute, lower-class group in a lodging house in Volga. Realistic depiction of this segment of Russian society was new and avant-garde at the turn of the century, in contrast to the age-old trend towards romanticizing the underclasses. Some critics at the time took issue with Gorki's subject matter, and his pessimistic, unredemptive presentation of the lower depths. Others disliked the ambiguity of the moral message about the human condition, and the unconventional structure of conversation around this. Most agreed, however, that the play's character sketches were powerful and moving, and the subject matter, at the very least, provocative. Debate over its chief theme, the merits of the ''truth'' versus the ''consoling lie,'' continues to engage audiences and scholars today, and it continues to be produced worldwide a century after its inception.

AUTHOR BIOGRAPHY

Maxim Gorki was born Alexei Maximovich Peshkov in Nizhy Novgorod, Russia, on March 16, 1868. His father died when Maxim was five years old, and he was raised by his maternal grandparents. His childhood was a brutal one; he was abused by his grandfather and forced to earn his own living from the age of eight. While he was still a child, Gorki became a menial laborer and a tramp, experiences that informed the works for which he is most famous. He was frequently beaten and abused by his employers, and to escape the miserable conditions of his life, he became an avid reader. In this way Gorki was self-educated, and came to see literature as a means of salvation for all people, as he details in his autobiographies and the essay collection, *On Literature*.

Gorki spent his early adulthood in Kazan, where, at 19, he attempted suicide by shooting himself in the chest. The event transformed the young man, and motivated him to begin his career as a writer. By 1892 he had published his first piece under his pseudonym, meaning Maxim the Bitter. His first major work, *Chelkash*, commenced his rise to recognition. In 1902 *The Lower Depths* was produced to enormous acclaim. The play was performed worldwide and established Gorki both at home and in the West.

Throughout this period Gorki was viewed with suspicion by Russian authorities, who saw his work as contributing to growing social unrest. He was briefly imprisoned in 1901 on account of his revolutionary poem, ''*Pesnya o Burevestnike*,'' and the following year his election to the Russian Academy of Sciences was rescinded. Gorki was active in the 1905 revolution, and after its defeat lived in exile, mostly in Capri. Mark Twain, who supported American intervention on behalf of the revolution, hosted him for a short period in the United States. When Gorki returned to Russia in 1913, he continued his political activities and supported the Bolshevik Revolution in 1917, although he disapproved of many of the new regime's unethical tactics.

During the early post-revolution years, on behalf of many intellectuals and in the interest of preserving works of art, Gorki complied with Lenin's demands that he cease speaking out against the new regime. After the revolution he returned to Capri, where he wrote his autobiographical trilogy: *Detstvo (My Childhood), V lyudyakh (In the World),* and *Mao universitety (My Universities)*. He entered a period of compliance with the new Soviet government, and, as Russia's foremost living writer, was used to promote Soviet views. He died on June 14, 1936, under suspicious circumstances amid speculation that he was assassinated.

Although Gorki has consistently received mixed criticism, his work marks the innovation of socialist realism and reflects tremendous advocacy on the part of Russia's oppressed people. While his work is compromised by adherence to ideology and an overly didactic tone, his sensitivity to character and environment are moving and powerful. The conflicting forces in his life, the socio-political movements in Russia with his emotional sensitivity to the plight of mankind, determine his work and make him very much a man of his time.

PLOT SUMMARY

Act I

The Lower Depths opens in a cavernous, underground lodging house. Kvaschnya, the Baron, Bubnoff and Kleshtch argue about whether or not Kvaschnya will marry again. In the course of the conversation, the Baron mocks Nastiah, who is engrossed in her romance novel. Meanwhile, Anna moans from bed about the noise and her ailment. Kvaschnya urges her to eat while her husband, Kleshtch, ignores her.

Sahtin rises and a conversation ensues over who will sweep the floor. The Actor claims he is too debilitated by alcohol poisoning to do it. In the course of what turns into an argument, the audience learns about Sahtin's former education, the Actor's flair for drama, and Bubnoff's past career as a faker of furs. Nobody sweeps the floor, and the Actor takes Anna outside for some air. All the while Kleshtch works away at an old lock.

Kostilioff comes downstairs in search of his wife, Wassilissa. Wordplay is exchanged between Kostiloff and several others over his status as a slumlord, and he appears to feign a Christian attitude. He wakes Pepel and they discuss money in a conversation revealing that they barter for stolen goods, even though Kostilioff professes innocence throughout. Shortly afterward, Natasha escorts in Luka, who is carrying a staff, a sack and a kettle. His role in the play is made immediately clear, as he declares he sees all men as equal and will be glad to sleep anywhere. Natasha urges Kleshtch and the

Maxim Gorki

others to have compassion for Anna as she approaches death. After she leaves, the men speculate on her, and Pepel's interest in her is revealed.

Luka begins to sing a song about how no path can be found in darkness. The song leads to a discussion about despair, and Luka restates his conviction that all men are equal. Alyoshka enters the scene drunk, carrying an accordian, and proceeds giddily to ramble on about caring about nothing. Wassilissa enters and berates him for spreading rumors about her. She tries to kick him out but he darts around, teasing her. When Luka laughs, Wassilissa turns on him, asking for his passport and calling him a vagabond. Bubnoff tells her that Pepel is not around and she bristles at the suggestion that she has any motives besides keeping order. As she leaves she demands the floor be swept, and Bubnoff and Nastiah explain that she is bitter because Pepel no longer loves her. Luka concedes to sweep the floor. Nastiah explains that Wassilissa is angry with Alyoshka for spreading rumors that Pepel is finished with her. She mentions her own misery and feelings of superfluousness, and Bubnoff says that all people are superfluous.

Medviedeff enters and introduces himself to Luka, and Luka lightly mocks him, reinforcing the impression that he tests authority. Medviedeff describes dealing with the drunken Alyoshka and the rumors he is spreading about his niece, Wassilissa, but nobody explains the situation to him. Kvaschnya enters and flirts with the policeman, but again says she will never remarry. Anna feebly makes her way back in, and when others joke about it, Luka wonders at how they can treat another human so. Medviedeff misinterprets him and points out that if she dies it will be legal trouble for all. There is noise from above as Wassilissa beats Natasha, and, as the others move to intervene, Anna and Luka make acquaintance.

Act II

It is evening in the same scene, and Sahtin, the Baron, Krivoi Zoba and the Tartar are playing cards while Kleshtch and the Actor watch. Bubnoff and Medviedeff play partidame, while Luka tends to Anna. Bubnoff and Krivoi Zoba sing a song about life as a prison while Anna moans about her life and Luka ministers to her. Luka comforts Anna with promises of peace and salvation while the players sing and argue, the Tartar advocating fair play. When the Actor bemoans his alcoholism, Luka tells him there is a clinic where he can be cured, although he cannot tell him where.

Pepel enters and asks Medviedeff about Natasha's condition, revealing his interest in her. They argue, and Pepel threatens to report the family for buying stolen goods. Medviedeff storms out and Luka urges Pepel to run away to Siberia with Natasha. Pepel accuses Luka of lying to give people hope. Luka responds that people believe what they need to believe.

Wassilissa enters to see Pepel, under the guise of seeing Anna. Luka conceals himself above the stove. Pepel makes clear he does not love Wassilissa. She offers to help him leave with Natasha if he will arrange to have her husband killed and free her from her life. Pepel refuses. Kostilioff enters and alternates between feigning courtesy and screeching hysterically. Kostilioff shakes Pepel by the collar, but is interrupted by noise that Luka makes from his hiding place. Kostilioff and Wassilissa leave. Luka emerges and explains that he didn't want Pepel to lose his head and kill Kostilioff. He warns Pepel away from Wassilissa and urges him to flee with Natasha. Their conversation is interrupted by Anna's death rattle, and they leave to find Kleshtch. The Actor enters and, newly inspired, recites a poem. Natasha enters and discovers Anna dead. The players enter and make callous remarks about the death. Kleshtch worries about funeral costs and the

Actor seeks Luka for more advice. Sahtin argues that Luka's advice is a hoax and declares that the dead neither hear nor feel.

Act III

Nastiah and Natasha sit in a vacant lot with Luka, the Baron and Kleshtch. Bubnoff looks out from a window in the house. Nastiah tells the story of her lost love, but the Baron interrupts her because of her shifting account of the lover's name. She gets upset, and Luka defends her right to some consideration while Natasha comforts her. Luka says he believes her, which opens a conversation on the merits of lying to oneself. Natasha admits to dreaming of being rescued. When Natasha tells Luka he is a good man, he tells a story of human potential, about two thieves he befriended after they tried to rob him. Kleshtch bursts out that his version of the truth is his terrible circumstance, and says he hates everyone.

Pepel enters and they continue the discussion about truth. Luka tells a story about a man who believed in a land of justice, but when he learned it did not exist he killed himself. Then Luka reports he intends to leave, and this provokes Pepel to declare his love for Natasha and ask her to leave with him. Wassilissa appears and overhears the conversation as Luka encourages the union. Kostilioff appears and berates Natasha for neglecting duties as Wassilissa makes a sinister promise of a wedding. Kostilioff warns Luka that he will set Medviedeff on him if he doesn't leave.

Luka says he will leave that night. Sahtin and the Actor enter, arguing about the rumored clinic. Luka questions Sahtin's motives in weakening the Actor's resolve, and Sahtin reports that prison changed him from a jolly man into the realist he is now. Their conversation about Sahtin's former life is interrupted by noise of Natasha being brutally beaten. The Actor runs to fetch Pepel. As the beating continues audibly, the Tartar and Krivoi Zoba enter, followed by Medviedeff, who is trying to retrieve his whistle from Alyoshka. Natasha enters, aided by Nastiah, with Wassilissa and Kostilioff in pursuit. Pepel bursts in and strikes Kostilioff, accidentally killing him. Natasha, hearing the commotion, accuses Pepel and Wassilissa of planning it all and conspiring to kill Kostilioff.

Act IV

The scene is an approximate recreation of the first. Kleshtch tinkers with an accordian and he, the Baron, Nastiah and Sahtin discuss Luka. The Tartar says he followed the law of his heart. Nastiah says she loved him and that she is disgusted with her companions. The Actor makes oblique reference to leaving forever. The Baron calls Luka a fool and a charlatan. Sahtin delivers monologues in which he appreciates Luka's motives for his lies, but advocates the truth as the inheritance of free men.

Nastiah reveals that Natasha has left town and that Pepel and Wassilissa are in prison. Nastiah continues to provoke the Baron and insult everyone, then leaves. Sahtin delivers a speech on the glory of man's potential. The Baron goes in search of Nastiah. The Actor takes a drink and rushes out. Medviedeff and Bubnoff enter with whiskey, followed by Alyoshka. It is revealed that he and Kvaschnya have married and now run the lodging house. Kvaschnya enters and confronts Alyoshka for spreading rumors that she beats her husband. Bubnoff and Krivoi Zoba begin their song about life as a prison, and the Baron and Nastiah burst in with news that the Actor has killed himself.

CHARACTERS

A Baron

The Baron is a slightly ridiculous, cynical character, once an aristocrat, now a resident of the lower depths who reminisces on his former status. His philosophy is "all is past", and he expects little from the world although he retains his aristocratic bearing. A great deal of animal imagery is associated with this aristocrat who has fallen to the level of beast.

A Tartar

The Tartar has little role until the final act, when his hand has been mashed and he has little hope of supporting himself without it. Before then he participates in a game of cards and repeatedly advocates fair play. He offers such practical insights as "someone can have the bed" when Anna dies. In Act IV he champions Luka's reputation and tells the others that the Koran leads his heart, while for Russians religion is law. When the actor asks him to pray for him, he replies, "Pray for yourself," suggesting both practical, personal advocacy and lack of brotherly love.

MEDIA ADAPTATIONS

- *The Lower Depths* was adapted as a Chinese film entitled *Ye 'dian* or *Night Lodging* in 1948. It was first performed on stage in 1946. Both stage and screen versions were banned in China during the Cultural Revolution.

- In 1957, Akira Kurosawa directed a Japanese film adaptation of *The Lower Depths* (translated as *Donzoko*) starring Toshiro Mifunge.

- In 1936, Jean Renoir directed a French film adaptation of *The Lower Depths* entitled *Les Bas*, or *The Underworld*. At the time the film was made, the French social climate resembled pre-Revolutionary Russia in its utopian yearnings.

The Actor

The actor is an alcoholic whose addiction has obliterated his memory. His hypochondria is humorous, and he shows compassion for the ailing Anna, but he is a pathetic character who pines for his past. He gets some false hope from Luka that his addiction can be cured, and attempts some restraint, but ultimately he fails and commits suicide at the end of the play.

Alyoshka

Alyoshka is a comic character, often drunk, who shows up largely for comic relief. He is provocative and tells rumors about people in authority, namely Wassilissa and, later, Kvaschnya.

Bubnoff

Bubnoff is a capmaker, whose first line in the play is a grunt of skepticism. This foreshadows his role as one of several cynical voices throughout the play. For example, when he hears that Anna is dead, his response is "There will be no more coughing." At more than one point in the play, Bubnoff and others sing about life as a prison, offering a sense of his world view.

Wassilissa Karpovna

Wassilissa is the young, bitter wife of Kostiloff. She wishes for freedom from her circumstances and tries to achieve it by coercing her lover Pepel to murder her husband. When Pepel refuses and she learns of Natasha's intent to run away with him, she brutally beats her sister. This leads to Pepel's accidental murder of her husband. Natasha accuses Wassilissa and Pepel of conspiring to the murder, and Wassilissa ends up in jail.

Anna Kleshtch

Anna is the terminally ill wife of Kleshtch. She both wants to die and escape the misery of her life, and is afraid to die, but she takes some consolation from the ministrations of Luka. When she dies nobody cares very much, aside from concern about the smell and the authorities.

Andrew Mitritch Kleshtch

Kleshtch is a locksmith who is always working on a lock that can't be mended. He sets himself apart from the others on account of his work ethic, which they do not share. He is extremely bitter, and claims he will be free from his circumstances when his wife, Anna, dies. When she finally does die, he has to sell his anvil and other tools to cover funeral costs, and so he can neither move on nor work. He is an angry man with no sense of brotherhood, and says in Act III, "I hate everyone."

Michael Ivanowitch Kostilioff

Kostilioff is the hypocritical, corrupt landlord of the lodging house. He preaches religion, salvation from hardship, and brotherly love, but he takes his tenants for all they are worth. Although he purchases stolen goods from Pepel, he treats him with suspicion and disdain, and is always trying to confirm the suspected affair with his wife. In Act III, Pepel comes to Natasha's defense when Kostilioff is beating her, and accidentally kills him.

Krivoi Zoba

Krivoi Zoba is part of the same chorus of skeptical voices as Bubnoff. He too sings the song of disaffection and life as a prison, and when Anna dies he asks, "Will she smell?"

Kvaschnya

Kvaschnya is a spirited middle aged woman who, at the opening of the play, sermonizes on why she will never marry again. She shows up sporadically, generally pouring forth on the same theme, but when the play closes she is married to the policeman and running the boardinghouse.

Luka

Luka is the central catalyst of the play. He is an old man, labeled a pilgrim, who arrives in Act I, greeting the decrepit lodgers with "Good day, honest folk." Throughout three of the four acts, he maintains this role of champion of mankind, but his methods of support are shifting and problematic. While he bolsters the Actor's hope and resolve with a story of a free clinic where he can be cured, for example, he can never tell him where it is, and thus appears to advocate self-deception. Because of his shifting messages, Luka is the most problematic character in the play. Having set in motion the conflict in Act III, Luka disappears, leaving the remaining characters, except for Sahtin, disheartened and changed for the worse.

Medviedeff

Medviedeff is a policeman and the uncle of Natasha and Wassilissa. He is generally ineffectual and some characters make a mockery of him, but he ends up marrying Kvaschnya and running the lodging house with her.

Nastiah

Nastiah is a prostitute who pines for a lover, real or imagined, left behind. She reads romance novels and tells improbable stories of this lost lover with shifting accounts of his name. Nastiah is strongly impacted by Luka, and in the course of the play her view of life grows increasingly dim. By the end of the play she says she is disgusted with everyone.

Natasha

Natasha is the younger sister of Wassilissa, who abuses her throughout the play because Pepel fancies her. While she wishes to be rescued from her life of drudgery, she is leery of Pepel's advances. In general she is a kind, compassionate character, but after she is beaten in Act III she turns on her protector, Pepel, and her accusations send him to jail. It is revealed that once she is released from the hospital, she disappears from the area.

Waska Pepel

Pepel is a young thief who sells his goods to his landlord and has an affair with Wassilissa, his landlord's wife. He is a good man at heart despite his life of crime, and aspires to marry Natasha and make a better life. When Wassilissa and Kostilioff brutally beat Natasha, he comes to her defense and accidentally kills the landlord. Natasha turns on him and accuses him of planning the murder with her sister. When the play ends, Pepel is jail.

Sahtin

Sahtin is a former convict who apparently was once well-educated and is a lover of words. At the opening of the play he has been beaten after losing a card game. Throughout most of the play he is drunk and gambling, but he generally offers witty, intelligent, and provocative wordplay. He challenges Luka for pacifying people with lies and philosophically is his opposite, but after Luka leaves he says he understands his impulse to comfort and soothe the troubled. In Act IV he delivers three monologues about the righteousness of mankind and the theme of "truth" versus the "consoling lie." His assertion is that compassion and the consoling lie are necessary for the weak, but the truth is the way of the free man. In the final act of the play, Sahtin is the only character who has not been changed by having given in to illusions of hope provided by Luka.

THEMES

The "Truth" vs. the "Consoling Lie"

The main philosophical issue in *The Lower Depths* is the central theme of the work, the merits of the truth versus the consoling lie. Luka, the pilgrim, embodies the philosophy that people need lies as buffers against the hardships of life. The first instance in which he demonstrates this conviction is when he soothes the dying Anna with promise of peace after death. His conversation later with Bubnoff and Pepel indicates that he may not believe in such an afterlife, but, rather, is committed to consoling one who suffers. Through Acts II and III Luka bolsters the hopes of characters who are downtrodden and suffering, by kindling hope with potentially insubstantial information. For example, he is quick to assure Nastiah that he believes her love story although it is clearly not true, in the interest of protecting her feelings. Similarly, he tells the Actor that he can be cured of his alcoholism at a free clinic in an unnamed town, if only he resolves to change. The Actor does achieve some personal change in the short term, and for a while he is inspired and can recite lines of poetry as in days of yore. In much the same way, Nastiah is comforted by Luka's moral support, and Anna dies more contented than she would have otherwise. However, once Luka disap-

TOPICS FOR FURTHER STUDY

- *The Lower Depths* was made into a French film in 1936, a Chinese film in 1948, and a Japanese film in 1957. What social, political, and economic factors in France, China and Japan might have contributed to the play's appeal at those respective times?

- *The Lower Depths* is considered a prime example of Socialist Realism. Research Socialist Realism and explain how and to what ends the play embodies this literary device.

- Research both Romanticism and Realism in literature. How did they evolve, and how are both manifested in *The Lower Depths?*

- Research the period preceding the Bolshevik Revolution. What social and political influences do you think the characters Luka and Sahtin represent?

- Consider social and economic conditions in the United States today. How might a contemporary American version of *The Lower Depths* look?

- Consider the central theme in *The Lower Depths*. Discuss the merits and problems of the "truth" and the "consoling lie," and argue your own moral stance on the issue.

- Very few props and stage instructions are provided by Gorki for *The Lower Depths*. If you could direct the play, how would you make the set support the thematic material of the text? Use plenty of detail and back up your reasoning.

---

pears, and with him his encouraging stories, the characters are disappointed and more downcast than they were before he came.

Different characters question Luka's soothing fabrications throughout the play. When he consoles Anna, Pepel asks Luka if he believes his own words. Bubnoff, Kleshtch, and Medviedeff also question Luka, but Sahtin most fully embodies his foil as a character in pursuit of the truth. During most of the first three acts, Sahtin operates as a background voice projecting skepticism and harsh realism, as at the end of Act II, when he responds to sentimentalism with "The dead hear not. The dead feel not." In Act IV, however, he is thrust into the foreground with three monologues concerning the power of the truth for mankind. Although he appreciates Luka's motives for showing compassion to people who suffer, he does not advocate compassion himself. Rather, he asserts that "The lie is the religion of the servant and master . . . the truth is the inheritance of free men!" He continues in this vein to praise man and credit him with the ability to advance himself through the pursuit of truth. The disparity between Sahtin's wild optimistic humanism associated with the truth and the human need for sympathy and compassion is the life-giving center of the play.

Hell/Prison

The theme of life in the lower depths as like prison or hell circulates throughout the text. The title is immediately telling; these scenes from Russian life are about what is dark, underground, buried. Lower depths, as opposed to height or the heavens, suggest hell by sheer proximity, and the miserable lives of the residents make this connection clear. Lack of light also suggests the dark side, or hell. So does lack of meaningful work, or progress, as suggested by Kleshtch's ceaseless scraping at a lock that can never be mended. In Acts II and IV, Bubnoff and Krivoi Zoba sing a song about being in prison, never seeing the sun rise or set, and this sets a tone for life in this underground cavern. Even in Act III, which is set outside, a brick wall is described as blocking out "the heavens." The fact that there is little or no private space, and that benches and bunks operate as beds further serve as prison imagery. Different characters throughout the play make reference to release from this life, as if they are serving time. Anna awaits death as relief from a life of suffering, Kleshtch waits for her to die so he can be free of the boardinghouse, and Natasha fantasizes that someone will come and rescue her. None of the characters are released except by death, and in fact two characters actually go to prison. Kleshtch in particular is even more firmly rooted in the lower depths once his wife dies, because he must sell his work materials to cover funeral costs. The song about prison is the last impression before the announcement of the Actor's suicide at the end of the play. The fact that Sahtin responds with, "He must spoil our song . . . the fool" suggests that, like the sinner condemned to an eternity in hell, he may not have any insight into his own condition.

Men as Animals

Degradation is a part of life in the lower depths, and the undercurrent theme of people as animals or beasts indicates this condition. Early in Act I the Baron calls Nastiah a "silly goose" for reading romances, humiliating her in front of the rest of the boarders. Moments later the former aristocrat dons a yoke for carrying containers to market, suggesting he is a workhorse. Shortly afterward, Kleshtch sarcastically suggests Kostilioff "Put a halter around my neck. . ." to use and degrade him further. All this imagery so early in the text sets the tone for the play, in which people are degraded and treated inhumanely. The lodgers' social and economic circumstances have reduced them to subservience to their landlord, but the way they behave toward each other also reflects inhumanity and a survivalist, animalistic mentality. For example, the fact that most characters are unmoved by Anna's suffering and death, aside from how it hurts or benefits them in a practical sense, reflects a lack of feeling that distinguishes human from other animals. In addition, much of the time the lodgers display a lack of intelligent insight into their own situations, but rather compound their problems by getting drunk and gambling away their money or getting beaten up. Subsisting in the underground cavern like animals in a den, the lodgers cannot see beyond their circumstances, but huddle together for survival.

STYLE

Realism

As a realistic play, characters, plot and setting are crucial components of *The Lower Depths*. Socialist realism entails lifelike depiction of characters' behavior and speech for purposes of conveying a political message. In *The Lower Depths*, characters speak and behave in somewhat fragmented, lifelike patterns and what they do and say are not romanticized to elicit audience emotions. Instead their various words and behaviors, however unappealing, are aimed at being realistic and provoking an impulse toward change or revolution. In *The Lower Depths*, some characters provoke contempt, others compassion, but the general sense at the end of the play is that social change is necessary. For example, when Nastiah complains that she feels superfluous, and Bubnoff confirms that everyone is superfluous, the response of the reader or audience is reflexively that a world should exist in which people do not feel superfluous.

Setting

Setting in *The Lower Depths* is minimal, as are stage directions. In Acts I, II, and IV, the set is dark and cavernous, with very little furniture aside from a few bunks and benches, suggesting a prison or a pit. The set in Act III is a depressing vacant lot, with various piles of rubbish and a wall which blocks out the sky. There is little or no color, and stage directions give the sense that characters are dressed in rags. Both settings convey a sense of the impoverished conditions of the lodgers, and attribute to them a feeling of desolation and despair. They generate in the audience the sense that these conditions are inhumane and should be changed.

Point of View

Throughout *The Lower Depths*, the audience gathers opinions about key characters, especially Luka, through the points of view of other characters. Every time Luka offers solace or tells a story, some character engages him or criticizes him, and especially in Act IV there is a detailed conversation analyzing him. In this way, the audience is offered multiple options for interpreting this provocative character, and for developing a personal opinion of the central moral question. This structure also keeps the audience from developing a strong emotional identification with any one character, which makes for more even-handed political assessment.

Monologue

Monologue is used to similar ends in the play. The most important monologues are delivered by Sahtin in Act IV to convey his opinion on the importance of the truth. Use of this device draws attention to the subject matter by making it stand out from the rest of the lines. In this case Sahtin voices a response to discussion of Luka's ethics, and in so doing establishes himself as Luka's moral foil. The monologues in this act depart from the realistic structure of the play in the sense that people tend not to speak in such substantial chunks in a conversation. In this case the author's moral agenda takes precedence over realism.

Foreshadowing

Foreshadowing is the use of symbols, lines or events to suggest something that will happen later in the play. In *The Lower Depths* the main events are foreshadowed before they occur. First, in Act II Pepel and Kostilioff are arguing heatedly, and as the conflict comes to a head, Luka makes his presence known, ostensibly to prevent Pepel from striking Kostilioff and getting himself into trouble. This foreshadows the fact that Pepel will in fact strike Kostilioff in Act III and inadvertently kill him. Earlier in the same scene, Luka tells a story of a man who believed in a land of justice, but when he learned it didn't exist, he killed himself. Later, in Act IV, the Actor interjects into the conversation that soon he will be gone, and quotes, "'this hole here . . . it shall be my grave. . .'" Shortly afterward he actualizes those words, and, like the disillusioned man in Luka's story, commits suicide.

Symbols

Gorki provides few physical props to serve as symbols in *The Lower Depths,* but those he does provide resonate with meaning. The lower depths themselves are symbolic of the conditions for the lodgers, as a grave, as prison, and as hell. The bunks and lack of furniture also speak of a prison or hell. One item stands out from the drab, minimalist setting, and that is an old Russian stove. The characters cluster around the ornate piece of antiquity for warmth in much the same way they gain solace from reminiscing about their pasts. The stove suggests a connection with the romantic Russia of the past.

Above and beyond the presence of physical objects, human characters serve as symbols in *The Lower Depths.* Luka and Sahtin represent the philosophies they embody and, some critics would conjecture, conflicting beliefs of the author. The ridiculous, ostentatious Baron stands for all of aristocracy, in much the way that Medviedeff's silliness pokes fun at law enforcement in general. Kostilioff stands for anyone who lords power over others, while the Actor plays a fool. The characters represent components of Russian society as well as the moral messages each advocates.

HISTORICAL CONTEXT

The period in which Gorki lived and wrote *The Lower Depths* was the end of a long period of repression and unrest in Russia, during which the czardom increasingly became an autocracy which governed by force. In 1861, under the Edict of Emancipation, Alexander II freed peasants from serfdom. Serfs were emancipated from servitude to nobles in much the same way blacks would soon be released from slavery in the American South: with little or no support to smooth the economic transition. Freedom afforded the peasantry was extremely limited, and although they were no longer considered chattel, peasants had access to even less farmland than they had before Emancipation. This new freedom imposed harsh economic conditions on the peasantry, and as a result, many moved to cities and centers of industry for work. Gorki's youth as a tramp on the move fits the description of many of the newly displaced, looking for work.

Emancipation effectively opened the doors for industrialization of Russia, and factories underwent phenomenal growth. Waves of peasants in an unfamiliar, urban environment, were, naturally, exploited. Factory work conditions into the turn of the century were far worse than those revealed in the famous investigations of English factories, including child labor, interminable workdays and unsafe, unhygienic conditions. Cities were newly crowded and could not accommodate the influx of people with suitable housing. Recurrent crop failure resulted in severe and widespread famine, which was at its peak in 1891. Poverty, already the norm in the days before Emancipation, was compounded by a severe trade depression in 1880, resulting in the dismissal of thousands of workers. Between 1880 and the turn of the century, unemployment was a huge problem, and created the community of drifters such as those depicted in *The Lower Depths.* In *Maxim Gorky The Writer, An Interpretation,* F. M. Borras points out that "Klesctch of all Kostylev's [Kostilioff's] lodgers most richly deserves compassion, because he does not dream of escape from the

COMPARE & CONTRAST

- **1861:** Alexander II emancipates serfs from landed nobility. Upon release, they are provided with less land than they previously held, and many were forced into the corrupt factory system and an even more brutal quality of life.

    Today: Virtually no signs of the antiquated class system of peasantry and nobility exist.

- **Mid-1860s:** Emancipation gives rise to industrialization and, as a result, the beginnings of capitalism in Russia. It is squelched by the Bolshevik Revolution, after which workers gained control of factory management.

    Today: Since the end of the Cold War in 1989, Russia has been moving in the direction of capitalism. Although some conditions have improved, Westernization of the former Soviet Union has recently been disastrous for its economy.

- **1917:** The Romanoff family, czarist heirs of the Russian Empire, along with many other heads of state, are executed as the Bolsheviks take power.

    Today: Boris Yeltsin resigns from power with diplomatic immunity.

- **1917:** Milyahov, the first foreign minister under the new government after the Bolshevik Revolution, is forced to resign based on his insistence on continuing the war effort.

    Today: Yeltsin is pressured to resign, and is replaced by Vladimir Putin, a former unknown, who is propelled into leadership based on his enthusiastic support of war in Chechnya.

---

depths through a miracle, but plans to achieve it by means of hard work and yields only when he realizes that this most reasonable of all purposes, because of social conditions, cannot be fulfilled. In the years of industrial recession, 1899-1903, such men as Kleshtch, wishing to work but unable to find jobs, would strike a chord with the audience.''

As a writer and an intellectual, Gorki was not among the working class who were so impacted by Russia's social conditions, but he was extremely sympathetic to the plight of the masses, having been a drifter as a child and a young man. His use of socialist realism in *The Lower Depths* is geared toward representing both the terrible living conditions and the feeling of unrest in the country at the time. The fantasies of release and escape, such as Pepel's dream of running away to make a new life with Natasha, reflect the utopian dream which was universal in Russia, especially among the working class, who were influenced by Marxism. The tension between the utopian fantasy that Luka instills and the brutal truths and self-reliance that Sahtin advocates reflects Gorki's view of forces at work in Russia. His didactic tone in Luka's and Sahtin's speeches, while characteristic of his own style, reflects his agenda of social reform. Around the same time, Tolstoy, another famous Russian author, had taken on a similar tone in what amounted to propagandistic writing.

Production of *The Lower Depths* preceded the Russian Revolution of 1905 by just over two years. This revolution was characterized by strikes, assassinations, and peasant outbreaks in protest of the corruption of the czarist government, although little reform resulted from the event. World War I resulted in massive food shortages and such widespread civilian suffering, however, that a new revolutionary climate was created by the end of 1916. Lenin and Trotsky led the Bolshevik Revolution of 1917, which resulted in many radical reforms, such as abolition of private property and introduction of workers' control into factories. The Russian Civil War followed, between the Bolsheviks (Reds) and anti-Bolsheviks (Whites), from 1918 to 1920. The Bolshevik party was victorious, but the country was devastated, and the Soviet regime which followed largely perpetuated Russia's legacy of repression and suffering.

CRITICAL OVERVIEW

When *The Lower Depths* was first presented in 1902, it was met with mixed criticism, but spectacular popular success. It was so successful, in fact, that the printed version of the play became a bestseller, with fourteen editions printed in 1903. Many critics took issue with the play's unconventional structure and lack of plot. Others criticized its preaching, didactic tone. Most agreed, however, that the Moscow Arts Theatre production was outstanding and amplified character sketches that were powerful and moving. Debate over the play's chief theme, the merits of "truth" verses "the consoling lie," continue today, and it is generally accepted that the play, although flawed, is considered a masterpiece.

At the time *The Lower Depths* was first performed, the vagabond life was in vogue, and realistic depiction of the lower classes was avant-garde. The play's presentation of the squalid underbelly of Russian society was the first of its kind and drew huge attention for its novelty. Much of the play's initial success was owed to the masterful work of Konstantin Stanislavsky and the Moscow Arts Theatre, which was then and continues to be considered one of the finest theater groups in the world. In *A History of Russia,* Jesse D. Clarkson notes that the play was a success "largely thanks to Stanislavsky's casting rather than to its author." Stanislavsky and Gorki insisted that the players spend time in dosshouses resembling the one in the play in preparation for their parts, and word of this approach also added to its novelty. Although Gorki himself gave the theater company credit for the scale of the play's initial success, it proved just as popular performed by German actors in Berlin. The play swept world capitals, and by 1903 Gorki's American publishers claimed his name was better known than Tolstoy.

Chekhov (as critic Sumie Jones records) was perhaps the most famous critic of *The Lower Depths,* and he took issue with some of Gorki's character choices. He claimed the characters that remain in Act IV are not interesting, and critics continue to take issue with this point today. Barry P. Scherr, in his essay "Gorky the Dramatist," asserts that "at least some of the characters do not seem entirely necessary. The Baron, the Actor, Bubnov, and the locksmith Kleshtch are all dwellers in the lower depths. Gorki manages to make individual characters out of each of them, yet the play would clearly be easier for audiences to follow had he combined these four figures into one or two, and the story-line would have remained intact." He also points out that "the characters who are most important for the play's intrigue—the thief Vaska Pepel, Kostilioff, owner of the lodging-house where the action takes place, and Kostilioff's wife and sister-in-law—have relatively little to do with the play's philosophical concerns."

Many critics disliked the structure of the play and its lack of driving action or plot. German critic F. Mering (as critic F. M. Borras records) wrote in a 1934 article that the only real conflict in the play took place between Kostilioff and Pepel, and that Act IV was unnecessary since all the action was completed in Act III. Chekhov declared Act IV superfluous as well, because all the stronger characters were absent from it. He also disliked that Act for what he felt was Gorki's preaching tone. Sumie Jones, in her essay, "Gorki, Stanislavsky, Kurosawa: Cinematic Translations of *The Lower Depths,*" quotes Stanislavsky in reporting that Chekov could not bear "to see Gorki mount the pulpit like a clergymen" to voice his opinions, as he does through Sahtin's monologues in Act IV. The play elicits the same criticism today, as in a review of a production at the Royal Lyceum Theatre in Edinburgh. Kate Bassett, in *The Daily Telegram* writes, ". . . several of Gorky's big speeches about the ineradicable worth of every individual and about man's responsibility for himself do verge on the wooden."

In the years after the first production of *The Lower Depths,* Gorki was his own chief critic. Over time, as his philosophical and political beliefs changed, he gave shifting interpretations of key characters, and suggested he intended them to be different than they were. According to Yevgeny Zamyatin in *A Soviet Heretic,* he called himself "a poor playwright" and suggested the play was even harmful in the time it was produced. Nevertheless, the play is, in Barry Scherr's words, "the prime example of a work that is an acknowledged masterpiece and yet contains several seemingly glaring weaknesses that would be enough to destroy a lesser work." He continues, ". . . the strength and originality of the secondary figures, the creation of a strange yet powerful central character, the very exotic quality of the lower depths that Gorky depicts, and the complexities of the play's theme largely account for its deserved success." *The Lower Depths* continues to be produced almost a century later as, for example, in Seattle in 1998, by the Vladivostok Chamber Theater. In the words of John Longenbaugh in a promotional piece in the *The*

Sanneke Bos (lying on the stage) from a production of Gorki's The Lower Depths.

Seattle Weekly, the work is still considered "a masterpiece of naturalism."

CRITICISM

Jennifer Lynch

Lynch teaches at the Potrero Hill After School Program and the Taos Literacy Program. Lynch also contributes to Geronimo, *a journal of politics and culture. In the following essay, Lynch argues that the flawed nature of Gorki's characters reveals the complexity both of the author and of humankind in general.*

The Lower Depths is typically characterized as a masterpiece, but one that is glaringly flawed. The flaws most often cited are Gorki's tendency to impose upon his characters language which rings false or is agenda-driven, and the fact that certain characters are viewed as unconvincing or unbelievable. Luka and Sahtin in particular generate these criticisms. From the first appearance of the play, critics have taken issue with inconsistencies in Luka's behavior, which weaken the moral objective around his character. Gorki himself gave conflicting interpretations of Luka's purpose in the story.

Critics have also questioned Sahtin as the mouthpiece for truth and mankind's potential, since this advocacy comes so late in the play and seems incongruous in a previously minor character.

Inconsistent as Luka and Sahtin may be, they are the most developed characters in Gorki's group portrait. As such, they are ambiguous, and in their ambiguity, quite human. Gorki has been criticized consistently for creating characters whose believability is compromised for the sake of his work's political messages. In this case, however, although Luka and Sahtin do convey strong political messages, and Sahtin delivers speeches which are slightly implausible, their ambiguous natures—the fact that they do not act in prescribed, consistent ways— make them more like real people, and thus more believable. In this way they also reflect the very ambiguous, conflicted nature of the author, who was known both for his political radicalism and for being profoundly sentimental. The conflicted nature of *The Lower Depths* is what has provoked debate and discussion over the years, and in so doing, kept both the characters and the play alive.

Richard Hare, in *Maxim Gorky: Romantic Realist and Conservative Revolutionary,* reports that "According to Gorky, Luka should have been a sly old fellow, who had become soft and pliable through

WHAT DO I READ NEXT?

- *Twenty-Six Men and a Girl,* published in 1902, is considered Gorki's best short story. It describes the brutal conditions of a provincial bakery.

- *Anna Karenina,* written By Leo Tolstoy in 1877, is one of the most widely read Russian novels ever, and considered an artisitic masterpiece. This story of love, romance, deceit and jealousy is characteristic of traditional Russian themes in literature.

- Anton Chekhov's *The Cherry Orchard* was, like *The Lower Depths,* produced by Stanislavsky's Moscow Arts Theatre. Written in 1904, Chekhov's characters are dominated by an atmosphere of hopelessness and disillusionment, much the way Gorki's characters are.

- Beween 1930 and 1937, reform-oriented John Dos Passos wrote his U.S.A. trilogy, *The 42nd Parallel, 1911,* and *The Big Money.* These experimental novels paint a portrait of America through stream of consciousness and news articles.

- Upton Sinclair's *The Jungle* (1906) shocked the world with its gruesome depiction of conditions in a meat-packing plant. Controversy over the novel colored the labor movement at the time.

- *Cesar Chavez: Labor Leader,* written by Maria E. Cedeno in 1993, details the life and times of America's most prominent labor leader of the late 20th century.

---

having been kicked around a lot." Hare continues, "Luka's rule of conduct was that men wanted to forget hard facts and be consoled; they had no need of truths which did not help them. If truths were so painful that they destroyed self-confidence, let them remain concealed." The Actor's experience with Luka exemplifies this; Luka comforts the alcoholic actor with promise of a clinic where he can be cured, although he cannot tell him where it is. The Actor is expected to gain solace from this promised clinic, without the benefit of actual, substantial support. As the advocate of the "consoling lie," Luka comforts characters with his stories, but leaves them even more disheartened after his departure. In the case of the Actor, he is so disheartened he kills himself.

In *Maxim Gorky, the Writer,* F.M. Borras suggests,

> The influence of Gorky's particular view of Tolstoy upon his concept of Luka is ... unmistakeable.... Gorky regarded Tolstoyan theories of self-perfection, self-simplification, and non-resistance to evil as spiritual opiates through which the great man encouraged thinking people to devote their attention to problems of personal life instead of to revolutionary activity; Luka appears from nowhere in the dark dosshouse of the brutal, tyrannical Maikhail Kostylev, filled with human wrecks, and indulges their fancy with dreams of escape from the unbearable reality of their lives, instead of urging them to overthrow the tyrant who exploits them.

Luka's promises of a utopian tomorrow suggest the dangers of such ideology; rather than incite the lodgers into action to change their circumstances, he lulls them into complacency. This is most clear when Luka consoles Anna with promise of peace after death. When Anna suggests that she might live a little longer, Luka laughs and replies, "For what? To fresh tortures." In effect, he dissuades her from hope for change.

History suggests that this is the Luka that Gorki intended. Dan Levin reports in *Stormy Petrel* that "Gorky himself insisted Luka was a charlatan." However, he continues, "the heart has its own reasons. Luka is extremely complex—as complex as his maker." He goes on to report the way Kachalov, one of the Moscow Art Theatre's stars, described a rehearsal of Act II with Gorki.

> "'When he began to read the scene,'' Kachalov wrote, "in which Luka consoles Anna on her deathbed, we held our breaths, and a wonderful stillness reigned. Gorky's voice trembled and broke. He stopped,

remained silent for a moment, wiped a tear with his finger, and tried to resume his reading, but after the first few words he stopped again and wept almost aloud, wiping his tears with a handkerchief. 'Ugh, devil,' he mumbled, smiling with embarrassment through his tears, 'well written, by God, well done.'"

From this description it is clear that Gorki was moved by a part of Luka and his ability for compassion. The scene with Anna does ring true, in a way that contrasts with, for example, Luka's means of comforting Nastiah in Act III. In this scene, Luka appears glib in his insistence that he believes her implausible story, and clearly only means to soothe her in the moment. However, at other points, Luka offers sound advice with solid motives, such as in Act II, when he urges Pepel to avoid Wassilissa and run away with Natasha. The advice is pragmatic, in that Wassilissa is a dangerous woman, and both Natasha's and Pepel's needs would be met by such a union. Luka also demonstrates some challenge to Wassilissa and Kostilioff, contrary to assertions that he is a model of non-resistance. When he and Wassilissa meet in Act I, he tells her, "You are not very hospitable, mother," and in Act III he counters Wassilissa and Kostilioff's threats with indicting sarcasm. This incongruity in Luka is characterized by Levin such that, "Both drives are in Gorky: rebellion, and holy wandering. This is why when seen from one angle Luka is a fraud, from another, Gorky's deepest projection."

Sahtin is admittedly a less developed and less complex character than Luka. F.M. Borrass supports this: "Sahtin plays a relatively small part in the conversations and discussions that make up the first three acts." For the most part Sahtin maintains a drunken, upbeat realism throughout the play, consistently challenging Luka for soothing the other tenants with stories. His realistic outlook verges on the harsh; in Act II he tries to dissuade the Actor that he will be cured of his alcoholism, and his only response to Anna's death is, "The dead hear not. The dead feel not." Although this is the strongest impression of him throughout the play, it is revealed in Act II in his conversation with Luka that he went to prison for killing a man in defense of his sister. This, and the fact that he protects Nastiah from a threatened assault from the Baron in Act IV, support some chivalric impression of Sahtin, which lends itself to the speeches he makes in that act.

Act IV begins with the remaining characters discussing Luka. Through their perspectives, the audience has another opportunity to assess his char-

" SAHTIN'S MONOLOGUES SUMMARIZE A RESPONSE, ADVOCATING TRUTH OUT OF RESPECT FOR MANKIND, TO LUKA'S MINISTRATIONS OF THE CONSOLING LIE."

acter; the Baron, for example, claims he was a charlatan, while the Tartar asserts he had a true heart. Sahtin launches into his first monologue with the imperative, "Be still! Asses! Say nothing ill of the old man. . . . He did tell them lies, but he lied out of sympathy, as the devil knows. There are many such people who lie for brotherly sympathy's sake. . . ." Although he validates Luka's motivation for lying, he counters it with his primary assertion in the play, "The lie is the religion of servant and master . . . the truth is the inheritance of free men!" He continues later with, "How loftily it sounds, M-a-n! We must respect man . . . not compassion . . . degrade him not with pity . . . but respect."

Sahtin's monologues summarize a response, advocating truth out of respect for mankind, to Luka's ministrations of the consoling lie. However, the power of these speeches is diminished by the fact that Sahtin is drunk when he delivers them, and the fact that they come from this seemingly minor character's mouth. Levin reports that "Gorky himself said that in Sahtin's mouth the lordly speech sounded 'pale' and 'strange,' but that there was no one else into whose mouth to put it." Borrass confirms, "Gorky revealed his disquiet at this ambivalence in a letter to K.A.Pyatnitsky dated 15 July 1902, in which he said that Sahtin's speech extolling Man 'sounded out of place in his mouth,' but that no other character in the play was suited to make it." Sahtin's statements about truth are in keeping with Gorki's political leanings in the sense that they credit the individual with the power to make change (and overthrow Czarism, for example). Yet the fact that they come from Sahtin suggests that the truth is not the unqualified answer to the problems of the lodgers, but perhaps that it is part of a larger, more complicated solution.

In his essay *How I Studied,* Gorki writes that as a child he learned from books that "All men were suffering in one way or another; all were dissatisfied with life and sought something that was better, and this made them closer and more understandable to me." He reports that they taught him "a sense of personal responsibility for all the evil in life and evoked in me a reverence for the human mind's creativity." In the same collection (*On Literature*) he writes to Leo Tolstoy, "I believe profoundly that there is nothing on earth better than man, and I even say—twisting Democritus' sentence to suit my own ends—that only man really exists, all the rest being merely opinion. I have always been, and will always be a Man-worshipper, only I am incapable of expressing this properly." Couched in these terms, his compassion for the human condition is not so incongruous with his advocacy for man's power through truth. As personifications of this two-sided, insoluble ethical question, Luka and Sahtin reflect not only the complexity of the author, but the complexity of character itself.

Source: Jennifer Lynch, for *Drama for Students,* Gale, 2000.

Victor Erlich

In the following essay, Erlich discusses Gorki's attitude toward truth and lying, suggesting that Gorki may have accepted the need to lie to further the truth but also realized the effect of lying upon people's perception of the truth.

The theme of truth versus illusion, of reality versus invention, haunts Maksim Gorky's oeuvre from his early story *"About the Siskin Who Lied and the Woodpecker Who Loved the Truth"* down to his interminable swan song *The Life of Klim Samgin,* whose unlovely hero is obsessed by the notion of having "invented" himself. Thus, what I will be offering here is no more than a few reflections on the Pushkinian dichotomy of "base truths" versus "the uplifting illusion" in Gorky's life and work or, to put it differently, no more than a gloss on Khodasevich's telling reference to Gorky's "extremely tangled attitude toward truth and lying, an attitude which was revealed early on and which exerted a crucial influence both on his work and on his life."

Lest this tack be construed as unduly invidious, let me offer, in haste, some admissions and distinctions. For one thing, Gorky is not alone among major Russian writers in allowing for the therapeutic value of illusion. Suffice it to mention that paragon of artistic integrity and clear-eyed lucidity, Anton Chekhov. The persistent pipe dream of the Prozorov sisters, "To Moscow, to Moscow!" is portrayed empathically as a way of coping with a profoundly dispiriting reality. And if we rephrase the dichotomy that is at the center of these remarks as "reality versus dream," is not the intrinsic superiority of the latter to the former one of the time-honored topoi of Romanticism? Nor is this stance necessarily a matter of seeking refuge from "revolting actuality" in dreams. (Need I recall here Gogol's Piskarev: "Oh, how revolting is reality! What is it compared to the dream?")

In a more active brand of Romanticism, clearly more germane to the young Gorky's "folly of the brave"-type rhetoric, "the given" is often seen as no more than a lump of inert matter, malleable and almost infinitely transformable by human will, commitment, and faith. Some of us will recall Adam Mickiewicz's early poetic manifesto "Piesn Filaretow": "For where hearts are on fire, where the spirit holds sway," the dead truths of science need not apply.

And yet Gorky's case is somewhat special, if not necessarily unique. For one thing, while Chekhov refuses to scorn the lovely sisters' daydreaming, he is not in the least implicated in their illusions. For another thing, in the early Gorky we are often confronted with the uneasy hybrid "romantic naturalism." To quote Khodasevich once more: "Gorky began to portray his none too real characters against the backdrop of thoroughly realistic stage sets." Moreover, and perhaps more important, his temperamental predisposition for romantic voluntarism coexisted rather precariously with other elements of the quasi-scientific worldview toward which he was groping—a philosophy that was too strongly tinged with historical materialism to be openly dismissive of the claims of material reality.

But let us dispense with generalities and get down to cases, or, to be exact, to the salient case in point: for *The Lower Depths* (*Na dne*), Gorky's most famous and, despite some glaring flaws, most arresting play, is a stark if strangely inconclusive dramatization of the theme first sounded in Gorky's early parable.

You will recall the siskin's unexpectedly bold challenge to the conventional wisdom of resignation and passivity. It rises to urge fellow birds to fly forward to the land of happiness that beckons from afar. The reality-oriented woodpecker sagely intervenes to point out that the land of happiness does not exist and that what lies ahead is either a bird trap or, at best, the world being round, a return to the same thicket. The defeated siskin muses: "The woodpecker may well be right, but who needs his truth if it weighs like a stone on one's wings?"

In *The Lower Depths* the role of the woodpecker is assumed by one of the inmates of Kostylev's squalid flophouse, the dour capemaker Bubnov: "Now I don't know how to tell lies. What good are they? What I say is—give 'em the whole truth just as it is." Luka, who enters the stage in the middle of act 1 only to exert a pervasive influence on the wretched assemblage until the end of act 3, takes a different view of the matter. When the spirited young thief, Pepel, whom he urges to seek a better life in Siberia, that land of golden opportunity, accuses the old man of fibbing, he answers in words that unmistakably echo the siskin's: "Anyway, what do you want the truth for? The truth might come down on you like an ax."

It is a matter of some moment that the champion of "truth" in *The Lower Depths* should be one of the bleakest among the derelicts. The epitome of weary resignation and grim adjustment to degrading reality, Bubnov—to echo another early Gorky dichotomy—is a "garden snake" (by contrast to the falcon of the oft-quoted parable) par excellence.

But how about Luka? Who is this professional "comforter" who offers to nearly everyone a word of solace or encouragement? Is he a holy wanderer or a fraud? To put it differently, is he a man of compassion and kindness or a canny purveyor of false hope, or both? Clearly, a tenable interpretation of *The Lower Depths* hinges on a more or less plausible answer to this query.

Predictably, Russian Marxist criticism, whether of prerevolutionary or of Soviet vintage, has had little use for Luka. (Though his message is at times elusive and equivocal, one thing is certain: it is a far cry from the clarion call to revolutionary struggle against the social order presumably responsible for the existence of such petty infernos as the Kostylev night lodging.) More noteworthy is the fact that Gorky himself arrived early on at a negative view of the play's chief protagonist and expressed it over the years with increasing vehemence.

There is no dearth of evidence that this was not his initial position or, in any case, not his initial attitude. M. F. Andreeva has recorded a moving scene. On September 6, 1902, Gorky read *The Lower Depths* to the actors of the Moscow Art Theater: "Gorky read splendidly, especially the

> "CLEARLY, WHERE THE MAIN REQUIREMENT IS NOT CONGRUENCE WITH SOME OBSERVABLE FACT BUT RATHER UPLIFT AND EDIFICATION, THE VERY NOTION OF TRUTH IS EFFECTIVELY SUBVERTED."

part of Luka. When he came to Anna's death, he couldn't contain himself and burst into tears. He tore himself away from the manuscript, looked at us all, and said, 'A good, a damned good job of writing!'" Another reading of *The Lower Depths* by Gorky elicited similar testimony from a Moscow writer, Teleshov: "He read very well and held his audience spellbound, especially by the part of the old man Luka." And V. A. Lunacharskii was clearly assuming that Gorky was strongly drawn to the old wanderer when adjudging *The Lower Depths* the author's temporary fall from grace.

It is a matter of record that shortly after the resounding success of *The Lower Depths* Gorky turned his back on what was arguably his most effective, certainly his most intriguing dramatic creation. As early as 1910, according to Piatnitskii, Gorky called Luka a "crook": "Luka is a crook. He actually does not believe in anything." The abuse escalates in a much later conversation with one D. Lutokhin: "What a crummy old man this Luka is! He deceives people by sweet lies and lives off them. From the outset, I conceived the wanderer as a con man and a crook, but Moskvin [who played Luka in the first Moscow Art Theater production of *The Lower Depths*] was so convincing that I did not want to argue with him." Parenthetically, this curious authorial self-effacement vis-a-vis the admittedly brilliant actor sounds a trifle unconvincing, the more so since Moskvin's interpretation of the part, though clearly engaging, was not as positive as it might have been. According to Iu. Iuzovskii, a number of reviewers took Moskvin to task for overemphasizing Luka's slyness at the expense of his kindness. The final authorial unmasking of Luka is found in Gorky's much-quoted 1933 article "On Plays" ("O p'esakh"). Luka, it turns out, represents the most harmful and most repelling kind of comforter—the type of cold, cunning, self-serving manipulator who tells suffering people comforting lies in order to get them off his back: "This is the kind of comforter Luka was intended to be, but apparently I did not carry it off." For once, it is difficult not to agree.

To suggest that this retrospective denigration finds scant support in the text is not to claim that Luka as he actually appears in the play is an unambiguously positive character, for he cuts a thoroughly unheroic figure. When the dying Anna compliments him on his "softness," he counters her praise with a candid pun: "I've been put through the wringer—that's why I'm soft" ("Miali mnogo— ottogo miagok"). Having been "pummeled" by life, he takes few chances. When Kostylev and Pepel fatally collide, Luka takes advantage of the turmoil and slips away quietly. He may or may not believe in the afterlife that he invokes while ministering to Anna, in the bright prospect he holds out to Pepel, or in the free-of-charge hospital for alcoholics that would cure the Actor of his addiction and restore to him his professional identity. But if Luka lies knowingly—which, in view of his scant concern with truth, is a strong possibility—he does so, I submit, not for his personal gain but out of compassion for his fellow humans.

Interestingly enough, this happens to be the contention of the protagonist, who comes as close as anyone in the play to being the authorial mouthpiece, notably Satin; conversely, it is the unspeakable Baron who, after Luka's quick getaway, declares him "a fake." To be sure, Satin is not uncritical of the "old man": at the beginning of the postmortem he likens him to "soft bread to the toothless." And in the course of his impassioned but rather incoherent monologue, he intones at some point: "Lies are the religion of slaves and bosses. Truth is the god of the free man." Yet, if act 4 was supposed to feature a post-factum unmasking of the false prophet, this does not quite come off. For in spite of a significant difference of emphasis, Satin's overquoted harangue is at least as much a consequence of Luka's intervention as it is a challenge to his message: "The old man had a head on his shoulders. He had the same effect on me as acid on the old, dirty coin—let us drink to his health." Also, "Don't touch her! Don't hurt another human being! I can't get that old man out of my head!" Shortly thereafter Satin revises the message: "We have to respect man, not pity him, not demean him with our pity!" Though the polemical intent here is obvious, it is equally apparent that Satin has been stirred by Luka's meeker preaching into his ringing—and at least to this reader somewhat hollow and unearned—celebration of man. (Whether one should be grateful to Luka for having triggered one of the most tiresome clichés in modern Russian literature—"Man! . . . It has such a proud ring!"— is quite another matter.)

More broadly, Luka's presence in the Kostylev flophouse proves as much a stimulant as a tranquilizer. However tame or "toothless" his gospel, it injects a discordant and humanizing note into the dark and brutish universe of the play. The notion that every human being, however lowly, destitute, or sinful, is worthy of concern, that, to quote Mrs. Willy Loman, "attention must be paid," may not set the world on fire, but for the profoundly demoralized and dispirited denizens of the Kostylev hellhole, it proves strangely catalytic.

That Luka is at his best or at his most demonstrably benign in dealing with a terminal case such as Anna's—that is, in comforting a dying woman, virtually abandoned by everyone, including her harsh, dejected husband—is as much a commentary on the nature of the situation into which the wanderer has stumbled as on the built-in limitations of his ministry. When at the conclusion of his wide-ranging and hitherto judicious essay "Ideas and Images" Iuzovskii speaks of Luka's "total bankruptcy" and his "catastrophic" impact on the proceedings, he clearly yields to the Soviet Gorky scholar's characteristic temptation—that of Luka-bashing. For as the critic admits earlier, no one, least of all a frail old man without a passport, could have prevented the bloody encounter between Pepel and Kostylev. True, the blame for the Actor's suicide could arguably be laid at Luka's door. After a brief moment of euphoria, the hapless Actor must have realized that he was too far gone to be able to shake off his crippling addiction. But even if in his case the attempt at rescue or cure proved counterproductive, indeed lethal, it simply pointed up the hopelessness of the patient's condition. Ironically, the purveyor of "exalting illusion" has produced a moment of truth.

Now this is no more than one possible diagnosis of the Luka syndrome. (One of the refreshingly un-Gorkyan qualities of *The Lower Depths* lies in its allowing, indeed encouraging, more than one reading.) What is incontestable and possibly significant is the avowed discrepancy between Gorky's alleged intentions vis-a-vis Luka and what he has actually wrought. So is the fact that, in looking back upon his most resounding dramatic success, Gorky should have been drawn into increasingly harsh and simplistic verdicts that were demonstrably at variance with the actual tenor of the play. Was his "protesting too much" a symptom of an unresolved inner conflict, of a struggle with a part of himself he was eager to submerge or control? Or is it that his instinctive attraction to any attempt to embellish and to inject color, spark, and hope into intolerably grimy and degrading reality was being overtaken and reduced to the status of a temporary "lapse from grace" by a more exacting, more doctrinaire, and more relentlessly activist mode of mythmaking?

At the time when Gorky found *The Lower Depths* unsuited for the Soviet repertory without drastic revisions, he was about to assume the mantle of the patron saint of Socialist Realism. He had already become the most authoritative and influential literary spokesman for Soviet culture and society. As some of us will recall, at the dawn of the Soviet system he had his differences with its architects, and he stated them with remarkable clarity and forthrightness. Yet en route to his triumphal homecoming, he stifled such lingering doubts as he may have had in order to commit himself with a quasi-religious fervor to what he saw primarily, I believe, as a grand and inevitably costly project of rousing Russia out of age-old inertia and of releasing and mobilizing the immense dormant energies of the Russian people for creative toil, for industrial and cultural construction (*stroitel'stvo.*).

Significantly enough, when Gorky recalled his initial "wavering," he spoke of it by referring to such dichotomies as personal observation versus a theorist's vision or the present versus the future. In a 1933 letter to the playwright A. Afinogenov, he avers: "In 1917 my empiricism served as a basis for my skeptical attitude toward the victorious proletariat. The theoretician [Lenin] turned out to be stronger than the empiricist, closer to the historical truth; I have made a costly mistake." Another major difference between himself and Lenin, claimed Gorky in a letter of April 13, 1933, to his biographer, Ilia Gruzdev, had to do with their respective vantage points: "It is impossible to reach the proper altitude of a vantage point without the *rare ability* to look at the present out of the future." Let me suggest at this point that this "rare ability"—a salient aspect of the utopian or millenarian frame of mind—has far-reaching consequences. For if what matters most, or if all that really matters, is a future whose total radiance is vouchsafed, indeed made imperative, by the total hatefulness of the past, then the ontological status of the immediate, the observable, is reduced accordingly. The present in this scheme is no more than a brief and necessarily unpleasant prelude to a preordained bliss. Its hardships, ordeals, or, if need be, horrors fade into insignificance or near irrelevance, as they are no more than way stations en route to the Promised Land. To put it differently, it is easy to construe what is demonstrably and bleakly but only provisionally there as somehow less real than what is dimly perceived, if at all, on the horizon.

Now it is my contention that, at the late stage of his far-flung career, Gorky's congenitally ambivalent or "tangled" attitude toward mere fact made him singularly vulnerable to the temptations of political utopianism and especially prone to deny recalcitrant realities or to explain them away. Perhaps the most dismal example of this tendency is the notorious collective volume in which, under Gorky's aegis, thirty-four gifted Soviet writers— Gorky was forever mindful of literary quality—cheerfully reinterpreted a major forced labor camp as an educational institution. And then there is a revealing outburst, briefly referred to by Khodasevich, in a 1929 letter to an incisive emigre essayist, E. G. Kuskova, who had just accused Gorky of taking a one-sidedly favorable view of the Soviet regime:

> The fact is that I hate with a passion the truth which for 99% of the people is an abomination and a lie. I know that reality is miserable for 50 million who make up the masses of the Russian people and that men have need of another truth which does not debase them but which lifts their energy in toil and creation. What is important for me is the rapid and general development of the human personality, the birth of a new . . . man. What is important for me is that a worker in a sugar refinery reads Shelley in the original. He is an excellent man, full of fervor and confidence. He does not need this impoverishing and lying truth in which he defeats himself and has need of a truth in which he creates himself.

It would be churlish and pettily empiricist to require statistics about Shelley-lovers at the Soviet sugar refineries. What is more serious is the hasty dismissal of the avowed misery of fifty million people. Yet especially unsettling and germane to my argument is the rhetorical manipulation of the word *truth,* the slippery distinction between two kinds of truth—the good (mobilizing, uplifting) and the bad (disheartening, paralyzing). Clearly, where the main requirement is not congruence with some observable fact but rather uplift and edification, the very notion of truth is effectively subverted.

It is this instrumental approach to truth that informs some of the advice that the grand old man of Soviet literature was dispensing to his younger confreres in the 1930s. Solicitude for talent, delight in genuine creativity, had always been one of Gorky's most admirable characteristics. His encouragement of, and empathy for, that spirited band of gifted and searching young writers, the Serapion Brothers, including their fiery spokesman, the irrepressible Lev Lunts, was first and foremost testimony to Gorky's concern with the quality of Russian prose fiction. Yet it was also a token of his regard for the freewheeling Russian literary imagination. Gorky the Socialist-Realist pundit is much more circumspect and pragmatic. The core of his already-quoted letter to A. Afinogenov is a sharply critical assessment of the younger man's then-current play, *The Lie*. According to the editors of the Gorky issue of *Literary Heritage*, *The Lie*, despite several revisions, incurred Stalin's displeasure; as a result, "Afinogenov asked the theaters to remove *The Lie* from their repertories."

Gorky's judgment is largely negative. Were the play, he opined, to be performed before a select and ideologically mature audience, it would not do much harm. Yet to show it to millions of Soviet citizens would not be appropriate. Gorky goes on to invoke the awesome resonance of Soviet literature: "We write not only for the proletarians of our land but for the world proletariat."

Let us note, on the run, the openly paternalistic variation rung here on the traditional Russian theme of the writer's social responsibility. A man who in 1917-18, aroused by the revolution, felt that nothing less than candor was owed to the people now seems to urge a distinction between two truths—the exoteric and the esoteric. As it happens, what is at issue here is precisely the legitimacy of tampering with the truth for the good of the cause. At some point in *The Lie* a Communist would-be intellectual (*intelligent*) declares: "The masses ought to trust us, without asking whether this is true or not." Another protagonist, apparently a well-intentioned but somewhat muddled activist, chimes in: "With a lie one can live snugly [lit. *teplee*, "warmly"]." Gorky is clearly unhappy about this: "If you intended to posit in this muddled fashion the necessity of lying in the struggle for the victory of the proletariat's universal truth, the effect of the way you have done it is to call into question the greatness of this truth."

I find it difficult to shake off the impression that what Gorky is objecting to here is not the nature of the sentiment expressed but infelicitous attribution. Gorky seems to allow that temporarily withholding from the masses the truth for which they are not ready, so as to hasten the triumph of "the proletariat's universal truth," may well be necessary. Yet in order to lend credibility to this proposition, Afinogenov would have to find a more impressive vehicle. By failing to do so, his play, if shown to a mass audience, would be apt to confuse an ideologically immature viewer, not to mention the fact that its inordinate candor might give aid and comfort to the "enemy."

Some Gorky watchers have claimed that he found it increasingly difficult to countenance this kind of moral double-bookkeeping. Presumably, the "base truths" of the terrible decade began to seep through the barrier of his insistent denials. Did he come to feel, as his long journey was coming to an end, that, to paraphrase his letter to Afinogenov, he "had made a costly mistake?" We may never know.

Source: Victor Erlich, "Truth and Illusion in Gorky: The Lower Depths and After: Essays in Honor of Robert Louis Jackson," in *Freedom and Responsibility in Russian Literature*, edited by Elizabeth Cheresh Allen and Gary Saul Morson, Northwestern University Press, Yale Center for International and Area Studies, 1995, pp. 191–98.

Paul G. Pickowicz

In the following excerpt, Pickowicz discusses Gorki's The Lower Depths *to show that the differences between it and the Chinese adaptation* Ye dian *are more significant than the similarities.*

Stage and screen productions of *Ye dian* [Night lodging] were quite familiar to urban Chinese born in the 1910s and early 1920s. The play was first performed in 1946 and won considerable acclaim. It must be regarded as one of the ten or twenty most important Chinese plays (*huaju*) of the first half of the twentieth century. The movie version was screened widely in China in spring 1948 and is generally viewed as one of the most serious films of the early post-war era. In the 1950s the play was staged in Singapore and other overseas Chinese communities. Both the play and the film were banned in China during the Cultural Revolution, but enjoyed a measure of renewed popularity in the early post-Mao period. Older people in particular expressed a strong nostalgic interest in Republican era works and thus were especially eager to see plays and films of this sort rehabilitated and relegitimized. In summer 1979 the play was restaged in Shanghai, and in fall 1983 the film was featured in Beijing and Shanghai in major retrospectives of notable pre-1949 movies (*Zhongguo dianying huigu.*)

Very little detailed scholarly attention has been paid to *Ye dian,* but short, glowing commentaries on its popularity and merits abound. Invariably these writings note that both the stage and film versions of *Ye dian* are "adapted" (*gaibian*) from Maxim Gorky's 1902 play entitled *The Lower Depths* (*Na dne.*) But what exactly does "adapted" mean? Almost nothing is said in such writings about the precise relationship between Gorky's work and the Chinese productions. Since critics have not been inclined to dwell upon the differences between the Chinese works and the Russian original, the impression is often left that the stage and screen versions of *Ye dian* strongly resemble what one finds in *The Lower Depths.* The distinguished film historian Cheng Jihua and his collaborators briefly discuss the film under the heading of "Ke Ling's adaptation based on Gorky's play." Jay Leyda goes so far as to refer to the movie as Huang Zuolin's "filming of Gorky's *[The] Lower Depths.*"

A related matter is the connection between the Chinese play and the Chinese movie. A biographical sketch of Ke Ling, who co-authored the stage play and single-handedly wrote the screenplay, observes that the film is a "cinematized" (*dianyinghua*) variation of the play, but that the "content [of the film] is basically the same as [the content of] the play." Cheng Jihua and his co-editors write that "With the exception of a reduction in the number of lines for [the character] Jin Buhuan, a comparison of the film *Ye dian* and the stage adaptation shows that the rest is basically the same. The film adopts (*caiqu*) some of the plot (*qingjie*) and characters (*renwu*) from the original Gorky work, but what it describes is Chinese social life. To be more precise, the film *Ye dian* is a new creation that refers to the original work." Vague as these characterizations may be, they share one thing in common: they underscore essential continuities that link all three works. In brief, the underlying spirit of Gorky's play was retained in the sinified stage and screen adaptations. Writing in 1947, director Huang Zuolin himself emphasized the commonality of "meaning" (*yisi*) that bound the Chinese play to the Russian original.

These types of commentaries simply do not prepare one for a comparative reading of the three texts. The Chinese play and movie most certainly brought Gorky's original work into the mainstream

> A SECOND BASIC POINT ABOUT THE PLAY IS ITS DEEPLY PESSIMISTIC IMPLICATIONS. GORKY'S PORTRAIT OF THE DOWNTRODDEN MASSES IS EXTREMELY DARK AND GRIM (OR, AS ONE CRITIC PUT IT, 'BLEAK AND SULLEN.')"

of twentieth-century Chinese stage and film culture, but the sinification process fundamentally altered the work. The discontinuities are far more pronounced than the continuities. Furthermore, as Ke Ling pointed out to me in a 1983 interview, the Chinese play and the Chinese movie are strikingly different. Gorky might have been able to recognize the contribution of his own work to the Chinese stage production, but he probably would have denied the existence of any substantive link between *The Lower Depths* and the remarkably sentimental Chinese movie.

The Lower Depths: A Russian Play

To understand better the relationship between *The Lower Depths* on the one hand and Ke Ling's screenplay and Huang Zuolin's film *Ye dian* on the other, it is necessary to begin with a discussion of Gorky's four-act play, which was first performed by the Moscow Art Theater in 1902. Two general points need to be underscored. First, there is not much of a plot in this play, and what there is of a plot is relatively unimportant to the communication of the play's moral message about the relationship between illusion and truth. Similarly, no single character becomes a central focus of attention or dominates the dialogues. Instead, the play offers a collective sketch of the pathetic inhabitants of a rundown lodging house in a Volga town at the turn of the century. The inn caters to a "*bosyak*" clientele, that is, an underclass of people "who did occasional odd jobs but mostly lived by their wits," a "motley, shiftless, and often criminal fringe" that was especially numerous in port towns.

A second basic point about the play is its deeply pessimistic implications. Gorky's portrait of the downtrodden masses is extremely dark and grim (or, as one critic put it, "bleak and sullen"). Indeed, Gorky seems to be indicting Russian culture and society in general when he highlights the profound backwardness of this repulsive corner of society. Daily life involves little more than endless cycles of drunkenness, violence, vulgarity, fear and persecution. No heroic figures emerge and there are no indications that meaningful change is ever going to take place. In *The Lower Depths* human beings resemble a pack of caged animals, each struggling to survive one more day.

Sympathetic and hostile critics alike generally agree with this assessment. Harold Segel, who liked the work, has observed that the play is "static and oppressive in atmosphere" and that "the total environment of the cellar flophouse lingers longer in the memory than any finely etched individual portrait." Writing in 1903, Max Beerbohm, who despised the play, complained bitterly that *The Lower Depths* had "no meaning, no unity, nothing but bald and unseemly horror." He added that the theater audience demands of the playwright who deals with "ugly things" something more than the mere "sight of his subject matter." F.M. Borras noted that "When *The Lower Depths* was first presented most critics regarded it as a static play, a series of sketches from life without internal links, a naturalistic work almost devoid of action and dramatic conflicts." Anton Chekov, who liked almost everything but the last act, wrote a letter to Gorky in which he said, "you can say goodbye to your reputation as an optimist." Critics also note that Gorky strongly discouraged sentimental renditions of the play.

There is virtually no action in the first act. Instead, a host of colorful characters who reside in the inn are overheard in detailed and animated conversation on a wide range of topics. These figures include a thief named Peppel, a capmaker, a locksmith and his sickly wife, a pudgy woman who sells dumplings, a cobbler, a broken-down actor, a fallen aristocrat and his female companion who works as a prostitute, an incompetent local policeman, a couple of longshoremen, an elderly wanderer, and a murderer named Satin.

The lodging is run by its miserly owner, an old man named Kostylyov, and his vicious young wife, Vassilissa. Their family unit includes Vassilissa's younger sister, Natasha.

Peppel, the thief, works closely with Kostylyov and Vassilissa, who support and encourage his criminal activities. They buy, at significantly discounted prices, many of the objects Peppel steals. Furthermore, Peppel is Vassilissa's lover. Kostylyov is suspicious of the relationship, but has no concrete evidence. Peppel, however, has grown tired of Vassilissa and has decided to terminate their romantic ties. He is now attracted to her unmarried younger sister, Natasha. Vassilissa is aware of his new interest and realizes she has no future with Peppel, but she is jealous of Natasha and abuses her. Natasha, for her part, distrusts Peppel.

The second and third acts of *The Lower Depths* are the important ones for the purposes of this discussion, because they constitute the raw material reprocessed by Chinese stage and screen artists more than forty years later. It is in these acts that something resembling a plot surfaces from time to time. By dwelling on these traces of a plot, however, I do not mean to contradict the view that the plot is of secondary importance in this play.

In the second act two relevant developments take place. First, Anna, the locksmith's sickly wife, comes increasingly closer to death. Her abusive husband ignores her suffering. Luka, the elderly, somewhat senile and highly religious wanderer, tries his best to comfort Anna. He reassures her that there is a heaven, that she will go to heaven, that there is no suffering in heaven, and that any additional suffering she has to endure on earth will be worth enduring because she can look forward to an eternity of peace. Gorky scholars have paid an enormous amount of attention to Luka, a figure who specializes in giving hope to desperate people by telling them sweet lies about the future. Luka is a peddlar of "illusionary truth." It is Peppel, the thief, who cruelly spoils Anna's momentary peace of mind by loudly ridiculing the old man's soothing commentary. This episode ends with Anna lying distraught on her bed.

A bit later Vassilissa wants to discuss a private matter with Peppel. She knows their relationship is almost over and that Peppel is attracted to her younger sister. She offers to facilitate the union of Peppel and Natasha and to pay Peppel 300 rubles if he will do her a favor: arrange at once to have her husband, the innkeeper Kostylyov, killed. Peppel immediately rejects the offer. Neither he nor Vassilissa knows that Luka, the old wanderer, has overheard the entire conversation. The meeting ends when Kostylyov walks in, curses his wife, engages in a minor scuffle with Peppel and withdraws with Vassilissa. Luka, who has seen everything, senses that there will be more trouble and advises Peppel to seek a happy future by running away with Natasha.

Immediately thereafter Luka and Peppel discover that Anna, the locksmith's suffering wife, has died. They depart in search of Anna's husband, and the body is discovered for a second time by Natasha, who fears that one day she will end up the same way. Act two ends with a discussion (that does not include Peppel or Luka) about what to do with the body. It is agreed it should be buried soon, otherwise it might begin to smell. The residents urge the locksmith to report the death to the police immediately, lest the authorities think foul play was involved. A few tenants agree to make minor contributions to cover funeral expenses, not because they feel compassion, but because they want to get rid of the body as soon as possible.

It is not until the third act that the relationship between Peppel and Natasha is treated in detail. This requires a long dialogue in which an uncharacteristically charming Peppel finally declares his love for Natasha. In the end she agrees to run away with Peppel, as the friendly wanderer has suggested, but her distrust and suspicion of Peppel never really disappear. Unfortunately for the couple, Vassilissa has overheard the conversation and suddenly intrudes on the scene. Before long Kostylyov shows up and gets into another shouting match with Peppel. Eventually Peppel exits and Natasha is taken back into the family quarters.

After a substantial delay, Natasha is subjected to a savage beating by her ruthless sister. Her screams fill the inn and draw a crowd. Before long Peppel shows up and, together with others, gets into a fist fight with Kostylyov. It is important to note here that Peppel is seen striking Kostylyov. Suddenly the old man collapses and dies.

In an extremely interesting turn of events, Vassilissa accuses Peppel of beating her husband to death and demands that the police be summoned. Peppel responds by saying that she should be pleased because she had been encouraging him to kill her husband. Natasha does not know what to believe and concludes at the end of the act that she has been lied to by Peppel and that Peppel and Vassilissa conspired all along to get rid of the old man so they could be together. Both Peppel and Vassilissa are jailed by the police.

The final act, the one Chekov disliked so much, is much like the first one. There is very little action. The dialogue is mainly among the other residents of the inn, who speak randomly on a variety of unrelated topics. In other words, life is back to normal after the recent commotion. Peppel, Vassilissa, and Natasha do not appear in the last act. Luka, the wanderer, has vanished into thin air. It is revealed, however, that both Peppel and Vassilissa are still in jail and that Natasha simply disappeared after a brief stay in a hospital. Just before the curtain falls, the rambling conversations of the residents are interrupted by the news that the drunken actor, realizing that he too was given false hopes by the old wanderer, has just hanged himself. No one seems to care.

Source: Paul G. Pickowicz, "Signifying and Popularizing Foreign Culture: From Maxim Gorky's *The Lower Depths* to Huang Zuolin's *Ye dian*," in *Modern Chinese Literature*, Fall, 1993, Vol. 7, no. 2, pp. 7–31.

SOURCES

Bassett, Kate. "The Arts: Modern Depths Hit Heights," in *The Daily Telegraph*, August 26, 1999.

Borras, F. M. *Maxim Gorky the Writer: An Interpretation*, Oxford University Press, 1967.

Clarkson, Jesse D. *A History of Russia*, Random House, 1961, p. 364.

Gorki, Maxim. *The Lower Depths*, Branden Publishing Company, 1906, pp. 7-108.

———. *On Literature*, University of Washington Press, 1973, pp. 16, 22, 363.

Jones, Sumie. "Gorki, Stanislavsi, Kurosawa: Cinematic Translations of *The Lower Depths*," in *Explorations: Essays in Comparative Literature*, University Press of America, 1986, p. 189.

Longenbaugh, John. "Diving the Depths," in *Seattle Weekly*, November 19-25, 1998.

Scherr, Barry P. "Gorky The Dramatist: A Reevaluation," in *50 Years On: Gorky and His Time*, Astra Press, 1987, pp. 40-41.

Zamyatin, E. I. *A Soviet Heretic*, University of Chicago Press, 1970.

FURTHER READING

Borras, F. M. *Maxim Gorky the Writer: An Interpretation*, Oxford University Press, 1967, pp. 167-177.
  Borras discusses much of Gorki's work, and *The Lower Depths* in particular, in detail.

Becker, George J. *Realism In Modern Literature,* Frederick Ungar Publishing Co., 1980, pp. 151-162.

> This book provides a short discussion of Gorki's work, and substantial information on Realism in Russian literature and the evolution of Realism in general.

Levin, Dan. *Stormy Petrel: The life and Work of Maxim Gorky,* Appleton-Century, 1965, pp.88-95.

> This book both provides analysis of Gorki's work and contextualization of that work in his life.

Hare, Richard. *Maxim Gorky: Romantic Realist and Conservative Revolutionary,* Greenwood Press, 1962, pp. 56-61.

> Hare discusses Gorki's work in the context of his life, with focus on the influences of Romanticism and Realism over his writing.

Mourning Becomes Electra

EUGENE O'NEILL
1931

Mourning Becomes Electra is considered O'Neill's most ambitious work. In the play, he adapts the Greek tragic myth *Oresteia* to nineteenth-century New England. Generally, critics praised the play as one of O'Neill's best. Even though performances ran almost six hours long, audiences seemed to agree; it ran for 150 performances.

Like *Oresteia,* O'Neill's play features themes of fate, revenge, hubris, adultery, and honor. Many critics note that the play reflects his recurring concerns about the unsuccessful struggle of an individual to escape a tragic fate and the dark nature of human existence. The play is structured as a trilogy, with three different plays—*The Homecoming, The Hunted, The Haunted*—comprising the story.

AUTHOR BIOGRAPHY

In 1888 Eugene O'Neill was born in New York City to a theatrical family. His father was the noted actor James O'Neill, who became famous for his starring role in Alexander Dumas's *Count of Monte Cristo.* During his childhood, Eugene traveled with his family on the theatre circuit.

In 1906 O'Neill attended Princeton University before being expelled for a drunken prank later that

year. In 1907, he moved to New York, where he held several jobs. In 1909 he sailed to Central America to prospect for gold. Critics believe that his experiences in Honduras provide the setting and background for one of his most successful plays, *The Emperor Jones.* Disillusioned with the work, O'Neill returned to New York.

O'Neill worked as a seaman on ships sailing to South America, Africa, and Europe. His experiences as a sailor and working odd jobs on foreign waterfronts became the basis of his early maritime plays, such as *Thirst* (1914), *Bound East for Cardiff* (1916), *The Long Voyage Home* (1917), and *The Hairy Ape* (1922).

O'Neill returned to New York in 1911 and supported himself working odd jobs and living among the poor and downtrodden. These experiences provided the background for such later plays as *The Iceman Cometh* (1946) and *Long Day's Journey into Night* (1956). He worked as an assistant stage manager and actor with his father's theatre company, which provided him with theater experience.

In 1912, O'Neill worked as a reporter for the *New London Telegraph.* Diagnosed with tuberculosis in 1913, he spent six months in the Gaylord Farm sanitarium.

During his convalescence, O'Neill decided to become a playwright. After recovery, he entered Harvard to study with George Pierce Baker. He became involved with an experimental theater group, the Provincetown Players, who in 1916 put on his first produced play, the one-act *Bound East for Cardiff.*

O'Neill won the Pulitzer Prize four times and received the Nobel Prize for literature in 1936. At the time, he was only the second American writer to receive that international honor, the first being novelist Sinclair Lewis.

Despite his financial and critical success, O'Neill retreated into seclusion in the late 1930s. Though he continued writing, theater companies infrequently performed his plays. He returned to the stage with *The Iceman Cometh* in 1946. He died in 1953.

It took the posthumous revival of *Long Day's Journey into Night* in 1956 to reestablish his esteemed position in the American theater. The success of O'Neill's plays since then proves his stature among the most prominent of American dramatists.

PLOT SUMMARY

Homecoming: Act I

In a small New England seaport town a group that functions as a Greek chorus—Seth Beckwith, Amos Ames, Louisa, and Minnie—sit in front of the Mannon home. They explain that the patriarch of the family, Ezra Mannon, serves as a general in Grant's army. A wealthy man, he is expected to return soon to rejoin his wife, Christine, and his two children, Lavinia and Orin.

As the scene progresses, Peter Niles asks Lavinia for her hand in marriage, which she refuses. Lavinia discloses that she followed her mother to New York, where she was carrying on an adulterous affair with Adam Brant. Seth, the family's elderly gardener, implies to Lavinia that Adam is David Mannon's son. The Mannon family disinherited David, Ezra's uncle, after he ran off with a French-Canadian nurse of humble origins, Marie Brantome.

Adam's arrival upsets Lavinia; they talk about "the Blessed Isles" of the South Pacific, which he has visited and describes as an early paradise. Lavinia tells Adam she knows the secret of his parentage. Adam informs Lavinia that he intends to take revenge on Ezra, who refused to help Adam's poor, sick mother when she was dying.

Homecoming: Act II

Talking in Ezra's study, Christine admits that she feels incapable of loving her daughter Lavinia, because she reminds her of her disastrous honeymoon and poor sexual relations with her husband. Christine states that she prefers her son Orin, because she was pregnant with him while Ezra was away fighting in the Mexican War.

Lavinia confronts her mother about her affair with Captain Brant. Christine agrees to stop seeing him. When Adam arrives, Christine tells him what has occurred and encourages him to get her some poison: she will kill her husband. She has already told others that Ezra has a weak heart, and she plans to poison him and claim that he had a heart attack.

Homecoming: Act III

One week later, Ezra returns home from the Civil War. He is obviously weak and dispirited from his war experiences. He tells his wife that he wants to try to start again and improve their marriage. She pretends to agree.

Homecoming: Act IV

The next morning Ezra and Christine make love. He suddenly realizes that she made love with him because she hoped he would have a heart attack and die. Christine tells Ezra the truth about her affair with Adam and his parentage. Ezra has a heart attack. Instead of giving him his medicine, Christine gives him the poison. Lavinia enters as Ezra gasps his dying words: "She's guilty—not medicine."

The Hunted: Act I

The second play in the trilogy opens outside the Mannon house two days after Ezra's death. Again, a group of five local people form a chorus, gossiping about what has occurred and repeating rumors.

Orin returns from the war. Lavinia is jealous over her mother's preferential treatment of Orin. Christine, who despised her husband and loves her son Orin, hates Lavinia; she blames Lavinia for convincing Orin to go off to war.

The Hunted: Act II

Ezra's body is laid out in the study. Lavinia tries to convince Orin that Christine murdered their father and shows her brother the box of poison. Orin refuses to believe her, though he takes the poison from her and hides the evidence. He does not seem to care that his mother has murdered her father— in his perverted mind, he considers it a chance to have a sexual relationship with his mother.

However, when Lavinia informs him of Christine's affair with Adam, Orin becomes jealous and threatens to kill him. Lavinia takes the poison back from Orin and places it on her father's body. Christine sees the poison and begs Lavinia not to tell Orin.

The Hunted: Act III

Lavinia enters and Orin tells her about his heroic deeds during the war. She tries to convince him that Christine murdered Ezra, but he will not believe until her until she reveals that their mother did so to cement her relationship with her lover, Adam Brant.

The Hunted: Act IV

At night on a clipper ship at an East Boston wharf, Adam Brant has a discussion with the Chantyman. The Chantyman reports that Lincoln and Mannon are dead. He states that though reports

Eugene O'Neill

indicate Ezra died of heart attack, he knows from working for him that he was too cheap to have a heart. Brant gives him money to continue drinking and the Chantyman leaves.

Christine arrives to tell Adam about Ezra's death. Lavinia and Orin spy on them, and when Orin sees his mother embrace Adam and overhears her declarations of love he resolves to kill him. After Christine leaves, Orin shoots Adam. Then Orin and Lavinia mess up the cabin to make it seem as though Adam was killed in a burglary.

The Hunted: Act V

The next night, Hazel comforts Christine, who is secretly worried about Adam. Hazel leaves and Orin arrives, telling Christine he has murdered her lover. Orin wants to run away with his mother. Christine goes inside and kills herself.

The Haunted: Act I, Scene One

One year later, a chorus of local residents discusses the rumors that the Mannon house is now haunted. Lavinia and Orin enter; she looks like her mother Christine, while he resembles his father Ezra. Lavinia claims that the dead have "forgotten" them.

The Haunted: Act I, Scene Two

Inside the Mannon house, Lavinia and Orin discuss their recent trip to the "blessed isles," where Lavinia hoped to free Orin of his feelings of guilt for Christine's death. It becomes clear that while on vacation Lavinia had a sexual experience with an island man. She claims to love Peter and expresses hope that they will be married. She asks Peter and Hazel to help console Orin, and "make allowances for any crazy thing he might say."

The Haunted: Act II

Alone in Ezra's study, Orin writes a letter describing the many sins of the Mannon family. When Lavinia enters, he criticizes her for not trusting him. Lavinia admits to her sexual relationship with Avahanni, one of the islanders; faced with Orin's jealousy, she then denies it.

Orin fears losing Lavinia to Peter; furthermore, he is afraid that Lavinia will kill Orin to marry Peter. Orin promises to give Peter the confession letter if Lavinia goes through with the wedding or if Orin should die.

The Haunted: Act III

Peter and Hazel discuss their concerns about Orin with Lavinia: his behavior is increasingly erratic. Orin gives Hazel the confession, telling her that Lavinia must never marry and be happy, for "She's got to be punished!"

When Lavinia realizes that Hazel has read the confession, Lavinia agrees to "do anything" if she will return it to Orin. Orin retrieves the manuscript. When the others leave, he makes Lavinia call off her marriage with Peter and insinuates that they should commit incest as a way to bind themselves to each other. Lavinia refuses, crying out, "You're too vile to live! You'd kill yourself if you weren't a coward!"

Orin goes off to clean his pistol as Peter arrives. Peter wants to take the gun from Orin, worrying about letting him clean a weapon in his confused mental state. Lavinia insists on discussing their upcoming marriage. As they hear a pistol shot, she hides Orin's confession manuscript.

The Haunted: Act IV

Three days later, Seth sings as Lavinia picks flowers in front of the Mannon house. Hazel arrives and accuses Lavinia of driving her brother to commit suicide. Hazel begs Lavinia to break off her engagement with Peter, or at least let him read what Orin had written.

Lavinia refuses. When Peter arrives, she begs him to make love with her immediately. She asks him to want her so badly he would kill to have her, because that is what she's done, telling him, "I did that—for you!" Then, she calls out, "Want me! Take me, Adam!"

Shocked, Peter calls off the wedding. He demands to read Orin's confession. Lavinia admits that she and the islander had sex, that she was his "fancy woman." Peter leaves her for good.

Lavinia, as "the last Mannon," decides that she must punish herself. She orders the shutters on the windows nailed up to keep out the light. As the play ends, Seth pulls the window shutters closed as Lavinia walks into the house, closing the door behind her.

CHARACTERS

Amos Ames

A middle-aged carpenter, Amos and his wife Louisa form part of the chorus in *Homecoming* and *The Haunted*.

Louisa Ames

Louisa is the wife of Amos. She appears as part of the chorus of local people in *Homecoming* and has a taste for vicious gossip.

Doctor Joseph Blake

Doctor Blake is a "stout," "self-important" family physician, who, as part of the chorus in *The Hunted*, provides background on Ezra's medical condition. After relating Ezra's symptoms, Christine has convinced the doctor of the seriousness of her husband's heart condition. This helps Christine conceal the actual cause of Ezra's death—murder by poison.

Josiah Borden

A manager of the Mannon family's shipping company, Josh and his wife Emma appear as part of the chorus of town folk in *The Hunted*, providing insight into the backgrounds of Christine and the family.

Captain Adam Brant

Brant is the black sheep of the Mannon family; it is his quest for revenge that propels the play. When his father, David Mannon, is exiled from his family for marrying Marie Brantome, Brant's family falls into ruin. When he is old enough, he runs off to sea. When he returns, he discovers his father has drunk himself to death, and, shockingly, David's nephew, Ezra, refused to help Brant's poor, sick mother.

After his mother's death, Adam vows revenge on the other Mannons. This desire for vengeance motivates his pursuit of Christine and ultimately drives the play's action.

Chantyman

The Chantyman chats with Brant near the ship in *The Hunted* and gives him information about Ezra. Brant gives him money to continue drinking, and the Chantyman leaves.

Hazel

Hazel is Peter Niles' sister and Orin's fiancee. She loves Orin and tries unsuccessfully to separate him from his sister Lavinia. Less naive than her brother Peter, Hazel sees the evil surrounding the Mannon family; her efforts to save Orin from that evil fail.

Everett Hills

Everett Hills is a Doctor of Divinity of the First Congregational Church and married to Mrs. Hills. Both appear as part of the chorus of local people in *The Hunted*.

Mrs. Hills

Mrs. Hills is married to Everett Hills, a Congregational minister. Both appear as part of the chorus of local people in *The Hunted*.

Ira Mackel

Ira is a member of the chorus of townsfolk in *The Haunted*. He is a whiskered farmer who walks with a cane. Believing the Mannon house to be haunted, he and others bet Abner Small ten dollars that he cannot spend the night there.

Christine Mannon

Christine is Ezra Mannon's wife and mother of Lavinia and Orin. She hates her husband and has an incestuous love for her son. While Ezra was away fighting in the Civil War, she began a passionate affair with Adam Brant. They plan to kill Ezra so they can be together.

MEDIA ADAPTATIONS

- In 1947, RKO Pictures released an adaptation of the play, which starred Raymond Massey, Rosalind Russell, and Michael Redgrave. The film compresses the play's six hours of action into three.

When Ezra returns from the war, he and Christine make love, but she does so in hopes that he will have a heart attack and die. When he realizes this, he does have a heart attack. When he demands his medicine, she gives him the poison. He realizes that she has poisoned him while he is dying. After Brant is murdered by Lavinia and Orin, Christine commits suicide.

Brigadier-General Ezra Mannon

Ezra is Christine's husband and father of Lavinia and Orin. He is the patriarch of the Mannon family. As the play opens, he returns from the Civil War.

A hardhearted businessman, Ezra refuses to help his brother's Canadian-Indian wife Marie Brantome when she really needs it. As a result, she dies and her son, Adam Brant, vows revenge.

Realizing the precarious nature of his marriage to Christine, he hopes to reconcile with her after he returns from the war. He is oblivious to her plans to murder him until they are making love—the realization that she wants to kill him causes him to have a heart attack. Christine gives him poison instead of medicine and he dies.

Lavinia Mannon

Lavinia is the daughter of Ezra and Christine Mannon and Orin's sister. She is meant to resemble the Electra figure in O'Neill's retelling of the *Orestia*. She is a manipulative, evil woman.

Although she is somewhat in love with Captain Brant, she convinces Orin to kill him. She then drives her mother Christine to suicide. The two siblings travel to the South Seas to escape their mutual guilt and Lavinia sleeps with a local man. Exploiting Orin's feelings of guilt over Brant's murder and their mother's suicide, she drives him to commit suicide too.

Toward the end of the play, Lavinia almost believes it possible for her to be happy and escape the guilt of her past. Ultimately, she realizes that as the last Mannon, she has sinned and must punish herself. In the last scene, she orders the flowers removed from the house, the windows shut up, and closes herself inside, presumably never to exit alive.

Lavinia presents a complex character, with strong and forbidden desires as well as powerful, if reprehensible, needs for revenge. In a sense, she seems trapped in a web of emotional and sexual desires—for her father Ezra, her brother Orin, and her mother's lover Brant. Moreover, she acts without conscience—until the end, when her conscience comes back to haunt her.

Orin Mannon

Orin is the youngest son of Ezra and Christine. A First Lieutenant of Infantry, he served in the Civil War under his father and is recognized as a courageous soldier. After getting wounded, he returns from the war overcome by the death and destruction.

In love with his mother, Orin helps Lavinia murder her mother's lover, Brant. He does this to revenge the murder of his father; also, he is jealous of Brant's relationship with his mother.

Orin is engaged to Hazel. She wants to take Orin away from Lavinia, perceiving the destructive and sick bond the two siblings have. Yet Orin will not allow this; he even suggests to Lavinia that they consummate their relationship as a way of binding themselves together in sin and guilt.

Orin writes his confession and history of Mannon family sins, which he threatens to give to Peter if Lavinia leaves him. Orin's guilt and incestuous feelings lead to his destruction. He feels he has lost the love of his mother and of his sister.

Eventually Orin breaks his engagement with Hazel and commits suicide, "accidentally" killing himself while cleaning his gun.

Minnie

Part of the chorus of townsfolk in *Homecoming*, Minnie is Louisa's cousin. She is known as a gossip.

Captain Peter Niles

A member of the U.S. Artillery, Peter is Hazel's brother and Lavinia's boyfriend. He wants to marry her, but she keeps him at a distance. He becomes uneasy when she resists handing over Orin's confession. Finally, Lavinia shocks Peter by suggesting that they have sex prior to marriage.

In an emotional fit of passion, she cries out to him—not his name, but that her mother's lover, Adam Brant. Horrified, Peter ends their engagement, condemns Lavinia, and storms off. Though not a bad person, Peter seems naive, unable to see Lavinia's dark, complex personality.

Joe Silva

Silva is a member of the chorus in *The Haunted*. A Portuguese fishing captain, he is one of those who bets Abner Small that he cannot stay overnight in the supposedly haunted Mannon house. They win the bet, though Abner refuses to pay.

Abner Small

Abner forms part of the chorus of local people in *The Haunted*. He is the hardware store clerk who accepts the bet that he can spend the night in the supposedly haunted Mannon house. He runs out after a short time, refusing to pay the ten dollars he has lost.

THEMES

Revenge

Revenge serves as a primary motivation for the play's actions. Seeking to revenge the death of his mother, Marie Brantome, Adam hopes to destroy the Mannon family, especially Ezra.

The Mannon family is a complex web of revenge scenarios: Christine wants revenge on her husband for her unhappy marriage; Lavinia wants revenge on her mother for killing her father; Orin wants revenge on Brant for sleeping with his mother.

Paradise

Paradise is an obsession for many of the play's characters. As a seafaring family, early generations of Mannons had sailed to beautiful South Pacific isles. Orin wants to run away with his mother Christine—an attempt to escape societal norms so that he can sleep with his mother. Christine wants to go with her lover, Adam.

Eventually, Orin does eventually go to the islands with his sister Lavinia. During their visit, she has sex with one of the islanders. In O'Neill's play, the island paradise—offering erotic possibilities and freedom from materialism—becomes a symbol of all that New England society is not.

Incest

Incest and incestuous desire lie behind most of the relationships central to *Mourning Becomes Electra*. Ezra's daughter Lavinia loves her father; Christine's son Orin loves his mother, and Lavinia and Orin love each other.

While O'Neill presents these relationships as unconsummated desires, Orin does urge Lavinia to sleep with him in act three of *The Haunted*, hoping that by committing incest that they will be bound together in sin and guilt. His sister refuses.

Sin and Guilt

O'Neill's work illustrates his fascination with sin, guilt, punishment, and redemption. In *Mourning Becomes Electra*, the sins include murder (Christine's killing of her husband; Lavinia and Orin's killing of Adam); adultery (Christine's with Brant); suicide (Christine's and Orin's); and premarital sex (Lavinia's with the islander).

In a sense, Ezra murders Brant's mother by refusing the sick woman money for food and medicine. Also, Lavinia "kills" Christine and Orin by driving them both to commit suicide.

Orin's feelings of guilt lead him to write his confession, which he threatens to give to Peter if Lavinia marries him. At the play's end, Lavinia's guilt forces her to give up hopes of happiness and to punish herself, as the last Mannon, by rejecting love and shutting herself in the house.

STYLE

Chorus

Traditionally in Greek tragedies, the chorus consists of masked actors who dance and chant. Generally, they do not participate in the action itself, which allows them to remain objective and offer advice or commentary. They often present background information and represent the community's position or traditional values. In the *Mourning Becomes Electra* trilogy, the groups of local people whose conversations and actions open the plays serve as the chorus.

TOPICS FOR FURTHER STUDY

- Consider how setting the play after the Civil War and in New England impacts the play's themes and meaning.

- Several times during the play, music serves to underscore the themes of *Mourning Becomes Electra*. Discuss the role music plays in O'Neill's play. What do the songs tell us about the characters who sing them, and about the play and the character's actions in general?

- Compare and contrast O'Neill's play to the original *Oresteia*. Other than the obvious changes in setting, what other alterations did the playwright make? How do these changes function to modernize and deepen the play? What changes would you make to set it in the 21st century?

Expressionism

Expressionism is a style of art that expresses internal experiences and psychological truth. Such art does not present a realistic image of world, but instead tries to create in the viewer a powerful "true" experience of a particular emotion, feeling, or state of mind.

Many of O'Neill's plays have expressionistic elements: masks, which conceal the actor's faces; and asides, in which actors address the audience without others on stage hearing. Expressionistic elements in *Mourning Becomes Electra* include the pairing of characters (Lavinia resembles Christine and Orin resembles Ezra) and the symbolism of the Mannon house, which resembles a Greek temple.

Naturalism

Naturalism is a nineteenth-century theory that developed in the wake of Darwin's theory of evolution. Naturalists perceived people as products of their heredity and environment. Naturalistic drama presents a vision of human life as akin to that of animal nature, in which these Darwinian drives motivate people. In many ways, these forces of nature minimize or even eliminate the individual's free will.

Naturalistic elements in *Mourning Becomes Electra* include the ways the characters' personal histories and environments determine their actions and motivations.

Realism

Realistic theater attempts to present realistic character actions, situations, and motivations. Furthermore, the stage recreates the experience of a real situation. Realistic drama avoids melodramatic acting, stagy effects, and dramatic conventions like a *deus ex machina,* character asides, and soliloquies.

Setting

The setting refers to the place in which the play's actions take place. Settings often have a symbolic value. For example, the neoclassical architecture of the Mannon mansion in *Mourning Becomes Electra* resembles a Greek temple, so the setting reminds us that the play itself offers a retelling of a cycle of Greek tragedies.

HISTORICAL CONTEXT

Born in 1888, Eugene O'Neill's life spanned some of the most important events of contemporary history. While he played no actual role in the events themselves, the issues involved—particularly those related to democracy and materialism—figure prominently in his plays.

O'Neill came of age during America's Progressive Era. Interested in politics and political philosophy, the young playwright associated with the radicals and reformers who comprised his Greenwich Village and Provincetown circle of Bohemian friends.

A close friend of John Reed, the journalist known for his book about the Russian Revolution, *Ten Days That Shook the World,* O'Neill had a longtime affair with Reed's wife, the journalist Louise Bryant. Many critics believe that O'Neill based *Strange Interlude*'s love triangle on this experience. O'Neill's writings explore the problems confronting American society, particularly rampant materialism, loss of individuality, and lack of spiritual values.

During the first twenty years of the twentieth century, more than ten million European immigrants arrived in America. O'Neill's father and his family had come to America during an earlier wave of immigration, arriving from Ireland in 1850. Factory jobs and mass transit drew millions of people to the cities, and America became an increasingly urban nation. Many immigrants brought with them a tradition of union activity and joined the American labor movement.

During his presidency, Theodore Roosevelt attempted to regulate large corporate interests and enforce anti-trust statutes. In 1902, he forced an arbitrated settlement during a major coal strike. President William Howard Taft, though less aggressive than Roosevelt, generally continued his predecessor's progressive policies, breaking up the Standard Oil Company's monopoly, and establishing a Children's Bureau and Department of Labor.

President Woodrow Wilson urged banking reform and anti-trust actions, supported farm loans and a ban on labor by children under fourteen—though the Supreme Court deemed this later action unconstitutional. In 1920 the 19th Amendment to the constitution gave women the right to vote.

Domestically, politicians did little to end segregation, halt the rising influence of the Klu Klux Klan, or curb the practices that prevented many African Americans from voting. In two plays, O'Neill created a leading role for a black man: *The Emperor Jones* (1920) and *All God's Chillun Got Wings* (1924). Both plays appeared as productions of the Provincetown Theatre.

This was also an era of American imperialism. Overseas, the United States fought a war with Spain in 1898 and gained colonial influence in places like Cuba and the Philippines. In 1903, American gained dominance over Panama and began the construction of the Panama Canal.

In Europe, industrialization, colonialism, and militarism resulted in World War I. Wilson tried to maintain American neutrality, restricting trade with the warring parties. However, the United States entered the war in 1917. After the war ended in

COMPARE & CONTRAST

- **1931:** America is in the midst of a severe economic depression, known as the Great Depression. Led by President Franklin Roosevelt, the federal government proposes and implements a series of social programs known as "The New Deal."

  Today: The country benefits from a robust and growing economy. Although there is still a wide chasm between the well-off and poor segments of society, most people enjoy low interest rates, low unemployment, a booming stock market, and cheap and accessible sources of fuel.

- **1931:** Most Americans travel by train or ship. Commercial aviation is very limited, and cars are becoming more popular and financially viable for the middle classes. This improved mobility allows people to move from the cities into surrounding suburbs.

  Today: Most Americans travel by car and airplane. Airline price wars decrease airline fares, allowing many Americans to travel frequently and cheaply.

- **1931:** Robert Frost's *Collected Poems* wins a Pulitzer Prize, philanthropist Albert Schweitzer publishes *My Life and Thoughts*, Disney releases its first color film, *Flowers and Trees,* and the "Star-Spangled Banner" becomes America's National Anthem.

  Today: Frost remains a popular and influential poet. Schweitzer's ideal of dedicating one's life to serving others inspired many, as seen in Mother Theresa's work with the sick and Jimmy Carter's work for Habitat for Humanity. Today, most films we see on television and in theaters are in color.

1919, Wilson worked for the formation of the League of Nations, precursor to today's United Nations.

Declining wages, farm economy problems, protectionist tariffs, and overproduction of manufactured goods contributed to the Stock Market Crash of 1929 and the Great Depression, which threw millions of people out of work. While President Franklin Roosevelt's New Deal policies of government spending to stimulate employment did improve conditions somewhat, the American economy did not fully recover until the Second World War.

In *Mourning Becomes Electra,* O'Neill's symbolic use of the post-Civil War setting reveals his understanding of American history and ideology, raising parallels between an earlier war fought for firm ideological beliefs and WWI, which was fought in large measure over colonial issues. He also compares New England's nineteenth-century Puritan heritage with contemporary America, in which conformity and materialism contribute to cultural relativism and the lack of a moral compass.

CRITICAL OVERVIEW

In adapting *Oresteia,* Eugene O'Neill set himself a challenging task. He explains he that hoped to create a "modern psychological approximation of [the] Greek sense of fate" and sets the play in New England because it evokes the "Puritan conviction of man born to sin and punishment." Critics continue to debate to what extent O'Neill succeeded in his project.

In its early reviews, Brooks Atkinson praised the play as "Mr. O'Neill's masterpiece," and John Mason Brown characterized it as "an achievement which restores the theatre to its high estate."

However, Eugene Burr derided the play as a "marathon by an author who takes himself too seriously... who wastes his own and his audiences' time by delving into morbid psychology that is just as unreal, just as fundamentally unimportant—and certainly as unentertaining—as the sentimentality which is *verboten* [forbidden] by his devotees."

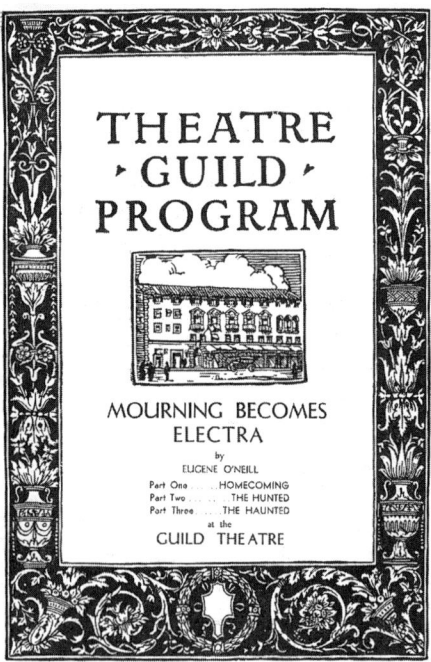

Playbill from O'Neill's Mourning Becomes Electra

According to George H. Jensen, O'Neill was an experimenter in technique who attempted ambitious projects; an "epigrammatic evaluation of O'Neill's career might be that he wrote some of the very best and some of the worst plays of the twentieth century."

Most critics consider the play one of O'Neill's best works. Some praise the piece for its insight into the human condition. Barrett H. Clark, for example, perceived the playwright's search "for a rational explanation of life and death, and what used to be called sin and evil."

Yet Clark also criticized *Mourning Becomes Electra* for a lack of emotion, describing it as "a tearless tragedy, remote, detached, august, artfully shaped, cunningly devised, skillfully related and magnificently conceived. It is concerned only indirectly with life as most of us see and feel it: it is comparable not so much to music or painting as to architecture."

Some critics characterize O'Neill's work as sensational, exploiting sex and violence without offering substantial motivation or explanation. For example, in *Mourning Becomes Electra,* his repeated use of incest shocks and promises some powerful thematic significance.

According to Clark, it instead lacked "complexity, darkness, or genuine passion . . . [it seems] the mentalized fantasy of an adolescent temperament, and totally incompatible with the portentous philosophical attitudes it is meant to support."

Frederic Carpenter concurred that the play suffers from excessive reliance on Freudian notions of the Oedipus complex (in which a male child loves the mother and wants to eliminate the father) and the Electra complex (in which the female child loves the father and wants to eliminate the mother):

> These protagonists [Orin, Christine, Lavinia, and Ezra] seem to have been born damned. Except for Electra [Lavinia], they do not achieve tragedy; they become merely the helpless victims of their inherited natures . . . this psychological equivalent of original sin.

While many critics perceive that Orin is motivated by jealous Oedipal rage against his mother's infidelity, Carpenter asserted that his acts were the product of his mad heroism during battle. This interpretation makes O'Neill's point more political than psychological, in that "Orin seems to be driven by the tortured conscience of all modern men, in their realization of the evil of world war."

According to Michael Manheim, *Mourning Becomes Electra* disguised the playwright's "compulsion to reveal (while carefully hiding) the personal melodrama of his family home." Manheim identified two key themes: the "events and emotions centering on Ella O'Neill's addiction and later death" and "O'Neill's hostility toward his mother."

Manheim maintained that these conflicts appear most prominently in the play with the "sinning" or "suicidal" Christine representing Ella, while the "outraged" Lavinia and "guilt-ridden" and Orin symbolize Eugene.

One reason for the contradictory nature of O'Neill's critical reception may stem from the stereotypically American notion that sees everything bigger as better. According to Brustein, O'Neill's work seemed "afflicted with the American disease of gigantism," which accounts for the playwright's epic ambitions.

Ideally, O'Neill hoped to see the six-hour trilogy performed one play a night over three nights. More than one critic believed the play would have benefited from cutting and compression. John Mason Brown no doubt expressed the thoughts of many when he wrote that parts of the play, particularly "*The Haunted,* seem overlong . . . That it is longer than it need be seems fairly obvious, as does the fact that, like so many of O'Neill's plays, it stands in need of editing.''

The other side in this debate about the epic pretensions of O'Neill's work, of course, claims that some stories—arguably that of the Mannon family—require a wealth of narrative detail and need to be told in epic fashion.

While praising *The Emperor Jones, Anna Christie,* and *Ah, Wilderness!,* Bernard De Voto found much of the playwright's other work—including *Mourning Becomes Electra*—falling short.

De Voto contended that at best O'Neill ''is only the author of some extremely effective pieces for the theatre. At worst he has written some of the most pretentiously bad plays of our time.''

De Voto also asserted: ''What he tells us is simple, familiar, superficial, and even trite—and because of a shallow misunderstanding of Freud and windy mysticism, sometimes flatly wrong.''

While admitting that O'Neill ''has given us many pleasurable evenings in the theatre,'' De Voto maintained that ''he has never yet given us an experience of finality, of genius working on the material proper to genius, of something profound and moving said about life. Just why, then, the Nobel Prize?''

While critics may debate the value of this play, almost all would agree that O'Neill has made important contributions toward today's American theatre. He moved beyond the early century's obsession with melodrama to embrace realism and naturalism, and lead the way for major dramatists to come, among them Edward Albee, Arthur Miller, and Tennessee Williams.

CRITICISM

Arnold Schmidt

In the following essay, Schmidt analyzes O'Neill's attempt to modernize Oresteia, *and how these changes affected the theme and structure of the play.*

Early in his composition of *Mourning Becomes Electra,* Eugene O'Neill stated his goal and problem: to create a ''modern psychological drama using one of the old legend plots of Greek tragedy for its basic theme,'' asking ''Is it possible to get [a] modern psychological approximation of the Greek sense of fate into such a play, which an intelligent audience of today, possessed of no belief in gods or supernatural retribution, could accept and be moved by.''

O'Neill also wanted to present a play with a uniquely American sensibility, and so he set the play in post-Civil War New England because it evoked the ''Puritan conviction of man born to sin and punishment.'' While O'Neill generally succeeded in his goal of adapting from an ancient Greek to a modern American viewpoint, in the process he changed the plays' character motivations, the ethical model, and the tragic ending. These changes have far-reaching thematic, psychological, and cultural implications.

To better understand *Mourning Becomes Electra,* we must examine the ancient Greek myth of *Oresteia.* The best-known retelling of the *Oresteia* might be the three-play cycle by Aeschylus.

The *Oresteia* myth concerns the house of Atreus, a doomed family cursed from its inception. According to legend, Atreus's grandfather, Tantalus, kills his son Pelops and serves the pieces of his body to the gods at a feast. Because of this atrocious crime, the gods restore Pelops to life and sentence Tantalus to eternal punishment in the underworld.

Atreus, one of the sons of Pelops and Hippodamia, becomes king of Mycenae. Cuckolded by his brother Thyestes, who covets his throne, Atreus seeks revenge. Atreus kills Thyestes's sons and serves them to their father at a banquet. Discovering Atreus' dastardly deed, Thyestes curses him and all his heirs.

Thyestes's son, Aegisthus, revenges his brothers' murder and kills Atreus. Thyestes takes over the throne of Mycenae, forcing Atreus' sons Agamemnon and Menaleus into exile. These events spark the tragic rivalry central to O'Neill's story between Agamemnon (Ezra Mannon) and Aegisthus (Adam Brant).

Agamemnon marries Clytemnestra (Christine), producing their daughters Iphegenia and Electra (Lavinia), and their son Orestes (Orin). Menaleus marries Helen. When Paris elopes with Helen, Agamemnon and Menaleus start the Trojan War to retrieve her.

While the Spartans (Menaleus is the king of Sparta) prepare their invasion fleet, Agamemnon goes hunting and kills a stag sacred to the goddess Diana, the virgin huntress. Angered by this

WHAT DO I READ NEXT?

- Aristophanes' *Lysistrata* (411 BC) is a comic—and perhaps the first—anti-war play.

- Stephen Crane's *Red Badge of Courage* (1895) describes the experiences of a young soldier during the Civil War.

- Jack London's *The Call of the Wild* (1903) considers whether people act the ways they do because of nature (genetics, hormones) or nurture (environment, family life, social experiences).

- Considered by many critics the perfect one-act play, John Millington Synge's *Riders to the Sea* (1904) chronicles the story of a mother who has lost her husband and all her sons to the sea.

---

act, Diane prevents the fleet from sailing unless Agamemnon sacrifices his daughter, Iphegenia. As a father, Agamemnon resists, but, believing Helen's rescue to be the will of the gods, he ultimately relents and agrees to Iphegenia's sacrifice. As the sacrifice begins, the goddess Diane changes her mind and spares Iphegenia, whisking her away to serve as a votive in a distant temple. Significantly, Agamemnon's family believes that Iphegenia is dead.

The role that Agamemnon plays in Iphegenia's death partly explains why Clytemnestra hates him and why she ultimately kills him. When Agamemnon departs for the Trojan War (As Ezra did for the Civil War), Clytemnestra (Christine) takes Aegisthus (Brant) as a lover, and plots her husband's murder.

After Agamemnon returns from the Trojan War, Clytemnestra and Aegisthus kill him. The rest of the *Oresteia* centers around Electra's and Orestes's plans, at Apollo's urging, to avenge their father's death by killing their mother and Aegisthus. Electra plays no part in the story's end, which tells of Orestes's persecution by the Furies for committing matricide.

A court eventually hears his case and, when the court deadlocks, Athena casts the deciding vote, freeing Orestes from the Furies.

As we can see, each trilogy—the Greek and the American—chronicles the tragic story of a family corrupted by the sins by its ancestors. Aeschylus' version differs from O'Neill's in ways that tell us much about the societies that produced them.

In Aeschylus' version of *Oresteia,* Electra and Orestes suffer because of the sins of their patriarch Tantalus, their grandparent Atreus, and his brother Thyestes. Thyestes's desire for power leads him to betray his brother's trust. The focus of Aeschylus' plot reveals the anxieties about political stability and legal due process which concerned Athens during the 4th and 5th centuries BCE.

Significantly, critics view the concluding play *Eumenides* as dramatizing the way the Athenian concept of justice evolved from a system based on revenge to one based on the rule of law.

O'Neill's work also tells us much about the society in which he lived. In many works, the playwright presents America's greatest failing as its materialism—of valuing money above all else and of seeing people and things only in terms of their material value. Perhaps most obviously, note how much "Mannon" resembles "mammon," the biblical term for worldly material concerns.

In *Mourning Becomes Electra,* the Mannon family's "sin" is its betrayal of the American ideal of being a classless society, one that rejects a caste system that defines people by their economic background. Lavinia's and Orin's suffering results from the struggle between their great-uncle David Mannon and the Mannon family.

When David marries Marie Brantome, a Canadian woman of lower social class, the Mannons drive him out of the family. When David needs money, Ezra Mannon—Lavinia's and Orin's father—cheats David out of his fortune and ultimately contributes to Marie's death. So, while the rivalry by the brothers in the *Oresteia* concerns sexual desire and power, the American trilogy explores common O'Neill themes—most specifically the violation of class boundaries.

When the Mannons ostracize David and Marie, they help destroy the newlyweds. Furthermore, Ezra Mannon, by swindling David, shows that he values money more highly than family. From O'Neill's perspective, then, the "sins" that set the action of the play in motion seem uniquely American.

O'Neill's interest in the attractions and dangers of materialism comes from his immediate family. Eugene believed that his father, the talented Shakespearean actor James O'Neill, exchanged commercial for artistic success. James spent most of his life performing the role of Edmond Dantes in Charles Fletcher's theatrical adaptation of Alexander Dumas's novel, the *Count of Monte Cristo,* a role which brought him fame and fortune.

When Eugene O'Neill retold the story of Aeschylus' *Oresteia* trilogy in *Mourning Becomes Electra,* he naturally made some changes. The first two plays in O'Neill's trilogy, *Homecoming* and *The Hunted,* rather closely follow the first two plays in Aeschylus' trilogy, *Agamemnon* and *The Libation Bearers.*

However, critics disagree as to how faithfully O'Neill follows Aeschylus' *Eumenides* in the third play in the trilogy, *The Haunted.* Some critics believe that he abandoned the Aeschylean model, but others contend that the dramatic symmetry remains intact, if only symbolically.

For example, O'Neill presents no actual trial scene that parallels that of the Athenian court in *The Eumenides.* In act II of *The Hunted,* however, Orin addresses the portrait of his father Ezra, a judge, as "Your Honor," creating a venue of crime, judgment, and punishment, and symbolically echoing the Aeschylean play.

Yet while there may be general similarities between the Greek and American trilogies, O'Neill's characters, their actions, and the play's overall message differ substantially from those of Aeschylus. Key among these is that Electra has disappeared from the *Eumenides,* but Lavinia plays the central role in *The Haunted* and arguably, as the last surviving Mannon, in the trilogy itself.

"WHERE AESCHYLUS RESOLVES THE BLOOD FEUD IN THE RULE OF LAW, REDEEMING THE SOCIETY IF NOT ALL THE INDIVIDUALS, O'NEILL WILL HAVE NONE OF THAT. BEYOND TWO DAMAGED INDIVIDUALS, PETER AND HAZEL, THE MANNONS LEAVE BEHIND NOTHING, CERTAINLY NOTHING THAT REDEEMS OR HEALS SOCIETY."

O'Neill explains that he intended in *The Haunted* to interpret the Electra story from a new perspective, presenting her in heroic terms. In his notes for the play, he tersely wrote: "Give modern Electra figure in play tragic ending worthy of character. In Greek story she peters out into undramatic married banality."

According to Frederic Carpenter, O'Neill's Electra (Lavinia) must confront the evils of her family and herself and live with that evil. I see Lavinia as adopting a rather existential or Byronic attitude toward her transgression. She identifies a law (matricide), which she has had the strength of will to violate. She knows herself to be guilty and could escape punishment, but she also questions the legitimacy of living in a world without values. She will not allow the world to punish her, though, and so punishes herself instead.

Another difference between the Greek and American versions of the *Oresteia* can be seen in O'Neill's characters, which differ sharply from those of Aeschylus. This changes the ways audiences view their psychological motivations and the nature of their crimes.

In the *Oresteia,* for example, Clytemnestra kills Agamemnon in part because she holds him responsible for the death of their daughter. While we may not agree with Clytemnestra's retaliation, we can sympathize with her as a grieving mother mourning the loss of her child at what she believes to be her husband's hand. This may not justify murder, but it makes revenge seem understandable, if not excusable.

In O'Neill's trilogy, Christine's reasons for murdering her husband Ezra seem venial and vague. In part, she no longer finds him sexually attractive, but this hardly seems ground for murder. When the audience meets Ezra, he seems sick and frail; while he may have done wrong to Marie and left Christine unsatisfied, he provokes pity.

O'Neill also changes the motivations behind the actions of Orin and Lavinia. While Orestes kills Aegisthus out of duty to revenge his father, Orin's motivations for killing Brant seem murky. True, he claims to be sorry at his father's death and does feel some responsibility to revenge him, but Orin really only acts when Lavinia points out to him that Christine chose Brant over Orin. Principally, Orin acts out of incestuous jealousy, not paternal feeling.

The same incestuous desires cloud the purity of Lavinia's motivations, who seems to love her father almost in a wifely way.

I do not intend to condemn the psychological aspects of O'Neill's play, but rather to show how these psychological motivations diminish the characters and their actions. While we may not admire Agamemnon, Clytemnestra, Aegisthus, Electra, or Orestes, Aeschylus presents them as bold, larger than life, of heroic proportions if not actually heroes. O'Neill's changes make his characters very different.

According to Carpenter, Ezra seems less a war hero than a broken old man. Christine's feelings toward her husband Ezra and her lover Brant seem driven less by mighty passions than by neurosis. Christine's death by suicide rather than by Orin's hand makes them both smaller and anti-heroic. Orin too appears diminished, since he cannot find release by struggling against the Furies as Orestes does in Aeschylus' *The Eumenides*. Instead, Orin commits suicide to escape his conscience.

It becomes difficult to view any of O'Neill's characters—Lavinia, Brant, Orin, and Christine—as sympathetic, heroic, or noble. They all seem weak, unethical, and evil.

Part of the problem here is that the *Oresteia* poses moral dilemmas but offers no real solutions. Both Agamemnon and Orestes must choose between obeying their duties to their families or to the gods.

Agamemnon consents to having his daughter Iphegenia sacrificed, but only because he believes he must follow the will of the gods. Orestes obeys Apollo in revenging his father and killing Clytemnestra and her lover. Neither faces an easy or obvious decision. Clytemnestra conspires to murder her husband because of his role in what she believes to be the death of their daughter.

All in all, their reasons seem justified—if not justifiable—certainly far more than the compulsions of the Mannon family. O'Neill's characters have options; they simply refuse to exercise them.

O'Neill makes another change: setting. By making the *Oresteia* American, critics contend that O'Neill changes the play's ethical basis from a shame culture (in which one's sense of right and wrong comes primarily from how one will be seen and judged by others) to a guilt culture (in which a one's ethical sense is internal, and one is judged by one's self).

O'Neill's shift from a Greek shame culture to an American guilt culture accounts for the ending. If shame—the opinion and judgment of others—characterizes Greek culture, public judgment by a court seems purely natural. If guilt characterizes American culture, then the self-punishment of O'Neill's characters (Christine's and Orin's suicides, Lavinia's self-imposed isolation) seems an extension of that guilt ethic.

This shift has consequences, however. Arguably, O'Neill's tragedy leaves audiences in some sense unsatisfied in comparison with the tragedies of Aeschylus. According to John Chioles, the Greek playwright balances tragedy's "inevitability" with its "containment," and by the end of his *Oresteia* trilogy, the world that has been torn asunder has been reassembled, "pieced together and healed anew."

No such healing occurs at the end of *Mourning Becomes Electra,* when we see instead "the ultimate pessimism of O'Neill's world." While O'Neill acknowledges the individual and family tragedies, his drama fails to reconcile the effects of these actions with their ramifications in the wider community.

Where Aeschylus resolves the blood feud in the rule of law, redeeming the society if not all the individuals, O'Neill will have none of that. Beyond two damaged individuals, Peter and Hazel, the Mannons leave behind nothing, certainly nothing that redeems or heals society.

This seems congruent with O'Neill's modernist vision, balanced with a healthy dose of romantic pessimism. In general, O'Neill's plays explore ethics in an early twentieth-century world which, in the wake of industrialism, materialism, and war, seems to lack values. His characters' actions reveal profound psychological complexity, questioning the nature of individual consciousness and human identity, ethics and spirituality.

Significantly, modernist art often remains fragmentary and introspective. In that sense, one key difference between the *Oresteia* and *Mourning Becomes Electra* comes from the ending, where O'Neill's play offers no sense of closure, no orderly universe. Yes, the individuals involved have been punished in one way or the other, but society remains unhealed, unlike the ending to Aeschylus' *Oresteia*.

That link between tragedy and social healing is missing, but it somehow seems more realistic or true in a society that has seen the atomic bomb and the Holocaust. In O'Neill, tragedy offers no social reintegration; instead, *Mourning Becomes Electra* remains modernist in its (ir)resolution.

Source: Arnold Schmidt, for *Drama for Students,* Gale, 2000.

Marc Maufort

In the following essay, Maufort argues that O'Neill used Melville's Pierre *as a source, and that together O'Neill and Melville show a criticism of Puritan American family relationships.*

O'Neill's dramatization of family relationships in *Long Day's Journey Into Night,* his culminating masterpiece, is admittedly autobiographical. Moreover, disguised portraits of the O'Neills abound throughout the entire canon, a feature which critics have repeatedly underlined. *Mourning Becomes Electra* undoubtedly represents a notable exception to that pattern. In this drama, O'Neill resorts to various artistic models to depict the conflicts besieging the house of the Mannons. Besides obvious references to Aeschylus and Shakespeare, there exists a more obscure literary allusion in *Mourning Becomes Electra:* muted reminders of Herman Melville's neglected novel, *Pierre, or the Ambiguities,* that have hitherto largely escaped critical attention.

At first glance, to assert that O'Neill may have been indebted to Melville in the composition of his trilogy would seem exaggerated. And yet I submit that a direct connection is highly probable, an impression reinforced by the many analogies linking the two works. Critic Joyce D. Kennedy, who first pointed out the possible kinship between the

> IN *PIERRE* AS IN *MOURNING BECOMES ELECTRA,* THEN, ONE WITNESSES A MOVEMENT TOWARDS AGNOSTICISM."

novel and the play, conjectured that O'Neill had been introduced to *Pierre* by his scholarly friend Carl Van Vechten. The latter, who had strongly contributed to the Melville revival of the twenties, visited the O'Neills at Le Plessis in the summer of 1929, a period during which the dramatist drafted his play. The fact that comparable plot incidents occur in both *Pierre* and *Mourning Becomes Electra* could therefore constitute a tangible result of O'Neill's and Van Vechten's conversations.

In addition, O'Neill appears to have nurtured a life-long admiration for Melville which concretized itself in a 1921 press interview. He then described the hero of *Diff'rent,* Caleb Williams, as an Ahab-like captain: "He belongs to the old iron school of Nantucket-New Bedford whalemen whose slogan was 'A dead whale or a stove boat.' The whale . . . is transformed suddenly into a malignant Moby Dick. . . .'' In a hitherto unpublished introduction to Hart Crane's *White Buildings,* the playwright further alluded to Melville's mystical vision of the sea: "In Crane's sea poems . . . there is something of Melville's intense brooding on the mystery of 'the high interiors of the sea.''' In a private communication, Louis Sheaffer informed me that, according to Agnes Boulton, O'Neill's second wife, the dramatist was fascinated by *Moby Dick.* Finally, it may not be purely coincidental that in *Mourning Becomes Electra* Orin Mannon evokes yet another romance by Melville, *Typee.* In a lyrical confession, he asks his mother, "Have you ever read a book called 'Typee'—about the South Sea Islands? . . . I read it and reread it until finally those Islands came to mean everything that was peace and warmth and security.''

In view of these hints, I regard the influence of *Pierre* upon *Mourning Becomes Electra* as plausible. The resemblance between the two works, however, resides primarily in a relationship of confluence, more than of influence, originating in the authors' affinity of vision. Considered in that perspective, *Pierre* offers a privileged observation post from which to examine the "Americanness" of the family feuds O'Neill delineates. Through such an analysis, the playwright emerges as a writer imbued with both the cultural and literary heritage of his nation.

I

As critics have remarked, *Pierre* and *Mourning Becomes Electra* possess features strongly reminiscent of the stories of Orestes and Hamlet. Both Orestes and Pierre, in attempting to avenge paternal honor, engage in conflictual relationships with their mothers. Isabel Banford, Pierre's half-sister, qualifies as a latter-day counterpart to Electra, for in leaving his manorial estate to live with Isabel as her husband, Pierre indirectly provokes the demise of his mother. Owing to his hesitations, Pierre can also be regarded as a replica of Shakespeare's romantic Hamlet.

The plot of *Mourning Becomes Electra*, like that of *Pierre,* owes a great deal to the myth of Orestes. Indeed, Lavinia Mannon urges her brother Orin to take the life of Adam Brant, Christine Mannon's lover. She thus hopes to punish her mother for plotting the death of the family head, Ezra Mannon. As a result of Orin's violent deed, Christine eventually commits suicide. Further, the action of O'Neill's play also recalls that of Shakespeare's *Hamlet.* Lavinia's first task consists of convincing her brother of Christine's guilt. Likewise, Hamlet must dispel his own doubts before deciding to act. In short, the plot incidents devised by the writers to portray the intricacies of their heroes's family crises derive their most strikingly identical features from Aeschylus and Shakespeare.

II

While in the works of these classical authors, the incest motif performs a restricted role, in *Pierre* and *Mourning Becomes Electra* it acquires a paramount importance. Melville's and O'Neill's male characters experience odd feelings towards their domineering mothers. In *Pierre,* Mrs. Glendinning adopts an authoritarian conduct when dealing with her son and praying that he may "remain all docility to me." However, Pierre lives with her in perfect harmony, giving her a "courteous lover-like adoration." In the opening pages, Saddle Meadows, the Glendinnings's estate, could even be decoded as a symbol of the Biblical paradise. Pierre enjoys there the beauty of a "scenery whose uncommon loveliness was the perfect mould of a delicate and poetic mind . . . ."

The buried incestual metaphor defining Pierre's link to his mother is duplicated in Orin's affection for Christine Mannon. As in Melville's novel, the mother's mixture of mild authority and loving gentleness forms an essential component of *Mourning Becomes Electra.* Indeed, Christine's tenderness is rooted in possession, as is evidenced in her exclamation, "Oh, Orin, you are my boy, my baby! I love you!" And yet, the male protagonist spontaneously confesses his erotic bond with the maternal heroine, while betraying his wish of living with her in the islands of *Typee:*

> ORIN. Someone loaned me the book . . . those Islands . . . I used to dream I was there. And later on all the time I was out of my head I seemed really to be there. There was no one there but you and me. And yet I never saw you, that's the funny part. I only felt you all around me. The breaking of the waves was your voice. The sky was the same color as your eyes. The warm sand was like your skin. The whole island was you. . . . A strange notion, wasn't it? But you needn't be provoked at being an island because this was the most beautiful island in the world—as beautiful as you, Mother!

If Saddle Meadows functions as an image of the celestial paradise on earth, where mother and son can enjoy unmitigated bliss, the islands of *Typee* play a comparable role in O'Neill's drama. Ironically, one might get the impression that the playwright uses Melville's *Typee* in order to reproduce in his trilogy an atmosphere of happiness comparable to the initial chapter of *Pierre.* This phenomenon inevitably leads one to consider the divergences separating O'Neill and Melville in their treatment of the mother/son relationship. As a typical writer of the twentieth century, O'Neill integrates his Melvillean model into a modified context, thereby distancing himself from the meaning of his source. He demonstrates his awareness of the limited value that Orin's projects can preserve in the terrible world of New England. Whereas Melville's Saddle Meadows actually shelters the characters, Orin's allusions to *Typee* remain purely abstract. Moreover, his hopes are threatened by Christine's love affair with Brant. That O'Neill should debunk his character's aspirations by applying the modernist technique of literary quotation testifies to the highly innovative nature of *Mourning Becomes Electra.*

III

The two authors' rendering of the brother/sister incest motif is even more unique than that of the mother/son relationship. This theme offers considerable insight into their concept of the American family. In *Pierre,* the hero declares his passion for his half-sister on the first night of their stay in the city:

> He moved nearer to her, and stole one arm around her; her sweet head leaned against his breast; each felt the other's throbbing . . . his whole frame was invisibly trembling. Then suddenly in a low tone of wonderful intensity, he breathed: "Isabel! Isabel!" . . . "Call me brother no more! . . . I am Pierre and thou Isabel, wide brother and sister in the common humanity . . . the demi-gods trample on trash, and Virtue and Vice are trash!. . ."

In a kindred manner, Orin Mannon suggests his secret love for Lavinia: "(. . . *He stares at her and slowly a distorted look of desire comes over his face*) . . . There are times when you don't seem to be my sister but some stranger with the same beautiful hair—(*He touches her hair caressingly*)."

Significantly, both Pierre and Orin prefer to regard their sisters as strangers bearing no kinship to them. Through these portrayals of perverted love affairs, the two writers obliquely indict the Puritan environment that allowed such a desecration of parental links to occur. *Pierre* and *Mourning Becomes Electra* focus on the doom of fated Puritan families whose members are stifled by a narrow code of moral principles. Being the unconscious victims of that background, Pierre and Orin adopt distorted sexual behaviors resulting in the disintegration of their lives. The Glendinning house is eventually shattered by murder and death, while the Mannons become prey to an implacable fate. Clearly, O'Neill and Melville reject the harsh set of Old Testament ethics underlying their heroes' religious system.

As with the mother/son incest motif, O'Neill seems simultaneously to adhere to Melville's view and to negate the validity of his philosophy. The dramatist's possible borrowing from Melville appears woven into a larger context, tending to complicate the situation detectable in *Pierre.* If in Melville's work the protagonist is motivated solely by his Oedipal longings, in *Mourning Becomes Electra* the source of the action proceeds from a more intricate design. At first, Peter Niles, prompted by Lavinia's indifference to his proposals, informs the young heroine of Adam Brant's affair with Christine Mannon. The report infuriates Lavinia and awakens her desire for revenge, thwarted as she feels in her secret loving admiration for Brant. She then seeks to bring Orin to murder the sea captain, after clearly evidencing Christine's guilt. Out of a thinly veiled love for his sister, Orin finally agrees to act according to her wishes.

In *Pierre,* that fatal step requires a lesser number of transactions. Indeed, Isabel's letter to the hero does not, as is the case in *Mourning Becomes Electra,* constitute the result of a series of events. With his method of amplifying the impact of his apparent model, O'Neill seems to indicate that the strange bond between Orin and Lavinia exceeds in horror and complexity that uniting Pierre and Isabel. In *Mourning Becomes Electra ,* the pressure of Puritanism, causing the degeneration of a genuine brother/sister relationship, deprives mankind of any hope of salvation.

IV

Not only do the two writers regard the disappearance of family cohesion as a product of American Protestantism; they also endow this gradual decline with tragic resonances. In *Pierre* and *Mourning Becomes Electra,* one discovers elements of an innovative tragic form, one that seeks to ennoble the American common man. Although they remain the hereditary proprietors of manorial estates, Glendinnings and Mannons alike are subjected to the psychological woes that any New World citizen could experience. It is precisely the magnitude of the heroes' sufferings that confers upon *Pierre* and *Mourning Becomes Electra* their tragic aura.

But in the end, one can only speak of near-tragedy when considering these two works. First, *Pierre* is written in a novelistic form which is generally not associated with pure tragedy. Second, the almost exclusively psychoanalytical nature of the characters' conflicts reduces the impact of the artists' tragic endeavors. Their creatures manifest marked Oedipal fixations, which, while they contain in themselves a tragic potential, tend to mitigate the social and metaphysical implications embedded in Aeschylus' and Shakespeare's dramas. Residing in the protagonists' psychological turmoil, the concept of fate displayed in *Pierre* and *Mourning Becomes Electra* acquires an inner shape. Orin and Pierre are literally imprisoned within their own soul and prove unwilling to assume the full consequences of their public acts. Indeed, they choose to commit suicide while Lavinia, unable to face the world, buries herself alive.

This testifies, in my opinion, to Melville's and O'Neill's ironical stance, which emerges with perhaps even darker pessimism in the playwright's work. Whereas at first, the authors seemingly confer a tragic nobility upon their heroes, they subsequently deny them the benefit of any spiritual enlightenment. The two artists imply that true tragedy cannot exist in the New World, owing to the exaggeratedly private—psychoanalytical, to use a modern critical term—quality of the crises characterizing American family relationships. Thus adopting a view that corresponds to the night side of Walt Whitman's *Leaves of Grass,* Melville and O'Neill offer us a bleak picture of the possibilities of tragic elevation in America.

V

A final point of confluence between *Pierre* and *Mourning Becomes Electra* consists of their common metaphysical import. In these works, O'Neill and Melville explore the essence of the connection between members of American families and the divinity presiding over their destinies. Both come to the bitter conclusion that no God can improve the tormented relationships in which such family members are engaged. The hero of *Pierre* never succeeds in understanding his link with the deity, a failure best expressed through his sudden discovery of Plotinus Plinlimmon's pamphlet, "Chronometricals and Horologicals." This treatise, advising the reader not to seek to interpret God, tells of the impossibility of reconciling the horror of the human plight and divine goodness. In other words, Plinlimmon suggests, "in things terrestrial (horological) a man must not be governed by ideas celestial (chronometrical)." Struck with the "Profound Silence" of God's voice, Pierre nearly "runs, like a mad dog, into atheism." God remains indifferent to the sufferings Pierre incurs while living with his half-sister Isabel. The hero qualifies as an American Enceladus, a character who, in his efforts to attain divine status, is confined to the earth:

> You saw Enceladus the Titan, the most potent of all the giants, writhing from out the imprisoning earth . . . still turning his unconquerable front toward that majestic mount eternally in vain assailed by him . . . Enceladus was both the son and grandson of an incest; and even thus, there had been born from the organic blended heavenliness and earthliness of Pierre, another mixed, uncertain, heaven-aspiring, but still not wholly earth-emancipated mood. . . .

Orin Mannon, another New World Enceladus, feels estranged from a heavenly God and consequently gropes in the darkness of the earth. He dimly realizes that he must rely on his own strength in order to survive the psychological crisis generated by his Oedipal desires:

> ORIN. And I find artificial light more appropriate for my work—man's light, not God's—man's feeble striving to understand himself, to exist for himself in the darkness! It's a symbol of his life—a lamp burning out in a room of waiting shadows!

In *Pierre* as in *Mourning Becomes Electra,* then, one witnesses a movement towards agnosticism. In his trilogy, with the aid of Melville's novel, O'Neill presents us with a portrait of a torn apart family bereft of the help of God, thus prefiguring the agnostic universe of *Long Day's Journey Into Night.*

VI

If one admits that O'Neill kept *Pierre* in mind while composing *Mourning Becomes Electra*, one is forced to note that the confluence between the two works resides in the moral, tragic, and metaphysical probings of their authors. Like James Joyce or Virginia Woolf, O'Neill apparently resorts to the technique of literary quotation, as defined by Jean Weisgerber, in order to structure his drama. *Mourning Becomes Electra* can be regarded as a mosaic of literary allusions, whether to Aeschylus, Shakespeare, or Melville. Moreover, comparing this trilogy with *Pierre* offers a new image of O'Neill as a writer belonging to the tradition of American literature. In addition, I have suggested that, in two instances, O'Neill qualifies Melville's notion of the family unit in America and amalgamates his borrowings within a highly personal framework. To this end, he manipulates ironic commentaries—his reference to *Typee*—and the device of amplification—evident in the complex structure in which Orin's murder is inserted. This double angle of vision reveals the profundity of the playwright's delineation of family relationships in *Mourning Becomes Electra*. In the process of translating the ancient patterns of Aeschylus' and Shakespeare's works to describe the American components of such conflicts, he was most probably aided by the legacy of Melville's *Pierre*.

Source: Marc Maufort, "The Legacy of Melville's *Pierre*: Family Relationships in *Mourning Becomes Electra*," in *The Eugene O'Neill Newsletter,* Summer-Fall, 1987, Vol. 11, no. 2, pp. 23–28.

Bette Charlene Werner

In the following essay, Werner contends that the theme of the islands in ONeill's play represents the recovery of the paradise of the original bond between mother and son.

In the plays of Eugene O'Neill, the breaking of the bond between a son and a mother is a common pattern, figuring an original fall from innocence. Just as O'Neill's biography can be read as a series of unsuccessful attempts to re-establish in adulthood the kind of exclusive attachment with a woman that would replicate and replace the broken filial-maternal bond, his plays can be seen as a series of imaginative struggles with the same need. In O'Neill's vision, maternal abandonment is the original sin, and life is a series of necessary, but futile, attempts of men always to try to remake in some way the original closed pairing of mother and child. This theme, dealt with explicitly in *Desire Under the Elms, The Iceman Cometh, Long Day's Journey into Night,* and *A Moon for the Misbegotten,* forms also the essential basis for understanding *Mourning Becomes Electra.* While critical attention to O'Neill's trilogy has tended to focus particularly on the character and point of view of Lavinia in the play (an emphasis explicable in terms of the title of the work), O'Neill's treatment, not of Electra's story, but of the Orestes myth can take us closer to the fructifying imaginative origins and meaning of *Mourning Becomes Electra.*

The theme of the Blessed Islands reveals O'Neill's central intention in the trilogy. The islands represent the paradisal world of prenatal existence, where a child, rocked in the warm lullaby of his mother's self, forms with her a perfect and unviolated unity. Birth is the first evil, a beginning of estrangement that the processes of living inevitably worsen. The child's sense of betrayal when he realizes that the woman he loves is not just his own pure mother, but also another man's mistress, impels him to retaliate, to punish her by attacking her lover and to abandon her, too—to leave and to seek out another. While her betrayal brings pain, his revenge stirs the more wrenching affliction of guilt. Seeking a new partner then, he attempts to find in adulthood a replication of the original island unity of love with a mother, an exclusive closed circle of two. But peace is impossible in Eden, given the nature of Eve. Woman is the first betrayer, who lets pure love turn to passion. She is the original deceiver, who is not only mother, but mistress.

O'Neill works out this pattern of human experience through three generations of the House of Mannon. The prototype for the women in the play is the Canuck nurse girl Marie Brantôme. Marie is first of all seen as a madonna image, then recognized in her passionate nature as a fallen woman. After her follow Christine Mannon and then Lavinia.

> THE IDYLLIC PEACE OF THE ISLANDS IS DECEPTIVE, THOUGH, AND IMPERMANENT. THE BLESSED ISLES DO NOT REMAIN THE INNOCENT HAVEN ORIN HOPED FOR—A PLACE OF NURTURING PEACE WITH A MOTHER. THEY PROVIDE SOMEHOW A CHANGING ATMOSPHERE FOR LAVINIA."

Each of these women first mothers and then deserts a Mannon son for a lover, as her own fatal femininity blossoms. The betrayed are Ezra and Orin. Adam Brant and Peter Niles embody the masculine potential to initiate the same kind of filial-maternal estrangement.

Seth's description of Marie Brantôme indicates the original of a pattern to be repeated throughout the chronicle. Ezra Mannon idealized Marie. Seth explains:

> He was only a boy then, but he was crazy about her, too, like a youngster would be. His mother was stern with him, while Marie, she made a fuss over him and petted him.

But besides being a mother-like nurse to him, Marie was alive to passion too, "always laughin' and singin'—frisky and full of life—with something free and wild about her like an animile" (*Homecoming,* III). Ezra's pained outrage when he realizes the implications of her womanly nature is clear. Seth says: "Ayeh—but he hated her worse than anyone when it got found out she was his Uncle David's fancy woman" (*Homecoming,* III). Ezra is the child furiously hurt by the discovery of his mother's passionate involvement with a lover.

The experience is repeated for him in marriage. It was apparently Christine's resemblance to Marie that first attracted Ezra to her. She has the same copper yellow hair. He strokes it with an attitude of awe, trembling, as he gropes mentally for its significance: "Only your hair is the same, your strange beautiful hair I always—" (*Homecoming,* III). While his own insight is never explicit, Ezra's attempt to understand the loneliness he feels in marriage suggests that what he longs for is actually a remaking of that exclusive and perfect union of a child with a mother.

The marriage has somehow failed to fulfill the hope he once held for it. Before their marriage, he says he felt sure Christine loved him, but afterwards he knew himself incapable of what he wanted most, "Able only to keep my mind from thinking of what I'd lost" (*Homecoming,* III). During their courtship her eyes spoke to him, but after their marriage they were only full of silence. He sensed there was always "some barrier between us—a wall hiding us from each other" (*Homecoming,* III). Death as the end to life's slow process of dying holds no terror for Ezra, but death in terms of her husband being killed seems somehow queer and wrong. He feels it would be "like something dying that had never lived" (*Homecoming,* III). His wish for an achieved union in love with her takes the form of a daydream of going off together on a voyage to find some island to be alone together. He promises, "You'll find I've changed, Christine. I'm sick of death! I want life" (*Homecoming,* III). The wish has a quality of desperation to it: "I've got to make you love me!" (*Homecoming,* III).

That Christine has provoked his passion is part of her betrayal. When she recalls to him his treatment of her as a wife, he answers with scorn: "Your body? What are bodies to me? I've seen too many rotting in the sun to make grass greener" (*Homecoming,* IV). The island-mother image of green earth is corrupted in association with her. He flails out against her:

> Is that your notion of love? Do you think I married a body? You made me appear a lustful beast in my own eyes!—as you've always done since our first marriage night! (*Homecoming,* IV)

While physical desire may have been sated, his deeper need for love remains somehow untouched. Ezra feels betrayed by Christine as he was before by Marie Brantôme.

Like Marie, Christine has also taken a lover. The transformation in her that makes the returned soldier Ezra instinctively uneasy is her awakened sensuality. She has filled the house with flowers in anticipation of Brant's arrival, not his. Her taunt to Lavinia indicates the nature of the outlook she has rejected: "Puritan maidens shouldn't peer too inquisitively into Spring! Isn't beauty an abomination and love a vile thing?" (*Homecoming,* III). Christine's blossoming womanhood is her affirmation of life, but it carries with it the seeds of death as well. It leads to her murder of Ezra and desertion of Orin, and finally to her own suicide.

Adam Brant's dialogue furthers the development of the island theme in the play. Brant's romantic descriptions of the South Sea islands he remembers establish their connection with a paradise before the fall, an Eden associated with existence as yet unspoiled, with life yet unborn. Lavinia recollects his talk about the native island women who "had found the secret of happiness because they had never heard that love can be a sin" (*Homecoming,* I). And Brant assures her "they live in as near the Garden of Paradise before sin was discovered as you'll find on this earth" (*Homecoming,* I). The island colors of green land, blue sky, and golden sun are the same colors associated with first Christine and then Lavinia, with their green velvet gowns, blue eyes, and strange golden hair. The quiet peace of Brant's description evokes prenatal slumber within the womb: ". . . the sun drowsing in your blood, and always the surf on the barrier reef singing a croon in your ears like a lullaby!" (*Homecoming,* I). He notes, "You can forget there all men's dirty dreams of greed and power!" (*Homecoming,* I). They are "The Blessed Isles" (*Homecoming,* I).

Lavinia's unsettling question put to him about whether one can forget there also men's "dirty dreams of love?" (*Homecoming,* I) indicates the precarious basis for this paradise. The islands are inhabited by the naked native women. And it is women with their capability for feeling and stirring passion that can obliterate the paradise of untainted and unbroken mother love.

In Brant's story too there are repetitions of the theme of desertion between a child and a mother. Brant says that when he was seventeen, he "ran away to sea—and forgot I had a mother" (*Homecoming,* I). The sea and his ship became substitutes for the mother he left. He says that women are always jealous of ships, they always suspect the sea (*Homecoming,* I); and his description of sailing vessels, "Tall, white clippers, . . . like beautiful, pale women" (*Homecoming,* I), establishes them as an image of feminine purity in his mind. Lavinia reminds Christine of how much his ship means to Adam, and he himself compares Christine to the *Flying Trades:* "You are like sisters" (*Homecoming,* II). Their plan for escape together after Ezra is murdered involves his desertion of his ship, an abandonment that destroys for him any hope for real happiness with her.

When Brant first spoke of going away with Christine, he had mentioned the islands: "By God, there's the right place for love and a honeymoon!" (*Homecoming,* II). But, as she reminded him, the closed circle was impossible as long as Ezra was alive. Christine hoped that their complicity in this murder would bind Adam to her irrevocably. Fearing the changes of time and her aging, she calculated on the crime sealing a permanent bond:

> You'll never dare leave me now, Adam—for your ships or your sea or your naked Island girls—when I grow old and ugly. (*Homecoming,* II)

For both of them finally the alliance is vile and grotesque. The attempt to remake somehow in adulthood a community of two can be based only on other betrayals.

The island imagery of prenatal union is fully developed in the description of Christine's relationship with her son Orin. Christine reminisces with Orin after his homecoming: "We had a secret little world of our own in the old days, didn't we?—which no one but us knew about" (*The Hunted,* II). She claims that Ezra hated his son because he knew that she loved the boy better than anything else in the world (*The Hunted,* II). The exclusion is something Ezra himself attested to: "You had turned to your new baby, Orin. I was hardly alive for you any more. I saw that" (*Homecoming,* III). But the original union is broken; mother and son have been separated. Orin's father took him away to a war, and he blames his mother now for the scarcity and coolness of her letters during his absence (*The Hunted,* II).

Upon his return, she attempts a reconciliation with him: "We'll make that little world of our own again, won't we?" (*The Hunted,* II). Her winding the bandage on his head wound is a symbolic gesture of swaddling and binding together again that recalls the earlier figure of the Canuck nurse girl. He leans against her knees, dreamily describing the South Sea islands again in a way that makes clear their maternal meaning for him:

> Those Islands came to mean everything that wasn't war, everything that was peace and warmth and security. I used to dream I was there.... There was no one there but you and me. And yet I never saw you, that's the funny part. I only felt you all around me. The whole island was you. (*The Hunted,* II)

To Orin the islands are mother.

Orin hoped to escape from the death of war by coming home again finally, but he curses his recovery from his battle injury when he recognizes his mother's guilty hand in his father's death:

> I should never have come back to life—from my island of peace! But that's lost now! You're my lost island, aren't you, Mother? (*The Hunted,* III)

He is willing to forgive her, though, the sin of this murder. Ezra was a threat to their own special love. Orin can still dream of a life with his mother, even if she has now become a lost island.

It is only when Lavinia convinces him of Christine's involvement with Brant that Orin finally breaks with his mother. It is Christine's and Brant's use of the island imagery that assures Orin of Christine's betrayal of him. As Lavinia and Orin eavesdrop during their shipboard meeting, Christine begins to talk about going away with Brant to the islands. Brant goes on, expressing the pull of hope he feels for something he no longer really believes in:

> Aye—the Blessed Isles—Maybe we can still find happiness and forget! ... The warm earth in the moonlight, the surf on the barrier reef singing a croon in your ears like a lullaby! Aye! There's peace, and forgetfulness for us there—if we can ever find those islands now! (*The Hunted,* IV)

Steeped in the guilt of murder and sick with the sense of failure to make good on his own aspirations in his calling at sea, Brant recognizes the islands for an unachievable daydream. But Orin, overhearing, is convinced now that his mother has been a traitor to him.

It is this conviction that enables him to resolve upon and accomplish Brant's murder. The motivation of revenge is clear in his furious comment to Lavinia, "And my island I told her about—which was she and I—she wants to go there—with him!" (*The Hunted,* IV). After Lavinia has arranged that he overhear the plans of Christine and her lover, it becomes easier for Orin to kill Brant. He shoots the man at close range and, in a scene of violation which follows, rips open drawers in the ship's cabin, rifles the place, tears things apart, goes through the dead man's pockets, and finally steals Brant's revolver. He destroys and attempts to take the place of this rival. Announcing Brant's death to his mother, Orin explains: "I heard you planning to go with him to the island I had told you about—our island—that was you and I!" (*The Hunted,* V). When she only moans with grief, he tells her that he will help her to forget:

> I'll make you forget him! I'll make you happy! We'll leave Vinnie here and go away on a long voyage—to the South Seas— (*The Hunted,* V)

Lavinia is right in recognizing her brother's goal as a retreat to infancy: "Are you becoming her crybaby again?" (*The Hunted,* V). Orin still wants to reestablish his exclusive childhood hold on his mother's affections.

When Christine kills herself, that hope is eliminated. Orin is beset with the guilt of having first killed Brant and then having taunted his mother with the murder. With her dead now, there is no further hope of a reconciliation. He recognizes his plight with despair: "I've got to make her forgive me! I—! But she's dead—She's gone—how can I ever get her to forgive me now?" (*The Hunted,* V). She has in a final act of betrayal now irrevocably left him.

To find some other way to live, some other hope, Orin turns to his sister Lavinia. It is Orin and Lavinia who actually sail off to the Islands. Lavinia becomes a mother to him, nursing him like a sick child to life.

The idyllic peace of the islands is deceptive, though, and impermanent. The Blessed Isles do not remain the innocent haven Orin hoped for—a place of nurturing peace with a mother. They provide somehow a changing atmosphere for Lavinia. A threatening aspect in her nature is awakened there. Orin tells Peter Niles:

> They turned out to be Vinnie's islands, not mine. They only made me sick—and the naked women disgusted me. I guess I'm too much of a Mannon, after all, to turn into a pagan. But you should have seen Vinnie with the men—! (*The Haunted,* I, ii)

Orin accuses Lavinia of admiring the handsome, romantic-looking island men and desiring their attentions:

> Oh, she was a bit shocked at first by their dances, but afterwards she fell in love with the Islanders. If we'd stayed another month, I know I'd have found her some moonlight night dancing under the palm trees—as naked as the rest. (*The Haunted,* I, ii)

He declares that it was his brotherly duty to take her away. He is jealous of the passionate nature he senses stirring in her and attempts to secure her unchanged for his own.

His sense of her awakening sexuality as the sin that will destroy their closeness becomes clear in his further accusations. He implies that she enjoyed the lustful looks of the native Avahanni and that something passed between the two. Although Lavinia avers it was only a kiss she shared with the islander, the moment marks the beginning of another betrayal for Orin. She shouts at him. "I'm not your property! I have a right to love!" (*The Haunted,* II). Lavinia explains that she loved the islands: "They finished setting me free" (*The Haunted,* I, ii). She has come to the conclusion that "Love is all beautiful" (*The Haunted,* I, ii). And with her new boldness she turns from Orin to Peter: "We'll be married soon.... We'll make an island for ourselves" (*The Haunted,* I, ii). Lavinia chooses to leave Orin just as Christine did before her.

Like Christine, she also tries to cover for her desertion of Orin by pushing him toward Hazel. Orin realizes by this time, however, the impossibility of any such hope of remaking the world of his childhood:

> No. I'm afraid myself of being too long alone with her—afraid of myself. I have no right in the same world with her. And yet I feel so drawn to her purity! Her love for me makes me appear less vile to myself! And, at the same time, a million times more vile, that's the hell of it! So I'm afraid you can't hope to get rid of me through Hazel. She's another lost island! (*The Haunted,* II)

His letter revealing all the crimes of the Mannon family is his last resort to prevent Lavinia from abandoning him to marry Peter. Lavinia has become Marie Brantôme to him (*The Haunted,* III). Just as Marie deserted Ezra, Lavinia is now bent upon leaving him. Recognizing the impossibility of ever recovering innocence and peace again in life, Orin turns to death for an answer. He determines upon suicide:

> Yes! It's the way to peace—to find her again—my lost island—Death is an island too—Mother will be waiting for me there—Mother! (*The Haunted,* III)

Lavinia persists in her hope for an earthly paradise just a while longer. She clings wildly to Peter as her brother goes out to shoot himself, talking with desperate hope of a time when they will be married and have a home and a garden with trees: "Hold me close, Peter! Nothing matters but love, does it? That must come first! No price is too great, is it?" (*The Haunted,* III).

Besides Lavinia's sending Orin to his death, it is clear that this marriage would be based on other desertions as well—Peter's abandonment of his mother and sister. Hazel tells how the plan has already broken his mother's heart and come between him and her too:

> You've changed him. He left home and went to the hotel to stay. He said he'd never speak to Mother or

me again. He's always been such a wonderful son before—and brother. (*The Haunted,* IV)

Hazel's jealous love for her brother prompts her to introduce the topic of Orin's letter. His last resort becomes hers as well, as she tries to stop with it the processes of changing and leaving that life invariably brings. Though Peter comes to her haggard and tormented with the guilt of his desertions, Lavinia still hopes to snatch from life some moment of bliss.

It is only when in her frantic appeal for love she slips the name of his predecessor in her affections, Adam, that she gives up the hopeful illusion: "Always the dead between! It's no good trying any more!" (*The Haunted,* IV). Lavinia throws away the lilacs she had brought into the thouse and lets the windows be boarded up again. The conclusion of the play confirms the Mannon outlook that Ezra had so much wanted to defy: "Life is dying. Being born was starting to die. Death was being born" (*Homecoming,* III). Christine once asked wistfully, looking at the fresh young girl Hazel, "Why can't all of us remain innocent and trustful?" (*The Hunted,* I). Persistence in innocence is an impossible hope, like the Blessed Isles, an irretrievable dream that exists only once for a while in prenatal slumber. The peace of Eden is precariously held as long as there is a "yaller-haired wench" in the garden ready to say, "Take me, Adam!" (*The Hunted,* IV and *The Haunted,* IV).

Source: Bette Charlene Werner, "Eugene O'Neill's Paradise Lost: The Theme of the Islands in *Mourning Becomes Electra,*" in *Forum,* Winter, 1986, Vol. 27, no. 1, pp. 46–52.

William Young

In the following essay, Young describes Lavinia as the "American Electra" but Christine as the "most tragic member of the Mannon family."

It is often an intellectual game among students of drama to debate who is the center of a play, whose story is being told. With some plays it's not much of a game: *Hedda Gabler,* for instance, is appropriately named since Hedda is, shall we say, the cornerstone of nearly all the triangular relationships in Ibsen's play. Ultimately all roads lead to Hedda (until of course the very end, when George and Thea get together). Eugene O'Neill's *Mourning Becomes Electra* is also, I think, properly named; but here, despite the title, it is not quite so clear to whom the play belongs. O'Neill set out to write a trilogy that would do for Electra what Aeschylus had done for Orestes, and in some ways he succeeds. In the end it is Lavinia, the American Electra, who must rid the world of the Mannons while simultaneously becoming a strange apotheosis of what it means to *be* a Mannon. Yet it is not Lavinia but her mother, Christine—Clytemnestra's counterpart—who is the most tragic member of the Mannon family because she more clearly wishes and strives to be free of the "Mannon curse."

The Mannon curse is to be forever bound to one's dead relatives; it is the fatal web which binds each character to the others and which ultimately binds the play together. The play is their cumulative ghost, and so of course it is not quite accurate to single out one character as the heart of the trilogy. But even within the inextricabilities of the Mannon web, the stories of the two women dominate the drama.

The main story is Vinnie's desire to be more like her mother. However, Vinnie never knows this is the story: even at the end she won't admit that she's never had a life of her own. And it is for this reason, this blindness, that Vinnie is more pathetic than tragic. Only at the very end does she take on tragic dimensions, when she realizes that there is no running from her punishment and indeed that she must punish herself.

But up until the final part of the trilogy it is Christine's play. Christine sees—she sees the oppressive nature of her Christian responsibilities; she sees her life slipping by—and she wants her freedom. The underside of American literature—the vast sensual wilderness underneath the Puritan ideal—that Lawrence describes in his *Studies in Classic American Literature,* becomes manifest in Christine's desire for Captain Adam Brant and a life on the virgin soil of a faraway island. Caught in what Lawrence calls "the mechanical bond of purposive utility," she feels she has a "right" to love, as her son Orin later says of her. Interestingly, when Vinnie virtually "becomes" her mother toward the end of the play, she *too* believes she has a "right to love." Vinnie cannot imagine another life without becoming someone other than herself. But once Christine gets a taste of love and freedom she will not give it up, and she will not be beholden to Vinnie. In the end, rather than submit to Vinnie's blackmail, she quite literally takes her life in her own hands. Christine's main failing, beyond a certain pathetic longing for youth and beauty, is that she doesn't see clearly enough that she's acted too late, and acting too late is the heart of tragedy.

> "BUT UP UNTIL THE FINAL PART OF THE TRILOGY IT IS CHRISTINE'S PLAY. CHRISTINE SEES—SHE SEES THE OPPRESSIVE NATURE OF HER CHRISTIAN RESPONSIBILITIES; SHE SEES HER LIFE SLIPPING BY—AND SHE WANTS HER FREEDOM."

Vinnie wants her mother to live according to the way things are, to live up to the traditional standards of mid-nineteenth century New England. Appalled at learning of her mother's adultery, she threatens to tell her father unless Christine gives up Brant: "You ought to see it's your duty to Father, not my orders—if you had any honor or decency." Vinnie is ever cognizant of her Puritan chores: "I'm not marrying anyone," she tells her mother. "I've got my duty to Father." Christine's immediate answer shows an awareness of responsibility as well as its traps, something Vinnie would never admit: "Duty! How often I've heard that word in this house! Well, you can't say I didn't do mine all these years. But there comes an end." There comes an end to "duty," and to life itself. Vinnie can only see the timeless portraits of the Mannon line and their stony pride reaching through history. Indeed, Vinnie is herself described as having the timeless quality of an "Egyptian statue."

But Christine has been married for twenty years to a man she doesn't love. She has become less and less her husband's lover and mate and more and more the person who takes care of the family. She is mother to all and yet finally rejects her role and family, and the Mannon "tomb," for her pagan Captain (who turns out, ironically, to have a fair share of Mannon in him) and the promise of romance and adventure in the South Seas, where the Christian doctrine of sin is unknown.

> I've been to the greenhouse to pick these. I felt our tomb needed a little brightening. (*She nods scornfully toward the house*) Each time I come back after being away it appears more like a sepulchre! The "whited" one of the Bible—pagan temple front stuck like a mask on Puritan gray ugliness! It was just like old Abe Mannon to build such a monstrosity—as a temple for his hatred. (*Then with a little mocking laugh*) Forgive me, Vinnie. I forgot you liked it. And you ought to. It suits your temperament.

Yes, mourning becomes Lavinia. Even in the end, when she nails shut the windows and retreats inside to punish herself and end the Mannon line, her sacrifice fulfills the Puritan creed. A noble act, perhaps; a necessary act; but still too willingly accepted. Why didn't she stay on the South Sea Islands where she had become a more natural woman? The answer, it seems, lies in the double edge of the play's message: consequences must be faced and in doing so you simultaneously fulfill and carry on the need for Puritan sacrifice. Vinnie's response to her mother's "there comes an end" is, "And there comes another end—and you must do your duty again!" Ad infinitum!

But even if one accepts Lavinia's sacrifice as an act of courage, and a moment of insight, on the whole she is more pathetic than tragic. She doesn't see, or if she does she won't admit what she sees. She won't admit what is obvious to others—that she is a poor imitation of her mother. Brant describes Vinnie's face as a "dead image" of Christine's. Orin realizes that Vinnie can never admit that she wanted Brant.

> ORIN: And that's why you suddenly discarded mourning in Frisco and bought new clothes—in Mother's colors!
>
> LAVINIA: (*furiously*) Stop talking about her! You'd think, to hear you, I had no life of my own!
>
> ORIN: You wanted Wilkins just as you'd wanted Brant!
>
> LAVINIA: That's a lie!

Only Vinnie's subconscious allows her to admit her desire for Brant. She mistakenly calls out for "Adam" when asking Peter to make love to her.

Christine is a tragic figure because she possesses more of a mind of her own and realizes, nevertheless, that she has wasted much of her life. She doesn't fully realize, however, what the past has done to her, how cruel she's become. For much of the play Christine underestimates the Mannon curse—to be forever tied to one's dead relatives because of an unwillingness to face the truth about one's living relatives. As Adam returns too late to his dying mother's bedside, and as Ezra tries too late to be open and loving with Christine, so Christine responds too slowly to years of bitterness toward Ezra and Lavinia. And bitterness is the handmaiden to cruelty. But it does not undermine Christine's victory as the central tragic figure of *Mourning Becomes Electra.*

Source: William Young, "Mother and Daughter in *Mourning Becomes Electra,*" in *The Eugene O'Neill Newsletter,* Summer-Fall, 1982, Vol. 6, no. 2, pp. 15–17.

Ronald T. Curran

In the following essay, Curran discusses how the concept of the islands fails for certain major characters in O'Neill's play, dominated as they are by Puritanism.

Approximately at midpoint in Eugene O'Neill's *Mourning Becomes Electra* (1929, 1931), Orin Mannon leans his head on his mother's knee and in a "dreamy and low and caressing" voice announces that Melville's *Typee* (1846) provided him with a sense of peace in the midst of the American Civil War and stimulated "wonderful dreams" about her:

> Someone loaned me the book. I read it and reread it until finally those Islands came to mean everything that wasn't war, everything that was peace and warmth and security. I used to dream I was there. And later on all the time I was out of my head I seemed really to be there. There was no one there but you and me. And yet I never saw you, that's the funny part. I only felt you all around me. The breaking of the waves was your voice. The sky was the same color as your eyes. The warm sand was like your skin. The whole island was you.

Orin did not read *Typee* critically. If he had, he would have recognized that Tommo's quest for a Polynesian retreat was a failure. The South Pacific contained no prelapsarian Eden. Like many of the early reviewers of *Typee,* Orin read his own interpretation of primitivism into the novel. For him Typee Valley, Tahiti or Imeeo became literally his mother.

> The nineteenth-century Rousseauistic yearning for uncorrupted civilizations and noble savages attracted readers to books about the South Seas; while this contributed to the popularity of *Typee* and *Omoo,* it banished Melville to premature obscurity. His barbed ambiguities troubled the delicate hearts of the American public which wanted to root in the past for the lost Golden Age. The popular sense of primitivism, like Orin's, was opposed to Melville's own more profound approach. The public sought escape while Melville looked for an explanation of his sense of culture failure.

James Baird has explained that primitivism attends a sense of culture failure expressed mainly in the disintegration of religious symbolism. In *Typee* Melville refutes the naive primitivism of Rousseau. His experience in the South Seas under-

> "O'NEILL RE-EMPLOYS IN VARIOUS FORMS THE CONVENTIONAL IMAGE OF EXOTIC ISLANDS IN ORDER TO GAIN A UNIVERSALLY-CONDITIONED RESPONSE FROM HIS AUDIENCE—ESCAPE FROM UNPLEASANT REALITY—, BUT THE ISLANDS FAIL FOR THREE IMPORTANT REASONS...."

mined the Frenchman's notion of the moral superiority of primitive peoples. Afterwards, as Baird has pointed out in *Ishmael,* Melville embraced an authentic primitivism, *"the mode of feeling which exchanges for traditional Christian symbols a new symbolic idiom referring to Oriental cultures of both Oceania and Asia ...* [Baird' italics]. Melville's nineteenth-century, New-England audience and O'Neill in *Mourning Becomes Electra* follow mainly in Rousseau's footsteps: encouraged by the collapse of the Puritan theological basis for the Protestantism of New England, they distort the past. Melville, on the other hand, uses the past — mainly Oriental culture — as a source of new symbols to replace those of Protestant Christianity. Thus Orin's South Pacific island offers an escape, while Melville's affords an opportunity to attempt a reintegration.

In *Mourning Becomes Electra* everyone has an island. Orin has his own vision of Melville's Marquesas, and Captain Brant cherishes his Blessed Isles and promotes their image for Christine and Lavinia. Even Ezra has one, although his more vague retreat closely resembles most people's image of a refuge, since it has no specific location and promises him the emotional luxuries which would damn nearly every one of us, were we to possess them all concurrently. Love. Peace. Happiness. Forgetfulness. Guiltlessness. Those common emotional wishes, which, if we could just get mind and heart to cooperate, would insure that equilibrium we never quite strike. In fact, towards the end of the trilogy, with merely a wag of the tongue, Orin makes an unattainable island of Hazel Niles, who is barely a body of emotions, let alone a piece of land. Lavinia, too, shows similar disregard for geography when she tells Hazel's brother, Peter, "We'll make an island for ourselves on land...."

It would be somewhat dishonest, however, to dismiss the significance of the various forms of Blessed Isles in *Mourning Becomes Electra* merely as popular metaphors for human wish-fulfillment. They acquire a deeper meaning when we look at them in the light of modern psychology and Rousseauistic primitivism. This is not to say that the play is heavily indebted to Freud or Rousseau. Neither its use of modern psychological insight nor its approach to primitivism is highly technical. Both, in fact, are employed much as they were in the nineteenth century by such writers as Hawthorne in *The Marble Faun* and Melville in *Typee*. A general knowledge of both the psychology and the peculiar form of primitivism in the trilogy adds a dimension to our understanding of the work. For in *Mourning Becomes Electra,* Eugene O'Neill reinterprets the failure of Rousseauistic primitivism in the light of twentieth-century psychological insight. The play is a modern version not only of the Oedipal tragedy in Aeschylus' Orestia trilogy but also of the failure of the doctrine of chronological primitivism in a culture dominated by Puritanism.

Rousseauistic primitivism underlies the various concepts of the Blessed Isles in *Mourning Becomes Electra,* but O'Neill's primary emphasis is upon the chronological aspect of Rousseau's mode of primitivism — that earlier stages in human existence were better or wholly good. By extending this naive concept to every major character in the trilogy, he emphasizes the sense of culture failure motivating each person's desire for escape.

Particularly, that culture failure is rooted in the destructive influence of Puritanism on the Mannon family. It distorts their relationships without providing a reassuring creed around which to structure their lives. This negative religious legacy descends from the father's side and inhibits Ezra, Orin and Lavinia, whom Christine refers to as a Puritan maiden and who questions whether Brant's Blessed Isles can make men forget their "dirty dreams" of love. Christine also refers to the "Puritan gray ugliness" of the Mannon home and claims that each time she goes away and returns it becomes "more like a sepulchre! The 'whited' one of the Bible...." *Mourning Becomes Electra,* like Hawthorne's "Young Goodman Brown," indicts Puritanism for encouraging neurotic sexual notions.

O'Neill, then, adds a few more lashes to the already striped carcass of Puritanism in American letters. In *Mourning Becomes Electra* he scores that religious legacy generally for reinforcing the Oedipal complexes which haunt Lavinia and Orin. Classical though it may be in its structure, O'Neill's trilogy employs a knowledge of modern psychology in order to explore a nineteenth-century theme and to pin the blame once again on Puritanism. Prudish attitudes toward sex underlie and strengthen the Freudian determinism which besets the Mannons. And the indirect effect of those attitudes on both Lavinia and Orin make chronological primitivism attractive to them as each wishes to go back in time in order to slough off the destructive sexual frustration they feel.

The Blessed Isles, however, fulfill different needs for both — renewal of Lavinia's basic sensuality and ultimately reinforcement of Orin's Puritan repression. Christine is Orin's Blessed Isle; naked Polynesian women only disgust him. Announcing his suicide, he exclaims: "Yes! It's the way to peace — to find her [mother] again — my lost island — Death is an island of peace too — Mother will be waiting for me there...."

O'Neill, of course, overemphasizes one facet of Rousseauistic primitivism — the sexual freedom of primitive peoples. The New-England Puritan preoccupation with the evil of sexual pleasure explains the majority of the emotional difficulties in *Mourning Becomes Electra*. The women in the play — and in O'Neill's plays generally — tend to be extreme types: good women (like mother) and bad or "fancy women" in the terminology of Seth, the caretaker; Minnie and Abbie in *Desire Under the Elms* or Marie Brantome and Christine Mannon in *Mourning Becomes Electra*. When even the good women shows signs of natural sensuality, they become, to use Orin's words, "whores". Once Eve is diddled by the serpent, it seems she becomes at the same time a fallen and a scarlet woman. In Nabokov's phrase, she contracts the "apple disease."

Orin, as his thoughts on *Typee* will reveal, wants to return to those prelapsarian days before the knowledge of sexual sin. In wanting to regress, he wishes not only to repudiate his individuality, but, more significantly, he wants to deny history — his own and his family's. Such a denial involves the destruction of one's identity. Ultimately, that denial means the disintegration of the self. For however doubtful the virtues of historical progress, the development of personality is inextricably bound to the forward movement of one's civilization. Irving's Rip Van Winkle attempted to deny history, sleeping through the Revolutionary War, and he awakened to find himself an anachronism. Captain Brant, who has not learned Tommo's lesson, shares Orin's belief in Rousseau's dream of escape by voyaging back in time to an island garden of Eden. Christine, not Fayaway, becomes his Eve, and he, like Tommo, leaves his island paradise. Brant finds his love among his own people and in his own time and place. But he is fated by the Mannon curse never to make his escape to the Blessed Isles where he feels he can play a trick on time.

For both Brant and Ezra Mannon, the islands represent mainly an escape from the present and an opportunity to turn back time. Ezra tells Christine, "I've got a notion if we'd leave the children and go off on a voyage together — to the other side of the world — find some island where we could be alone for a while. You'll find I have changed." Brant had told Christine earlier that he admired the naked native women because they had found the secret of happiness — "they had never heard that love can be a sin." "They live in as near the Garden of Paradise before sin was discovered as you'll find on earth." Each feels that the islands will enable him to shed the stigma of sin which his New-England Puritanism had bequeathed to sensual love. They want to regress, however, to unlearn rather than to modify. Change for them means a return to the innocence of childhood, for Orin almost a prenatal existence. Brant's repeated reference to "the surf on the barrier reef singing a croon in your ears like a lullaby!" pairs him with Orin, whose Blessed Isle is his mother. Unable to come to terms with their Puritan legacy, they wish instead to recover the purity of childhood, not of the supposedly uninhibited adulthood of the noble savage.

They associate inhibition with immaturity. Each interprets chronological primitivism naively, supposing that relationships with primitive peoples, isolation from their Puritan environment, and communion with nature will dissolve religious inhibitions. This error precipitates their tragic fate because they wrongly associate psychic with historical time. The Mannons believe that visiting peoples living in an earlier period of historical development can change their unconscious minds. They mistake the nostalgia aroused by a pleasant vacation for a spontaneous cure for their psychological condition. They wish to begin again with a clean slate in the Lockian sense because they do not realize that the noble savages they admire bear the markings of their own unique culture. Primitives' consciences are not without guilt either; they contain indigenous forms of "sin," and so-called primitive men are not the children of Eden whom Ezra and Brant wish to become again and can only become with the loss of their respective selves. All of the Mannons ultimately accept some form of this delusion. Even though Lavinia seems to have made a partial recovery during her vacation in a South Pacific Eden and an innocent affair with Avahanni, she too is forced to accept her self and her place in the New England of her day.

Hazel and Peter Niles act as foils to Lavinia and Orin: they become an ironic pair of noble savages in New England. Their childlike innocence affirms the ideals of purity and wholesomeness in contrast to the guilty Mannon consciences of Orin and Lavinia. These uncorrupted neighbors embody the elemental values of the Blessed Isles. Nonetheless, Orin recognizes the impossibility of attaining expiation and happiness through marriage to Hazel when he admits that "She's another lost island!" Lavinia, too, accepts finally that Peter can never be the Adam she mistakingly calls him, and she can never be his Biblical wife. No one returns to the prelapsarian garden in *Mourning Becomes Electra,* for O'Neill makes the simplemindedness of brother and sister Niles almost as unattractive as the Mannon guilt.

Orin's allusion to *Typee* in the play suggests that O'Neill is telling the same tale of paradise lost as Melville had told eighty-three years before. Like Melville, O'Neill recounts not only the failure of Rousseauistic primitivism, but also illustrates clearly in his ironic treatment of the various forms of Blessed Isles that any such wish is at best illusory. O'Neill, however, criticizes Puritanism, not missionaries, for developing a destructive guilt syndrome. When sex and sin are equated, love relationships are frustrated and they intensify our sense of isolation instead of our feelings of mutuality. Guilt isolates all the Mannons, and its source can be traced to the effect of Puritanism on their lives. To each successive generation of Mannons the fathers bequeath a sense of sexual sin, and the consequences of that inheritance far outstrip the influence of any more palpable wrongdoing such as that of which Hawthorne's Pyncheons were gulty. The sins of the fathers in the Mannon family are the result of their collective acceptance of that aspect of Puritanism which considers sexual pleasure in or outside of marriage as sinful.

In *Mourning Becomes Electra,* Captain Brant, a figure of renewal like Holgrave in *The House of the Seven Gables,* is murdered. His death ends any chance of atonement and regeneration for the Mannon family. The destructive effects of Puritanism kill Ezra, Captain Brant, Christine, and Orin as surely as does the psychological fate born of the Oedipus complexes of Orin and Lavinia. O'Neill re-employs in various forms the conventional image of exotic islands in order to gain a universally-conditioned response from his audience — escape from unpleasant reality —, but the islands fail for three important reasons: first of all, guilt is best relieved through some form of public confession in one's own community rather than privately and in isolation from it; second, Brant's epithet, ''Blessed Isles,'' borrows an adjective the Christian connotations of which belie the islands' efficacy: these can never be given divine approval because the sexual license they suggest cannot be sanctified by the Puritan god of the Mannons. Finally, the islands must fail because they represent a happiness that can be gained only through the sacrifice of one's identity.

In *Mourning Becomes Electra,* O'Neill both updates the Orestia trilogy with his knowledge of modern psychology and localizes the universal Oedipal pattern which Aeschylus depicted by showing that for one part of the American character at least that pattern is reinforced by New-England Puritanism. Writing in this thematic tradition, O'Neill shows his kinship with the major writers of the American Renaissance, especially Melville and Hawthorne.

Source: Ronald T. Curran, ''Insular Typees: Puritanism and Primitivism in *Mourning Becomes Electra,*'' in *Revue Des Langues Vivantes,* Summer, 1975, Vol. 4, pp. 371–77.

Horst Frenz and Martin Mueller

In the following essay, Frenz and Mueller argue that Hamlet *and* Mourning Becomes Electra *''show similarities in plot wherever there are plot differences between* Hamlet *and the* Oresteia*'' and that a comparison of the plays of Shakespeare and O'Neill ''help to define the fundamentally different concept of action that separates O'Neill's trilogy from the* Oresteia.*''*

There has been general critical agreement that *Mourning Becomes Electra* was modeled on the *Oresteia,* and the publication of O'Neill's work diary has strengthened this assumption. On closer investigation, however, the similarities between the two plays are superficial, and more fundamental parallels may be found in O'Neill's trilogy and Shakespeare's *Hamlet.* The latter play shares its basic plot with *Mourning Becomes Electra,* and it can be shown that in other ways, too, O'Neill owes more to Shakespeare and less to Aeschylus and to a genuine experience of Greek drama. One may indeed speak of a direct influence of *Hamlet,* but it is quite possible that the American playwright was not aware of it. The comparison of *Hamlet* and *Mourning Becomes Electra* will not only prove that these two plays show similarities in plot wherever there are plot differences between *Hamlet* and the *Oresteia* but also help to define the fundamentally different concept of action that separates O'Neill's trilogy from the *Oresteia.*

First of all, the murder of Ezra Mannon resembles the murder of Hamlet's father more closely than that of Agamemnon. Ezra Mannon is poisoned. It is easy to see the reason for this change. Since the crime had to remain undetected for the family drama to unfold free from outside interference, open violence was irreconcilable with the setting O'Neill had chosen for his trilogy. In the *Oresteia,* the murder of Agamemnon makes Clytemnaestra and Aegisthus the absolute rulers of Argos. At the end of the *Agamemnon,* after Clytemnaestra has proudly acknowledged her deed to the helpless Chorus, tyranny is established in Argos. Clytemnaestra's shameless confession, which indicates the absence of any authority to punish her, is crucial to the trilogy, since it justifies Orestes's revenge. In the *Oresteia,* as well as in the Electra plays of Sophocles and Euripides, secrecy surrounds the return of the avenger. Intrigue is restricted to the concealment of the avenger's identity until the moment of retribution. In *Mourning Becomes Electra,* on the other hand, the crime itself is the secret, and the plot necessarily deals with the story of its discovery. That is to say, *Mourning Becomes Electra* shares its basic plot with *Hamlet.*

There are other differences between the *Oresteia* and *Mourning Becomes Electra* that have been overlooked because O'Neill's identification of Lavinia with Electra has been accepted too readily. In the Greek tragedies Electra is the disinherited princess and her humiliation is the result of her father's death. In *Mourning Becomes Electra* the order is reversed. According to its position in the American trilogy, *Homecoming* should be an Agamemnon tragedy; actually, the play is dominated by the conflict between mother and daughter. The death of the father is only one episode in an

Electra drama. Far from causing the humiliation of Electra-Lavinia, the death of Agamemnon-Mannon actually terminates it. In Lavinia's and Christine's struggle for power, the daughter's discovery of the poison is the decisive event. The last remnant of Christine's doubtful ascendancy over Lavinia has now disappeared: Lavinia, casting off the role of the disinherited princess, assumes that of the avenger. There is no comparable situation in the *Oresteia;* for a parallel we have to turn to *Hamlet.* It has been suggested that Hamlet is both Electra and Orestes, and it may be argued that the discovery of his father's murder effects in Hamlet the change from Electra to Orestes. The frustration and the humiliation for which he lacked an "objective correlative" in the first court scene are absorbed by his new duty and his will to revenge.

In *Hamlet* the ghost scene achieves all at once the reversal that takes up the entire first part of O'Neill's trilogy. The discovery of the murder suddenly gives direction to Hamlet's profound but aimless disgust at his mother's "adultery." In *Mourning Becomes Electra* this reversal occurs gradually. *Homecoming* shows Lavinia at various stages of knowledge; each increase in knowledge is a step toward ascendancy, which she finally achieves with the discovery of the poison. The Lavinia who squabbles with her mother about the right to show the garden to strangers and who wilfully shuts herself off in her room is as contumacious as Electra; she is stronger than her mother, but she still lacks the power to break her authority. The quarrel, however, points to a change. Lavinia knows something about Christine that will give her power. At the end of the brief conversation she throws down the gauntlet:

> LAVINIA (*harshly*): I've got to have a talk with you, Mother—before long!
>
> CHRISTINE (*turning defiantly*): Whenever you wish. Tonight after the Captain leaves you, if you like. But what is it you want to talk about?
>
> LAVINIA: You'll know soon enough!
>
> CHRISTINE (*staring at her with a questioning dread—forcing a scornful smile*): You always make such a mystery of things, Vinnie.

The unexpected revelation of Brant's identity turns Lavinia's knowledge of her mother's adultery into an even more effective weapon than she had thought. It gives her a superiority that is only seemingly and temporarily offset by the return of Mannon, who lends fatal support to his wife's authority. Mannon's dying words and the discovery of the poison make Christine the helpless victim of Lavinia's revenge.

> "THUS IT IS NOT ACCIDENTAL THAT O'NEILL REPLACES THE MURDER OF CLYTEMNAESTRA WITH THE SUICIDE OF CHRISTINE. THE CHANGE WAS NOT MERELY DUE TO THE SETTING OF THE TRILOGY AND THE EXIGENCIES OF THE PLOT; IT TELLS SOMETHING ABOUT O'NEILL'S IDEA OF ACTION. IN *MOURNING BECOMES ELECTRA* A SUICIDAL ELEMENT IS CONTAINED IN ALL ACTION; ONE MIGHT ALMOST SAY THAT ACTION IS SUICIDE."

Ashley Dukes, one of the critics of the London premiere of *Mourning Becomes Electra,* maintains that Mannon's return from war is like the return of Hamlet's father from the realm of death. But Mannon's death more closely parallels the ghost scene. Mannon's dying words: "She's guilty—not medicine" (I,iv) are like the "Remember me" of Hamlet's father. Hamlet's reaction to his father's command is this:

> Remember thee!
> Yea, from the table of my memory
> I'll wipe away all trivial fond records,
> All saws of books, all forms, all pressures past
> That youth and observation copied there:
> And the commandment all alone shall live
> Within the book and volume of my brain,
> Unmix'd with baser matter.
>
> (I,v)

He confirms his vow by jilting Ophelia. Lavinia, too, rejects Peter's proposal from a sense of duty to her father. The parallel is valid if we consider that the sudden discovery is replaced in *Mourning Becomes Electra* by a series of partial revelations.

In this lives of Lavinia and Hamlet the call to revenge is the turning point that ends the humiliations of the past. Orestes's revenge takes a different course. His chief obstacle is the power of

Clytemnaestra and Aegisthus, represented by the bodyguard at the end of the Agamemnon, and indirectly by the status of Electra at the opening of the Choephoroe. Lavinia lacks no opportunity to execute her revenge, but she wants to do it without arousing the suspicion of outsiders. Again Hamlet is the model, for the similar character of the crime entails a similar course of revenge. When Hamlet first hears the truth from his father he exclaims:

> Haste me to know't, that I, withe wings as swift
> As meditation or the thoughts of love,
> May sweep to my revenge (I,v)

But as soon as he meets his friends he realizes the difficulty of action: the need for secrecy forces Hamlet to modify his desire for instantaneous revenge.

The motif recurs in *Mourning Becomes Electra,* most explicitly when Christine initiates Brant into her plan. Brant has all sorts of ideas how he might "sweep" to his revenge: "If I could catch him alone, where no one would interfere, and let the best man come out alive as I've often seen it done in the West!" (I, ii). Christine replies succintly: "This isn't the West." Indeed, it is not. The house of the Mannons reminds one far more of the court of Denmark.

The need for secrecy and "indirections" (*Hamlet*) guides Lavinia's revenge. Her first task is to convince her brother of her mother's guilt just as Hamlet has to dispel his own doubts. Both of them decide to become actors and stage situations in which the criminal will betray himself. However, some time elapses before an opportunity arises. Hamlet mystifies the court by his antic disposition. In *Mourning Becomes Electra* Lavinia "mystifies" her mother who, like Claudius, recognizes the threat in her daughter's behavior. Later, when the roles are reversed and Lavinia has identified herself with her mother, she is terrified by Orin's deliberate mystification (I, i; II, i; III, ii). Hamlet's pretended madness furnishes Claudius with a pretext to remove the prince from the court; in *Mourning Becomes Electra*. Christine tries to convince Orin that Lavinia is mad (II, ii). The struggle between Christine and Lavinia corresponds to that of Claudius and Hamlet, but it takes very different forms. The two women fight for the possession of Orin, and it is during the intrigues which this struggle involves that Orin becomes a true Mannon. The spoiled child of whom we had heard in *Homecoming* and who at his first appearance in *Hunted* is still associated with Peter and Hazel undergoes a change as he is drawn into the tragic circle. He exemplifies the truth of Christine's outburst: "Why can't all of us remain innocent and loving and trusting? But God won't leave us alone. He twists and wrings and tortures our lives with others' lives until—we poison each other to death" (II, i). The spread of poison once corrupted Christine herself, and in the final play of the trilogy its all-pervasive power is again revealed in Lavinia's frantic but hopeless attempts to rid herself of it. Even Peter and Hazel are almost infected by it. At one point Hazel implores Lavinia not to marry Peter, who is already showing signs of her baneful influence (III, iv). The theme of poisoning thus develops a motif of the plot in a manner very similar to that of *Hamlet*. There the theme of poisoning occurs with many variations. The corruption of Laertes by Claudius is perhaps the best parallel to the corruption of Orin. Laertes runs into Claudius's trap with pathetic eagerness. His corruption, which he himself realizes only in his death, is conveyed to the audience much earlier. To Claudius's suggestion that he should fight Hamlet with an unbuttoned rapier Laertes replies:

> I will do't:
> And, for that purpose, I'll anoint my sword.
> I bought an unction of a mountebank
> So mortal that but dip a knife in it,
> Where it draws blood no cataplasm so rare,
> Collected from all simples that have virtue
> Under the moon, can save the thing from death
> That is but scratched withal. (IV, vii)

The Laertes who carries poison with him is very different from the young man who set out for France.

Christine fails to keep Orin on her side. She does not want Orin to be alone with Lavinia before she has spoken to him; hence, her anger at Peter: "Why didn't you call me, Peter? You shouldn't have left him alone!" (II, i). But Lavinia literally intercepts Orin, and her few words with him are enough to undermine Orin's trust in his mother. For a moment, indeed, Christine seems to win. It is with great reluctance that Orin tears himself from his mother to follow Lavinia to see his father's corpse (II, ii). The dialogue of Lavinia and Orin in the presence of the dead father is superficially modeled on the *kommos* of the *Choephoroe,* where the dead king is also "present." But unlike Orestes, Orin cannot be incited to action by Lavinia's words alone. Christine has too cleverly anticipated her accusations. Therefore, Lavinia suggests that they give Christine and Brant a chance to meet again at a place where Orin and Lavinia can overhear their conversation (II, iii). That meeting in the following act bears some resemblance to the scene in which Ophelia is used as a decoy. While Lavinia and Orin are plotting, Christine has followed Orin and is terrified to find the door locked. Lavinia seizes at her chance and on the spur of the moment stages a "mouse-trap." She places the medicine bottle on the dead man's chest and tells Orin to watch Christine closely. In like manner, Hamlet and Horatio resolve not to take their eyes off the king. Both times the "play" succeeds. The similarity extends even to the reactions of Hamlet and Orin. Hamlet loses his control and forfeits half his triumph. Orin, too, is tempted to forget himself and is only restrained by Lavinia's warnings. Even so, the revelation is too much for him: he "stumbles blindly" out of the room (II, iii). His breakdown and his savage irony may be compared to Hamlet's hysterical behavior after Claudius's exit.

Like Lavinia, Orin is a descendant of Hamlet; actually, each represents a different interpretation of Hamlet. Lavinia lacks the reflection and irresolution of the popular Hamlet; she does not hesitate to act with speed and determination. She is very much like the Hamlet of Wilson Knight's "Embassy of Death." In fact, Knight's portrait really fits Lavinia better than Hamlet. Lavinia may well be called a superman even among the Mannons, who are all in their own way superhuman. Her obsession with truth and her strength of will lead her to reject escape in any disguise. Escape in *Mourning Becomes Electra* takes two forms: it is either illusion or death. Mannon's public career, Christine's affair with Brant, and Orin's dreams of a South Sea island belong to the former; the suicides of Christine and Orin, to the latter. Now Lavinia does not differ from the others in her attempt to escape into illusion; she tries harder than anyone else. She differs from the other characters in being herself the obstacle to her own happiness. Her penetrating intellect ultimately prevents any self-deception; it can bear the truth. Mannon, Orin, and Christine come to see the truth and realize the futility of illusion only to escape into death. Lavinia alone survives. She is the incarnation of the Mannon evil, "the most interesting criminal of us all," as Orin calls her (III, i, 2), and in this respect, too, she resembles Knight's Hamlet from whom death emanates.

Orin is a much less original creation. He is the disillusioned Romantic. Like the popular Hamlet, he is weak and oversensitive. He is either bullied by his mother or by his sister. He is given to reflection and is by nature unwilling to act; when he acts he does so in a state of blind excitement, a trait considered an essential feature of Hamlet by critics who think of him as the melancholy Dane.

Orin's share in the action is much slighter than Lavinia's; he does not come to the fore until *Haunted,* the plot of which is a pale echo of the preceding events. He is a portrait rather than a character revealed in action, except for his relation to Hazel, which may well be modeled on Hamlet's relation to Ophelia. Hamlet turns from his thoughts about suicide when he sees Ophelia:

Soft you now!
The fair Ophelia. Nymph, in thy orisons
Be all my sins remember'd. (III, i)

Likewise, Orin is attracted to Hazel—whether he has just returned from war or wishes to escape the burden of his guilt—because she is an unchanging image of peace. But Hazel's innocence also provokes Orin's cynicism. His bitter remarks about war (II, ii) are meant to shock Hazel; in this regard they resemble Hamlet's obscenities in the play scene. In *Haunted,* Orin is led by his sense of duty to jilt Hazel just as Hamlet jilts Ophelia. Something of the intensity of Hamlet's feeling for Ophelia shows through her report of his farewell. His savage insults in the decoy scene are but the other side of these feelings. The same contrast is found in Orin:

I have no right in the same world with her. And yet I feel so drawn to her purity! Her love for me makes me appear less vile to myself! (*Then with a harsh laugh*) And, at the same time, a million times more vile, that's the hell of it! (III, ii)

When he finally jilts Hazel, he first asks her gently not to love him any more (III, iii), but then changes to taunting cruelty to make the farewell final (III, iii).

Hazel offers the key to Christine's tragedy, for in a sense Christine is never so much herself as in the two short scenes with Hazel (II, i, v), which are modeled on the relationship of Gertrude with Ophelia. To compare Christine and Gertrude may seem strange at first. Gertrude is neither guilty of murder nor is it clear whether she has committed adultery. Hatred is foreign to her nature; in all she says and does she reveals her sincere affection for Ophelia and her great love for Hamlet. But above all, there is something very vague about her. Only once, in the closet scene, does she come to the fore, and then only to recede into a shadowy and ambiguous background. It is in this scene that Gertrude is shown lacking parental authority, just as Christine, in her various confrontations with her daughter, is handicapped by the loss of this authority.

There is a deliberate contrast between Gertrude's pale portrait in the play and the violent colors in which Hamlet and his father paint her offense. Christine, on the other hand, is a Gertrude with the merciful veil of ambiguity torn from her face; in a sense she is the woman one would expect from what Hamlet and his father say about Gertrude. There is no doubt about her adultery: we see her as she abandons a respectable husband to "prey on garbage," in favor of the "son of a low Canuck nurse girl" (I, i). We do not know whether Hamlet's imagination is accurate when he describes Gertrude's passion for Claudius, but Lavinia is an eyewitness of the clandestine rendezvous of Brant and Christine in a squalid New York hotel, and she dwells on it with the perverted pleasure Hamlet at times takes in sordid details (I, ii).

Although the events at Elsinore are concerned with Gertrude, she hardly takes part in them. Her only active interest seems to be the match between Hamlet and Ophelia; it is typical of her remoteness that she should continue to talk about it when it has long ceased to matter. When she hears from Claudius that Polonius has found the reason of Hamlet's madness, she replies:

> I doubt it is no other but the main;
> His father's death, and our o'erhasty marriage. (II, ii)

Polonius's news fascinates her. It is she, not Claudius, who asks him to come to the point, and when Claudius and Polonius have only the success of their scheme in mind, Gertrude looks to the future and addresses Ophelia:

> And for your part, Ophelia, I do wish
> That your good beauties be the happy cause
> Of Hamlet's wildness: so shall I hope your virtues
> Will bring him to his wonted way again,
> To both your honours. (III, i)

The link between Gertrude and Ophelia is maintained in the following act. It is Gertrude who first receives the mad Ophelia; she also reports her death. At Ophelia's funeral Gertrude once more returns to the match in words whose quietness contrasts with the ranting of Hamlet:

> Sweets to the sweet! Farewell.
> I hoped thou shouldst have been my
>   Hamlet's wife:
> I thought thy bride-bed to have decked,
>   sweet maid,
> And not have strew'd thy grave. (V, i)

The constant association of Gertrude and Ophelia in the spectator's mind balances the slanders of Hamlet and his father; her kindness to Ophelia belies at least their more extreme accusations. Gertrude looks at Ophelia with a twofold regret. She knows that she has offended Hamlet and seizes at the prospect of the match in order to secure his happiness as well as to regain his affection. It is understandable why marriage should appeal to her as the best means to this end: she herself had once experienced happiness in marriage. Her vision of the future is nostalgic; it attempts to regain the past.

The queen is choosing a young court lady as a match for her difficult son: so far the plot fits both *Hamlet* and *Mourning Becomes Electra*. But Christine acts from fear rather than from solicitude for Orin. Also, she thinks primarily of her own interest; she uses Hazel as Claudius uses Ophelia. Whether Gertrude's plan is quite unselfish it is impossible to tell. Christine hopes that by furthering the romance between Orin and Hazel, which she had hitherto obstructed, she can isolate Lavinia and prevent her from winning Orin to her side. Thus she proposes a "conspiracy" between Hazel and herself, insinuating the danger that lies in Lavinia's jealousy. But the innocence with which Hazel at once goes into the trap and yet refuses to believe anything evil about Lavinia surprises and touches her, and a well of affection springs up for Hazel in whom she sees her own past reflected:

> Hazel: Poor Vinnie! She was so fond of her father. I don't wonder she—
>
> Christine (*staring at her—strangely*): You are genuinely good and pure of heart, aren't you?
>
> Hazel (*embarrassed*): Oh, no! I'm not at all—
>
> Christine: I was like you once—long ago—before— (*then with bitter longing*) If I could only have stayed as I was then! (II, i)

Just as Gertrude may see her former happiness in the mirage of a happy marriage between Hamlet and Ophelia, so the thought of Hazel makes Christine recall her time of courtship, which she describes to Lavinia: "No. I loved him once—before I married him —incredible as that seems now! He was handsome in his lieutenant's uniform! He was silent and mysterious and romantic! But marriage soon turned his romance into—disgust!" (I, ii). Then her eyes spoke and were full of life, as Mannon says in his clumsy attempt to break the barrier between them (I, iii). There was a time when she resembled Marie Brantome, the nurse girl, whose memory is invoked in the scene before Mannon's entrance in order to make the contrast between past and present as poignant as possible. Christine wants nothing so much as to be young Christine again. Her affection for Hazel and her longing for innocent youth spring from her desperate fear of growing old: "I can't let myself get ugly! I can't!" (II, v).

A portrait of Gertrude would be incomplete without mention of her timidity and lack of initiative. In these respects, too, Christine resembles her; for her actions, premeditated as they may appear, are actually reactions to forces over which she has no control. And it is blind fear that makes her commit her fatal mistakes. The fearful Clytemnaestra is, of course, known to Sophocles and Euripides, but Aeschylus shows her as a woman of immense courage. O'Neill's Christine commits the crime of the Aeschylean Clytemnaestra, although by nature she is much more like Gertrude.

One must keep in mind the fact that O'Neill's idea of action is quite different from that of the *Oresteia*. In Aeschylus the problem of necessity always presents itself as a fateful choice: Agamemnon makes a decision "when he put on the yoke of necessity" (*Agamemnon*); Orestes *decides* to kill his mother. Aeschylus has no abstract concept of fate, let alone a fate that deprives action of its meaning or relieves the agent of his responsibility. He even lets his Chorus speak out against a determinism that denies responsibility and thinks of crime as something that merely happens (*Agamemnon*). The consequences of an action are determined by the original choice, and this choice may not in our sense be "free," but Aeschylus would never have denied its existence.

In *Mourning Becomes Electra,* and to a certain extent in *Hamlet,* we find a very different concept of action. It is summarized by Horatio:

> So shall you hear
> Of carnal, bloody, and unnatural acts,
> Of accidental judgments, casual slaughters,
> Of deaths put on by cunning and forced cause,
> And, in this upshot, purposes mistook
> Fall'n on the inventor's heads. (V, ii)

A contrast between deliberate actions that miscarry and rash or intuitive actions that are decisive runs through the whole tragedy of Hamlet. While Orestes asks: "What shall I do?" before proceeding to kill his mother, Hamlet comes to rely on intuition. His attitude toward action is exemplified by his account of his adventures at sea:

> Rashly
> And praised be rashness for it, let us know,
> Our indiscretion sometime serves us well
> When our deep plots do pall....
> ....
> Up from my cabin,
> My sea-gown scarf'd about me, in the dark
> Groped I to find out them....
> ....
> Being thus benetted round with villainies,
> Ere I could make a prologue to my brains,
> They had begun the play—I sat me down. (V, ii)

It is a corollary of such an intuitive view of action that the agent becomes a sufferer: the events happen to him as well as to the person he acts on. Hamlet dies with Claudius; their deaths are one action, as the deaths of Agamemnon and Clytemnaestra are not. In *Mourning Becomes Electra,* such ideas are carried to an extreme. Action is no longer the result of choice and loses all significance; it becomes a stage in some pathological process that ends in death. Orin committed his "heroic" deeds in a kind of trance, in which he saw a blurred face—his own, his father's?—which he had to kill over and over again. He sees this face again when he looks at Brant whom he has just killed:

> Orin: By God, he does look like father!
> Lavinia: No. Come along!
> Orin (*as if talking to himself*): This is like my
>   dream. I've killed before—over and over.
> Lavinia: Orin!
> Orin: Do you remember me telling you how the
>   faces of the men I killed came back and
>   changed to Father's face and finally became
>   my own? (*He smiles grimly*) He looks like
>   me, too! Maybe I've committed suicide....
>   It's queer! It's a rotten dirty joke on
>   someone! (II, iv)

Thus it is not accidental that O'Neill replaces the murder of Clytemnaestra with the suicide of Christine. The change was not merely due to the setting of the trilogy and the exigencies of the plot; it tells something about O'Neill's idea of action. In *Mourning Becomes Electra* a suicidal element is contained in all action; one might almost say that action is suicide. There is a telling ambiguity in the account of Mannon's death which will illustrate this paradoxical statement. Christine's plan is easily summarized. Shortly after she hears of Mannon's imminent return, Christine begins to plan the murder of her husband should it become necessary. She spreads a rumor of his heart disease and chooses what seems a safe way of acquiring the poison with which to do the murder. The confrontation with Lavinia convinces her that the time to act has come. She dispatches Brant to get the poison, and in the night of Mannon's return she deliberately provokes a heart attack and gives him the poison instead of his medicine. In this outline each step of the action appears to be initiated by a decision on the part of Christine, but this is not the way things happen in the play. Christine never decides to kill Mannon; the encounter with Lavinia rather pushes her into a situation in which she suddenly realizes that her plan has started moving. At first everything works surprisingly smoothly, particularly since it emerges that Mannon's disease is more serious than he had cared to admit. But Christine had not considered the nature of the victim. The Mannon whom she planned to murder was the man of whom Orin will later say:

> Death sits so naturally on you! Death becomes the Mannons! You were always like a statue of an eminent dead man—sitting on a chair in a park or straddling a horse in a town square—looking over the head of life without a sign of recognition—cutting it dead for the impropriety of living! (II, iii)

There is something innocent about Christine's plan, simply because it had never occurred to her that the man whom she was going to murder was not already "dead." When Mannon in his awkward fashion tries to remove the barrier between them and reveals that behind his mask he is alive and suffering, Christine realizes with growing dread what her plan really involves. For a moment Mannon has doffed his mask and beneath it she sees a man who in his way loves her deeply. In helpless terror she exclaims:

> For God's sake, stop talking. I don't know what you're saying. Leave me alone. What must be, must be! You make me weak! (*Then abruptly*) It's getting late. (I, iii)

Mannon, "terribly wounded," dons his mask and becomes once more a pale ghost: Christine can proceed with her plan. She *decides* to bring on his heart attack. But at the beginning of the following act we see a timid Christine moving away from her husband's bed and the scene of the fateful action. Mannon calls back, turns on the light, and insists on talking to her. For the quarrel that develops between them it is important to remember what Christine had earlier said to Brant:

> I couldn't fool him long. He's a strange, hidden man. His silence always creeps into my thoughts. Even if he never spoke, I would feel what was in his mind and some night, lying beside him, it would drive me mad and I'd have to kill his silence by screaming out the truth! (I, ii)

Something similar is happening now, only it is not Mannon's silence that drives her toward the murder. Far from pursuing her plan, Christine is persecuted by Mannon's insinuations and coarse insults until she breaks under the strain: she tells the truth. That this collapse enables her to carry out her plan no longer matters. O'Neill does not say explicitly that Mannon would have died of his heart attack, but he strongly suggests that Christine's murder is supererogatory. Christine and Mannon tear off one another's masks and the truth that appears is more deadly than any poison could be. The only certain victim of the poison is Christine herself, for it provides Lavinia with the weapon that will drive Christine into suicide. If one insists on calling Christine's death premeditated murder, one might just as well argue that Mannon commits suicide. Both arguments assume that every action requires a responsible agent, but that is precisely the assumption which is denied in O'Neill's trilogy.

Finally, in Aeschylus the form of the trilogy has a meaning: Orestes is the third man in a chain of tragic events. He belongs to the third generation after the original crime of Thyestes; his fate is the third to be decided after the deaths of Agamemnon and Clytemnaestra. As the "third savior" he is unobtrusively compared to Zeus, who is king in the third generation after Ouranos and Kronos. Will he succeed in breaking the chain of crime and retribution? That is the question the Chorus asks with great anxiety at the end of the *Choephoroe*; it is answered in the third play, the *Eumenides*. The three parts of *Mourning Becomes Electra*, on the other hand, are like the progressive stages of a disease. The form of the trilogy has lost its meaning; *Mourning Becomes Electra* is really one very long play that does not end until the pathological process has come to an end.

The traditional assumptions about the relationship of *Mourning Becomes Electra* and the *Oresteia*, then, should be revised. O'Neill misled himself and his critics by maintaining that the *Oresteia* was a blueprint for his trilogy. *Mourning Becomes Electra* significantly departs from the *Oresteia*, and wherever it does so it goes parallel with *Hamlet*. The murder of Ezra Mannon follows the poisoning of Hamlet's father, and the revenge plot based on the secrecy of crime and revenge rather than on the concealment of the avenger's identity also has *Hamlet* as its model. Lavinia and Orin are both descended from Hamlet rather than from Electra and Orestes, respectively. The relationship of Hamlet and Ophelia is the pattern for the relations of Peter and Hazel to Lavinia and Orin, and the relationship of Hazel and Christine is strikingly similar to that of Ophelia and Gertrude.

The comparison between *Hamlet* and *Mourning Becomes Electra* throws a new light on the "Greekness" of O'Neill's trilogy. Critics commonly contrast the "happy end" of the *Oresteia* with the grim pessimism of *Mourning* and then either condemn O'Neill for his extreme pessimism or—as

Roger Asselineau has done recently —praise him for the deeper insight and greater daring with which he carried the story to its bitter end. But the difference is not one of degree or of mood. We have seen that the *Oresteia* and *Mourning Becomes Electra* employ entirely different concepts of action. It is simply not true that O'Neill, as he said himself, psychologized Greek fate. For the "fate" that O'Neill considers so typical of Greek tragedy does not exist. There is no evidence that O'Neill's approach to Greek drama ever freed itself from the critical prejudices that persist even to this day; he saw Greek tragedy through the spectacles of a popular determinism. There is nothing in *Mourning Becomes Electra* which would suggest that O'Neill ever had an original experience of Greek drama in general, or of the *Oresteia* in particular. No doubt, he knew Aeschylus's trilogy well, but he must have read it with a notion, at once very strong and rather vague, of what a Greek tragedy ought to be like. He never penetrated to the Greekness of it; nor was he inspired by it. O'Neill's trilogy is no more Greek than the house of the Mannons: it only has a Greek facade.

Source: Horst Frenz and Martin Mueller, "More Shakespeare and Less Aeschylus in Eugene O'Neill's *Mourning Becomes Electra,*" in *American Literature,* 1966, Vol. 38, pp. 85–100.

Joseph Wood Krutch

In this favorable review of O'Neill's play, Krutch appraises the original production of Mourning Becomes Electra *as possessing all the "virtues . . . which one expects in the best contemporary dramatic writing."*

Except for a dinner intermission Eugene O'Neill's new trilogy, *Mourning Becomes Electra* (Guild Theater), runs from five o' clock in the afternoon until about eleven-fifteen in the evening. Seldom if ever has any play received a reception so unreservedly enthusiastic as this one was accorded by the New York newspapers and, to begin with, I can only say that I share the enthusiasm to the full. Here, in the first place, are those virtues—intelligence, insight, and rapid, absorbing action—which one expects in the best contemporary dramatic writing. But here also are a largeness of conception and a more than local or temporary significance which put to rest those doubts which usually arise when one is tempted to attribute a lasting greatness to any play of our generation. O'Neill, though thoroughly "modern," is not dealing with the accidents of contemporary life. He has managed to give his—I am almost tempted to say "our"—version of a tale which implies something concerning the most permanent aspects of human nature, and it is hard to imagine how the play could lose its interest merely because of those superficial changes which take place from generation to generation. For this reason it may turn out to be the only permanent contribution yet made by the twentieth century to dramatic literature.

As the title suggests, O'Neill's fable follows, almost incident for incident, the main outlines of the Greek story. Though he has set the action in New England just after the Civil War, his Clytemnestra murders Agamemnon and his Electra persuades Orestes to bring about the death of their common mother. Nor do such changes as are necessarily made in the motivation of the characters so much modify the effect of the story as merely restore that effect by translating the story into terms which we can fully comprehend. It is true that Electra loves her father and that Orestes loves his mother in a fashion which the Greeks either did not understand or, at least, did not specify. It is true also that the play implies that the psychological quirks responsible for the tragedy are the result of a conflict between puritanism and healthy love. But this is merely the way in which we understand such situations, and the fact remains that these things are *merely* implied, that the implications exist for the sake of the play, not the play for the sake of the implications. It is, moreover, this fact more than any other which indicates something very important in the nature of O'Neill's achievement.

Hitherto most of our best plays have been—of necessity perhaps—concerned primarily with the exposition and defense of their intellectual or moral or psychological backgrounds. They have been written to demonstrate that it was legitimate to understand or judge men in the new ways characteristic of our time. But O'Neill has succeeded in writing a great play in which a reversal of this emphasis has taken place at last. Because its thesis is taken for granted, it has no thesis. It is no more an exposition or defense of a modern psychological conception than Aeschylus is an exposition or defense of the tenets of the Greek religion, even though it does accept the one as Aeschylus accepts the other. It is on the other hand—and like all supremely great pieces of literature—primarily about the passions and primarily addressed to our interest in them. Once more we have a great play which does not "mean" anything in the sense that the plays of Ibsen or Shaw or Galsworthy usually mean something, but one which does, on the contrary, mean the

> WHAT WE DO IS MERELY TO ACCEPT THESE FABLES AS THOUGH THEY WERE FACTS AND SIT AMAZED BY THE HEIGHT AND THE DEPTH OF HUMAN PASSIONS, BY THE GRANDEUR AND MEANNESS OF HUMAN DEEDS."

same thing that "Oedipus" and "Hamlet" and "Macbeth" mean—namely, that human beings are great and terrible creatures when they are in the grip of great passions, and that the spectacle of them is not only absorbing but also and at once horrible and cleansing. Nineteenth-century critics of Shakespeare said that his plays were like the facts of nature, and though this statement has no intellectual content it does imply something concerning that attitude which we adopt toward *Mourning Becomes Electra* as well as toward Shakespeare. Our arguments and our analyses are unimportant as long as we attempt to discover in them the secret of our interest. What we do is merely to accept these fables as though they were facts and sit amazed by the height and the depth of human passions, by the grandeur and meanness of human deeds. Perhaps no one knows exactly what it means to be "purged by pity and terror," but for that very reason, perhaps, one returns to the phrase.

To find in the play any lack at all one must compare it with the very greatest works of dramatic literature, but when one does compare it with "Hamlet" or "Macbeth" one realizes that it does lack just one thing and that that thing is language—words as thrilling as the action which accompanies them. Take, for example, the scene in which Orin (Orestes) stands beside the bier of his father and apostrophizes the body laid there. No one can deny that the speech is a good one, but what one desires with an almost agonizing desire is something not merely good but something incredibly magnificent, something like "Tomorrow and tomorrow and tomorrow . . ." or "I could a tale unfold whose lightest word . . . ." If by some miracle such words could come, the situation would not be unworthy of them. Here is a scenario to which the most soaring eloquence and the most profound poetry are appropriate, and if it were granted us we should be swept aloft as no Anglo-Saxon audience since Shakespeare's time has had an opportunity to be. But no modern is capable of language really worthy of O'Neill's play, and the lack of that one thing is the penalty we must pay for living in an age which is not equal to more than prose. Nor is it to be supposed that I make this reservation merely for the purpose of saying that Mr. O'Neill's play is not so good as the best of Shakespeare; I make it, on the contrary, in order to indicate where one must go in order to find a worthy comparison.

Space is lacking to pay fitting tribute to the production and acting of the play. It must suffice to say that both they and the setting do it justice. Both Nazimova as Christine (Clytemnestra) and Alice Brady as Lavinia (Electra) contribute performances hardly less notable in their own way than the play, and, indeed, everyone concerned in the production may be said to share somewhat in the achievement. *Mourning Becomes Electra* reads well; when it comes to life on the stage of the Guild Theater it is no less than tremendous.

Source: Joseph Wood Krutch, "Our Electra," in the *Nation*, Vol. CXXXIII, no. 3463, November 18, 1931, pp. 551–52.

Richard Dana Skinner

Claiming that the playwright "has at last written a straightforward tragedy of major proportions," Skinner offers a positive review of the debut production of O'Neill's play.

Eugene O'Neill has at last written a straightforward tragedy of major proportions. For reasons which I shall try to explain later on, it would be lacking in a true sense of proportion to call it a "great" tragedy—in spite of the fact that many of its passages are infused with the true greatness of the tragic spirit, and in spite of the further fact that in structure, in sequence and in rhythm, the three plays composing the trilogy, "*Mourning Becomes Electra,*" contain, by all odds, the finest dramatic writing of O'Neill's career.

As to the general character of this ambitious trilogy, it is already widely understood that O'Neill has made the deliberate experiment of transposing the basic legend of several of the most important Greek tragedies into the atmosphere and period of New England immediately after the Civil War. One can see clearly that O'Neill has felt, in the perfect outer form and inner emotional turmoil of New

England, the modern counterpart of ancient Greece. Essentially, however, he is not writing a tragedy of New England, but a tragedy of universal proportions expressing one of the oldest psychological problems of the tragic spirit, and merely using terms and circumstances sufficiently close to the present day to give it an immediate and understandable quality for modern audiences.

''*Mourning Becomes Electra*'' is a restatement for our own century of the story of the house of Atreus, of the murder of Agamemnon by his wife, Clytemnestra, of the vengeance wreaked upon her by Agamemnon's children, Electra and Orestes, and of their further pursuit by the Furies for having committed the sin of matricide. The core of Greek tragedy obviously lay in just such conflicts of obligation. Electra and Orestes were caught between the obligation to avenge their father's murder and the unspeakable horror of being forced, as part of that vengeance, to kill their own mother, thus piling crime upon crime through generations. The Greeks, always highly objective in their expression of such problems, made their tragic characters chiefly the victims of fate. Revenge was ordered by a god. But, in executing that revenge, another god was offended, and demanded in turn further punishment for the new crime.

O'Neill now restates this classic tragic dilemma, but in a spirit which is far removed from Greek objectivity. He summons up, instead of fate and factious gods, those mysterious inner impulses of the neurotic mind which modern psychologists have attempted to chart and label under the names of various "complexes." He summons them in terms of a mother's jealousy of her own daughter, of a son's jealousy of his father, and of a daughter's unconscious desire to occupy in the household the triple mental rôle of wife, mother and sister.

In all fairness to modern psychologists, it should be said that these explanations of tragic motives represent merely one school of thought, and a rather extreme and partly discredited one at that. When a young man shows signs of moral weakness, for example, and is unable to face the independent responsibilities of manhood, the more advanced psychologists are content to say that he is regressing to a childish attitude and to a time when all decisions were made for him and when any rebuffs of the world could soon be forgotten at a mother's knee. Such a man might easily prefer for a wife the maternal type of woman who mothers him in difficulties, to a more independent type who forces him

> "O'NEILL NOW RESTATES THIS CLASSIC TRAGIC DILEMMA, BUT IN A SPIRIT WHICH IS FAR REMOVED FROM GREEK OBJECTIVITY. HE SUMMONS UP, INSTEAD OF FATE AND FACTIOUS GODS, THOSE MYSTERIOUS INNER IMPULSES OF THE NEUROTIC MIND WHICH MODERN PSYCHOLOGISTS HAVE ATTEMPTED TO CHART AND LABEL UNDER THE NAMES OF VARIOUS 'COMPLEXES.'"

to face responsibilities squarely. He might also resent a domineering father who tried to drive him from his mother's apron strings. All these weaknesses and hidden resentments might easily result in a neurotic state of mind, in violent excesses of rage and remorse and in a perpetual inner conflict leading to a tragic outcome. The other and older school of psychologists would attribute the same neurotic symptoms to the young man's unadmitted and abnormal attachment to his own mother and to a definite jealousy of his own father. O'Neill uses the explanations of this latter school to describe the motives for his tragedy. Every one of his main characters is tied to a definite incestuous desire. This is more than evident at each successive stage of the trilogy, even though O'Neill carefully avoids using any of the modern psychological jargon.

Electra (Lavinia Mannon in the play) is doubly moved to avenge her father's death by the fact of her jealousy of her mother in relation to two men, her dead father and her mother's lover, who is also a cousin of her father, with many of her father's personal traits. Again, Orestes (Orin Mannon in the play) seeks in Electra (Lavinia) a substitute for the morbid love of his dead mother, and then, in the horror of his discovery, commits suicide. A dozen such deep and sinister currents of perverted emotion fill the course of the play, logically enough if you once accept the premise of O'Neill's school of mental analysis, but without any of the subtler modifying influences which a broader and less heavily sexualized interpretation would bring.

O'Neill departs still further from the Greek tradition and feeling in quailing before the possibility of matricide. Lavinia and Orin are content to avenge their father's death by killing their mother's lover. Nevertheless, when the shock of his death leads their mother to commit suicide, Orin feels as guilty as if he had killed her. Lavinia does not share this sense of guilt. But when Orin, too, kills himself, then, at last, Lavinia shuts herself up in the house of tragic memories, to expiate through years of silent though proud seclusion, the sins of her family. Symbolically, at least, O'Neill has chosen to end with the theme of the outcast and blind Oedipus, Lavina shutting out the sight of the world and living in it no more.

Essentially, then, ''*Mourning Becomes Electra*'' is not a Greek tragedy except in the bare outlines of the plot. Even the plot avoids the Greek culmination of matricide. The play is utterly modern (though hardly up to date) in its analysis of motives, and as far removed from the Greek spirit as Freud from Aristotle. What we have is a deeply involved story of abnormal desires transmitting themselves bit by bit into a chain of tragic and terrible consequences, into an overwhelming sense of guilt for each character in turn and at last into the lonely expiation and pride of Lavinia—a pride which lets her say ''I ask forgiveness of no one. I forgive myself!'' In the very height and stature of this pride we fail to discover the rumor of resurrection which alone could lend the note of great lyric tragedy to this dark story. The trilogy is written with restrained intensity, with superb emotional power and with tremendous climactic pace. It holds both emotions and interest with unrelenting firmness. It is a work of greatness in playwriting but it fails to emerge as a great tragedy. It is limited by the proud self-pity of its ending and by that symbolic blindness which does not presage resurrection from the house of the dead.

The Theatre Guild has given a production of extraordinary beauty and austerity to this group of three plays. In selecting Robert Edmond Jones to create the settings, and Alice Brady, Alla Nazimova, Earl Larimore and Thomas Chalmers for the leading parts, the Guild has shown rare aptitude in putting together exactly the qualities of artistry needed to bring the utmost of beauty and distinction from the sinister material of the plays themselves. No matter what one may think of the play material, there can be no question that, as the Guild has mounted it, it becomes one of the most distinguished exhibits we have had in many years of the power of the theatre to create and sustain illusion. The three plays of the trilogy are given in one day, the first play in the afternoon and the second and third in the evening. It might be added, at this point, that O'Neill has abandoned for the purposes of this trilogy the entire bag of theatrical tricks with which he has distorted so many of his plays. There are none of the asides of *Strange Interlude,* and there are no masks. In consequence, every moment is used to advance the dramatic action without the impediment of theatrical padding. The plays run through swiftly and directly in the writing as well as in the production.

Philip Moeller has directed this trilogy with consummate artistry and finely disciplined restraint. It is easily the best work of his career. The stage settings by Robert Edmond Jones catch the spirit of the plays with extraordinary fidelity. The stage curtain shows the Greek-Colonial façade of the gloomy house of Mannon and shows, more strikingly than any words could possibly explain, what is in O'Neill's mind—namely, the sense of identity between the spirit of New England and the spirit of Greece. Both the interior and the exterior scenes of the house itself, and the scene of a chipper ship at its dock in Boston, are typical expressions of Mr. Jones's finest artistry, that is, his ability to combine realism with an overpowering atmosphere of universal suggestion.

But it is the acting cast, after all, which deserves the maximum amount of praise for its complete mastery of one of the most difficult tasks ever assigned to a group of actors. The Lavinia of Alice Brady is one of the truly astonishing figures of the modern theatre. The way in which she manages to convey a torrent of interior emotions through an exterior of calm austerity is an achievement almost without parallel. The part of the mother, as played by Alla Nazimova, is also a performance of unquestioned greatness. Her sea-captain lover is played by Thomas Chalmers with downrightness and clear understanding, and Earl Larimore brings to the part of the weakling, Orin, the full terror of growing insanity.

In general, it is still true that O'Neill exhibits through this trilogy the picture of volcanic emotions violently at war with his intellect. These emotions, which might become his greatest creative gift, still lack utterly the disciplined direction of an informed will. Certainly it is the character of Lavinia who seems to be the creative artist in O'Neill, just as it is the distracted Orin who represents his lack of intellectual stability. There is no question that O'Neill is a true artist, and with true artists it is never possible to separate completely the artist from his work. There is still nothing to indicate that O'Neill, as an artist, has yet achieved that self-mastery which, if once united with his creative power, might easily make him one of the great playwrights of all time. There is too much in this "*Electra*" trilogy to recall the futile search and the ultimate tragedy of "Dynamo," and yet—if Lavinia, as a symbol of O'Neill's power, should ever emerge from her darkened house of the dead, we would unquestionably witness something of astonishing beauty.

Source: Richard Dana Skinner, Review of *Mourning Becomes Electra*, in the *Commonweal*, Vol. XV, no. 2, November 11, 1931, pp. 46–47.

SOURCES

Brustein, Robert. "Eugene O'Neill," in *The Theatre of Revolt: An Approach to the Modern Drama*, Little, Brown, & Co. 1964, pp. 329-59.

Carpenter, Frederic I. *Eugene O'Neill*, Twayne Publishers, 1979.

Clark, Barrett H. *Eugene O'Neill: The Man and His Plays*, Dover, 1947.

De Voto, Bernard. "Minority Report," in *Playwright's Progress: O'Neill and the Critics*, edited by Jordan Miller, Scott, Foresman, & Co., 1965, pp. 108-12.

Jensen, George H. "Eugene O'Neill," in *Dictionary of Literary Biography, Volume 7*, edited by John MacNicholas, Gale Research, 1981, pp. 141-63.

FURTHER READING

Black, Stephen A. *Eugene O'Neill: Beyond Mourning and Tragedy*, Yale University Press, 1999, 480 p.
    A comprehensive, well-documented biography of O'Neill.

Bloom, Harold, ed. *Eugene O'Neill* Chelsea House, 1988, 183 p.
    Collection of critical essays on O'Neill's work.

Bogart, Travis, ed. *Selected Letters of Eugene O'Neill*, Yale University Press, 1988, 602 p.
    O'Neill's collected letters provide insight into his life and work.

Stroupe, John H., ed. *Critical Approaches to O'Neill*, AMS Press, 1988.
    Comprised of critical essays on O'Neill's work.

The Philadelphia Story

PHILIP BARRY

1939

Philip Barry was one of the more popular and successful American playwrights of the 1920s and 1930s. He wrote more than twenty plays, but is best remembered for *The Philadelphia Story,* a comedy of manners set in Philadelphia high society during the late 1930s.

Tracy Lord, the wealthy heroine of *The Philadelphia Story,* divorces her husband, C.K. Dexter Haven, and is about to marry a man named George Kittredge. However, their wedding preparations are interrupted by meddlesome reporters, her ex-husband, and her estranged father; she is also disconcerted by the growing realization that she still has feelings for her ex-husband, Dexter. Amidst the situation comedy and fast-paced dialogue, Barry explores several contemporary social issues, such as society's perception of class differences in America and contemporary attitudes towards adultery and divorce.

The play was enthusiastically reviewed by critics and enjoyed a successful Broadway run for over a year. During that period, more people saw *The Philadelphia Story* than had seen all of Barry's other plays combined. In fact, the success of the play effectively rescued the troubled Shubert Theater in New York (otherwise known as the Theater Guild) from bankruptcy. Barry had written the role especially for the actress Katherine Hepburn, and the play's success simultaneously launched Hepburn's career on the stage and film.

The Philadelphia Story has remained a popular staple of regional theater companies since its debut. Although social attitudes towards adultery and divorce have changed, the play endures because of its compelling characterization of Tracy Lord, a young woman whose self-discoveries still speak to younger generations of theatergoers and movie fans.

AUTHOR BIOGRAPHY

Philip Barry was born on June 18, 1896, in Rochester, New York, to a wealthy Irish-Catholic family. He was educated in both Roman Catholic and secular schools before attending Yale University in 1913. Rejected for military service during the World War I, Barry worked for the U.S. Department of State at home and abroad during 1918–1919.

He returned to Yale in 1919 for his senior year, and became involved in the Dramatic Club. He contributed short stories and poetry to the *Yale Literary Magazine* and the college newspaper; later, he wrote a one-act play for the Dramatic Club.

After graduating from Yale he attended George Pierce Baker's famous 47 Workshop at Harvard University. The 47 Workshop was a course in playwrighting and producing that taught several renowned writers.

Barry spent the early years of the 1920s working for an advertising firm. When his third play, *The Jilts,* was produced on Broadway as *You and I* (1923), he quit his job and became a full-time playwright. *You and I* depicted a young man's decision to forsake security for the stage, and it became an immense success. He divided his time between New York and Cannes, although America remained the setting of most of his dramas and comedies.

Barry was a prolific writer: he wrote nineteen major plays and a novel. He wanted to be recognized for his serious dramas as well as his comedies, but his dramas were invariably commercial flops; although critics have subsequently pointed to his innovative and early use of psychoanalysis on the stage, his dramatic works remain unappreciated to this day.

Consequently, Barry's reputation primarily rests on his three most successful comedies, *Holiday* (1928), *Paris Bound* (1927), and *The Philadelphia Story* (1939). These three plays are set in upper-class New England, and all of them concern marriage and status in contemporary America. In *Holiday,* the happy-go-lucky protagonist is engaged to a wealthy woman; she and her family want to squeeze him into the family firm, but he resists, and eventually abandons her to pursue his dreams.

In *Paris Bound,* a young, rich, newly married couple embrace liberal ideas about a free marriage, but find their bohemian attitudes are soon challenged. In *The Philadelphia Story,* a young heiress discards one husband and chooses another she believes is more suitable, only to discover that her first husband is in fact the right man for her.

Barry died at age fifty-five from a heart attack. His reputation as a fine writer of American comedy remains solid, and has been bolstered by the continuing popularity of both the stage and film versions of his best play, *The Philadelphia Story.*

PLOT SUMMARY

Act I

The play opens with an intimate family scene between the long-suffering Margaret Lord and her two daughters, Tracy and Dinah. The three women are busy planning Tracy's wedding to George Kittredge. She is marrying in style, with a prenuptial party and a stylish reception for five hundred people.

When Tracy briefly exits, Dinah tells her mother that Dexter is in town. Dinah is clearly fond of Dexter, and seems to regret her sister's divorce. Later in the scene, Dinah telephones Dexter and issues him an invitation to the festivities.

Tracy's impending marriage and her past alliance are discussed in light of the failed marriage of her parents. Tracy despises her father for his poor treatment of her mother, but her mother tends to blame herself. Their disagreement seems to parallel Tracy's attitude towards her own failed first marriage. Was her first husband, Dexter, at fault? Or was she? Should she be more forgiving, like her mother? Tracy dismisses the idea of shared blame, commenting that she and her mother "just picked the wrong first husbands."

Tracy exits. Dinah has been proofreading; she now reveals that the proof sheets are a magazine story about her father's adultery. Dinah innocently

Philip Barry

believes the story is false; Margaret inadvertently reveals that the story is true.

Sandy, Tracy's elder brother, arrives. He works as an editor at *The Saturday Evening Post.* Margaret asks him whether the story can be stopped. Tracy learns about the story. Sandy announces that he has "fixed" the problem: instead of printing the story, the magazine will instead cover Tracy's wedding. Tracy is furious with this "trade" to "save" her "Father's face," pointing out that he doesn't deserve it. Yet she agrees to cooperate.

Tracy realizes that the reporters will suspect something is suspicious when her father is not present for the wedding. (Tracy has refused to invite him.) Sandy responds by saying that he already thought of this possibility and arranged a telegram announcing that their father cannot attend the wedding due to illness. This is not good enough for Tracy: she decides to pretend that her Uncle Willie is her father and that her family is a bunch of pretentious snobs.

Liz Imbrie and Mike Connor arrive to write the story. Dinah greets them, speaking in French and singing ditties. Mike concludes that she is "an idiot . . . They happen in the best of families, especially the best."

Tracy enters and dismisses her sister, then proceeds to play out the even more ridiculous part of charming, flattering hostess. When Mike says, "I'm 'Mike' to my friends," Tracy replies, all sweetness and light, "Of whom you have many, I'm sure." Her interrogative manner takes Liz and Mike by surprise.

Tracy reenters with Kittredge and introduces him. Uncle Willie arrives, and Tracy pretends he is her "Papa!" Unexpectedly, Dexter arrives. The charade is further complicated when Tracy's real father, Seth, arrives. She promptly pretends that he is Uncle Willie.

Act II

As Act II opens, Mike and Liz provide another perspective on Lord family history. After Liz leaves with Uncle Willie, Tracy enters and strikes up a conversation with Mike. She has read Mike's books and enjoyed them, and they soon realize they understand each other in unexpected ways.

When Mike explains that he is a reporter in order to support his career as a writer, Tracy generously offers him the use of her country cottage, but he ungraciously refuses. "Well, you see—er—you see the idea of artists having a patron has more or less gone out [of fashion]."

Suddenly, Dexter appears. The atmosphere becomes tense as Dexter jokes about his poor treatment of Tracy in the past and then criticizes Tracy in front of Mike. He accuses her of being insensitive to his alcoholism and impatient with "any kind of human imperfection."

Obviously uncomfortable, Mike exits. Continuing his conversation with Tracy, Dexter criticizes Kittredge, arguing that "he's just not for you."

Kittredge enters and Dexter leaves. Their conversation makes it clear that many of Dexter's statements are true. Kittredge views Tracy as "marvelous, distant . . . cool" and feels she possesses "a kind of beautiful purity." He wants "to build" her "an ivory tower with my own two hands."

It seems that Kittredge may indeed not be the right man for Tracy, who wants to be "really loved," not "worshipped." This is even more apparent when Kittredge voices his approval for the *Destiny* magazine article.

Kittredge exits, and Margaret and Seth enter. Tracy confronts her father about his infidelity. Her mother insists that the only person it concerns is

Seth, who then responds, "That's very wise of you, Margaret. What most wives won't seem to realize is that their husband's philandering—particularly the middle-aged kind—has nothing to do with them."

Incredulous, Tracy questions her father's statement. Seth replies that he was reluctant to "grow old" and wishes he had "the right kind of daughter . . . One who loves him blindly." Without such a daughter, he claims, "he's inclined to go in search of it . . ." In short, he blames her for his affair.

Liz and Mike try to reveal that they are in fact from *Destiny* magazine. Their attempt is foiled by the arrival of the telegram announcing Seth's sickness. The subsequent confusion makes clear to Mike and Liz that the Lords have been duplicitous.

Uncle Willie and Seth resume their correct identities, and the entire group leaves for the pre-nuptial party. As they exit, however, Tracy gulps down a glass of champagne, and pours herself another.

Act II Scene II takes place in the early hours of the morning after the pre-nuptial party. Sandy and Tracy, both drunk, scheme to write an expose of *Destiny*'s publisher, Sidney Kidd, in order to blackmail him into stopping the story about the wedding.

During the course of their conversation it becomes clear that Tracy is very drunk and that she has already spent two hours alone with Mike that evening. Mike, who imagines himself in love with Tracy, then enters, and Sandy exits to write the article on Kidd.

Tracy and Mike flirt. Mike delights Tracy by proclaiming that he sees her as "made of flesh and blood . . . full of love and warmth." She is pleased and relieved that a man finally sees her as warmly human rather than as a remote goddess. They kiss, then run off to the swimming pool for a naked dip.

Sandy and Liz enter. Sandy has already guessed that Liz is in love with Mike, and asks her why she doesn't marry him. Liz replies that "he's still got a lot to learn, and I don't want to get in his way yet." Liz leaves, and Dexter enters.

Sandy hints that there may be "complications" to the wedding. Kittredge enters and Dexter hints that Tracy and Mike may be interested in each other. Mike enters, with Tracy in his arms. Kittredge is horrified to realize that "she—she hasn't any clothes on!" Mike carries her up to bed then returns. Dexter knocks him down before Kittredge can.

Act III

Uncle Willie and Dinah misinterpret Mike's presence in Tracy's bedroom. At first, she does not remember her escapades, but starts to recall her behavior. Tracy, forced to realize that she has "feet of clay," apologizes to her father for her unforgiving attitude.

Mike enters and Tracy explains that she is not interested in him. She mistakenly believes that they have slept together. Tracy confesses her misbehavior to her ex-husband. He reveals that Kittredge left a note for her; Tracy is relieved to find out that he has broken off the wedding.

Kittredge appears and says that he will go ahead with the marriage if she can offer him an explanation. Tracy refuses and contemptuously dismisses him. However, a wedding does go ahead: the play ends with Tracy, who finally feels "like a human being," remarrying Dexter.

CHARACTERS

Mike (Macauly) Connor

Mike Connor is the author of a novel and a collection of short stories. Yet because creative writing does not earn enough money, Mike is reduced to writing "cheap stuff for expensive magazines," such as his present assignment to cover the Lord-Kittredge wedding.

Although he is initially hostile to the Lord family, his feelings soon change. He warms to Sandy, who joins forces with him in attacking Sidney Kidd, and he is attracted to Tracy's charm and beauty. At play's end, Mike even offers to marry Tracy, who gently but firmly rebuffs him. Although his future is left uncertain, it seems plain that Mike will leave his job at *Destiny* and perhaps become involved with Liz.

C.K. Dexter Haven

Dexter is a young, good-looking man. Wealthy and privileged, he has a passion for designing and racing yachts. He is still in love with his ex-wife, Tracy. At one point in the play, Dexter harshly attacks Tracy for her judgmental and unforgiving attitude when he was battling alcoholism, and criticizes her choice of Kittredge for a husband.

However, these attacks do not really resolve the unspoken question, which is never adequately addressed in the play: how abusive was Dexter to

MEDIA ADAPTATIONS

- *The Philadelphia Story* was adapted as a film in 1940. The film was directed by George Cukor and produced by Joseph L. Mankiewicz for MGM. It starred Katharine Hepburn as Tracy Lord, Cary Grant as C. K. Dexter Haven, and James Stewart as Macaulay Connor. Donald Ogden Stewart adapted Barry's play into a screenplay. This highly successful adaptation is still the best-known version of Barry's play.

- In 1956 MGM produced a musical re-make of *The Philadelphia Story* entitled *High Society*. It was faithful to the original plot but was set during the Newport Jazz Festival and featured the playing and singing of Louis Armstrong. *High Society* was directed by Charles Walters and included a star-studded cast: Bing Crosby starred as C. K. Dexter Haven, Frank Sinatra as Macaulay Connor, Grace Kelley as Tracy Lord, and Celeste Holm as Liz Imbrie.

Tracy? Nonetheless, with some skillful targeting of his rival's weak points, Dexter manages to get rid of his rival for Tracy's affections; consequently, he proposes to her for a second time, and she promptly accepts.

Liz Imbrie

Liz Imbrie is the photographer who accompanies Mike to do a story on the Lord family. A young career woman, she provides a contrast to Tracy Lord's privileged but somewhat vacant existence. She is in love with Mike.

George Kittredge

George Kittredge is a handsome, industrious self-made millionaire. His fiancee, Tracy, admires him because she views him as "a great man and good man; already he's of national importance." Tracy is attracted by the qualities that made him so newsworthy in the past: his "rags to riches" life history, his popularity, and his charismatic speaking power. Yet she fails to see that Kittredge's rapid rise through the ranks owes much to his own ambition and class aspirations.

Tracy represents high society for Kittredge, and he believes that his marriage to her will signal his acceptance by upper-class society. His subsequent rejection of Tracy, on the most pompous terms possible, suggests that he still has much to learn about love and perception.

Dinah Lord

Dinah is the younger of the two Lord sisters. She is a precocious young woman, prone to occasional malapropisms, and rather assured of her own maturity—when she is in fact, at times, quite strikingly innocent. Dinah is fond of her brother and sister as well as Dexter. She clearly wishes that Tracy and Dexter had remained together, and she impulsively invites Dexter to come over, hoping that his presence will remind Tracy of past happiness.

Dinah joins Tracy in pretending to the *Destiny* reporters that the Lord family is eccentric and pretentious. Her most entertaining moment, however, comes at the play's end when she misinterprets Mike's presence in Tracy's bedroom and melodramatically marshals the family's resources in order to save Tracy from her "illikit passion" and marriage to Kittredge.

Margaret Lord

Margaret is the mother of Tracy, Dinah, and Sandy. An attractive woman, she has put up with her husband's philandering for many years. They are separated at the time of the play.

Sandy Lord

Sandy is Tracy's younger brother. A newspaper editor working for the *Saturday Evening Post,* he is light-hearted and witty. Unlike Tracy, he has made a happy marriage; in fact, his wife has just given birth to their first child. Sandy, like Tracy, is concerned about the family's reputation, and arranges a deal with *Destiny* editor Sidney Kidd: the magazine will suppress its planned expose of Seth Lord's affairs and instead print a story about Tracy's marriage.

However, Sandy decides to write an expose on Kidd with Mike and Liz. In part, the expose is intended as revenge for the intrusive prying into the family business; in addition, it is meant as punishment to the man who has sold out Liz's and Mike's creative talents for a few dollars.

Seth Lord

Seth Lord is Tracy's father. A wealthy and successful man, he has long been involved with a colorful dancer named Tara Maine. This seems to have been the cause of his separation from his long-suffering wife, Margaret. However, Seth has other explanations for his adultery and for the collapse of his marriage: he blames Tracy's critical attitude for his pursuit of the youthful dancer, and argues that the "ideal daughter" would be one who "blindly" loves her father and believes that "he can do no wrong." Tracy and her father reconcile by the end of the play.

Tracy Lord

Tracy Lord is the eldest daughter of Margaret and Seth Lord. Her beauty, wealth, wit, and cleverness hide a somewhat static interior. As a young woman, she eloped with her childhood friend, the equally wealthy and leisured C.K. Dexter Haven. They divorced after just ten months because of his excessive drinking and abuse. As the play opens, she is just a day away from marrying a self-made and industrious man named George Kittredge.

However, the situation is not as rosy as it seems. Tracy still has feelings for her ex-husband, and is deeply hurt by his bitter criticism of her as unfeeling and intolerant. Furthermore, she is profoundly alienated from her philandering father, Seth Lord. She starts to believe that she has made a mistake with Kittredge; she realizes that he has views and dreams that are strikingly different from her own. Lastly, Tracy finds herself attracted to the attractive, liberal writer Mike Connor, who sees past her brittle facade and tough manner. Tracy's final decision—to remarry her ex-husband—represents an attempt to recapture the happiness they once shared together.

Mac

Mac is the night watchman.

Uncle Willie

Uncle Willie is Tracy's good-natured uncle. He is a philanderer and pinches women's bottoms when he has the chance.

TOPICS FOR FURTHER STUDY

- Compare and contrast the stage and film versions of *The Philadelphia Story*. Discuss the advantages of film versions over stage productions.

- Some critics have claimed that Barry tried to rescue the upper-classes from the overwhelmingly negative portrayal of them in contemporary theater. Do you think *The Philadelphia Story* is just such an attempt, or is it critical of high society?

- Discuss Tracy Lord's maturation during the play. If the play had been written in the 1990s, would it have ended with her remarrying Dexter Haven? Write an ending for the play that you think is realistic for contemporary times.

- Choose two minor characters in the play—for instance, Margaret Lord and Liz Imbrie, or Seth and Willie Lord—and contrast them. Consider the values and ideals these characters represent, and how their presence influences the audience's perception of Tracy Lord.

THEMES

Prejudice and Tolerance

Tracy Lord believes that her uncompromising morals are part of her strong character: she expects "exceptionally high standards for herself" and "lives up to them." She is disappointed when others fail to live up to her standards. In fact, her father's behavior caused a deep schism in their relationship, as she was unable to forgive him. Also, her husband's alcoholism led to their estrangement; instead of trying to help him, she had rejected him for his weakness.

Tracy's brief fling with Mike, which becomes the source of many comic misunderstandings in Act III, enables her to break free of her own self-imposed moral straitjacket and become more sensitive to human weakness. By the end of the play, she has cast off her prejudices and embraced a more tolerant standard from which to judge herself and others.

Public vs. Private Life

The stimulus for much of the comedy in *The Philadelphia Story* is the impending revelation of Seth Lord's adulterous affair with Tina Mara. The forthcoming article in *Destiny* horrifies the Lord family, for they value their reputation highly, particularly Tracy.

Moreover, they value their status as members of the Philadelphia elite, and members of this group were expected to be discreet. Thus much of the original impetus for the comedy of manners hinges upon the Lord family's attempt to cover up past misdeeds.

The Lord family's concern about their public reputation is cleverly emphasized in their playful decision to act out a stereotype in front of reporters. Tracy acts the part of simpering hostess, while Dinah acts like an eccentric and pretentious "idiot." In fact, the entire Lord family presents a false facade of their private life to the reporters: each member wants to maintain the illusion that the Lords are still happily married and that the family is fully functional.

The tension between public reputation and private behavior is of course the source of much of the play's comedy, but it also represents a growing concern among the leisured classes about the tabloid frenzy for scandal and gossip. Barry portrayed this increasing tension through his presentation of the lives of the rich and famous.

STYLE

Stage Directions

Detailed stage directions are a very noticeable feature of *The Philadelphia Story*. There are three simple reasons for this. First, although the dialogue was strong in itself, it depends upon staging. Imprecise staging and inappropriate gestures detract from the impact of the dialogue.

Second, Barry was a consummate producer of plays: he understood much about stagecraft, and knew that if he wanted to replicate the success of one play all over the country, he had to give directors of amateur companies precise guidance.

Third, *The Philadelphia Story* is written realistically, and Barry worked hard to give the audience the impression that the action unfolding in front of their eyes was, indeed, an accurate representation of "the real thing."

Also, Barry's stage directions enable the actors to add nuance to their characterizations. For instance, when Mike strikes a match, Tracy offers him a light from her lighter. The action is amusing because of Tracy's pretense, but, because it is also a classic gesture of attraction between men and women, it is also a nice hint to the audience that Mike and Tracy may be interested in each other.

Comedy of Manners

By and large, the great American playwrights of the twentieth century are dramatists such as Arthur Miller, August Wilson, and Eugene O'Neill. Drama often appears more resonant and universal; in contrast, comedy is invariably limited to themes such as marriage, adultery, and sex, and reflects contemporary society. These qualities can date comedy faster than drama.

The comedy of manners, a distinct sub-genre within the light comic tradition, is better able to survive the vagaries of time and fashion because its humor depends upon character foibles and upon situation humor, such as misunderstandings and identity switches.

The great nineteenth-century master of the comedy of manners was Oscar Wilde, whose plays included the masterpiece, *The Importance of Being Earnest* (1895). In this popular play, comedy is created not only by Wilde's dazzling wit, but also by numerous confusions of identity and revelations of double lives. Philip Barry owes a great debt to Wilde in his use of intricate plots, confused identities, and comic misunderstandings.

HISTORICAL CONTEXT

World War II

The rise of totalitarian regimes in Germany, Italy, and Japan during the 1930s tipped the scales toward a world war. These dictatorships—known as the Axis alliance—began to forcibly expand into neighboring countries. For instance, in 1936 Benito Mussolini's Italian troops took over Ethiopia, which gave them a strong foothold in Africa. In 1938 Germany annexed Austria; a year later, German

COMPARE & CONTRAST

- **1939:** America feels the continuing effects of the Great Depression. Unemployment remains high and industrial production is low.

    Today: The American economy booms: the Dow Jones Industrial Index passes the 10,000 mark, unemployment is at a record low, and inflation is under control.

- **1939:** Europe erupts into full-scale war, pitting Nazi Germany and Italy against France and England. By the year's end, Germany has taken control of Poland, partitioning it with Russia, while Russia has seized Lithuania, Latvia, Estonia, and is preceding in its invasion of Finland.

    Today: The conflict in the former Yugoslavia escalates. In the wake of widespread killing, NATO launches a peace-keeping mission and commits to air and ground warfare against Serbia.

- **1939:** Scientists announce that they have succeeded in splitting uranium, thorium, and protactinium atoms by bombarding them with neutrons. Their success paves the way for the invention of the H-bomb in the final years of World War II.

    Today: After the escalation of the nuclear arms race during the Cold War, the 1980s and 1990s were marked by attempts to reduce the superpowers' arsenal of nuclear weapons. Developing world nations such as India and Pakistan, however, are keen to acquire nuclear weapons, and recently each nation has announced the successful testing of nuclear weapons.

- **1939:** Color television is demonstrated for the first time. Black-and-white televisions are sold to millions of households in the 1950s.

    Today: Most American households own two televisions, and have access to over one hundred cable channels.

- **1939:** American labor organizations unionize employees from mass-production industries such as the steel and automobile industries, and force employers to accept the validity of strike action and collective bargaining power.

    Today: American labor organizations struggle to maintain their traditional membership, as mass-production industries move to Mexico or overseas. They also strive to unionize the massive (and often non-English speaking and itinerant) labor force of the textile, agricultural, and service industries.

- **1939:** President Franklin D. Roosevelt maintains his commitment to liberal "New Deal" social programs and announces American neutrality in the European War. The following year, he is reelected president for a third term.

    Today: Second-term Democratic President Bill Clinton survives an impeachment vote, and continues to enjoy strong popularity despite the impeachment vote and Lewinsky scandal.

---

forces occupied Czechoslovakia. Italy took control of Albania in 1939.

On September 1, 1939, Germany invaded Poland and World War II began. On September 3, 1939, a German U-boat sank the British ship *Athenia* off the coast of Ireland. Another British ship, *Courageous,* was sunk on September 19. All the members of the British Commonwealth, except Ireland, soon joined Britain and France in their declaration of war.

The Great Depression

Contrary to popular belief, the stock market crash of 1929 did not trigger the Great Depression of the 1930s; rather, many economic analysts attribute the depressed economy to problems within the international stock market and investment banks. In fact, it seems that Great Depression owed more to the legacy of the First World War (in particular Britain and America's punitive reparation policy) and to technological advances that increased profits but made many workers redundant. Agricultural, mining, and textile markets, traditionally the source of great profit, were also depressed.

From 1929 to 1932, unemployment in America rose from about 1.5 million to about fifteen million. This extraordinarily rapid rise in unemployment placed tremendous strains upon social services. Farmers were also suffering. By the mid-1930s, drought and bank foreclosures had driven farm prices down by more than 50% and many tenant-farmers were forced off their land.

In the face of this unprecedented social and economic crisis, the American president, Herbert Hoover, held out for the upswing in "market forces" that he felt sure would put an end to the escalating crisis. The voters were not so confident, and in 1933 they elected the Democratic presidential candidate, Franklin D. Roosevelt, to office. He immediately began implementing his "New Deal" reform plan: relief for the unemployed, fiscal reform, and stimulating measures to boost economic recovery. With the escalation of arms production in the late 1930s, America finally began to recover from the Great Depression.

CRITICAL OVERVIEW

The Philadelphia Story was well received when the play first premiered on Broadway at the Shubert Theater on March 28, 1939. *The New York Times* praised the playwright and the Theater Guild company for their "top form" and called the play a "gay and sagacious comedy." That review was typical of the critical response.

The play has remained popular for several decades. It was made into a successful movie in 1940, which starred Katherine Hepburn. However, in the 1960s and 1970s, American critics were more interested in social protest drama and tended to overlook Barry's writing as light entertainment. When they did turn to Barry with a serious eye, they explored several elements of his work.

Francis Wyndham, writing in the *Times Literary Supplement,* focused on the father-daughter relationship that figures as a background theme in some of Barry's plays. His somewhat unusual argument hinted at "incestuous undertones" in Barry's writing.

Moreover, Wyndham evidenced a prejudice against Barry's style of light comedy: "Barry was himself prouder of his serious flops than of his tailor-made successes, but . . . the verdict of *Variety* and the Broadway public has been sadly justified by the passage of time . . . the frankly artificial framework of drawing-room comedy was necessary to preserve the frail but genuine spark of Barry's talent."

Unable to appreciate Barry's mastery of the comedy of manners, he chose to concentrate on the more obscure and unconventional elements of Barry's writing and to dismiss the very things that were Barry's strengths.

Albert Wertheim, writing a few years later in *Educational Theatre Journal,* was able to appreciate Barry in his own right. He recognized Barry as "one of the few masters of the American comedy of manners," and contended that Barry had surmounted the inherent challenges in the genre: "As all comedies of manners do, Philip Barry's demand a great sense of style from actors and actresses who must demonstrate the wit and urbanity that wealth and social position can foster, yet at the same time show the foibles and failures that exist despite social prominence and material well-being."

Wertheim praised the play mainly because of Barry's compelling characterization of Tracy Lord and in particular because of her development as a character. He asserted that the major "business of Barry's play [is] to bring Tracy Lord a comic insight that will enable her to harmonize her social poise with her inner humanity . . . to produce, in short, something akin to Barry's idea of true human grace." Tracy must soften her "morally uncompromising" attitude towards people's behavior, and she does this through her own personal experience of a fall from grace.

Wertheim's essay, written after the sexual revolution of the 1960s and 1970s, virtually ignores the question of whether the play was still relevant in such changed times. Why, for instance, should Tracy's journey of self-discovery end in a return to her abusive ex-husband?

Wertheim also emphasized the more conservative representation of class in the play: "Barry's aim was at least in part a revaluation of the merits and basic humanity of the upper class after the

George Cukor directing The Philadelphia Story, *with John Howard as George Kittredge, Katharine Hepburn as Tracy Lord, and Cary Grant as C. K. Dexter Haven.*

flogging it received at the hands of the social revolutionary playwrights of the Depression years.'' Yet, he did not discuss Barry's representation of the Depression era in the play, nor offer an explanation of precisely what the supposed ''merits'' of the upperclass were.

In 1988 Gary Green echoed Wertheim's praise of the play. Green maintained that beneath the ''wittily and elegantly presented portrait of Philadelphia's mainline society,'' Barry questioned ''class mores and conventional ideas about marriage'' and advocated ''the value of tolerance.''

Also like Wertheim, Green accepted the play's surface representation of class, particularly Barry's apparent redemption of the alternately despised and idolized upper class. Mike and George are Tracy's ''social inferiors.'' Mike is crippled by ''the inverted snobbery of the proletarian intellectual'' and perceives ''the rich as non-productive, social parasites.'' George is a ''parvenu who has embraced the restricted conventionality of the moneyed upper class to which he aspires.''

Yet some critics assert that the ''moneyed upper class'' in *The Philadelphia Story*, just as in other Barry comedies, have a remarkably flexible set of moral standards, and George's problem is that his moral standards are out of kilter with the Lord family values. Moreover, although Barry celebrates the Lords' urbanity and wit, he does not present them as productive members of society.

Although Barry is considered one of America's best writers of comedies of manners, the true complexity of his writing is underappreciated. The best comic writers can speak to their own times and to later generations: it is this rare skill that makes their work enduring. Barry is one such writer.

CRITICISM

Helena Ifeka,

Ifeka is a Ph.D. specializing in American and British literature. In this essay, she analyzes Barry's treatment of class issues in The Philadelphia Story.

Barry's comedies are almost all set in the world of ''high society'' and feature characters who are rich,

WHAT DO I READ NEXT?

- *Paris Bound* (1927) is one of Barry's most successful comedy of manners. It concerns the fashionable and rich Jim and Mary Hutton. On their wedding day, the couple decides that they will be tolerant of extramarital affairs. Their bohemian ideals come under pressure when Mary learns that Jim has visited an old sweetheart when traveling abroad.

- Barry's *Holiday* (1928) is an enjoyable comedy that depicts the relationship between Julia Seton, a millionaire's daughter, and Johnny Case, a hardworking young man. The Seton family cannot tolerate Case's determination to enjoy life when young and try to force him to join the family firm.

- John Steinbeck's *The Grapes of Wrath* (1939) displays Steinbeck's characteristic social realism and his determination to depict the lives of rural people with sympathy and understanding. He won the Pulitzer Prize for his epic novel about the struggles of an emigrant farming family who leave the dust bowl of the Midwest for the promised land of California.

- Bernard Shaw's *Pygmalion* (1913) remains a popular comedy. It is about a professor, Henry Higgins, who decides that he can pass off a young Cockney flower-seller, Eliza Doolittle, as a society lady. Shaw's depiction of Eliza's rise to social acceptance allows him to comment upon the British class system while also providing his audience with light-hearted entertainment.

- Royall Tyler was one of the first major American playwrights. His best-known play remains *The Contrast* (1787), a social comedy that contrasts the simply dignity of American mores with the foppery and pretensions of British fashion. Tyler drew upon Restoration comedy to create one of America's first comedy of manners.

---

privileged, and educated. This does not mean, however, that he sets out to celebrate the upper-class; in fact, Barry subtly explores class conflict in many of his comedies, including *The Philadelphia Story*.

Barry is no radical, however, and while he presents his audiences with hints of the conflicts that underscored the myth of American egalitarianism, he never moves beyond this gentle thematization of class conflict. In fact, his endings usually reinforce rather than challenge the status quo.

The Lords, as their surname boldly asserts, are so firmly entrenched as leaders of Philadelphia society as to almost be American aristocrats. Pennsylvania, the home of so much revolutionary activity during the American Revolution, is home to an established social hierarchy that would have made the American Loyalists proud.

Barry emphasizes this ironic twist of history in a tense exchange between Sandy and Mike early in the play. The two men discuss the present Democratic Roosevelt administration, and Mike asks—assuming the Sandy is a conservative—"I suppose you're all of you opposed to the Administration." Sandy wittily responds, "No—as a matter of fact we're Loyalists."

Sandy's word play hints that the Lords *may* be liberal supporters of the Roosevelt Administration, but also suggests that their sympathies would have been "Loyalist" (or pro-British, anti-Revolutionary) during the American Revolution.

The same exchange between Mike and Sandy is critical to Barry's development of the theme of class conflict. In it, Sandy reveals himself to be sensitive about his family's wealth and privilege: "I think you ought to give us a break ... in spite of certain of our regrettably inherited characteristics, we just might be fairly decent." Mike, however, is not so quick to set aside his suspicions.

These suspicions are confirmed when Sandy admits that although he, like Mike, does work in the newspaper industry, the two men are on opposite sides of the divide: Mike, a journalist, represents the working man, whereas Sandy, an editor, organizes and dictates policy and is therefore management. Mike announces brusquely that he is "opposed to everything" Sandy represents, but Sandy responds coolly that Mike's magazine "is hardly a radical sheet," and asks him snidely, "what is it you're doing—boring from within?"

A moment later, he adds that Mike's idol, Thomas Jefferson, was never a man of the people, but rather, like the Lords, came from a background of wealth and privilege: "Have you ever seen his house at Monticello?"

The two men's opposing interests and perspectives are only reconciled in their joint—and somewhat underhanded—decision to collude in the blackmailing of Mike's editor, Sidney Kidd. Sandy acts in the interests of the Lord family to reveal Kidd's own dirty past; Mike, only half-aware of what he is doing, reveals the necessary information, because he believes that Kidd is degrading his creative talent. Their action is hardly one of class resistance: rather, each man is inspired to strike out at Kidd for his own reasons, and each man joins forces with the other only in order to achieve this goal. However, it suggests that they have reached a rapprochement.

Barry's ambivalent attitude towards class difference is most apparent in the characterization of George Kittredge. George, whom Tracy describes as an "angel," was once a dirty angel: a coalminer who worked in the mines and rose through the ranks to the head of the company. Early in the play, Sandy asks Tracy whether George was "sore" about a recent newspaper article about him, in which he was identified as a "former coal miner." The audience never hears Tracy's response to this question, but they are alerted to George's *nouveau riche* status and to the possibility of tension arising in the family about his recent shift from miner to boss.

Mike seems to share Sandy's somewhat snide attitude to George's social elevation, albeit in a different way. He describes George as "up from the bottom," a word choice that perhaps inadvertently links the low depths of the mine shafts with poverty's negative associations. Sandy's response shows that he, for once, is aware of the word's dual meanings: "Just exactly—and of the mine."

Mike then makes plain why he is suspicious of Kittredge: "National hero, new model: makes drooping family incomes to revive again." Kittredge may

" THE LESSON THAT AFFECTS MIKE—APPEARANCES CAN BE DECEIVING—CONCEALS A REAL UNDERCURRENT OF CONSERVATISM IN BARRY'S PLOT. TRACY'S REJECTION OF KITTREDGE FOR HAVEN IS CERTAINLY A REJECTION OF IDEALIZATION AND OF CONSTRICTIVE MIDDLE-CLASS MORALITY, BUT IT IS ALSO A REJECTION OF THE SOCIAL INFIDEL, AND A CONFIRMATION OF THE RIGIDITY OF THE EXISTING CLASS HIERARCHY."

---

well have done a tremendous job of reorganizing the failing mines, but at what cost? The mine may well run better in its "new model," but the only people whose fortunes seemed to have revived in the wake of its reorganization are the owners, "the drooping family."

No mention is made of the workers—the miners themselves—and the question hangs in the air: who suffered, who benefited, who was laid off in order to revitalize the mines? This ominous question is answered a short time later, when Kittredge announces that his plans to reform the mines extend to reforming the unions: there is a lot, he says, that is "yet to be done with Labor relations."

Kittredge is crucial to the overall plot development—in particular to Tracy's developing ambivalence about her impending marriage—and it is worth examining his character in more detail. The first time he appears on stage, Tracy introduces him as "my beau," Liz compliments him on his appearance, and Kittredge himself announces that "I've shaken quite a lot of coal-dust from my feet in the last day or two." Tracy, who firmly believes her fiancee is angelically handsome, responds to Kittredge's self-conscious attempt at a joke with one herself, but one that comes out sounding a little patronizing: "Isn't he beautiful? Isn't it wonderful what a little soap and water will do?"

This early suggestion that Kittredge is self-conscious and perhaps uncomfortable about his recent rise from rags to riches, and that their different backgrounds could cause problems between the couple, is evident later in the play. Kittredge, in a long conversation with Tracy, displays a concern about appearances and good taste that marks him as *nouveau riche:* as aspiring to the respectability and status of the upper classes. Dexter, on the other hand, who is born to wealth, "never concerns himself much with taste."

The difference between the two men comes down to being born into a certain class, and consequently being certain of one's station in life. For Kittredge, this means cutting certain "unimportant people" out of his social calendar, and establishing a circle which others will aspire to join, just as he, too, once longed to join Tracy in her golden shadow. "Our little house on the river up there . . . I'd like people to consider it an honor to be asked there. We're going to represent something, Tracy—something straight and sound and fine.—And then perhaps young Mr. Haven may be somewhat less condescending."

Kittredge's social insecurity leads him inevitably into the disastrous trap of comparing himself with someone who is inherently secure and confident. While this study in contrasts might be of interest simply in itself, it becomes significant because Kittredge has pursued and won someone who is from Haven's background, and who consequently shares his easy confidence and contempt for such *nouveau riche* concerns.

The play's ending is foreshadowed in these early scenes. It is also, however, something of a foregone conclusion that the couple are not suited, for in Barry's somewhat conservative worldview, like must marry like, and the great, the talented, the creative, must join forces with their equals.

The conclusion that like must marry like is inherently a conservative one. No one could fault Barry's characterization of Tracy Lord or Dexter Haven: both are charismatic, smart, witty people, and are clearly suited. But Haven's merits are contrasted with those of two working-class men: one of whom labors industriously in a socially acceptable (and hardly radical) profession, writing, and the other of whom rises from dirt to wealth.

The first, Mike Connor, seems at first glance the more radical and challenging of the two men: he identifies himself as a liberal in the Jeffersonian tradition, and is hostile to upper-class interests. Yet Mike's threat is considerably softened as a result of his romantic entanglement with Tracy: he proves himself a "true gentleman" by refusing to "take advantage" of her and offering, with an almost Victorian attitude, to marry her since he has been implicated in her damaged honor. Finally, he makes the "funny discovery" that "in spite of the fact that someone's up from the bottom, he may be quite a heel. And that even though someone else's born to the purple, he still may be quite a guy."

Kittredge, the "heel," may have raised himself by his bootstraps, but he disturbed Philadelphia's tranquil social hierarchy by aspiring above his class, and, moreover, by clinging to what are essentially middle-class moral values, rather than embracing the more accommodating liberal values of the upper class.

Barry's *The Philadelphia Story* is for the most part a frothy social comedy, but its sweet exterior masks darker themes—not least of all amongst them the tensions between the social classes in the 1930s. Barry explores this tension firstly through the presence of Mike, an intruder with a chip on his shoulder, and secondly through the play's central event, the impending marriage of Tracy Lord and George Kittredge.

The lesson that affects Mike—appearances can be deceiving—conceals a real undercurrent of conservatism in Barry's plot. Tracy's rejection of Kittredge for Haven is certainly a rejection of idealization and of constrictive middle-class morality, but it is also a rejection of the social infidel, and a confirmation of the rigidity of the existing class hierarchy.

Source: Helena Ifeka, for *Drama for Students,* Gale, 2000.

Christian H. Moe

Calling The Philadelphia Story *"one of Barry's most accomplished works," Moe offers an overview of the play and discusses its place within the genre of class comedy.*

Philip Barry's social comedy in three acts is set in the house of a rich, high-society Philadelphia family in the 1930's. Tracy Lord, the mercurial, oldest daughter of the family's separated parents, is a divorcee who will, on the morrow, embark on a second marriage to a stuffy, self-made millionaire named George Kittredge. Puritanical about the frailties of others, Tracy has recently divorced a childhood friend, Dexter Haven, for his past alcoholic weakness, and holds no sympathy for her father, whose escapades with a dancer are to be made the feature of a popular magazine. To avoid public disclosure of a family scandal, Tracy's brother has persuaded the magazine's editor to suppress the story in return for letting two reporters do an inside story on Tracy's wedding. The journalists soon arrive: Mike Connor, an idealistic writer unafraid of venting disapproval of mainline society, and a young woman journalist clearly in love with her colleague. To render their observations harmless, Tracy assumes a deceptive facade and falsely identifies her uncle as her father, whom she has not asked to the wedding. Equilibrium tumbles when the father arrives along with her uninvited first husband, Dexter. When both men are reprimanded by Tracy for showing up, each accuses her of being coldly unforgiving of others' frailties. Disturbed by the accusation, the heroine gives way to a mutually shared attraction with Mike, leading to a kiss and a champagne-inebriated, midnight swim without suits. In realizing that she too is capable of lapses which demonstrate warm, human feelings, Tracy gains a truer measure of herself and a larger tolerance of others. Her bridegroom-to-be learns of the incident, suspects the worst, and demands an explanation on the wedding morning. Fully recognizing his pompousness, Tracy breaks off the engagement and happily accepts Dexter's offer of remarriage, and the wedding takes place with a new bridegroom.

One of Barry's most accomplished works, *The Philadelphia Story* belongs to a small group of his social comedies, *Holiday* among them, dealing with the nature of marriage and the life of the upper classes—the stratum of society from which the author sprang and which he knew well. These refined comedies represent the most successful category of Barry's work, departing from his larger group of plays treating serious religious, moral, and psychological questions often developed in symbolic or fantastic form as in *Hotel Universe*. However, moral concerns remain essential ingredients in his comedies, including *The Philadelphia Story*.

Underlying the wittily and elegantly presented portrait of Philadelphia's mainline society, there is a theme which questions class mores and conventional ideas about marriage, advocating the value of tolerance. Tracy, the focal character, only has the possibility of self-fulfillment and hope for a happy marriage if she fully realizes that her nature is

> "A FINE EXAMPLE OF ITS GENRE, *THE PHILADELPHIA STORY* DEMONSTRATES ITS AUTHOR'S SKILLED CRAFTSMANSHIP IN CREATING THE MILIEU OF HIGH SOCIETY PEOPLED BY THREE-DIMENSIONAL, INTERESTING CHARACTERS WITHIN A WELL-STRUCTURED AND HIGHLY POLISHED COMIC PLOT"

humanly frail and her lack of tolerance (and that in others) reprehensible. Having been quick to condemn the human frailties of her former husband and her father, she is shaken when told by them individually that her intolerance of weakness renders her a cold "Virgin Goddess" whose sinless high standards only spur on transgressions by others. When, however, she recalls her affectionately intoxicated, unrestrained "skinny-dipping" escapade with Mike on the eve of the wedding, from which she had emerged chaste owing only to Mike's gentlemanly behavior, she learns that she too is capable of the same lively, hedonistic impulses she has condemned in others.

Embodying the thematic thrust of the play, Tracy's growth forms the spine of the action. The intolerant heroine is surrounded by several people committed to their prejudices and a refusal to accept ideas or behavior that differ from their own. Together with her class and family, she shares a suspicion and dislike of reporters, whom she sees, initially, as spying intruders with no manners or sensitivity until she realizes Mike's dimension as a writer and human being. Yet Mike, who like her fiancé George is her social inferior, has the inverted snobbery of the proletarian intellectual who perceives the rich as non-productive, social parasites. George is a parvenu who has embraced the restrictive conventionality of the moneyed, upper class to which he aspires, and he expects the unconventional Tracy to fit his image of a wife. Upon discovering his fiancée's behavior with Mike, and shocked by it, his nasty reaction and demand for explanation reveal him to Tracy as the stuffed shirt he is. She then breaks off the engagement and kindly rejects a marriage proposal from Mike to accept that of Dexter, her tolerant first husband who has always understood and loved her. Her final decision reflects the central character's culmination of a journey toward self-understanding, tolerance, and humanity.

A fine example of its genre, *The Philadelphia Story* demonstrates its author's skilled craftsmanship in creating the milieu of high society peopled by three-dimensional, interesting characters within a well-structured and highly polished comic plot. The plot, whose humorous action arises from an attempt to keep a private scandal from exposure by the press, richly provides comic complications, confrontations, and revelations typical of an effective comedy of manners. In terms of characterization, the figure of Tracy Lord (which was written for, and was the springboard to fame for, Katharine Hepburn, both in the original and successful Broadway production and the subsequent motion picture version) remains a stunning portrait of an intelligent young woman who discovers tolerance and humanity. Reversing a typical pattern of the genre, the author shows in George Kittredge a man risen from the ranks who turns out to be a prig, and in Dexter Haven a man from society's upper crust who proves himself to be gallant and understanding. Also interestingly drawn are such characters as reporter Mike Connor, Tracy's unpredictable and hoydenish younger sister, and an uncle fond of pinching ladies' bottoms.

A successful 1980 Broadway revival gave proof of the play's durability, as have its frequent productions in regional theatre. With *The Philadelphia Story,* Barry has earned a firm place in American letters as an elegant writer of social comedy.

Source: Christian H. Moe, ''*The Philadelphia Story*'' in *The International Dictionary of Theatre,* Volume 1: *Plays,* edited by Mark Hawkins-Dady, St. James Press, 1992, pp. 604–06.

John Mason Brown

Focusing on the charms of Katherine Hepburn, the actress playing Tracy in the original production, Brown offers a mixed, though mostly favorable appraisal of Barry's play.

That there have always been two Philip Barrys has long since been well known to those who have followed Mr. Barry's double life as a dramatist. One of these has been the cosmic Mr. Barry who has fought an anguishing, often arresting, inner struggle as he has gone searching for his God in such scripts as *John, Hotel Universe, The Joyous Season,* and this winter's *Here Come the Clowns.* The other Mr. Barry, the first to be heard from and the one his largest public has always doted upon, is the dramatist who has shown a genuine flair for badinage and written such perceptive tearful comedies as *You and I, White Wings, Paris Bound, In a Garden, Tomorrow and Tomorrow,* and *The Animal Kingdom.*

It is this second Mr. Barry, the smiling one with a lump in his throat, who has tossed off *The Philadelphia Story,* that play, so pleasant at times but so unimportant throughout, which can boast as its truest and most commanding virtue the fact that it brings Katharine Hepburn triumphantly back to our stage. Although Mr. Barry's new script is not in his best comic vein, through it shine those qualities, literate and ingratiating, which have distinguished his better comedies. It is the work of a man, sensitive and witty, who, even when he has embarked upon what proves to be something of a dramatist's holiday, turns up bearing his special gifts.

As he relates how a rich young Philadelphia divorcee, a chill perfectionist, a married virgin who has no understanding in her heart, is awakened to love and life by a drunken incident with a writer the night before she is to marry another man, Mr. Barry has difficulty starting his fable and nods at times, in the best Greek fashion, while keeping it going. Yet when once he has established his wealthy family, and abruptly indicated that they are supposed to be on their best behavior because their country home is being invaded by a writer and a lady photographer representing a magazine thinly disguised as *Destiny,* Mr. Barry's play begins to show agreeable signs of his authorship.

If his comedy is not a good one, if it forces one to think back to the superiority of *Paris Bound* which it often brings to mind, it has its commendable points. At least it passes the time, often very pleasantly. It bristles with amusing lines. It has scenes which indicate Mr. Barry's surety as a comic dramatist. It makes clear what a gay and intuitive mind is his and how polished can be his gift for dialogue. Even at its feeblest and most aimless, it is warmed by a winning sense of tolerance. Once again Mr. Barry may be turning Congreve into a cardinal, and advancing his old argument that a single transgression is no justification for divorce between two people who really love one another. But to this he adds a welcome and timely plea to the effect that people, not classes, are what matter; that poverty does not spell virtue any more than riches necessarily spell meanness.

At its best Mr. Barry's play is no more than a rich cloak which Mr. Barry, in a moment of Raleighesque gallantry, has spread wide for Miss Hepburn to walk upon. Miss Hepburn is not an actress easy to describe. It is difficult to distinguish between what she is and what she does. It is more than difficult; it is irrelevant. To an almost unmatched extent what she is, is also what she does.

What she is, as playgoers came to know in *The Warrior's Husband,* and as movie-goers realized in such films as *Morning Glory, Little Women,* and *Alice Adams,* is one of the most beautiful young women on our stage and screen and also one of the most fascinating. That on the screen she has wavered between performances of high excellence and those which have been said to be downright embarrassing by people who have had the heart to see them, only indicates, as does her more recent stage record of failure in *The Lake* and triumph in *The Philadelphia Story,* that Miss Hepburn is a performer who, more than most, needs to find the right script, to be protected by expert direction, and to have her very special gifts displayed to equally special advantage. As an actress she bears a greater resemblance than the majority of her rivals to the little girl with the curl in the middle of her forehead. Certainly when she is good, she can be very, very good indeed.

That she is blessed with uncommon endowments no one can deny who has seen her at her best or at her worst. She has intelligence, breeding, fire, a voice which in its emotional scenes can be satin, a body Zorina might look upon with envy, and a personality of such compulsion that, without meaning to do so, she can make the center of the stage wherever she happens to be. There is grace—a lovely and arresting grace—about her very awkwardness; about the tomboyish attitudes she strikes from time to time; and, most especially, about that free-limbed quality of hers which can turn her very crosses into the poetry of motion.

Most of all, there is Miss Hepburn's beauty. Dramatic critics, of course, have a way of pretending that an actress' beauty is of no importance either to them or to her art. What has led them to do this is at once a desire to seem judicial when appraising technique, and the fact—the melancholy fact—that

> AT ITS BEST MR. BARRY'S PLAY IS NO MORE THAN A RICH CLOAK WHICH MR. BARRY, IN A MOMENT OF RALEIGHESQUE GALLANTRY, HAS SPREAD WIDE FOR MISS HEPBURN TO WALK UPON."

so many of our actresses have had to get along (and done very nicely, thank you) unaided by beauty.

Miss Hepburn is not one of these. Beauty is decidedly in league with her. Nor is her loveliness of that languid, bovine sort so dear to the elder Edward with his well-known fondness for Lilys who, though eye-filling in their serenity, were apt to be more Jersey than Lily. Miss Hepburn's face is as interesting as it is pretty, as flexible as it is well-modeled. It has strength no less than temperament behind it. Above all, its decisive modeling enables Miss Hepburn to project her expressions onstage with the clarity of a close-up. With its high cheek bones, its almost equine spread, its generous mouth, and its sculptured features, it is the mask of a Bryn Mawr Garbo whose visual fascinations are endless. Moreover, Miss Hepburn can act. And act she does with agreeable results, not only by being what she is but by doing very nicely what she is called upon to do in Mr. Barry's script when, in the last act, he gets around to asking her.

Source: John Mason Brown, "Miss Hepburn in *The Philadelphia Story*" in his *Broadway in Review,* Norton, 1940, pp. 127–31.

SOURCES

Moe, Christian H. "*The Philadelphia Story*" in *The International Dictionary of Theatre, Vol. 1: Plays,* edited by Mark Hawkins-Dady, St. James Press, 1992.

Wertheim, Albert. "*The Philadelphia Story,*" in *Educational Theater Journal,* Vol. 30, No. 2, May, 1978, pp. 273-74.

Wyndham, Francis. "Dreams and Drawing Rooms," in *Times Literary Supplement,* December 19, 1975, p. 1507.

FURTHER READING

Brown, John Mason. "The American Barry," in *Still Seeing Things,* McGraw-Hill, 1950, pp. 30-7.

> Brown includes reminiscences of Barry.

Gross, Robert F. "Servants of Three Masters: Realism, Idealism, and 'Hokum' in American High Comedy," in *Realism and the American Dramatic Tradition,* edited by William W. Demastes, University of Alabama Press, 1996, pp. 71-90.

> Contends that scholars have overlooked the realism of American high comedy and have focused too much upon drama and social realism at the expense of American comedy.

Meredith, George. *Essay on Comedy,* Chapman and Hall, 1877, 99 p.

> British poet and novelist George Meredith was also known as a literary critic. His *Essay on Comedy* was one of the most influential critical texts on high comedy during the late nineteenth century and continued to influence critics and writers during the first decades of the twentieth century.

Wolfe, Thomas. *Of Time and the River,* C. Scribner's, 1935, 892 p.

> Wolfe attended the infamous 47 Workshop of George Baker Pierce in the 1920s. His semi-autobiographical novel includes a portrait of Baker in the character of Professor Hatcher.

Right You Are, If You Think You Are

LUIGI PIRANDELLO
1917

As with many of Pirandello's plays, *Right You Are, If You Think You Are* is an adaptation of one of his short stories, "Signora Frola and Signor Ponza, Her Son-in-Law," published in 1915. The story concerns the conflicting versions of the truth told by the characters of the title, and comes right to the point by declaring that one of them is mad. Determining which one is mad, and where fantasy meets reality, is the focus of the play and of the townspeople. Signora Frola explains that her son-in-law went mad when her daughter, his wife, died four years ago, then remarried but fantasizes that the new wife is his old wife. For his part, Ponza claims that Signora Frola could not accept her daughter's death, went mad, and only survives by believing that his second wife is in actuality her living daughter; it is for this reason, he says, that he guards his wife so jealously. In the play, as Renate Matthei describes in her 1973 work on Pirandello, "the social role built up by one character for himself is continually destroyed by another, devaluated into a sick sham existence that outsiders accept as real only out of pity." Neither the short story nor the play gives the satisfaction of an answer; in fact, the ambiguities expand as the townspeople press for more data in their vain attempts to fix reality through the unreliable medium of perception. Both the play and the short story are representative of Pirandello's obsession with the fine line between fantasy and reality as they are experienced in human consciousness. As

he explained to his son in a 1916 letter, the plot is a "great deviltry."

AUTHOR BIOGRAPHY

Luigi Pirandello was born to affluent parents in 1867 in a small provincial town in Sicily. He was sensitive and ill-suited to follow his robust and occasionally violent father into the family business of sulphur mining, and led a rather sheltered life until he went to college, first in Rome, and then in Bonn, Germany. There he began to bloom intellectually, and he led an active social life, though he longed for his own sunny climate. His happiness lasted until his arranged marriage with the daughter of one his father's business partners. Antonietta was an unsuitable wife for Pirandello, but he immediately fastened his illusions of love onto her. Early in their marriage, Pirandello's father's firm failed, forcing Pirandello to take a teaching job to support his young family. Antonietta had been jealously overprotected by her father, and with the added financial stress, she, in her own turn, tortured her new husband with insane jealousy. For seventeen years she haunted his and their three children's lives until Pirandello committed her to an asylum. He continued to teach school, without enjoying it, until his literary career took hold. In 1925, Pirandello fell in love with a beautiful young actress named Marta Abba. Marta kept the older man at arm's length as she pursued her acting career. A recently published volume of his letters to her show him vacillating wildly between suicidal depression and euphoric mania for the rest of his life.

Pirandello was fairly well known for his short stories and novels before he turned to the theatre and made his name with *Six Characters in Search of an Author* (1921). Many of his works concern the self, or more specifically, consciousness. For this he was called the founder of modern theatre, since modernism, too, is concerned with the instability and fabrication of the self. Pirandello portrayed consciousness as fleeting, unreliable, and idiosyncratic, affected as it is by memory, personality, and mood. Once Pirandello discovered the theatre, he devoted himself to modernizing Italian theater through new kinds of repertoire and acting, and then educating his audiences to appreciate it. Unfortunately, the impoverished years following World War I and the rise of Fascism in Italy during the years before World War II made the success of his experimental theater, Teatro d'Arte, all but impossible (even with Mussolini's patronage), though similar projects were flourishing elsewhere in Europe. A fascist sympathizer, Pirandello publicly joined the party in 1924 to help boost Mussolini's popularity. When his Teatro d'Arte di Roma closed in 1928 due to lack of funds, Pirandello left for Germany to participate in the newly invented cinema, to adapt several of his plays for the "talkies." He became more popular in Germany and the rest of Europe than in Italy. He resented Italy's aloofness, and determined not to return, saying, "I am a foreigner in Italy." However, he returned to Rome in 1933 to be near Marta, and was awarded the Nobel Prize for Literature in 1934, still admired everywhere but in Italy. He died of pneumonia in 1937.

PLOT SUMMARY

Act One

The play opens in the parlor of Commendatore Agazzi. Agazzi's wife Amalia, their daughter Dina, and Amalia's brother Laudisi are arguing about an affront the ladies have suffered from Signora Frola, a newcomer to the town who refused to see them when they called. On a second visit, Ponza, her son-in-law, coolly answered the door and again frustrated their visit. To top it off, the town is curious about Ponza's wife, because she never goes out and never visits her mother, although Ponza does daily. Ladisi accuses the women of nosiness, and is incensed that they intend to have Signor Agazzi complain to Ponza's boss, the Prefect, about his behavior. While they debate whether Ponza has actually done anything wrong, the butler announces visitors. Three town gossips, Sirelli, his wife, and Signora Cini, join in the fray, also eager to know the truth about the newcomers. Laudisi finds their obsession laughable, since as he demonstrates, he himself is "a different person for each of [them]." Signora Sirelli calls his pessimism "dreadful." The new gossips mention that Ponza and company's village was destroyed by an earthquake recently, which may explain why they all dress in black. Agazzi arrives to announce that he has arranged a visit from Signora Frola herself, and soon thereafter, the old lady is announced.

Signora Frola, a sweet, sad, older lady, apologizes for her negligence of her "social duties," defends her strange family relations, and tells of having lost all of her relatives in the village earthquake. The group pursues her with questions, and they worm out of her that Ponza loves her daughter so jealously that he insists on their communicating only through him. Despite this, she considers him a loving son-in-law. After she leaves, the group condemns Ponza for his cruelty. Now, Ponza himself arrives, and is coldly received. But he throws everyone off with a complex explanation that his mother-in-law is insane, that her daughter is really dead, that his present wife is his second wife, although Signora Frola thinks she is her daughter. Ponza keeps them separated to protect his new wife. Now Ponza's story is accepted.

They are processing new attitudes when the butler announces another visitor: Signora Frola again. After mildly chastising them for interfering with her family, she reveals that it is not she, but Ponza who is mad, with delusions that his wife had died. Signora Frola claims that the daughter actually survived, but to go along with Ponza's delusions, she remarried him. Signora Frola insists that Ponza keeps her locked up out of fear of losing her. For herself, Signora Frola feigns madness to sustain Ponza's delusion. The curtains falls with Laudisi laughing at the stunned busybodies.

Act Two

Act Two opens in Agazzi's study. Agazzi is on the phone with police commissioner, Centuri, asking if he has found anything in his investigation of the Ponza story. Centuri reports that all the village records had been destroyed by the earthquake. Laudisi advises Agazzi and Sirelli to believe both stories, or neither. He sums up the essence of the play's conflict:

> She [signora Frola] has created for him, or he for her, a world of fancy which has all the earmarks of reality itself. And in this fictitious reality they get along perfectly well, and in full accord with each other; and this world of fancy, this reality of theirs, no document can possibly destroy because the air they breathe is of that world—if you could get a death certificate or a marriage certificate or something of the kind, you might be able to satisfy that stupid curiosity of yours. Unfortunately, you can't get it. And the result is that you are in the extraordinary fix of having before you, on the one hand, a world of fancy, and on the other, a world of reality, and you, for the life of you, are not able to distinguish one from the other.

They ignore him. Now, Sirelli hatches the idea to bring Ponza and his mother-in-law together, so they can sort out the truth. Even though Laudisi finds this laughable, a ruse is undertaken to bring them to Agazzi's house without letting on that the

Luigi Pirandello

other will be there. All depart except Laudisi, who looks into a mirror and wonders aloud whether he or the image is the lunatic. "What fools these mortals be, as old Shakespeare said," he muses. The butler sees Laudisi talking to himself and wonders if the man is crazy, then announces the arrival of two more gossips, Signora Cini and Nenni. Laudisi has some fun with the butler by asking whether he is the version of Laudisi they want to see, and the ladies are shown in. Laudisi teases them with the thought that a certificate of the second marriage has been found, but bursts their bubble by adding it may be a fraud. Dina arrives with news of other documents: Signora Frola has shown her and Amalia letters written to her by her daughter. Arguments ensue until Ponza and the old lady arrive; the men and women stay in separate rooms. Suddenly, Ponza hears Signora Frola playing a piano piece that his wife, Lena, used to play. He becomes agitated, and the ladies are brought in. Not only is the mystery is not solved, but it is only further complicated by another name, Julia, his name for his second wife, Julia. Signora Frola pretends to go along with Ponza's delusions, and then goes home. By now all are convinced that he is mad, but then he explains to them that he was only acting agitated to sustain her delusions that her daughter is really dead. When he departs, they all stand "in blank amazement," except for Laudisi, who once again is laughing as the curtain falls.

Act Three

Back in Agazzie's study, Laudisi is reading a book when Police Commissioner Centuri arrives with the news that he has proof at last. Laudisi reads it and announces that it proves nothing, then proposes that the commissioner make up something more "precise," for the sake of peace in the town. Centuri refuses, not realizing that his findings are equally uncertain. A witness has stated that he *thinks* that the "Frola woman" was in a sanitorium. Not knowing which Frola woman is meant makes the evidence valueless. Laudisi now hits upon a foolproof solution—to interview the wife. Sirelli, with growing skepticism, suggests that an interview will work only if the prefect himself conducts the interview. The commissioner goes off to arrange it. Everyone feels certain that the truth is at hand, but Laudisi spoils their hope by casting doubt on the existence of the wife; after all, no one has ever seen her!

The prefect arrives. Although trustful of Ponza (his secretary), he agrees to conduct the interview. As a formality, he asks Ponza's permission first. But Ponza surprises him by offering his resignation before the words are barely out of the prefect's mouth. The Prefect offers assurances of his trust, adding that he is performing the interview only to assure the others. Ponza refuses "to submit to such an indignity." His anxiety and protests succeed in making the prefect skeptical. Finally, Ponza relents and goes to get his wife. He plans to keep his mother-in-law out of the way himself, during the interview.

Unfortunately, Signora Frola comes to visit just at the wrong moment. She wants to say goodbye, for she plans to leave town. Agazzi tells her that her son-in-law is about to arrive. She begs the townspeople to stop tormenting her family, and begins to weep. As the prefect tries to console her, a woman dressed in deep mourning, her face concealed by a thick veil, appears at the door. Signora Frola shrieks, "Lena!" and Ponza dashes into the room shrieking "No! Julia!" He is too late to stop Signora Frola from grasping the woman in an embrace, just the event he had wanted to avoid. The veiled woman dismisses them both coldly, and they depart arm in arm, weeping. The final twist to the plot comes when the veiled woman proclaims to the group that she is both "the daughter of Signora Frola and the second wife of Signor Ponza" but for herself, "nobody." She exits, and the curtain falls on Laudisi, saying "you have the truth! But are you satisfied?" He laughs ironically.

CHARACTERS

Amalia Agazzi

Amalia is wife to Agazzi and sister to Laudisi. She and her daughter Dina feel rebuffed by Signora Frola because she does not answer the door or return their visit when they call on her. Their interest in the gossip about Signora Frola is part human concern, but mostly provincial curiosity. Signora Agazzi enjoys and is quite comfortable with the prestige that comes of being wife to the councilor.

Commendatore Agazzi

Agazzi is a provincial councilor, or lawyer, husband to Amalia, Laudisi's sister. Agazzi is close to fifty years old, accustomed to the authority of his status in a small town. He participates fully in gossiping about Signora Frola and Ponzo.

Dina Agazzi

Dina, at nineteen, acts very grown up about her role in detecting the true details of gossip.

Centuri

Centuri is the Police Commissioner who is brought in to investigate the history of Ponzo, Ponzo's wife, and his mother-in-law. He is around forty, very serious, and single-minded about his duties. He presents his findings with an air of having solved the mystery, failing, however, to comprehend that facts are insignificant in this case. He is quite relieved to be given the duty to call in his superior, the Prefect, since that puts him once again in the realm of concrete action.

Signora Cini

Signora Cini is one of the ladies of the town, an old woman with affected manners and an air of surprise about the misdeeds she loves to hear of in others. She, along with Signora Nenni and the

Sirellis operate similarly to the Greek chorus, as a group of normal citizens who react to the events of the play. Unlike the Greek chorus, however, they do not guide the audience, but rather serve as a foil to the audience's hoped-for reaction.

Commisioner

See Centuri

Signora Frola

Signora Frola is the mysterious older woman who is stationed in a fashionable apartment by her son-in-law. The townspeople cannot decide whether to believe her or her son-in-law. Either she is quite mad, delusional about her dead daughter, or quite sane, and foolishly going along with Ponza's delusions, and thus play-acting at being insane, to mollify his insanity. Her pleas to be left alone are ignored.

Governor

See The Prefect

Lamberto Laudisi

Laudisi (''Nunky'' to Dina, because he is her uncle) good-naturedly plays the devil's advocate in the gossip ring, using a Socratic kind of probing and jibing. He tries but fails to convince the others of the futility of discovering the truth about Ponza and his mother-in-law. He tells the Sirellis from the very beginning that they are both right, explaining that he himself ''is a different person for each of [them].'' When they think they have solid data in the form of Centuri's investigative report, he proves to them that it is ambiguous (*which* Signora Frola was in a sanitarium?) and hints that the record may have been forged. He encourages them to bring in the wife for questioning, then laughs when her appearance complicates, rather than solves, the mystery. He acts as a *raisonneur,* a character who, in contrast to the others, behaves reasonably and makes sense of the messy facts; he is similar to Sherlock Holmes in this respect. He is also the alter ego of the playwright, who has fashioned a puzzle and withholds the conventional solution. His solution is a meta-solution, aimed not at solving the problem, but at endowing a better appreciation for awareness itself.

Signora Nenni

Signora Nenni is another town gossip, similar to Signora Cini, who comes in toward the end of the play.

Nunky

See Lamberto Laudisi

Ponza

Ponza is the new secretary to the town's prefect, recently moved to town with lodgings for himself and wife, and a separate apartment for his mother-in-law. He presents a mystery to the townspeople, because he stays away from them and keeps his wife concealed in their fifth-story apartment, yet pays daily visits to his mother-in-law without allowing her to visit his wife, her daughter. Ponza's dark, swarthy complexion and nervous demeanor undermine his credibility, but his version of things competes well enough with Signora Frola's version to confuse the townspeople completely. He claims that his first wife is dead, and that he keeps his deluded mother-in-law away from his second wife to protect the latter from the mother's caresses. He claims to feign craziness as a way of soothing his mother-in-law.

Signora Ponza

Ponza's wife appears in the very last scene, dressed in mourning, and heavily veiled in black. After Ponza and his mother-in-law stumble weeping out of the room, affected by the wife's public appearance, Signora Ponza announces that she is daughter to Signora Frola, wife to Ponza, and to herself, ''nobody.'' This last statement throws uncertainty on everything that has been conjectured and verified about her, since it implies that she has allowed herself to be formed by others, and thus she cannot be speaking ''the truth.'' As such, she is the perfect emblem of Laudisi's theory that every person is exactly as others perceive her to be; however she undermines even his theory too, in denying his corollary at the same time, that she is still herself.

The Prefect

The Prefect, Ponza's superior, and the person of highest rank in the town, is called in to mediate the gossip crisis, which he will do by interrogating Signora Ponza himself. He is about sixty, competent, and good-natured, and perfectly confident in his ability to take charge and set things aright. However, he has to threaten Ponza with dismissal to force him to bring in his wife. Up to this point, the Prefect has trusted Ponza, but even his trust also is undermined by a surfeit of information.

Sirelli

A pretentious and overdressed provincial who, with his wife, gets into the thick of the gossip ring.

Signora Sirelli

Signora Sirelli is a provincial gossip, young and pretty, who cannot understand Laudisi's demonstration that she can be many things to many people. Her argument is that she is "always the same, yesterday, today, and forever!"

THEMES

Relativism

Relativism is the theory that "truth and moral values are not absolute but are [pertinent] to the persons or groups holding them" (*American Heritage Dictionary, 3rd Edition*). The idea of relativism is a core concept of 20th century modernism. At the turn of the century, it was a new idea, just gaining coinage. It followed on the crisis of faith that had occurred during the nineteenth century, spurred on by Darwin's discoveries. Relativism suggests that rather than seek an overarching, absolute truth, such as that previously held forth by the Church, each person might in his or her own conscious discover a relevant truth. At the end of the nineteenth century, philosophers like Matthew Arnold theorized that the way to make the conscious "worthy" of such responsibility was to cultivate genius, to fill the mind with "the best that has been known and said in the world" (as Arnold phrased it in 1873). But who would arbitrate what was the best? The two dimensions of this idea, what was right, and how much weight the conscious could bear, became the burning questions that attended the theory of relativism. Artists and writers tried out the new theory in different contexts, plumbing its depths and testing its fit. So did Pirandello. In an 1893 essay called "Art and Consciousness Today," he wrote,

> In minds and consciousnesses an extraordinary confusion reigns. In their interior mirror the most disparate figures, all in disordered attitudes, as if weighed down with insupportable burdens, are reflected, and each gives a different counsel. To whom should we listen? To whom should we cling? The insistence of one counsel overrides for a moment the voices of all the others, and we give ourselves to him for a time with the unhealthy impulsiveness of someone who wants an escape and doesn't know where it is—we feel bewildered, lost in an immense, blind labyrinth surrounded on all sides by impenetrable mystery. There are many paths, but which is the true one?—The old norms have crumbled, and the new ones haven't arisen and become well established. It's understandable that the idea of the relativity of all things has spread so much within us to deprive us almost altogether of the faculty for judgement.

The term "relativity" does not appear directly in Pirandello's play *Right You Are, If You Think You Are,* but it undergirds its plot, placing it in the context of perceptions about other persons. Amalia, Dina, Agazzi and the others are obsessed with finding the absolute truth about Sigonora Frola and Ponza. But an earthquake has destroyed their past, and they give conflicting stories. Laudisi accepts relativism; he is modern, a man in tune with new ideas. None of the other characters is "ready" to accept that there is no absolute truth. Thus Laudisi is a vanguard of modernist thought, while the other characters are blind (or veiled, like the wife at the end of the play) to reality, or rather, realities.

Privacy

Along with the modernist theme of relativism in *Right You Are, If You Think You Are* lies a more conservative theme. Signora Frola makes a heartfelt plea for the townspeople to leave her family in peace. She insists that they do not realize the harm they are doing with their persistent questioning and prying into her family's affairs. Pirandello himself, who was at the time of writing this play suffering from the presence of his severely mentally ill wife in his home, certainly understood the need for privacy and peace. His wife Antonietta exhibited paranoia and severe jealousy, and her outbursts embarrassed Pirandello, who was shy and reserved. He therefore cloistered himself from prying eyes, and fabricated reasons for his many separations from his wife, when either she left him or drove him and the children away from their home. Everyone in *Right You Are, If You Think You Are* except for Laudisi (the playwright's alter ego) commits the social crime of overstepping the boundaries of conventional propriety in asking questions of Signora Frola and Ponza. The truth is not even revealed to the audience, as if forcing their respect for privacy. Although moralist plays were no longer fashionable in 1917, Pirandello's play is moralist in the sense that it conveys the theme of respecting personal privacy as a maxim of proper human relations.

STYLE

Parable

Parables, like the stories told by Christ in the *Bible,* are simple stories designed to teach a lesson. The simple, flat characters and rather thin plot serve to illustrate an important idea. Thus, the characters do not need to seem realistic, nor does the plot need intrinsic interest. In this way, the parable is a kind of allegory, which Coleridge defined as "a translation of abstract notions into picture-language." Pirandello's *Right You Are, If You Think You Are* is a parable in the sense that it is not really about a specific man, Laudisi, who has trouble convincing his family and friends that they cannot discover the real truth about their new neighbors. Rather, it is an illustrative example of the theme that all truth is relative; it is an example of the concept, with multiple reminders (through Laudisi's theorizing) to pay attention to the larger ideas at play, and not the story itself. On another level, the play also addresses the moral, Pirandello's corollary to the principle of relativism, to respect people's privacy, for if there is no absolute truth, then we have no right to judge others according to our truths. It is the modernist version of the biblical moral, "He that is without sin among you, let him cast the first stone."

The Raisonneur

In some parables or plays of ideas, a *raisonneur* plays the role of guiding the audience to comprehend a moral or intellectual message. The *raisonneur* must have credibility, which he gains through his actions, words, and attitude, but he can also be playful as he chides the other characters for their blindness to the central idea. Laudisi is the *raisonneur* in *Right You Are, If You Think You Are,* but like the prophet Cassandra of the Greek tragedies, his words of warning are destined to be ignored. In his role of chiding the other characters, Laudisi is also a kind of clown, trickster, or *harlequin* figure, seen as foolish by those who cannot hear his message.

Coup de Theatre

A *coup de theatre* is a surprising and usually unmotivated stroke in a drama that produces a

TOPICS FOR FURTHER STUDY

- Which is more important in *Right You Are, If You Think You Are* the theme of relativism, or the moral to respect the privacy of others? Support your claim with evidence from the play.

- How does Laudisi's role as *raisonneur* affect the audience's appreciation of the quandary faced by his relatives and friends concerning Ponza and Signora Frola?

- Of what significance is the final speech by Signora Ponza?

sensational effect; by extension, any piece of claptrap or anything designed solely for effect" (Holman and Harmon *A Handbook to Literature, 6th edition*). The hand thrusting from the grave at the end of the thriller film *Carrie* was a *coup de theatre;* so was Hamlet's sudden stab at the tapestry in his mother's rooms, when he thought he had discovered the King spying on him, but killed Polonius instead. The *coups de theatre* at the ends of each scene in *Right You Are, If You Think You Are* may be less physically dramatic, but they are intellectually dramatic. In the first act, Laudisi's friends and family stand stunned after Signora Frola explains that Ponza's wife is not, after all, her daughter, thus overturning Ponza's explanation that Signora Frola is mad, which had just overturned *her* explanation that Ponza kept her daughter locked up because he loved her so much. The drama lies in stretching the listener's credibility to the maximum. The townspeople stand in "blank astonishment." At the end of Act Two, "they stand in blank amazement," after Ponza explains that he feigned his insane rage at Signora Frola as a palliative to her insanity. The *coup* here is the ingenuity of Pirandello's tortuous plot construction. At the end of Act Three, the crowd simply looks in "profound silence" at Signora Ponza, who has stunned them all by admitting to being both Signora's daughter and Ponza's second wife. Her bizarre dress and sudden appearance conform to conventionally shocking *coups de theatre,* but once again, Pirandello shows dramatic mastery by not relying on the surprise effect as much as on the unusual intellectual twist that her speech confers on the play's meaning. For someone who came rather late to the theater, Pirandello had a flair for dramatic elements such as the *coup de theatre*.

HISTORICAL CONTEXT

Pirandello & World War I

World War I raged while Pirandello wrote his play, *Right You Are, If You Think You Are*. Pirandello later said that "It was war that revealed theatre to me. Mine is a theatre of war." War between Germany and France had been considered inevitable since at least 1905, and finally broke out in 1914. What began in a nationalist frenzy soon stalemated in a 350-mile line of trenches where thousands of lives were sacrificed to gain or lost a single mile. Euphoria was replaced by nihilism as it became evident that a whole generation was going to slaughter. To many writers and thinkers, the war was proof of the crisis in consciousness that was separate but intricately linked with the political problems that plagued Europe. Italy joined the war in 1915, and Pirandello's son Stefano enlisted, interrupting his university studies. Stefano was immediately was sent to the front, where he was wounded and taken prisoner. Pirandello's younger son Fausto was called up, but was so weak from an intestinal operation that Pirandello had to intervene to get him released to convalesce; however, Fausto had already contracted tuberculosis. Then Stefano contracted tuberculosis as well. Pirandello lobbied for a trade of prisoners, and the Austrian government demanded three prisoners in return for Stefano. Caught between his patriotic duty and his love for his son, Pirandello refused. Stefano was released at the end of the war. During the war years, with both sons in danger, Pirandello's wife Antonietta, who was already mentally unstable, grew unpredictable and violent. The war years were a time of disillusion and danger to all, but of particular torment for Pirandello. After the war, Pirandello joined the Fascist movement, both because it promised to bring backward Italy into the twentieth century, and because of his desperate need to feel connected as well as his attraction to the allure of revolution and dramatic change. Fascism ultimately disappointed him.

Relativism

It is difficult to place exactly when in time the idea of relativism first took root. Certainly it hit its stride when Einstein published his General Theory of Relativity in 1905, but that event merely gave a scientific example of a way of thinking that already existed; in fact, the term "relativity" was already in use. Further back, Darwin's publication of *The Origin of Species* in 1859 started a cataclysmic shift in allegiance away from religion, God was "dead," and the idea of progress became an end to itself. Of course, the idea of progress, too, was already extant at this time, in the form of Imperialism and its notion that growth was necessary for survival. Darwin's theories seemed to support nineteenth century imperialism, yet were unsettling to his age because they suggested that humankind may not have been destined to rule, but developed power through a random series of trials and error. Even though the human species sat at top of the "Great Chain of Being," humanity's divine sponsorship was called into question. Then Freud came along with his *The Interpretation of Dreams* (1899) and accelerated the sense of displacement, by proving that emotion and unconscious forces were as strong as, if not stronger than, logic and reason. The confidence of the Age of Enlightenment was eroding, and the self-adulation of the Romantic Age seemed inappropriate. World War I would prove to the Allies that the fittest who survived were not necessary morally better. The "Lost Generation," led by Ernest Hemingway and his friends in Europe, mourned this realization. The acceptance of relativism thus came about more as a slow, layer-by-layer removal of outdated arrogances than as a sudden, bright epiphany. If humans could not put their confidence in god, they could at least put it into their own consciousness, whatever that might be. Consciousness could be the new "god," or rather, gods, since each person's view was different, or relative.

CRITICAL OVERVIEW

Right You Are, If You Think You Are opened on June 18, 1917 at the Teatro Olimpia in Milan. Pirandello had sent the script to director Virgilio Talli describing the play as "a parable, which is truly original, new in both its conception and development, and

COMPARE & CONTRAST

- **1917:** A network of "ententes" or political alliances between European countries had been signed wherein each promised to help its allies in case of war. Europe was divided by paper loyalties. As warring countries coerced their neutral allies to join in the war according to their agreements, there was a "domino" effect as the new aggressors called upon their neutral allies.

    Today: Europe is attempting to create a universal agreement among its nations on several levels: economically through the "eurodollar," and politically through the European Union (Europa), a multinational European parliament.

- **1917:** Europe was embroiled in a full-scale war that left no country, even those like Belgium that claimed neutrality, safe from invasion.

    Today: Although the Kosovo crisis of 1998 threatened stability in Eastern Europe, decisive action on the part of NATO prevented the conflict from spreading to other countries.

- **1917:** Influenza killed more people during and just after World War I than did weapons and bombs, and tuberculosis was an incurable and devastating disease that often led to death.

    Today: A simple annual flu shot can prevent most strains of influenza, and the millions who do not receive inoculations can get relief from its symptoms with antibiotics. Flu can still be fatal, if not treated adequately. Tuberculosis, though still incurable, is rare in developed countries. Skin tests are used to screen for its presence so that the disease can be managed if contracted.

---

very daring." Talli wrote back saying that although he loved the dialogue, he thought the play might not hold together on stage, that it seemed more suitable to be "enjoyed in solitude," through reading. However, Talli did stage the play, and it won the attention that Pirandello's previous seven plays had not garnered. His success initiated a productive writing period that saw thirteen more Pirandello plays appear over the next six years. Of the debut of *Right You Are,* Pirandello reported in a letter to his son that "it was performed very successfully," and that he was received "very warmly." After a tour of major Italian cities, the play reached Rome the following year, to much acclaim. His popularity increased after the arrival in 1921 of his best-known play, *Six Characters in Search of an Author* (1925), but then waned in Italy a few short years later. A German reviewer of a 1925 production of *Right You Are, If You Think You Are* called it a "terrifying play," in which "both sides were equally crazy—and—all the other characters held their own in a quiet craziness of their own." Another German reviewer called the play "bluff—clever bluff at times—but bluff all the same." Nevertheless, Pirandello's renown in the rest of Europe was firmly established, and the term *Pirandellisme* came to signify his style of dramatic intellectual games.

During the height of his fame, *Right You Are, If You Think You Are* was first played in New York at the Guild Theater February 21, 1927, with Edward G. Robinson as Ponza. Reviewer Stark Young deemed this production "at least passable," for a play with an "exhilarating game of motives and ideas," one that put *Right You Are* in a league with the *commedia dell'arte,* or improvisation with a clown, or harlequin, character. Brooks Atkinson of the *New York Times* hailed it as a good run from "satire to metaphysics and on to melodrama" that is "ingeniously exciting and amusing by turns." Helen Hayes played Signora Frola in a 1966 production at the Lyceum Theater in New York City, following the stage directions and translation of Eric Bentley, again to good acclaim. A 1972 production in New York earned high praise from *New York Post* critic Jerry Tallmer, who especially liked the stage design that included a wall of mirrors to emphasize the shifting perspectives. Clive Barnes considered the same production with less enthusiasm, though he fully approved of Bentley's translation, which he deemed as having "just the right primed and provincial seediness to it."

For many decades scholarly treatments of his work appeared only in Italian, though these were, and continue to be, numerous. The 1950s brought about a revival of his work, as it corresponds well with Existentialism and the Theater of the Absurd. Once the copyright of his works expired and the centenary of his death was celebrated (in 1986), his plays experienced a resurgence in popularity, and since then new anthologies of his works and new volumes of literary criticism in English have appeared with some regularity.

Like George Bernard Shaw, Pirandello felt oppressed by publicity. In 1935, he complained of "the many Pirandellos in circulation in the world of international literary criticism, lame, deformed, all head and no heart, erratic, gruff, insane, and obscure, in whom no matter how hard [he tried, he could not] recognize himself even for a moment." To some, his was an intellectual art, lacking feeling. The term "Pirandellisme," as it was applied to Jean Giraudoux and Jean Anouilh, meant "pure intellectual game," a trait that was much appreciated in French theater. Pirandello objected to this label as suggesting he was merely a "juggler of ideas." It was not until after World War II that audiences appreciated his seriousness.

CRITICISM

Carole Hamilton

Hamilton is an English teacher at Cary Academy, an innovative private school in Cary, North Carolina. In this essay she examines the themes of privacy and relative truth in Right You Are, If You Think You Are, *especially in light of Pirandello's tormented personal life.*

Pirandello's *Right You Are, If You Think You Are* is one of many of his plays and essays that concerns relativism, a feature of the modern consciousness. Pirandello described his own version of the theory in *Umorismo,* [*On Humor*] (1908):

> Life is a continuous flux that we seek to arrest and to fix in stable and determinate forms, within and outside ourselves—But within ourselves, in what we call the spirit—the flux continues, indistinct, flowing under the banks, beyond the limits that we impose as we compose a consciousness for ourselves and construct a personality.

Not surprisingly, many critics have focused on the theme of relativism as it appears in *Right You Are, If You Think You Are*. The play concerns "flux" of shifting truths in the several explanations that Ponza and Signora Frola proclaim about Signora Ponza. Each of their revelations supercedes the last, and each new truth seems final, until the next one is presented. For example, Signora Frola's story that Ponza keeps her away from her daughter out of love melts away when Ponza explains that she is insanely perpetuating a myth that her daughter is alive. With each turn of events, it is as though the solid background of the theater gives way to another curtain, and then, impossibly, to another.

Against the overlaying of multiple truths, Laudisi, Pirandello's alter ego in the play, insists that all of the explanations are simultaneously true, and thus there is no ultimate truth to uncover. To prove his case he tells them, "I am really what you take me to be; though—that does not prevent me from also being really what your husband, my sister, my niece, and Signora Cini take me to be—because they are all absolutely right!" Each perspective is "right" in its own way, although incomplete. The friends and family ignore him, however, and continue their quest for the ultimate truth. In doing so, they fail to grasp the metaphysical truth that Laudisi represents and that underpins the play. Thus on one level, Pirandello's play simply illustrates his theory of multiple coexisting truths, i.e., relativism, and its consequences.

Relativism's effect on human relations, Pirandello's play suggests, leads to frustration, because humans continue to search for absolute truth. As Anthony Caputi points out in *Pirandello and the Crisis of Modern Consciousness,* the play also concerns itself with "the implications of living with fictions created with a full awareness that they are fictions." When people understand, with Laudisi, that truth is relative, they feel unmoored, lacking the comforting anchor of absolute truth. The sensation can be as unsettling as madness, and so Laudisi asks his image in the mirror, "Who is the lunatic, you or I?" He goes on, "What are you for other people? What are you in their eyes? An image, my dear sir, just an image in the glass!" In other words, relativism reduces truth to a play of surfaces, where conflicting interpretations compete for viability in a world that refuses to offer confirmation. The family

WHAT DO I READ NEXT?

- Pirandello's most famous play, *Six Characters in Search of an Author* (1922), provides another perspective on his theories of self and consciousness. George Bernard Shaw's *Man and Superman* (1905) is another "drama of ideas," in which the characters debate Shaw's ideas about social philosophy. The modernist poem "Portrait d'une Femme" (1912) by Ezra Pound comes close to representing consciousness in the way that Pirandello presents it, as a source of many interpretations. Pound was an American expatriate living in Italy from 1924 until 1944, when he was arrested for treason (for making Fascist remarks) by the United States. Other modernists concerned with consciousness are James Joyce (especially in his novel, *Ulysses*, 1922, where he experiments with "stream of consciousness" writing) and Marcel Proust (in his seven-part novel about memory, *A La Recherche de Temps Perdue*, translated as *Remembrance of Things Past*, 1913-1927). "The Falling Girl" by Italian Dino Buzzati is an example of a postmodern parable. Argentine writer Jorge Luis Borges wrote many poem and short story parables on themes of self and reality, such as "The Circular Ruins" and "The Aleph." Colombian Gabriel Garcia Marquez's parable, "A Very Old Man with Enormous Wings" also concerns differing interpretations of reality.

---

and friends base their assessment of Ponza and Signora Frola on their explanations, which they cannot verify because Signora Ponza is hidden away and an earthquake has destroyed the family's documents. As a last resort, the townspeople force a confrontation between Ponza and Signora Frola, to force the truth out. But the confrontation proves no more fruitful than Laudisi's conversations with his mirror image. This is because the problem lies not in the facts or words, but within themselves. Laudisi laughs, "'What fools these mortals be!' as old Shakespeare said." As Pirandello's spokesperson indicates, the problems of relativism are personal, and therefore it is necessary to consider Pirandello's personal relationship to the theme of relativism. In doing so, the related moral theme of respect for human privacy becomes paramount.

Drama critic and director Eric Bentley notes in *The Pirandello Commentaries* that Pirandello is not simply interested in the philosophy of relativism, but in the moral dilemma that accompanies it. He asserts that, "the play is not about thinking, but about suffering, a suffering that is only increased by those who give understanding and enquiry precedence over sympathy and help." Suffering is a thread that quietly winds its way through the play.

Signora Frola and her family are mourning the effects of losing many members of their family, and under these conditions, the townspeople's insistent questioning is "cruel." Although they accuse Ponza of cruelty and selfishness, they are blind to the cruelty they impose on her, in their relentless crusade to uncover her truths. In the end of Act Three, Signora Ponza cries, "You must stop all this. You must let us alone. You think you are helping me. You are trying to do me a favor; but really, what you're doing is working me a great wrong." According to Bentley, a key detail is the fact that in spite of their efforts, the truth about Signora Ponza never comes to light. Bentley emphatically says, "The truth, Pirandello wants to tell us again and again, is concealed, *concealed*, CONCEALED!" It is as though Pirandello is demonstrating not that truth is impossible to perceive, tricky or shifting, but that it is, and should be, private. Bentley concludes, "The solution of the problem, the cure for these sick human beings, is to leave their problem unsolved and unrevealed."

The theme of suffering at the hands of nosy gossips could easily derive from Pirandello's tormented life. From an insane wife who tormented him with her jealous rages to his own obsessive

> IN PIRANDELLO'S CASE, HE WANTED TO OBSCURE THE REALISTIC APPRAISALS OF OUTSIDERS, SO THAT THEY WOULD NOT INTERFERE WITH HIS FANTASIES. HIS FANTASIES OCCLUDED A PROPER ASSESSMENT OF HIS MAD WIFE, SUCH THAT HE LET HIS FAMILY SUFFER FOR SEVENTEEN YEARS. THEY ALSO ALLOWED HIM TO BURN FOR TEN YEARS IN FUTILE PASSION FOR AN ACTRESS HALF HIS AGE."

dependency on her and then on a much younger actress, Pirandello's personal life was something he needed to obscure from public view. Former students of his attest to a man who "always kept to himself," who cared to befriend neither his students nor his colleagues. Perhaps he was ashamed of his marriage. In catholic Italy, divorce was impossible, as was abandonment, especially since he felt he could not live without his wife, despite her madness. To ease the agony, he wrote about it. In his novel, *Her Husband,* he describes a man tormented as "the target of madness" from a wife who "knew nothing of his ideal life, his superior talents" but only saw "the phantom she had made of him." He was "two people: one for himself, another for her." Perhaps there was, too, a side of Pirandello that aggravated her madness, or that somehow thrived on it. Most biographers cast Pirandello as the victim of his mad wife's behavior. But Renate Matthaei suggests that "His mad wife was an inspiration. She showed him all the symptoms of a disturbance that he recognized in himself but had managed to conceal, being more robust than she." For years Pirandello managed to conceal his own obsessive nature behind the mask of his wife's madness. He brought it to the light in the relative safety of stories and plays that explored the boundaries of such relationships. In *Right You Are* he plays with various readings of the Ponza-Frola relationship, with killing off the wife, or simply fantasizing her death. It is as though he cannot bear to reach a resolution with it, just as he could not bear to resolve his own marriage's difficulties. It took seventeen years of torment before, with the support of their children, he had her institutionalized. He must have felt both relief and great guilt when he finally took that step.

Not to have made a decision about his wife was a way of keeping all of the options alive, all truths simultaneously true. Bentley is correct to point out that the mystery character's secret truth stays concealed, even at the end of the play when a resolution is fervently expected. Furthermore, Signora Ponza verifies *every* interpretation of her, by claiming to be both wife to Ponza and daughter to Signora Frola, and "nothing" to herself. This final intellectual turn shockingly reveals that Signora Ponza has allowed herself to be molded by her husband. Her veiled existence, a product of other's perspectives of her, makes an eloquent appeal for human privacy. The viewer is left feeling that she should somehow have resisted their interpretations, and kept true to herself, as Pirandello often urged Marta Abba to be. To stay true to oneself is to resist and lock out other people's interpretations so that one's own ideas may survive. In Pirandello's case, he wanted to obscure the realistic appraisals of outsiders, so that they would not interfere with his fantasies. His fantasies occluded a proper assessment of his mad wife, such that he let his family suffer for seventeen years. They also allowed him to burn for ten years in futile passion for an actress half his age.

Pirandello's sentiments concerning truth are given voice by Laudisi, who argues for keeping alive all of the possible interpretations of Ponza, his wife, and his mother-in-law, and their tortuous relations. Laudisi could equally well have been arguing for keeping alive all the fantasies that Pirandello used to negotiate his complex and troubled life. The theory of relativism, for Pirandello, is a means to maintaining his internal fictional world. The play's title, *Right You Are, If You Think You Are,* could be directed at the Laudisi's friends, at Pirandello's friends, or even, at Pirandello himself.

Source: Carole Hamilton, for *Drama for Students,* Gale, 2000.

A. Petrusso

In this essay, Petrusso discusses how social values and the theme of truth shape Right You Are!.

In Luigi Pirandello's *Right You Are! (If You Think So),* many of the primary characters are on a quest for the truth about newcomers to their community. The Agazzis, Lamberto Laudisi, and their friends want to know several things about Signor Ponza, his wife, and his mother-in-law, Signora Frola. They are curious about the unusual living situation among the Ponzas and Frola, as well as what happened to them in their previous home. This nosy interest leads to much speculation, gossip, and trickery, but the group never really finds out the "real" truth about the Ponzas and Frola. Pirandello shows how relative "truth" can be, and how such an investigation can harm those concerned.

At the end of *Right You Are! (If You Think So)*, the primary protagonists—Commendatore Agazzi, his wife Amalia, their daughter Dina, and their friends the Sirellis, among others—end up forcing a face-to-face confrontation between Signor Ponza, his wife, and his mother-in-law, Signora Frola, to get at the truth about them. Over the course of the play, it is stated several times that Signora Ponza and Frola have not talked in such a face-to-face manner because of something that happened in the past. The only way the alleged mother and daughter have communicated is by letter. Frola would visit the Ponzas' tenement apartment, and Signora Ponza would drop a basket from her fifth floor balcony for the exchange of notes. Yet the forced meeting does not answer any of the protagonists' questions about the Ponzas and Frola. Signora Ponza tells them that the contradictory stories that Signor and Signora Frola have told them are both true. The previously unseen Signora Ponza solves the play by not solving it, thus giving *Right You Are!* its primary theme: the truth about people differs based on point of view. Much of the time, what is believed to be a truth is irrelevant.

The reason for the protagonists' quest for the truth is understandable. The more they find out about the Ponzas and Frola, the more their interest is piqued. In addition to the letter-only communication between mother and daughter, the Ponzas live in a tenement on the edge of town, while Frola lives in the same upscale building as the Agazzis. Signor Ponza does not want Frola to have a normal social life with anyone, including her neighbors. Yet Frola and Signor Ponza spend much time together. Though Frola manages to have some social contact, her alleged daughter has none at all. No one in the village has seen her outside the home until the end of *Right You Are!*, and the only reason she has been brought there is because the village's Prefect has ordered it.

" WHAT THE GROUP WANTED WAS A CLEAR TRUTH SO THEY COULD JUDGE THE SOCIAL ACCEPTABILITY OF THE PONZAS AND FROLA. WHAT EMOTIONAL DAMAGE AND DISTRESS THEY CAUSED IN THEIR EXPLANATION WAS IRRELEVANT, THOUGH THAT IS ALSO A BREACH OF SOCIAL MORES."

But what starts the Agazzis, their relatives and friends on their quest is a breach of perceived social mores by Frola. Before this major transgression, it seems the protagonists merely noticed and gossiped about the minor social oddities of the Ponzas and Frola. A major transgression opens a floodgate, and gives the protagonists a license to dig deeper and create confrontational situations. This transgression is Frola's refusal to receive the social call of Signora Agazzi and her daughter Dina just before the action of Act I begins. This infuriates Signora Agazzi and Dina because, as Signora Agazzi states, "We were trying to do her a favor." The truth becomes important to them because of their values. Their social mores must be upheld, and the only way to do that is to discover the truth. The truth would explain why Frola refused to (or was not allowed to) receive them, which would allow the social mistake to be acceptable.

Nothing less than what the protagonists perceive to be the truth will do to counteract this social misstep by Frola. They go to great lengths to find out the truth, without respect for the privacy of the Ponzas and Frola or other social mores. Some of their group goes as far as to call for the firing of Ponza from his governmental job based on speculation and rumor, even before explanations can be given by Ponza and Frola. Like the truth at the end of *Right You Are!*, social graces are portrayed as relative, at least for established citizens of the village.

Thus when Frola calls upon the Agazzis in Act I to apologize and relate her story, they conveniently deny their already stated abhorrence of her social transgression so that more information can be obtained. Signora Agazzi herself says, "Oh, we are just neighbors, Signora Frola! Why stand on ceremony?" This statement comforts Frola and makes her more open to answering their questions. Frola tells them about an earthquake in which she and Ponza lost their families, which should sufficiently explain away why they act differently. But the group gathered push Frola to the limit with their persistent, torturous questions. There is no regard for sociability here. The group cannot accept Frola's feeble explanations nor her statements of happiness. When she says, "We all have our weaknesses in this world, haven't we! And we get along best by having a little charity, a little indulgence for one another," they ignore her implied plea and decide to dig deeper for a more "real," socially acceptable truth.

Soon after Frola leaves in Act I, Ponza makes a social call to the Agazzis and relates his version of events to counteract anything Frola may have said. Ponza is flustered and controlling, explaining that Frola must be left alone. When the group does not like this, Ponza reveals that she is insane. He claims that he was married to Frola's daughter at one time, but she died and the woman he is married to now is his second wife. Frola has mistaken the second wife for her own daughter, and lives in obsessed denial about who the woman Ponza is married to really is. This is Ponza's reason for essentially keeping Frola under lock and key, and not allowing social mores to be followed. Some of the group of protagonists accepts most of this explanation, while others are not so sure.

Their quest for truth takes another unexpected turn when Frola returns. She tells them that while Ponza is an excellent worker, he is the one who is a lunatic. Frola's version of the story is that her daughter became ill with a contagious disease and had to be isolated and hospitalized. Ponza believed that his wife had died in the hospital, and when she recovered, he would not believe it was her. A second wedding was held for the couple, so Ponza still believes that Frola's daughter is dead. Frola assures them that this is the only way Ponza can survive his day-to-day life. She also says that she pretends to be insane for his benefit. As Frola tells the group during her second visit, "Oh, my dear Signora Agazzi, I wish I had left things as they were. It was hard to feel that I had been impolite to you by not answering the bell when you called the first time; but I could never have supposed that you would come back and force me to call upon you."

Throughout Acts II and III, the group of protagonists, led by the Agazzis, try to discern the truth of these statements: Who is really insane, Frola or Ponza? Which is telling the truth about their past? The quest for the truth only gets more confusing, not less. When they resort to trickery in Act II, they find out that Frola calls Signora Ponza by the name of Julia, while Ponza insists that her name is Lena. They end up hurting Ponza desperately. The group also arranges for a background investigation by the police which leads nowhere. Their quest ends in the manner described above, by involving the town's Prefect and arranging a confrontation between all three which does nothing to fulfill their need to know. When forced, the mysterious Signora Ponza asks of the group, "And what can you want of me now, after all this, ladies and gentlemen?" What the group wanted was a clear truth so they could judge the social acceptability of the Ponzas and Frola. What emotional damage and distress they caused in their explanation was irrelevant, though that is also a breach of social mores.

There is one voice of reason in *Right You Are!*, Signora Agazzi's brother, Lamberto Laudisi. Though he is aligned with the group of protagonists, he is a skeptic who questions their every statement, every motive, and every move. Laudisi sees the narrowness of their vision, how they perceive that everything must be true or false, with no other possible explanation. From the beginning of the play, he says things like "It was none of your damned business" when Dina Agazzi tried to rationalize their visit to Frola. Laudisi is aware of the importance of privacy, and implicitly sees how the group is using social mores to further their quest. He tries to show them the futility of their task, but he is ridiculed, and, at one point, banned from the room. Still, he maintains a sense of humor which serves him well. And at the end of each act, including the end of *Right You Are!*, Laudisi gets the last laugh because he has known the truth about their "real" truth all along.

Source: A. Petrusso, for *Drama for Students*, Gale, 2000.

Robert S. Dombroski

The following is Dombroski's aim in this essay: "Rather than interpreting Laudisi's laughter as a sign of Pirandello's satirical aims, I should like to suggest the possibility of viewing it simply as a spontaneous show of approval for a humorous situation, a favorable response to a rather elaborate joke."

Criticism has more or less agreed that Pirandello's intention in writing *Right You Are (If You Think So)* was to illustrate his conviction that truth does not exist absolutely, but merely as a product of the individual mind. From here it became a question of whether the play was successful as drama and to what extent the thesis may be said to either enhance or diminish the work's emotional content. Is *Right You Are* a "sensitive" and "provoking" expression of Pirandello's philosophy? Or is it nothing more than—as Gramsci would have it—"a superficial fact of literature: a pure and simple mechanical aggregate of words"? (*AVANTI!,* Oct. 5, 1917) Contemporary criticism has rescued the play from a type of discussion based on whether Pirandello did or did not succeed in dramatizing his relativist *Weltanschauung* by shifting the perspective from the work's philosophical content to its social bearings and the existential turmoil of its main characters; that is, from Laudisi's arid reasoning about the relativity of truth to the sufferings of the Ponza-Frola group. Eric Bentley, for example, views the play as a social satire, Pirandello's aim being to demonstrate how the "idle curiosity" and "nosiness" of the townspeople is detrimental to the sufferers' struggle for life in its inner essence and private depths. And Robert Brustein goes a step further, describing the work as a "drama of social revolt." According to him, "the play is a protest against [he quotes Bentley] the 'scandalmonger, the prying reporter, and the amateur psychoanalyst' and [he himself adds] the sob sister, the candid cameraman, and the Congressional investigator—those who recklessly probe the secrets of others."

For Bentley and Brustein, therefore, the drama consists in the play's emotional content, that is, in Signora Frola's and Signor Ponza's struggle for survival against the onslaught of the townspeople's destructive curiosity. Although convincing in many ways and certainly supported by the characters' awareness of conflict, interpretations of this sort do not take sufficiently into account the function of the "intellectual" frame in which the drama develops: they focus on the dramatic or dialectical process as if this process were free from the imposing presence of Laudisi and thus ignore the importance of the relationship between structural elements in determining the play's total meaning.

Those readers to whom *Right You Are* appeared as too intellectually contrived had good reasons on which to base their assumptions. For it is clear that the conflict between the townspeople and the Ponza-Frola group is a dramatic actualization of Laudisi's

"REGARDLESS OF WHAT THEORY WE CHOOSE TO EXPLAIN LAUDISI'S LAUGHTER, WE ARE DEALING BASICALLY WITH A PLAY ON FORM, AN ATTACK ON SOMETHING FORMAL BY SOMETHING INFORMAL; THE TOWNSPEOPLE'S ESTABLISHED, LOGICALLY CONTROLLED APPROACH TO REALITY IS OVERTURNED BY THE VITALITY AND IRRATIONALITY OF THE PONZA-FROLA GROUP."

relativist convictions. From the standpoint of the play's thematic organisation *Right You Are* appears unequivocally as a *dramma a tesi*. It begins simply with man's natural desire to know the things around him (the townspeople's wanting to understand the reasons for the Ponza-Frola group's strange living arrangement). It concludes with the discovery that things have not an absolute, but a relational existence (the meaning of Signora Ponza's final words "Io sono colei che mi si crede"). The play develops in a way that the thesis is proved in each of the acts and in the final act it becomes impossible to disprove. From the standpoint of action, the reader follows a circular schema whereby he sees the townspeople move from a state of unsatisfied curiosity through several intense moments of expectation and disillusionment back to that same state; while thematically he proceeds from the lack of knowledge through a series of demonstrations to the awareness that truth beyond appearance is unattainable. In addition to Laudisi and Signora Ponza, who express their relativist beliefs directly to the townspeople, Signora Frola and Signor Ponza illustrate perfectly Pirandello's thesis: they both tell equally convincing stories and each is aware of the role the other is playing.

At the same time, however, the play's emotional nucleus does consist in the struggle of the Ponza-

Frola group to preserve their illusions, although we may sincerely wonder if this theme could not have been expressed in a less mechanical way. Is the character of Laudisi really necessary to the drama? Why did Pirandello choose such an "unrealistic" story to illustrate his convictions? It might be that the artist is at fault. Professor Brustein believes that Pirandello, by not fusing the "spokesman-sufferer" (Laudisi) with the pathetic sufferers (the Ponza-Frola group), has not yet perfected his dramatic structure. But the work's flawless technique suggests that Pirandello has willingly created an ambiguous dramatic structure, which in itself is perfect. The ambiguity lies in the figure of Laudisi who, on the one hand, tells us that truth is equal to appearance and laughs at those who seek "objective facts," and on the other, goes no further than showing abstract sympathy for the sufferings of the Ponza-Frola family. That is to say, Laudisi relates to Signora Frola and Signor Ponza through his epistemological considerations which are potentially beneficial to their lives. But his involvement in their drama ends there. He does not, for instance, act directly to help them; nor does he voice more than mild objections at the townspeople's tactics. Thus, as an element of structure, Laudisi does not have the status of a character belonging to one of the dialectical forces in the play. Rather he is a sort of device whose function lies in establishing the emotional and intellectual relationships between the playwright and the dialectical oppositions he is representing.

The role of Laudisi in *Right You Are* may be better understood if we consider for a moment the short story on which the play is based, *"La signora Frola e il signor Ponza suo genero"* (1915). The story is related by an anonymous speaker in the form of a dramatic monologue. The speaker of the monologue addresses an audience of readers, telling them how the entire citizenry of Valdana is perplexed at not being able to distinguish which of the two eccentric strangers, Mrs. Frola or Mr. Ponza, has gone mad. The speaker then goes on to recount the events (repeated for the most part in the play) leading to the townspeople's suspicion that "reality is just as bad as fantasy, and that every reality can quite well be fantasy and vice versa." Ulrich Leo, in a well known article, has argued convincingly that the "persona" of the monologue may be described as an "embryonic" Laudisi, "a Laudisi *avant la lettre,"* essentially because he utters in direct discourse much of the same Pirandellian epistemology contained in the play. However true this may be, there are perhaps reasons for establishing a more binding relationship between the *raisonneur* of *Right You Are* and the nameless speaker of the story. Laudisi and the speaker of the monologue, in my view, share the same structural peculiarities within the context of their respective genres; and they perform basically the same function as dramatic devices. Only, in the story, on account of a more elementary structure, the function is more clearly seen and understood. Like Laudisi, the "persona" partakes of the dialectical oppositions in the story and, at the same time, conveys directly the author's thoughts. Pirandello's choice of the dramatic monologue doubtless facilitates this scheme and his use of free indirect discourse makes it possible. In the story's opening sentence, for instance, the speaker states sympathetically the townspeople's chief preoccupation which reappears in the play on the lips of Signora Sirelli:

> Well, just imagine what it's like! It really *is* enough to drive you out of your mind to be completely unable to find out which of these two people is mad....
>
> SIGNORA SIRELLI. But how can you escape the curiosity we all feel to get to the bottom of this mystery which is enough to drive us all mad?

But he also goes on to speak in behalf of Signora Frola and Signor Ponza, uttering the very words that their counterparts will express in the drama. Here is one of many possible examples:

> Oh, no, for pity's sake! He's not cruel! There's just this: he wants her all, he wants that darling little wife all for himself, even to such an extent that her love for her mother, well, he wants it to reach her not directly, but through him, by way of him.
>
> SIGNORA FROLA. Jealous of me, her mother? I don't think you can say that.... You see, he wants his wife's heart all for himself, to the extent that the love which my daughter must have for me, her mother (...). He wants that it should reach me through him, that's it!

In addition, the speaker conveys Pirandello's reaction to the situation by interjecting, from time to time, his thoughts into the monologue, such as, "Even if it is true that they have undergone a terrible disaster, it is nonetheless true that at least one of them has had the good luck to go mad...." The similarities between the anonymous speaker and Laudisi as elements of structure suggest that Laudisi was mainly conceived as personage-replacement for the "persona": that is, as a character-device which betrays, as we shall see, the author's uncertain position with respect to his drama.

When the play begins, the Agazzi household is in a turmoil because Signora Frola, the mother-in-law of Signor Ponza, the new provincial secretary, has not welcomed in her home Agazzi's wife and daughter. The visit has been prompted by their desire to understand why the Ponza-Frola family, having come to town as the sole survivors of an earthquake, should live divided: the man and his wife sharing the top floor of a tenement at the edge of town while the mother lives at her son-in-law's expense in a fashionable apartment. It is also known that the wife never leaves the tenement and that the mother never sees her face to face. This situation leads to the townspeople's investigation, their aim being to unite mother and daughter according to accepted standards of social behaviour.

Immediate suspicion as to who is at fault falls on Signor Ponza, and Signora Frola confirms the people's assumption, stating that she lives separated from her daughter because of Ponza's need for absolute possession of his wife. She adds, however, that she is in perfect agreement with the arrangement and that by living this way the family is very happy. Signora Frola having exited, Ponza himself enters to vouch for the fact that it was he who prevented his mother-in-law from carrying out her social obligations. The reason is because Signora Frola is mad. Her madness—he says—consists in her believing that her daughter is alive, when in fact she has been dead for several years. The mother is therefore deluded in thinking that the husband's second wife is actually her daughter. Her illusion, nevertheless, must be preserved in order that she not suffer from the truth. Now public opinion has shifted in Ponza's favor, but not for long. Signora Frola, aware of her son-in-law's version of the story, returns to tell the townspeople that it is really Ponza who is deluded. His love for his wife—she explains—was so overpowering that it was necessary for reasons of health to commit her to a sanatorium. Ponza, thinking she was dead, would no longer accept her as his wife. To reunite the couple a second wedding had to be staged. Ponza's wife, therefore, according to the mother, is really her daughter who, in order not to unmask her husband's beneficial illusion, pretends to be his second wife. At this point, after having heard two equally plausible, but contradictory accounts of why the family must live divided, the astonished townspeople stand looking at each other, while Laudisi, who all along has argued that there is no key to the mystery, has a hearty laugh at their expense.

In the second act, the dialectical pattern repeats itself. Disappointed because there are no documents to prove who is telling the truth, Agazzi plans to have Ponza and Frola meet face to face, believing that the encounter would force the hand of one of them. It appears, in fact, to be the case when the husband becomes furiously angry with the mother and tries to convince her before the others that his wife is not her daughter. But as soon as the mother leaves, his rage subsides. He was just pretending to be mad in order to verify her impression of him. Once again the spectators remain dumbfounded and once again Laudisi bursts out laughing.

In the final act, the pattern is repeated again. Now the townspeople have no other recourse than to call the wife to unravel the mystery. Signora Ponza, however, is of little help to them. She confesses that she is both Signora Frola's daughter and Signor Ponza's second wife and that for herself she is nobody. Now thoroughly foiled in their quest for *the* truth, Agazzi and Co. stand baffled as Laudisi's laughter once again fills the stage.

Inasmuch as Laudisi functions as a *raisonneur,* he shares the playwright's convictions and states them as universal premises, i.e. truth is equal to appearance. But more important is the fact that he reacts as a spectator to the dramatic events by laughing in every crucial moment of the play's development. His recurring laughter, I believe, is a clear sign of the way Pirandello himself interprets his drama, and only through an understanding of the psychology of his laughter can we arrive at an understanding of Pirandello's point of view.

Laudisi's laughter is generally seen as being "caustically sardonic," intended to deride the philistine attitudes and pretentions of the townspeople and thus viewed as an expression of "social revolt." To quote again Robert Brustein:

> Pirandello exercises [in *Right You Are*] the animus of his social revolt; and the tragedy which threatens is averted at the end. Their right to privacy affirmed, their secret still hidden from the gossips and busybodies, the *pharmakoi* [the pathetic sufferers] depart into darkness, while the *alazones* [buffoons] stand lost in amazement, whipped by the savage laughter of the *eiron* [sufferer-spokesman].

One possible objection to this view is the lack of textual evidence that might reveal the "sardonic" quality of Laudisi's laughter. On the contrary, although the stage directions do not divulge the nature of his laughter ("Laudisi," Pirandello indicates simply, "Scoppiera a ridere—Ah! Ah! Ah! Ah!"), the dialogue between him and his family clarifies his attitude toward their actions as being somewhat less than contemptuous. Like Pirandello, Laudisi is sympathetic to human foibles. His manner of reacting to the townspeople's naivete is at most benevolently ironical, as when he tells them:

> I enjoy hearing you talk. I'll be quiet, don't fear. At the very most, I shall indulge in a laugh or two, and if I really burst out laughing, please forgive me.

In other words, Laudisi amuses himself at their expense, laughing when reality proves to be at odds with their ambitions. This sort of relationship between the author's spokesman and his would-be antagonists would seem inappropriate in a dramatic context where the message is one of either social or existential revolt. Rather than interpreting Laudisi's laughter as a sign of Pirandello's satirical aims, I should like to suggest the possibility of viewing it simply as a spontaneous show of approval for a humorous situation, a favorable response to a rather elaborate joke.

Laudisi's laughter alone does not establish sufficiently the presence in the play of a joke pattern, for the acid test of a joke is not whether it provokes laughter or not. What does, however, is his awareness of a humorous situation:

> AGAZZI. Some of the talk had reached him [the Prefect] and even he feels that it's time to clear up this mystery, so that we shall know the truth.
>
> LAUDISI. [*bursts out laughing*] Ha! Ha! Ha! Ha!
>
> AMALIA. All we need now is for you to laugh.
>
> AGAZZI. And why is he laughing?
>
> SIGNORA SIRELLI. Because he says that no one can ever know the truth!

The joke implied in this instance is that the townspeople know the truth already, since whatever seems to each of them true is true.

Translated into terms compatible with Pirandello's reflections on humor, Laudisi's laughter would derive from his perception of something incongruous ("L'avvertimento del contrario"): that is, he laughs because the townspeople make fools of themselves by trying to control logically something uncontrollable and, in doing so, appear ludicrously distorted, frozen in their futile ambition. Bergson would say that Laudisi has perceived something mechanical encrusted on something living (for Pirandello, *Form* imposed on *Life*), the townspeople thus being automata who threaten to deprive the Frola-Ponza group of its spontaneity and freedom, while Laudisi's actual laughter results from his observing the spiritual rigidity and lifelessness of Agazzi and Co. To Freud the Ponza-Frola group would probably appear as the symbolic expression of the subconscious that has succeeded in breaking down the control imposed on it by the conscious mind, symbolized by the townspeople. Laudisi's laughter in this case would be a sign of freedom experienced in the face of a momentary release of psychic energy.

Regardless of what theory we choose to explain Laudisi's laughter, we are dealing basically with a play on form, an attack on something formal by something informal; the townspeople's established, logically controlled approach to reality is overturned by the vitality and irrationality of the Ponza-Frola group. Why then does the subversion of form not indicate the animus of revolt? The answer lies in the joke form itself which implies that the upsetting of formal values or thought patterns is only *temporary,* and that the laugh it elicits is a sign of *momentary* freedom from the burden of reality. Although Signora Frola and Signor Ponza challenge the accepted pattern of structuring reality throughout the play, they succeed only at the end of each act in tilting the scales in their favor. The joke also implies a congenial relationship between the joker and the societal group in which the joke is told and accepted. Mary Douglas, who has made several studies of jokes and their relationship to social experience, argues that the joker "has a firm hold on his own position in the social structure and the disruptive comments which he makes upon it are in a sense the comments of the social group upon itself. *He merely expresses consensus.* Safe within *the permitted range of attack* he lightens for everyone the oppressiveness of social reality, demonstrates its arbitrariness by making light of formality in general." (Italics mine).

Right You Are (If You Think So) contains three distinct structural elements, two of which (the townspeople and the Ponza-Frola group) represent the terms of the joke pattern; the third (Laudisi) embodies an ideal audience of listeners. Pirandello relates to the townspeople and family through Laudisi, whose rapport with the members of his family and their friends reflects in a sense Pirandello's own position within the social structure of his time. Laudisi is an evolved part of the provincial bourgeois society he ridicules. Aware of the problematic nature of human existence, he challenges the townspeople's claim to objective truth, but rather than offending their values, he is really only causing a nuisance, a minor hindrance to their investigation. In other words, the epistemological relativism that Pirandello conveys through his *raisonneur* is not meant to undermine the social structure represented by Agazzi and Co., but rather to define a drama in which everyone participates: the drama of man's depersonalization, of his life as a role actor on the stage of society. Signora Frola and Signor Ponza literally act out this drama in their conflict with the townspeople. On stage, they perform according to the demands created by the social context. The more accentuated the demands become (the more the townspeople push ahead in their quest for "truth") the more they challenge each other's role in the face of the investigators, until Signora Ponza, herself the personification of man's identity crisis, arrives to declare that her appearance *is* her existence: she is whoever she appears to be—"Cosi e (se vi pare)." For Pirandello the Frola-Ponza group has a dual function. As dramatic characters they illustrate the crisis of the divided self, while as the major term of the joke pattern they afford the opportunity for realizing that the townspeople's way of structuring reality may be arbitrary and subjective, and therefore without necessity.

As for the townspeople, they exemplify the element of control against which the vital, uncontrolled Ponza-Frola group combats. In their ranks, we can certainly find the busybody or buffoon type: the Signoras Sirelli, Nenni, and Cini, for example, and Agazzi and the Prefect are unquestionably persistent enough to be likened to "congressional investigators," but there are characters such as Amalia and Sirelli who appear more humane and compassionate. Their motives for carrying out the investigation are somewhat less selfish than those of their fellow citizens. On the whole, it is a diversified group representing various types and degrees of curiosity. The character of Laudisi bridges the gap between the two groups. Socially he is one of the townspeople, but in his epistemological reflections, he speaks for the Ponza-Frola family. His laugh is the effect of an exhilarating sense of being liberated from conventional thought patterns. For a moment *Life* has subverted *Form:* the human spirit has been released from the limitations imposed on it by logical discourse.

The social message concealed in *Right You Are (If You Think So),* as in any joke or humorous situation, is not one of satire or revolt (both of which necessitate contempt for reality, and, at least, an implicit display of objective values); rather what we have can be best described as the mild ridicule a society imposes upon itself as a way of censoring its belief in the objective world constructed by its own reason. *Right You Are* is a play written for a confused, disoriented society, spiritually uprooted by the havoc and catastrophes of war; a society whose members have lost confidence in its institutions and are questioning the rational foundations on which those very institutions are built. It is a play of crisis in which a solution is only hinted at.

With *Henry IV* and *Six Characters in Search of an Author,* Pirandello begins to emerge from the structural ambiguity manifested in *Right You Are (If You Think So).* The momentary liberation from the official categories of thought crystallized in the relationship between Laudisi and the Ponza-Frola group becomes an extended escape that springs from the development of a counter-logic (the logical paradoxes of Laudisi) and terminates in the creation of a new and eternal form of existence. Henry's willed decision to accept as *his* reality the mask of madness indicates his desire to live apart from his social group in the timelessness of history where his identity has already been accounted for as a Holy Roman Emperor. The six characters who wander on to the set of *The Rules of the Game* are in search of an author who will eternalize their masks and thereby confer on their problematic lives the timelessness of art. The elaboration of myth in the dramatist's later phase signals the exasperation of his quest for existential cohesion.

If *Right You Are (If You Think So)* reflects, as I believe it does, a crisis of values and the consciousness the society has of the crisis, I should like to suggest going a step further to note how the evolution of Pirandello's theater from *Right You Are* to the later plays is analogous to the political and social evolution that took place in Italy in the aftermath of the First World War. The movement from the dialectics of crisis (i.e. Pirandello's relativism) to the compensations offered by existence apart from the social group parallels the movement from the state of uncertainty and confusion of post-war society to the acceptance of a new, mystical form of civil life embodied in the "Fascist revolution" which, as it is known, presented itself as a substitute for the inadequacies of political reason. Pirandello's acceptance of Fascism should be viewed within the perspective of this historical crisis and the irrational solutions which the regime glorified.

Source: Robert S. Dombroski, "Laudisi's Laughter and the Social Dimension of *Right You Are (If You think So),* " in *Modern Drama,* Vol. 16, 1973, pp. 337–46.

Orazio Costa

The following essay contains Orazio Costa's comments regarding the attitudes seen in the play: "In fact, one is suggested here, which I attempted to

> "A CRUELLY COMIC CHOIR, CROWDED AROUND A VERY SMALL SPACE—THE ONLY SPACE SUBSEQUENTLY PROVIDED FOR THE CHARACTERS, SEEMINGLY QUESTIONED WITH MUCH RESPECT, IN FACT, PILLORIED."

realize scenically: analogous to the prying attitude of the provincial society gathered in a typical drawing-room, and facing a group of shy and secret creatures who refuse the principle of "sociability."

[Introduction]
Ever since 1945, many of Orazio Costa's productions have stood out as landmarks in the development of the Italian theatre.

It is hardly surprising, therefore, that he has staged a good many of Pirandello's plays and even staged some of them several times over. A fascinating experience for such a recognized "perfectionist"!

One of Orazio Costa's most characteristic features is the combination of extreme rigour in the analysis of the text—the sure sign of the philologist—with a constant, but never completely fulfilled aspiration towards the highest summits of spirituality. And while equally fitted to make his mark at a University or to devote himself to meditation, he decided to consecrate his talents to the theatre, that is to say to the task of conveying literature to the stage and of embodying his aspirations in the most concrete of plastic forms.

This is what gives outstanding value to the study he has kindly sent us. On receiving the latter, we realized at once that lack of space would unfortunately prevent us from bringing it out in full.

We have therefore decided to publish only the first part and to omit, to our deep regret, Orazio Costa's commentaries on other Pirandello plays and notably on *The Giants of the Mountain*, the spirit of which he brought out to such excellent effect. [Costa directed Pirandello's plays several times, and was recognized for his intellectual rigor in interpreting dramatic texts.]

[Costa's Remarks]
Even before I realized my first staging, I was convinced, from the study of *Six Characters in Search of an Author* and of *Right You Are—If You Think You Are,* that Pirandello had taken the European theatre to the end of its bourgeois cycle by renovating it totally: plot, characters, settings. Pirandello, fully aware of the futility of the plot, reduced the argument to an interchangeable canvas; he rediscovered, in the characters' sufferings, the only dignity worthy of containing and expressing life; he stripped the stage of its decorative tinsel and restored it to the nudity of its primary function, that of a machine. Thus, he came to the theatre in a state of absolute virginity, perfectly conscious of his part as a renovator and even perhaps—all considered—the only poet of his time in such a position. . . .

I am coming now to the interpretation of *Right You Are—If You Think You Are,* a play I have also been able to stage twice, first with the Piccolo Teatro della Citta di Roma, in 1952, then with the Theatre National de Belgique, in 1959. . . . The provincial town tallies with the theatre company and its presumption of having all its "recognized titles"; and the three unfortunates—Mme Frola and the Ponza couple—are effectively "characters" kneaded out of the same dough as the Son's character: they tend to be demure, to refuse to make an exhibition of themselves.

It must be admitted that, up to Pirandello, dramatic poetry tended, by its own nature, to confirm the existence of characters eager to manifest themselves, with the result of making creditable a vision of the world easy to read, transparent and, in its exuberance, wide open.

In *Right You Are* clearly appears the modern trend which consists in proposing for the audience, in each drama, a particular attitude. In fact, one is suggested here, which I attempted to realize scenically: analogous to the prying attitude of the provincial society gathered in a typical drawing-room, and facing a group of shy and secret creatures who refuse the principle of "sociability." A cruelly comic choir, crowded around a very small space—the only space subsequently provided for the characters, seemingly questioned with much respect, in fact, pilloried.

In view of obtaining the greatest possible opposition between the cruel circle and the "mourning" central group, during all the rehearsals I kept apart the actors of the grotesque choir and the tragic characters, so that their tones—aggressive questioning on the one hand, tragic panicking on the other—would not, from the beginning, tend towards an insufferable unification, but that, fixed on distinct registers, they would only in the end reach that minimum of common tuning demanded by the necessity of establishing a colloquy, however hostile. . . .

Source: Orazio Costa, "*Six Characters; Right You Are . . .* and *Henry IV,*[with introduction]" in *World Theatre,* Vol. 16, 1967, pp. 248–55.

SOURCES

Bentley, Eric. *The Pirandello Commentaries,* Northwestern University Press, 1986.

Bloom, Harold, ed. *Luigi Pirandello: Modern Critical Views,* Chelsea House, 1989.

Caputi, Anthony. *Pirandello and the Crisis of Modern Consciousness,* University of Illinois Press, 1988.

Matthaei, Renate. *Luigi Pirandello,* Frederick Ungar Publishing Co., 1973.

FURTHER READING

Bassanese, Fiona. *Understanding Luigi Pirandello (Understanding Modern European and Latin American Literature),* University of South Carolina Press, 1997.
    Considers Pirandello in the light of the modernist crises of consciousness and of the self.

Bentley, Eric. *The Pirandello Commentaries,* Northwestern University Press, 1986.
    A collection of Eric Bentley's incisive essays on Pirandello, as written over a thirty-year period.

Biasin, Gian-Paolo and Manuela Gieri. *Luigi Pirandello,* University of Toronto Press, 1999.
    An anthology of recent literary criticism on Pirandello's works, responding to a renewed interest in him.

Bassnet, Susan and Jennifer Lorch. *Luigi Pirandello in the Theatre: a Documentary Record,* Harwood Academic Publishers, 1993.
    Excerpts of reviews and letters, with photographs of play productions, chronicling Pirandello's impact on Italian theater and film.

Bini, Daniela. *Pirandello and His Muse : The Plays for Marta Abba (Crosscurrents),* University Press of Florida, 1998.
    Explores how Pirandello's perception of women and his relationship with Marta Abba influenced and subliminally shaped his plays (*Right You Are, If You Think You Are* is not treated).

Bloom, Harold, ed. *Luigi Pirandello: Modern Critical Views,* Chelsea House, 1989.
    An anthology of recent scholarship on Pirandello, with a brief commentary by Bloom in which he dubs Pirandello a "'playwright-as-sophist' leading us to the relativity of all truth."

Caesar, Ann. *Characters and Authors in Luigi Pirandello,* Oxford University Press, 1998.
    Examines issues of self, family, society, and narrative space in Pirandello's work.

Cambon, Glauco. *Pirandello: A Collection of Critical Essays,* Prentice-Hall, Inc., 1967.
    An early collection of criticism on his work as a whole, rather than on specific plays.

Caputi, Anthony. *Pirandello and the Crisis of Modern Consciousness,* University of Illinois Press, 1988.
    Explores the role of relativity as a theme of modernism that finds expression in Pirandello's works.

Dashwood, Julie (ed.). *Luigi Pirandello: The Theater of Paradox,* Edwin Mellen Press, 1997.
    An anthology of recent literary criticism on issues of gender, genre, and language, among others, in Pirandello's dramatic works.

Digaetani, John, ed. *A Companion to Pirandello Studies,* Greenwood Publishing Group, 1991.
    An anthology of recent literary criticism by acknowledged experts on Pirandello, concerning his life, work, and influence on the theater.

Guidice, Gaspare. *Pirandello: A Biography,* Oxford University Press, 1975.
    Covers his early life, his tempestuous marriage, his love for actress Marta Abba, and attempts to justify his association with the Fascist movement.

Matthaei, Renate. *Luigi Pirandello,* Frederick Ungar Publishing Co., 1973.
    Brief but insightful biography and synopses of the major plays.

The Nobel Foundation. *The Electronic Nobel Prize Project* [web page], September, 1999. http://www.nobel.se/enm-index.html
    Contains a copy of Pirandello's acceptance speech for the Nobel Prize for Literature, awarded in 1934.

Paolucci, Anne. *Pirandello's Theater: The Recovery of the Modern Stage for Dramatic Art,* Southern Illinois University Press, 1974.
    A scholarly analysis of Pirandello's plays, finding in them dramatic value that can withstand the test of time better than his theme of relativity alone.

Serjeant Musgrave's Dance

JOHN ARDEN

1959

Serjeant Musgrave's Dance is regarded as John Arden's first important play. Yet interestingly, its initial British run at the Royal Court Theatre in 1959 was not particularly successful; it ran for only twenty-eight performances and was a financial disaster.

In 1966 *Serjeant Musgrave's Dance* came to New York City for an Off-Broadway run. Appearing at the Theatre de Lys, the play ran for 135 performances and eventually won the Vernon Rice Award. As a result, Arden's reputation as an innovative dramatist was firmly established.

Serjeant Musgrave's Dance is set in a northern British mining town in 1880, but it draws from several contemporary sources for inspiration. Arden's pacifist theme and depiction of the negative aspects of army life on soldiers is seen to have universal significance.

AUTHOR BIOGRAPHY

On October 26, 1930, Arden was born in Barnsley, Yorkshire, England. The son of Charles Alwyn Arden, a glass factory manager, and Annie Elizabeth (nee Layland), a schoolteacher, Arden attended local schools until the beginning of World War II. For his safety, he was then sent to a public school in Sedbergh, Yorkshire.

After graduation, Arden served in the Army's Intelligence Corps for eighteen months. He then entered King's College at Cambridge University to study architecture. In 1953 he earned his B.A. and continued to study architecture at Edinburgh College of Art in Scotland.

In Edinburgh, Arden wrote his first play, *All Fall Down,* for a college drama group. After receiving his diploma in 1955, he moved to London to work as an architect's assistant.

By 1957 Arden's plays were being produced. The first was *The Waters of Babylon,* an experimental piece that utilized verse and song. With the initial success of his playwrighting career, Arden quit architecture and became a full-time writer. He also married Margaretta D'Arcy, an actress and political activist. Under D'Arcy's influence, Arden's plays took on a more political bent.

After completing a commission for the Royal Court Theatre, *The Waters of Babylon* (1958), he wrote what was arguably his most important stage play, *Serjeant Musgrave's Dance* (1959). Though it was not initially successful, many critics and scholars came to view the play as a prime example of Arden's style.

Many of Arden's subsequent plays were historical in nature. They included his first truly successful play, *Armstrong's Last Goodnight* (1964), as well as *The Hero Rises Up: A Romantic Melodrama* (1969), and *The Island of the Might* (1972).

Today he continues to write plays as well as novels and radio plays. He and his family live in Ireland.

John Arden

PLOT SUMMARY

Act I: Scene One
Serjeant Musgrave's Dance opens on a wharf in the north of England in 1880. Three British Army soldiers—Hurst, Attercliffe, and Sparky—are nervously waiting for the arrival of their superior officer, Serjeant Musgrave. The Bargee (barge driver) appears first, ready to drive the three soldiers to their destination on his barge. Musgrave arrives and the men depart.

Act I: Scene Two
At a public house in a small mining town, the Bargee enters and announces the soldiers' arrival to the pub's owner, Mrs. Hitchcock, and the Parson. The Parson infers that the soldiers have been sent to intercede in the local miner's strike. The Bargee tells him that they have come to recruit soldiers.

After the Parson leaves, the Bargee tells Mrs. Hitchcock and her barmaid, Annie, that the soldiers will stay at the pub or a nearby barn. Annie is apprehensive of the soldier's presence.

The soldiers enter. While they relax, the Mayor (who also owns the mine), Constable, and Parson enter the pub. The Mayor decides to use the soldiers to recruit the men who have caused trouble in his mine. The Constable wants to use the soldiers against the strikers, but the Mayor refuses.

After the officials leave, Musgrave asks Mrs. Hitchcock if she knew Billy Hicks. She tells him that Hicks had impregnated Annie before leaving to join the military and fight overseas. Eventually the baby died. Musgrave and his men leave to explore the town.

Act I: Scene Three
The four soldiers meet up in the churchyard and compare notes on the town. They agree that the townspeople are resentful and fearful of them. Three colliers (coal miners) threaten the soldiers, accusing

them of coming to break the miner's strike. Musgrave assures them that they are not.

When the colliers leave, Musgrave begins to reveal his true plan—take revenge on the town for Hicks's death and to drive home the hardships of military life. The soldiers are worried that they will be arrested before they can achieve their goal. Musgrave draws a parallel between their cause and the corruption in the town.

After filling them in on the plan, he tells them to remain relatively sober during their recruiting party that night. The Bargee overhears the truth about Musgrave's mission.

Act II: Scene One

At Mrs. Hitchcock's pub, the recruiting party is in full swing. Sparky hits on Annie but she rebuffs him; his fellow soldiers warn him that he has had enough to drink. Hurst shows up, still unsure of their mission. Annie showers attention on him, offering herself for the night. He accepts.

The Constable closes the party, but the colliers do not want the bar to close. One of the colliers attacks the Constable. The soldiers intercede, and the colliers and Bargee are removed from the pub. Sparky's drunken actions annoy the other soldiers, who start arguing among themselves. Sparky begs Annie to come to bed with him that night. Musgrave tells Annie to leave his men alone.

Act II: Scene Two

On the street the Bargee tries to lead the drunken colliers in military drills. Musgrave watches them. When Walsh, a leader of the colliers, passes by and makes fun of the soldiers, the Bargee tells Walsh he knows where to get weapons.

Act II: Scene Three

Inside the barn, Annie tries to get into bed with Hurst. He rebuffs her, and she becomes angry. When Attercliffe appears, she begs for his affections. After kissing her several times, he also snubs her. Annie begins to cry.

Sparky tries to comfort her, but Annie is not interested in him until he admits he is scared. She tells him about Hicks and their baby. As they share their fears, they become passionate.

He confides to Annie the real reason they are in town and tries to convince her to run away with him.

Hurst overhears and confronts Sparky. As the argument escalates, Attercliffe gets involved and accidentally stabs Sparky to death with his own bayonet. Attercliffe is horrified by his actions.

Musgrave and Mrs. Hitchcock enter the barn. Musgrave orders Attercliffe and Hurst to bury Sparky in the backyard. He has Mrs. Hitchcock lock Annie up in a safe place.

The Bargee arrives and informs Musgrave that someone is breaking the windows of the coachhouse where their weapons are located. Alarmed, the soldiers leave and then return with Walsh. The soldiers beg Musgrave to change the plan because of Sparky's death, but he will not.

The Mayor and Parson arrive. The Mayor says that the telegraph has been fixed and the dragoons are coming in twelve hours to quell violence. Musgrave proposes a recruitment rally in the streets to distract everyone.

Act III: Scene One

The next morning, the rally begins and Musgrave takes the stage to talk about the life of a soldier. He shows the crowd a Gatling gun, and has Attercliffe load it. Musgrave describes the horrible conditions that soldiers live in, and how duty comes before all else. In a dramatic sequence, the skeleton of Billy Hicks is revealed, hung by a noose from a flagpole. Everyone present is shocked.

Musgrave informs the crowd that they have to stay or his men will shoot them. Musgrave chronicles the story of how Hicks was killed by civilians, and in retaliation, five civilians were killed. Musgrave invites Walsh up to speak, assuming he will be sympathetic—but he is not. The town does not understand his message.

Musgrave announces that killing twenty-five townspeople will be a just revenge for Hicks's death. Attercliffe is repulsed by Musgrave's words—this had not been part of the original plan. No one is sure about Musgrave's message except Annie, who reveals the circumstances of Sparky's death.

Dragoons kill Hurst. Musgrave and Attercliffe are arrested.

Act III: Scene Two

In prison, Musgrave refuses food. He is still haunted by Hicks's death and the death of the five civilians. Mrs. Hitchcock tells him that his message will be remembered by the townspeople.

CHARACTERS

Annie

Annie is the barmaid who works in Mrs. Hitchcock's pub. She earned a bad reputation by becoming impregnated by Billy Hicks, a soldier who later died. Their baby died soon after birth.

She reinforces her bad reputation by flirting with the British soldiers. Initially Annie is attracted to Hurst, refusing Sparky's amorous advances. However, after being rebuffed by both Hurst and Attercliffe, she finds comfort with Sparky.

Only Annie understands Musgrave's obsession with truth. It is she who reveals what really happened to Sparky.

Private Attercliffe

Attercliffe is one of the four soldiers who have deserted the English army to seek revenge for Billy Hicks. He is the peacemaker of the group. Attercliffe truly believes in Musgrave's cause, and follows his directives to the letter. He is also adamantly against killing anyone.

Yet he is the one who accidentally kills Sparky. This incident tears Attercliffe apart, and he wants Musgrave to change their plan. When Musgrave refuses, this marks a shift in their relationship.

During Musgrave's speech at the rally, Attercliffe tries to promote nonviolence and refuses to kill anyone. He prevents Hurst from killing them as well. At the end of the play, he is imprisoned with Musgrave. In many ways, Attercliffe is Musgrave's conscience.

The Bargee

The Bargee is the barge driver who transports the soldiers to the town. A merry fellow, he is always working an angle—even to the point of selling out the soldiers to make a little money.

He does not seem to like soldiers, and generally regards Musgrave and his mission with contempt. The Bargee is only interested in attention or financial reward. It is he who sticks a gun in Musgrave's back as the dragoons enter the town; he wants credit for capturing them.

Joe Bludgeon
See The Bargee

The Constable

The Constable is the chief law enforcer in the town. He hopes to use the soldiers as reinforcements against the strikers.

Mrs. Hitchcock

Mrs. Hitchcock runs the pub where the soldiers stay. She is a large, good-natured woman who can defend herself effectively. Primarily, she is out to protect her own (primarily economic) interests. Yet she shows much kindness to Annie and the soldiers during the play.

Private Hurst

Hurst is one of Musgrave's soldiers. He is a murderer, having killed an officer with good reason. Impatient and tense, he can be mean and spends much of his time brooding. Yet Annie believes Hurst is the most handsome of the soldiers, and offers to spend the night with him. He ultimately rejects her.

Though Hurst follows most of Musgrave's orders, he is full of doubt about their mission. He threatens to kill Sparky when Hurst finds out that he was going to leave. At the climax of the play, Hurst rejects some of Musgrave's ideas and is ready to kill the townspeople. He is killed when the dragoons shoot him.

MEDIA ADAPTATIONS

- *Serjeant Musgrave's Dance* was adapted for television by Granada Television for the BBC in 1961.

The Mayor

The Mayor runs the small town: in addition to being its highest officer, he also owns the coal mines. He is despised by most of the townspeople. Throughout the play, the Mayor tries to use the soldiers' presence to his own advantage.

Serjeant Musgrave

Also known by the nickname Black Jack, Musgrave is the protagonist of the play. He is the leader of the group of four soldiers; it is his plan they are implementing.

His true intentions are unclear for most of the play. Like the other soldiers, he has deserted the army while stationed in a foreign land. Several incidents prompted the desertion, particularly the death of Billy Hicks and the killing of some civilians. To fund his plan, Musgrave stole money from the army.

Musgrave wants to communicate the negative aspects of army life, especially the corruption and how it wastes lives. He wants to avenge the deaths that haunt his consciousness. Yet no one realizes how mentally ill he is until he reveals his true plan: killing twenty-five townspeople. He ends up in prison, worrying that his message will be forgotten.

The Parson

The Parson is the supposed moral center of the town. He is clearly on the side of the Mayor, and does not have much sympathy for the colliers and their plight. When the soldiers arrive, he is most concerned that they do not act drunk and disorderly.

Private Sparky

Sparky is the youngest and most volatile of the soldiers. He seems to have known Hicks the best.

At the recruiting party, he gets drunk and tries to get together with Annie. Sparky becomes jealous when she picks Hurst. Though he does not win her over immediately, he is the only soldier who shows her real kindness in the barn. With Annie, Sparky decides to leave.

For his disloyalty to the plan he is killed by Attercliffe and Hurst. Annie uses his senseless death as a symbol of truth during the play's climax.

Walsh

A leader among the colliers, Walsh is suspicious of Musgrave's true intentions. His paramount concerns are with the labor problems in the town.

THEMES

Guilt

Guilt and remorse underscore much of *Serjeant Musgrave's Dance*. Musgrave is overcome by guilt over the death of Billy Hicks as well as the five civilians who were killed in retaliation. Two of his fellow deserters, Attercliffe and Sparky, also knew Hicks and share these feelings. In part, guilt prompted them to desert their posts in order to travel to this coal-mining town.

Musgrave wants to force England to share responsibilities for these deaths. To that end, he makes a public display of Hicks's skeleton, showing the townspeople how one of their sons died in vain. Musgrave also plans to shoot twenty-five of the town's leading citizens, but his dastardly scheme is fortunately stopped.

Ghosts

The ghost of Billy Hicks haunts many of the characters of *Serjeant Musgrave's Dance*. Musgrave and two of the three soldiers, Attercliffe and Sparky, have deserted their regular posts in order to do something so that Hicks's death was not in vain.

The soldiers assume that the rally will be a peaceful display of Hicks's skeleton and an explanation of the horrors of army life—but Musgrave has other ideas. He wants to kill in order to exorcise Hicks's ghost from his head and drive his point home in a very dramatic fashion.

In a way, Hicks's ghost represents the futility of war for Musgrave and his men. At the end of the play, the ghost still haunts Musgrave and Attercliffe.

Hicks's ghost also haunts Annie. He was her lover and the father of her baby. After Hicks left town to join the army and the baby died, Annie was left alone and rejected as an outcast. Unlike the soldiers, Annie gets a chance to excise Hicks' ghost during the rally at the end of the play. She uses his death to tell the truth about Sparky's untimely demise at the hands of Attercliffe. This gives her the strength and insight to reveal questionable aspects of Musgrave's beliefs.

Hurst is being haunted by another ghost—not that of Billy Hicks. Hurst deserted the army because he was accused of killing an officer. In an attempt to escape his fate he runs away with Musgrave, only to be killed by the dragoons late in the play.

Loyalty

Serjeant Musgrave demands absolute loyalty from his fellow soldiers. He is their leader and believes that he has God on his side. Although Musgrave has deserted the British Army, he still adheres to some of its values. While he believes that unnecessary killing is wrong and that troops often live and work in abysmal conditions, Musgrave is not above callousness to his own men.

For example, after Sparky is accidentally killed by Attercliffe, the Serjeant writes off his death as "immaterial" when he learns that Sparky was going to desert them.

Similarly, Musgrave expects Attercliffe to help kill twenty-five civilians, despite the fact that he knows Attercliffe is totally opposed to killing.

All the soldiers remain loyal to Musgrave through much of the play—although they all question his values at some point. Sparky dies the moment he considers disloyalty. Hurst dies taking loyalty to an extreme by preparing to kill innocent civilians.

One of the moral lessons of *Serjeant Musgrave's Dance* is that loyalty can be abused and should have its limits.

STYLE

Setting

Serjeant Musgrave's Dance is a realistic drama set in the north of England in 1880. Much of the action takes place in a public house (pub) in a small mining town torn apart because of a miner's strike.

There are also a few outdoor settings, such as the churchyard and the town's marketplace.

The settings add to the realism of the play. Both the pub and the marketplace are places where different kinds of people come together, from town officials to common colliers. The other settings emphasize the cold harshness of life in the northern town.

Songs, Verse and Dance

Arden utilizes various dramatic techniques to emphasize the time and place of the action as well as develop characters. The most prominent of these are songs, poetic verse, and dances.

Many of the main characters sing folk-type songs and recite verse. Sparky sings many times,

TOPICS FOR FURTHER STUDY

- Compare and contrast the character of Serjeant Musgrave with Mother Courage from Bertolt Brecht's play *Mother Courage and her Children*. How does armed conflict impact the lives of these characters?

- Research psychological and sociological writings on army life and desertion. How do the military characters in the play embody these theories? Why do Hurst, Attercliffe, and Sparky follow Musgrave's orders as long as they do?

- What was the state of the British economy at the time of the play, particularly in the north of England? Focus on the impact of labor strikes. Does this give you a new perspective on the characters of the colliers? Are economic conditions part of the reason why the colliers are not as sympathetic to Musgrave's message as he expects them to be?

- Pick one of the dances, songs, or poems in *Serjeant Musgrave's Dance*. Research its origin and history. You might choose "Michael Finnegan," the song often whistled by the Bargee. What does the song or dance add to the play and how does it reflect the play's themes?

commenting on the action and revealing much about himself and his attitude towards life. Mrs. Hitchcock, Annie, and the Bargee also sing, while Walsh, other colliers, and Attercliffe (especially at the very end of the play) chime in with enlightening verse. The Bargee is always whistling the song "Michael Finnegan."

During the recruiting party, everyone but Musgrave sings and dances. Two of the colliers do a clog dance while the Bargee and others provide the music. This creates a festive atmosphere that belies the true meaning for the soldiers' visit, and gives a sense of the culture of Northern England.

Musgrave lets loose only in the play's climax, in which he both sings and—as the title of the play indicates—dances. His furious words and movements are a release from his tight-lipped presence throughout the play. The song and dance allow him to express the true meaning of his appearance in town: to display the skeleton of Billy Hicks, avenge Hicks's death, and educate the townspeople about the horrors of war.

Audience Participation

In the climactic scene of *Serjeant Musgrave's Dance,* the audience becomes part of the drama. In the marketplace, a small crowd gathers to hear the speeches. Yet because there is no crowd of townspeople beyond the handful of characters, everything is addressed to the audience. It is as if Arden is making his argument directly to the audience.

The Bargee is especially important in this scene. He is the link between the audience and the action on stage. The directions call for him to "create crowd-reactions." When Musgrave and his men pull out their rifles and Gatling gun, they aim them at the audience, emphasizing that this message is addressed directly to them—the townspeople of the world.

HISTORICAL CONTEXT

In the late 1950s and early 1960s, British society was in transition. Yet one consistent factor was the dominance of the Conservative Party. From 1951–1964 they would remain in power.

The British economy had greatly recovered from World War II. Overall, British citizens were more prosperous and affluent. Average earnings increased. While unemployment declined on the whole, it increased at the beginning and again at the end of 1959.

Labor issues came to the forefront during this period of British history. In June 1959, for example, there was a major printing strike involving 100,000 workers in London and the provinces. As a result, most provincial presses did not operate for much of the summer.

There had been a trend towards nationalization of major industries, like printing, that had begun in the immediate postwar period. This continued, though most of these industries lost money at the end of the 1950s.

Great Britain declined to join the European Economic Community (EEC) in 1957, but soon regretted the decision. They joined a rival economic group, the European Free Trade Association, in 1960, and lobbied to join the EEC in the mid-1960s.

Foreign affairs were very important in this time period. Britain had been a colonial power in the nineteenth century, but by the middle of the twentieth century, their influence was waning. Several British colonies and protectorates were seeking independence to some extent.

One historical incident inspired Arden to write *Serjeant Musgrave's Dance.* Great Britain had controlled the island of Cyprus for many years, but both Greek and Turkish Cypriots wanted to rule the island by the late 1950s. In 1958, a Greek Cypriot, intent on overthrowing the British, killed the wife of a British Army sergeant.

As a result, locals were rounded up and three Cypriots were killed. Two years later, Great Britain conceded control of much of the island to the Greek Cypriot majority.

There were also significant disturbances in Malta and Nyasaland in 1959.

British colonial holdings directly affected life in the home country. There was significant immigration to England. Immigration would have a great impact on Great Britain for the rest of the twentieth century.

CRITICAL OVERVIEW

From its first production, *Serjeant Musgrave's Dance* has been controversial. Reviewers of the initial British productions found flaws with the play's structure. Hilary Spurling of the *Spectator* contended: "There is no conflict. I defy anyone to explain the plot, except perhaps as a series of expedients to stave off the grand climax until the last act. . ."

Only a few critics favorably assessed Arden's play. Alan Brien asserted that "I have never seen a play which created its own mad, obsessed, otherworld so completely as *Serjeant Musgrave's Dance.*"

American critics offered mixed reviews of the drama. Stanley Kauffmann of *The New York Times* maintained, "*Serjeant Musgrave's Dance . . .* has been hailed as the best postwar English play and has

COMPARE & CONTRAST

- **1880:** Queen Victoria rules Great Britain; she is in the forty-third year of her rule. She has significant political power.

  1959: Queen Elizabeth II is in the seventh year of her reign. Her political role is small; instead, the parliamentary system sets policy.

  Today: Queen Elizabeth II continues her rule. She is basically a figurehead with minimal political influence.

- **1880:** Great Britain is a significant world power, with significant colonial holdings in Asia and Africa.

  1959: Many of Great Britain's colonial holdings had gained or were seeking independence. India had gained independence in 1947.

  Today: Great Britain has a few colonial holdings and protectorates.

- **1878:** Great Britain acquires Cyprus at the Congress of Berlin.

  1959: Greek and Turkish Cypriots demand their independence from Great Britain. Within a year, the request is granted although Britain retains the areas around their military bases.

  Today: Internal strife between Greek and Turkish Cypriots has resulted in a split on the island. While an independent country of Cyprus covers most of the island, one-third of the island is the Turkish Republic of Northern Cyprus.

---

been derogated as murky. To me, there seems to be good argument on both sides.''

An anonymous critic in *Newsweek* asserted: ''There is no single 'point' to *Musgrave*. Read by some as a muddled pacifist tract and by others as an equally muddled anti-imperialist one, its real dramatic vision is that of the horror of single-mindness, of ends determining means and even more crucially of abstraction in moral life.''

Only a few American commentators praised Arden's work, such as Henry Hewes of *The Saturday Review*. He found ''*Serjeant Musgrave's Dance* . . . a deeply evocative and earth-rich dramatic experience.''

Most critics took the tone of Harold Clurman. He claimed: ''One cannot see *Serjeant Musgrave's Dance* . . . without realizing that one is in the presence of a real dramatist, a man of passion and power. A cross-grained poetry emerges from his work. Yet one is not wholly satisfied. . .''

Many American critics delineated the many problems they found in Arden's text. Kauffmann composed a list: ''Control of the central image is dissipated; tensions slacken; the theme is unclear and unresolved, even somewhat arbitrarily tied up.''

Along similar lines, Edith Oliver of *The New Yorker* maintained: ''Mr. Arden's writing is not the clearest on earth, and he certainly is a relentless man with an obvious point, hammering away long after it has reached home. Sifting out his subsidiary ideas and the twists of his plot from all the clatter and clutter becomes a problem.''

Thematic concerns were the focus of several reviews. The anonymous *Time* critic asserted: ''He tries to practice consensus drama, a contradiction in terms. For *Serjeant Musgrave's Dance* to possess any intrinsic vitality, there would have to be a respectable body of thought holding that war is heavenly. As it is, Arden is merely preaching to the converted. . .''

Oliver also considered *Serjeant Musgrave's Dance*'s lack of vitality. She contended: ''For all the noise and movement, the play has little real vitality, being neither moving nor stirring. Underneath its jumpy surface, *Serjeant Musgrave's Dance* seems to me . . . conventional, sentimental, and,

Albert Finney in the title role in Serjeant Musgrave's Dance *by John Arden.*

what is worse, condescending to its own characters, most of whom are of the working class and could have been assembled from old *Punch* cartoons.''

Between the 1960s and 1980s, Arden and his play were closely scrutinized by scholars. He came to be viewed as an icon in British theater, as *Serjeant Musgrave's Dance* was interpreted and studied from every angle.

By the time the play was revived in Great Britain in 1984, *Serjeant Musgrave's Dance* was an integral part of England's theater history. Many reviews acknowledged its iconic status. As Michael Billington of the *Manchester Guardian Weekly* asserted, ''But, when all one's reservations have been registered, the blunt fact is that Arden's work is one of the best post-war political plays and deserves to be seen as well as studied.''

CRITICISM

A. Petrusso

In this essay, Petrusso contends that though most critics and scholars maintain that Serjeant Musgrave's Dance *promotes pacifism, the play is actually a pro-war and pro-army drama.*

Although *Serjeant Musgrave's Dance* has been extremely controversial from its first production in 1959, most critics and scholars agree that the play is pacifist in nature. That is, they believe the play depicts armed conflict and army life in very negative, futile terms.

Yet to accomplish this, Arden explores both the positive and negative aspects of military life. Many critics point to this duality as a hallmark of Arden's developing style—though they also claim that it bogs down the play's true meaning.

However, I contend that Arden implicitly supports violence, the army, and war throughout the play. Pacifism loses in *Musgrave,* and while the audience could walk away believing that pacifism should triumph, Arden does not do much to give hope that it will. Indeed, he seems to be illustrating that the military is important—and that there is a point to fighting.

In this essay, I explore the elements of the play that could be defined as pacifist; counter these points with examples of Arden's pro-violence message; and finally, provide a new perspective on the end of the play.

Many critics maintain that *Serjeant Musgrave's Dance* promotes pacifism. They believe that

WHAT DO I READ NEXT?

- *The Royal Pardon: The Soldier Who Became an Actor* (1966) is a play written by Arden and his wife. It also concerns a soldier who deserts the army.

- *Voices from the Ranks: A Personal Narrative of the Crimean Campaign by a Serjeant of the Royal Fusiliers* is a memoir written by Timothy Gowling and edited by Kenneth Fenwich. Published in 1954, the book reflects on the conditions of army life during the Crimean War.

- Arden's 1960 play entitled *Happy Haven* features characters who question and rebel against authority.

- Written by Bertolt Brecht in 1941, *Mother Courage and Her Children* is an antiwar epic that illustrates the devastating effects of violence and war.

Musgrave has led the soldiers to this coal-mining town in order to show the citizens how war has negatively impacted one of their own citizens—Billy Hicks.

Billy Hicks was a soldier who died unnecessarily while serving in the army. His death in an unnamed British colony inspired controversy and anger against the civilians in the area. To avenge Hicks' death, some locals were rounded up and five were killed, including a young girl.

Hicks served with Musgrave, Sparky, and Attercliffe. Shocked at their friend's death and the army's response to it, these soldiers deserted their posts, picked up Hurst (who had killed an officer under circumstances Musgrave could rationalize), and traveled to Hicks's hometown to settle the score.

The soldiers have different reactions to the violence of military life: Attercliffe does not want to kill anyone; Sparky tries to desert the deserters; and Hurst is ready to kill at an instant.

Yet Musgrave is the most seriously affected of the four men. Believing that he is on some sort of mission from God to avenge the deaths, he plans to kill twenty-five prominent citizens of the town (five times the number of civilians killed) as retribution. He is stopped before he can go through with it, but all these components are perceived to underscore the idea that the play is pacifist.

Another pacifist aspect of *Serjeant Musgrave's Dance* is the character of Annie. The barmaid in Mrs. Hitchcock's pub, Annie was Hicks's lover. In fact, she was pregnant with his child, but he left for the army before the child's birth. When the baby was born, it was deformed and sickly. The child died before it was two months old, around the same time Hicks was killed.

So Annie is a victim of the violence of war. An outcast because of her bad reputation and her out-of-wedlock child, Annie is taken in by Mrs. Hitchcock.

At the climax of the play, Annie takes possession of Hicks's skeleton. When Musgrave tries to write off Sparky's murder (after Hurst discovers that Sparky intends to leave, Hurst threatens to kill Sparky, though Attercliffe accidentally does the deed) as "barely materi[al]" to his antiwar and antiarmy message, Annie relates the truth about Sparky's death. To Annie, Sparky's death is just as important in terms of revealing the truth about the army, violence, and soldiers.

Despite the power of these pacifist elements of *Serjeant Musgrave's Dance,* Arden subversively champions violence, war, and the military. Violence is an inherent part of all the lives depicted in the play. There were violent tensions even before the arrival of the soldiers, which depicts violence as a way of life.

> "THE CLIMAX OF THE PLAY IS THE PINNACLE OF ARDEN'S ANTI-PACIFISM: MUSGRAVE DISPLAYS HICKS'S SKELETON, PROVIDES THE CIRCUMSTANCES OF HIS DEATH, DESCRIBES THE HARSH LIFE OF A SOLDIER, AND THEN PREPARES TO TAKE HIS REVENGE."

The town officials fear violence from the colliers, and rightfully so. These workers are on strike or have been locked out of their workplace, and are quite angry about how they have been treated. Violence is one of the only ways they can express themselves.

At first, the colliers also hate the soldiers, believing they represent the same kind of authority as management. The colliers resort to violence to intimidate the authorities. They throw stones at soldiers and the Constable's office. They try to steal the Gatling gun (a precursor to the machine gun). Colliers also physically attack the Constable when he tries to close the bar.

The climax of the play—the recruiting rally—occurs as town officials hope to prevent violence by the colliers. Musgrave has other plans; they involve the murder of twenty-five relatively innocent people. More violence seems to be his answer for everything. This is hardly pacifist.

As depicted in the play, army life has many positive points. Though Hicks lost his life and Musgrave is arguably insane, neither is necessarily a direct result of the army. Mrs. Hitchcock describes Hicks as this: "Not what you'd call a bad young feller, you know—but he weren't no good either." Who is to say he would not have had problems if he had stayed at home—perhaps he would have died in a colliers' strike.

In the military, Musgrave gained discipline, organizational skills, and a moral compass. He learned how to be in charge of men and have them execute his plan. Throughout the play, Musgrave uses the army and its methods to prove his point, though he ultimately fails. Yet that is because of his deficiency of character. Without the army, Musgrave would not be the same man.

The army represents authority and order. The colliers hate the soldiers because they believe that they have been called by management to break the strike. While this is not true, the town's officials believe that the soldiers have come to recruit new soldiers. To that end, they try to identify troublemakers for the soldiers to recruit.

While this would directly benefit management, it might also be good for the colliers as well. There would be less competition for jobs, and the soldiers who join up would have the opportunity to become authority figures themselves. They will get the chance to learn important life skills that will only help them when they return. The colliers even allow themselves to be led in a drunken drill by the Bargee in an attempt to put themselves in authority's shoes.

Arden implies that wars are continuous, though not always with men in bright uniforms or on foreign soil. Every time there is an economic crisis in the coal industry, there will probably be a war between management and colliers. There can be no pacifists in this war, because both sides have too much to lose. Musgrave believes that all wars are the same—but they are not. The rally at the marketplace utterly fails to prove their point.

The climax of the play is the pinnacle of Arden's anti-pacifism: Musgrave displays Hicks's skeleton, provides the circumstances of his death, describes the harsh life of a soldier, and then prepares to take his revenge. He asserts that he wants to end war, but his methods work in an opposite manner. He plans to take twenty-five innocent lives as revenge for Hicks' death, hoping to drive his message home.

Yet if the townspeople are threatened, there is no reason why they would listen to this pacifist message. If Musgrave and Hurst had begun firing, many of those gathered would have fought them. Defending one's self is not particularly pacifist. Musgrave tries to draw a parallel between his war against war and the colliers' struggle against management, but they see through it. The kind of wars Musgrave is talking about cannot compare to their daily fight to survive.

At the conclusion of the play, the authorities restore order: the dragoons arrive, killing Hurst and arresting Attercliffe and Musgrave. After the arrests, the Mayor does not use the dragoons on the colliers, at least right away. He tells an officer,

"Well, I'd say it was about all over now, young man—wouldn't you?"

Musgrave and Attercliffe are imprisoned. Mrs. Hitchcock tries to give Musgrave hope that their message will be remembered—but there is nothing to hope for anymore. It seems that pacifism does not get one very far.

Source: A. Petrusso, for *Drama for Students,* Gale, 2000.

Helena Forsas-Scott

In the following essay, Forsas-Scott examines the conflict between the plot structure of the play and Musgrave's message.

Serjeant Musgrave's Dance is probably John Arden's best-known play. It is also a play which has generated much critical argument, the focal point tending to be Black Jack Musgrave himself. Frequently, however, the Serjeant has been interpreted in conventional naturalistic terms, the reasons for his failure being traced to his outlook, his personality, and his mind. When John Russell Taylor asserted, in *Anger and After,* that "this is a play about individual, complicated human beings, . . .'' he defined a view of *Serjeant Musgrave's Dance* which has continued to play an important part in the critical discussion.

The most notable divergent approach to the play—and indeed to Arden's play-writing as a whole—is that which has been advocated by Albert Hunt. Hunt sees Arden's work as belonging, not to the naturalistic theatre of illusion, but to a broader and more ancient tradition which he exemplifies with theatre as different as British pantomime and the dramas of Shakespeare and Brecht. The theatre of illusion, Hunt argues, is "a theatre of persuasion''; the tradition to which Arden's plays belong, in contrast, "has precisely the opposite aim: to question appearances.'' Consequently, *Serjeant Musgrave's Dance* , if "Played for identification with the audience, . . . becomes incomprehensible. For the true statement of the play lies in the way Musgrave's pacifist message is judged against the action of the play and found inadequate. If you're too close to Musgrave, this judgement is never seen.''

Hunt's view of Arden's drama is, I believe, essentially correct. In this essay, I want to investigate more closely what Hunt calls "the action of the play'' and demonstrate how Arden uses a given plot structure as a means of making a statement in artistic terms. As Hunt indicates, the central conflict is between this plot structure and Musgrave's message, but Musgrave's particular brand of pacifism is

> **MORE IMPORTANTLY, THE SONGS AND VERSE BRING OUT AND ENHANCE THE STYLIZATION OF THE CHARACTERS WHICH IS SO CENTRAL TO THE OVERALL DESIGN OF THE PLAY, SETTING THE FEMALE CHARACTERS SHARPLY AGAINST THE MALES."**

compounded of elements which have a special historical significance with regard to drama as well as politics. It seems to me that only when these dimensions become clear to us, can the full implications of the play's confrontation begin to emerge.

In an illuminating essay on *Macbeth,* Glynne Wickham has shown that the structure of Shakespeare's tragedy can be seen as a combination of two famous sequences from the medieval Cycle Plays: the story of Herod the Great and the Harrowing of Hell. According to Wickham, "The essentials that [Shakespeare] . . . drew from the [Herod] play are the poisoning of a tyrant's peace of mind by the prophecy of a rival destined to eclipse him, the attempt to forestall that prophecy by the hiring of assassins to murder all potential rivals and the final overthrow and damnation of the tyrant.'' With Macbeth as a Scottish Herod, his eventual damnation foreshadowed by frequent references to him as the Devil, Macduff, his chief protagonist, plays the role of Christ. "As Christ harrowed Hell and released Adam from Satan's dominion,'' Wickham explains, "so afflicted subjects of mortal tyranny will find a champion who will release them from fear and bondage. This Macduff does for Scotland. . . .''

Wickham begins his analysis with a detailed examination of the familiar Porter scene, often so strangely out of place to a modern audience, but to the Elizabethan theatre-goer, a well-nigh unmistakable reference to the Harrowing of Hell. Like Shakespeare, Arden draws on a popular dramatic tradition for the plot of *Serjeant Musgrave's Dance* and brings this tradition sharply into focus at a crucial point in the dramatic action. The type of popular drama which Arden uses has survived into the present time, and in Act III, Scene I of *Serjeant Musgrave's Dance* it surfaces with full force and all of its customary paraphernalia, the significant details being underlined by the Bargee who sets the scene in the market-place:

> Here they are on a winter's morning, you've got six kids at home crying out for bread, you've got a sour cold wife and no fire and no breakfast: and you're too damn miserable even to fight—if there's owt else at all to take your mind off it—so here you are, you lucky people, in your own old market-place, a real live lovely circus, with real live golden sovereigns in somebody's pocket and real live taddy ale to be doled out to the bunch of you!

This is the setting for a Mummers' Play. Mary B. O'Connell, in an article published in *Modern Drama* in 1971, has pointed to certain parallels between *Serjeant Musgrave's Dance* and the Mummers' Play, more especially the type known as the Wooing Ceremony or the Plough Play. In O'Connell's opinion, the Plough Play has served Arden "as his model for characterization and plot development," and she has convincingly identified several of the characters in *Serjeant Musgrave's Dance* with their prototypes in the ancient folk-play. But with regard to the plot, it seems to me that Arden's consistent use of the Wooing Ceremony as the basis of the dramatic action in *Serjeant Musgrave's Dance* invites us to make rather more far-reaching comparisons than the ones presented by O'Connell. Once this has been done, it also becomes apparent that Arden has taken the liberty of giving the Mummers' Play a personal but highly significant twist which I believe to be central to the overall message of the play. O'Connell has concluded that Arden, in dealing with "the problems of our contemporary world," has "attempted to use a ritual pattern which helped previous generations to cope with their particular world structures." To my mind, however, Arden's employment of this ritual pattern aims far beyond the passive concept of coping; ultimately, it charges the action of *Serjeant Musgrave's Dance* with revolutionary dynamism. Let us take a closer look, therefore, first at the Wooing Ceremony and then at its application in Arden's play.

There is no definitive version of the Wooing Ceremony, just as there is no standard Sword Play or Hero Combat; what we have is simply a number of individual plays which, although they often vary considerably, can be recognized as constituting a distinctive group. To illustrate my argument here, I have chosen the well-known Wooing Ceremony called the Bassingham Play, reproduced by Chambers in *The English Folk-Play* and used by Brody in *The English Mummers and their Plays* to exemplify the Wooing Ceremony as a type. In the Bassingham Play, the action consists of a Prologue; a threefold wooing of the Lady; the appearance of Old Dame Jane, who brings a baby allegedly fathered by the Fool; a continuation of the wooing action; a fight between St. George and the Fool, in which the Fool falls; the revival of the Fool by the Doctor; and the Lady's acceptance of the Fool. In the so-called Children's version of the Bassingham Play, the action concludes with the Fool's invitation to the wedding. Significantly, a number of Wooing Ceremonies involve a Recruiting Sergeant as a principal figure. These plays follow a pattern similar to the one outlined above, but they also include the Lady's repeated rejection of a young recruit, and frequently the Sergeant himself proceeds to woo the Lady.

O'Connell has identified Sparky as the Fool and the Bargee as the Devil in Arden's play, and she has also pointed to the significance of Annie and Mrs. Hitchcock, Arden's equivalents of the Lady who woos the Fool and the Old Woman connected with the bastard child. To this list we can then add the Recruiting Sergeant, who dances and sings, moreover, just as Musgrave does in the market-place. Further, numerous details in Arden's drama reinforce the parallels with the Mummers' Play. Like true mummers, the soldiers are visitors to the community. Their all-important anonymity, traditionally achieved by means of disguise, has been expanded into the circumstantial disguise provided by the confusion surrounding the soldiers' mission. Their peace mission can be seen, in fact, as a modern reflection of the very function of the Mummers' Play, making explicit its concern with overcoming death and destruction for the sake of ensuring the continuation of life. The soldiers' role as mummers is further underlined by the Mayor's questions on first meeting Musgrave: "How do you propose to work?" he asks, "... I mean, d'you tramp around the streets drumming, or set on your fannies in a pub—or what?" The image of the men tramping around the streets drumming clearly conjures up the Mummers' Play. *Serjeant Musgrave's Dance* also contains direct verbal echoes of the Mummers' Play; perhaps the most striking is the Bargee's irreverent stanza about the Constable:

Constable Constable alive or dead
His head is of leather and his belly's of lead.

Chambers quotes a range of similar lines which are part of the dispute preceding the fight between the two combatants, and he also demonstrates, most convincingly, that the reference originally was to a dragon. With the Constable being a feeble and helpless man, the implicit comparison would seem to add to the disrespectful irony of the Bargee's words, but it can also be taken as a more direct indication of the true power which the Constable is ultimately seen to represent.

Having thus noted that Arden's play has obvious similarities with the Mummers' Play in general and the Wooing Ceremony in particular, we shall turn to the application of this traditional pattern in *Serjeant Musgrave's Dance*. To begin with, the Mummers' Play customarily ends with a collection of money among the spectators. In *Serjeant Musgrave's Dance*, however, the pattern is inverted. Virtually as soon as the soldiers have arrived, they are offered money, and not by the community at large, but by the Mayor, who uses bribery as a means of assisting Musgrave in what he takes to be a recruiting campaign. The soldiers are thus to be rewarded, not for ensuring the fertility and prosperity of the community, but for taking away as many of its young and able men as they can to the death and destruction of war.

This inversion of the traditional pattern is not a unique occurrence, but a consistent feature which assumes a profound significance in Arden's play. Thus, for example, we would normally expect the Recruiting Sergeant to woo the Lady himself. But clearly the man who treats Annie to a long speech about the dangers of interfering with the soldiers in his charge would never even contemplate behaving in accordance with the traditional pattern:

> Look, lassie, anarchy: now, we're soldiers. Our work isn't easy, no and it's not soft: it's got a strong name— duty. And it's drawn out straight and black for us, a clear plan. But if you come to us with what you call your life or love—*I'd call it your indulgence* —and you scribble all over that plan, you make it crooked, dirty, idle, untidy, *bad*—there's anarchy. I'm a religious man. I know words, and I know deeds, and I know how to be strong. So do these men. You will not stand between them and their strength! Go on now: take yourself off.

Obviously, this emphatic effort to ward off the threat posed by women undermines the very strength which Musgrave is claiming for the soldiers. But even more important is the fact that here the Serjeant, quite deliberately and explicitly, separates his men and himself from the Lady. This amounts to a violation of the pattern of the Wooing Ceremony and, indeed, of the Mummers' Play as a whole. For with the Mummers' Play being a fertility ritual, the role of the women is crucial. When Musgrave attempts to banish Annie to the very fringe of the dramatic action, the traditional pattern is quite blatantly inverted.

At the centre of the action in the Mummers' Play is a symbolic killing followed by a revival. And just as in the Wooing Ceremony, the Fool in *Serjeant Musgrave's Dance* is killed: Sparky dies as the result of a fight. The quarrel begins in truly farcical style as a battle over a pair of trousers, and the killing occurs quite inadvertently with Attercliffe, the pacifist, happening to hold the bayonet which pierces Sparky's body. A central sequence of the ritual is thus presented as taking place by mistake, an impression which is reinforced by Musgrave's reaction: "Desertion. Fornication. It's not material. He's dead. Hide him away."

Sparky has a double in his friend Billy Hicks, killed overseas and brought back by the soldiers to his home town, where they eventually display his skeleton as their own crude means of communicating the futility of their trade. The skeleton in its box throws an ever-present shadow over Sparky's life, pointing ahead to the death of the Fool. The parallel is emphasized by the fact that both men die as a consequence of their profession, Sparky actually provoking the fatal quarrel with his decision to desert. And the deaths of these Army men are final. Billy Hicks is carried around as a skeleton, the very emblem of Death; and Sparky, in sharp contrast to the pattern of the Mummers' Play, cannot be brought back to life. The Doctor, indispensable in the Mummers' Play as the figure who revives the dead, simply does not exist in *Serjeant Musgrave's Dance*.

As a result, the Mummers' Play for which the Bargee sets the scene in the market-place can never be performed. This section of *Serjeant Musgrave's Dance*, so often criticized, is a deliberate hiatus. The situation of the community and the arrangements in the market-place add up to a perfect setting for a Mummers' Play, but on closer inspection, several of the central figures are missing. The Fool lies buried in Mrs. Hitchcock's midden, the Lady has been locked away, and the bastard child whom the Old Woman ought to bring is dead too, for Annie's baby with Billy "came a kind of bad shape, pale, sick: it wor dead and in the ground in no more nor two month." And with no Doctor to revive the dead, there can be no invitation to the wedding as the action draws to a close; all we get is a pathetic reminder of the events that ought to have occurred as we watch Annie cradling Billy's skeleton.

The scene which opens with promises of the ancient ritual degenerates into a confused sequence of speeches, preaching, and demonstrations of weapons, eventually disintegrating into arguments and chaos. This is the great opportunity to convey his message for which Musgrave has been waiting — blind to the fact that in the meantime the ritual which is an inherent refutation of death and a celebration of life has been enacted around him. For the first two acts of *Serjeant Musgrave's Dance* contain the traditional Wooing Ceremony, albeit in a stunted form. Sparky's magnificent entry into Mrs. Hitchcock's pub announces the beginning of a performance; Billy Hicks is the play's equivalent of the young man who has enlisted after making advances to the Lady; and the story of the bastard child is told by Mrs. Hitchcock. There is a threefold wooing, with the Fool being the final and successful suitor, and as in the Wooing Ceremony, the Fool is killed after an exchange of challenges. But here the similarities end, the scene in the market-place confirming the collapse of the ritual.

The reasons for this collapse are brought into focus by the inversions of the traditional pattern. The Mayor, who bribes Musgrave with golden sovereigns, is using the recruiting party to solve his own problems. His coal-mine is at a standstill, lay-offs and wage-cuts having provoked a strike, and the simplest solution, in the words of the Mayor, is to "clear out half the population, stir up a diversion, turn their minds to summat else. The Queen's got wars, she's got rebellions. Over the sea. . . . Get rid o' the trouble-makers." It has been pointed out that the wintry weather in *Serjeant Musgrave's Dance* is of a piece with the traditional setting for a Mummers' Play, but clearly the real strangle-hold on this community is that which is exerted not by the winter, but by the Mayor, as Mrs. Hitchcock stresses poignantly in her stanza about him:

> I am a proud coalowner
> And in scarlet here I stand.
> Who shall come or who shall go
> Through all my coal-black land?

Being a fertility ritual, the Mummers' Play revolves around the community's fundamental relationship with the powers of nature. In *Serjeant Musgrave's Dance,* by contrast, the pattern of the Mummers' Play throws into relief the deep divisions within the community and the consequent shift of focus on to man's relationship with his powerful fellow men. The livelihood of the community in Arden's play depends not on "the eternal pattern of the seasons," but on the actions of the Mayor and owner of the colliery—who inevitably has his own interests at heart.

The arrival of Musgrave and his men does not merely confirm these divisions within the community: it contributes to making them wider still. The Serjeant is instrumental in achieving this greater divisiveness, his most conspicuous measure being his banishment of Annie. Musgrave's treatment of the Lady in the Mummers' Play adds up to a deliberate suppression of the ancient fertility ritual with its inherent power of revitalizing the community. Instead, this community is left entirely in the hands of men. Their rule, Arden emphasizes, can be only sterile, divisive, and destructive.

Musgrave's impact on the course of the Mummers' Play is not the result of mere personal eccentricity. The inclusion of the Recruiting Serjeant in the Wooing Ceremony in the first place is a good illustration of that capacity for adaptation and expansion which has been one of the conditions for the survival of the Mummers' Play into the present century, and Arden has shrewdly exploited this capacity by turning *his* Recruiting Sergeant into a member of Cromwell's New Model Army. In an apparently casual remark in the Introduction to the play, Arden himself has hinted at this significance of his Serjeant: "he could well have served under Cromwell" is his concluding comment on Musgrave. It seems to me that the hint is worth taking seriously; indeed, I believe that the Cromwellian dimension is fundamental to the interpretation of Arden's Serjeant. Thus, Musgrave's strictness and rigidity, his preoccupation with discipline and duty, and last but not least, his religious fanaticism, are all of a piece with the image of the Cromwellian soldier. The Serjeant, who reads his pocket Bible in the pub, chewing his supper of dry bread and cheese after having declined the offer of a drink—and annoyed the landlady into the bargain—is an unmistakable Puritan. The point is made again, in terms which are equally immediate, when Musgrave wakes up the house with his nightmares: like so many seventeenth-century Puritans, he is convinced that the end of the world is imminent. And what might be taken for personal hesitation and uncertainty at a critical juncture in the market-place, just before the appearance of Annie, is more properly a reflection of the Puritan soldier's habit of waiting for the guidance of God, the suspended dramatic illustration of the words with which Musgrave has concluded his prayer in the churchyard: ". . . I know it is Your Logic, and You will provide-"

To Arden, the combination of a Puritan and an ancient dramatic tradition such as that of the Mummers' Play has profound significance. In a letter published in *Encore* in 1959, Arden refers to the fact that the Elizabethan and Jacobean theatre could appeal to virtually the entire range of social classes as a result of "the still extraordinarily powerful popular tradition which informed that Theatre as a whole." After a brief sketch of this tradition, with references to medieval Moralities and Buffooneries as well as Mummers' Plays, he continues: "The true tradition is still with us, but it is buried deep down under several hundred years of puritanical falsification. . . ." Arden's ideal is theatre as the central concern of the community; yet during much of his career as a playwright, he has been attempting to convey this ideal through the conventional modern theatre, geared towards providing what he would regard as no more than entertainment for a mere section of the community. His solution has been to adopt, theatrically and dramatically, the style of the old popular tradition, and to demonstrate, on the stage, how this tradition is being quenched by a new order which turns the theatre into a place for speech-making and sermonizing. Again and again this confrontation is enacted in Arden's drama, one of the most elaborate examples being the forcible removal of the drunken Butterthwaite from the respectable art gallery, formerly the notorious Copacabana Club, in *The Workhouse Donkey*. In *Serjeant Musgrave's Dance*, when the Gatling gun with its capacity of three-hundred-and-fifty rounds a minute is trained on to the spectators in the auditorium—who are doubling, significantly, as the crowd in Arden's market-place—the true role of this modern theatre is revealed: it is, by Arden's standards, essentially a tool of oppression.

The fate of the Fool in *Serjeant Musgrave's Dance* illustrates the joint consequences of all that for which the Serjeant and the local magistrates stand. Sparky may belong to a group of deserters who have chosen to turn their original role on its head by spreading the gospel of pacifism, but he still dies for the sake of the Army—not, as would befit the Fool in the Mummers' Play, for the sake of the community. And the Army, the cause of this sterile and meaningless death, is the very embodiment of Musgrave's ideas. The Queen's Book, he explains, "which eighteen years I've lived, it's turned inside out for *me*," but this reversal alters little: the Serjeant's strategy for his peace mission is in true military style, the intended climax being the crudely primitive and only too familiar measure of large-scale retaliation. Arden is saying that the Army, by definition, breeds nothing but violence and death. The same point is made in contrasting, deliberately farcical terms in the scene where the Bargee drills the drunken colliers. What starts as a comic send-up of the stern Serjeant and his men ends as a condensed and almost over-explicit illustration of what Arden regards as the inevitable consequences of the presence of an army: the Bargee's mock soldiers pick a quarrel among themselves and start fighting each other.

The Army is the basis of the power of the local magistrates. Musgrave and his men may be rebellious deserters, but nevertheless it is Army men who finally return the community to law and order. In terms of the life of the community, the wheel is brought full circle, as one of the colliers emphasizes in his summary: "The community's been saved. Peace and prosperity rules. We're all friends and neighbours for the rest of today. We're all sorted out. We're back where we were." But clearly this is not peace and prosperity of the kind that the Mummers' Play would promote: it is peace and prosperity dependent on rule through the barrel of a gun. As the officer in charge of the dragoons points out significantly, his troopers are at the Mayor's disposal; and Arden has stressed that if he were able to produce the play in a large theatre employing an enormous cast of supernumeraries, "the stage would be full of dragoons and the dance would take place in front of them. Then the impression given would be that even the most sympathetic of the colliers, who nearly sides with Musgrave, has no alternative but to take part in the dance, and that law and order have been re-established by force."

The qualities of the control that is re-established are epitomized by the Bargee, whose sole motive for taking action is personal advantage. Being totally unscrupulous, the Bargee sides with whoever is in power, and the fact that he plays the role of the Devil in the Mummers' Play adds a poignantly ironic dimension to his activities. "[G]ive me some room to swing me tiller . . ." he shouts significantly as his barge is being loaded and the Devil himself prepares to bring the recruiting party to the strikebound community; but the figure who eventually sticks a rifle into Musgrave's back and boasts to the dragoons and the magistrates that, "*I* caught him, *I* caught him, *I* used me strategy!" clearly is not in charge to the extent that he wants us to believe. He emerges, however, as a most illuminating reflection of the figures who do come out on top, namely those members of the community who can truly greet the dragoons as saviours.

In *Serjeant Musgrave's Dance*, then, Arden presents a story—or a fable, to use a Brechtian term sometimes also employed by Arden—which derives its basic structure from the clash between the type of Mummers' Play known as the Wooing Ceremony and the ideas promoted by a Cromwellian Recruiting Sergeant. By setting the action in Victorian times, Arden achieves a perspective which heightens the effect of his fable, bringing it closer to the modern spectator and yet leaving it at a certain distance where its overall significance is more easily discerned. Any attempts by the spectator to identify with the character of Musgrave are plainly doomed to end in frustration and confusion: this Serjeant needs to be seen in the context of the fable as a whole. As Arden has stated in an article published only a couple of years after *Serjeant Musgrave's Dance*:

> A play that is a sermon and no more will be in danger of preaching only to the converted. But if the sermon is expressed in terms of a poetic statement (either of the bad life that is, or the good life that could be, or of both contrasted) and given to the audience to hold, as it might be a ripe apple, so that they could look at it all round and decide for themselves by touch and feel whether it is sound or not—then one may have some hope of effecting a change in somebody's heart.

The bad life that is, contrasted with the good life that could be, all expressed in terms of a poetic statement ... the description neatly encapsulates the action and form of *Serjeant Musgrave's Dance*. Here an ostensibly simple clash of opposites is endowed with archetypal dimensions as a result of the application of the pattern of the Mummers' Play, and the poetic impact of this conflict is heightened by Arden's extensive use of ballad-style songs and verse. *Serjeant Musgrave's Dance* offers very good examples of the playwright's technique of employing songs and verse as a means of reaching through to his spectators and involving them emotionally in a conflict which subsequently unfolds also at a more intellectual level. In strikingly immediate terms, moreover, the songs and verse transmit that pulse of death and rebirth which beats with such vigour not only in early drama but in a whole range of twentieth-century writings besides Arden's play.

The verse in *Serjeant Musgrave's Dance* helps to crystallize the significance of the primary colours, black and white, red and green, which pervade the play like a visual echo of its basic rhythm. More importantly, the songs and verse bring out and enhance the stylization of the characters which is so central to the overall design of the play, setting the female characters sharply against the males. As the themes of the songs and verse revolve around woman as the provider of life and love, while man is seen as her transient partner, the cycle of life and death is in effect condensed in the verse used in the play. This cycle is epitomized by the life of the soldier, which is a recurring subject of the ballads and the verse in *Serjeant Musgrave's Dance* and which, invariably, is depicted as a brief spell of vigour and aggressive virility in the looming shadow of death. By contrast, the unique and mysterious powers of the women are mirrored in poetic utterances which are remarkably perceptive and even prophetic, while the limitations of the magistrates are underlined by the fact that songs and verse are quite beyond their reach: the dour men in charge of this community can express themselves only in prose.

In the case of Shakespeare's *Macbeth*, the combination of two sections from the medieval Cycle Plays provides a distinctive form for the tragedy and adds a significant moral dimension to the story of the Scottish usurper. In *Serjeant Musgrave's Dance*, the Mummers' Play fulfils the equivalent functions, but it also plays a third role which is at least as important as the other two. The Mummers' Play is, by definition, an expression of the life of the community. Arden's employment of this ancient pattern enables him not only to pinpoint what he sees as the causes of its distortion, but, more immediately, to bring into focus the inherent potential of the community. "[B]egin again" is the recurring call at the end of the scene in the marketplace, and any spectator who has followed the plot of Arden's play will be able to perceive the negative implications of this new beginning. When the underlying patterns are taken into account, however, the call also acquires a more challenging note. Arden is not an irresponsible romantic making a plea for a return to the distant past when the ritual of the Mummers' Play had a central communal function; but he is making a plea for the community, and more especially for the ordinary people who have the capacity to maintain it as a living organism. *Serjeant Musgrave's Dance* is thus not merely a story of life and love and their oppression. With its combination of historical scope, dramatic effectiveness, and poetic impact, this fable is ultimately designed to impart to the spectator some of that awareness which is the first prerequisite for change.

Source: Helena Forsas-Scott, "Life and Love and Serjeant Musgrave: An Approach to Arden's Play," in *Modern Drama*, March, Vol. 26, 1983, no. 1, pp. 1–11.

Fernand Lagarde

In the following essay, Lagarde discusses similarities between Serjeant Musgrave's Dance *and various plays by Shakespeare, notably* Julius Caesar, Macbeth, *and* Romeo and Juliet.

Serjeant Musgrave's Dance, no doubt, may be considered first and foremost as a twentieth century reworking of *The Recruiting Officer,* inspired or influenced by Brecht's vision of Farquhar's comedy, the 1955 Berlin repertoire production of *Pauken und Trompeten,* with a few touches from Brecht's own *Mutter Courage.* Yet, whatever the international influences at play in the world of theatre nowadays, an English dramatist cannot forget he was nurtured on a national tradition which began in the Renaissance and John Arden, who acknowledged his debt to Ben Jonson in *The Waters of Babylon,* cannot be an exception. Indeed the reader of *Serjeant Musgrave's Dance* more than once gathers the impression that Shakespeare was pent up in Arden's mind, ready to gush forth, from the moment of the inception to that of the definitive draft.

The turning-point in the plot, when the soldiers lose all hope of gaining the support of the colliers, comes, everyone will agree, after Annie has revealed the hole in Sparky's tunic which confounds Musgrave and indicts the Army:

> (holding up the tunic). Hey, here's the little hole where they let in the bayonet. Eee, aie, easily in. His blood's on my tongue, so hear what it says. A bayonet is a raven's beak. This tunic's a collier's jacket. The scarecrow's a birdcage. (*SMD*, III.1.101)

Now this sounds like a clear recollection of Antony's speech and tactics to move the Roman plebians. The situation is the same; Brutus has explained that Caesar's ambition constituted a threat to the citizens' liberties and that death was the only solution; so Musgrave has tried to convince the colliers that British ambition, greed and callousness were the causes of the rebellion in the distant protectorate and consequently that the Mayor, the Parson and the Constable are guilty of Billy's death as well as of the natives' sufferings at the hands of Her Majesty's soldiers; on both occasions the orator at first carries the conviction of his listeners (though a modern audience demands nuances and Arden's earnest collier, Walsh, provides the necessary dissenting voice). As Antony leaves the pulpit and 'descends' into the midst of his fellow-Romans, so Annie has ceremoniously 'come down the ladder', taken possession of the centre of the platform and mixed with her fellow-citizens the better to move

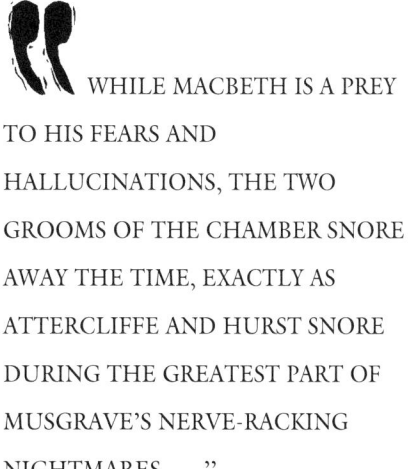

"WHILE MACBETH IS A PREY TO HIS FEARS AND HALLUCINATIONS, THE TWO GROOMS OF THE CHAMBER SNORE AWAY THE TIME, EXACTLY AS ATTERCLIFFE AND HURST SNORE DURING THE GREATEST PART OF MUSGRAVE'S NERVE-RACKING NIGHTMARES. . . ."

them; as Antony plucks the mantle off Caesar's corpse, so Annie has Mrs Hitchcock throw her the 'bundle' and reveals the rent tunic of the Army's other victim to incense the lookers-on. Actually the words *His blood's on my tongue* spring from the same rhetorical trick of introducing the blood and wounds as orators and the speaker as a mere mouthpiece for a dead friend; though Antony's cultivated mind may resort to more elaborate language and prompt the revolt that the forlorn barmaid cannot even wish for, consciously or unconsciously:

> Show you sweet Caesar's wounds, poor
>   dumb mouths,
> And bid them speak for me [. . .]
> [. . .] and put a tongue
> In every wound of Caesar, that should move
> The stones of Rome to rise and mutiny
> (*Julius Caesar,* III.2.227–8, 229–31),

there exists a great similarity in the technique of the two characters as well as in the end result. Not only does Arden remember and reproduce the circumstances and details of how a crowd switch their support, but he makes the back-drop of the mining town resemble that of Caesar's Rome: the rumours of wars and rebellions, the presence of the army at the gates. After the arrival of the dragoons and the restoration of law and order, Walsh bitterly remarks that being *saved* means that *We're back where we were* (*SMD,* III.1.105); one might say as much of Rome after the check on tyranny devised by Brutus and Cassius, for the shadow of dictatorship has not fled the city. One might also argue that the liberator of the mining town, the officer, the *young man* (*SMD,* III.1.1.04), is the very apt counterpart of Octavius, whom Shakespeare conceived of as a young man, in opposition to Antony. Furthermore, the Bargee, a modern avatar of the Lord of Misrule, who changes sides as easily as a weather-cock and whose mind constantly dwells on drinks and destruction, stands as a good epitome of the crowds that Shakespeare paints in *Julius Caesar* and elsewhere. The title-hero, however, is the character that gains most from a contamination by the Roman play; his profession and his illicit return to the mother-country may, at first sight, suggest a resemblance with Julius Caesar, his death being the only means of exorcizing fear; on second thought, though, it is with Brutus that Musgrave has greater affinities, for both evince idealism, self-control and relentlessness of purpose and both for the first half of the play subjugate other characters, forcing them to endorse their vision of things. Moreover, during their abortive attempt to murder the men in office, the conspirators and liberators, Musgrave and Hurst, quarrel, not unlike Brutus and Cassius after Caesar's death, because they disagree on their deeper motives.

True, Brutus is haunted by the ghost of Caesar before and during the battle at Philippi, whereas Musgrave never flinches after his defeat. If the serjeant feels the panges of remorse, it is before he embarks upon the final stage of his mission, at the time of Sparky's murder in the stable, and scene 3 of act II seems to owe more to *Macbeth* than to any other play. First, Mrs Hitchcock visits Musgrave when the latter is oppressed by nightmares and not only re-lives the ordeal of the repression but lives the revenge to come—since the number of victims, twenty-five, fits either situation equally well. Mrs Hitchcock brings him a grog, just as Lady Macbeth has been expected to prepare a drink for her husband on the fatal night. Like Macbeth, Musgrave should have been 'against the deed' in both the foreign and the mining town, since in both places he was welcomed as the man bearing the weapons to protect others, not to kill his hosts. While Macbeth is a prey to his fears and hallucinations, the two grooms of the chamber snore away the time, exactly as Attercliffe and Hurst snore during the greatest part of Musgrave's nerve-racking nightmares; for like Macbeth the serjeant *hath murdered sleep, the innocent sleep*. Keeping Macbeth's hallucinations in mind, the public better understands Musgrave's part in the scene, Musgrave who follows the book (the Bible and the Queen's Book) as irresistibly as the Scottish felon follows the dagger of the mind. The infernal concatenation of murders, which is masterfully illustrated in *Macbeth,* is also one of the lessons of *Serjeant Musgrave's Dance,* in this scene especially. The final hecatomb in Shakespeare's tragedy is ushered in by the apparition of Lady Macbeth sleepwalking in her nightgown; Mrs Hitchcock, in her nightgown also, heralds the many deaths, the first of which, that of Sparky, is concomitant with her visit; no matter if it is the woman who is wide awake and the man a near somnambulist here, the resemblance forces itself upon the minds of the audience, all the more easily as Arden stresses, thanks to the two distinct acting areas, downstage and upstage, the incongruity of the bar-owner's proffered comfort for the serjeant's metaphysical anxiety, the two characters living then on as surely different planes as Lady Macbeth and her husband in the last act of the tragedy—*Musgrave (now shouting in his sleep)* (*SMD,* II.3.70) being reminiscent of the *night-shriek* in Dunsinane.

In the same scene (II.3) there remains one echo of *Macbeth,* a very distinct verbal echo, which seems to fit the dramatic situation far less satisfactorily; Attercliffe, after rejecting the advances of Annie, looks at his hands and quotes Musgrave:

> Our Black Jack'd [...] say there's blood on these two hands. (He looks at his hands with distaste.) You can wipe 'em as often as you want on a bit o' yellow hair, but it still comes blood the next time so why bother, he'd say (*SMD,* II.3.67),

which must remind everyone of Lady Macbeth's obsession with the *damned spot* on her hand (*Macbeth,* V.1.34), rather than of Macbeth's horror earlier in the play (*Macbeth,* II.1.59–63), for the possibility no longer exists of 'clearing' the guilty one of his 'deed' with a little water; Attercliffe's reflection comes at a moment when a woman's love can no longer assuage his sorrow, which can compare with the Shakespearian heroine's predicament in act V. Now the scene in *Serjeant Musgrave's Dance* also evokes *Romeo and Juliet,* in reverse as it were; Hurst has repelled Annie, because instead of anticipating the pleasures of the night he fears the cold of the morning (*SMD,* II.3.64–5): *As far as my mind goes, it's morning already. Every one alone—that's all;* one at once thinks of Juliet's passionate longing for the night and of her plea in favour of Romeo's prolonging their happiness together in defiance of the morning's threats. Once the resemblance has been taken for granted, the scene between Sparky and Annie appears in a new light and recalls that of the Verona lovers who also fight against a hostile environment and resort to ruse and concealment. Indeed in the eyes of Juliet's Nurse, the heroine's sentiments seem to waver, to favour Tybalt, then Romeo and, why not, Paris by turns; Annie may give the same impression to the casual observer, Mrs Hitchcock for instance and all those that take her for *a whoor-to-the-soldiers,* when she comes to settle her affections on Sparky for good, though she has passed from one box to the other, from one soldier to the next. When Annie comes down the ladder to be reunited with the skeleton of her former lover, one is almost tempted to associate it with the ladder which the Nurse procures and

> by the which your love [i.e. Romeo]
> Must climb a bird's nest soon when it is dark
> (*Romeo and Juliet,* II.5.73–4),

the descent towards death having replaced the ascent towards life, though it is equally prompted by love, and the winter morning has replaced the summer night.

If all these similitudes and analogies are accepted, Annie's 'song-ballad' to describe Musgrave's parentage:

> *The North Wind in a pair of millstones*
> Was your father and your mother
> They got you in a cold grinding (*SMD,* I.3.32)

expresses the same 'stricture and abstinence' and savours of the same wit as Lucio's tales of Angelo's begetting:

> *They say, this Angelo was not made by man and woman, after the downright way of creation [. . .]. Some report a sea-maid spawned him. . .some, that he was begot between two stock-fishes. . .But it is certain, that when he makes water, his urine is congealed ice.* (*Measure for Measure,* III.2.101–3, 105–8)

Again, when Annie portrays Hurst wandering *down by the canal, all alone and wretched* and, to tease him, *sings with fierce emphasis:*

> *All round his hat he wore the green willow—!*
> (*SMD,* II.3.65),

one instinctively thinks of Desdemona's song of the willow and its evocation of a forsaken lover. Later, the Bargee's ballad, *Hark hark the drums do bark* (*SMD,* III.1.83), suggests Ariel's song when the spirit leads Ferdinand along the *yellow sands:*

> *The burthen. . . Hark!*
> Hark!
> 'Burthen dispersedly.' Bow-wow!
> Ariel. The watch-dogs bark:
> Burthen. Bow-wow!
> Ariel. Hark, hark, I hear
> The strain of strutting chanticleer
> Cry-.
> (*The Tempest,* I.2.382–9)

Although Arden's prose does not echo Shakespeare's verse so obviously as it does nursery rhymes at times ('Baa, baa, black sheep', II.1.56 and II.3.69, or 'London's burning, London's burning!', II.3.70), it would no doubt be quite easy to discover other Shakespearian traces. What must be asserted is that no one can read or see *Serjeant Musgrave's Dance* without calling to mind the great model that Shakespeare has remained, even after the 1956 bang of *Look Back in Anger*. Dissociated from his Renaissance counterparts or ancestors, the Bargee loses much of his fascination; the very title of Arden's plays suggests a typically Elizabethan and Jacobean convention, for to Musgrave's dance there responds the Bargee's dance, which closes the 'un-historical parable' proper—III.2 is hardly more than an epilogue—and in which the spectators on the stage join the professional merrymaker as the assassins joined hands at the end of a revenge tragedy or as courtiers and professional dancers joined in masques and antimasques. Quite naturally, borrowing, which ranges from unconscious reminiscence to patent imitation, may turn to parody, witness the officer's proclamation:

> *The winter's broken up. Let normal life begin again*
> (*SMD,* III.1.105),

promising the dawn of a new golden age when everything points to unchanged and unchangeable misery for all but the representatives of the powers that be. Irony does not detract from indebtedness or from adhesion to a tradition; irony and parody are only methods of adaptation.

Source: Fernand Lagarde, "Shakespearian Reminiscences in *Serjeant Musgrave's Dance*," in *Cahiers Elisabethains,* Vol. 17, 1980, pp. 77–81.

Thomas P. Adler

In the following essay, Adler suggests that Musgrave's first dance partakes of ritual elements in "a grotesque parody of the Christian 'slaying of winter'—the Crucifixion—and a perversion of its essential meaning."

In a recent article, Mary B. O'Connell suggests that John Arden's *Serjeant Musgrave's Dance* is "a contemporary folk ritual" whose "characterization and plot development" are modeled on the medieval Mummers Play of Plough Monday, which traditionally was "a mime slaying of winter." The purpose here is not to dispute Miss O'Connell's suggestion, since the Plough Monday play might well be the inspiration behind some elements in Arden's drama, especially the second dance near the end during which "Each man takes his drink, swigs a large gulp, then links wrists with the previous one, until all are dancing around the centre-piece in a chorus, singing." I suggest, however, that the first dance in the play, undertaken near the beginning of Act III by Musgrave alone, partakes of ritual elements of a more specifically religious nature. Here Musgrave, "waving his rifle, his face contorted with demonic fury," dances around "an articulated skeleton dressed in a soldier's tunic and trousers," hanging from "the cross-bar" in the town square, in what is obviously a grotesque parody of the Christian "slaying of winter"—the Crucifixion—and a perversion of its essential meaning.

Arden's debt to medieval drama is well-known: his modern mystery play, *The Business of Good Government,* written for performance during Christmastime, is, as John Russell Taylor says, "of a radiant grace and simplicity which make clear some of the lessons Arden has learned from a study of the medieval stage. . ."; and Robert John Jordan has rightly singled out certain aspects of the characterization and conflict in *Musgrave's Dance* as "almost morality-play in style." Although there was never any literal dance around the cross in the Crucifixion plays in the medieval mystery cycles, Christ's death was seen as the climactic event in the sacred history of mankind from the Creation to the Last Judgment in that it reconciled man with God and was thus the culmination of God's salvific dance of grace on earth.

Arden's stage directions specify a number of visual images and gestures which would suggest to the audience a re-enactment of the Crucifixion—albeit in a parodic way—in the hoisting of the skeleton and Musgrave's demonic dance around it. The description of the stage set for Act III, Scene One, states that "In the centre of the stage is a practicable feature—the centre-piece of the market place. It is a sort of Victorian clock-tower-cum-lamppost-cum-market-cross, and stands on a raised plinth. There is a ladder leaning against it." (The last two photographs of the English production which are published at the back of the Grove Press edition of the play show very well how the crosslike formation of this centre-piece dominates the setting.) Two other stage directions dictating gesture and movement by the actors would also play on the audience's awareness of Christian symbology and call to mind Christ's crucifixion: when Attercliffe, the pacifist follower of Musgrave, jumps in front of Hurst's gatling gun to prevent him from opening fire on the crowd, he "stands on the step of the plinth . . . with his arms spread out" in a Christlike pose; and when the skeleton of Billy Hicks is removed from the cross-bar, his former mistress Annie "sits with it on her knees," cradling it in her arms in a visual image reminiscent of the Pieta.

If the central message of Christ's crucifixion is one of love and reconciliation—the inauguration of a new dispensation of forgiveness—, then Musgrave's fanatical plan for revenge—a throwback to the old dispensation of "an eye for an eye" vengeance—is antithetical to the meaning of the cross. Musgrave is correct in his original assumption that his gospel of no more war coincides with the Word of God, particularly as expressed by Christ in the Sermon on the Mount; as Musgrave says, "without God" such a proclamation of peace is but "a bad belch and a hiccup." He desires to "Let the word dance," but, ignoring the lesson of the Crucifixion, errs in his conviction that "God's dance on this earth" must be a thing of fear and trembling; "The Word alone is terrible: the Dance must be worse." Arden dramatically underscores Musgrave's failure to perceive that God's dance is one of mercy rather than of strict, retributive justice. When Musgrave prays, "keep my mind clear so I can weigh Judgement against the Mercy and Judgement against the Blood, and make this Dance as terrible as You have put it into my brain," the Bargee undercuts the Serjeant's petition as he "parodies his attitude behind his back" and at the end "gives a sanctimonious smirk and breathes 'Amen'."

Seen against the backdrop of Christ's life-bringing death on the Cross, Musgrave's "crucifixion" of the skeleton of the dead Hicks is life-denying, thus perverting a symbol of mercy and love into an embodiment and justification of vengeance. As Annie, the force of life and love in the play, perceives, this is the "old true-love gone twisted," malformed and transformed into something akin to hate. This is supported by the recurrent symbol of the "twisted little dead" baby which she conceived just before Hicks went off to war: "when it wor born, it came a kind of bad shape, pale, sick: it wor dead and in the ground in no more nor two month. About the time they called *him* [Billy] dead, y'see." The baby buried in the ground and Billy's skeleton hanging from the cross-bar are the two most pervasive *momento mori* emblems in a play filled with the aura of death—with the cold of winter rather than the warmth of spring.

For the movement from death to life, from winter to spring, which is an important motif in both the Mummers Play of Plough Monday and the Christian observance of the Crucifixion and Resurrection each Eastertime, is really quite muted in *Musgrave's Dance*. Hicks' "crucifixion" has not led to a new era of peace; as the innkeeper Mrs. Hitchcock says, the townspeople's dance at the end is "not a dance of joy." And Attercliffe knows why this is so: "you can not end it [war] by its own rules: no bloody good." Musgrave tried to unmask the absurdity of war by extending the reign of bloodshed and terror. Now Musgrave's own folly is unmasked, for no shedding of blood in the name of peace is good.

But Mrs. Hitchcock does suggest the tentative hope that what Musgrave attempted to achieve through the wrong means will someday be accomplished through the right means: "Let's hope it, any road, Eh." The ballad that Attercliffe sings to conclude the play makes the contrast between "a blood-red rose-flower"—a symbol for the soldiers throughout the play—and "the apple [which] holds a seed will grow / In live and lengthy joy / To raise a flourishing tree of fruit / For ever and a day." The apple, significantly enough, becomes the major symbol of life and hope in the play. Popularizations of the Biblical story of the Fall in Genesis 3 identify the fruit of the forbidden tree as the apple; and according to Apocryphal legends, which influenced much medieval literature, seeds from that same fruit sprung up into the tree from which Christ's cross is hewn. Thus, as the Catholic liturgy for Passiontide emphasizes, man's salvation is accomplished upon the tree of the cross so that life might be restored through the very same instrument that brought death. So, too, Attercliffe and Musgrave, hanging "higher nor most apple-trees grow," might someday "start an orchard." Their deaths, dancing from a noose in expiation for using bloody means to end war, may be one step closer than Hicks' "crucifixion" to inaugurating God's dance of love and peace on earth.

Source: Thomas P. Adler, "Religious Ritual in *Serjeant Musgrave's Dance*," in *Modern Drama*, Vol. 16, 1973, pp. 163–66.

Barry Thome

In the following essay, Thome describes Musgrave as an "Old Testament avenger" in a morality play indebted to the Elizabethan romantic and dramatic tradition.

Next to Harold Pinter, John Arden is perhaps the most respected contemporary English playwright. And this despite the fact he has made a break with realism which carries his work back in method to

> "SEEN AGAINST THE BACKDROP OF CHRIST'S LIFE-BRINGING DEATH ON THE CROSS, MUSGRAVE'S 'CRUCIFIXION' OF THE SKELETON OF THE DEAD HICKS IS LIFE-DENYING, THUS PERVERTING A SYMBOL OF MERCY AND LOVE INTO AN EMBODIMENT AND JUSTIFICATION OF VENGEANCE."

the Renaissance. His best known play, written in 1959 and signalling his break with kitchen sink realism, is *Serjeant Musgrave's Dance*. But Arden's acceptance has not been instantaneous, nor have his plays lasted long at the box office on their first run.

Musgrave, for example, lasted 28 performances, largely because its initial audiences could fathom neither its medium nor its message. The liberal spectators saw in the play a tract about pacifism which seemed to show that pacifism does not work. The conservatives saw a statement that human weakness and evil confound the liberal idealism of the naive.

One of the problems with the play is that Arden does not take sides; he merely presents the humanity of a series of contradictory points of view on the same issue. Unfortunately, he loses the thread briefly toward the end of *Serjeant Musgrave's Dance*, and like his main character scribbles on the orderly tablet of his plot and theme.

As a result, the confused message of this modern morality play leaves not only the angry men of the cast but also the audience unsure of what has been accomplished by the action of the plot. Surprisingly, however, the play has actually worked on stage for subsequent audiences, especially after the B.B.C. television production of 1962. Its emotional impact seems heightened rather than lessened by the folk stylization, particularly the choric role played by the women and the enigmatic Bargee. And though the moral is blurred in the final scene, the audience's emotional reaction remains strongly positive.

> THE BARGEE IS THEN A MOCKING FIGURE OF INTRIGUE REMINISCENT OF THE VICE FIGURE OF RENAISSANCE MORALITY PLAYS. SYMBOLIZING THE POTENTIAL EVIL OF MAN'S NATURE, HE THEREFORE EXTENDS THE MEANING OF THE PLAY BEYOND CONVENTIONAL WARFARE...."

Arden's depiction of the protest crusade of Musgrave, Sparky, Hurst, and Attercliffe seems more than commonly indebted to the Elizabethan dramatic tradition. The play appears to deliberately incorporate the Elizabethan romantic tradition in plot structure and incidental device, for example in the use of songs and comic dance and action, thereby producing a modern Elizabethan hybrid, a tragicomedy. The romantic plot structure and the folk stylization serve to relieve the sombre quality of the basic action and the Jehovian madness of the central character, Black Jack Musgrave. Like Osborne's *The Entertainer* and several of Pinter's plays, *Musgrave* owes a good deal as well to the British music hall tradition.

Arden portrays Serjeant Musgrave as an Old Testament avenger stirred out of his habitual guidelines for living (the Book of Regulations) by the inconsistencies of a colonial war.

Unable to reconcile the book and the fact, Musgrave substitutes books, the Book of the Lord for the Book of Regulations. With the power of a new set of regulations, the Word and hence the Power of the Lord, Musgrave convinces himself that military tactics and Old Testament reprisal should be used to force the people at home to see the evil of his "Colonial War."

Of his three confederates, only Private Attercliffe sees the error of Musgrave's ways, though Attercliffe, too, is limited by the torture of conscience.

> To end it by its own rules: no bloody good. She's right, you're wrong. You can't cure the pox by further whoring. Sparky died of those damned rules. And so did the other one.

Attercliffe's discovery during the play is that all war, not just a particular colonial war, is evil. The individual life and the individual death, contrary to the philosophy of Musgrave's perverted evangelism, are very much "material."

Musgrave has adopted without question the role of a military Messiah, bringing the word of the Lord by the doctrine of "measure for measure" as a panacea for ending his war. Obsessed with the brutality and inhumanity of a colonial war, Musgrave sees himself as an instrument of God sent to punish sinners. But he is tragically unaware that he has become an extension of the very thing he has come to defeat. As Attercliffe hysterically cries to him in Act Two, scene one, "We've come to stop it, not to start it . . ."

Confusing his motives and methods, Musgrave attempts to use the methods of the army in crushing a colonial rebellion to bring his message to the people at home. To appease his own conscience, he is willing to create a bloodbath by turning a gatling gun on a square full of civilians. This device simply restates in symbolic dramatic terms Musgrave's point that "their riots and our war are the same one corruption." And it makes clear that Musgrave's motive is to work the guilt for the slaughter of particular people back to the individual at home.

The tragic irony in the play, then, is that the Serjeant's method for curing the ills of the world is just as confused and evil as anyone else's despite the suggestion that his motivation was initially just. Though only Attercliffe sees all war as sin Sparky comes very, close in his halting suggestion of "paying through love," a New Testament conversion of Musgrave's measure for measure.

The women, of course, indict the tragic domestic results of war and poverty. Through his use of the folk songs and the choric function of Annie and Mrs. Hitchcock, Arden makes clear that the women condemn violence as a means of social protest or political change.

By means of carefully developed parallels between representatives of Management, Labour, Church, and State, *Serjeant Musgrave's Dance* becomes more than an anti-war document, for it depends on the coordinating function of the Bargee to establish its composite meaning. The Bargee is primarily a personification of crooked, distorted human nature! Crooked Old Joe Bludgeon tempts, is tempted, and finally leads the gothically grotesque dance around the centrepiece upon which Billy Hicks has been gruesomely resurrected. In his use of the Bargee as an "interlocutor" figure, Arden cleverly melds the classical and folk dramatic traditions. Old Joe Bludgeon simulates crowd reactions, recounts action off stage, adds a refrain dimension to the plot, and initiates action by playing on the weaknesses and desires of the Parson, the Mayor, Walsh, and the women.

The Bargee is then a mocking figure of intrigue reminiscent of the Vice figure of Renaissance morality plays. Symbolizing the potential evil of man's nature, he therefore extends the meaning of the play beyond conventional warfare, beyond the battle of the pitmen and the Establishment, to the violence, the heart of darkness, which may afflict all men. As Arden points out in his introduction to the Evergreen edition of the play, "The Bargee is something of a grotesque, a hunchback . . . very rapid in his movements, with a natural urge towards intrigue and mischief." That the Bargee represents the very thing Musgrave is battling against is made clear in Mrs. Hitchcock's speech in Act Three, scene two, when she exclaims despairingly, "All I can see is Crooked Joe Bludgeon having his dance out in the middle of fifty Dragoons!"

The Bargee's mockery of the main figures is designed to supply exposition, but his temptation of the Parson to use soldiers to control the colliers also suggests his similarity to the Vice tradition. He represents the self-seeking egotism of man which precipitates not only battles between coal-owners and pitmen, but colonial wars as well. The Bargee's temptation of Walsh, to use the gatling gun in forcing the mine owners to capitulate, establishes a clear parallel between Walsh and Musgrave. Walsh, the union leader, has been stung into action by injustice, but he is just as willing as Musgrave to allow the end to justify any means used.

Equally single-minded, he also wishes to force the whole of society to accept the rules for a single group, in fact to foster anarchy. Ironically, both these reform leaders live to see crooked human nature defeat their idealism. Walsh's capitulation and eventual joining of the beer dance therefore symbolize the triumph of egotistic self-interest.

The folk stylization of the play is integrated with the role of the Bargee to coordinate the action. The ballads themselves, of course, pick up major themes and sections of the action to counterpoint or restate them. This folk device, characteristic of traditional mummer's plays, the British music hall, or musical comedy in general, adds colour and variety to the play, despite the stark setting and the stripped stage. And ritual elements introduced into the play also increase the strength of its message. At the end of Act One, scene three, Musgrave delivers his stylized "Let the world dance" speech. In the following act, the Bargee acts as a refrain to Musgrave's address to the colliers. Earlier the incantatory delivery of the cemetery scene accentuates the red and black symbolism in the dialogue. Red is the color of the "blood-red rose flower" which is the central image of the play, and dominates the black and white of the winter coal town. As Arden explains, black is for death and the coal mines. Red is for murder and the red coat the collier puts on to escape his black.

The humour of the songs, as well as that of Sparky and the Bargee, extends the scope of the play and cushions its action. The songs and dialogue are so obviously reminiscent of Rudyard Kipling's *Barrack Room Ballads* as to give the impression of what Ronald Bryden calls "the black North and red-coated imperialism." The Bargee's song at the beginning of Act Three, for example, is typical of the play's satirical attacks upon the Establishment:

Hip hip hooroar
Hark hark the drums do bark
The Hungry Army's coming to town
Lead 'em in with a Holy Book
A golden chain and a scarlet gown.

And the chant-like delivery of the theme "A soldier's duty is a soldier's life" is heightened by punctuating drum rolls and the maniacal dance of Musgrave. The song he sings complements the theme of death and duty.

Though Arden is certainly criticizing the methods of British imperialism, the colour imagery of the play generates meaning beyond simple indictment of war in general or the British colonial Raj in particular. In fact the play envelopes all of its characters in its controlling irony and leaves none unscathed by its searching scrutiny of human nature.

At the level of political allegory, *Serjeant Musgrave's Dance* seems to play no favourites. Both Management and Labour become self-seeking and ludicrous in their struggle to advance an egocentric point of view. In the "angry" tradition of British drama, Arden moves from the principle of corrupt human nature to corrupt society. Motivated by the self-interest symbolized by the Bargee, workers and managers meet in conflict, so that "war" is presented as a basic fact of the human condition.

Like Jimmy Porter and the other prototypal anger figures of the sixties, Serjeant Musgrave's "hurt" has angered him into violence. Emotion by-passing reason, he lashes out at a system he cannot reconcile with the "materialities" of life as he experiences it.

The point has been made elsewhere that what began "with the power and sureness of a legend or ballad peters out in discussion." The judgement that the final working out of the moral is clouded and confused in the "apple orchard scene" between Musgrave and Mrs. Hitchcock seems a just criticism of *Serjeant Musgrave's Dance*. For the balletic quality of the play is lost here in a debate during which the audience cannot see the woods for the trees. The Christian Soldiers, confused and launched on a vendetta to clear mind and conscience, have ended lost in a trackless wood.

Though Eden's taint seems in the background of the apple orchard song at the end of the play, Arden's intention is unclear. Will the ritual gesture of self-sacrifice and the wildwood madness of Musgrave bear fruit? Will it be remembered? Probably not! For the implication of the play is that, when the "blood-dimmed tide is loosed," all the world goes wild-wood mad.

That violence begets only more violence is underscored by the central irony of the play—Sparky's accidental death. Again Attercliffe is the incidental cause and carries the taint of guilt despite his good intentions. Guilt by association, of course, is exactly what they have come to prove. Ironically, however, they prove it only on themselves. The villagers remain substantially untouched by their sacrificial gesture, forced into foolish acquiescence by economic circumstances and a solid ring of red coated dragoons.

Source: Barry Thome, "*Serjeant Musgrave's Dance :* Form and Meaning," in *Queen's Quarterly,* Vol. 78, 1971, pp. 567–71.

SOURCES

Billington, Michael. "Finney as Musgrave," in *Manchester Guardian Weekly,* June 3, 1984, p. 20.

"Black Jack's Prayer," in *Newsweek,* March 21, 1966, p. 98.

Brien, Alan. "Disease of Violence," in the *Spectator,* October 30, 1966.

Clurman, Harold. A review of *Sergeant Musgrave's Dance* in *The Nation,* March 28, 1966, p. 372.

Hewes, Henry. "Journey Into a North Wind," in *Saturday Review,* March 26, 1966, p. 45.

Kauffmann, Stanley. "Colicos in Title Role of John Arden's Play," in *The New York Times,* March 9, 1966, p. 44.

———. "The Art of John Arden," in *The New York Times,* March 20, 1966, section 2, p. 1.

Oliver, Edith. "Doleful Dance," in *The New Yorker,* March 19, 1966, p. 162-63.

Spurling, Hilary. "Royal Fortress," in the *Spectator,* December 17, 1965.

A review in *Time,* March 18, 1966, p. 80.

FURTHER READING

Arden, John. "John Arden," in *Contemporary Authors Autobiography Series,* Volume 4, Gale Research, 1986, pp. 29-47.
    This autobiographical essay reveals much about Arden's background, family, and childhood.

Page, Malcolm. *John Arden,* Twayne Publishers, 1984, 175 p.
    Full-length critical analyses of Arden's work, including *Serjeant Musgrave's Dance.*

Trussler, Simon. *John Arden,* Columbia University Press, 1973, 48 p.
    A critical overview of Arden's work, including *Serjeant Musgrave's Dance.*

Glossary of Literary Terms

A

Abstract: Used as a noun, the term refers to a short summary or outline of a longer work. As an adjective applied to writing or literary works, abstract refers to words or phrases that name things not knowable through the five senses. Examples of abstracts include the *Cliffs Notes* summaries of major literary works. Examples of abstract terms or concepts include "idea," "guilt" "honesty," and "loyalty."

Absurd, Theater of the: See *Theater of the Absurd*

Absurdism: See *Theater of the Absurd*

Act: A major section of a play. Acts are divided into varying numbers of shorter scenes. From ancient times to the nineteenth century plays were generally constructed of five acts, but modern works typically consist of one, two, or three acts. Examples of five-act plays include the works of Sophocles and Shakespeare, while the plays of Arthur Miller commonly have a three-act structure.

Acto: A one-act Chicano theater piece developed out of collective improvisation. *Actos* were performed by members of Luis Valdez's Teatro Campesino in California during the mid-1960s.

Aestheticism: A literary and artistic movement of the nineteenth century. Followers of the movement believed that art should not be mixed with social, political, or moral teaching. The statement "art for art's sake" is a good summary of aestheticism. The movement had its roots in France, but it gained widespread importance in England in the last half of the nineteenth century, where it helped change the Victorian practice of including moral lessons in literature. Oscar Wilde is one of the best-known "aesthetes" of the late nineteenth century.

Age of Johnson: The period in English literature between 1750 and 1798, named after the most prominent literary figure of the age, Samuel Johnson. Works written during this time are noted for their emphasis on "sensibility," or emotional quality. These works formed a transition between the rational works of the Age of Reason, or Neoclassical period, and the emphasis on individual feelings and responses of the Romantic period. Significant writers during the Age of Johnson included the novelists Ann Radcliffe and Henry Mackenzie, dramatists Richard Sheridan and Oliver Goldsmith, and poets William Collins and Thomas Gray. Also known as Age of Sensibility

Age of Reason: See *Neoclassicism*

Age of Sensibility: See *Age of Johnson*

Alexandrine Meter: See *Meter*

Allegory: A narrative technique in which characters representing things or abstract ideas are used to convey a message or teach a lesson. Allegory is typically used to teach moral, ethical, or religious lessons but is sometimes used for satiric or political purposes. Examples of allegorical works include Edmund Spenser's *The Faerie Queene* and John Bunyan's *The Pilgrim's Progress*.

Allusion: A reference to a familiar literary or historical person or event, used to make an idea more easily understood. For example, describing someone as a ''Romeo'' makes an allusion to William Shakespeare's famous young lover in *Romeo and Juliet*.

Amerind Literature: The writing and oral traditions of Native Americans. Native American literature was originally passed on by word of mouth, so it consisted largely of stories and events that were easily memorized. Amerind prose is often rhythmic like poetry because it was recited to the beat of a ceremonial drum. Examples of Amerind literature include the autobiographical *Black Elk Speaks,* the works of N. Scott Momaday, James Welch, and Craig Lee Strete, and the poetry of Luci Tapahonso.

Analogy: A comparison of two things made to explain something unfamiliar through its similarities to something familiar, or to prove one point based on the acceptedness of another. Similes and metaphors are types of analogies. Analogies often take the form of an extended simile, as in William Blake's aphorism: ''As the caterpillar chooses the fairest leaves to lay her eggs on, so the priest lays his curse on the fairest joys.''

Angry Young Men: A group of British writers of the 1950s whose work expressed bitterness and disillusionment with society. Common to their work is an anti-hero who rebels against a corrupt social order and strives for personal integrity. The term has been used to describe Kingsley Amis, John Osborne, Colin Wilson, John Wain, and others.

Antagonist: The major character in a narrative or drama who works against the hero or protagonist. An example of an evil antagonist is Richard Lovelace in Samuel Richardson's *Clarissa,* while a virtuous antagonist is Macduff in William Shakespeare's *Macbeth.*

Anthropomorphism: The presentation of animals or objects in human shape or with human characteristics. The term is derived from the Greek word for ''human form.'' The fables of Aesop, the animated films of Walt Disney, and Richard Adams's *Watership Down* feature anthropomorphic characters.

Anti-hero: A central character in a work of literature who lacks traditional heroic qualities such as courage, physical prowess, and fortitude. Anti-heros typically distrust conventional values and are unable to commit themselves to any ideals. They generally feel helpless in a world over which they have no control. Anti-heroes usually accept, and often celebrate, their positions as social outcasts. A well-known anti-hero is Yossarian in Joseph Heller's novel *Catch-22*.

Antimasque: See *Masque*

Antithesis: The antithesis of something is its direct opposite. In literature, the use of antithesis as a figure of speech results in two statements that show a contrast through the balancing of two opposite ideas. Technically, it is the second portion of the statement that is defined as the ''antithesis''; the first portion is the ''thesis.'' An example of antithesis is found in the following portion of Abraham Lincoln's ''Gettysburg Address''; notice the opposition between the verbs ''remember'' and ''forget'' and the phrases ''what we say'' and ''what they did'': ''The world will little note nor long remember what we say here, but it can never forget what they did here.''

Apocrypha: Writings tentatively attributed to an author but not proven or universally accepted to be their works. The term was originally applied to certain books of the Bible that were not considered inspired and so were not included in the ''sacred canon.'' Geoffrey Chaucer, William Shakespeare, Thomas Kyd, Thomas Middleton, and John Marston all have apocrypha. Apocryphal books of the Bible include the Old Testament's Book of Enoch and New Testament's Gospel of Peter.

Apollonian and Dionysian: The two impulses believed to guide authors of dramatic tragedy. The Apollonian impulse is named after Apollo, the Greek god of light and beauty and the symbol of intellectual order. The Dionysian impulse is named after Dionysus, the Greek god of wine and the symbol of the unrestrained forces of nature. The Apollonian impulse is to create a rational, harmonious world, while the Dionysian is to express the irrational forces of personality. Friedrich Nietzche uses these terms in *The Birth of Tragedy* to designate contrasting elements in Greek tragedy.

Apostrophe: A statement, question, or request addressed to an inanimate object or concept or to a nonexistent or absent person. Requests for inspiration from the muses in poetry are examples of apostrophe, as is Marc Antony's address to Caesar's corpse in William Shakespeare's *Julius Caesar*: ''O, pardon me, thou bleeding piece of earth, That I am meek and gentle with these butchers!... Woe to the hand that shed this costly blood!...''

Archetype: The word archetype is commonly used to describe an original pattern or model from which all other things of the same kind are made. This term was introduced to literary criticism from the psychology of Carl Jung. It expresses Jung's theory that behind every person's "unconscious," or repressed memories of the past, lies the "collective unconscious" of the human race: memories of the countless typical experiences of our ancestors. These memories are said to prompt illogical associations that trigger powerful emotions in the reader. Often, the emotional process is primitive, even primordial. Archetypes are the literary images that grow out of the "collective unconscious." They appear in literature as incidents and plots that repeat basic patterns of life. They may also appear as stereotyped characters. Examples of literary archetypes include themes such as birth and death and characters such as the Earth Mother.

Argument: The argument of a work is the author's subject matter or principal idea. Examples of defined "argument" portions of works include John Milton's *Arguments* to each of the books of *Paradise Lost* and the "Argument" to Robert Herrick's *Hesperides.*

Aristotelian Criticism: Specifically, the method of evaluating and analyzing tragedy formulated by the Greek philosopher Aristotle in his *Poetics.* More generally, the term indicates any form of criticism that follows Aristotle's views. Aristotelian criticism focuses on the form and logical structure of a work, apart from its historical or social context, in contrast to "Platonic Criticism," which stresses the usefulness of art. Adherents of New Criticism including John Crowe Ransom and Cleanth Brooks utilize and value the basic ideas of Aristotelian criticism for textual analysis.

Art for Art's Sake: See *Aestheticism*

Aside: A comment made by a stage performer that is intended to be heard by the audience but supposedly not by other characters. Eugene O'Neill's *Strange Interlude* is an extended use of the aside in modern theater.

Audience: The people for whom a piece of literature is written. Authors usually write with a certain audience in mind, for example, children, members of a religious or ethnic group, or colleagues in a professional field. The term "audience" also applies to the people who gather to see or hear any performance, including plays, poetry readings, speeches, and concerts. Jane Austen's parody of the gothic novel, *Northanger Abbey,* was originally intended for (and also pokes fun at) an audience of young and avid female gothic novel readers.

Avant-garde: A French term meaning "vanguard." It is used in literary criticism to describe new writing that rejects traditional approaches to literature in favor of innovations in style or content. Twentieth-century examples of the literary *avant-garde* include the Black Mountain School of poets, the Bloomsbury Group, and the Beat Movement.

B

Ballad: A short poem that tells a simple story and has a repeated refrain. Ballads were originally intended to be sung. Early ballads, known as folk ballads, were passed down through generations, so their authors are often unknown. Later ballads composed by known authors are called literary ballads. An example of an anonymous folk ballad is "Edward," which dates from the Middle Ages. Samuel Taylor Coleridge's "The Rime of the Ancient Mariner" and John Keats's "La Belle Dame sans Merci" are examples of literary ballads.

Baroque: A term used in literary criticism to describe literature that is complex or ornate in style or diction. Baroque works typically express tension, anxiety, and violent emotion. The term "Baroque Age" designates a period in Western European literature beginning in the late sixteenth century and ending about one hundred years later. Works of this period often mirror the qualities of works more generally associated with the label "baroque" and sometimes feature elaborate conceits. Examples of Baroque works include John Lyly's *Euphues: The Anatomy of Wit,* Luis de Gongora's *Soledads,* and William Shakespeare's *As You Like It.*

Baroque Age: See *Baroque*

Baroque Period: See *Baroque*

Beat Generation: See *Beat Movement*

Beat Movement: A period featuring a group of American poets and novelists of the 1950s and 1960s—including Jack Kerouac, Allen Ginsberg, Gregory Corso, William S. Burroughs, and Lawrence Ferlinghetti—who rejected established social and literary values. Using such techniques as stream of consciousness writing and jazz-influenced free verse and focusing on unusual or abnormal states of mind—generated by religious ecstasy or the use of drugs—the Beat writers aimed to create works that were unconventional in both form and subject matter. Kerouac's *On the Road* is perhaps the best-known example of a Beat Generation novel, and Ginsberg's *Howl* is a famous collection of Beat poetry.

Black Aesthetic Movement: A period of artistic and literary development among African Americans in the 1960s and early 1970s. This was the first major African-American artistic movement since the Harlem Renaissance and was closely paralleled by the civil rights and black power movements. The black aesthetic writers attempted to produce works of art that would be meaningful to the black masses. Key figures in black aesthetics included one of its founders, poet and playwright Amiri Baraka, formerly known as LeRoi Jones; poet and essayist Haki R. Madhubuti, formerly Don L. Lee; poet and playwright Sonia Sanchez; and dramatist Ed Bullins. Works representative of the Black Aesthetic Movement include Amiri Baraka's play *Dutchman,* a 1964 Obie award-winner; *Black Fire: An Anthology of Afro-American Writing,* edited by Baraka and playwright Larry Neal and published in 1968; and Sonia Sanchez's poetry collection *We a BaddDDD People,* published in 1970. Also known as Black Arts Movement.

Black Arts Movement: See *Black Aesthetic Movement*

Black Comedy: See *Black Humor*

Black Humor: Writing that places grotesque elements side by side with humorous ones in an attempt to shock the reader, forcing him or her to laugh at the horrifying reality of a disordered world. Joseph Heller's novel *Catch-22* is considered a superb example of the use of black humor. Other well-known authors who use black humor include Kurt Vonnegut, Edward Albee, Eugene Ionesco, and Harold Pinter. Also known as Black Comedy.

Blank Verse: Loosely, any unrhymed poetry, but more generally, unrhymed iambic pentameter verse (composed of lines of five two-syllable feet with the first syllable accented, the second unaccented). Blank verse has been used by poets since the Renaissance for its flexibility and its graceful, dignified tone. John Milton's *Paradise Lost* is in blank verse, as are most of William Shakespeare's plays.

Bloomsbury Group: A group of English writers, artists, and intellectuals who held informal artistic and philosophical discussions in Bloomsbury, a district of London, from around 1907 to the early 1930s. The Bloomsbury Group held no uniform philosophical beliefs but did commonly express an aversion to moral prudery and a desire for greater social tolerance. At various times the circle included Virginia Woolf, E. M. Forster, Clive Bell, Lytton Strachey, and John Maynard Keynes.

Bon Mot: A French term meaning "good word." A *bon mot* is a witty remark or clever observation. Charles Lamb and Oscar Wilde are celebrated for their witty *bon mots.* Two examples by Oscar Wilde stand out: (1) "All women become their mothers. That is their tragedy. No man does. That's his." (2) "A man cannot be too careful in the choice of his enemies."

Breath Verse: See *Projective Verse*

Burlesque: Any literary work that uses exaggeration to make its subject appear ridiculous, either by treating a trivial subject with profound seriousness or by treating a dignified subject frivolously. The word "burlesque" may also be used as an adjective, as in "burlesque show," to mean "striptease act." Examples of literary burlesque include the comedies of Aristophanes, Miguel de Cervantes's *Don Quixote,*, Samuel Butler's poem "Hudibras," and John Gay's play *The Beggar's Opera.*

C

Cadence: The natural rhythm of language caused by the alternation of accented and unaccented syllables. Much modern poetry—notably free verse—deliberately manipulates cadence to create complex rhythmic effects. James Macpherson's "Ossian poems" are richly cadenced, as is the poetry of the Symbolists, Walt Whitman, and Amy Lowell.

Caesura: A pause in a line of poetry, usually occurring near the middle. It typically corresponds to a break in the natural rhythm or sense of the line but is sometimes shifted to create special meanings or rhythmic effects. The opening line of Edgar Allan Poe's "The Raven" contains a caesura following "dreary": "Once upon a midnight dreary, while I pondered weak and weary...."

Canzone: A short Italian or Provencal lyric poem, commonly about love and often set to music. The *canzone* has no set form but typically contains five or six stanzas made up of seven to twenty lines of eleven syllables each. A shorter, five- to ten-line "envoy," or concluding stanza, completes the poem. Masters of the *canzone* form include

Petrarch, Dante Alighieri, Torquato Tasso, and Guido Cavalcanti.

Carpe Diem: A Latin term meaning "seize the day." This is a traditional theme of poetry, especially lyrics. A *carpe diem* poem advises the reader or the person it addresses to live for today and enjoy the pleasures of the moment. Two celebrated *carpe diem* poems are Andrew Marvell's "To His Coy Mistress" and Robert Herrick's poem beginning "Gather ye rosebuds while ye may. . . ."

Catharsis: The release or purging of unwanted emotions— specifically fear and pity—brought about by exposure to art. The term was first used by the Greek philosopher Aristotle in his *Poetics* to refer to the desired effect of tragedy on spectators. A famous example of catharsis is realized in Sophocles' *Oedipus Rex,* when Oedipus discovers that his wife, Jacosta, is his own mother and that the stranger he killed on the road was his own father.

Celtic Renaissance: A period of Irish literary and cultural history at the end of the nineteenth century. Followers of the movement aimed to create a romantic vision of Celtic myth and legend. The most significant works of the Celtic Renaissance typically present a dreamy, unreal world, usually in reaction against the reality of contemporary problems. William Butler Yeats's *The Wanderings of Oisin* is among the most significant works of the Celtic Renaissance. Also known as Celtic Twilight.

Celtic Twilight: See *Celtic Renaissance*

Character: Broadly speaking, a person in a literary work. The actions of characters are what constitute the plot of a story, novel, or poem. There are numerous types of characters, ranging from simple, stereotypical figures to intricate, multifaceted ones. In the techniques of anthropomorphism and personification, animals—and even places or things—can assume aspects of character. "Characterization" is the process by which an author creates vivid, believable characters in a work of art. This may be done in a variety of ways, including (1) direct description of the character by the narrator; (2) the direct presentation of the speech, thoughts, or actions of the character; and (3) the responses of other characters to the character. The term "character" also refers to a form originated by the ancient Greek writer Theophrastus that later became popular in the seventeenth and eighteenth centuries. It is a short essay or sketch of a person who prominently displays a specific attribute or quality, such as miserliness or ambition. Notable characters in literature include Oedipus Rex, Don Quixote de la Mancha, Macbeth, Candide, Hester Prynne, Ebenezer Scrooge, Huckleberry Finn, Jay Gatsby, Scarlett O'Hara, James Bond, and Kunta Kinte.

Characterization: See *Character*

Chorus: In ancient Greek drama, a group of actors who commented on and interpreted the unfolding action on the stage. Initially the chorus was a major component of the presentation, but over time it became less significant, with its numbers reduced and its role eventually limited to commentary between acts. By the sixteenth century the chorus—if employed at all—was typically a single person who provided a prologue and an epilogue and occasionally appeared between acts to introduce or underscore an important event. The chorus in William Shakespeare's *Henry V* functions in this way. Modern dramas rarely feature a chorus, but T. S. Eliot's *Murder in the Cathedral* and Arthur Miller's *A View from the Bridge* are notable exceptions. The Stage Manager in Thornton Wilder's *Our Town* performs a role similar to that of the chorus.

Chronicle: A record of events presented in chronological order. Although the scope and level of detail provided varies greatly among the chronicles surviving from ancient times, some, such as the *Anglo-Saxon Chronicle,* feature vivid descriptions and a lively recounting of events. During the Elizabethan Age, many dramas— appropriately called "chronicle plays"—were based on material from chronicles. Many of William Shakespeare's dramas of English history as well as Christopher Marlowe's *Edward II* are based in part on Raphael Holinshead's *Chronicles of England, Scotland, and Ireland.*

Classical: In its strictest definition in literary criticism, classicism refers to works of ancient Greek or Roman literature. The term may also be used to describe a literary work of recognized importance (a "classic") from any time period or literature that exhibits the traits of classicism. Classical authors from ancient Greek and Roman times include Juvenal and Homer. Examples of later works and authors now described as classical include French literature of the seventeenth century, Western novels of the nineteenth century, and American fiction of the mid-nineteenth century such as that written by James Fenimore Cooper and Mark Twain.

Classicism: A term used in literary criticism to describe critical doctrines that have their roots in ancient Greek and Roman literature, philosophy, and art. Works associated with classicism typically exhibit restraint on the part of the author, unity of design and purpose, clarity, simplicity, logical organization, and respect for tradition. Examples of literary classicism include Cicero's prose, the dramas of Pierre Corneille and Jean Racine, the poetry of John Dryden and Alexander Pope, and the writings of J. W. von Goethe, G. E. Lessing, and T. S. Eliot.

Climax: The turning point in a narrative, the moment when the conflict is at its most intense. Typically, the structure of stories, novels, and plays is one of rising action, in which tension builds to the climax, followed by falling action, in which tension lessens as the story moves to its conclusion. The climax in James Fenimore Cooper's *The Last of the Mohicans* occurs when Magua and his captive Cora are pursued to the edge of a cliff by Uncas. Magua kills Uncas but is subsequently killed by Hawkeye.

Colloquialism: A word, phrase, or form of pronunciation that is acceptable in casual conversation but not in formal, written communication. It is considered more acceptable than slang. An example of colloquialism can be found in Rudyard Kipling's *Barrack-room Ballads:* When 'Omer smote 'is bloomin' lyre He'd 'eard men sing by land and sea; An' what he thought 'e might require 'E went an' took—the same as me!

Comedy: One of two major types of drama, the other being tragedy. Its aim is to amuse, and it typically ends happily. Comedy assumes many forms, such as farce and burlesque, and uses a variety of techniques, from parody to satire. In a restricted sense the term comedy refers only to dramatic presentations, but in general usage it is commonly applied to nondramatic works as well. Examples of comedies range from the plays of Aristophanes, Terrence, and Plautus, Dante Alighieri's *The Divine Comedy,* Francois Rabelais's *Pantagruel* and *Gargantua,* and some of Geoffrey Chaucer's tales and William Shakespeare's plays to Noel Coward's play *Private Lives* and James Thurber's short story "The Secret Life of Walter Mitty."

Comedy of Manners: A play about the manners and conventions of an aristocratic, highly sophisticated society. The characters are usually types rather than individualized personalities, and plot is less important than atmosphere. Such plays were an important aspect of late seventeenth-century English comedy. The comedy of manners was revived in the eighteenth century by Oliver Goldsmith and Richard Brinsley Sheridan, enjoyed a second revival in the late nineteenth century, and has endured into the twentieth century. Examples of comedies of manners include William Congreve's *The Way of the World* in the late seventeenth century, Oliver Goldsmith's *She Stoops to Conquer* and Richard Brinsley Sheridan's *The School for Scandal* in the eighteenth century, Oscar Wilde's *The Importance of Being Earnest* in the nineteenth century, and W. Somerset Maugham's *The Circle* in the twentieth century.

Comic Relief: The use of humor to lighten the mood of a serious or tragic story, especially in plays. The technique is very common in Elizabethan works, and can be an integral part of the plot or simply a brief event designed to break the tension of the scene. The Gravediggers' scene in William Shakespeare's *Hamlet* is a frequently cited example of comic relief.

Commedia dell'arte: An Italian term meaning "the comedy of guilds" or "the comedy of professional actors." This form of dramatic comedy was popular in Italy during the sixteenth century. Actors were assigned stock roles (such as Pulcinella, the stupid servant, or Pantalone, the old merchant) and given a basic plot to follow, but all dialogue was improvised. The roles were rigidly typed and the plots were formulaic, usually revolving around young lovers who thwarted their elders and attained wealth and happiness. A rigid convention of the *commedia dell'arte* is the periodic intrusion of Harlequin, who interrupts the play with low buffoonery. Peppino de Filippo's *Metamorphoses of a Wandering Minstrel* gave modern audiences an idea of what *commedia dell'arte* may have been like. Various scenarios for *commedia dell'arte* were compiled in Petraccone's *La commedia dell'arte, storia, technica, scenari,* published in 1927.

Complaint: A lyric poem, popular in the Renaissance, in which the speaker expresses sorrow about his or her condition. Typically, the speaker's sadness is caused by an unresponsive lover, but some complaints cite other sources of unhappiness, such as poverty or fate. A commonly cited example is "A Complaint by Night of the Lover Not Beloved" by Henry Howard, Earl of Surrey. Thomas Sackville's "Complaint of Henry, Duke of Buckingham" traces the duke's unhappiness to his ruthless ambition.

Conceit: A clever and fanciful metaphor, usually expressed through elaborate and extended comparison, that presents a striking parallel between two seemingly dissimilar things—for example, elaborately comparing a beautiful woman to an object like a garden or the sun. The conceit was a popular device throughout the Elizabethan Age and Baroque Age and was the principal technique of the seventeenth-century English metaphysical poets. This usage of the word conceit is unrelated to the best-known definition of conceit as an arrogant attitude or behavior. The conceit figures prominently in the works of John Donne, Emily Dickinson, and T. S. Eliot.

Concrete: Concrete is the opposite of abstract, and refers to a thing that actually exists or a description that allows the reader to experience an object or concept with the senses. Henry David Thoreau's *Walden* contains much concrete description of nature and wildlife.

Concrete Poetry: Poetry in which visual elements play a large part in the poetic effect. Punctuation marks, letters, or words are arranged on a page to form a visual design: a cross, for example, or a bumblebee. Max Bill and Eugene Gomringer were among the early practitioners of concrete poetry; Haroldo de Campos and Augusto de Campos are among contemporary authors of concrete poetry.

Confessional Poetry: A form of poetry in which the poet reveals very personal, intimate, sometimes shocking information about himself or herself. Anne Sexton, Sylvia Plath, Robert Lowell, and John Berryman wrote poetry in the confessional vein.

Conflict: The conflict in a work of fiction is the issue to be resolved in the story. It usually occurs between two characters, the protagonist and the antagonist, or between the protagonist and society or the protagonist and himself or herself. Conflict in Theodore Dreiser's novel *Sister Carrie* comes as a result of urban society, while Jack London's short story "To Build a Fire" concerns the protagonist's battle against the cold and himself.

Connotation: The impression that a word gives beyond its defined meaning. Connotations may be universally understood or may be significant only to a certain group. Both "horse" and "steed" denote the same animal, but "steed" has a different connotation, deriving from the chivalrous or romantic narratives in which the word was once often used.

Consonance: Consonance occurs in poetry when words appearing at the ends of two or more verses have similar final consonant sounds but have final vowel sounds that differ, as with "stuff" and "off." Consonance is found in "The curfew tolls the knells of parting day" from Thomas Grey's "An Elegy Written in a Country Church Yard." Also known as Half Rhyme or Slant Rhyme.

Convention: Any widely accepted literary device, style, or form. A soliloquy, in which a character reveals to the audience his or her private thoughts, is an example of a dramatic convention.

Corrido: A Mexican ballad. Examples of *corridos* include "Muerte del afamado Bilito," "La voz de mi conciencia," "Lucio Perez," "La juida," and "Los presos."

Couplet: Two lines of poetry with the same rhyme and meter, often expressing a complete and self-contained thought. The following couplet is from Alexander Pope's "Elegy to the Memory of an Unfortunate Lady": 'Tis Use alone that sanctifies Expense, And Splendour borrows all her rays from Sense.

Criticism: The systematic study and evaluation of literary works, usually based on a specific method or set of principles. An important part of literary studies since ancient times, the practice of criticism has given rise to numerous theories, methods, and "schools," sometimes producing conflicting, even contradictory, interpretations of literature in general as well as of individual works. Even such basic issues as what constitutes a poem or a novel have been the subject of much criticism over the centuries. Seminal texts of literary criticism include Plato's *Republic*, Aristotle's *Poetics,* Sir Philip Sidney's *The Defence of Poesie,* John Dryden's *Of Dramatic Poesie,* and William Wordsworth's "Preface" to the second edition of his *Lyrical Ballads.* Contemporary schools of criticism include deconstruction, feminist, psychoanalytic, poststructuralist, new historicist, postcolonialist, and reader- response.

D

Dactyl: See *Foot*

Dadaism: A protest movement in art and literature founded by Tristan Tzara in 1916. Followers of the movement expressed their outrage at the destruction brought about by World War I by revolting against numerous forms of social convention. The Dadaists presented works marked by calculated madness and flamboyant nonsense. They stressed total freedom of expression, commonly through primitive displays of emotion and illogical, often senseless, poetry. The movement ended shortly after the war, when it was replaced by surrealism. Proponents of Dadaism include Andre Breton, Louis Aragon, Philippe Soupault, and Paul Eluard.

Decadent: See *Decadents*

Decadents: The followers of a nineteenth-century literary movement that had its beginnings in French aestheticism. Decadent literature displays a fascination with perverse and morbid states; a search for novelty and sensation—the "new thrill"; a preoccupation with mysticism; and a belief in the senselessness of human existence. The movement is closely associated with the doctrine Art for Art's Sake. The term "decadence" is sometimes used to denote a decline in the quality of art or literature following a period of greatness. Major French decadents are Charles Baudelaire and Arthur Rimbaud. English decadents include Oscar Wilde, Ernest Dowson, and Frank Harris.

Deconstruction: A method of literary criticism developed by Jacques Derrida and characterized by multiple conflicting interpretations of a given work. Deconstructionists consider the impact of the language of a work and suggest that the true meaning of the work is not necessarily the meaning that the author intended. Jacques Derrida's *De la grammatologie* is the seminal text on deconstructive strategies; among American practitioners of this method of criticism are Paul de Man and J. Hillis Miller.

Deduction: The process of reaching a conclusion through reasoning from general premises to a specific premise. An example of deduction is present in the following syllogism: Premise: All mammals are animals. Premise: All whales are mammals. Conclusion: Therefore, all whales are animals.

Denotation: The definition of a word, apart from the impressions or feelings it creates in the reader. The word "apartheid" denotes a political and economic policy of segregation by race, but its connotations— oppression, slavery, inequality—are numerous.

Denouement: A French word meaning "the unknotting." In literary criticism, it denotes the resolution of conflict in fiction or drama. The *denouement* follows the climax and provides an outcome to the primary plot situation as well as an explanation of secondary plot complications. The *denouement* often involves a character's recognition of his or her state of mind or moral condition. A well-known example of *denouement* is the last scene of the play *As You Like It* by William Shakespeare, in which couples are married, an evildoer repents, the identities of two disguised characters are revealed, and a ruler is restored to power. Also known as Falling Action.

Description: Descriptive writing is intended to allow a reader to picture the scene or setting in which the action of a story takes place. The form this description takes often evokes an intended emotional response—a dark, spooky graveyard will evoke fear, and a peaceful, sunny meadow will evoke calmness. An example of a descriptive story is Edgar Allan Poe's *Landor's Cottage,* which offers a detailed depiction of a New York country estate.

Detective Story: A narrative about the solution of a mystery or the identification of a criminal. The conventions of the detective story include the detective's scrupulous use of logic in solving the mystery; incompetent or ineffectual police; a suspect who appears guilty at first but is later proved innocent; and the detective's friend or confidant— often the narrator—whose slowness in interpreting clues emphasizes by contrast the detective's brilliance. Edgar Allan Poe's "Murders in the Rue Morgue" is commonly regarded as the earliest example of this type of story. With this work, Poe established many of the conventions of the detective story genre, which are still in practice. Other practitioners of this vast and extremely popular genre include Arthur Conan Doyle, Dashiell Hammett, and Agatha Christie.

Deus ex machina: A Latin term meaning "god out of a machine." In Greek drama, a god was often lowered onto the stage by a mechanism of some kind to rescue the hero or untangle the plot. By extension, the term refers to any artificial device or coincidence used to bring about a convenient and simple solution to a plot. This is a common device in melodramas and includes such fortunate circumstances as the sudden receipt of a legacy to save the family farm or a last-minute stay of execution. The *deus ex machina* invariably rewards the virtuous and punishes evildoers. Examples of *deus ex machina* include King Louis XIV in Jean-Baptiste Moliere's *Tartuffe* and Queen Victoria in *The Pirates of Penzance* by William Gilbert and Arthur Sullivan. Bertolt Brecht parodies the abuse of such devices in the conclusion of his *Threepenny Opera.*

Dialogue: In its widest sense, dialogue is simply conversation between people in a literary work; in its most restricted sense, it refers specifically to the speech of characters in a drama. As a specific literary genre, a "dialogue" is a composition in which characters debate an issue or idea. The Greek philosopher Plato frequently expounded his theories in the form of dialogues.

Diction: The selection and arrangement of words in a literary work. Either or both may vary depending on the desired effect. There are four general types of diction: "formal," used in scholarly or lofty writing; "informal," used in relaxed but educated conversation; "colloquial," used in everyday speech; and "slang," containing newly coined words and other terms not accepted in formal usage.

Didactic: A term used to describe works of literature that aim to teach some moral, religious, political, or practical lesson. Although didactic elements are often found in artistically pleasing works, the term "didactic" usually refers to literature in which the message is more important than the form. The term may also be used to criticize a work that the critic finds "overly didactic," that is, heavy-handed in its delivery of a lesson. Examples of didactic literature include John Bunyan's *Pilgrim's Progress,* Alexander Pope's *Essay on Criticism,* Jean-Jacques Rousseau's *Emile,* and Elizabeth Inchbald's *Simple Story.*

Dimeter: See *Meter*

Dionysian: See *Apollonian and Dionysian*

Discordia concours: A Latin phrase meaning "discord in harmony." The term was coined by the eighteenth-century English writer Samuel Johnson to describe "a combination of dissimilar images or discovery of occult resemblances in things apparently unlike." Johnson created the expression by reversing a phrase by the Latin poet Horace. The metaphysical poetry of John Donne, Richard Crashaw, Abraham Cowley, George Herbert, and Edward Taylor among others, contains many examples of *discordia concours.* In Donne's "A Valediction: Forbidding Mourning," the poet compares the union of himself with his lover to a draftsman's compass: If they be two, they are two so, As stiff twin compasses are two: Thy soul, the fixed foot, makes no show To move, but doth, if the other do; And though it in the center sit, Yet when the other far doth roam, It leans, and hearkens after it, And grows erect, as that comes home.

Dissonance: A combination of harsh or jarring sounds, especially in poetry. Although such combinations may be accidental, poets sometimes intentionally make them to achieve particular effects. Dissonance is also sometimes used to refer to close but not identical rhymes. When this is the case, the word functions as a synonym for consonance. Robert Browning, Gerard Manley Hopkins, and many other poets have made deliberate use of dissonance.

Doppelganger: A literary technique by which a character is duplicated (usually in the form of an alter ego, though sometimes as a ghostly counterpart) or divided into two distinct, usually opposite personalities. The use of this character device is widespread in nineteenth- and twentieth- century literature, and indicates a growing awareness among authors that the "self" is really a composite of many "selves." A well-known story containing a *doppelganger* character is Robert Louis Stevenson's *Dr. Jekyll and Mr. Hyde,* which dramatizes an internal struggle between good and evil. Also known as The Double.

Double Entendre: A corruption of a French phrase meaning "double meaning." The term is used to indicate a word or phrase that is deliberately ambiguous, especially when one of the meanings is risque or improper. An example of a *double entendre* is the Elizabethan usage of the verb "die," which refers both to death and to orgasm.

Double, The: See *Doppelganger*

Draft: Any preliminary version of a written work. An author may write dozens of drafts which are revised to form the final work, or he or she may write only one, with few or no revisions. Dorothy Parker's observation that "I can't write five words but that I change seven" humorously indicates the purpose of the draft.

Drama: In its widest sense, a drama is any work designed to be presented by actors on a stage. Similarly, "drama" denotes a broad literary genre that includes a variety of forms, from pageant and spectacle to tragedy and comedy, as well as countless types and subtypes. More commonly in modern usage, however, a drama is a work that treats serious subjects and themes but does not aim at the grandeur of tragedy. This use of the term originated with the eighteenth-century French writer Denis Diderot, who used the word *drame* to designate his plays about middle- class life; thus "drama" typically features characters of a less exalted stature than those of tragedy. Examples of classical dramas include Menander's comedy *Dyscolus* and Sophocles' tragedy *Oedipus Rex.* Contemporary dramas include Eugene O'Neill's *The Iceman Cometh,* Lillian Hellman's *Little Foxes,* and August Wilson's *Ma Rainey's Black Bottom.*

Dramatic Irony: Occurs when the audience of a play or the reader of a work of literature knows something that a character in the work itself does not know. The irony is in the contrast between the intended meaning of the statements or actions of a character and the additional information understood by the audience. A celebrated example of dramatic irony is in Act V of William Shakespeare's *Romeo and Juliet,* where two young lovers meet their end as a result of a tragic misunderstanding. Here, the audience has full knowledge that Juliet's apparent "death" is merely temporary; she will regain her senses when the mysterious "sleeping potion" she has taken wears off. But Romeo, mistaking Juliet's drug-induced trance for true death, kills himself in grief. Upon awakening, Juliet discovers Romeo's corpse and, in despair, slays herself.

Dramatic Monologue: See *Monologue*

Dramatic Poetry: Any lyric work that employs elements of drama such as dialogue, conflict, or characterization, but excluding works that are intended for stage presentation. A monologue is a form of dramatic poetry.

Dramatis Personae: The characters in a work of literature, particularly a drama. The list of characters printed before the main text of a play or in the program is the *dramatis personae.*

Dream Allegory: See *Dream Vision*

Dream Vision: A literary convention, chiefly of the Middle Ages. In a dream vision a story is presented as a literal dream of the narrator. This device was commonly used to teach moral and religious lessons. Important works of this type are *The Divine Comedy* by Dante Alighieri, *Piers Plowman* by William Langland, and *The Pilgrim's Progress* by John Bunyan. Also known as Dream Allegory.

Dystopia: An imaginary place in a work of fiction where the characters lead dehumanized, fearful lives. Jack London's *The Iron Heel,* Yevgeny Zamyatin's *My,* Aldous Huxley's *Brave New World,* George Orwell's *Nineteen Eighty-four,* and Margaret Atwood's *Handmaid's Tale* portray versions of dystopia.

E

Eclogue: In classical literature, a poem featuring rural themes and structured as a dialogue among shepherds. Eclogues often took specific poetic forms, such as elegies or love poems. Some were written as the soliloquy of a shepherd. In later centuries, "eclogue" came to refer to any poem that was in the pastoral tradition or that had a dialogue or monologue structure. A classical example of an eclogue is Virgil's *Eclogues,* also known as *Bucolics.* Giovanni Boccaccio, Edmund Spenser, Andrew Marvell, Jonathan Swift, and Louis MacNeice also wrote eclogues.

Edwardian: Describes cultural conventions identified with the period of the reign of Edward VII of England (1901-1910). Writers of the Edwardian Age typically displayed a strong reaction against the propriety and conservatism of the Victorian Age. Their work often exhibits distrust of authority in religion, politics, and art and expresses strong doubts about the soundness of conventional values. Writers of this era include George Bernard Shaw, H. G. Wells, and Joseph Conrad.

Edwardian Age: See *Edwardian*

Electra Complex: A daughter's amorous obsession with her father. The term Electra complex comes from the plays of Euripides and Sophocles entitled *Electra,* in which the character Electra drives her brother Orestes to kill their mother and her lover in revenge for the murder of their father.

Elegy: A lyric poem that laments the death of a person or the eventual death of all people. In a conventional elegy, set in a classical world, the poet and subject are spoken of as shepherds. In modern criticism, the word elegy is often used to refer to a poem that is melancholy or mournfully contemplative. John Milton's "Lycidas" and Percy Bysshe Shelley's "Adonais" are two examples of this form.

Elizabethan Age: A period of great economic growth, religious controversy, and nationalism closely associated with the reign of Elizabeth I of England (1558-1603). The Elizabethan Age is considered a part of the general renaissance—that is, the flowering of arts and literature—that took place in Europe during the fourteenth through sixteenth centuries. The era is considered the golden age of English literature. The most important dramas in English and a great deal of lyric poetry were produced during this period, and modern English criticism began around this time. The notable authors of the period—Philip Sidney, Edmund Spenser, Christopher Marlowe, William Shakespeare, Ben Jonson, Francis Bacon, and John Donne—are among the best in all of English literature.

Elizabethan Drama: English comic and tragic plays produced during the Renaissance, or more narrowly, those plays written during the last years of and few years after Queen Elizabeth's reign. William Shakespeare is considered an Elizabethan dramatist in the broader sense, although most of his work was produced during the reign of James I. Examples of Elizabethan comedies include John Lyly's *The Woman in the Moone,* Thomas Dekker's *The Roaring Girl, or, Moll Cut Purse,* and William Shakespeare's *Twelfth Night.* Examples of Elizabethan tragedies include William Shakespeare's *Antony and Cleopatra,* Thomas Kyd's *The Spanish Tragedy,* and John Webster's *The Tragedy of the Duchess of Malfi.*

Empathy: A sense of shared experience, including emotional and physical feelings, with someone or something other than oneself. Empathy is often used to describe the response of a reader to a literary character. An example of an empathic passage is William Shakespeare's description in his narrative poem *Venus and Adonis* of: the snail, whose tender horns being hit, Shrinks backward in his shelly cave with pain. Readers of Gerard Manley Hopkins's *The Windhover* may experience some of the physical sensations evoked in the description of the movement of the falcon.

English Sonnet: See *Sonnet*

Enjambment: The running over of the sense and structure of a line of verse or a couplet into the following verse or couplet. Andrew Marvell's "To His Coy Mistress" is structured as a series of enjambments, as in lines 11-12: "My vegetable love should grow/Vaster than empires and more slow."

Enlightenment, The: An eighteenth-century philosophical movement. It began in France but had a wide impact throughout Europe and America. Thinkers of the Enlightenment valued reason and believed that both the individual and society could achieve a state of perfection. Corresponding to this essentially humanist vision was a resistance to religious authority. Important figures of the Enlightenment were Denis Diderot and Voltaire in France, Edward Gibbon and David Hume in England, and Thomas Paine and Thomas Jefferson in the United States.

Epic: A long narrative poem about the adventures of a hero of great historic or legendary importance. The setting is vast and the action is often given cosmic significance through the intervention of supernatural forces such as gods, angels, or demons. Epics are typically written in a classical style of grand simplicity with elaborate metaphors and allusions that enhance the symbolic importance of a hero's adventures. Some well-known epics are Homer's *Iliad* and *Odyssey,* Virgil's *Aeneid,* and John Milton's *Paradise Lost.*

Epic Simile: See *Homeric Simile*

Epic Theater: A theory of theatrical presentation developed by twentieth-century German playwright Bertolt Brecht. Brecht created a type of drama that the audience could view with complete detachment. He used what he termed "alienation effects" to create an emotional distance between the audience and the action on stage. Among these effects are: short, self-contained scenes that keep the play from building to a cathartic climax; songs that comment on the action; and techniques of acting that prevent the actor from developing an emotional identity with his role. Besides the plays of Bertolt Brecht, other plays that utilize epic theater conventions include those of Georg Buchner, Frank Wedekind, Erwin Piscator, and Leopold Jessner.

Epigram: A saying that makes the speaker's point quickly and concisely. Samuel Taylor Coleridge wrote an epigram that neatly sums up the form: What is an Epigram? A Dwarfish whole, Its body brevity, and wit its soul.

Epilogue: A concluding statement or section of a literary work. In dramas, particularly those of the seventeenth and eighteenth centuries, the epilogue is a closing speech, often in verse, delivered by an actor at the end of a play and spoken directly to the audience. A famous epilogue is Puck's speech at the end of William Shakespeare's *A Midsummer Night's Dream.*

Epiphany: A sudden revelation of truth inspired by a seemingly trivial incident. The term was widely used by James Joyce in his critical writings, and the stories in Joyce's *Dubliners* are commonly called "epiphanies."

Episode: An incident that forms part of a story and is significantly related to it. Episodes may be either self-contained narratives or events that depend on a larger context for their sense and importance. Examples of episodes include the founding of Wilmington, Delaware in Charles Reade's *The Disinherited Heir* and the individual events comprising the picaresque novels and medieval romances.

Episodic Plot: See *Plot*

Epitaph: An inscription on a tomb or tombstone, or a verse written on the occasion of a person's death. Epitaphs may be serious or humorous. Dorothy Parker's epitaph reads, "I told you I was sick."

Epithalamion: A song or poem written to honor and commemorate a marriage ceremony. Famous examples include Edmund Spenser's

"Epithalamion" and e. e. cummings's "Epithalamion." Also spelled Epithalamium.

Epithalamium: See *Epithalamion*

Epithet: A word or phrase, often disparaging or abusive, that expresses a character trait of someone or something. "The Napoleon of crime" is an epithet applied to Professor Moriarty, arch-rival of Sherlock Holmes in Arthur Conan Doyle's series of detective stories.

Exempla: See *Exemplum*

Exemplum: A tale with a moral message. This form of literary sermonizing flourished during the Middle Ages, when *exempla* appeared in collections known as "example-books." The works of Geoffrey Chaucer are full of *exempla*.

Existentialism: A predominantly twentieth-century philosophy concerned with the nature and perception of human existence. There are two major strains of existentialist thought: atheistic and Christian. Followers of atheistic existentialism believe that the individual is alone in a godless universe and that the basic human condition is one of suffering and loneliness. Nevertheless, because there are no fixed values, individuals can create their own characters—indeed, they can shape themselves—through the exercise of free will. The atheistic strain culminates in and is popularly associated with the works of Jean-Paul Sartre. The Christian existentialists, on the other hand, believe that only in God may people find freedom from life's anguish. The two strains hold certain beliefs in common: that existence cannot be fully understood or described through empirical effort; that anguish is a universal element of life; that individuals must bear responsibility for their actions; and that there is no common standard of behavior or perception for religious and ethical matters. Existentialist thought figures prominently in the works of such authors as Eugene Ionesco, Franz Kafka, Fyodor Dostoyevsky, Simone de Beauvoir, Samuel Beckett, and Albert Camus.

Expatriates: See *Expatriatism*

Expatriatism: The practice of leaving one's country to live for an extended period in another country. Literary expatriates include English poets Percy Bysshe Shelley and John Keats in Italy, Polish novelist Joseph Conrad in England, American writers Richard Wright, James Baldwin, Gertrude Stein, and Ernest Hemingway in France, and Trinidadian author Neil Bissondath in Canada.

Exposition: Writing intended to explain the nature of an idea, thing, or theme. Expository writing is often combined with description, narration, or argument. In dramatic writing, the exposition is the introductory material which presents the characters, setting, and tone of the play. An example of dramatic exposition occurs in many nineteenth-century drawing-room comedies in which the butler and the maid open the play with relevant talk about their master and mistress; in composition, exposition relays factual information, as in encyclopedia entries.

Expressionism: An indistinct literary term, originally used to describe an early twentieth-century school of German painting. The term applies to almost any mode of unconventional, highly subjective writing that distorts reality in some way. Advocates of Expressionism include dramatists George Kaiser, Ernst Toller, Luigi Pirandello, Federico Garcia Lorca, Eugene O'Neill, and Elmer Rice; poets George Heym, Ernst Stadler, August Stramm, Gottfried Benn, and Georg Trakl; and novelists Franz Kafka and James Joyce.

Extended Monologue: See *Monologue*

F

Fable: A prose or verse narrative intended to convey a moral. Animals or inanimate objects with human characteristics often serve as characters in fables. A famous fable is Aesop's "The Tortoise and the Hare."

Fairy Tales: Short narratives featuring mythical beings such as fairies, elves, and sprites. These tales originally belonged to the folklore of a particular nation or region, such as those collected in Germany by Jacob and Wilhelm Grimm. Two other celebrated writers of fairy tales are Hans Christian Andersen and Rudyard Kipling.

Falling Action: See *Denouement*

Fantasy: A literary form related to mythology and folklore. Fantasy literature is typically set in nonexistent realms and features supernatural beings. Notable examples of fantasy literature are *The Lord of the Rings* by J. R. R. Tolkien and the Gormenghast trilogy by Mervyn Peake.

Farce: A type of comedy characterized by broad humor, outlandish incidents, and often vulgar subject matter. Much of the "comedy" in film and television could more accurately be described as farce.

Feet: See *Foot*

Feminine Rhyme: See *Rhyme*

Femme fatale: A French phrase with the literal translation "fatal woman." A *femme fatale* is a sensuous, alluring woman who often leads men into danger or trouble. A classic example of the *femme fatale* is the nameless character in Billy Wilder's *The Seven Year Itch,* portrayed by Marilyn Monroe in the film adaptation.

Fiction: Any story that is the product of imagination rather than a documentation of fact. characters and events in such narratives may be based in real life but their ultimate form and configuration is a creation of the author. Geoffrey Chaucer's *The Canterbury Tales,* Laurence Sterne's *Tristram Shandy,* and Margaret Mitchell's *Gone with the Wind* are examples of fiction.

Figurative Language: A technique in writing in which the author temporarily interrupts the order, construction, or meaning of the writing for a particular effect. This interruption takes the form of one or more figures of speech such as hyperbole, irony, or simile. Figurative language is the opposite of literal language, in which every word is truthful, accurate, and free of exaggeration or embellishment. Examples of figurative language are tropes such as metaphor and rhetorical figures such as apostrophe.

Figures of Speech: Writing that differs from customary conventions for construction, meaning, order, or significance for the purpose of a special meaning or effect. There are two major types of figures of speech: rhetorical figures, which do not make changes in the meaning of the words, and tropes, which do. Types of figures of speech include simile, hyperbole, alliteration, and pun, among many others.

Fin de siecle: A French term meaning "end of the century." The term is used to denote the last decade of the nineteenth century, a transition period when writers and other artists abandoned old conventions and looked for new techniques and objectives. Two writers commonly associated with the *fin de siecle* mindset are Oscar Wilde and George Bernard Shaw.

First Person: See *Point of View*

Flashback: A device used in literature to present action that occurred before the beginning of the story. Flashbacks are often introduced as the dreams or recollections of one or more characters. Flashback techniques are often used in films, where they are typically set off by a gradual changing of one picture to another.

Foil: A character in a work of literature whose physical or psychological qualities contrast strongly with, and therefore highlight, the corresponding qualities of another character. In his Sherlock Holmes stories, Arthur Conan Doyle portrayed Dr. Watson as a man of normal habits and intelligence, making him a foil for the eccentric and wonderfully perceptive Sherlock Holmes.

Folk Ballad: See *Ballad*

Folklore: Traditions and myths preserved in a culture or group of people. Typically, these are passed on by word of mouth in various forms—such as legends, songs, and proverbs— or preserved in customs and ceremonies. This term was first used by W. J. Thoms in 1846. Sir James Frazer's *The Golden Bough* is the record of English folklore; myths about the frontier and the Old South exemplify American folklore.

Folktale: A story originating in oral tradition. Folktales fall into a variety of categories, including legends, ghost stories, fairy tales, fables, and anecdotes based on historical figures and events. Examples of folktales include Giambattista Basile's *The Pentamerone,* which contains the tales of Puss in Boots, Rapunzel, Cinderella, and Beauty and the Beast, and Joel Chandler Harris's Uncle Remus stories, which represent transplanted African folktales and American tales about the characters Mike Fink, Johnny Appleseed, Paul Bunyan, and Pecos Bill.

Foot: The smallest unit of rhythm in a line of poetry. In English-language poetry, a foot is typically one accented syllable combined with one or two unaccented syllables. There are many different types of feet. When the accent is on the second syllable of a two syllable word (con- *tort*), the foot is an "iamb"; the reverse accentual pattern (*tor* -ture) is a "trochee." Other feet that commonly occur in poetry in English are "anapest", two unaccented syllables followed by an accented syllable as in inter-*cept*, and "dactyl", an accented syllable followed by two unaccented syllables as in *su*-i- cide.

Foreshadowing: A device used in literature to create expectation or to set up an explanation of later developments. In Charles Dickens's *Great Expectations,* the graveyard encounter at the beginning of the novel between Pip and the escaped convict Magwitch foreshadows the baleful atmosphere and events that comprise much of the narrative.

Form: The pattern or construction of a work which identifies its genre and distinguishes it from other genres. Examples of forms include the different genres, such as the lyric form or the short story form, and various patterns for poetry, such as the verse form or the stanza form.

Formalism: In literary criticism, the belief that literature should follow prescribed rules of construction, such as those that govern the sonnet form. Examples of formalism are found in the work of the New Critics and structuralists.

Fourteener Meter: See *Meter*

Free Verse: Poetry that lacks regular metrical and rhyme patterns but that tries to capture the cadences of everyday speech. The form allows a poet to exploit a variety of rhythmical effects within a single poem. Free-verse techniques have been widely used in the twentieth century by such writers as Ezra Pound, T. S. Eliot, Carl Sandburg, and William Carlos Williams. Also known as *Vers libre*.

Futurism: A flamboyant literary and artistic movement that developed in France, Italy, and Russia from 1908 through the 1920s. Futurist theater and poetry abandoned traditional literary forms. In their place, followers of the movement attempted to achieve total freedom of expression through bizarre imagery and deformed or newly invented words. The Futurists were self-consciously modern artists who attempted to incorporate the appearances and sounds of modern life into their work. Futurist writers include Filippo Tommaso Marinetti, Wyndham Lewis, Guillaume Apollinaire, Velimir Khlebnikov, and Vladimir Mayakovsky.

G

Genre: A category of literary work. In critical theory, genre may refer to both the content of a given work—tragedy, comedy, pastoral—and to its form, such as poetry, novel, or drama. This term also refers to types of popular literature, as in the genres of science fiction or the detective story.

Genteel Tradition: A term coined by critic George Santayana to describe the literary practice of certain late nineteenth- century American writers, especially New Englanders. Followers of the Genteel Tradition emphasized conventionality in social, religious, moral, and literary standards. Some of the best-known writers of the Genteel Tradition are R. H. Stoddard and Bayard Taylor.

Gilded Age: A period in American history during the 1870s characterized by political corruption and materialism. A number of important novels of social and political criticism were written during this time. Examples of Gilded Age literature include Henry Adams's *Democracy* and F. Marion Crawford's *An American Politician*.

Gothic: See *Gothicism*

Gothicism: In literary criticism, works characterized by a taste for the medieval or morbidly attractive. A gothic novel prominently features elements of horror, the supernatural, gloom, and violence: clanking chains, terror, charnel houses, ghosts, medieval castles, and mysteriously slamming doors. The term "gothic novel" is also applied to novels that lack elements of the traditional Gothic setting but that create a similar atmosphere of terror or dread. Mary Shelley's *Frankenstein* is perhaps the best-known English work of this kind.

Gothic Novel: See *Gothicism*

Great Chain of Being: The belief that all things and creatures in nature are organized in a hierarchy from inanimate objects at the bottom to God at the top. This system of belief was popular in the seventeenth and eighteenth centuries. A summary of the concept of the great chain of being can be found in the first epistle of Alexander Pope's *An Essay on Man,* and more recently in Arthur O. Lovejoy's *The Great Chain of Being: A Study of the History of an Idea.*

Grotesque: In literary criticism, the subject matter of a work or a style of expression characterized by exaggeration, deformity, freakishness, and disorder. The grotesque often includes an element of comic absurdity. Early examples of literary grotesque include Francois Rabelais's *Pantagruel* and *Gargantua* and Thomas Nashe's *The Unfortunate Traveller,* while more recent examples can be found in the works of Edgar Allan Poe, Evelyn Waugh, Eudora Welty, Flannery O'Connor, Eugene Ionesco, Gunter Grass, Thomas Mann, Mervyn Peake, and Joseph Heller, among many others.

H

Haiku: The shortest form of Japanese poetry, constructed in three lines of five, seven, and five syllables respectively. The message of a *haiku* poem usually centers on some aspect of spirituality and provokes an emotional response in the reader. Early masters of *haiku* include Basho, Buson,

Kobayashi Issa, and Masaoka Shiki. English writers of *haiku* include the Imagists, notably Ezra Pound, H. D., Amy Lowell, Carl Sandburg, and William Carlos Williams. Also known as *Hokku.*

Half Rhyme: See *Consonance*

Hamartia: In tragedy, the event or act that leads to the hero's or heroine's downfall. This term is often incorrectly used as a synonym for tragic flaw. In Richard Wright's *Native Son,* the act that seals Bigger Thomas's fate is his first impulsive murder.

Harlem Renaissance: The Harlem Renaissance of the 1920s is generally considered the first significant movement of black writers and artists in the United States. During this period, new and established black writers published more fiction and poetry than ever before, the first influential black literary journals were established, and black authors and artists received their first widespread recognition and serious critical appraisal. Among the major writers associated with this period are Claude McKay, Jean Toomer, Countee Cullen, Langston Hughes, Arna Bontemps, Nella Larsen, and Zora Neale Hurston. Works representative of the Harlem Renaissance include Arna Bontemps's poems "The Return" and "Golgotha Is a Mountain," Claude McKay's novel *Home to Harlem,* Nella Larsen's novel *Passing,* Langston Hughes's poem "The Negro Speaks of Rivers," and the journals *Crisis* and *Opportunity,* both founded during this period. Also known as Negro Renaissance and New Negro Movement.

Harlequin: A stock character of the *commedia dell'arte* who occasionally interrupted the action with silly antics. Harlequin first appeared on the English stage in John Day's *The Travailes of the Three English Brothers.* The San Francisco Mime Troupe is one of the few modern groups to adapt Harlequin to the needs of contemporary satire.

Hellenism: Imitation of ancient Greek thought or styles. Also, an approach to life that focuses on the growth and development of the intellect. "Hellenism" is sometimes used to refer to the belief that reason can be applied to examine all human experience. A cogent discussion of Hellenism can be found in Matthew Arnold's *Culture and Anarchy.*

Heptameter: See *Meter*

Hero/Heroine: The principal sympathetic character (male or female) in a literary work. Heroes and heroines typically exhibit admirable traits: idealism, courage, and integrity, for example. Famous heroes and heroines include Pip in Charles Dickens's *Great Expectations,* the anonymous narrator in Ralph Ellison's *Invisible Man,* and Sethe in Toni Morrison's *Beloved.*

Heroic Couplet: A rhyming couplet written in iambic pentameter (a verse with five iambic feet). The following lines by Alexander Pope are an example: "Truth guards the Poet, sanctifies the line,/ And makes Immortal, Verse as mean as mine."

Heroic Line: The meter and length of a line of verse in epic or heroic poetry. This varies by language and time period. For example, in English poetry, the heroic line is iambic pentameter (a verse with five iambic feet); in French, the alexandrine (a verse with six iambic feet); in classical literature, dactylic hexameter (a verse with six dactylic feet).

Heroine: See *Hero/Heroine*

Hexameter: See *Meter*

Historical Criticism: The study of a work based on its impact on the world of the time period in which it was written. Examples of postmodern historical criticism can be found in the work of Michel Foucault, Hayden White, Stephen Greenblatt, and Jonathan Goldberg.

Hokku: See *Haiku*

Holocaust: See *Holocaust Literature*

Holocaust Literature: Literature influenced by or written about the Holocaust of World War II. Such literature includes true stories of survival in concentration camps, escape, and life after the war, as well as fictional works and poetry. Representative works of Holocaust literature include Saul Bellow's *Mr. Sammler's Planet,* Anne Frank's *The Diary of a Young Girl,* Jerzy Kosinski's *The Painted Bird,* Arthur Miller's *Incident at Vichy,* Czeslaw Milosz's *Collected Poems,* William Styron's *Sophie's Choice,* and Art Spiegelman's *Maus.*

Homeric Simile: An elaborate, detailed comparison written as a simile many lines in length. An example of an epic simile from John Milton's *Paradise Lost* follows: Angel Forms, who lay entranced Thick as autumnal leaves that strow the brooks In Vallombrosa, where the Etrurian shades High over-arched embower; or scattered sedge Afloat, when with fierce winds Orion armed Hath vexed the Red-Sea coast, whose waves o'erthrew Busiris and his Memphian chivalry, While with perfidious hatred they pursued The sojourners of

Goshen, who beheld From the safe shore their floating carcasses And broken chariot-wheels. Also known as Epic Simile.

Horatian Satire: See *Satire*

Humanism: A philosophy that places faith in the dignity of humankind and rejects the medieval perception of the individual as a weak, fallen creature. "Humanists" typically believe in the perfectibility of human nature and view reason and education as the means to that end. Humanist thought is represented in the works of Marsilio Ficino, Ludovico Castelvetro, Edmund Spenser, John Milton, Dean John Colet, Desiderius Erasmus, John Dryden, Alexander Pope, Matthew Arnold, and Irving Babbitt.

Humors: Mentions of the humors refer to the ancient Greek theory that a person's health and personality were determined by the balance of four basic fluids in the body: blood, phlegm, yellow bile, and black bile. A dominance of any fluid would cause extremes in behavior. An excess of blood created a sanguine person who was joyful, aggressive, and passionate; a phlegmatic person was shy, fearful, and sluggish; too much yellow bile led to a choleric temperament characterized by impatience, anger, bitterness, and stubbornness; and excessive black bile created melancholy, a state of laziness, gluttony, and lack of motivation. Literary treatment of the humors is exemplified by several characters in Ben Jonson's plays *Every Man in His Humour* and *Every Man out of His Humour*. Also spelled Humours.

Humours: See *Humors*

Hyperbole: In literary criticism, deliberate exaggeration used to achieve an effect. In William Shakespeare's *Macbeth,* Lady Macbeth hyperbolizes when she says, "All the perfumes of Arabia could not sweeten this little hand."

I

Iamb: See *Foot*

Idiom: A word construction or verbal expression closely associated with a given language. For example, in colloquial English the construction "how come" can be used instead of "why" to introduce a question. Similarly, "a piece of cake" is sometimes used to describe a task that is easily done.

Image: A concrete representation of an object or sensory experience. Typically, such a representation helps evoke the feelings associated with the object or experience itself. Images are either "literal" or "figurative." Literal images are especially concrete and involve little or no extension of the obvious meaning of the words used to express them. Figurative images do not follow the literal meaning of the words exactly. Images in literature are usually visual, but the term "image" can also refer to the representation of any sensory experience. In his poem "The Shepherd's Hour," Paul Verlaine presents the following image: "The Moon is red through horizon's fog;/ In a dancing mist the hazy meadow sleeps." The first line is broadly literal, while the second line involves turns of meaning associated with dancing and sleeping.

Imagery: The array of images in a literary work. Also, figurative language. William Butler Yeats's "The Second Coming" offers a powerful image of encroaching anarchy: Turning and turning in the widening gyre The falcon cannot hear the falconer; Things fall apart. . . .

Imagism: An English and American poetry movement that flourished between 1908 and 1917. The Imagists used precise, clearly presented images in their works. They also used common, everyday speech and aimed for conciseness, concrete imagery, and the creation of new rhythms. Participants in the Imagist movement included Ezra Pound, H. D. (Hilda Doolittle), and Amy Lowell, among others.

In medias res: A Latin term meaning "in the middle of things." It refers to the technique of beginning a story at its midpoint and then using various flashback devices to reveal previous action. This technique originated in such epics as Virgil's *Aeneid.*

Induction: The process of reaching a conclusion by reasoning from specific premises to form a general premise. Also, an introductory portion of a work of literature, especially a play. Geoffrey Chaucer's "Prologue" to the *Canterbury Tales,* Thomas Sackville's "Induction" to *The Mirror of Magistrates,* and the opening scene in William Shakespeare's *The Taming of the Shrew* are examples of inductions to literary works.

Intentional Fallacy: The belief that judgments of a literary work based solely on an author's stated or implied intentions are false and misleading. Critics who believe in the concept of the intentional fallacy typically argue that the work itself is sufficient matter for interpretation, even though they may concede that an author's statement of purpose can be useful. Analysis of William Wordsworth's *Lyri-*

cal Ballads based on the observations about poetry he makes in his "Preface" to the second edition of that work is an example of the intentional fallacy.

Interior Monologue: A narrative technique in which characters' thoughts are revealed in a way that appears to be uncontrolled by the author. The interior monologue typically aims to reveal the inner self of a character. It portrays emotional experiences as they occur at both a conscious and unconscious level. images are often used to represent sensations or emotions. One of the best-known interior monologues in English is the Molly Bloom section at the close of James Joyce's *Ulysses.* The interior monologue is also common in the works of Virginia Woolf.

Internal Rhyme: Rhyme that occurs within a single line of verse. An example is in the opening line of Edgar Allan Poe's "The Raven": "Once upon a midnight dreary, while I pondered weak and weary." Here, "dreary" and "weary" make an internal rhyme.

Irish Literary Renaissance: A late nineteenth- and early twentieth-century movement in Irish literature. Members of the movement aimed to reduce the influence of British culture in Ireland and create an Irish national literature. William Butler Yeats, George Moore, and Sean O'Casey are three of the best-known figures of the movement.

Irony: In literary criticism, the effect of language in which the intended meaning is the opposite of what is stated. The title of Jonathan Swift's "A Modest Proposal" is ironic because what Swift proposes in this essay is cannibalism—hardly "modest."

Italian Sonnet: See *Sonnet*

J

Jacobean Age: The period of the reign of James I of England (1603-1625). The early literature of this period reflected the worldview of the Elizabethan Age, but a darker, more cynical attitude steadily grew in the art and literature of the Jacobean Age. This was an important time for English drama and poetry. Milestones include William Shakespeare's tragedies, tragi-comedies, and sonnets; Ben Jonson's various dramas; and John Donne's metaphysical poetry.

Jargon: Language that is used or understood only by a select group of people. Jargon may refer to terminology used in a certain profession, such as computer jargon, or it may refer to any nonsensical language that is not understood by most people. Literary examples of jargon are Francois Villon's *Ballades en jargon,* which is composed in the secret language of the *coquillards,* and Anthony Burgess's *A Clockwork Orange,* narrated in the fictional characters' language of "Nadsat."

Juvenalian Satire: See *Satire*

K

Knickerbocker Group: A somewhat indistinct group of New York writers of the first half of the nineteenth century. Members of the group were linked only by location and a common theme: New York life. Two famous members of the Knickerbocker Group were Washington Irving and William Cullen Bryant. The group's name derives from Irving's *Knickerbocker's History of New York.*

L

Lais: See *Lay*

Lay: A song or simple narrative poem. The form originated in medieval France. Early French *lais* were often based on the Celtic legends and other tales sung by Breton minstrels—thus the name of the "Breton lay." In fourteenth-century England, the term "lay" was used to describe short narratives written in imitation of the Breton lays. The most notable of these is Geoffrey Chaucer's "The Minstrel's Tale."

Leitmotiv: See *Motif*

Literal Language: An author uses literal language when he or she writes without exaggerating or embellishing the subject matter and without any tools of figurative language. To say "He ran very quickly down the street" is to use literal language, whereas to say "He ran like a hare down the street" would be using figurative language.

Literary Ballad: See *Ballad*

Literature: Literature is broadly defined as any written or spoken material, but the term most often refers to creative works. Literature includes poetry, drama, fiction, and many kinds of nonfiction writing, as well as oral, dramatic, and broadcast compositions not necessarily preserved in a written format, such as films and television programs.

Lost Generation: A term first used by Gertrude Stein to describe the post-World War I generation of American writers: men and women haunted by a sense of betrayal and emptiness brought about by the destructiveness of the war. The term is commonly applied to Hart Crane, Ernest Hemingway, F. Scott Fitzgerald, and others.

Lyric Poetry: A poem expressing the subjective feelings and personal emotions of the poet. Such poetry is melodic, since it was originally accompanied by a lyre in recitals. Most Western poetry in the twentieth century may be classified as lyrical. Examples of lyric poetry include A. E. Housman's elegy ''To an Athlete Dying Young,'' the odes of Pindar and Horace, Thomas Gray and William Collins, the sonnets of Sir Thomas Wyatt and Sir Philip Sidney, Elizabeth Barrett Browning and Rainer Maria Rilke, and a host of other forms in the poetry of William Blake and Christina Rossetti, among many others.

M

Mannerism: Exaggerated, artificial adherence to a literary manner or style. Also, a popular style of the visual arts of late sixteenth-century Europe that was marked by elongation of the human form and by intentional spatial distortion. Literary works that are self-consciously high-toned and artistic are often said to be ''mannered.'' Authors of such works include Henry James and Gertrude Stein.

Masculine Rhyme: See *Rhyme*

Masque: A lavish and elaborate form of entertainment, often performed in royal courts, that emphasizes song, dance, and costumery. The Renaissance form of the masque grew out of the spectacles of masked figures common in medieval England and Europe. The masque reached its peak of popularity and development in seventeenth-century England, during the reigns of James I and, especially, of Charles I. Ben Jonson, the most significant masque writer, also created the ''antimasque,'' which incorporates elements of humor and the grotesque into the traditional masque and achieved greater dramatic quality. Masque-like interludes appear in Edmund Spenser's *The Faerie Queene* and in William Shakespeare's *The Tempest*. One of the best-known English masques is John Milton's *Comus*.

Measure: The foot, verse, or time sequence used in a literary work, especially a poem. Measure is often used somewhat incorrectly as a synonym for meter.

Melodrama: A play in which the typical plot is a conflict between characters who personify extreme good and evil. Melodramas usually end happily and emphasize sensationalism. Other literary forms that use the same techniques are often labeled ''melodramatic.'' The term was formerly used to describe a combination of drama and music; as such, it was synonymous with ''opera.'' Augustin Daly's *Under the Gaslight* and Dion Boucicault's *The Octoroon, The Colleen Bawn,* and *The Poor of New York* are examples of melodramas. The most popular media for twentieth-century melodramas are motion pictures and television.

Metaphor: A figure of speech that expresses an idea through the image of another object. Metaphors suggest the essence of the first object by identifying it with certain qualities of the second object. An example is ''But soft, what light through yonder window breaks?/ It is the east, and Juliet is the sun'' in William Shakespeare's *Romeo and Juliet*. Here, Juliet, the first object, is identified with qualities of the second object, the sun.

Metaphysical Conceit: See *Conceit*

Metaphysical Poetry: The body of poetry produced by a group of seventeenth-century English writers called the ''Metaphysical Poets.'' The group includes John Donne and Andrew Marvell. The Metaphysical Poets made use of everyday speech, intellectual analysis, and unique imagery. They aimed to portray the ordinary conflicts and contradictions of life. Their poems often took the form of an argument, and many of them emphasize physical and religious love as well as the fleeting nature of life. Elaborate conceits are typical in metaphysical poetry. Marvell's ''To His Coy Mistress'' is a well-known example of a metaphysical poem.

Metaphysical Poets: See *Metaphysical Poetry*

Meter: In literary criticism, the repetition of sound patterns that creates a rhythm in poetry. The patterns are based on the number of syllables and the presence and absence of accents. The unit of rhythm in a line is called a foot. Types of meter are classified according to the number of feet in a line. These are the standard English lines: Monometer, one foot; Dimeter, two feet; Trimeter, three feet; Tetrameter, four feet; Pentameter, five feet; Hexameter, six feet (also called the Alexandrine); Heptameter, seven feet (also called the ''Fourteener'' when the feet are iambic). The most common English meter is the iambic pentameter, in which each line contains ten syllables, or five iambic feet, which individually are composed of an unstressed syllable followed by an accented syllable. Both of the following lines from Alfred, Lord Tennyson's

"Ulysses" are written in iambic pentameter: Made weak by time and fate, but strong in will To strive, to seek, to find, and not to yield.

Mise en scene: The costumes, scenery, and other properties of a drama. Herbert Beerbohm Tree was renowned for the elaborate *mises en scene* of his lavish Shakespearean productions at His Majesty's Theatre between 1897 and 1915.

Modernism: Modern literary practices. Also, the principles of a literary school that lasted from roughly the beginning of the twentieth century until the end of World War II. Modernism is defined by its rejection of the literary conventions of the nineteenth century and by its opposition to conventional morality, taste, traditions, and economic values. Many writers are associated with the concepts of Modernism, including Albert Camus, Marcel Proust, D. H. Lawrence, W. H. Auden, Ernest Hemingway, William Faulkner, William Butler Yeats, Thomas Mann, Tennessee Williams, Eugene O'Neill, and James Joyce.

Monologue: A composition, written or oral, by a single individual. More specifically, a speech given by a single individual in a drama or other public entertainment. It has no set length, although it is usually several or more lines long. An example of an "extended monologue"—that is, a monologue of great length and seriousness—occurs in the one-act, one-character play *The Stronger* by August Strindberg.

Monometer: See *Meter*

Mood: The prevailing emotions of a work or of the author in his or her creation of the work. The mood of a work is not always what might be expected based on its subject matter. The poem "Dover Beach" by Matthew Arnold offers examples of two different moods originating from the same experience: watching the ocean at night. The mood of the first three lines— The sea is calm tonight The tide is full, the moon lies fair Upon the straights. . . . is in sharp contrast to the mood of the last three lines— And we are here as on a darkling plain Swept with confused alarms of struggle and flight, Where ignorant armies clash by night.

Motif: A theme, character type, image, metaphor, or other verbal element that recurs throughout a single work of literature or occurs in a number of different works over a period of time. For example, the various manifestations of the color white in Herman Melville's *Moby Dick* is a "specific" *motif,* while the trials of star-crossed lovers is a "conventional" *motif* from the literature of all periods. Also known as *Motiv* or *Leitmotiv.*

Motiv: See *Motif*

Muckrakers: An early twentieth-century group of American writers. Typically, their works exposed the wrongdoings of big business and government in the United States. Upton Sinclair's *The Jungle* exemplifies the muckraking novel.

Muses: Nine Greek mythological goddesses, the daughters of Zeus and Mnemosyne (Memory). Each muse patronized a specific area of the liberal arts and sciences. Calliope presided over epic poetry, Clio over history, Erato over love poetry, Euterpe over music or lyric poetry, Melpomene over tragedy, Polyhymnia over hymns to the gods, Terpsichore over dance, Thalia over comedy, and Urania over astronomy. Poets and writers traditionally made appeals to the Muses for inspiration in their work. John Milton invokes the aid of a muse at the beginning of the first book of his *Paradise Lost:* Of Man's First disobedience, and the Fruit of the Forbidden Tree, whose mortal taste Brought Death into the World, and all our woe, With loss of Eden, till one greater Man Restore us, and regain the blissful Seat, Sing Heav'nly Muse, that on the secret top of Oreb, or of Sinai, didst inspire That Shepherd, who first taught the chosen Seed, In the Beginning how the Heav'ns and Earth Rose out of Chaos. . . .

Mystery: See *Suspense*

Myth: An anonymous tale emerging from the traditional beliefs of a culture or social unit. Myths use supernatural explanations for natural phenomena. They may also explain cosmic issues like creation and death. Collections of myths, known as mythologies, are common to all cultures and nations, but the best-known myths belong to the Norse, Roman, and Greek mythologies. A famous myth is the story of Arachne, an arrogant young girl who challenged a goddess, Athena, to a weaving contest; when the girl won, Athena was enraged and turned Arachne into a spider, thus explaining the existence of spiders.

N

Narration: The telling of a series of events, real or invented. A narration may be either a simple narrative, in which the events are recounted chronologically, or a narrative with a plot, in which the account is given in a style reflecting the author's artistic concept of the story. Narration is sometimes used as a synonym for "storyline." The recounting of scary stories around a campfire is a form of narration.

Narrative: A verse or prose accounting of an event or sequence of events, real or invented. The term is also used as an adjective in the sense "method of narration." For example, in literary criticism, the expression "narrative technique" usually refers to the way the author structures and presents his or her story. Narratives range from the shortest accounts of events, as in Julius Caesar's remark, "I came, I saw, I conquered," to the longest historical or biographical works, as in Edward Gibbon's *The Decline and Fall of the Roman Empire,* as well as diaries, travelogues, novels, ballads, epics, short stories, and other fictional forms.

Narrative Poetry: A nondramatic poem in which the author tells a story. Such poems may be of any length or level of complexity. Epics such as *Beowulf* and ballads are forms of narrative poetry.

Narrator: The teller of a story. The narrator may be the author or a character in the story through whom the author speaks. Huckleberry Finn is the narrator of Mark Twain's *The Adventures of Huckleberry Finn.*

Naturalism: A literary movement of the late nineteenth and early twentieth centuries. The movement's major theorist, French novelist Emile Zola, envisioned a type of fiction that would examine human life with the objectivity of scientific inquiry. The Naturalists typically viewed human beings as either the products of "biological determinism," ruled by hereditary instincts and engaged in an endless struggle for survival, or as the products of "socioeconomic determinism," ruled by social and economic forces beyond their control. In their works, the Naturalists generally ignored the highest levels of society and focused on degradation: poverty, alcoholism, prostitution, insanity, and disease. Naturalism influenced authors throughout the world, including Henrik Ibsen and Thomas Hardy. In the United States, in particular, Naturalism had a profound impact. Among the authors who embraced its principles are Theodore Dreiser, Eugene O'Neill, Stephen Crane, Jack London, and Frank Norris.

Negritude: A literary movement based on the concept of a shared cultural bond on the part of black Africans, wherever they may be in the world. It traces its origins to the former French colonies of Africa and the Caribbean. Negritude poets, novelists, and essayists generally stress four points in their writings: One, black alienation from traditional African culture can lead to feelings of inferiority. Two, European colonialism and Western education should be resisted. Three, black Africans should seek to affirm and define their own identity. Four, African culture can and should be reclaimed. Many Negritude writers also claim that blacks can make unique contributions to the world, based on a heightened appreciation of nature, rhythm, and human emotions—aspects of life they say are not so highly valued in the materialistic and rationalistic West. Examples of Negritude literature include the poetry of both Senegalese Leopold Senghor in *Hosties noires* and Martiniquais Aime-Fernand Cesaire in *Return to My Native Land.*

Negro Renaissance: See *Harlem Renaissance*

Neoclassical Period: See *Neoclassicism*

Neoclassicism: In literary criticism, this term refers to the revival of the attitudes and styles of expression of classical literature. It is generally used to describe a period in European history beginning in the late seventeenth century and lasting until about 1800. In its purest form, Neoclassicism marked a return to order, proportion, restraint, logic, accuracy, and decorum. In England, where Neoclassicism perhaps was most popular, it reflected the influence of seventeenth- century French writers, especially dramatists. Neoclassical writers typically reacted against the intensity and enthusiasm of the Renaissance period. They wrote works that appealed to the intellect, using elevated language and classical literary forms such as satire and the ode. Neoclassical works were often governed by the classical goal of instruction. English neoclassicists included Alexander Pope, Jonathan Swift, Joseph Addison, Sir Richard Steele, John Gay, and Matthew Prior; French neoclassicists included Pierre Corneille and Jean-Baptiste Moliere. Also known as Age of Reason.

Neoclassicists: See *Neoclassicism*

New Criticism: A movement in literary criticism, dating from the late 1920s, that stressed close textual analysis in the interpretation of works of literature. The New Critics saw little merit in historical and biographical analysis. Rather, they aimed to examine the text alone, free from the question of how external events—biographical or otherwise—may have helped shape it. This predominantly American school was named "New Criticism" by one of its practitioners, John Crowe Ransom. Other important New Critics included Allen Tate, R. P. Blackmur, Robert Penn Warren, and Cleanth Brooks.

New Negro Movement: See *Harlem Renaissance*

Noble Savage: The idea that primitive man is noble and good but becomes evil and corrupted as he becomes civilized. The concept of the noble savage originated in the Renaissance period but is more closely identified with such later writers as Jean-Jacques Rousseau and Aphra Behn. First described in John Dryden's play *The Conquest of Granada,* the noble savage is portrayed by the various Native Americans in James Fenimore Cooper's "Leatherstocking Tales," by Queequeg, Daggoo, and Tashtego in Herman Melville's *Moby Dick,* and by John the Savage in Aldous Huxley's *Brave New World.*

O

Objective Correlative: An outward set of objects, a situation, or a chain of events corresponding to an inward experience and evoking this experience in the reader. The term frequently appears in modern criticism in discussions of authors' intended effects on the emotional responses of readers. This term was originally used by T. S. Eliot in his 1919 essay "Hamlet."

Objectivity: A quality in writing characterized by the absence of the author's opinion or feeling about the subject matter. Objectivity is an important factor in criticism. The novels of Henry James and, to a certain extent, the poems of John Larkin demonstrate objectivity, and it is central to John Keats's concept of "negative capability." Critical and journalistic writing usually are or attempt to be objective.

Occasional Verse: poetry written on the occasion of a significant historical or personal event. *Vers de societe* is sometimes called occasional verse although it is of a less serious nature. Famous examples of occasional verse include Andrew Marvell's "Horatian Ode upon Cromwell's Return from England," Walt Whitman's "When Lilacs Last in the Dooryard Bloom'd"— written upon the death of Abraham Lincoln—and Edmund Spenser's commemoration of his wedding, "Epithalamion."

Octave: A poem or stanza composed of eight lines. The term octave most often represents the first eight lines of a Petrarchan sonnet. An example of an octave is taken from a translation of a Petrarchan sonnet by Sir Thomas Wyatt: The pillar perisht is whereto I leant, The strongest stay of mine unquiet mind; The like of it no man again can find, From East to West Still seeking though he went. To mind unhap! for hap away hath rent Of all my joy the very bark and rind; And I, alas, by chance am thus assigned Daily to mourn till death do it relent.

Ode: Name given to an extended lyric poem characterized by exalted emotion and dignified style. An ode usually concerns a single, serious theme. Most odes, but not all, are addressed to an object or individual. Odes are distinguished from other lyric poetic forms by their complex rhythmic and stanzaic patterns. An example of this form is John Keats's "Ode to a Nightingale."

Oedipus Complex: A son's amorous obsession with his mother. The phrase is derived from the story of the ancient Theban hero Oedipus, who unknowingly killed his father and married his mother. Literary occurrences of the Oedipus complex include Andre Gide's *Oedipe* and Jean Cocteau's *La Machine infernale,* as well as the most famous, Sophocles' *Oedipus Rex.*

Omniscience: See *Point of View*

Onomatopoeia: The use of words whose sounds express or suggest their meaning. In its simplest sense, onomatopoeia may be represented by words that mimic the sounds they denote such as "hiss" or "meow." At a more subtle level, the pattern and rhythm of sounds and rhymes of a line or poem may be onomatopoeic. A celebrated example of onomatopoeia is the repetition of the word "bells" in Edgar Allan Poe's poem "The Bells."

Opera: A type of stage performance, usually a drama, in which the dialogue is sung. Classic examples of opera include Giuseppi Verdi's *La traviata,* Giacomo Puccini's *La Boheme,* and Richard Wagner's *Tristan und Isolde.* Major twentieth- century contributors to the form include Richard Strauss and Alban Berg.

Operetta: A usually romantic comic opera. John Gay's *The Beggar's Opera,* Richard Sheridan's *The Duenna,* and numerous works by William Gilbert and Arthur Sullivan are examples of operettas.

Oral Tradition: See *Oral Transmission*

Oral Transmission: A process by which songs, ballads, folklore, and other material are transmitted by word of mouth. The tradition of oral transmission predates the written record systems of literate society. Oral transmission preserves material sometimes over generations, although often with variations. Memory plays a large part in the recitation and preservation of orally transmitted material. Breton lays, French *fabliaux,* national epics (including the Anglo- Saxon *Beowulf,* the Spanish *El Cid,* and the Finnish *Kalevala*), Native American myths and legends, and African folktales told by plantation slaves are examples of orally transmitted literature.

Oration: Formal speaking intended to motivate the listeners to some action or feeling. Such public speaking was much more common before the development of timely printed communication such as newspapers. Famous examples of oration include Abraham Lincoln's ''Gettysburg Address'' and Dr. Martin Luther King Jr.'s ''I Have a Dream'' speech.

Ottava Rima: An eight-line stanza of poetry composed in iambic pentameter (a five-foot line in which each foot consists of an unaccented syllable followed by an accented syllable), following the abababcc rhyme scheme. This form has been prominently used by such important English writers as Lord Byron, Henry Wadsworth Longfellow, and W. B. Yeats.

Oxymoron: A phrase combining two contradictory terms. Oxymorons may be intentional or unintentional. The following speech from William Shakespeare's *Romeo and Juliet* uses several oxymorons: Why, then, O brawling love! O loving hate! O anything, of nothing first create! O heavy lightness! serious vanity! Mis-shapen chaos of well-seeming forms! Feather of lead, bright smoke, cold fire, sick health! This love feel I, that feel no love in this.

P

Pantheism: The idea that all things are both a manifestation or revelation of God and a part of God at the same time. Pantheism was a common attitude in the early societies of Egypt, India, and Greece—the term derives from the Greek *pan* meaning ''all'' and *theos* meaning ''deity.'' It later became a significant part of the Christian faith. William Wordsworth and Ralph Waldo Emerson are among the many writers who have expressed the pantheistic attitude in their works.

Parable: A story intended to teach a moral lesson or answer an ethical question. In the West, the best examples of parables are those of Jesus Christ in the New Testament, notably ''The Prodigal Son,'' but parables also are used in Sufism, rabbinic literature, Hasidism, and Zen Buddhism.

Paradox: A statement that appears illogical or contradictory at first, but may actually point to an underlying truth. ''Less is more'' is an example of a paradox. Literary examples include Francis Bacon's statement, ''The most corrected copies are commonly the least correct,'' and ''All animals are equal, but some animals are more equal than others'' from George Orwell's *Animal Farm*.

Parallelism: A method of comparison of two ideas in which each is developed in the same grammatical structure. Ralph Waldo Emerson's ''Civilization'' contains this example of parallelism: Raphael paints wisdom; Handel sings it, Phidias carves it, Shakespeare writes it, Wren builds it, Columbus sails it, Luther preaches it, Washington arms it, Watt mechanizes it.

Parnassianism: A mid nineteenth-century movement in French literature. Followers of the movement stressed adherence to well-defined artistic forms as a reaction against the often chaotic expression of the artist's ego that dominated the work of the Romantics. The Parnassians also rejected the moral, ethical, and social themes exhibited in the works of French Romantics such as Victor Hugo. The aesthetic doctrines of the Parnassians strongly influenced the later symbolist and decadent movements. Members of the Parnassian school include Leconte de Lisle, Sully Prudhomme, Albert Glatigny, Francois Coppee, and Theodore de Banville.

Parody: In literary criticism, this term refers to an imitation of a serious literary work or the signature style of a particular author in a ridiculous manner. A typical parody adopts the style of the original and applies it to an inappropriate subject for humorous effect. Parody is a form of satire and could be considered the literary equivalent of a caricature or cartoon. Henry Fielding's *Shamela* is a parody of Samuel Richardson's *Pamela*.

Pastoral: A term derived from the Latin word ''pastor,'' meaning shepherd. A pastoral is a literary composition on a rural theme. The conventions of the pastoral were originated by the third-century Greek poet Theocritus, who wrote about the experiences, love affairs, and pastimes of Sicilian shepherds. In a pastoral, characters and language of a courtly nature are often placed in a simple setting. The term pastoral is also used to classify dramas, elegies, and lyrics that exhibit the use of country settings and shepherd characters. Percy Bysshe Shelley's ''Adonais'' and John Milton's ''Lycidas'' are two famous examples of pastorals.

Pastorela: The Spanish name for the shepherds play, a folk drama reenacted during the Christmas season. Examples of *pastorelas* include Gomez

Manrique's *Representacion del nacimiento* and the dramas of Lucas Fernandez and Juan del Encina.

Pathetic Fallacy: A term coined by English critic John Ruskin to identify writing that falsely endows nonhuman things with human intentions and feelings, such as "angry clouds" and "sad trees." The pathetic fallacy is a required convention in the classical poetic form of the pastoral elegy, and it is used in the modern poetry of T. S. Eliot, Ezra Pound, and the Imagists. Also known as Poetic Fallacy.

Pelado: Literally the "skinned one" or shirtless one, he was the stock underdog, sharp-witted picaresque character of Mexican vaudeville and tent shows. The *pelado* is found in such works as Don Catarino's *Los effectos de la crisis* and *Regreso a mi tierra.*

Pen Name: See *Pseudonym*

Pentameter: See *Meter*

Persona: A Latin term meaning "mask." *Personae* are the characters in a fictional work of literature. The *persona* generally functions as a mask through which the author tells a story in a voice other than his or her own. A *persona* is usually either a character in a story who acts as a narrator or an "implied author," a voice created by the author to act as the narrator for himself or herself. *Personae* include the narrator of Geoffrey Chaucer's *Canterbury Tales* and Marlow in Joseph Conrad's *Heart of Darkness.*

Personae: See *Persona*

Personal Point of View: See *Point of View*

Personification: A figure of speech that gives human qualities to abstract ideas, animals, and inanimate objects. William Shakespeare used personification in *Romeo and Juliet* in the lines "Arise, fair sun, and kill the envious moon,/ Who is already sick and pale with grief." Here, the moon is portrayed as being envious, sick, and pale with grief—all markedly human qualities. Also known as *Prosopopoeia.*

Petrarchan Sonnet: See *Sonnet*

Phenomenology: A method of literary criticism based on the belief that things have no existence outside of human consciousness or awareness. Proponents of this theory believe that art is a process that takes place in the mind of the observer as he or she contemplates an object rather than a quality of the object itself. Among phenomenological critics are Edmund Husserl, George Poulet, Marcel Raymond, and Roman Ingarden.

Picaresque Novel: Episodic fiction depicting the adventures of a roguish central character ("picaro" is Spanish for "rogue"). The picaresque hero is commonly a low-born but clever individual who wanders into and out of various affairs of love, danger, and farcical intrigue. These involvements may take place at all social levels and typically present a humorous and wide-ranging satire of a given society. Prominent examples of the picaresque novel are *Don Quixote* by Miguel de Cervantes, *Tom Jones* by Henry Fielding, and *Moll Flanders* by Daniel Defoe.

Plagiarism: Claiming another person's written material as one's own. Plagiarism can take the form of direct, word-for- word copying or the theft of the substance or idea of the work. A student who copies an encyclopedia entry and turns it in as a report for school is guilty of plagiarism.

Platonic Criticism: A form of criticism that stresses an artistic work's usefulness as an agent of social engineering rather than any quality or value of the work itself. Platonic criticism takes as its starting point the ancient Greek philosopher Plato's comments on art in his *Republic.*

Platonism: The embracing of the doctrines of the philosopher Plato, popular among the poets of the Renaissance and the Romantic period. Platonism is more flexible than Aristotelian Criticism and places more emphasis on the supernatural and unknown aspects of life. Platonism is expressed in the love poetry of the Renaissance, the fourth book of Baldassare Castiglione's *The Book of the Courtier,* and the poetry of William Blake, William Wordsworth, Percy Bysshe Shelley, Friedrich Holderlin, William Butler Yeats, and Wallace Stevens.

Play: See *Drama*

Plot: In literary criticism, this term refers to the pattern of events in a narrative or drama. In its simplest sense, the plot guides the author in composing the work and helps the reader follow the work. Typically, plots exhibit causality and unity and have a beginning, a middle, and an end. Sometimes, however, a plot may consist of a series of disconnected events, in which case it is known as an "episodic plot." In his *Aspects of the Novel,* E. M. Forster distinguishes between a story, defined as a "narrative of events arranged in their time- sequence," and plot, which organizes the events to a "sense of causality." This definition closely mirrors Aristotle's discussion of plot in his *Poetics*.

Poem: In its broadest sense, a composition utilizing rhyme, meter, concrete detail, and expressive language to create a literary experience with emotional and aesthetic appeal. Typical poems include sonnets, odes, elegies, *haiku,* ballads, and free verse.

Poet: An author who writes poetry or verse. The term is also used to refer to an artist or writer who has an exceptional gift for expression, imagination, and energy in the making of art in any form. Well-known poets include Horace, Basho, Sir Philip Sidney, Sir Edmund Spenser, John Donne, Andrew Marvell, Alexander Pope, Jonathan Swift, George Gordon, Lord Byron, John Keats, Christina Rossetti, W. H. Auden, Stevie Smith, and Sylvia Plath.

Poetic Fallacy: See *Pathetic Fallacy*

Poetic Justice: An outcome in a literary work, not necessarily a poem, in which the good are rewarded and the evil are punished, especially in ways that particularly fit their virtues or crimes. For example, a murderer may himself be murdered, or a thief will find himself penniless.

Poetic License: Distortions of fact and literary convention made by a writer—not always a poet—for the sake of the effect gained. Poetic license is closely related to the concept of "artistic freedom." An author exercises poetic license by saying that a pile of money "reaches as high as a mountain" when the pile is actually only a foot or two high.

Poetics: This term has two closely related meanings. It denotes (1) an aesthetic theory in literary criticism about the essence of poetry or (2) rules prescribing the proper methods, content, style, or diction of poetry. The term poetics may also refer to theories about literature in general, not just poetry.

Poetry: In its broadest sense, writing that aims to present ideas and evoke an emotional experience in the reader through the use of meter, imagery, connotative and concrete words, and a carefully constructed structure based on rhythmic patterns. Poetry typically relies on words and expressions that have several layers of meaning. It also makes use of the effects of regular rhythm on the ear and may make a strong appeal to the senses through the use of imagery. Edgar Allan Poe's "Annabel Lee" and Walt Whitman's *Leaves of Grass* are famous examples of poetry.

Point of View: The narrative perspective from which a literary work is presented to the reader. There are four traditional points of view. The "third person omniscient" gives the reader a "godlike" perspective, unrestricted by time or place, from which to see actions and look into the minds of characters. This allows the author to comment openly on characters and events in the work. The "third person" point of view presents the events of the story from outside of any single character's perception, much like the omniscient point of view, but the reader must understand the action as it takes place and without any special insight into characters' minds or motivations. The "first person" or "personal" point of view relates events as they are perceived by a single character. The main character "tells" the story and may offer opinions about the action and characters which differ from those of the author. Much less common than omniscient, third person, and first person is the "second person" point of view, wherein the author tells the story as if it is happening to the reader. James Thurber employs the omniscient point of view in his short story "The Secret Life of Walter Mitty." Ernest Hemingway's "A Clean, Well-Lighted Place" is a short story told from the third person point of view. Mark Twain's novel *Huck Finn* is presented from the first person viewpoint. Jay McInerney's *Bright Lights, Big City* is an example of a novel which uses the second person point of view.

Polemic: A work in which the author takes a stand on a controversial subject, such as abortion or religion. Such works are often extremely argumentative or provocative. Classic examples of polemics include John Milton's *Aeropagitica* and Thomas Paine's *The American Crisis.*

Pornography: Writing intended to provoke feelings of lust in the reader. Such works are often condemned by critics and teachers, but those which can be shown to have literary value are viewed less harshly. Literary works that have been described as pornographic include Ovid's *The Art of Love,* Margaret of Angouleme's *Heptameron,* John Cleland's *Memoirs of a Woman of Pleasure; or, the Life of Fanny Hill,* the anonymous *My Secret Life,* D. H. Lawrence's *Lady Chatterley's Lover,* and Vladimir Nabokov's *Lolita.*

Post-Aesthetic Movement: An artistic response made by African Americans to the black aesthetic movement of the 1960s and early '70s. Writers since that time have adopted a somewhat different tone in their work, with less emphasis placed on the disparity between black and white in the United States. In the words of post-aesthetic authors such as Toni Morrison, John Edgar Wideman, and Kristin Hunter, African Americans are portrayed as looking inward for answers to their own questions, rather than always looking to the outside world. Two well-known examples of works produced as part of the post-aesthetic movement are the Pulitzer Prize-winning novels *The Color Purple* by Alice Walker and *Beloved* by Toni Morrison.

Postmodernism: Writing from the 1960s forward characterized by experimentation and continuing to apply some of the fundamentals of modernism, which included existentialism and alienation. Postmodernists have gone a step further in the rejection of tradition begun with the modernists by also rejecting traditional forms, preferring the anti-novel over the novel and the anti-hero over the hero. Postmodern writers include Alain Robbe-Grillet, Thomas Pynchon, Margaret Drabble, John Fowles, Adolfo Bioy-Casares, and Gabriel Garcia Marquez.

Pre-Raphaelites: A circle of writers and artists in mid nineteenth-century England. Valuing the pre-Renaissance artistic qualities of religious symbolism, lavish pictorialism, and natural sensuousness, the Pre-Raphaelites cultivated a sense of mystery and melancholy that influenced later writers associated with the Symbolist and Decadent movements. The major members of the group include Dante Gabriel Rossetti, Christina Rossetti, Algernon Swinburne, and Walter Pater.

Primitivism: The belief that primitive peoples were nobler and less flawed than civilized peoples because they had not been subjected to the tainting influence of society. Examples of literature espousing primitivism include Aphra Behn's *Oroonoko: Or, The History of the Royal Slave,* Jean-Jacques Rousseau's *Julie ou la Nouvelle Heloise,* Oliver Goldsmith's *The Deserted Village,* the poems of Robert Burns, Herman Melville's stories *Typee, Omoo,* and *Mardi,* many poems of William Butler Yeats and Robert Frost, and William Golding's novel *Lord of the Flies.*

Projective Verse: A form of free verse in which the poet's breathing pattern determines the lines of the poem. Poets who advocate projective verse are against all formal structures in writing, including meter and form. Besides its creators, Robert Creeley, Robert Duncan, and Charles Olson, two other well-known projective verse poets are Denise Levertov and LeRoi Jones (Amiri Baraka). Also known as Breath Verse.

Prologue: An introductory section of a literary work. It often contains information establishing the situation of the characters or presents information about the setting, time period, or action. In drama, the prologue is spoken by a chorus or by one of the principal characters. In the "General Prologue" of *The Canterbury Tales,* Geoffrey Chaucer describes the main characters and establishes the setting and purpose of the work.

Prose: A literary medium that attempts to mirror the language of everyday speech. It is distinguished from poetry by its use of unmetered, unrhymed language consisting of logically related sentences. Prose is usually grouped into paragraphs that form a cohesive whole such as an essay or a novel. Recognized masters of English prose writing include Sir Thomas Malory, William Caxton, Raphael Holinshed, Joseph Addison, Mark Twain, and Ernest Hemingway.

Prosopopoeia: See *Personification*

Protagonist: The central character of a story who serves as a focus for its themes and incidents and as the principal rationale for its development. The protagonist is sometimes referred to in discussions of modern literature as the hero or anti-hero. Well-known protagonists are Hamlet in William Shakespeare's *Hamlet* and Jay Gatsby in F. Scott Fitzgerald's *The Great Gatsby.*

Protest Fiction: Protest fiction has as its primary purpose the protesting of some social injustice, such as racism or discrimination. One example of protest fiction is a series of five novels by Chester Himes, beginning in 1945 with *If He Hollers Let Him Go* and ending in 1955 with *The Primitive.* These works depict the destructive effects of race and gender stereotyping in the context of interracial relationships. Another African American author whose works often revolve around themes of social protest is John Oliver Killens. James Baldwin's essay "Everybody's Protest Novel" generated controversy by attacking the authors of protest fiction.

Proverb: A brief, sage saying that expresses a truth about life in a striking manner. "They are not all cooks who carry long knives" is an example of a proverb.

Pseudonym: A name assumed by a writer, most often intended to prevent his or her identification as the author of a work. Two or more authors may work together under one pseudonym, or an author may use a different name for each genre he or she publishes in. Some publishing companies maintain "house pseudonyms," under which any number of authors may write installations in a series. Some authors also choose a pseudonym over their real names the way an actor may use a stage name. Examples of pseudonyms (with the author's real name in parentheses) include Voltaire (Francois-Marie Arouet), Novalis (Friedrich von Hardenberg), Currer Bell (Charlotte Bronte), Ellis Bell (Emily Bronte), George Eliot (Maryann Evans), Honorio Bustos Donmecq (Adolfo Bioy-Casares and Jorge Luis Borges), and Richard Bachman (Stephen King).

Pun: A play on words that have similar sounds but different meanings. A serious example of the pun is from John Donne's "A Hymne to God the Father": Sweare by thyself, that at my death thy sonne Shall shine as he shines now, and hereto fore; And, having done that, Thou haste done; I fear no more.

Pure Poetry: poetry written without instructional intent or moral purpose that aims only to please a reader by its imagery or musical flow. The term pure poetry is used as the antonym of the term "didacticism." The poetry of Edgar Allan Poe, Stephane Mallarme, Paul Verlaine, Paul Valery, Juan Ramoz Jimenez, and Jorge Guillen offer examples of pure poetry.

Q

Quatrain: A four-line stanza of a poem or an entire poem consisting of four lines. The following quatrain is from Robert Herrick's "To Live Merrily, and to Trust to Good Verses": Round, round, the root do's run; And being ravisht thus, Come, I will drink a Tun To my *Propertius*.

R

Raisonneur: A character in a drama who functions as a spokesperson for the dramatist's views. The *raisonneur* typically observes the play without becoming central to its action. *Raisonneurs* were very common in plays of the nineteenth century.

Realism: A nineteenth-century European literary movement that sought to portray familiar characters, situations, and settings in a realistic manner. This was done primarily by using an objective narrative point of view and through the buildup of accurate detail. The standard for success of any realistic work depends on how faithfully it transfers common experience into fictional forms. The realistic method may be altered or extended, as in stream of consciousness writing, to record highly subjective experience. Seminal authors in the tradition of Realism include Honore de Balzac, Gustave Flaubert, and Henry James.

Refrain: A phrase repeated at intervals throughout a poem. A refrain may appear at the end of each stanza or at less regular intervals. It may be altered slightly at each appearance. Some refrains are nonsense expressions—as with "Nevermore" in Edgar Allan Poe's "The Raven"—that seem to take on a different significance with each use.

Renaissance: The period in European history that marked the end of the Middle Ages. It began in Italy in the late fourteenth century. In broad terms, it is usually seen as spanning the fourteenth, fifteenth, and sixteenth centuries, although it did not reach Great Britain, for example, until the 1480s or so. The Renaissance saw an awakening in almost every sphere of human activity, especially science, philosophy, and the arts. The period is best defined by the emergence of a general philosophy that emphasized the importance of the intellect, the individual, and world affairs. It contrasts strongly with the medieval worldview, characterized by the dominant concerns of faith, the social collective, and spiritual salvation. Prominent writers during the Renaissance include Niccolo Machiavelli and Baldassare Castiglione in Italy, Miguel de Cervantes and Lope de Vega in Spain, Jean Froissart and Francois Rabelais in France, Sir Thomas More and Sir Philip Sidney in England, and Desiderius Erasmus in Holland.

Repartee: Conversation featuring snappy retorts and witticisms. Masters of *repartee* include Sydney Smith, Charles Lamb, and Oscar Wilde. An example is recorded in the meeting of "Beau" Nash and John Wesley: Nash said, "I never make way for a fool," to which Wesley responded, "Don't you? I always do," and stepped aside.

Resolution: The portion of a story following the climax, in which the conflict is resolved. The resolution of Jane Austen's *Northanger Abbey* is neatly summed up in the following sentence: "Henry and Catherine were married, the bells rang and everybody smiled."

Restoration: See *Restoration Age*

Restoration Age: A period in English literature beginning with the crowning of Charles II in 1660 and running to about 1700. The era, which was characterized by a reaction against Puritanism, was the first great age of the comedy of manners. The finest literature of the era is typically witty and urbane, and often lewd. Prominent Restoration Age writers include William Congreve, Samuel Pepys, John Dryden, and John Milton.

Revenge Tragedy: A dramatic form popular during the Elizabethan Age, in which the protagonist, directed by the ghost of his murdered father or son, inflicts retaliation upon a powerful villain. Notable features of the revenge tragedy include violence, bizarre criminal acts, intrigue, insanity, a hesitant protagonist, and the use of soliloquy. Thomas Kyd's *Spanish Tragedy* is the first example of revenge tragedy in English, and William Shakespeare's *Hamlet* is perhaps the best. Extreme examples of revenge tragedy, such as John Webster's *The Duchess of Malfi,* are labeled "tragedies of blood." Also known as Tragedy of Blood.

Revista: The Spanish term for a vaudeville musical revue. Examples of *revistas* include Antonio Guzman Aguilera's *Mexico para los mexicanos,* Daniel Vanegas's *Maldito jazz,* and Don Catarino's *Whiskey, morfina y marihuana* and *El desterrado.*

Rhetoric: In literary criticism, this term denotes the art of ethical persuasion. In its strictest sense, rhetoric adheres to various principles developed since classical times for arranging facts and ideas in a clear, persuasive, appealing manner. The term is also used to refer to effective prose in general and theories of or methods for composing effective prose. Classical examples of rhetorics include *The Rhetoric of Aristotle,* Quintillian's *Institutio Oratoria,* and Cicero's *Ad Herennium.*

Rhetorical Question: A question intended to provoke thought, but not an expressed answer, in the reader. It is most commonly used in oratory and other persuasive genres. The following lines from Thomas Gray's "Elegy Written in a Country Churchyard" ask rhetorical questions: Can storied urn or animated bust Back to its mansion call the fleeting breath? Can Honour's voice provoke the silent dust, Or Flattery soothe the dull cold ear of Death?

Rhyme: When used as a noun in literary criticism, this term generally refers to a poem in which words sound identical or very similar and appear in parallel positions in two or more lines. Rhymes are classified into different types according to where they fall in a line or stanza or according to the degree of similarity they exhibit in their spellings and sounds. Some major types of rhyme are "masculine" rhyme, "feminine" rhyme, and "triple" rhyme. In a masculine rhyme, the rhyming sound falls in a single accented syllable, as with "heat" and "eat." Feminine rhyme is a rhyme of two syllables, one stressed and one unstressed, as with "merry" and "tarry." Triple rhyme matches the sound of the accented syllable and the two unaccented syllables that follow: "narrative" and "declarative." Robert Browning alternates feminine and masculine rhymes in his "Soliloquy of the Spanish Cloister": Gr-r-r—there go, my heart's abhorrence! Water your damned flower-pots, do! If hate killed men, Brother Lawrence, God's blood, would not mine kill you! What? Your myrtle-bush wants trimming? Oh, that rose has prior claims— Needs its leaden vase filled brimming? Hell dry you up with flames! Triple rhymes can be found in Thomas Hood's "Bridge of Sighs," George Gordon Byron's satirical verse, and Ogden Nash's comic poems.

Rhyme Royal: A stanza of seven lines composed in iambic pentameter and rhymed *ababbcc*. The name is said to be a tribute to King James I of Scotland, who made much use of the form in his poetry. Examples of rhyme royal include Geoffrey Chaucer's *The Parlement of Foules,* William Shakespeare's *The Rape of Lucrece,* William Morris's *The Early Paradise,* and John Masefield's *The Widow in the Bye Street.*

Rhyme Scheme: See *Rhyme*

Rhythm: A regular pattern of sound, time intervals, or events occurring in writing, most often and most discernably in poetry. Regular, reliable rhythm is known to be soothing to humans, while interrupted, unpredictable, or rapidly changing rhythm is disturbing. These effects are known to authors, who use them to produce a desired reaction in the reader. An example of a form of irregular rhythm is sprung rhythm poetry; quantitative verse, on the other hand, is very regular in its rhythm.

Rising Action: The part of a drama where the plot becomes increasingly complicated. Rising action leads up to the climax, or turning point, of a drama. The final "chase scene" of an action film is generally the rising action which culminates in the film's climax.

Rococo: A style of European architecture that flourished in the eighteenth century, especially in France. The most notable features of *rococo* are its extensive use of ornamentation and its themes of lightness, gaiety, and intimacy. In literary criticism, the term is often used disparagingly to refer to a decadent or over-ornamental style. Alexander Pope's "The Rape of the Lock" is an example of literary *rococo.*

Roman a clef: A French phrase meaning "novel with a key." It refers to a narrative in which real persons are portrayed under fictitious names. Jack Kerouac, for example, portrayed various real-life beat generation figures under fictitious names in his *On the Road.*

Romance: A broad term, usually denoting a narrative with exotic, exaggerated, often idealized characters, scenes, and themes. Nathaniel Hawthorne called his *The House of the Seven Gables* and *The Marble Faun* romances in order to distinguish them from clearly realistic works.

Romantic Age: See *Romanticism*

Romanticism: This term has two widely accepted meanings. In historical criticism, it refers to a European intellectual and artistic movement of the late eighteenth and early nineteenth centuries that sought greater freedom of personal expression than that allowed by the strict rules of literary form and logic of the eighteenth-century neoclassicists. The Romantics preferred emotional and imaginative expression to rational analysis. They considered the individual to be at the center of all experience and so placed him or her at the center of their art. The Romantics believed that the creative imagination reveals nobler truths—unique feelings and attitudes—than those that could be discovered by logic or by scientific examination. Both the natural world and the state of childhood were important sources for revelations of "eternal truths." "Romanticism" is also used as a general term to refer to a type of sensibility found in all periods of literary history and usually considered to be in opposition to the principles of classicism. In this sense, Romanticism signifies any work or philosophy in which the exotic or dreamlike figure strongly, or that is devoted to individualistic expression, self-analysis, or a pursuit of a higher realm of knowledge than can be discovered by human reason. Prominent Romantics include Jean-Jacques Rousseau, William Wordsworth, John Keats, Lord Byron, and Johann Wolfgang von Goethe.

Romantics: See *Romanticism*

Russian Symbolism: A Russian poetic movement, derived from French symbolism, that flourished between 1894 and 1910. While some Russian Symbolists continued in the French tradition, stressing aestheticism and the importance of suggestion above didactic intent, others saw their craft as a form of mystical worship, and themselves as mediators between the supernatural and the mundane. Russian symbolists include Aleksandr Blok, Vyacheslav Ivanovich Ivanov, Fyodor Sologub, Andrey Bely, Nikolay Gumilyov, and Vladimir Sergeyevich Solovyov.

S

Satire: A work that uses ridicule, humor, and wit to criticize and provoke change in human nature and institutions. There are two major types of satire: "formal" or "direct" satire speaks directly to the reader or to a character in the work; "indirect" satire relies upon the ridiculous behavior of its characters to make its point. Formal satire is further divided into two manners: the "Horatian," which ridicules gently, and the "Juvenalian," which derides its subjects harshly and bitterly. Voltaire's novella *Candide* is an indirect satire. Jonathan Swift's essay "A Modest Proposal" is a Juvenalian satire.

Scansion: The analysis or "scanning" of a poem to determine its meter and often its rhyme scheme. The most common system of scansion uses accents (slanted lines drawn above syllables) to show stressed syllables, breves (curved lines drawn above syllables) to show unstressed syllables, and vertical lines to separate each foot. In the first line of John Keats's *Endymion,* "A thing of beauty is a joy forever:" the word "thing," the first syllable of "beauty," the word "joy," and the second syllable of "forever" are stressed, while the words "A" and "of," the second syllable of "beauty," the word "a," and the first and third syllables of "forever" are unstressed. In the second line: "Its loveliness increases; it will never" a pair of vertical lines separate the foot ending with "increases" and the one beginning with "it."

Scene: A subdivision of an act of a drama, consisting of continuous action taking place at a single time and in a single location. The beginnings and endings of scenes may be indicated by clearing the stage of actors and props or by the entrances and exits of important characters. The first act of William Shakespeare's *Winter's Tale* is comprised of two scenes.

Science Fiction: A type of narrative about or based upon real or imagined scientific theories and technology. Science fiction is often peopled with alien creatures and set on other planets or in different dimensions. Karel Capek's *R.U.R.* is a major work of science fiction.

Second Person: See *Point of View*

Semiotics: The study of how literary forms and conventions affect the meaning of language. Semioticians include Ferdinand de Saussure, Charles Sanders Pierce, Claude Levi-Strauss, Jacques Lacan, Michel Foucault, Jacques Derrida, Roland Barthes, and Julia Kristeva.

Sestet: Any six-line poem or stanza. Examples of the sestet include the last six lines of the Petrarchan sonnet form, the stanza form of Robert Burns's "A Poet's Welcome to his love-begotten Daughter," and the sestina form in W. H. Auden's "Paysage Moralise."

Setting: The time, place, and culture in which the action of a narrative takes place. The elements of setting may include geographic location, characters' physical and mental environments, prevailing cultural attitudes, or the historical time in which the action takes place. Examples of settings include the romanticized Scotland in Sir Walter Scott's "Waverley" novels, the French provincial setting in Gustave Flaubert's *Madame Bovary,* the fictional Wessex country of Thomas Hardy's novels, and the small towns of southern Ontario in Alice Munro's short stories.

Shakespearean Sonnet: See *Sonnet*

Signifying Monkey: A popular trickster figure in black folklore, with hundreds of tales about this character documented since the 19th century. Henry Louis Gates Jr. examines the history of the signifying monkey in *The Signifying Monkey: Towards a Theory of Afro-American Literary Criticism,* published in 1988.

Simile: A comparison, usually using "like" or "as", of two essentially dissimilar things, as in "coffee as cold as ice" or "He sounded like a broken record." The title of Ernest Hemingway's "Hills Like White Elephants" contains a simile.

Slang: A type of informal verbal communication that is generally unacceptable for formal writing. Slang words and phrases are often colorful exaggerations used to emphasize the speaker's point; they may also be shortened versions of an often-used word or phrase. Examples of American slang from the 1990s include "yuppie" (an acronym for Young Urban Professional), "awesome" (for "excellent"), wired (for "nervous" or "excited"), and "chill out" (for relax).

Slant Rhyme: See *Consonance*

Slave Narrative: Autobiographical accounts of American slave life as told by escaped slaves. These works first appeared during the abolition movement of the 1830s through the 1850s. Olaudah Equiano's *The Interesting Narrative of Olaudah Equiano, or Gustavus Vassa, The African* and Harriet Ann Jacobs's *Incidents in the Life of a Slave Girl* are examples of the slave narrative.

Social Realism: See *Socialist Realism*

Socialist Realism: The Socialist Realism school of literary theory was proposed by Maxim Gorky and established as a dogma by the first Soviet Congress of Writers. It demanded adherence to a communist worldview in works of literature. Its doctrines required an objective viewpoint comprehensible to the working classes and themes of social struggle featuring strong proletarian heroes. A successful work of socialist realism is Nikolay Ostrovsky's *Kak zakalyalas stal* (*How the Steel Was Tempered*). Also known as Social Realism.

Soliloquy: A monologue in a drama used to give the audience information and to develop the speaker's character. It is typically a projection of the speaker's innermost thoughts. Usually delivered while the speaker is alone on stage, a soliloquy is intended to present an illusion of unspoken reflection. A celebrated soliloquy is Hamlet's "To be or not to be" speech in William Shakespeare's *Hamlet.*

Sonnet: A fourteen-line poem, usually composed in iambic pentameter, employing one of several rhyme schemes. There are three major types of sonnets, upon which all other variations of the form are based: the "Petrarchan" or "Italian" sonnet, the "Shakespearean" or "English" sonnet, and the "Spenserian" sonnet. A Petrarchan sonnet consists of an octave rhymed *abbaabba* and a "sestet" rhymed either *cdecde, cdccdc,* or *cdedce*. The octave poses a question or problem, relates a narrative, or puts forth a proposition; the sestet presents a solution to the problem, comments upon the narrative, or applies the proposition put forth in the octave. The Shakespearean sonnet is divided into three quatrains and a couplet rhymed *abab cdcd efef gg*. The couplet provides an epigrammatic comment on the narrative or problem put forth in the quatrains. The Spenserian sonnet uses three quatrains and a couplet like the Shakespearean, but links their three rhyme schemes in this way: *abab bcbc cdcd ee*. The Spenserian sonnet develops its theme in two parts like the Petrarchan, its final six lines resolving a problem, analyzing a narrative, or applying a proposition put forth in its first eight lines. Examples of sonnets can be found in Petrarch's *Canzoniere,* Edmund Spenser's *Amoretti,* Elizabeth Barrett

Browning's *Sonnets from the Portuguese,* Rainer Maria Rilke's *Sonnets to Orpheus,* and Adrienne Rich's poem "The Insusceptibles."

Spenserian Sonnet: See *Sonnet*

Spenserian Stanza: A nine-line stanza having eight verses in iambic pentameter, its ninth verse in iambic hexameter, and the rhyme scheme ababbcbcc. This stanza form was first used by Edmund Spenser in his allegorical poem *The Faerie Queene.*

Spondee: In poetry meter, a foot consisting of two long or stressed syllables occurring together. This form is quite rare in English verse, and is usually composed of two monosyllabic words. The first foot in the following line from Robert Burns's "Green Grow the Rashes" is an example of a spondee: Green grow the rashes, O

Sprung Rhythm: Versification using a specific number of accented syllables per line but disregarding the number of unaccented syllables that fall in each line, producing an irregular rhythm in the poem. Gerard Manley Hopkins, who coined the term "sprung rhythm," is the most notable practitioner of this technique.

Stanza: A subdivision of a poem consisting of lines grouped together, often in recurring patterns of rhyme, line length, and meter. Stanzas may also serve as units of thought in a poem much like paragraphs in prose. Examples of stanza forms include the quatrain, *terza rima, ottava rima,* Spenserian, and the so-called *In Memoriam* stanza from Alfred, Lord Tennyson's poem by that title. The following is an example of the latter form: Love is and was my lord and king, And in his presence I attend To hear the tidings of my friend, Which every hour his couriers bring.

Stereotype: A stereotype was originally the name for a duplication made during the printing process; this led to its modern definition as a person or thing that is (or is assumed to be) the same as all others of its type. Common stereotypical characters include the absent-minded professor, the nagging wife, the troublemaking teenager, and the kindhearted grandmother.

Stream of Consciousness: A narrative technique for rendering the inward experience of a character. This technique is designed to give the impression of an ever-changing series of thoughts, emotions, images, and memories in the spontaneous and seemingly illogical order that they occur in life. The textbook example of stream of consciousness is the last section of James Joyce's *Ulysses.*

Structuralism: A twentieth-century movement in literary criticism that examines how literary texts arrive at their meanings, rather than the meanings themselves. There are two major types of structuralist analysis: one examines the way patterns of linguistic structures unify a specific text and emphasize certain elements of that text, and the other interprets the way literary forms and conventions affect the meaning of language itself. Prominent structuralists include Michel Foucault, Roman Jakobson, and Roland Barthes.

Structure: The form taken by a piece of literature. The structure may be made obvious for ease of understanding, as in nonfiction works, or may obscured for artistic purposes, as in some poetry or seemingly "unstructured" prose. Examples of common literary structures include the plot of a narrative, the acts and scenes of a drama, and such poetic forms as the Shakespearean sonnet and the Pindaric ode.

Sturm und Drang: A German term meaning "storm and stress." It refers to a German literary movement of the 1770s and 1780s that reacted against the order and rationalism of the enlightenment, focusing instead on the intense experience of extraordinary individuals. Highly romantic, works of this movement, such as Johann Wolfgang von Goethe's *Gotz von Berlichingen,* are typified by realism, rebelliousness, and intense emotionalism.

Style: A writer's distinctive manner of arranging words to suit his or her ideas and purpose in writing. The unique imprint of the author's personality upon his or her writing, style is the product of an author's way of arranging ideas and his or her use of diction, different sentence structures, rhythm, figures of speech, rhetorical principles, and other elements of composition. Styles may be classified according to period (Metaphysical, Augustan, Georgian), individual authors (Chaucerian, Miltonic, Jamesian), level (grand, middle, low, plain), or language (scientific, expository, poetic, journalistic).

Subject: The person, event, or theme at the center of a work of literature. A work may have one or more subjects of each type, with shorter works tending to have fewer and longer works tending to have more. The subjects of James Baldwin's novel *Go Tell It on the Mountain* include the themes of father-son relationships, religious conversion, black life, and sexuality. The subjects of Anne Frank's

Diary of a Young Girl include Anne and her family members as well as World War II, the Holocaust, and the themes of war, isolation, injustice, and racism.

Subjectivity: Writing that expresses the author's personal feelings about his subject, and which may or may not include factual information about the subject. Subjectivity is demonstrated in James Joyce's *Portrait of the Artist as a Young Man,* Samuel Butler's *The Way of All Flesh,* and Thomas Wolfe's *Look Homeward, Angel.*

Subplot: A secondary story in a narrative. A subplot may serve as a motivating or complicating force for the main plot of the work, or it may provide emphasis for, or relief from, the main plot. The conflict between the Capulets and the Montagues in William Shakespeare's *Romeo and Juliet* is an example of a subplot.

Surrealism: A term introduced to criticism by Guillaume Apollinaire and later adopted by Andre Breton. It refers to a French literary and artistic movement founded in the 1920s. The Surrealists sought to express unconscious thoughts and feelings in their works. The best-known technique used for achieving this aim was automatic writing—transcriptions of spontaneous outpourings from the unconscious. The Surrealists proposed to unify the contrary levels of conscious and unconscious, dream and reality, objectivity and subjectivity into a new level of ''super-realism.'' Surrealism can be found in the poetry of Paul Eluard, Pierre Reverdy, and Louis Aragon, among others.

Suspense: A literary device in which the author maintains the audience's attention through the build-up of events, the outcome of which will soon be revealed. Suspense in William Shakespeare's *Hamlet* is sustained throughout by the question of whether or not the Prince will achieve what he has been instructed to do and of what he intends to do.

Syllogism: A method of presenting a logical argument. In its most basic form, the syllogism consists of a major premise, a minor premise, and a conclusion. An example of a syllogism is: Major premise: When it snows, the streets get wet. Minor premise: It is snowing. Conclusion: The streets are wet.

Symbol: Something that suggests or stands for something else without losing its original identity. In literature, symbols combine their literal meaning with the suggestion of an abstract concept. Literary symbols are of two types: those that carry complex associations of meaning no matter what their contexts, and those that derive their suggestive meaning from their functions in specific literary works. Examples of symbols are sunshine suggesting happiness, rain suggesting sorrow, and storm clouds suggesting despair.

Symbolism: This term has two widely accepted meanings. In historical criticism, it denotes an early modernist literary movement initiated in France during the nineteenth century that reacted against the prevailing standards of realism. Writers in this movement aimed to evoke, indirectly and symbolically, an order of being beyond the material world of the five senses. Poetic expression of personal emotion figured strongly in the movement, typically by means of a private set of symbols uniquely identifiable with the individual poet. The principal aim of the Symbolists was to express in words the highly complex feelings that grew out of everyday contact with the world. In a broader sense, the term ''symbolism'' refers to the use of one object to represent another. Early members of the Symbolist movement included the French authors Charles Baudelaire and Arthur Rimbaud; William Butler Yeats, James Joyce, and T. S. Eliot were influenced as the movement moved to Ireland, England, and the United States. Examples of the concept of symbolism include a flag that stands for a nation or movement, or an empty cupboard used to suggest hopelessness, poverty, and despair.

Symbolist: See *Symbolism*

Symbolist Movement: See *Symbolism*

Sympathetic Fallacy: See *Affective Fallacy*

T

Tale: A story told by a narrator with a simple plot and little character development. Tales are usually relatively short and often carry a simple message. Examples of tales can be found in the work of Rudyard Kipling, Somerset Maugham, Saki, Anton Chekhov, Guy de Maupassant, and Armistead Maupin.

Tall Tale: A humorous tale told in a straightforward, credible tone but relating absolutely impossible events or feats of the characters. Such tales were commonly told of frontier adventures during the settlement of the west in the United States. Tall tales have been spun around such legendary heroes as Mike Fink, Paul Bunyan, Davy Crockett, Johnny Appleseed, and Captain Stormalong as well as the real-life William F. Cody and Annie Oakley. Literary use of tall tales can be found in Washington Irving's *History of New York,* Mark Twain's *Life on the Mississippi,* and in the German R. F. Raspe's *Baron Munchausen's Narratives of His Marvellous Travels and Campaigns in Russia.*

Tanka: A form of Japanese poetry similar to *haiku.* A *tanka* is five lines long, with the lines containing five, seven, five, seven, and seven syllables respectively. Skilled *tanka* authors include Ishikawa Takuboku, Masaoka Shiki, Amy Lowell, and Adelaide Crapsey.

Teatro Grottesco: See *Theater of the Grotesque*

Terza Rima: A three-line stanza form in poetry in which the rhymes are made on the last word of each line in the following manner: the first and third lines of the first stanza, then the second line of the first stanza and the first and third lines of the second stanza, and so on with the middle line of any stanza rhyming with the first and third lines of the following stanza. An example of *terza rima* is Percy Bysshe Shelley's "The Triumph of Love": As in that trance of wondrous thought I lay This was the tenour of my waking dream. Methought I sate beside a public way Thick strewn with summer dust, and a great stream Of people there was hurrying to and fro Numerous as gnats upon the evening gleam,...

Tetrameter: See *Meter*

Textual Criticism: A branch of literary criticism that seeks to establish the authoritative text of a literary work. Textual critics typically compare all known manuscripts or printings of a single work in order to assess the meanings of differences and revisions. This procedure allows them to arrive at a definitive version that (supposedly) corresponds to the author's original intention. Textual criticism was applied during the Renaissance to salvage the classical texts of Greece and Rome, and modern works have been studied, for instance, to undo deliberate correction or censorship, as in the case of novels by Stephen Crane and Theodore Dreiser.

Theater of Cruelty: Term used to denote a group of theatrical techniques designed to eliminate the psychological and emotional distance between actors and audience. This concept, introduced in the 1930s in France, was intended to inspire a more intense theatrical experience than conventional theater allowed. The "cruelty" of this dramatic theory signified not sadism but heightened actor/audience involvement in the dramatic event. The theater of cruelty was theorized by Antonin Artaud in his *Le Theatre et son double* (*The Theatre and Its Double*), and also appears in the work of Jerzy Grotowski, Jean Genet, Jean Vilar, and Arthur Adamov, among others.

Theater of the Absurd: A post-World War II dramatic trend characterized by radical theatrical innovations. In works influenced by the Theater of the absurd, nontraditional, sometimes grotesque characterizations, plots, and stage sets reveal a meaningless universe in which human values are irrelevant. Existentialist themes of estrangement, absurdity, and futility link many of the works of this movement. The principal writers of the Theater of the Absurd are Samuel Beckett, Eugene Ionesco, Jean Genet, and Harold Pinter.

Theater of the Grotesque: An Italian theatrical movement characterized by plays written around the ironic and macabre aspects of daily life in the World War I era. Theater of the Grotesque was named after the play *The Mask and the Face* by Luigi Chiarelli, which was described as "a grotesque in three acts." The movement influenced the work of Italian dramatist Luigi Pirandello, author of *Right You Are, If You Think You Are.* Also known as *Teatro Grottesco.*

Theme: The main point of a work of literature. The term is used interchangeably with thesis. The theme of William Shakespeare's *Othello*—jealousy—is a common one.

Thesis: A thesis is both an essay and the point argued in the essay. Thesis novels and thesis plays share the quality of containing a thesis which is supported through the action of the story. A master's thesis and a doctoral dissertation are two theses required of graduate students.

Thesis Play: See *Thesis*

Three Unities: See *Unities*

Tone: The author's attitude toward his or her audience may be deduced from the tone of the work. A formal tone may create distance or convey politeness, while an informal tone may encourage a friendly, intimate, or intrusive feeling in the reader. The author's attitude toward his or her subject matter may also be deduced from the tone of the words he or she uses in discussing it. The tone of John F. Kennedy's speech which included the appeal to "ask not what your country can do for you" was intended to instill feelings of camaraderie and national pride in listeners.

Tragedy: A drama in prose or poetry about a noble, courageous hero of excellent character who, because of some tragic character flaw or *hamartia*, brings ruin upon him- or herself. Tragedy treats its subjects in a dignified and serious manner, using poetic language to help evoke pity and fear and bring about catharsis, a purging of these emotions. The tragic form was practiced extensively by the ancient Greeks. In the Middle Ages, when classical works were virtually unknown, tragedy came to denote any works about the fall of persons from exalted to low conditions due to any reason: fate, vice, weakness, etc. According to the classical definition of tragedy, such works present the "pathetic"—that which evokes pity—rather than the tragic. The classical form of tragedy was revived in the sixteenth century; it flourished especially on the Elizabethan stage. In modern times, dramatists have attempted to adapt the form to the needs of modern society by drawing their heroes from the ranks of ordinary men and women and defining the nobility of these heroes in terms of spirit rather than exalted social standing. The greatest classical example of tragedy is Sophocles' *Oedipus Rex.* The "pathetic" derivation is exemplified in "The Monk's Tale" in Geoffrey Chaucer's *Canterbury Tales.* Notable works produced during the sixteenth century revival include William Shakespeare's *Hamlet, Othello,* and *King Lear.* Modern dramatists working in the tragic tradition include Henrik Ibsen, Arthur Miller, and Eugene O'Neill.

Tragedy of Blood: See *Revenge Tragedy*

Tragic Flaw: In a tragedy, the quality within the hero or heroine which leads to his or her downfall. Examples of the tragic flaw include Othello's jealousy and Hamlet's indecisiveness, although most great tragedies defy such simple interpretation.

Transcendentalism: An American philosophical and religious movement, based in New England from around 1835 until the Civil War. Transcendentalism was a form of American romanticism that had its roots abroad in the works of Thomas Carlyle, Samuel Coleridge, and Johann Wolfgang von Goethe. The Transcendentalists stressed the importance of intuition and subjective experience in communication with God. They rejected religious dogma and texts in favor of mysticism and scientific naturalism. They pursued truths that lie beyond the "colorless" realms perceived by reason and the senses and were active social reformers in public education, women's rights, and the abolition of slavery. Prominent members of the group include Ralph Waldo Emerson and Henry David Thoreau.

Trickster: A character or figure common in Native American and African literature who uses his ingenuity to defeat enemies and escape difficult situations. Tricksters are most often animals, such as the spider, hare, or coyote, although they may take the form of humans as well. Examples of trickster tales include Thomas King's *A Coyote Columbus Story,* Ashley F. Bryan's *The Dancing Granny* and Ishmael Reed's *The Last Days of Louisiana Red.*

Trimeter: See *Meter*

Triple Rhyme: See *Rhyme*

Trochee: See *Foot*

U

Understatement: See *Irony*

Unities: Strict rules of dramatic structure, formulated by Italian and French critics of the Renaissance and based loosely on the principles of drama discussed by Aristotle in his *Poetics.* Foremost among these rules were the three unities of action, time, and place that compelled a dramatist to: (1) construct a single plot with a beginning, middle, and end that details the causal relationships of action and character; (2) restrict the action to the events of a single day; and (3) limit the scene to a single place or city. The unities were observed faithfully by continental European writers until the Romantic Age, but they were never regularly observed in English drama. Modern dramatists are typically more concerned with a unity of impression or emotional effect than with any of the classical unities. The unities are observed in Pierre Corneille's tragedy *Polyeuctes* and Jean-Baptiste Racine's *Phedre.* Also known as Three Unities.

Urban Realism: A branch of realist writing that attempts to accurately reflect the often harsh facts of modern urban existence. Some works by Stephen Crane, Theodore Dreiser, Charles Dickens, Fyodor Dostoyevsky, Emile Zola, Abraham Cahan, and Henry Fuller feature urban realism. Modern examples include Claude Brown's *Manchild in the Promised Land* and Ron Milner's *What the Wine Sellers Buy.*

Utopia: A fictional perfect place, such as "paradise" or "heaven." Early literary utopias were included in Plato's *Republic* and Sir Thomas More's

Utopia, while more modern utopias can be found in Samuel Butler's *Erewhon,* Theodor Herzka's *A Visit to Freeland,* and H. G. Wells' *A Modern Utopia.*

Utopian: See *Utopia*

Utopianism: See *Utopia*

V

Verisimilitude: Literally, the appearance of truth. In literary criticism, the term refers to aspects of a work of literature that seem true to the reader. Verisimilitude is achieved in the work of Honore de Balzac, Gustave Flaubert, and Henry James, among other late nineteenth-century realist writers.

Vers de societe: See *Occasional Verse*

Vers libre: See *Free Verse*

Verse: A line of metered language, a line of a poem, or any work written in verse. The following line of verse is from the epic poem *Don Juan* by Lord Byron: "My way is to begin with the beginning."

Versification: The writing of verse. Versification may also refer to the meter, rhyme, and other mechanical components of a poem. Composition of a "Roses are red, violets are blue" poem to suit an occasion is a common form of versification practiced by students.

Victorian: Refers broadly to the reign of Queen Victoria of England (1837-1901) and to anything with qualities typical of that era. For example, the qualities of smug narrowmindedness, bourgeois materialism, faith in social progress, and priggish morality are often considered Victorian. This stereotype is contradicted by such dramatic intellectual developments as the theories of Charles Darwin, Karl Marx, and Sigmund Freud (which stirred strong debates in England) and the critical attitudes of serious Victorian writers like Charles Dickens and George Eliot. In literature, the Victorian Period was the great age of the English novel, and the latter part of the era saw the rise of movements such as decadence and symbolism. Works of Victorian literature include the poetry of Robert Browning and Alfred, Lord Tennyson, the criticism of Matthew Arnold and John Ruskin, and the novels of Emily Bronte, William Makepeace Thackeray, and Thomas Hardy. Also known as Victorian Age and Victorian Period.

Victorian Age: See *Victorian*

Victorian Period: See *Victorian*

W

Weltanschauung: A German term referring to a person's worldview or philosophy. Examples of *weltanschauung* include Thomas Hardy's view of the human being as the victim of fate, destiny, or impersonal forces and circumstances, and the disillusioned and laconic cynicism expressed by such poets of the 1930s as W. H. Auden, Sir Stephen Spender, and Sir William Empson.

Weltschmerz: A German term meaning "world pain." It describes a sense of anguish about the nature of existence, usually associated with a melancholy, pessimistic attitude. *Weltschmerz* was expressed in England by George Gordon, Lord Byron in his *Manfred* and *Childe Harold's Pilgrimage,* in France by Viscount de Chateaubriand, Alfred de Vigny, and Alfred de Musset, in Russia by Aleksandr Pushkin and Mikhail Lermontov, in Poland by Juliusz Slowacki, and in America by Nathaniel Hawthorne.

Z

Zarzuela: A type of Spanish operetta. Writers of *zarzuelas* include Lope de Vega and Pedro Calderon.

Zeitgeist: A German term meaning "spirit of the time." It refers to the moral and intellectual trends of a given era. Examples of *zeitgeist* include the preoccupation with the more morbid aspects of dying and death in some Jacobean literature, especially in the works of dramatists Cyril Tourneur and John Webster, and the decadence of the French Symbolists.

Cumulative Author/Title Index

Anonymous
  Everyman: V7

A

Aeschylus
  Prometheus Bound: V5
Ajax (Sophocles): V8
Albee, Edward
  Three Tall Women: V8
  Who's Afraid of Virginia Woolf?: V3
  The Zoo Story: V2
The Alchemist (Jonson): V4
All My Sons (Miller): V8
American Buffalo (Mamet): V3
Angels in America (Kushner): V5
Anouilh, Jean
  Antigone: V9
Antigone (Anouilh): V9
Antigone (Sophocles): V1
Arcadia (Stoppard): V5
Arden, John
  Serjeant Musgrave's Dance: V9
Ayckbourn, Alan
  A Chorus of Disapproval: V7

B

The Bacchae (Euripides): V6
The Bald Soprano (Ionesco): V4
Baraka, Amiri
  Dutchman: V3
Barnes, Peter
  The Ruling Class: V6
Barrie, J(ames) M.
  Peter Pan: V7

Barry, Philip
  The Philadelphia Story: V9
The Basic Training of Pavlo Hummel (Rabe): V3
Beckett, Samuel
  Krapp's Last Tape: V7
  Waiting for Godot: V2
Behan, Brendan
  The Hostage: V7
The Birthday Party (Pinter): V5
Blood Relations (Pollock): V3
Blue Room (Hare): V7
Boesman & Lena (Fugard): V6
Bolt, Robert
  A Man for All Seasons: V2
Bond, Edward
  Lear: V3
  Saved: V8
Brecht, Bertolt
  The Good Person of Szechwan: V9
  Mother Courage and Her Children: V5
  The Threepenny Opera: V4
Brighton Beach Memoirs (Simon): V6
The Browning Version (Rattigan): V8
Buried Child (Shepard): V6
Burn This (Wilson): V4
Bus Stop (Inge): V8

C

Capek, Karel
  R.U.R.: V7
Carballido, Emilio
  I, Too, Speak of the Rose: V4

The Caretaker (Pinter): V7
Cat on a Hot Tin Roof (Williams): V3
The Chairs (Ionesco): V9
Chekhov, Anton
  The Cherry Orchard: V1
  Uncle Vanya: V5
The Cherry Orchard (Chekhov): V1
Children of a Lesser God (Medoff): V4
The Children's Hour (Hellman): V3
Childress, Alice
  Trouble in Mind: V8
  The Wedding Band: V2
A Chorus of Disapproval (Ayckbourn): V7
Christie, Agatha
  The Mousetrap: V2
Come Back, Little Sheba (Inge): V3
Coward, Noel
  Hay Fever: V6
  Private Lives: V3
Crimes of the Heart (Henley): V2
The Crucible (Miller): V3
Cyrano de Bergerac (Rostand): V1

D

Death and the Maiden (Dorfman): V4
Death of a Salesman (Miller): V1
Delaney, Shelagh
  A Taste of Honey: V7
Doctor Faustus (Marlowe): V1
A Doll's House (Ibsen): V1
Dorfman, Ariel
  Death and the Maiden: V4

Dutchman (Baraka): V3

E

Edward II (Marlowe): V5
Electra (Sophocles): V4
The Elephant Man (Pomerance): V9
Eliot, T. S.
   Murder in the Cathedral: V4
The Emperor Jones (O'Neill): V6
Entertaining Mr. Sloane (Orton): V3
Equus (Shaffer): V5
Euripides
   The Bacchae: V6
   Iphigenia in Taurus: V4
   Medea: V1
Everyman (): V7

F

Fences (Wilson): V3
Fiddler on the Roof (Stein): V7
Fierstein, Harvey
   Torch Song Trilogy: V6
Fool for Love (Shepard): V7
for colored girls who have considered suicide/when the rainbow is enuf (Shange): V2
Ford, John
   'Tis Pity She's a Whore: V7
The Foreigner (Shue): V7
The Front Page (Hecht and MacArthur): V9
Fugard, Athol
   Boesman & Lena: V6
   "Master Harold". . . and the Boys: V3
Fuller, Charles H.
   A Soldier's Play: V8
Funnyhouse of a Negro (Kennedy): V9

G

Garcia Lorca, Federico
   The House of Bernarda Alba: V4
The Ghost Sonata (Strindberg): V9
Gibson, William
   The Miracle Worker: V2
Glaspell, Susan
   Trifles: V8
The Glass Menagerie (Williams): V1
Glengarry Glen Ross (Mamet): V2
Goldsmith, Oliver
   She Stoops to Conquer: V1
The Good Person of Szechwan (Brecht): V9
Gorki, Maxim
   The Lower Depths: V9
Guare, John
   The House of Blue Leaves: V8

H

The Hairy Ape (O'Neill): V4
Hammerstein, Oscar
   The King and I: V1
Hansberry, Lorraine
   A Raisin in the Sun: V2
Hare, David
   Blue Room: V7
   Plenty: V4
Hart, Moss
   You Can't Take It with You: V1
Hay Fever (Coward): V6
Hedda Gabler (Ibsen): V6
The Heidi Chronicles (Wasserstein): V5
Hecht, Ben
   The Front Page: V9
Hellman, Lillian
   The Children's Hour: V3
   The Little Foxes: V1
Henley, Beth
   Crimes of the Heart: V2
Highway, Tomson
   The Rez Sisters: V2
The Homecoming (Pinter): V3
The Hostage (Behan): V7
Hot L Baltimore (Wilson): V9
The House of Bernarda Alba (Garcia Lorca): V4
The House of Blue Leaves (Guare): V8
Hughes, Langston
   Mule Bone: V6
Hurston, Zora Neale
   Mule Bone: V6

I

I, Too, Speak of the Rose (Carballido): V4
Ibsen, Henrik
   A Doll's House: V1
   Hedda Gabler: V6
   Peer Gynt: V8
The Iceman Cometh (O'Neill): V5
The Importance of Being Earnest (Wilde): V4
Inge, William
   Bus Stop: V8
   Come Back, Little Sheba: V3
   Picnic: V5
Inherit the Wind (Lawrence and Lee): V2
Ionesco, Eugène
   The Chairs: V9
Ionesco, Eugene
   The Bald Soprano: V4
Iphigenia in Taurus (Euripides): V4

J

Jarry, Alfred
   Ubu Roi: V8

Jesus Christ Superstar (Webber and Rice): V7
Jonson, Ben(jamin)
   The Alchemist: V4

K

Kaufman, George S.
   You Can't Take It with You: V1
Kennedy, Adrienne
   Funnyhouse of a Negro: V9
The King and I (Hammerstein and Rodgers): V1
Kopit, Arthur
   Oh Dad, Poor Dad, Mamma's Hung You in the Closet and I'm Feelin' So Sad: V7
Krapp's Last Tape (Beckett): V7
Kushner, Tony
   Angels in America: V5

L

Lady Windermere's Fan (Wilde): V9
Lawrence, Jerome
   Inherit the Wind: V2
Lear (Bond): V3
Lee, Robert E.
   Inherit the Wind: V2
The Little Foxes (Hellman): V1
Long Day's Journey into Night (O'Neill): V2
Look Back in Anger (Osborne): V4
The Lower Depths (Gorki): V9

M

MacArthur, Charles
   The Front Page: V9
Major Barbara (Shaw): V3
Mamet, David
   American Buffalo: V3
   Glengarry Glen Ross: V2
   Speed-the-Plow: V6
Man and Superman (Shaw): V6
A Man for All Seasons (Bolt): V2
Marat/Sade (Weiss): V3
Marlowe, Christopher
   Doctor Faustus: V1
   Edward II: V5
"Master Harold". . . and the Boys (Fugard): V3
McCullers, Carson
   The Member of the Wedding: V5
Medea (Euripides): V1
Medoff, Mark
   Children of a Lesser God: V4
The Member of the Wedding (McCullers): V5
Miller, Arthur
   All My Sons: V8
   The Crucible: V3
   Death of a Salesman: V1
The Miracle Worker (Gibson): V2

Miss Julie (Strindberg): V4
A Month in the Country
    (Turgenev): V6
Mother Courage and Her Children
    (Brecht): V5
Mourning Becomes Electra
    (O'Neill): V9
The Mousetrap (Christie): V2
Mule Bone (Hurston and
    Hughes): V6
Murder in the Cathedral (Eliot): V4

N

'night, Mother (Norman): V2
The Night of the Iguana
    (Williams): V7
No Exit (Sartre): V5
Norman, Marsha
    'night, Mother: V2

O

The Odd Couple (Simon): V2
Odets, Clifford
    Waiting for Lefty: V3
Oedipus Rex (Sophocles): V1
Oh Dad, Poor Dad, Mamma's Hung
    You in the Closet and I'm
    Feelin' So Sad (Kopit): V7
O'Neill, Eugene
    The Emperor Jones: V6
    The Hairy Ape: V4
    The Iceman Cometh: V5
    Long Day's Journey into
        Night: V2
    Mourning Becomes Electra: V9
Orton, Joe
    Entertaining Mr. Sloane: V3
    What the Butler Saw: V6
Osborne, John
    Look Back in Anger: V4
Our Town (Wilder): V1

P

Peer Gynt (Ibsen): V8
Peter Pan (Barrie): V7
The Philadelphia Story (Barry): V9
The Piano Lesson (Wilson): V7
Picnic (Inge): V5
Pinter, Harold
    The Birthday Party: V5
    The Caretaker: V7
    The Homecoming: V3
Pirandello, Luigi
    Right You Are, If You Think You
        Are: V9
    Six Characters in Search of an
        Author: V4
Plenty (Hare): V4
Pollock, Sharon
    Blood Relations: V3

Pomerance, Bernard
    The Elephant Man: V9
Private Lives (Coward): V3
Prometheus Bound (Aeschylus): V5
Pygmalion (Shaw): V1

R

R.U.R. (Capek): V7
Rabe, David
    The Basic Training of Pavlo
        Hummel: V3
    Streamers: V8
A Raisin in the Sun (Hansberry): V2
Rattigan, Terence
    The Browning Version: V8
The Real Thing (Stoppard): V8
The Rez Sisters (Highway): V2
Rice, Tim
    Jesus Christ Superstar: V7
Right You Are, If You Think You Are
    (Pirandello): V9
Rodgers, Richard
    The King and I: V1
Rosencrantz and Guildenstern Are
    Dead (Stoppard): V2
Rostand, Edmond
    Cyrano de Bergerac: V1
The Ruling Class (Barnes): V6

S

Salome (Wilde): V8
Sartre, Jean-Paul
    No Exit: V5
Saved (Bond): V8
School for Scandal (Sheridan): V4
Serjeant Musgrave's Dance
    (Arden): V9
Shaffer, Peter
    Equus: V5
Shange, Ntozake
    for colored girls who have
        considered suicide/when the
        rainbow is enuf: V2
Shaw, George Bernard
    Major Barbara: V3
    Man and Superman: V6
    Pygmalion: V1
She Stoops to Conquer
    (Goldsmith): V1
Shepard, Sam
    Buried Child: V6
    Fool for Love: V7
    True West: V3
Sheridan, Richard Brinsley
    School for Scandal: V4
Shue, Larry
    The Foreigner: V7
Simon, Neil
    Brighton Beach Memoirs: V6
    The Odd Couple: V2
Six Characters in Search of an
    Author (Pirandello): V4

The Skin of Our Teeth (Wilder): V4
Smith, Anna Deavere
    Twilight: Los Angeles, 1992: V2
A Soldier's Play (Fuller): V8
Sophocles
    Ajax: V8
    Antigone: V1
    Electra: V4
    Oedipus Rex: V1
Speed-the-Plow (Mamet): V6
Stein, Joseph
    Fiddler on the Roof: V7
Stoppard, Tom
    Arcadia: V5
    The Real Thing: V8
    Rosencrantz and Guildenstern Are
        Dead: V2
Streamers (Rabe): V8
A Streetcar Named Desire
    (Williams): V1
Strindberg, August
    The Ghost Sonata: V9
    Miss Julie: V4

T

A Taste of Honey (Delaney): V7
Three Tall Women (Albee): V8
The Threepenny Opera (Brecht): V4
'Tis Pity She's a Whore (Ford): V7
Torch Song Trilogy (Fierstein): V6
Trifles (Glaspell): V8
Trouble in Mind (Childress): V8
True West (Shepard): V3
Turgenev, Ivan
    A Month in the Country: V6
Twilight: Los Angeles, 1992
    (Smith): V2

U

Ubu Roi (Jarry): V8
Uncle Vanya (Chekhov): V5

V

Valdez, Luis
    Zoot Suit: V5
Vidal, Gore
    Visit to a Small Planet: V2
Visit to a Small Planet (Vidal): V2

W

Waiting for Godot (Beckett): V2
Waiting for Lefty (Odets): V3
Wasserstein, Wendy
    The Heidi Chronicles: V5
Webber, Andrew Lloyd
    Jesus Christ Superstar: V7
The Wedding Band (Childress): V2
Weiss, Peter
    Marat/Sade: V3
What the Butler Saw (Orton): V6

Who's Afraid of Virginia Woolf?
    (Albee): V3
Wilde, Oscar
    The Importance of Being
        Earnest: V4
    Lady Windermere's Fan: V9
    Salome: V8
Wilder, Thornton
    Our Town: V1
    The Skin of Our Teeth: V4

Williams, Tennessee
    Cat on a Hot Tin Roof: V3
    The Glass Menagerie: V1
    The Night of the Iguana: V7
    A Streetcar Named Desire: V1
Wilson, August
    Fences: V3
    The Piano Lesson: V7
Wilson, Lanford
    Burn This: V4

    Hot L Baltimore: V9

Y

You Can't Take It with You
    (Kaufman and Hart): V1

Z

The Zoo Story (Albee): V2
Zoot Suit (Valdez): V5

Nationality/Ethnicity Index

Anonymous
  Everyman: V7

African American

Baraka, Amiri
  Dutchman: V3
Childress, Alice
  Trouble in Mind: V8
  The Wedding Band: V2
Fuller, Charles H.
  A Soldier's Play: V8
Hansberry, Lorraine
  A Raisin in the Sun: V2
Hughes, Langston
  Mule Bone: V6
Hurston, Zora Neale
  Mule Bone: V6
Kennedy, Adrienne
  Funnyhouse of a Negro: V9
Shange, Ntozake
  for colored girls who have considered suicide/when the rainbow is enuf: V2
Smith, Anna Deavere
  Twilight: Los Angeles, 1992: V2
Wilson, August
  Fences: V3
  The Piano Lesson: V7

American

Albee, Edward
  Three Tall Women: V8
  Who's Afraid of Virginia Woolf?: V3
  The Zoo Story: V2
Baraka, Amiri
  Dutchman: V3
Barry, Philip
  The Philadelphia Story: V9
Childress, Alice
  Trouble in Mind: V8
  The Wedding Band: V2
Eliot, T. S.
  Murder in the Cathedral: V4
Fierstein, Harvey
  Torch Song Trilogy: V6
Fuller, Charles H.
  A Soldier's Play: V8
Gibson, William
  The Miracle Worker: V2
Glaspell, Susan
  Trifles: V8
Guare, John
  The House of Blue Leaves: V8
Hammerstein, Oscar
  The King and I: V1
Hansberry, Lorraine
  A Raisin in the Sun: V2
Hart, Moss
  You Can't Take It with You: V1
Hellman, Lillian
  The Children's Hour: V3
  The Little Foxes: V1
Henley, Beth
  Crimes of the Heart: V2
Hurston, Zora Neale
  Mule Bone: V6
Inge, William
  Bus Stop: V8
  Come Back, Little Sheba: V3
  Picnic: V5
Kaufman, George S.
  You Can't Take It with You: V1
Kopit, Arthur
  Oh Dad, Poor Dad, Mamma's Hung You in the Closet and I'm Feelin' So Sad: V7
Kushner, Tony
  Angels in America: V5
Lawrence, Jerome
  Inherit the Wind: V2
Lee, Robert E.
  Inherit the Wind: V2
MacArthur, Charles
  The Front Page: V9
Mamet, David
  American Buffalo: V3
  Glengarry Glen Ross: V2
  Speed-the-Plow: V6
McCullers, Carson
  The Member of the Wedding: V5
Medoff, Mark
  Children of a Lesser God: V4
Miller, Arthur
  All My Sons: V8
  The Crucible: V3
  Death of a Salesman: V1
Norman, Marsha
  'night, Mother: V2
Odets, Clifford
  Waiting for Lefty: V3
O'Neill, Eugene
  The Emperor Jones: V6
  The Hairy Ape: V4
  The Iceman Cometh: V5
  Long Day's Journey into Night: V2
  Mourning Becomes Electra: V9

Pomerance, Bernard
   The Elephant Man: V9
Rabe, David
   The Basic Training of Pavlo Hummel: V3
   Streamers: V8
Rodgers, Richard
   The King and I: V1
Shange, Ntozake
   for colored girls who have considered suicide/when the rainbow is enuf: V2
Shepard, Sam
   Buried Child: V6
   Fool for Love: V7
   True West: V3
Shue, Larry
   The Foreigner: V7
Simon, Neil
   Brighton Beach Memoirs: V6
   The Odd Couple: V2
Smith, Anna Deavere
   Twilight: Los Angeles, 1992: V2
Stein, Joseph
   Fiddler on the Roof: V7
Valdez, Luis
   Zoot Suit: V5
Vidal, Gore
   Visit to a Small Planet: V2
Wasserstein, Wendy
   The Heidi Chronicles: V5
Wilder, Thornton
   Our Town: V1
   The Skin of Our Teeth: V4
Williams, Tennessee
   Cat on a Hot Tin Roof: V3
   The Glass Menagerie: V1
   The Night of the Iguana: V7
   A Streetcar Named Desire: V1
Wilson, August
   Fences: V3
   The Piano Lesson: V7
Wilson, Lanford
   Burn This: V4
   Hot L Baltimore: V9

Argentinian

Dorfman, Ariel
   Death and the Maiden: V4

Canadian

Highway, Tomson
   The Rez Sisters: V2
Pollock, Sharon
   Blood Relations: V3

Chilean

Dorfman, Ariel
   Death and the Maiden: V4

Czechoslovakian

Capek, Karel
   R.U.R.: V7

English

Arden, John
   Serjeant Musgrave's Dance: V9
Ayckbourn, Alan
   A Chorus of Disapproval: V7
Barnes, Peter
   The Ruling Class: V6
Bolt, Robert
   A Man for All Seasons: V2
Bond, Edward
   Lear: V3
   Saved: V8
Christie, Agatha
   The Mousetrap: V2
Coward, Noel
   Hay Fever: V6
   Private Lives: V3
Delaney, Shelagh
   A Taste of Honey: V7
Ford, John
   'Tis Pity She's a Whore: V7
Goldsmith, Oliver
   She Stoops to Conquer: V1
Hare, David
   Blue Room: V7
   Plenty: V4
Jonson, Ben(jamin)
   The Alchemist: V4
Marlowe, Christopher
   Doctor Faustus: V1
   Edward II: V5
Orton, Joe
   Entertaining Mr. Sloane: V3
   What the Butler Saw: V6
Osborne, John
   Look Back in Anger: V4
Pinter, Harold
   The Birthday Party: V5
   The Caretaker: V7
   The Homecoming: V3
Rattigan, Terence
   The Browning Version: V8
Rice, Tim
   Jesus Christ Superstar: V7
Shaffer, Peter
   Equus: V5
Stoppard, Tom
   Arcadia: V5
   The Real Thing: V8
   Rosencrantz and Guildenstern Are Dead: V2
Webber, Andrew Lloyd
   Jesus Christ Superstar: V7

French

Anouilh, Jean
   Antigone: V9

Jarry, Alfred
   Ubu Roi: V8
Rostand, Edmond
   Cyrano de Bergerac: V1
Sartre, Jean-Paul
   No Exit: V5

German

Brecht, Bertolt
   The Good Person of Szechwan: V9
   Mother Courage and Her Children: V5
   The Threepenny Opera: V4
Weiss, Peter
   Marat/Sade: V3

Greek

Aeschylus
   Prometheus Bound: V5
Euripides
   The Bacchae: V6
   Iphigenia in Taurus: V4
   Medea: V1
Sophocles
   Ajax: V8
   Antigone: V1
   Electra: V4
   Oedipus Rex: V1

Hispanic

Valdez, Luis
   Zoot Suit: V5

Irish

Beckett, Samuel
   Krapp's Last Tape: V7
   Waiting for Godot: V2
Behan, Brendan
   The Hostage: V7
Shaw, George Bernard
   Major Barbara: V3
   Man and Superman: V6
   Pygmalion: V1
Sheridan, Richard Brinsley
   School for Scandal: V4
Wilde, Oscar
   The Importance of Being Earnest: V4
   Lady Windemere's Fan: V9
   Salome: V8

Italian

Pirandello, Luigi
   Right You Are, If You Think You Are: V9
   Six Characters in Search of an Author: V4

Mexican
Carballido, Emilio
I, Too, Speak of the Rose: V4

Native Canadian
Highway, Tomson
The Rez Sisters: V2

Norwegian
Ibsen, Henrik
A Doll's House: V1
Hedda Gabler: V6
Peer Gynt: V8

Romanian
Ionesco, Eugène
The Chairs: V9

Ionesco, Eugene
The Bald Soprano: V4

Russian
Chekhov, Anton
The Cherry Orchard: V1
Uncle Vanya: V5
Gorki, Maxim
The Lower Depths: V9
Turgenev, Ivan
A Month in the Country: V6

Scottish
Barrie, J(ames) M.
Peter Pan: V7

South African
Fugard, Athol
Boesman & Lena: V6
"Master Harold"... and the Boys: V3

Spanish
Garcia Lorca, Federico
The House of Bernarda Alba: V4

Swedish
Strindberg, August
The Ghost Sonata: V9
Miss Julie: V4

Subject/Theme Index

1930s
- *The Philadelphia Story:* 292, 298-300

1960s
- *Funnyhouse of a Negro:* 104, 109-111

A

Abandonment
- *The Elephant Man:* 70, 74
- *The Ghost Sonata:* 131, 135, 139
- *The Good Person of Szechwan:* 186-187, 191, 194
- *Hot L Baltimore:* 208-209
- *Mourning Becomes Electra:* 271-272

Absurdity
- *The Chairs:* 30

Absurdity
- *The Chairs:* 38-39
- *The Elephant Man:* 70, 72-73, 77-78

Adultery
- *Mourning Becomes Electra:* 253-254, 262, 281, 283-284
- *The Philadelphia Story:* 293-294

Africa
- *Funnyhouse of a Negro:* 106, 108, 110, 120, 122

Alienation and Loneliness
- *The Elephant Man:* 45
- *Funnyhouse of a Negro:* 108

Alienation
- *The Philadelphia Story:* 304

Allegory
- *Antigone:* 5, 8

The Elephant Man: 69-74, 77-81
The Ghost Sonata: 161, 164
The Good Person of Szechwan: 169, 176, 188, 191-193
Right You Are, If You Think You Are: 316

American Northeast
- *The Elephant Man:* 41, 47-48, 74, 76, 79-80
- *The Front Page:* 86, 88, 90-91
- *The Good Person of Szechwan:* 179
- *Mourning Becomes Electra:* 253-254, 261

American South
- *Funnyhouse of a Negro:* 110

Anger
- *The Elephant Man:* 70, 73, 76
- *Mourning Becomes Electra:* 262-263, 282, 289
- *Serjeant Musgrave's Dance:* 331-332, 340

Appearances and Reality/ Truth and Falsehood
- *Funnyhouse of a Negro:* 108

Asia
- *The Chairs:* 32-33
- *The Good Person of Szechwan:* 170, 176-178

Atonement
- *The Front Page:* 99, 101
- *The Ghost Sonata:* 143, 146, 162-164
- *Mourning Becomes Electra:* 259, 266

Authoritarianism
- *Antigone:* 1, 5, 7

Avant-garde
- *The Ghost Sonata:* 128, 138, 140

B

Beauty
- *The Elephant Man:* 45

Beauty
- *The Elephant Man:* 45, 71-76, 81
- *The Ghost Sonata:* 130-132, 137-138, 152-153, 166-167
- *Mourning Becomes Electra:* 268-269

Betrayal
- *The Ghost Sonata:* 136

Betrayal
- *Lady Windermere's Fan:* 222
- *Mourning Becomes Electra:* 271-274

Buddhism
- *The Ghost Sonata:* 150-153, 164

C

Charity
- *The Good Person of Szechwan:* 172, 176

Choices and Consequences
- *The Front Page:* 88
- *Hot L Baltimore:* 199

Christianity
- *The Elephant Man:* 72, 76, 78-79

Civil Rights
- *Funnyhouse of a Negro:* 109-110

Comedy
- *The Front Page:* 97-99

Hot L Baltimore: 196, 201, 208-209
The Philadelphia Story: 298, 300-301, 305-306

Coming of Age
The Ghost Sonata: 137

Communication (or the Lack Thereof)
The Chairs: 31

Communism
The Good Person of Szechwan: 185, 192-194

Courage
Antigone: 24

Creativity and Imagination
The Elephant Man: 45

Crime and Criminals
The Elephant Man: 56, 59, 63, 71, 73-74, 77
The Front Page: 83-86, 89, 91, 98-100, 103
The Ghost Sonata: 130-132, 136-140, 160-161, 164
Hot L Baltimore: 197, 201-202
The Lower Depths: 232-233, 245, 249-251
Mourning Becomes Electra: 282-286

Cruelty
Antigone: 14-15
The Elephant Man: 55-56, 63, 73-80
The Lower Depths: 237, 239
Serjeant Musgrave's Dance: 338-340, 353-354

Curiosity
The Elephant Man: 52, 56, 58-59
Right You Are, If You Think You Are: 323-324

Cynicism
The Elephant Man: 70-71, 77-78
Lady Windermere's Fan: 220-222

D

Dance
Serjeant Musgrave's Dance: 335-336, 350-353

Death
Antigone: 1-3, 10-22, 25
The Elephant Man: 52-54, 66-68, 73, 77-80
The Front Page: 86, 88-89
Funnyhouse of a Negro: 105-106, 109, 112-124
The Ghost Sonata: 127, 129-132, 136-138, 142, 144-151, 156-164
Hot L Baltimore: 207-208
Lady Windermere's Fan: 225
The Lower Depths: 232-233, 236-238
Mourning Becomes Electra: 255-256, 262, 264-266, 273-275, 281-286, 290-291
Right You Are, If You Think You Are: 311, 315-318
Serjeant Musgrave's Dance: 332, 334-336, 340, 342-351

Deceit
Lady Windermere's Fan: 215-216

Deception
The Front Page: 88

Depression and Melancholy
The Ghost Sonata: 142, 145-146
The Lower Depths: 246-248

Description
Mourning Becomes Electra: 271-273

Devil
Serjeant Musgrave's Dance: 341-342

Dialogue
The Front Page: 101-102
The Ghost Sonata: 155-156
Hot L Baltimore: 203
The Lower Depths: 249, 251
The Philadelphia Story: 292, 298

Disease
Mourning Becomes Electra: 282, 285-286
Right You Are, If You Think You Are: 317

Disillusionment
Antigone: 6

Divorce
The Ghost Sonata: 137, 139-140
The Philadelphia Story: 293

Drama
Antigone: 1, 5-8, 17, 20-26
The Elephant Man: 48, 52-54, 59-63, 69-75, 78, 80-81
The Front Page: 88, 90-91, 95, 98, 101
Funnyhouse of a Negro: 120-121
The Ghost Sonata: 127-128, 139-142, 147, 149, 151, 153-156, 159
The Good Person of Szechwan: 169-170, 179, 185-188, 191-194
Hot L Baltimore: 200-202, 209
The Lower Depths: 230-231
Mourning Becomes Electra: 260-261, 266-270, 281, 287, 290
The Philadelphia Story: 292-293, 300, 306
Right You Are, If You Think You Are: 315-318, 324-328
Serjeant Musgrave's Dance: 335-338, 342, 345-347

Dreams and Visions
The Elephant Man: 55, 59, 61-63, 74-79
Funnyhouse of a Negro: 117-118, 121-122
The Ghost Sonata: 128, 130, 137-138, 141, 147-149, 153-154, 157
Mourning Becomes Electra: 271-273

Duty and Responsibility
Mourning Becomes Electra: 276, 281, 283, 285

E

Economic Circumstances/Wealth & Poverty
The Good Person of Szechwan: 176

Emotions
Antigone: 8, 15, 20, 25
The Chairs: 37
The Elephant Man: 43, 45, 54-56, 66, 68, 73, 76, 81
Funnyhouse of a Negro: 109, 112, 116, 119-120
The Ghost Sonata: 138, 167
The Good Person of Szechwan: 180, 183-185, 189, 191
Lady Windermere's Fan: 225, 227
The Lower Depths: 237
Mourning Becomes Electra: 259, 262, 277-278, 289-290
Right You Are, If You Think You Are: 323-324

Epic
The Good Person of Szechwan: 185-188, 191-194

Eternity
Antigone: 24-26
The Elephant Man: 68-69

Europe
Antigone: 1, 5-8
The Chairs: 33
The Elephant Man: 41-42, 47-48, 53-56, 60-64, 70-71, 74-75, 79-80
The Ghost Sonata: 128-129, 138-141
The Good Person of Szechwan: 170, 177-178
Lady Windermere's Fan: 213-214, 218
The Lower Depths: 230, 238-245
The Philadelphia Story: 298-300
Right You Are, If You Think You Are: 317
Serjeant Musgrave's Dance: 331, 334-338, 349

Evil
The Elephant Man: 54-55, 59-60, 75-76
The Ghost Sonata: 137, 144, 149, 157, 159, 161-163, 167

Subject/Theme Index

The Good Person of Szechwan:
 186, 188, 191
Lady Windermere's Fan: 223-225
Mourning Becomes Electra: 256,
 262, 265-266, 272-274,
 283-285
Serjeant Musgrave's Dance:
 351-353
Execution
 The Front Page: 83-85, 90
 Serjeant Musgrave's Dance:
 350-351
Exile
 The Elephant Man: 54-55
 Hot L Baltimore: 203-204
Exploitation
 The Elephant Man: 53, 62-63, 75
 The Good Person of Szechwan:
 188, 190, 192
Exposition
 The Ghost Sonata: 137-138,
 158-159
Expressionism
 The Ghost Sonata: 128, 138,
 140-142, 164
 Mourning Becomes Electra: 259

F

Family Life
 The Ghost Sonata: 140
 Mourning Becomes Electra:
 264, 271, 283
Farm and Rural Life
 The Philadelphia Story: 299-300
Fate and Chance
 Antigone: 16-19
 Funnyhouse of a Negro: 114
 Mourning Becomes Electra: 282-
 283, 286-287
 Serjeant Musgrave's Dance:
 344-345
Fatherhood
 The Ghost Sonata: 161-162
Fear
 The Elephant Man: 45
Fear and Terror
 Antigone: 17-18
 The Ghost Sonata: 131, 135, 138
 Mourning Becomes Electra:
 284-286
Feminism
 The Good Person of Szechwan:
 185-186, 193-194
Film
 The Elephant Man: 41, 49,
 52-54, 57-61
 The Front Page: 91, 97-101
 The Ghost Sonata: 141
 The Lower Depths: 248-249
Folklore
 Antigone: 21
 The Elephant Man: 53

The Ghost Sonata: 153, 164-167
Mourning Becomes Electra: 288
Foreshadowing
 The Lower Depths: 238
Forgiveness
 Mourning Becomes Electra:
 273-274
Freedom
 The Elephant Man: 45

G

Generosity
 The Ghost Sonata: 130, 135, 137
 The Good Person of Szechwan:
 175-176, 181, 186-188
Ghost
 The Ghost Sonata: 127, 129-132,
 138, 144-145
 Mourning Becomes Electra:
 281, 286
 Serjeant Musgrave's Dance: 334
Ghosts
 Serjeant Musgrave's Dance: 334
God
 The Chairs: 39
 The Elephant Man: 66-67, 70,
 72-73, 76-80
 Serjeant Musgrave's Dance:
 350-351
Goodness
 The Good Person of Szechwan:
 180-182
 Lady Windermere's Fan: 225
Great Depression
 The Philadelphia Story: 299-301
Greed
 The Ghost Sonata: 155, 157
Grief and Sorrow
 Antigone: 18-19
Grotesque
 The Ghost Sonata: 155, 159
Guilt
 Serjeant Musgrave's Dance: 334
Guilt
 The Ghost Sonata: 132, 136-138,
 145-146, 166
 Mourning Becomes Electra: 255-
 256, 262, 265-266, 273-
 275, 280

H

Happiness and Gaiety
 Antigone: 24-25
 Mourning Becomes Electra: 273,
 275, 283-284
Hatred
 Antigone: 10-14
 The Elephant Man: 56-57, 73-74
 The Good Person of Szechwan:
 186-187, 194
 Mourning Becomes Electra:
 281, 283-284

Heaven
 The Elephant Man: 76
 The Ghost Sonata: 127, 132, 136,
 138, 143-146, 152-153
Hell/Prison
 The Lower Depths: 236
Hell
 The Ghost Sonata: 148, 151, 153
 The Lower Depths: 236-238
Heritage and Ancestry
 Funnyhouse of a Negro: 116-120
Heroism
 Antigone: 10-11, 25
 The Elephant Man: 54-59, 68
 Funnyhouse of a Negro: 117
 The Ghost Sonata: 165-166
 Mourning Becomes Electra:
 268-270
History
 The Elephant Man: 52, 54-55, 63
 Funnyhouse of a Negro: 118-119
 The Philadelphia Story: 294
 Serjeant Musgrave's Dance:
 336, 338
Homelessness
 Hot L Baltimore: 208-209
Honor
 The Philadelphia Story: 304
Hope
 The Elephant Man: 69, 72-73, 78
 Funnyhouse of a Negro:
 115, 119-120
 The Ghost Sonata: 136-138
 The Good Person of Szechwan:
 190-191
 Hot L Baltimore: 204-205
 Mourning Becomes Electra: 256,
 258-259, 262, 272-275
 Serjeant Musgrave's Dance:
 340-341
Human Condition
 The Elephant Man: 46
 The Ghost Sonata: 137
 Hot L Baltimore: 199
Human Condition/Isolation
 The Chairs: 31
Human Condition
 The Lower Depths: 230
Humiliation and Degradation
 Mourning Becomes Electra:
 280-281
Humility
 The Elephant Man: 56-60
Humor
 The Chairs: 28, 33-34, 38
 The Front Page: 88-91, 97,
 99, 101
 The Good Person of Szechwan:
 179, 187-189
 Hot L Baltimore: 209
 The Philadelphia Story: 294, 297-
 298, 301, 306

Subject/Theme Index

Right You Are, If You Think You Are: 326-327
Hypocrisy
Lady Windermere's Fan: 215

I

Idealism
Lady Windermere's Fan: 227-228
Identity
Funnyhouse of a Negro: 107
The Good Person of Szechwan: 176
Ignorance
Antigone: 18
The Elephant Man: 61-62
Illusion vs. Reality
The Ghost Sonata: 135
Imagery and Symbolism
Antigone: 12-13
The Elephant Man: 57-58, 64
Funnyhouse of a Negro: 109, 111, 118-119
The Ghost Sonata: 132, 138, 141, 148-152, 158, 163-165
The Good Person of Szechwan: 186, 192, 194
The Lower Depths: 236-238
Mourning Becomes Electra: 261-262
Serjeant Musgrave's Dance: 352-353
Imagination
Lady Windermere's Fan: 226-228
Imperialism
The Elephant Man: 52, 60-61
Incest
Mourning Becomes Electra: 259
Incest
Mourning Becomes Electra: 256, 259, 262
Insanity
Funnyhouse of a Negro: 106, 108
Right You Are, If You Think You Are: 311, 315, 317-320
Irony
Antigone: 19, 21
The Chairs: 32
The Elephant Man: 71, 78, 80
The Front Page: 97, 99-100
The Good Person of Szechwan: 188-190
Lady Windermere's Fan: 222
Serjeant Musgrave's Dance: 352-354

K

Killers and Killing
Antigone: 17-18
The Elephant Man: 62, 78, 80
The Front Page: 84-85
Funnyhouse of a Negro: 106, 108, 110, 115, 119-120, 125
Lady Windermere's Fan: 224
The Lower Depths: 232-233
Mourning Becomes Electra: 254-256, 263-266, 273-274, 286, 289-290
Serjeant Musgrave's Dance: 334-336, 351
Kindness
The Elephant Man: 53, 55-57, 62, 70-73, 76
Knowledge
The Elephant Man: 52, 61, 63, 71, 78
Lady Windermere's Fan: 226-229
Right You Are, If You Think You Are: 324, 326-327

L

Landscape
Antigone: 18-19, 22
Funnyhouse of a Negro: 124-125
Mourning Becomes Electra: 268-269, 272-273
Law and Order
The Elephant Man: 56, 58-63, 75, 77, 79, 81
The Front Page: 83-86, 89-90, 99-100
Funnyhouse of a Negro: 110
The Ghost Sonata: 139-140
The Good Person of Szechwan: 172-173, 177-178, 184
The Lower Depths: 232-233, 240, 250-251
Mourning Becomes Electra: 264-266, 282, 284
Right You Are, If You Think You Are: 309-312
Serjeant Musgrave's Dance: 343, 345-346
Literary Criticism
Antigone: 21
Right You Are, If You Think You Are: 318
Literary Movements
The Ghost Sonata: 140
Loneliness
The Chairs: 28, 30-32
The Elephant Man: 43, 45, 55, 80
Funnyhouse of a Negro: 124-125
The Ghost Sonata: 158
Hot L Baltimore: 208-209
Love and Passion
Antigone: 12-14
The Elephant Man: 73-74, 78-79
The Front Page: 92-96
Funnyhouse of a Negro: 117-120, 125
The Ghost Sonata: 142, 144-146, 150-151, 166-167
The Good Person of Szechwan: 172, 176-177, 184-189
Lady Windermere's Fan: 220-225, 228
The Lower Depths: 232-233
Mourning Becomes Electra: 254-256, 259-260, 264, 266, 268-269, 272-279, 283-284, 288
The Philadelphia Story: 295, 298
Serjeant Musgrave's Dance: 332, 334, 337, 342-344, 348-351
Lower Class
The Lower Depths: 230, 238-239, 248
Loyalty
The Front Page: 88
Serjeant Musgrave's Dance: 335
Loyalty
Antigone: 2, 5
The Front Page: 88
The Philadelphia Story: 302
Serjeant Musgrave's Dance: 335

M

Marriage
The Ghost Sonata: 139-141
The Good Person of Szechwan: 184-185, 189-190
Mourning Becomes Electra: 256, 258, 271-272, 284
The Philadelphia Story: 292-295, 301, 304-306
Memory and Reminiscence
Hot L Baltimore: 200
Men as Animals
The Lower Depths: 237
Mental and Physical Infirmity
The Elephant Man: 52-53, 61, 63
Mental Instability
The Ghost Sonata: 142
Right You Are, If You Think You Are: 314
Middle Ages
Serjeant Musgrave's Dance: 349-351
Middle East
The Ghost Sonata: 161-163
Serjeant Musgrave's Dance: 337
Modernism
Mourning Becomes Electra: 266-267
Right You Are, If You Think You Are: 315
Monarchy
Antigone: 12-17
Funnyhouse of a Negro: 105-106, 109-110, 113-114, 117-118
The Ghost Sonata: 166-167
Mourning Becomes Electra: 281-284
Money and Economics
The Elephant Man: 52, 61, 63
The Ghost Sonata: 132, 139-140

The Good Person of Szechwan: 170-172, 176-178, 181-187, 192
Lady Windermere's Fan: 212, 214, 216-217
The Lower Depths: 237-239
The Philadelphia Story: 300

Monologue
Funnyhouse of a Negro: 105-106, 115-117
The Lower Depths: 233, 236-238, 243
Right You Are, If You Think You Are: 324

Mood
Antigone: 16, 19, 21-22
The Ghost Sonata: 151

Morality
Hot L Baltimore: 200

Morals and Morality
The Elephant Man: 53-55, 58-59, 64, 69, 72-77, 80
The Ghost Sonata: 131, 135, 147, 149-150, 159, 163-164
The Good Person of Szechwan: 190-194
Lady Windermere's Fan: 224-225
Mourning Becomes Electra: 260-263, 266-267, 270, 277, 279, 282
The Philadelphia Story: 297, 301
Serjeant Musgrave's Dance: 351-354

Murder
The Elephant Man: 52-61, 64
Funnyhouse of a Negro: 106, 108-110
Mourning Becomes Electra: 259, 263-266, 273-274, 281, 283, 285-286, 290

Music
The Elephant Man: 42, 44, 48
The Ghost Sonata: 127-128, 131, 137-138, 154-156, 159, 165, 167
The Good Person of Szechwan: 177, 185-192
The Lower Depths: 233, 236-237
Mourning Becomes Electra: 271-273
Serjeant Musgrave's Dance: 336, 342, 346, 352-354

Mystery and Intrigue
The Elephant Man: 69, 71-73, 81
The Ghost Sonata: 127, 130-131, 144-145
Mourning Becomes Electra: 281-284

Myth
Antigone: 5

Myths and Legends
Antigone: 1, 5, 7, 18-19

The Elephant Man: 52-53, 59-60, 71-72, 75-78
The Ghost Sonata: 127, 130, 132, 138, 150-152, 166-167
Mourning Becomes Electra: 264-266, 270, 275, 280-283, 286-289

N

Naivete
Lady Windermere's Fan: 223-225

Narration
Antigone: 8-9
The Elephant Man: 53, 55, 57, 61
Funnyhouse of a Negro: 122-123
The Ghost Sonata: 157, 159

Naturalism
Antigone: 6-7
Mourning Becomes Electra: 260, 263

Nature
Antigone: 12-15
The Elephant Man: 59, 63, 69, 71, 73, 76-77
The Front Page: 99
The Ghost Sonata: 146, 150-153
The Good Person of Szechwan: 189-192
Mourning Becomes Electra: 253, 260, 262, 264, 268-269, 272, 274

Nomadic Life
The Lower Depths: 232, 238-240, 246, 250-251

North America
Funnyhouse of a Negro: 104, 106-107, 111, 118
The Ghost Sonata: 139, 141
The Good Person of Szechwan: 169, 177-180

Nuclear War
The Philadelphia Story: 299

O

Oedipus Complex
The Elephant Man: 53, 59-60

Old Age
The Chairs: 28-37
The Ghost Sonata: 130-132, 136-138, 144-145
The Good Person of Szechwan: 171-172, 176-177
The Lower Depths: 246, 248, 250-251

P

Painting
The Ghost Sonata: 154, 156, 158-159

Paradise
Mourning Becomes Electra: 258

Paranoia
Funnyhouse of a Negro: 115

Paranormal
Serjeant Musgrave's Dance: 334

Parody
The Ghost Sonata: 164-166

Patience
The Elephant Man: 55, 57, 61-62, 66-68

Perception
The Elephant Man: 55, 58, 60-63, 68
Right You Are, If You Think You Are: 323, 325-326

Permanence
The Elephant Man: 53, 61, 67-68

Persecution
The Elephant Man: 53-56, 74, 76, 78-79
Funnyhouse of a Negro: 116-117, 120
Mourning Becomes Electra: 281, 286

Personal Identity
Funnyhouse of a Negro: 104, 107-109, 120-122
Lady Windermere's Fan: 227-229

Personality Traits
Hot L Baltimore: 201

Personification
Antigone: 12, 15
Funnyhouse of a Negro: 116-117
The Ghost Sonata: 156-157
The Good Person of Szechwan: 191-192
The Lower Depths: 235-236
Right You Are, If You Think You Are: 326-327

Philosophical Ideas
The Elephant Man: 69, 78-79
The Ghost Sonata: 150, 152
Mourning Becomes Electra: 260, 262, 269-270

Pleasure
The Elephant Man: 52, 54, 58-61

Plot
The Front Page: 97-98
The Good Person of Szechwan: 189-191
Hot L Baltimore: 202-203
Lady Windermere's Fan: 220, 222, 227-230
The Lower Depths: 240, 249-250
Mourning Becomes Electra: 268, 280, 282-286
The Philadelphia Story: 304, 306
Right You Are, If You Think You Are: 310, 312, 314-315
Serjeant Musgrave's Dance: 342, 346, 351-353

Poetry
Serjeant Musgrave's Dance: 346

Point of View
   Antigone: 13-15
   The Good Person of Szechwan: 191, 194
Politicians
   The Front Page: 84-86, 89-90
   Mourning Becomes Electra: 260-261
   The Philadelphia Story: 300
   Serjeant Musgrave's Dance: 331-332, 342-345
Politics
   The Front Page: 89
Politics
   Antigone: 1, 5, 7-8, 13-15
   The Elephant Man: 47-48, 55, 61-63
   The Front Page: 89-91
   Funnyhouse of a Negro: 109-110
   The Ghost Sonata: 139-141
   The Good Person of Szechwan: 177-178, 192, 194
   Hot L Baltimore: 196-197, 201-202
   The Lower Depths: 239-240
   Mourning Becomes Electra: 261-262
   The Philadelphia Story: 300
   Right You Are, If You Think You Are: 316-317
   Serjeant Musgrave's Dance: 337-338, 343
Pornography
   The Elephant Man: 59-61, 64
Poverty
   The Good Person of Szechwan: 170, 176-177
Prejudice and Tolerance
   The Philadelphia Story: 297
Pride
   Mourning Becomes Electra: 290
Primitivism
   Mourning Becomes Electra: 277-279
Privacy
   Right You Are, If You Think You Are: 314
Prostitution
   The Good Person of Szechwan: 170-171, 183-187
   Hot L Baltimore: 197-201, 209
Protestantism
   Mourning Becomes Electra: 277-280
Psychology and the Human Mind
   The Elephant Man: 52, 58-59, 67-68
   Funnyhouse of a Negro: 107, 111, 115-116, 120-124
   The Ghost Sonata: 138, 140-142, 147, 149-151, 164, 167
   Lady Windermere's Fan: 226-228
   Mourning Becomes Electra: 261-263, 266-267, 270, 278-280, 290
   Right You Are, If You Think You Are: 311, 314, 316, 323, 325-326
   Serjeant Musgrave's Dance: 353
Public vs. Private Life
   The Philadelphia Story: 298
Punishment
   Mourning Becomes Electra: 256, 259, 261, 263, 265-267

R

Race
   Funnyhouse of a Negro: 104-108, 111-112, 120-123
Realism
   Antigone: 5-8, 21
   The Ghost Sonata: 138-141, 147
   The Lower Depths: 230, 236-239
Recreation
   The Front Page: 90-91
Relativism
   Right You Are, If You Think You Are: 314
Religion and Religious Thought
   The Chairs: 39
   The Elephant Man: 42-43, 47-48, 67, 69-70, 74-76, 79-81
   The Ghost Sonata: 143, 146, 154, 160, 164
   The Good Person of Szechwan: 170-173, 176-177, 182, 186-187, 191-192
   Mourning Becomes Electra: 269, 277-279
   Serjeant Musgrave's Dance: 344, 350-351
Revenge
   Mourning Becomes Electra: 258
Revenge
   The Ghost Sonata: 131, 135-136
   Mourning Becomes Electra: 253-254, 263-266, 273, 280-282, 289
   Serjeant Musgrave's Dance: 332, 334, 339-340

S

Sadism and Masochism
   The Elephant Man: 54, 56, 59-61
Saints
   Antigone: 24-25
Satire
   Lady Windermere's Fan: 220, 222
   Right You Are, If You Think You Are: 323, 326-327
Schizophrenia
   Funnyhouse of a Negro: 115-116
Science and Technology
   The Elephant Man: 49-50, 60-63, 71, 73, 75, 77
Sculpture
   Funnyhouse of a Negro: 117-118
Search For Knowledge
   Right You Are, If You Think You Are: 320-322, 326-327
Selfless*
   The Elephant Man: 53, 57, 64
Sentimentality
   Antigone: 15, 17, 19
   The Elephant Man: 52-59, 63-64
   The Front Page: 103
   Hot L Baltimore: 206-207
Setting
   The Elephant Man: 46-47
   The Front Page: 99
   The Good Person of Szechwan: 187, 190, 192
   Hot L Baltimore: 201-202
   The Lower Depths: 237-238
   Mourning Becomes Electra: 261, 280, 285
   Serjeant Musgrave's Dance: 335, 342-344
Sex and Sexuality
   The Elephant Man: 50-53, 57-58, 61-64
   Funnyhouse of a Negro: 116-117
   The Good Person of Szechwan: 189-191
   Mourning Becomes Electra: 254-256, 262, 278-280
Sickness
   Right You Are, If You Think You Are: 309, 314, 317
Sin and Guilt
   Mourning Becomes Electra: 259
Sin
   The Elephant Man: 54-55, 58-59, 71-72, 76-77
   The Front Page: 90
   The Ghost Sonata: 131-132, 137-140, 144-146, 150, 157, 164-165
   Lady Windermere's Fan: 223-225
   Mourning Becomes Electra: 259, 261-265, 272-274, 279, 282-283
   Serjeant Musgrave's Dance: 352-353
Social Order
   The Elephant Man: 62, 71
   Lady Windermere's Fan: 218
   The Lower Depths: 239, 245, 247-248
   The Philadelphia Story: 304
Socialism
   The Good Person of Szechwan: 185, 190-191, 194

Solitude
    The Ghost Sonata: 155, 158
Soothsayer
    Funnyhouse of a Negro: 124, 126
Soul
    The Elephant Man: 70-72
    The Ghost Sonata: 150-151
Spirituality
    The Elephant Man: 76, 78-80
Storms and Weather Conditions
    Antigone: 12-13
Structure
    The Elephant Man: 52-53, 62, 72
    The Ghost Sonata: 153-154, 159-160
    Hot L Baltimore: 200
    Lady Windermere's Fan: 219-220
    The Lower Depths: 230, 237-238
    Right You Are, If You Think You Are: 324, 326
    Serjeant Musgrave's Dance: 341, 346
Success and Failure
    The Good Person of Szechwan: 175
Success and Failure
    The Lower Depths: 230, 238, 240
    Mourning Becomes Electra: 277-279
Suicide
    The Chairs: 28, 30-32
    The Elephant Man: 78
    Mourning Becomes Electra: 283, 285-286
Supernatural
    The Ghost Sonata: 130, 143

T
The Bad Mother
    Lady Windermere's Fan: 216

The Individual and Society
    Funnyhouse of a Negro: 110
The "Truth" vs. the "Consoling Lie"
    The Lower Depths: 235
Time and Change
    The Elephant Man: 52, 55, 57, 62, 64, 69, 71-72, 75, 77, 79-80
    The Ghost Sonata: 149, 151-153
    The Good Person of Szechwan: 190-191
    Hot L Baltimore: 208
Tolerance
    The Philadelphia Story: 305-306
Tone
    The Lower Depths: 236-237, 240
Tragedy
    Antigone: 16-22, 25-26
    Mourning Becomes Electra: 266-267, 283, 285, 287-291

U
Ugliness
    Antigone: 14-15
Uncertainty
    The Elephant Man: 72-73, 79-80
    Lady Windermere's Fan: 221-222
Understanding
    The Elephant Man: 62, 67, 72, 75
    The Good Person of Szechwan: 185, 193
    Right You Are, If You Think You Are: 324-325
Upper Class
    The Ghost Sonata: 135, 137, 141
    Lady Windermere's Fan: 211, 215-218

Utopianism
    The Ghost Sonata: 148, 151-153, 166-167
    Mourning Becomes Electra: 272, 274-275, 278-279

V
Victorian Age
    Funnyhouse of a Negro: 115-118, 124-126

W
War, the Military, and Soldier Life
    Antigone: 1, 7
    The Chairs: 29, 32
    The Ghost Sonata: 130-132, 136-137, 144-145, 149-150, 165-166
    The Good Person of Szechwan: 178
    Mourning Becomes Electra: 254-255, 261-264, 267
    The Philadelphia Story: 298-300
    Right You Are, If You Think You Are: 317-318
    Serjeant Musgrave's Dance: 331-332, 335-340, 343-347, 350-354
Wealth and Poverty
    Hot L Baltimore: 200
Wildlife
    Antigone: 12, 14
    The Elephant Man: 52-54, 59, 69-81
    The Front Page: 98, 100-101
World War II
    The Good Person of Szechwan: 169, 177-178

WITHDRAWN